READING MEDIEVAL LATIN

Praesidi et Magistro et ceteris Collegii Sancti Patricii apud Maynooth studiosis hoc opus, ducentesimo anno a Collegio condito primis curis editum, libens dedico.

I have pleasure in dedicating this work, first published in the college's bicentenary year, to the President, Master and other scholars of St Patrick's College, Maynooth

READING MEDIEVAL LATIN

KEITH SIDWELL

Professor of Latin and Greek,
University College Cork

 CAMBRIDGE
UNIVERSITY PRESS

CAMBRIDGE
UNIVERSITY PRESS

University Printing House, Cambridge CB2 8BS, United Kingdom

Cambridge University Press is part of the University of Cambridge.

It furthers the University's mission by disseminating knowledge in the pursuit of education, learning and research at the highest international levels of excellence.

www.cambridge.org
Information on this title: www.cambridge.org/9780521447478

First published 1995
17th printing 2013

A catalogue record for this publication is available from the British Library

Library of Congress Cataloguing in Publication data
Sidwell, Keith C.
   Reading medieval Latin / Keith Sidwell
      p. cm.
   ISBN 0 521 44239 7 (hardback) ISBN 0 521 44747 X (paperback)
   1. Latin language, Medieval and modern - Readers. 2. Latin language,
   Medieval and modern - grammer. I. Title.
   PA2825.S53   1995 95 - 10864
   477 - dc20   CIP

ISBN 978-0-521-44239-8 Hardback
ISBN 978-0-521-44747-8 Paperback

Contents

Maps and plans

Names of some monasteries and sees mentioned in texts and introductions will be found on maps 2, 3 and 4. For a general orientation in the political geography of the Middle Ages, see C. McEvedy, *The Penguin Atlas of Medieval History*, Harmondsworth, 1961. For further geographical details of the spread of Christianity, see F. van der Meer and Christine Mohrmann, *Atlas of the Early Christian World*, London, 1958 and *Atlas zur Kirchengeschichte*, ed. H. Jedin, K. S. Latourette and J. Martin, revised J. Martin, Fribourg/Basle/Rome/Vienna, 1988.

Note on cover illustration

Miniature from a handmade vellum facsimile of a twelfth-century MS of the *Sciuias* of Hildegard of Bingen produced between 1927 and 1933 by the Benedictine nuns of the Abbey of St Hildegard at Eibingen. The original (Wiesbaden, Hessische Landesbibliothek, Hs. 1), lost since 1945, was probably the work of monks from Trier working at Rupertsberg under Hildegard's direction. See p. 289 for the text which it illustrates.

Preface

Verum quia haec tam copiosa...sunt...ut uix nisi a locupletioribus tot
uolumina adquiri, uix tam profunda nisi ab eruditioribus ualeant
perscrutari, placuit uestrae sanctitati id nobis officii iniungere ut de
omnibus his, uelut de amoenissimis late florentis paradisi campis, quae
infirmorum uiderentur necessitati sufficere decerperemus.

But since these are so numerous that only the rich could buy so many
volumes and so deep that they could only be read by the more advanced
scholars, your holiness has decided to enjoin upon me the task of excerpting
from all of these, as though from the loveliest meadows of an expansively
flowering garden, what seemed to serve the purposes of the weak.

Bede, *Praefatio ad Accam Episcopum* to *In Genesim* (CC 118A, p. 1)

This volume fulfils a promise made to users of *Reading Latin* as long ago as
1986 (*Text*, p. vii). Those who care to look up that passage and compare
what is offered here will see that in the years which have elapsed since the
pledge was made, the author has changed his mind about the plan.
Nonetheless, the idea of a Latin course which would take beginners from
Classical Latin through to the Middle Ages is now a reality. The need for
such a course to serve the English-speaking world is certainly greater even
than it was when *Reading Latin* was published. Fewer and fewer students
arrive at the university with as much as a year or two of Latin under their
belt and many can now graduate, even in medieval history, without having
to acquire a working knowledge of the language. This has led to the need
for crash courses as late as MA level. The requirement here and at earlier
stages to get on with the primary aim as quickly as possible has led to a
tendency to misrepresent Medieval Latin as something without roots in and
relation to Classical Latin. It cannot be stated strongly enough that Latin is
Latin. It retained its identity throughout the period when it was the main
medium for the transmission of intellectual culture. Medieval writers

learned it from Late Classical grammars and with a mixture of pagan and Christian texts mostly composed before the collapse of the Roman Empire. Some did not have enough training. Others used it in close interaction with vernacular languages. None of this makes Medieval Latin an independent language. Consequently, it remains my view that a sound knowledge of Classical Latin is even for today's rushed students an indispensable first step towards a good grasp of Medieval Latin texts.

It is my pleasure to thank here those who have contributed materially or spiritually to this venture. Peter Walsh kindly gave initial suggestions for the outline of the book and cast an eye over a very early and rough draft. I have benefited enormously at various times from discussions with Brian Scott, Robert Coleman, Jim Binns, Carlotta Dionisotti and Robert Ireland. Brian Scott read and commented on several drafts and Robert Ireland drove a finely sharpened pencil through the final draft, as well as heroically undertaking the proofreading. Robert Thomson helped me with written comments on the early sections and the grammar. Jo Wallace-Hadrill read a large part of the commentary and gave guidance about the level of help. Lorna Kellett used drafts of some material with adult classes which had been weaned on *Reading Latin* and gave valuable advice. Clare Woods set me straight about the vocabulary and Richard Cooper answered at a sitting some niggling queries which would have taken days of laborious research. Ann Gleeson typed much of an earlier draft from spidery manuscript and has helped unstintingly with the technical difficulties of producing a final version. The book would have been delayed even longer had it not been for the year's sabbatical leave granted me by Maynooth College. I am deeply grateful to King's College London, where I spent that year as a Visiting Lecturer, for the stimulating environment the Classics Department there provided for the final push.

To students at Lancaster University, who (alas, long ago) used trial versions of the book, my gratitude is due for their forbearance of the role of guinea pig. Peter Jones has been a constant presence at my elbow, urging me not to allow the minutiae to distract my attention for too long. The memory of the pleasure gained during my introduction to Medieval Latin under the direction of Peter Dronke and then to Neo-Latin under Robert Bolgar urges me to mention them as continuing sources of inspiration. Finally (and not least), Sue and Jessica deserve a special mention. The space in which this book was made was given by them without demur, without stint and with love.

Keith Sidwell
St Patrick's College, Maynooth

Sources

Abbreviations

CC	Corpus Christianorum, Series Latina
CCCM	Corpus Christianorum, Continuatio Medievalis
CIL	*Corpus Inscriptionum Latinarum*
CSEL	Corpus Scriptorum Ecclesiasticorum Latinorum
MGH	Monumenta Germaniae Historica
DL	*MGH, De Lite*, I–III, Hanover, 1891–7
SRLI	*MGH, Scriptores Rerum Langobardicarum et Italicarum*
SRM	*MGH, Scriptores Rerum Merovingicarum*
PL	Patrologia Latina (ed. J.-P. Migne)
PLAC	*MGH, Poetae Latini Aevi Carolini*
RHC HO	Recueil des historiens des Croisades: historiens occidentaux, Paris, 1841–1906 (reprinted 1967)
SRGUS	MGH, *Scriptores Rerum Germanicarum in Usum Scholarum*

Texts

1.1 (a)	St Benedict, *Regula* 38; ed. R. Hanslik, CSEL 75, Vienna, 1977 (2nd edn)
1.1 (b)	St Isidore, *Regula Monachorum* 8; ed. F. Arévalo, PL 83/6, col. 867
1.2	Cassiodorus, *Institutiones* I.30.1–3; ed. R. A. B. Mynors, Oxford, 1937
2.1	St Benedict, *Regula* 16, 17, 19 (see 1.1 (a) above)
2.2	Vulgate, Psalm 22; *Biblia Sacra Iuxta Latinam Vulgatam Versionem ad codicum fidem iussu Pii PP. XII...edita. Liber Psalmorum ex recensione Sancti Hieronymi*, pp. 81–2 (= vol. X of continuous series), Rome, 1953

2.3	St Ambrose, *In nocte natalis Domini*; Analecta Hymnica, 50, no. 8, pp. 13f.
2.4	Egeria, *Itinerarium*, 24.1–6; ed. A. Franceschini and R. Weber, CC CLXXV, pp. 29–90, Turnhout, 1965
3.1	Vulgate, 1 Kings (= 1 Samuel) 17.1–54; *Biblia Sacra* (see above 2.2), vol. V, pp. 150–61, Rome, 1944
3.2	Vulgate, *Canticum Canticorum* I.1–16; *Biblia Sacra* (see 2.2 above), vol. XI, pp. 179–80, Rome, 1957
3.3	Vulgate, Luke 23; *Biblia Sacra Iuxta Vulgatam Versionem adiuvantibus Bonifatio Fischer etc.*, revised R. Weber, Stuttgart, 1969
3.4	Vulgate, 1 Corinthians 13; see 3.3 above
4.1 (a)	St Augustine, *Confessiones* 8.12; ed. L. Verheijen, CC XXVI, Turnhout, 1981
4.1 (b)	St Augustine, *De civitate Dei* 11.10; ed. B. Dombart and A. Kalb, = CC XLVIII, Turnhout, 1955
4.2	St Jerome, *Epistulae* I; ed. I. Hilberg, CSEL LIV, pp. 1–9, Vienna/Leipzig, 1910
5.1	Caesarius of Arles, *Sermo* 238; ed. D. G. Morin, CC CIV, pp. 949–53, Turnhout, 1953
5.2	Prudentius, *Psychomachia* 310–43; ed. M. P. Cunningham, CC CXXVI, Turnhout, 1966
6.1	St Columba, *Altus prosator*, ed. F. Raby, *Oxford Book of Medieval Latin Verse*, no. 48, Oxford, 1959
6.2	St Columbanus, *Epistulae* 2.7; ed. G. S. M. Walker, Dublin Institute for Advanced Studies, Scriptores Latini Hibernici, Dublin, 1970, pp. 18, 20
6.3	St Adomnan, *Vita Sancti Columbae* II.27, 33; ed. A. O. and M. O. Anderson, London, 1961
7.1 (a)	Aldhelm, *De Virginitate* 26; ed. R. Ehwald, MGH, *Scriptores Antiquissimi* 15, Berlin, 1919
7.1 (b)	Aldhelm, *Aenigmata* 46, 89, 90; ed. F. Glorie, CC CXXXIII, Turnhout, 1968
7.2 (a)	Bede, *Ecclesiastical History* II.1–2; ed. B. Colgrave and R. A. B. Mynors, Oxford, 1969
7.2 (b)	Bede, *In Lucae Evangelium Expositio* VI, xiii.13–19 (lines 1341–85); ed. D. Hurst, CC CXX, Turnhout, 1960
7.3	*Miracula Nynie Episcopi* 150–82; ed. K. Strecker, PLAC IV.2, pp. 943–61, Berlin, 1923
7.4	Hygeburg of Heidenheim, *Vita Willibaldi Episcopi*

18.2   Bernard of Clairvaux, *Sermones super Cantica Canticorum* 40.1–2; ed. J. Leclercq, C. H. Talbot, H. M. Rochais, vol. II, pp. 24–6, Rome, 1958

18.3   Peter Abelard, *Theologia 'Scholarium'* II.112–13; ed. E. M. Buytaert and C. J. Mews, CCCM XIII, Turnhout, 1987

18.4   Alan of Lille, *Anticlaudianus* IX.149–206; ed. R. Bossuat, Paris, 1955

19.1   William FitzStephen, *Vita S. Thomae*; ed. J. G. Robertson, *Materials for the History of Thomas Becket*, vol. III, pp. 138–43, London, 1877

19.2   Giraldus Cambrensis, *Expugnatio Hibernica* I.46; ed. A. B. Scott and F. X. Martin, Dublin, 1978

19.3   Rahewin, *Gesta Friderici Imperatoris*, III.8–10, 16, 23; ed. G. Waitz, SRGUS 7, Hanover and Leipzig, 1912

20.1   Andreas Capellanus, *De Amore* I.8, 11; ed. P. G. Walsh, London, 1982

20.2   *Carmina Burana*, I.2, nos. 90 (p. 86), 158 (p. 268), 130 (p. 215); ed. A. Hilka, O. Schumann, B. Bischoff, Heidelberg, 1930–70

20.3   Peter of Blois, *Quod amicus suggerit*; ed. P. Dronke, *The Medieval Poet and his World*, pp. 304–7, Rome, 1984

20.4   The Archpoet, VIII; ed. K. Langosch, Stuttgart, 1965

20.5   Walter of Châtillon, *Alexandreis* VII. 235–52, 294–347; ed. Marvin L. Colker, Padua, 1978

20.6   Nigel Whiteacre, *Speculum stultorum* 2413–64; ed. J. H. Mozley and R. R. Raymo, Berkeley/Los Angeles, 1960

Abbreviations

abl.(ative)
abl.(ative) abs.(olute)
acc.(usative)
adj.(ective)
adv.(erb)
b.(orn)
c. circa
cf. compare (Latin *confer*)
ch.(apter)
CL Classical Latin
d.(ied)
dat.(ive)
dep.(onent)
dim.(inutive)
f.(eminine)
f.(ollowing)
fl.(oruit)
Fr.(ench)
fut.(ure)
G Grammar (p. 362)
gen.(itive)
Gen.(esis)
imper.(ative)
impf. (imperfect)
indecl.(inable)
indir.(ect)
inf.(initive)
intrans.(itive)
Intro.(duction)
It.(alian)
Jo John's gospel

l./ll. line(s)
lit.(erally)
Lk Luke's gospel
LL Late Latin
m.(asculine)
Mk Mark's gospel
ML Medieval Latin
ms./mss. manuscript(s)
Mt Matthew's gospel
n.(euter)
n.(ote)
NIV New International Version
nom.(inative)
O Orthography (p. 373)
obj.(ect)
OFr Old French
p./pp. page(s)
part.(iciple)
pf. (perfect)
pl.(ural)
plupf. pluperfect
pres.(ent)
Ps.(alm)
q.v. *quod vide* (see this)
Rev.(elation)
RL Reading Latin: Text
RLGVE Reading Latin: Grammar,
   Vocabulary and Exercises
RLRGr Reading Latin: Reference
   Grammar (= *RLGVE* pp. 448–
   556)

s.(ingular)

sc.   *scilicet* (presumably)

Sp.(anish)

subj.(unctive)

sup.(erlative)

tr.(anslate/anslation)

trans.(itive)

v./vv.   verse(s)

Vlg.   Vulgate

Introduction

The name of the book

Reading Medieval Latin is designed to follow on from *Reading Latin* (P. V. Jones and K. C. Sidwell, Cambridge University Press, 1986). But it can be used by any student who has learned the basic morphology and syntax of Classical Latin taught in *Reading Latin* sections 1–5.

How the book is arranged

The book is in four parts, each part being divided into five sections. Part one presents texts to illustrate the culture in which Medieval Latin (ML) developed and the sources on which its writers were nurtured. Part two presents selections of Latin written between *c.*500 and 1000. Parts three and four give fuller treatment of the Latin writing of the eleventh and twelfth centuries. A list of sources can be found on pp. xi–xvi.

Each part, section and text has introductory material, with suggestions for further reading. Each text has a commentary with help on language and content. In most cases, reference to text is by line number. However, reference is sometimes by numbered paragraph (e.g. in section 3). The linguistic help is keyed in to two brief appendices on Orthography and Grammar, which are referred to by O.0 etc. and G.1 etc. respectively. Other grammar references are to *Reading Latin: Grammar, Vocabulary and Exercises* (*RLGVE*) or Reading Latin: Reference Grammar (RLRGr), found at *RLGVE* pp. 448–56.

For vocabulary, the reader is advised to use a Classical Latin dictionary (say Cassell's) in the first place. The word-list at the end of the book aims to help with items not included there and with non-classical spellings. Names of people and places are in the main glossed in the commentaries. See further Note on vocabulary (pp. 376–7).

The texts

The texts have been printed as found in the sources (see pp. xif.), without changes of spelling. This means that there is no consistent convention for the consonantal vowels, which are written u or v, i or j according to the policy of the editor of the source. Vowel length has not been marked, but unclassical quantities in poems using classical metres are indicated by the use of ¯ and ˘.

The texts have been selected for their intrinsic interest and for the way they illustrate important aspects of medieval culture, history, philosophy, religion, literature or language. The book may be used as a historical introduction to ML writing in its cultural and historical context, or excerpted as a reader to accompany courses on philosophy, history or literature.

The texts are not arranged in order of difficulty, but the commentaries are designed to give the same level of help at every point. Hence the book may be begun anywhere and selections made on the basis of the reader's specific interests. Readers interested in classicizing poetry are strongly advised to read the verse selections and metrical explanations in *Reading Latin* section 6 before moving on to this book. Those looking for the simplest passages to begin with are advised to start with section 3 (the Vulgate). Some very difficult passages (e.g. section 7.1(a)) have been inserted (with appropriate help) to underline the fact that much ML writing is highly complex and sophisticated.

In general, an attempt has been made to avoid passages already anthologized.

Medieval Latin

Ludwig Traube once said: 'There is no such thing as Medieval Latin. Consequently there will never be a dictionary or a grammar of Medieval Latin.' He meant that ML has no separate *linguistic* existence. It is *Latin*, learned from late classical grammars, with variations in spelling, occasional errors in morphology, a syntax influenced by external phenomena (e.g. other languages, or the creation of equivalences between different CL conjunctions (*dum* for *cum* etc.)) and a vocabulary expanded to meet the needs of a changed environment, both external and intellectual.

In this book, for this and for purely practical reasons, ML is treated as a series of divergences from CL, whether in orthography or grammar. The principle is *discitur ambulando*. No consistent attempt is made to give an account of the reasons for changes. For that the reader is referred in the

first place to E. Löfstedt, *Late Latin*, Oslo, 1959. A fuller account of
divergences without a linguistic explanation can be found in A. Blaise,
Manuel du Latin Chrétien, Turnhout, 1955 (now available in English, tr. G.
C. Roti, *A Handbook of Christian Latin: Style, Morphology, and Syntax*
Georgetown U. Press, Washington, D.C., 1992). For dictionaries, see the
Note on vocabulary, pp. 376–7.

Further study

Some of the texts have been taken from sources such as the Oxford
Medieval Texts series, which are accompanied by facing-page translations.
These are a good next step from this anthology.

   There are series of ML texts specifically designed for students.
Particularly useful and accessible are:

> Toronto Medieval Latin Texts (published for the Centre for
>   Medieval Studies by the Pontifical Institute of Mediaeval Studies,
>   Toronto)
> Reading University Medieval and Renaissance Texts (published now
>   by Bristol Classical Press, a subsidiary of Duckworth)

Study of the material by genre will be made easier by a forthcoming
anthology by F. A. C. Mantello and A. G. Rigg, which will accompany
the new *Medieval Latin: An Introduction and Bibliographical Guide* replacing
McGuire and Dressler, *Introduction to Medieval Latin Studies*, Washington,
D.C., 1977.

PART ONE

The foundations of Christian Latin

The term 'Christian Latin' has no linguistic validity. There was no 'special language' which only Christians used, distinguished clearly from that employed by pagans. The various registers of Latin, from 'vulgar' at the lowest end to the sophisticated and complex language of high literary products at the other, were always clearly distinguished from each other as far as their function was concerned, whether used by pagans or Christians. The only linguistic feature which united the registers as employed specifically by Christians was the specialized Christian vocabulary (e.g. *baptizo* 'I baptize'; *sinaxis* 'Divine Office'). This was also the only feature which distinguished pagan writings in the various registers from Christian. The possibility of making such a distinction soon vanishes anyway, since the decree of the emperor Theodosius in 394 which made Christianity the official religion of the Roman Empire also led inexorably to the Christianization of all Latin writing.

The usefulness of the term lies in its definition of a cultural phenomenon. After the final dissolution of its centralized secular power structure in the fifth century, the Western Roman Empire was supplanted as the 'universal empire' by the Catholic Church. As an expression of this continuing universality, the Church adopted and retained Latin. This, then, was the language of its sacred texts, its liturgy, its ecclesiastical administration, and therefore of its education system. To maintain this universality, it was necessary to keep unbroken the links with the vital core of Christian thought. This was expressed by the inspired writings of the Bible and the Fathers of the Church. It was essential continually to praise God through the *opus Dei* ('Divine Office'), whose central texts were the Psalms. These factors combined to ensure the survival of Latin as an unchanging language. Unchanging, that is, in its morphology and, by and large, in its syntax. Its vocabulary was added to constantly as new needs arose (e.g. *bombarda* 'cannon', in the fifteenth century), or words changed their meaning (e.g. *rotulus* CL 'little wheel'; ML 'roll' – see section 15.3), or were transferred from the vernacular language (e.g. *sopa* 'shop').

Children – male and (early on especially) female (for 'in Christ there is no male and female', Galatians 3.28) – learned Latin if they were dedicated to the Church. What they studied, after the painful process of basic grammar learning was over, were, on the whole, Christian texts. What they produced, if they ever gained enough proficiency, were works in one way or another associated with the propagation of the Church's message. These factors were always central. There were increasingly moments when the secular power began once more to use learning as a tool to propagate its own agenda (e.g. during the 'Carolingian Renaissance' – see section 9), and this pattern led eventually to a more secular use of Latin, both as an administrative tool and for other purposes. Even so, until the advent of 'humanism' in the fourteenth century in Italy there was no idea of a Latin education which was not firmly based upon the centrality of the core Christian texts.

What we call 'Medieval Latin' is Latin written after the end of the Roman Empire until the Italian Renaissance (fourteenth–sixteenth centuries), when we change to the term 'Neo-Latin'. There is vast diversity within this corpus of writing, because it covers a period in which enormous political and social changes occur and a geographical region which incorporates many ethnic groups with diverse approaches even to Christianity. Nonetheless, Latin and Latin learned through and with the foundation texts of the monastic rules, the liturgy, the Bible, the Church Fathers and the legacy of earlier Christian writing, binds it together. So this first part focuses on what most medieval writers would have known and expected their audience to know, and attempts to illustrate the impact of Christianity on the formation of new literary genres.

Section 1
Education

The Roman education system was geared to producing speakers. In both its practical and theoretical aspects, it reflected a world where the word and its presentation were central to civic life. Even under the imperial system, where real power was effectively removed from the aristocratic élite which had frequented the oratorical schools, the basis remained the same. In the late first century AD, Quintilian (*Institutiones*) attempted to argue for an oratorical education which was essentially encyclopaedic and general. But rhetoric was losing its practical usefulness. It was not until the fifth century that educators tried to push things in a different direction. For the first time the seven liberal arts are set as the basis for the new school curriculum: Grammar, Logic and Rhetoric (later known as the *Trivium*), Music, Geometry, Arithmetic and Philosophy (or Astronomy – the later *Quadrivium*). The first treatise of this type was Martianus Capella's *De Nuptiis Mercurii et Philologiae* 'On the marriage of Mercury and Philology', revised a century later by the Christian rhetorician Memor Felix. In the sixth century, Cassiodorus wrote the *Institutiones*, to provide a safe equivalent of traditional education – both Christian and pagan – for his monks. Both treatises were immensely influential during the Middle Ages, along with the *Etymologiae* of Isidore of Seville (602–36).

Works like those of Cassiodorus and Isidore were models for later educators' expanded compilations. In the first part of his work, Cassiodorus gives a sort of bibliography of biblical studies. When he moves to the liberal arts, he gives a précis of knowledge derived from various authorities. For example, in the section on Logic (*Dialectica*) he gives an outline of the *Isagoge* ('Introduction') of Porphyry, the *Categoriae* ('Categories') of Aristotle, the *De Interpretatione* ('On Interpretation') of Aristotle, and so on. Isidore's compilation gives the definitions and origins of words (often highly fancifully). For example:

Mare est aquarum generalis collectio. Omnis enim congregatio aquarum, sive salsae sint, sive dulces, abusive maria nuncupantur, iuxta illud: Et congregationes aquarum vocavit maria. Proprie autem mare appellatum, eo quod aquae eius amarae sint.

(Etymologiae 13.1, ed. W. M. Lindsay, Oxford, 1911)

A sea is a general collection of waters. For every congregation of waters, whether salt or fresh, is called a sea, inaccurately, on the following authority: 'And the congregations of waters he called seas' [Genesis 1.10]. Now *mare* is properly so called because its waters are *amarae* (bitter).

It must be said, however, that what actually happened in schools did not fit the theoretical structures envisaged by the manuals. A child (normally a boy, though nuns were in some traditions required to know some Latin – see sections 2.4, 7.4, 10.4, 17.5) would enter a monastery as an oblate at seven. In the later period, he might instead attend a cathedral school. He would begin with an elementary course which aimed to teach reading and writing in Latin, singing (*cantus*) and calculation (*computus*). The first texts to which he would be exposed were the Psalms, which doubled as a chant textbook. The *computus* was not only an introduction to basic arithmetic, but also included the study of time and especially the annual and liturgical calendars. This elementary curriculum was followed by the intensive study of *grammatica*, which was pursued with the help of the late Roman textbooks by Donatus and Priscian. Here they learned, for example, that the perfect passive could be *lectum est* or *lectum fuit*, the pluperfect *lectum erat* or *lectum fuerat* (Donatus *Ars Minor* 4.361), and that the passive has two participles, a past (*lectus*) and a future (*legendus*). There are many examples of these Late Latin forms in this book. Later, new compilations were composed, such as that of the Mercian Tatwine (d. 734), from which the following passage comes:

DE CONPARATIONE

Conparatio est eloquutio quae ex alterius conlatione alterum praefert; nam de uno numquam dicitur 'doctior' nisi ad alterius conparationem respiciatur. Conparatio autem aut auget aut minuit et ipsud quod minuit ad sensum auget, ceterum ad sonum minuit, ut 'doctus, doctior, doctissimus': ecce hic auxit; item 'stultus, stultior, stultissimus': minuit, sed tamen auxit, ut si dicas 'mendicus' qui parum habet, 'mendicior' qui minus habet, 'mendicissimus' qui minimum: sed tamen auxit sensum, nam paupertatis augmentum per gradus creuit.

(Ars Tatuini, chapter 26, ed. M. de Marco, CCCM cxxxiii, p. 13,
Turnhout, 1968)

COMPARISON

Comparison is a way of speaking which expresses a preference for one of a pair by comparison with the other; for the word 'more learned' is never used of one person unless it refers to comparison with a second. Comparison either increases or diminishes and that which it diminishes it increases as regards the sense, but diminishes as regards the sound, for example 'clever, cleverer, cleverest': here, as you see, it has increased it; likewise 'stupid, stupider, stupidest': it has diminished it, but yet it has increased it, as if you were to call 'mendicant' him who has little, 'more mendicant' him who has less, and 'most mendicant' him who has the least: but nonetheless it has increased the sense, since the increase in poverty grew by stages.

As this excerpt shows, *grammatica* was an analytical tool as much as a linguistic aid, and it dominated the way in which language was perceived and used. Fluency in both speaking and writing Latin was aided by puzzles (see section 7.1(b)), jokes, set speeches and dialogues like this colloquium written for his school by Aelfric, abbot of Eynsham from 1005:

MAGISTER: Fuisti hodie verberatus?
PUER: Non fui, quia caute me tenui.
MAGISTER: Et quomodo tui socii?
PUER: Quid me interrogas de hoc? Non audeo pandere secreta nostra. Unusquisque scit si flagellatus erat an non.

MASTER: Were you beaten today?
PUPIL: No, I wasn't, because I was careful.
MASTER: And what about your friends?
PUPIL: Why are you asking me about that? I don't dare reveal our secrets. Each one knows whether he was beaten or not.

Those who were able then pursued a further course of *grammatica*, which included the study of Roman poets such as Virgil, Horace, Lucan, Ovid and Juvenal, early ML poets such as Claudian, Prudentius (section 5.2) and Venantius Fortunatus (section 8.4(a)–(b)), and prose authors. The method was pedestrian. The master would read the text and analyse it word by word, explaining the grammar and the references and commenting on the meaning. The texts read covered the fields of law, rhetoric and logic, though the fact that they often led into other areas such as geometry or medicine allowed discussion of those too. The focus did not stay the same throughout the Middle Ages. Grammar dominated the curriculum of the

ninth century, while dialectic became predominant in the twelfth. Rhetoric
was not important until Alcuin of York's time (see section 9.2(b)).

The goal of this training was the preservation and propagation of the
Christian religion. As a decree of Charlemagne (see section 9 Intro.) put it,
'there must be schools in monasteries or cathedrals consisting of boys who
study the psalms, orthography, chant, *computus* and *grammatica*, and well-
corrected catholic books'.

The repositories of learning during the early Middle Ages were the
monasteries. In these often isolated fastnesses, books were hoarded and
copied, and new books written (especially commentaries on the liberal arts
or on parts of the Bible). What could be known was entirely a matter of
which books the monastery's library possessed. Later, the monasteries were
joined by the cathedrals. We have some catalogues from the later period,
like the twelfth-century list from Durham. Here is a sample of its contents:

1.2. Vetus et novum testamentum in duobus voluminibus et 3.4. item vetus et
novum testamentum in duobus minoribus voluminibus. – 5. Iosephus
antiquitatum. – 6–9. duo paria decretorum Ivonis. – 10. epistolae Ivonis. –
11. decreta pontificum. – 12. excerpta canonum. ... 14. epistolae sancti
Ieronimi. – 15. Ieronimus super Isaiam. – 16. Ieronimus super duodecim
prophetas...

1.2. Old and new testament in two volumes and 3.4. Likewise an old and new
testament in two smaller volumes. – 5. Josephus' *Antiquities*. – 6–9. Two sets of
the decrees of Ivo [of Chartres, who wrote on Canon Law: see section 16.3
Intro.]. – 10. Ivo's Letters. 11. Papal decrees. – 12. Excerpts from the canons. –
14. St Jerome's Epistles. – 15. Jerome on Isaiah. – 16. Jerome on the Twelve
prophets...'

The list is dominated by copies of the sacred texts, biblical commentaries,
ecclesiastical law and the Church Fathers. Now and again, pagan classical
texts occur and in some places they may even form a significant portion of
the collection. It is rare, however, for this proportion to be more than one
fifth of the whole. Throughout our period, the work of God is at the heart
of the library as of the rest of the educational establishment.

See further: P. Riché, *Education and Culture in the Barbarian West, Sixth
Through Eighth Centuries*, tr. J. J. Contreni, Columbia, S.C., 1976 and *Les
écoles et l'enseignement dans l'occident chrétien de la fin du Ve siècle au milieu du
XIe siècle*, Paris, 1979; R. R. Bolgar, *The Classical Heritage and its
Beneficiaries*, Cambridge, 1954.

1. Rules of St Benedict and St Isidore

Monasteries were organized as self-sufficient communities, whose work supported the process of learning. Early on, the Rules of such communities were formulated. There were several, including the Rule of Pachomius, translated into Latin by Jerome, Augustine's Letter 211 (later the basis of the Rule of St Augustine) and the *Regula magistri* ('Rule of the master'). This latter was the basis for the most influential Rule of all, that of St Benedict, composed *c*.530–60, which became the guide to the Benedictine Order. Benedict's date of birth is traditionally put in 480 and his birthplace was Nursia, around sixty miles north-east of Rome. His life coincided with the wars fought by the Emperor Justinian against the Ostrogothic rulers of the West. Nothing is known of him except what Pope Gregory the Great records in the second book of his *Dialogues*. This reveals him as the head of several monastic communities. Gregory, who wrote before the end of the sixth century, elsewhere quotes the Rule, which had clearly become known and respected very soon after its composition.

The following excerpts are from Benedict's Rule and another – perhaps somewhat later – Rule (before 613) ascribed to St Isidore of Seville. The language of both rules is marked by elements of 'vulgar' usage (e.g. *comparare* for *emere* 'to buy', *meminere* for *meminisse* 'to remember', *paruissimus* for *minimus* 'smallest', *ab Idus* for *ab Idibus* 'from the Ides', the use of nom. or acc. for abl. abs. etc.).

1(a) *St Benedict's Rule* (Benedicti Regula)

Benedict enunciates the rules governing readings at meals, which are to be done by a 'weekly reader' to a silent refectory.

XXXVIII DE EBDOMADARIO LECTORE

1. Mensis fratrum lectio deesse non debet, nec fortuito casu qui arripuerit codicem legere ibi, sed lecturus tota ebdomada dominica ingrediatur.
2. Qui ingrediens post missas et communionem, petat ab omnibus pro se orari, ut auertat ab ipso Deus spiritum elationis.
3. Et dicatur hic uersus in oratorio tertio ab omnibus, ipso tamen incipiente, Domine, labia mea aperies, et os meum annuntiabit laudem tuam.
4. Et sic accepta benedictione, ingrediatur ad legendum.
5. Et summum fiat silentium, ut nullius musitatio uel uox nisi solius legentis ibi audiatur.

6.   Quae uero necessaria sunt comedentibus et bibentibus, sic sibi uicissim ministrent fratres, ut nullus indigeat petere aliquid.

7.   Si quid tamen opus fuerit, sonitu cuiuscumque signi potius petatur quam uoce.

8.   Nec praesumat ibi aliquis de ipsa lectione aut aliunde quicquam requirere, ne detur occasio,

9.   nisi forte prior pro aedificatione uoluerit aliquid breuiter dicere.

10. Frater autem lector ebdomadarius accipiat mixtum, priusquam incipiat legere, propter communionem sanctam et ne forte grabe sit ei ieiunium sustinere.

11. Postea autem cum coquinae ebdomadariis et seruitoribus reficiat.

12. Fratres autem non per ordinem legant aut cantent, sed qui aedificant audientes.

---

1 **nec...qui...legere:** 'And let no one pick up...to read' (*nec qui* = *et ne quis*). For *legere* (inf. of purpose) see G.17(a), 27(a).
lecturus: 'the person who is going to read'.
tota ebdomada: 'for the whole week' (abl. instead of acc. See G.16(c)).
dominica: sc. *die*.

2 **Qui:** i.e. 'the reader'.
petat...pro se orari: 'let him ask that prayers be said' (the infinitive is impersonal 'that it be prayed': see RLGVE 155 Note 2. See also G.23(a)).
ipso: 'him' (see G.11(a)(i)–(ii)).

3 **ipso:** see n. above.
Domine...tuam: Ps. 50.17. *aperies* is future used as imperative 'open'.

6 **sibi uicissim:** 'to one another' (see G.11(e)(ii)).
aliquid: 'anything' (see G.11(f)).

7 **Si...fuerit:** 'If there is...'.
sonitu cuiuscumque signi: 'by the sound of some sign' (*quicumque* is used for *aliquis*, cf. G.11(f)). *sonitu* is being used metaphorically, since signs make no noise, and even banging the cutlery would disturb the reading. Later on, at Cluny (founded 910), silence became a

more integral part of monastic life and an intricate sign-language was developed. Bread was requested by a circular motion made with the thumbs and first two fingers of both hands. Some such system was clearly already in use in Benedict's day.
aliquis: 'anyone' (see G.11(f)).
ipsa: 'the' (see G.11(a)(i)–(ii)).
aliunde quicquam: 'about anything else' (see G.13).
ne detur occasio: sc. *loquendi*.

9 **nisi...uoluerit:** 'unless...wishes'.
prior: 'the prior'.

10 **mixtum:** 'a small portion of bread and wine'.
propter communionem sanctam: i.e. because he might commit an involuntary irreverence (such as spitting out the host) if he reads without ingesting anything after the mass.
grabe: i.e. *graue* (see O.13).

11 **reficiat:** 'refresh himself'.

12 **qui aedificant:** '(only those) who edify'. Indistinct, badly phrased, mispronounced or monotonous reading would not fulfil the requirement that the *lectio* should instruct the monks.

1(b) The Rule of St Isidore

Rules for the borrowing and return of books, the asking of questions and forbidden reading.

DE CODICIBUS

1. Omnes codices custos sacrarii habeat deputatos, a quo singulos singuli fratres accipiant, quos prudenter lectos vel habitos semper post vesperam reddant. Prima autem hora codices singulis diebus petantur; qui vero tardius postulat, nequaquam accipiat.

2. De his autem quaestionibus, quae leguntur, nec forte intelliguntur, unusquisque fratrum aut in collatione aut post vesperam abbatem interroget, et, recitata in loco lectione, ab eo expositionem suscipiat, ita ut, dum uni exponitur, caeteri audiant.

3. Gentilium libros vel haereticorum volumina monachus legere caveat; melius est enim eorum perniciosa dogmata ignorare, quam per experientiam in aliquem laqueum erroris incurrere.

1 **habeat deputatos:** 'let him have assigned', 'let him assign'.
  habitos: 'and (properly) looked after'.
  vesperam: 'Vespers' (see section 2 Intro. for the monastic day).
  qui: 'he who...'.
2 **his:** 'those' (see G.11(c)).
  collatione: 'supper' (so called from the reading during the meal of Cassianus' *Collationes*).

3 **legere caveat:** 'take care not to read' (the more normal construction is with *ne* + subj. or subj. alone. Seé RLRGr p. 413 on Section 6A(iii) ll.18–19). The reason given in Isidore's *Sententiae* III. 12–13, is that to 'read the inventions of the poets draws the mind by way of delight in empty stories towards the inducements of lust'.

2. Cassiodorus, *Institutiones*

Flavius Magnus Aurelius Cassiodorus Senator (*c.*490–583), a Roman aristocrat and contemporary with St Benedict, retired to a monastery which he created on his own estate at Vivarium in southern Italy, after service with the Ostrogothic king Theodoric. Here he composed a programme of studies for the monks, including classical orators and Aristotle's logic. It was in two parts, dealing with divine and secular letters. The purpose of studying the latter was to prepare the student for a better grasp of sacred Scripture. The survival and popularity of his *Institutiones* ('Institutes') was one of the forces which kept alive the possibility of a revival of classical learning. In this passage, he stresses the importance of studying orthography, the only way of keeping the texts pure at a time when the spoken language was affecting the phonology and so the spelling of Latin.

See further: J. J. O'Donnell, *Cassiodorus*, Berkeley/Los Angeles/London, 1979

(i) *The justification for placing scribal activity at the centre of the monastic work.*

Ego tamen fateor votum meum, quod, inter vos quaecumque possunt corporeo labore compleri, antiquariorum mihi studia, si tamen veraciter scribant, non immerito forsitan plus placere, quod et mentem suam relegendo Scripturas divinas salutariter instruunt et Domini praecepta scribendo longe lateque disseminant. Felix intentio, laudanda sedulitas, manu hominibus   5
praedicare, digitis linguas aperire, salutem mortalibus tacitum dare, et contra diaboli subreptiones illicitas calamo atramentoque pugnare. Tot enim vulnera Satanas accipit, quot antiquarius Domini verba describit. Uno itaque loco situs, operis sui disseminatione per diversas provincias vadit; in locis sanctis legitur labor ipsius; audiunt populi unde se a prava voluntate convertant, et Domino   10
pura mente deserviant; operatur absens de opere suo. Nequeo dicere vicissitudinem illum de tot bonis non posse percipere, si tamen non cupiditatis ambitu sed recto studio talia noscatur efficere. Verba caelestia multiplicat homo, et quadam significatione contropabili, si fas est dicere, tribus digitis scribitur quod virtus sanctae Trinitatis effatur. O spectaculum bene conside-   15
rantibus gloriosum! Arundine currente verba caelestia describuntur, ut, unde diabolus caput Domini in passione fecit percuti, inde eius calliditas possit extingui. Accidit etiam laudibus eorum, quod factum Domini aliquo modo videntur emitari, qui legem suam, licet figuraliter sit dictum, omnipotentis digiti operatione conscripsit. Multa sunt quidem quae de tam insigni arte   20
referantur, sed sufficit eos dici librarios, qui librae Domini iustitiaeque deserviunt.

1f. **Ego...disseminant:** 'I confess my preference, that of all the things that can...., the studies of the scribes (provided they write correctly) please me most, because they (the scribes)...' The structure is: *Ego fateor uotum meum* (namely) *quod* (that) *quaecumque* (of all the things that)...*compleri* (understand *inter uos* with *compleri*), *antiquariorum...studia* (continuing the *quod* clause), *si tamen* (provided that...)...*scribant, non immerito ...placere* (back to the *quod* clause: he has slipped into acc. + inf. - so understand *placere* as the verb), *quod* (because) ... *instruunt*.

5f. **Felix...praedicare:** '(It is) a happy purpose...to...'.

6 **tacitum:** 'silently' (acc. agreeing with the unstated subject of the inf. *dare*).

8 **situs:** i.e. the *antiquarius*.

10 **ipsius:** 'his' (see G.11(a)(ii)).

unde...convertant: 'by what means to...' (lit. 'from where...').

11 **operatur absens de opere suo:** 'he works (or serves God) although absent from his work'. Note the pun in *operatur...opere*.

12 **si tamen:** 'if nonetheless', i.e. 'provided that' (CL *dum, dummodo*).

12f. **cupiditatis ambitu:** 'from the vanity of ambition', i.e. 'from vain ambition' (abl. of cause, RLRGr L(f)4(iii)).

14 **contropabili:** 'figurative' (a hybrid word, composed from Greek *tropos* 'figure', 'trope'. Cf. the common words *tropologia, tropologice* 'figurative language', 'figuratively').

15 **quod:** 'that which', 'what'

15f. **bene considerantibus:** 'to those who think (about it) properly'

16f. **unde...inde:** 'by the (same) means with which the devil..., by those means...'. This is a reference to the reed (*arundo*) first used mockingly as a sceptre for Jesus by his executioners and then to strike his head (Mt 27.29–30). The Christian scribe uses the *arundo* (pen) to undo the harm done by the devil through the Roman soldiers' reed.

17 **fecit percuti:** 'caused to be struck' (see G.17(c)).

18 **Accidit...quod:** 'It happens...that' (see G.26(b)).
laudibus eorum: 'through their praises' (sc. of God, i.e. their work of writing).

19 **emitari:** i.e. *imitari* (see O.11).

19f. **qui...conscripsit:** cf. e.g. Exodus 31.18: *deditque Dominus Moysi...duas tabulas testimonii scriptas digito Dei* 'And the Lord gave Moses... the two tablets of the Testimony, written by the finger of God.' Cassiodorus remarks that these tablets

had not literally been engraved by God's finger!

20f. **quae...referantur:** 'such as might be said' (generic *qui* clause: see RLRGr Q2(a))

21 **sufficit...dici:** 'it is enough for them to be called...'

librarios...librae: another pun (see above *operatur...opere*). *librarii* are scribes (from *liber* 'book'), while *libra* is the 'balance of God', a symbol of justice (cf. e.g. Proverbs 16.11: *Pondus et statera iudicia Domini sunt* 'The weight and the balance are God's justice'; Daniel 5.27: *appensus es in statera et inventus es minus habens* 'You have been weighed in the balance and found wanting'). Tr. '*penmen*', '*dispensations*'.

(ii) *A bibliography for orthographic studies.*

Sed ne tanto bono mutatis litteris scriptores verba vitiosa permisceant aut ineruditus emendator nesciat errata corrigere, orthographos antiquos legant, id est, Velium Longum, Curtium Valerianum, Papirianum, Adamantium Martyrium de V et B, eiusdem de primis mediis atque ultimis syllabis, eiusdem de B littera trifariam in nomine posita, et Eutychen de aspiratione, sed et Focam de 5
differentia generis; quos ego quantos potui studiosa curiositate collegi. Et ne quempiam memoratorum codicum obscuritas derelicta turbaret, quoniam antiquarum declinationum permixtione pro maxima parte confusi sunt, magno studio laboris incubui, ut in libro sequestrato atque composito, qui inscribitur de Orthographia, ad vos defloratae regulae pervenirent, et dubietate 10
sublata liberior animus viam emendationis incederet. Diomedem quoque et Theoctistum aliqua de tali arte scripsisse comperimus; qui si inventi fuerint, vos quoque eorum deflorata colligite. Forte et alios invenire possitis, per quos notitia vestra potius instruatur. Isti tamen qui memorati sunt, si assiduo studio relegantur, omnem vobis caliginem ignorationis abscidunt, ut quod hactenus 15
ignoratum est habeatur ex maxima parte notissimum.

1 **ne tanto bono...verba vitiosa permisceant:** 'so that they don't mix wrong words with such good' (i.e. corrupt the message by making spelling mistakes or grammatical errors).

3f. **Velium Longum ... Adamantium Martyrium:** very little has survived of the works of the late grammarians (e.g. Adamantius Martyrius a writer of the first half of the sixth century AD) mentioned in this passage. Velius Longus

was a grammarian of the early second century AD (his *De Orthographia* survives); nothing is known of Curtius Valerianus; Papirianus, who was known also to Priscian, wrote a (lost) *De Orthographia* in the late fourth or early fifth century AD; Adamantinus Martyrius belongs to the early sixth century AD. His *De B muta et V vocali* survives.

4 **de V et B:** When to write which had become a

problem, since the phonemes represented by these letters were not totally distinct any more (see O.13).

de...ultimis syllabis: The final syllable, containing the crucial syntactical information (case, number, gender, person, tense, voice, etc.), was generally given less emphasis now that the spoken language had stress accent rather than pitch accent. But words in the spoken language close to their written counterparts might trap unsuspecting scribes into misspellings at other points too. They might, for example, write *hispatium* for *spatium* (prosthesis – see O.22), or *caldus* for *calidus* (syncope – see O.9).

4f. **de B littera trifariam...posita:** i.e. *b* pronounced *b, p* or *v*. In the intervocalic position, the spellings *-b-* and *-u-/-v-* are often morphologically crucial (*abibit* is future tense, *abivit* perfect). It was essential, therefore, not to allow the uncertain distinction between the phonemes to befog the meaning of a written text.

5 **Eutychen:** Greek acc. (see RLR.Gr H6).

de aspiratione: The letter h represents aspiration in initial position (e.g. *hortus*) and was used elsewhere with *c, p, t* to represent the Greek letters χ, φ, θ in words of Greek origin (e.g. *philosophus*). In speech, the aspirate disappeared early. But in writing, it produced semantic distinctions (such as *os/hos* 'mouth'/'these'; *ortus/hortus* 'having arisen'/'garden'), and it was important to retain it. Once the acquisition of Greek was not automatic (Cassiodorus knows it, but expects that many of his monks might not), the position of *-h-* with the consonants also became a source of difficulty, requiring manuals. See O.3.

5f. **de differentia generis:** in the spoken language, the neuter had probably disappeared (see G.2: e.g. *vinum* 62 *vinus* probably covers *vino*). A scribe needed to learn the correct genders carefully to avoid misconstruing agreements and altering endings to produce wrong sense.

7 **obscuritas derelicta:** 'the inherent obscurity' (lit. 'bequeathed'; sc. 'with the mss.').

8 **antiquarum declinationum permixtione:** 'because of the mixing up of the old inflections', i.e. nobody could tell e.g. 3rd conjugation from 2nd and 4th declension from 2nd, and feminines from neuter plurals. Lack of education led to confusion in Latin. This problem became even greater as educational institutions declined over the next two centuries (see section 8 Intro.).

9 **magno studio laboris:** 'with great zeal of labour' (i.e. 'with hard work enthusiastically undertaken').

sequestrato atque composito: 'separate and compiled' (i.e. 'a separate volume of my own composition').

10 **de Orthographia:** Orthography continued to be a central concern of Latin teachers. It was at the heart of the Carolingian reforms (see section 9). The architect of these, Alcuin of York, also composed a treatise with the same name in the late eighth century.

defloratae regulae: 'selected rules' (lit. 'the pick of the bunch', plucked like flowers).

11 **viam emendationis:** 'the path of emendation', i.e. once they know the proper rules, they will more easily be able to correct the errors in their mss.

12 **aliqua:** 'some things' n.pl.

inventi fuerint: see G.4(a).

13 **deflorata:** 'selections' (see note above on **defloratae regulae**). Selection from authorities was a fundamental literary activity of the Middle Ages. Such compilations were called *florilegia* 'bunches of flowers'. They were often the direct source for quotations or *exempla* from both patristic and classical writers.

14f. **si...relegantur, ...abscidunt:** 'if they are read... they will/can...'.

16 **habeatur...notissimum:** 'may be for the most part very well known' (*habeo* in the passive in CL can mean 'I am'. So also *se habere*.).

(iii) *A sacred book is judged by its cover.*

His etiam addidimus in codicibus cooperiendis doctos artifices, ut litterarum pulchritudinem facies desuper decora vestiret, exemplum illud Dominicae

figurationis ex aliqua parte forsitan imitantes, qui eos quos ad cenam aestimat
invitandos in gloria caelestis convivii stolis nuptialibus operuit. Quibus
multiplices species facturarum in uno codice depictas, ni fallor, decenter   5
expressimus, ut qualem maluerit studiosus tegumenti formam ipse sibi possit
elegere.

1 **his etiam:** i.e. 'to scribes'.
in codicibus cooperiendis: i.e. 'in bookbinding'. The codex, a ms. organized in pages like our book, was now the standard form of written document. It had replaced the more cumbersome roll (see text 4.1(a) for Augustine's use of one).

2 **facies desuper decora:** 'a beautiful external form' (if *desuper* qualifies the noun, it is a Graecism, see G.10). The phrase may be modelled on Song of Songs 2.14: *et facies tua decora* 'And your face is beautiful'.

2f. **Dominicae figurationis:** 'of the Lord's parable'. At Mt 22.1ff., Jesus likens the kingdom of Heaven to a wedding-feast, to which only those properly dressed are admitted. In the same way, codices containing the sacred texts must show by their beautiful bindings where they truly belong.

4 **Quibus:** 'for them', i.e. 'the bookbinders'.

4f. **multiplices species facturarum:** 'many styles of work' (i.e. 'of binding').

5 **ni:** = *nisi*.

6 **qualem maluerit...formam:** 'the sort of binding he prefers' (pf. subj.: 'he has expressed a preference for', or fut. pf. 'he will have...'. But translate as present. See G. 24(b)).

Section 2
Liturgy and Divine Office

Education was in the first instance a by-product of the Church's central purpose, to celebrate the Eucharist and to keep up a constant stream of prayer to God. These two functions were fulfilled by the Mass and the Divine Office respectively. In the Western Church from the latter part of the fourth century, these were conducted in Latin. In the early period, two distinct types of liturgy were used in different areas, the Roman, which ultimately became standard, and the Gallican, which probably originated in the East.

The chants used in the Ordinary of the Mass consisted of Kyrie eleison, Gloria, Credo, Sanctus and Agnus Dei, and those of the Proper of Introit, Gradual, Alleluia (or Tract), Offertory and Communion. From the tenth century onwards, various items appear in mss. with additional texts plus music. Two important types are the 'sequence' (*prosa*; see section 10.2 Intro.) and the 'trope' (*tropus*), a composition of new music and text used as an introduction to or insert into an introit, offertory or communion chant. One of these (the *Quem quaeritis in sepulchro* dialogue), which was performed before the introit for the Mass on Easter morning, probably led eventually to the development of the liturgical drama.

From the earliest period onwards, the prayer function was divided into two basic types of Office, the cathedral and the monastic. Most is known about the monastic Office, because it is described in detail in the monastic Rules, such as those of Caesarius of Arles (see section 5.1) and St Benedict of Nursia (see section 1.1(a) and 2.1 below). However, there was wide variation throughout the Middle Ages in the structure of the Office and its performance. This became less so with the development of the *breviarium* ('breviary'), which by the thirteenth century had regularized the Office and collected the materials within the covers of one book.

The Office was performed at certain times of the day and night known as *horae* ('hours'). The night Office (*matutini* 'matins', also called 'nocturns' or 'vigils') might begin around 2.10 a.m. and end at 3.30 a.m. The day

Office contained seven *horae*, lauds, prime, terce, sext, none, vespers and
compline. Each service contained a mixture of Psalms (see 2.2) antiphons,
verses (recited from the Bible), Old and New Testament canticles (e.g. the
Benedictus from Lk 1.68–79, the Magnificat from Lk 1.46–55 and the
Nunc dimittis from Lk 2.29–32), hymns (see 2.3), collects, *capitula* (short
readings, often from Paul's Epistles), and readings from the Bible (see
section 3), the Church Fathers (see section 4), or saints' lives. In the
Benedictine Rule, the Office was so organized as to complete the cycle of
the Psalms once every week. It is no wonder that the writings of monks in
particular drip with citations from and reminiscences of the Psalter (see e.g.
section 17.2).

There were other elements to liturgical observance, of course, covering
the principal secular rites of passage, baptism and burial, as well as such
areas as ordinations to the offices of deacon, priest and bishop. It is
important to note the complete interpenetration of sacred and secular in
this world. A good example would be the ecclesiastical ceremonies for the
coronation of kings (see section 10.3) and the emperor (see section
12.3(iii)).

1. St Benedict (*fl. c.530*)

For details about St Benedict, see above, section 1.1(a) Intro. After a
number of general precepts concerning the types of the monastic life, the
nature of the abbot, consultation, obedience, silence and humility, the Rule
turns to a detailed prescription of the *opus Dei*. It covers the number of
psalms to be sung during the night office, in winter and summer, the
conduct of vigils on Sundays, of matins on Sundays and weekdays, of vigils
on saints' days and the times for the singing of 'Alleluia'. Then come the
following chapters.

(i) *Rules for the frequency of psalm-singing.*

XVI. QUALITER DIUINA OPERA AGANTUR.

1.   Ut ait propheta, *Septies in die laudem dixi tibi.*
2.   Qui septenarius sacratus numerus a nobis sic implebitur, si matutino,
     primae, tertiae, sextae, nonae, uesperae, completoriique tempore nostrae
     seruitutis officia persolbamus,
3.   quia de his diurnis horis dixit, *Septies in die laudem dixi tibi.*   5
4.   Nam de nocturnis uigiliis idem ipse propheta ait, *Media nocte surgebam ad
     confitendum tibi.*
5.   Ergo his temporibus referamus laudes creatori nostro *super iudicia iustitiae*

suae, id est matutinis, prima, tertia, sexta, nona, uespera, completorio;
sed et nocte surgamus ad confitendum ei. 10

Title **AGANTUR:** 'should be...'.
1 **Septies....tibi:** Ps. 118.164 (it concludes *super iudicia iustitiae tuae* 'because of the judgements of your justice').
2 **Qui...:** 'and this...'.
   si looks forward to *officia persolbamus* (= *persoluamus* (see O.13): tr. as though indicative: see G.28(b)).
3 **primae...completorii** all depends on *tempore*, but *matutino* is abl. of time (tr. 'at'), if it is not an error for *matutini*.

5 **dixit:** subject is 'he', i.e. *propheta*.
6 **Nam:** 'but'.
   idem ipse: tr. only *idem* (though *ipse* may mean 'the': see G.11(a)(i)).
6f. **Media...tibi:** Ps. 118.62.
8 **referamus:** 'let us...' (jussive subj.: see *RLGVE* 152).
   super...suae: adapted from Ps.118.164 (see note on line 1 above).

(ii) *Rules for the number of psalms and their distribution over the canonical hours.*

XVII. QUOT PSALMI PER EASDEM HORAS CANENDI SUNT.

1. Iam de nocturnis uel matutinis digessimus ordinem psalmodiae; nunc de sequentibus horis uideamus.

2. Prima hora dicantur psalmi tres singillatim et non sub una *gloria*,

3. hymnum eiusdem horae post uersum: *Deus in adiutorium* antequam psalmi incipiantur. 5

4. Post expletionem uero trium psalmorum recitetur lectio una, uersu et *quirie eleison*, et missas.

5. Tertia uero, sexta et nona idem eodem ordine celebretur oratio, id est uersu, hymnos earundem horarum, ternos psalmos, lectione et uersu, *quirie eleison*, et missas sunt.

6. Si maior congregatio fuerit, cum antiphonas; si uero minor, in directum psallantur. 10

7. Uespertina autem sinaxis quattuor psalmis cum antiphonis terminetur.

8. Post quibus psalmis lectio recitanda est; inde responsorium, ambrosianum, uersu, canticum de euangelia, litania, et oratio dominica fiant missae.

9. Completorios autem trium psalmorum dictione terminentur; qui psalmi directanei sine antiphona dicendi sunt. 15

10. Post quos hymnum eiusdem horae, lectionem unam et uersu, *quirie eleison*, et benedictione missae fiant.

Title **CANENDI SUNT:** 'are to be...' (for mood of verb see G.24(b))
2 **uideamus:** 'let us...' (jussive subj., see *RLGVE* 152): so also 2 *dicantur*, 4 *recitetur*, 5 *celebretur*, 6 *psallantur*, 7, 9 *terminentur*, 8, 10 *fiant*.

3 **singillatim...gloria:** that is, each psalm is to be finished with a 'Gloria'.
4 **hymnum** (acc.) is also a *subject* of *dicantur* in 2.
   Deus...adiutorium (sc. 'intende'): Ps. 69.2 'Lord, attend to my aid'.

6 **una:** 'a' (so also in 10; see G.10(d)).

uersu (= acc. *uersum*, see O.10), *quirie eleison* and *missas* (acc.) are *subjects* of *recitetur* along with *lectio una*.

7 **quirie eleison:** 'Lord have mercy' (Greek).

missas: here and in lines 12 and 13, 'prayers of dismissal'.

8 **Tertia...nona** are abl. of time (tr. 'at').

idem = *item* (see O. 19).

9f. **uersu** (= acc. *uersum*, see O.10), **hymnos** (acc.), **psalmos** (acc.), **quirie eleison, uersu** (= *uersum*: see above), **lectione** (acc. = *lectionem*, see O.10), **missas** (acc.) are all *subjects* of *sunt*.

9 **cum antiphonas:** sc. 'let the service be celebrated...' (see G.15(c)(i) for *cum* + acc.).

in directum psallantur (sc. subject *psalmi*): 'directly', i.e. 'without antiphons between verses'). The directives relate to the size of

the community. Antiphons require a split choir, which is not possible in a small community.

12 **Post...psalmis:** 'after' (cf. *cum* + acc. and see G.15(c)(i)).

12f. **inde...litania:** sc. 'are to be recited...' (*uersu* = acc. *uersum*, see O.10, is also a *subject*).

13 **de euangelia:** 'from...' (cf. *cum* + acc. and see G.15(c)(i)).

oratio (= *oratione*) **dominica fiant missae:** 'let the dismissal be with the Lord's prayer'

14 **Completorios** (acc.) is the *subject* of *terminentur*

trium psalmorum depends on *dictione*

16f. **hymnum** (acc.), **lectionem unam** (acc.), **uersu** (acc. = *uersum*, see O.10), *quirie eleison* are all *subjects*, sc. 'are to be said...'.

17 **benedictione missae fiant:** 'let the dismissal be with the benediction'

(iii) *The chapter omitted (XVIII) specifies the order in which the psalms have to be sung. This chapter deals with rules governing behaviour and attitude during psalm-singing.*

XVIIII. DE DISCIPLINA PSALLENDI.

1. Ubique credimus diuinam esse praesentiam et *oculos Domini in omni loco speculari bonos et malos;*

2. maxime tamen hoc sine aliqua dubitatione credamus, cum ad opus diuinum adsistimus.

3. Ideo semper memores simus, quod ait propheta: *Seruite domino in timore;* 5

4. et iterum, *Psallite sapienter;*

5. et *In conspectu angelorum psallam tibi.*

6. Ergo consideremus qualiter oporteat in conspectu diuinitatis et angelorum eius esse,

7. et sic stemus ad psallendum, ut mens nostra concordet uoci nostrae. 10

1 **diuinam** (= *Dei*) goes with *praesentiam* (subject of *esse*).

oculos...malos: Proverbs 15.3..

in omni loco: see G.15(a)(i).

3 **aliqua** = *ulla* (see G.11(f)).

credamus: 'let us...' (jussive subj., see RLGVE 152); so also 5 *simus*, 8 *consideremus*, 10 *stemus*.

5 **Ideo** = 'therefore'.

memores...quod: 'mindful of what...'.

Seruite...timore: Ps. 2.11.

6 **Psallite sapienter:** Ps. 46.8.

7 **In...tibi:** Ps. 137.1.

8 **oportet** looks forward to *esse* (tr. 'how one ought to behave').

2. Psalm 22 (23)

In the Benedictine Office, this psalm would have been chanted at the
nocturnae uigiliae on Sundays. Note that this is the unrevised version (not
Jerome's translation), known as 'Gallican', and its peculiarities come
through from the Septuagint's attempt to render literally the Hebrew text
(see further section 3 Intro.).

1.   Dominus reget me, et nihil mihi deerit.
2.   In loco pascuae ibi me collocavit. Super aquam refectionis educavit me.
3.   Animam meam convertit. Deduxit me super semitas iustitiae, propter
     nomen suum.
4.   Nam, et si ambulavero in medio umbrae mortis, non timebo mala,   5
     quoniam tu mecum es. Virga tua et baculus tuus, ipsa me consolata
     sunt.
5.   Parasti in conspectu meo mensam, adversus eos, qui tribulant me.
     Inpinguasti in oleo caput meum: et calix meus inebrians quam prae-
     clarus est.
6.   Et misericordia tua subsequitur me omnibus diebus vitae meae et ut
     inhabitem in domo Domini in longitudinem dierum.   10

2 **In loco pascuae ibi:** 'in...there' (*ibi* is redundant).
super: 'by', 'beside'.
aquam refectionis: 'the waters of comfort', i.e.
'the comforting waters'.
3 **super:** (also v. 3) 'in', 'along'.
6 **Virga tua et baculus tuus, ipsa:** 'your....these'
(*ipsa* is redundant: this is a Hebraism, see G.10).
8 **in oleo:** 'with oil' (see G.15(a)(ii)).

calix meus inebrians quam praeclarus est:
'my intoxicating cup is very glorious' (copied
from the Greek: see G.10).
10f. **ut inhabitem:** 'the fact that I will dwell...', 'my
dwelling...'. This clause is a second subject of
the verb *subsequitur* with *misericordia*.
11 **in longitudinem dierum:** 'for ever' (lit. 'for the
length of days'. Another Hebraism, see G.10).

3. St Ambrose (340–97)

St Ambrose was Bishop of Milan. St Augustine (see section 4.1 Intro.) tells
us that Ambrose influenced him to Catholicism away from Manicheism (a
belief in two gods, one good and one evil, the latter being the creator of
the world). He has been described as 'the real father of Western hymnody'
and this judgement can be seen as early as the Rule of St Benedict, where
ambrosianum is a general word for 'hymn'. His hymns remained in the
liturgy throughout the Middle Ages. The following, Hymn for Christmas
Eve, is one which (at least from verse 2) is still used today in the English
translation of J. M. Neale (and others). It is composed in a classical metre,

the iambic dimeter (two measures of - -ˇ- or ˇ-ˇ- with various resolutions such as ˇˇ-ˇ- or ˇ-ˇˇ-).

'Come thou redeemer of the earth'

IN NOCTE NATALIS DOMINI

Intende, qui regis Israel,
super Cherubim qui sedes,
appare Ephrem coram, excita
potentiam tuam et veni.

Veni, redemptor gentium,   5
ostende partum virginis;
miretur omne saeculum,
talis decet partus Deum.

Non ex virili semine,
sed mystico spiramine   10
verbum Dei factum est caro
fructusque ventris floruit.

Alvus tumescit virginis,
claustrum pudoris permanet,
vexilla virtutum micant,   15
versatur in templo Deus.

Procedat e thalamo suo
pudoris aula regia
geminae gigas substantiae,
alacris ut currat viam.   20

Egressus eius a patre,
regressus eius ad patrem,
excursus usque ad inferos,
recursus ad sedem Dei.

Aequalis aeterno patri,   25
carnis tropaeo cingere,
infirma nostri corporis
virtute firmans perpeti.

> Praesepe iam fulget tuum,
> lumenque nox spirat suum,   30
> quod nulla nox interpolet
> fideque iugi luceat.

1 **intende:** 'Listen...', 'Give ear...'.
qui regis: 'you who...'.
Israel (acc.), **Cherubim** (acc.), **Ephrem** (abl.)
(see G.6(a)).
This first verse is a metrical version of Vlg. Ps. 80
(79). 2–3: *qui regis Israel, intende. qui sedes super
Cherubim, manifestare coram Ephraim, Beniamin et
Manasse. excita potentiam tuam, et veni ut salvos
facias nos.*

5 **gentium:** 'of the nations' or 'of the gentiles'.

6 **ostende partum virginis:** i.e. 'show that a
virgin has given birth'.

7 **miretur:** 'let...' (jussive subj.: RLRGr 152).

10 **mystico spiramine:** 'from the Holy Spirit' (abl.
of cause: RLRGr L(f)4(iii)).

11 **verbum:** Cf. John 1.14: *Et verbum caro factum est.*
Here 'Word' = 'Christ'.

12 **ventris:** i.e. Mary's womb.

14 **claustrum pudoris:** 'the lock (or barrier) of her
chastity', i.e. 'her virginity'.

15 **vexilla virtutum:** 'the standards of the virtues',
i.e. 'standards displaying the Virgin's virtues'.

16 **in templo:** i.e. Mary's body (cf. 1 Cor. 6.19: *An
nescitis quoniam corpus vestrum templum est Spiritus sancti* 'Do you not know that your body is
a temple of the Holy Spirit?').

17 **procedat:** 'let...' (jussive subj.: RLRGr 152).
thalamo: i.e. Mary (cf. Ps. 18.6 *tamquam sponsus
procedens de thalamo suo*: 'like a bridegroom
coming from his chamber').

18 **pudoris:** 'of chastity', i.e. 'where chastity resides'.
aula regia: abl. in apposition to *thalamo*.

19 **geminae gigas substantiae:** i.e. Christ (identified with the giant of Ps. 19(18).6 *exsultavit ut
gigas ad currendam viam* 'He exulted like a giant
to run his course'; and 'of double substance'
refers to his combination of humanity and
divinity).

20 **alacris:** 'keenly', 'eagerly' (m. CL *alacer*).

21 **egressus...regressus** etc.: sc. *est* (but they are
nouns, not verbs).

23 **usque ad inferos:** it was a basic tenet of
medieval Christianity (reported in the Gospel
of Nicodemus) that Jesus descended to Hell
between his death and Resurrection and
released from there the righteous (this is
known as the 'harrowing of Hell').

26 **carnis tropaeo:** 'the trophy of flesh', because
Christ's incarnation signals victory over death.
cingere: 'be clothed' (passive 2nd s. imperative).

27 **infirma:** 'weaknesses' (note the word play in
infirma...firmans).

28 **firmans:** almost final, 'to strengthen' (see
G.20(b)).
perpeti: adj. with *virtute*.

29 **praesepe:** 'crib' (i.e. the manger of Jesus).

30 **lumenque nox spirat suum:** 'and the night
breathes (i.e. reveals) its light', i.e. the star over
the stable.

31f. **quod:** the antecedent is *lumen* and the subjunctives potential (*RLGVE* 153.2): tr. 'a light
which no night shall obscure...'. But the
syntax shifts in l.32, and *quod* has to be seen
as nom. 'and which shall shine with constant
faith'.

4. Egeria (*fl.* 380)

The author of the following passage was a nun, probably called Egeria,
who visited the East between 381 and 384. She came from one of the far
western provinces, perhaps Aquitaine in Gaul or Galicia in Spain. She
recorded her travels in a work called *Itinerarium*.

It is highly significant that early Christianity produces some female prose

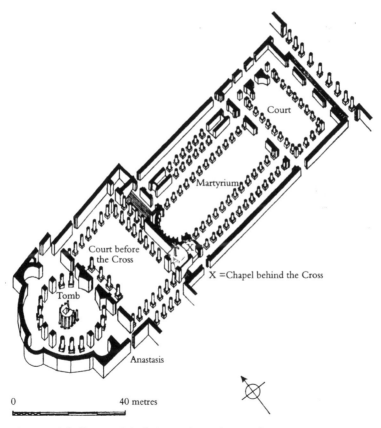

Court

Martyrium

Court before
the Cross

X = Chapel behind the Cross

Tomb

Anastasis

0   40 metres

1 Constantine's buildings on Golgotha in Jerusalem in the time of Egeria.

writing (cf. the Passion of St Perpetua). Women had to have Latin too, in order to be Christians. Already, we have here many of the familiar aspects of medieval culture. There is the pilgrimage to the holy places, the veneration of the Bible, the idea of the solitary life as hermit or monk, the co-operation of state with Church (where the pilgrim is protected by soldiers of the empire as she approaches dangerous territory), the liturgy of the Church, articulated around the chief points of its creed, together with its potent new symbolism.

Here she describes daily services in Jerusalem. She is one of the main sources for the cathedral Office of the Eastern Church, though what she describes is of a mixed monastic and cathedral type. There was particular emphasis upon the ceremonial lighting of lamps (mentioned here) and the offering of incense.

The Latin of this text is strongly marked by 'vulgarisms', such as the omission of final -*m* in accusatives of the 1f. declension (*intro spelunca*) and the substitution of -*e*- for -*i*- (*dicet*). See also section 1 Intro.

See further: J. Wilkinson, *Egeria's Travels*, London, 1971.

(i) *The pre-dawn service at the Anastasis.*

Vt autem sciret affectio uestra, quae operatio singulis diebus cotidie in locis sanctis habeatur, certas uos facere debui, sciens, quia libenter haberetis haec cognoscere. Nam singulis diebus ante pullorum cantum aperiuntur omnia hostia Anastasis et descendent omnes monazontes et parthene, ut hic dicunt, et non solum hii, sed et laici preter, uiri aut mulieres, qui tamen uolunt maturius   5
uigilare. Et ex ea hora usque in luce dicuntur ymni et psalmi responduntur, similiter et antiphonae: et cata singulos ymnos fit oratio. Nam presbyteri bini uel terni, similiter et diacones, singulis diebus uices habent simul cum monazontes, qui cata singulos ymnos uel antiphonas orationes dicunt.

1 **affectio uestra:** 'your kindness', addressed to Egeria's sisters (cf. *tua magnificentia* 'your magnificence' in section 19.3(vi)).

2f. **quia libenter haberetis haec cognoscere:** 'that you would be glad to know these things' (see G.4(c)).

3 **pullorum:** i.e. *gallorum* 'cockerels'.

4 **hostia:** i.e. *ostia* 'doors' (see O.3(c)).
  Anastasis: gen. s. (Greek 'resurrection'). This is the Tomb of Christ, a cavern (*spelunca*) in the rock, from which he is believed to have arisen on Easter Day. It was at the western end of a

site which Egeria calls Golgotha. In Constantine's time, the cave had been isolated by the removal of all the surrounding rock. But in Egeria's day it was surrounded by a colonnaded building. The Tomb had a porch at the eastern end surrounded by a screen (here called *cancellus* or *cancelli*). See further Wilkinson, *op. cit.* pp. 242–52 and map 1.

descendent: i.e. *descendunt* (2nd for 3rd conjugation. See G.2).

parthene: 'virgins' (Greek word adapted to Latin 1f. declension: -*e* is for -*ae*. See O.1).

5 **hii** = *hi.*

preter: 'besides'.

6 **usque in luce:** i.e. *usque in lucem* (see O.10).

dicuntur ymni (= *hymni*: see O.3(c)): *dico* here means (virtually) 'sing'.

7 **cata singulos ymnos:** 'after each hymn' (*cata* is Greek), 'between the individual hymns' (so also later *cata...antiphonas*).

8f. **simul cum monazontes:** 'together with...' (see G.15(c)(i)).

(ii) *The dawn service at the Anastasis.*

Iam autem ubi ceperit lucescere, tunc incipiunt matutinos ymnos dicere. Ecce et superuenit episcopus cum clero et statim ingreditur intro spelunca et de intro cancellos primum dicet orationem pro omnibus; commemorat etiam ipse nomina, quorum uult, sic benedicet cathecuminos. Item dicet orationem et benedicet fideles. Et post hoc exeunte episcopo de intro cancellos omnes ad manum ei   5 accedunt, et ille eos uno et uno benedicet exiens iam, ac sic fit missa iam luce.

1 **ubi ceperit** (= *coeperit*: see O.1) **lucescere:** note the perfect subjunctive here and below at section 2.4 (iv), contrary to CL usage.

2 **intro spelunca:** i.e. *intra speluncam* 'into the cavern' (see O.10). For the cavern, see note in 2.4 (i) above on *Anastasis*.

de intro: 'from inside'. See note in 2.4 (i) above on *Anastasis* for *cancelli*.

3 **dicet:** i.e. *dicit* (see O.11 and G.2).

ipse: 'he' (see G.11(a)(i)).

4 **benedicet, dicet:** i.e. *dicit...benedicit* (see O.11, G.2).

5f. **ad manum ei accedunt:** 'they approach his hand' (so also in (iii) and (iv) below).

6 **uno et uno:** 'one by one'.

fit missa: 'there comes the dismissal' (cf. section 2.1(ii), 5, 8, 10).

iam luce: 'it now being daylight' (abl. abs.).

(iii) *The midday service.*

Item hora sexta denuo descendent omnes similiter ad Anastasim et dicuntur psalmi et antiphonae, donec commonetur episcopus; similiter descendet et non sedet, sed statim intrat intra cancellos intra Anastasim, id est intra speluncam, ubi et mature, et inde similiter primum facit orationem, sic benedicet fideles, et sic exiens de intro cancellos similiter ei ad manum acceditur. Ita ergo et hora   5 nona fit sicuti et ad sexta.

1 **hora sexta:** i.e. midday.

descendent: i.e. *descendunt* (see G.2).

Anastasim: Latin accusative of Greek *Anastasis* (lit. 'resurrection': here 'the shrine of the Resurrection').

2 **commonetur:** 'is given the signal'.

descendet: i.e. *descendit* (see O.11, G.2).

4 **ubi et mature:** 'where (sc. he was) in the morning also'.

benedicet: i.e. *benedicit* (see O.11, G.2).

5 **sic:** 'then' (= *tum*).

exiens de intro...ei ad manum acceditur: 'when he has come out from inside...people come to touch his hand' (the construction changes in mid-clause).

5f. **hora nona:** i.e. three o'clock.

6 **ad sexta:** i.e. *ad sextam* (sc. *horam*) = midday (see O.10).

(iv) *The four o'clock service, 'Licinicon' or 'Lucernare'.*

Hora autem decima, quod appellant hic licinicon, nam nos dicimus lucemare, similiter se omnis multitudo colliget ad Anastasim, incenduntur omnes

candelae et cerei et fit lumen infinitum. Lumen autem de foris non affertur, sed
de spelunca interiori eicitur, ubi noctu ac die semper lucerna lucet, id est de
intro cancellos. Dicuntur etiam psalmi lucernares, sed et antiphonae diutius.   5
Ecce et commonetur episcopus et descendet et sedet susum, nec non etiam et
presbyteri sedent locis suis, dicuntur ymni uel antiphonae.

Et ad ubi perdicti fuerint iuxta consuetudinem, lebat se episcopus et stat ante
cancellum, id est ante speluncam, et unus ex diaconibus facit commemo-
rationem singulorum, sicut solet esse consuetudo. Et diacono dicente singulo-   10
rum nomina semper pisinni plurimi stant respondentes semper: *kyrie eleyson*
(quod dicimus nos: *miserere, Domine*), quorum uoces infinitae sunt.

Et at ubi diaconus perdixerit omnia, quae dicere habet, dicet orationem
primum episcopus et orat pro omnibus; et sic orant omnes, tam fideles quam et
cathecumini simul. Item mittet uocem diaconus, ut unusquisque, quomodo   15
stat, cathecuminus inclinet caput; et sic dicet episcopus stans benedictionem
super cathecuminos. Item fit oratio et denuo mittet diaconus uocem et
commonet, ut unusquisque stans fidelium inclinent capita sua; item benedicet
fideles episcopus et sic fit missa Anastasi. Et incipient episcopo ad manum
accedere singuli.   20

At the end of this service, they conduct the bishop to the Cross (see map 1), then to
a chapel behind the Cross. In both places prayers and blessings are said. Dusk is
falling as the services end.

1 **Hora...decima:** i.e. four o'clock.
   licinicon: 'Lamptime' (Greek 2nd declension
   acc.).
2 **colliget:** i.e. *colligit* (see O.11, G.2).
4 **interiori:** i.e. *interiore* (see G.7(a)).
6 **descendet:** i.e. *descendit* (see O.11, G.2).
   susum (= *sursum*): i.e. 'in the chief seat'.
7 **uel:** possibly 'and'.
8 **ad ubi:** 'when'.
   perdicti fuerint: 'have been...'.
   lebat: i.e. *leuat* (see O.13).
11 *kyrie eleyson:* 'Lord, have mercy' (Greek).
12 **quod...nos:** 'what *we* call'.

13 **at ubi:** i.e. *ad ubi* 'when' (see O.19).
   dicere habet: 'he is going to say' (see G.4(c)),
   'has to say', or 'must say'.
   dicet (also l.16): i.e. *dicit* (see O.11, G.2).
15 **mittet** (also l.17): i.e. *mittit* (see O.11, G.2).
15f. **ut unusquisque...inclinent:** 'that all should..'
   (construction by sense).
   quomodo stat: lit. 'how he stands', i.e. 'just as
   he is'.
18 **benedicet:** i.e. *benedicit* (see O.11, G.2).
19 **fit missa:** see note on 2, 1 (ii), l.7.
   Anastasi: 'at the Anastasis': for this, see note on
   section 2.4(i) l.4 above.

Section 3
The Bible

The Jewish idea of sacred texts was carried over into Christianity, which set the 'New Covenant' between God and his people alongside the 'Old Covenant'. The 'New Covenant' was embodied by Jesus and expressed in the – at first fluctuating – body of writings which we call the 'New Testament'. The 'Old Covenant' was expressed in the law of Moses and the other books which make up what we call the 'Old Testament' (not excluding what some parts of the Christian Church now set aside as the 'Apocrypha'). This body of writings was translated into Latin by the second century. Then the factors mentioned in the general introduction to this part (above, pp. 5–6) led to the retention of this form of the text, despite the spread of the gospel message well outside the area of the Roman Empire. Here we will focus on two important aspects of the Bible, its language and its interpretation.

The earliest Latin translations were those known as the *Vetus Latina* ('Old Latin'). Their renditions of the Old Testament were made directly from the Septuagint, the Greek version of the Hebrew scriptures made in the third century BC at Alexandria. St Jerome (d. 420) produced a new, partially revised, text, the so-called Vulgate, which eventually became the standard text. Some of the books he left unrevised (Wisdom, Ecclesiasticus, 1 and 2 Maccabees, Baruch). Some he revised slightly (Acts, Epistles, Revelations). Others he rapidly translated 'from the Chaldee' (Tobit, Judith). For the Gospels he revised and corrected the *Vetus Latina* from the oldest Greek mss. available. The Psalter (Psalms) he did translate directly from the Hebrew, but this version was never accepted, and the Vulgate contains the older 'Gallican' version. His great contribution was the direct translation from Hebrew of the rest of the Canonical books of the Old Testament. It is the earlier versions which are used in Egeria (section 2.4), in Augustine (section 4.1(a)), Jerome's contemporary, and in Caesarius of Arles (section 5.1).

The *Vetus Latina* follows the Septuagint closely. The main feature of the version is its retention at second hand of a number of features of the original Hebrew. Jerome did not have to rely on the Septuagint, since he was a Hebrew scholar as well. Even so, where Jerome was merely revising rather than translating anew, his version retains substantial numbers of peculiarities. These include: (1) the copying of Hebrew syntax, (2) the retention of Hebrew word order, (3) the introduction of Hebrew words, (4) the copying of Greek syntax, (5) the inclusion (as in Egeria) of some erroneous (spoken?) Latin forms (e.g. the conjugation of the defective verb *odi* as though it had the form *odire*: so *odibunt* in Proverbs 1.22). The net effect of the process is a singular language which is unlike anything else in Latin.

Jerome's Vulgate is quoted extensively, of course, and had a great effect upon subsequent Latin writing, especially after it was adopted as the official text by Charlemagne at the end of the eighth century. It sanctified usages such as changes in the use of the cases and the subjunctive, and the more frequent use of *quod/quia* clauses in reported speech. Because it never became the source for the teaching of *grammatica*, it was not the only influence upon writers. But it is linguistically a central text.

It was also regarded as the 'Word of God' and as such its every phrase was deemed to be meaningful. Throughout the Middle Ages one of the chief tasks of monasteries and cathedral schools was the interpretation of the Bible. St Paul had pointed to one method by reinterpreting the Old Testament allegorically in terms of the New (e.g. Galatians 4.24–31). This was developed further by Origen (d. *c.*254), who argued that the text had three main senses, literal, moral and spiritual. His ideas reached the West through the Latin Church Fathers (see section 4), Ambrose, Hilary, Augustine and Jerome and through Rufinus' translation. Gregory the Great (d. 604) is generally credited with the development of the fourfold scheme, in which the senses are the literal (or historical), allegorical, moral (or tropological) and spiritual (or anagogical). In practice, twofold (literal and spiritual), threefold and fourfold interpretations are found. Not all passages yield to all senses.

Commentary came in a number of forms. It could be a set of notes interleaved with the text (e.g. Bede's commentary on Luke, section 7.2(b)). It might be in the form of a treatise based on *quaestiones* (such as Alcuin of York's *Interrogationes in Genesim*). It might be in the form of a sermon (such as those of St Bernard of Clairvaux on the Song of Songs: see section 18.2). By the beginning of the twelfth century there was a complete gloss of the Bible, which soon became the standard commentary, the *Glossa ordinaria*.

See further: W. E. Plater and H. J. White, *A Grammar of the Vulgate*, Oxford, 1926; B. Smalley, *The Study of the Bible in the Middle Ages*, 2nd edn, Oxford, 1952.

1. 1 Kings (= 1 Samuel) 17.1–54

Bede (see section 7.2) wrote a strongly allegorical commentary on the First Book of Samuel, in which David is seen as a figure of Christ. The Books of Kings became very useful during the eleventh- and twelfth-century battles between the centralized monarchies and the Papacy (see sections 12 and 19). But they could also be brought into play allegorically to serve the Church against those whom it deemed heretics. In this way St Bernard of Clairvaux uses the story of David and Goliath in his attack on Peter Abelard (section 17.2). The conflict between Israel and the Philistines becomes transposed into the battle between Christianity and paganism.

David and Goliath

1. Congregantes vero Philisthim agmina sua in proelium, convenerunt in Soccho Iudae: et castrametati sunt inter Soccho et Azeca, in finibus Dommim.
2. Porro Saul et viri Israhel congregati venerunt in Valle terebinthi, et direxerunt aciem ad pugnandum contra Philisthim.
3. Et Philisthim stabant super montem ex hac parte, et Israhel stabat super montem ex altera parte: vallisque erat inter eos.
4. Et egressus est vir spurius de castris Philisthinorum, nomine Goliath, de Geth, altitudinis sex cubitorum et palmo.
5. Et cassis aerea super caput eius et lorica hamata induebatur; porro pondus loricae eius quinque milia siclorum aeris.
6. Et ocreas aereas habebat in cruribus: et clypeus aereus tegebat umeros eius.
7. Hastile autem hastae eius erat quasi liciatorium texentium: ipsum autem ferrum hastae eius sescentos siclos habebat ferri: et armiger eius antecedebat eum.
8. Stansque clamabat adversum falangas Israhel, et dicebat eis: 'Quare venitis parati ad proelium? Numquid ego non sum Philistheus, et vos servi Saul? Eligite ex vobis virum, et descendat ad singulare certamen.
9. Si quiverit pugnare mecum et percusserit me, erimus vobis servi: si autem ego praevaluero et percussero eum, vos servi eritis et servietis nobis.'
10. Et aiebat Philistheus: 'Ego exprobravi agminibus Israhelis hodie. Date mihi virum et ineat mecum singulare certamen.'

11. Audiens autem Saul et omnes Israhelitae sermones Philisthei huiusce-
     modi, stupebant et metuebant nimis.
12. David autem erat filius viri Ephrathei, de quo supra dictum est, de
     Bethleem Iuda, cui erat nomen Isai, qui habebat octo filios, et erat vir in
     diebus Saul senex, et grandevus inter viros.
13. Abierunt autem tres filii eius maiores post Saul in proelium: et nomina
     trium filiorum eius qui perrexerant ad bellum, Heliab primogenitus, et
     secundus Abinadab tertiusque Samma.
14. David autem erat minimus. Tribus ergo maioribus secutis Saulem,
15. abiit David et reversus est a Saul, ut pasceret gregem patris sui in
     Bethleem.
16. Procedebat vero Philistheus mane et vespere, et stabat quadraginta
     diebus.
17. Dixit autem Isai ad David filium suum: 'Accipe fratribus tuis oephi
     polentae et decem panes istos et curre in castra ad fratres tuos.
18. Et decem formellas casei has deferes ad tribunum: et fratres tuos visitabis
     si recte agant, et cum quibus ordinati sint, disce.'
19. Saul autem et illi et omnes filii Israhel in Valle terebinthi pugnabant
     adversum Philisthim.
20. Surrexit itaque David mane et commendavit gregem custodi et onustus
     abiit sicut praeceperat ei Isai. Et venit ad locum Magala et ad exercitum,
     qui egressus ad pugnam vociferatus erat in certamine.
21. Direxerat enim aciem Israhel, sed et Philisthim ex adverso fuerant
     praeparati.
22. Derelinquens ergo David vasa quae adtulerat, sub manu custodis ad
     sarcinas, cucurrit ad locum certaminis et interrogabat si omnia recte
     agerentur erga fratres suos.
23. Cumque adhuc ille loqueretur eis, apparuit vir ille spurius ascendens,
     Goliath nomine Philistheus de Geth, ex castris Philisthinorum: et
     loquente eo haec eadem verba audivit David.
24. Omnes autem Israhelitae cum vidissent virum, fugerunt a facie eius
     timentes eum valde.
25. Et dixit unus quispiam de Israhel: 'Num vidisti virum hunc qui ascendit.
     Virum ergo qui percusserit eum ditabit rex divitiis magnis et filiam suam
     dabit ei et domum patris eius faciet absque tributo in Israhel.'
26. Et ait David ad viros qui stabant secum, dicens: 'Quid dabitur viro qui
     percusserit Philistheum hunc et tulerit obprobrium de Israhel? Quis est
     enim hic Philistheus incircumcisus qui exprobravit acies Dei viventis?'
27. Referebat autem ei populus eundem sermonem, dicens: 'Haec dabuntur
     viro qui percusserit eum.'
28. Quod cum audisset Heliab frater eius maior, loquente eo cum aliis, iratus

est contra David et ait: 'Quare venisti et quare dereliquisti pauculas oves illas in deserto? Ego novi superbiam tuam et nequitiam cordis tui, quia ut videres proelium descendisti.'

29. Et dixit David: 'Quid feci? Numquid non verbum est?'

30. Et declinavit paululum ab eo ad alium dixitque eundem sermonem. Et respondit ei populus verbum sicut et prius.

31. Audita sunt autem verba quae locutus est David et adnuntiata in conspectu Saul.

32. Ad quem cum fuisset adductus, locutus est ei: 'Non concidat cor cuiusquam in eo: ego servus tuus vadam et pugnabo adversus Philistheum.'

33. Et ait Saul ad David: 'Non vales resistere Philistheo isti nec pugnare adversus eum, quia puer es. Hic autem vir bellator ab adulescentia sua.'

34. Dixitque David ad Saul: 'Pascebat servus tuus patris sui gregem et veniebat leo vel ursus tollebatque arietem de medio gregis.

35. Et sequebar eos et percutiebam eruebamque de ore eorum. Et illi consurgebant adversum me et adprehendebam mentum eorum et suffocabam interficiebamque eos.

36. Nam et leonem et ursum interfeci ego servus tuus. Erit igitur et Philistheus hic incircumcisus quasi unus ex eis, quia ausus est maledicere exercitum Dei viventis?'

37. Et ait David: 'Dominus qui eruit me de manu leonis et de manu ursi, ipse liberabit me de manu Philisthei huius.' Dixit autem Saul ad David: 'Vade et Dominus tecum sit.'

38. Et induit Saul David vestimentis suis et inposuit galeam aeream super caput eius et vestivit eum lorica.

39. Accinctus ergo David gladio eius super veste sua coepit temptare si armatus posset incedere: non enim habebat consuetudinem. Dixitque David ad Saul: 'Non possum sic incedere, quia nec usum habeo.' Et deposuit ea

40. et tulit baculum suum, quem semper habebat in manibus, et elegit sibi quinque limpidissimos lapides de torrente et misit eos in peram pastoralem, quam habebat secum et fundam manu tulit et processit adversum Philistheum.

41. Ibat autem Philistheus incedens et adpropinquans adversum David et armiger eius ante eum.

42. Cumque inspexisset Philistheus et vidisset David, despexit eum. Erat enim adulescens, rufus et pulcher aspectu.

43. Et dixit Philistheus ad David: 'Numquid ego canis sum, quod tu venis ad me cum baculo?' Et maledixit Philistheus David in diis suis.

44.   Dixitque ad David: 'Veni ad me et dabo carnes tuas volatilibus caeli et bestiis terrae.'

45.   Dixit autem David ad Philistheum: 'Tu venis ad me cum gladio et hasta et clypeo. Ego autem venio ad te in nomine Domini exercituum, Dei agminum Israhel, quibus exprobrasti.

46.   Hodie et dabit te Dominus in manu mea et percutiam te et auferam caput tuum a te, et dabo cadaver castrorum Philisthim hodie volatilibus caeli et bestiis terrae, ut sciat omnis terra quia est Deus in Israhel,

47.   et noverit universa ecclesia haec quia non in gladio nec in hasta salvat Dominus. Ipsius est enim bellum et tradet vos in manus nostras.'

48.   Cum ergo surrexisset Philistheus et veniret et adpropinquaret contra David, festinavit David et cucurrit ad pugnam ex adverso Philisthei.

49.   Et misit manum suam in peram, tulitque unum lapidem et funda iecit et percussit Philistheum in fronte. Et infixus est lapis in fronte eius et cecidit in faciem suam super terram.

50.   Praevaluitque David adversus Philistheum in funda et lapide, percussumque Philistheum interfecit. Cumque gladium non haberet in manu David,

51.   cucurrit et stetit super Philistheum, et tulit gladium eius et eduxit eum de vagina sua et interfecit eum praeciditque caput eius. Videntes autem Philisthim, quod mortuus esset fortissimus eorum, fugerunt.

52.   Et consurgentes viri Israhel et Iuda vociferati sunt et persecuti sunt Philistheos usquedum venirent in vallem et usque ad portas Accaron, cecideruntque vulnerati de Philisthim in via Sarim usque ad Geth et usque Accaron.

53.   Et revertentes filii Israhel postquam persecuti fuerant Philistheos, invaserunt castra eorum.

54.   Adsumens autem David caput Philisthei adtulit illud in Hierusalem. Arma vero eius posuit in tabernaculo suo.

---

1 **congregantes:** 'having gathered together' (see G.20(a)). Other examples of the present participle as past in sense here are: 22 *Derelinquens*, 51 *Videntes*, 53 *revertentes*, 54 *Adsumens*.

 Philisthim: nom.pl. 'Philistines' (also nom. in 3). For the use of Hebrew names and other words, see G.6.

 Soccho: abl.

 Azeca: acc.

 Dommim: gen. pl.

2 **Israhel:** gen.

 Philisthim: acc. pl.

4 **spurius:** 'illegitimate' (an error of interpretation;

the Hebrew word can mean 'man of the between' and was rendered *vir inter duos* 'man between two' in earlier versions. It means 'between two armies', and refers to skirmishers, but Jerome took it to mean 'between two fathers', i.e. a bastard!).

 Goliath: nom.

 Geth: abl.

 altitudinis...palmi: lit.'of the height of...'. Tr. 'six...high'.

5 **cassis aerea super caput eius:** supply *erat*.

 induebatur: 'he was clothed in...'.

6 **clypeus:** i.e. *clipeus* (see O.5).

8 **Numquid:** indicates a question (see G.24(a)).
Saul: gen.
11 **Saul:** nom.
nimis: 'very much' (CL 'too much').
12 **David:** nom.
Bethleem: abl.
Iuda: gen. (cf. *Iudae* in v.1).
Isai: i.e. Jesse.
Saul: gen.
13 **Saul:** acc.
nomina: sc. 'were'.
Heliab... Abinadab...Samma: nom.
14, 15 **David:** nom.
15 **Saul:** abl.
Bethleem: abl.
16 **quadraginta diebus:** 'for forty days' (see G.16(c)).
17 **Isai:** nom.
David: acc.
oephi: n. acc. 'an ephah' (a measure for corn etc.).
istos: 'these' (see G.11(c)).
19 **Saul:** nom.
Israhel: gen.
Philisthim: acc. pl.
20 **David:** nom.
ei: i.e. David.
Magala: acc.
vociferatus erat in certamine: 'had made its battle cry' (lit. 'had shouted in combat', possibly '*for* combat').
21 **Israhel:** nom. (i.e. 'the Israelites').
Philisthim: nom. pl.
fuerant praeparati: 'were prepared' (see G.4(a)).
22 **David:** nom.
si: 'whether' (see G.24(c)).
erga: 'as regards' (CL 'towards').
23 **Goliath:** nom.
Geth: abl.
loquente eo: abl. abs. Supply 'him' after *audivit*.
David: nom.
24 **a facie eius:** 'away from him' (a Hebraism: see G.10).
25 **Israhel:** abl. (also in 26).
26 **David:** nom.
exprobravit acies: CL + dat. (cf. v. 10), see G.16.
27 **populus:** 'people' (see v. 30).

28 **Heliab:** nom.
iratus...contra: 'angry with' (see G.15(b)).
David: acc.
quia: 'that' (see G.22(a)).
29 **David:** nom.
numquid...est: 'Can't I even speak?' (see G.24(a)).
30 **populus:** 'the person'.
31 **David:** nom.
Saul: gen.
32 **quem:** *David* is the subject of both clauses.
33 **Saul:** nom.
David: acc.
vales: 'you can' (+ infin.) (see G.17(d)).
34 **David:** nom.
Saul: acc.
37 **David:** (1) nom. (2) acc.
ipse: 'he' (see G.11(a)(ii)).
37, 38 **Saul:** nom.
38 **David:** acc.
39 **David:** nom.
Saul: acc.
41, 42 **David:** acc.
43 **David:** 1) acc. 2) dat. (after *maledixit*). See G.15(b).
in diis (= deis) suis: 'in the name of his gods'.
44 **David:** acc.
45 **David:** nom.
exercituum: 'of hosts' (Hebrew *Sabaoth*).
Israhel: gen.
46 **in manu mea:** i.e. 'into my hand' (see G.15(c)(ii)).
castrorum: i.e. 'of the troops'.
Philisthim: gen. pl. (depends on *castrorum*).
Israhel: abl.
47 **noverit:** pf. subj. after ut in v.46.
quia: 'that' (see G.22(a)).
non in gladio nec in hasta: 'not by the sword nor by the spear' (see G.15(a)(ii); a Hebraism, see G.10).
Ipsius: 'his' (see G.11(a)(ii)).
48 **David:** 1) acc. 2) nom.
ex aduerso: 'from the opposite side (to)'.
49 **cecidit:** sc. *Goliath*
50 **in funda et lapide:** 'with sling and stone' (see G.15(a)(ii); a Hebraism, see G.10).
51 **de vagina sua:** i.e. 'from its sheath' (see G.11(e)(iii)).
Philisthim: nom.

quod: 'that' (see G.22(a)).
52 **Israhel... Iuda:** gen.
usquedum: 'until'.
Accaron: gen.
de Philisthim: 'of the Philistines' (see
    G.15(a))(ii).
Sarim: gen.

Geth: acc.
Accaron: acc.
53 **Israhel:** gen.
persecuti fuerant: 'they had pursued' (see
    G.4(a)).
54 **David:** nom.
Hierusalem: acc.

2. *Canticum Canticorum* (The Song of Songs) 1.1–16

The Song of Songs or Song of Solomon is a dialogue of great sensual
beauty between two lovers. Christian interpreters were deeply appreciative
of the fine language of the poem, but could not allow its literal meaning
any sway. Hence dubious phrases such as 'A flask of myrrh is my love unto
me; he shall lie between my breasts' were allegorized. The male lover is
Christ and the female is the Church, absorbing the fragrance of its master's
doctrine in this image of close contact. Bede (see section 7.2) wrote an
influential gloss. But in the twelfth century in particular, this text was often
commented (see section 18.2). It also had in various versions a profound
influence upon medieval love lyric.

See further: P. Dronke, 'The Song of Songs and Medieval Love-Lyric', in
The Medieval Poet and his World, Rome, 1984, pp. 209–36.

(i) *The beloved speaks of her lover and a chorus interjects.*

1. ·Osculetur me osculo oris sui: quia meliora sunt ubera tua vino,
2. fraglantia unguentis optimis. Oleum effusum nomen tuum: ideo
    adulescentulae dilexerunt te.
3. Trahe me: post te curremus. Introduxit me rex in cellaria sua:
    exultabimus et laetabimur in te, memores uberum tuorum super
    vinum: recti diligunt te.

1 **osculetur:** 'let him...' (jussive subj.: *RLGVE*
    152).
meliora looks forward to *vino* ('than...': abl. of
    comparison).
2 **oleum...tuum:** sc. *est*.
3 **exultabimus...vinum:** modern translations take

these as the words of 'friends'; *super vinum* is
loosely attached to *uberum tuorum* – tr. '(which
are) better than...'.
recti...te: in modern editions, this is ascribed to
the beloved; *recti* tr. 'rightly'.

(ii) *The beloved speaks of her dark skin and asks her lover where he keeps his sheep at midday.*

4.   Nigra sum sed formonsa, filiae Hierusalem, sicut tabernacula Cedar, sicut pelles Salomonis.

5.   Nolite me considerare quod fusca sim, quia decoloravit me sol: filii matris mei pugnaverunt contra me, posuerunt me custodem in vineis: vineam meam non custodivi.

6.   Indica mihi, quem diligit anima mea, ubi pascas, ubi cubes in meridie, ne vagari incipiam post greges sodalium tuorum.

4 **Hierusalem:** 'of...' (gen.: see G.6 for Hebrew words).

Cedar: 'of Kedar' (gen.).

6 **quem...mea:** tr. '(you) whom...'.

(iii) *The lover tells her, likens her to a mare and promises a gift.*

7.   Si ignoras te, o pulchra inter mulieres, egredere et abi post vestigia gregum, et pasce hedos tuos iuxta tabernacula pastorum.

8.   Equitatui meo in curribus Faraonis adsimilavi te, amica mea.

9.   Pulchrae sunt genae tuae sicut turturis: collum tuum sicut monilia.

10.   Murenulas aureas faciemus tibi, vermiculatas argento.

7 **si...te:** lit. 'if you do not know yourself', i.e. 'if you do not know'.

8 **equitatui meo** ('to...') is constructed with

adsimilavi te.

9 **collum...monilia:** sc. *pulchrum est* (with *collum tuum*).

(iv) *The beloved speaks in images of her lover.*

11.   Dum esset rex in accubitu suo, nardus mea dedit odorem suum.

12.   Fasciculus murrhae dilectus meus mihi, inter ubera mea commorabitur.

13.   Botrus cypri dilectus meus mihi, in vineis Engaddi.

12 **fasciculus...mihi:** sc. *est.*

13 **botrus...mihi:** sc. *est.* Tr. 'cluster of henna-

flowers'.

Engaddi: gen. (see G.6(a)) 'En-Gedi'.

(v) *The lover praises the beloved's beauty and she his. He speaks of their house.*

14.   Ecce tu pulchra es, amica mea, ecce tu pulchra, oculi tui columbarum.

15.   Ecce tu pulcher es, dilecte mi, et decorus. Lectulus noster floridus:

16.   tigna domorum nostrarum cedrina, laquearia nostra cypressina.

14 **oculi...columbarum:** sc. *sunt oculi* before *columbarum.*

15 **lectulus...floridus:** sc. *est.*

16 **tigna...cedrina** and **laquearia...cypressina:** sc. *sunt* with each part.

3. Luke 23

The Gospel accounts of the Crucifixion were central texts for literal
interpretation. In particular it is worth noting how the behaviour of the
Jews was treated. The basis for their persecution in later medieval Europe is
to be found in the exegetical tradition. A section of Bede's commentary on
this passage is printed at section 7.2(b).

The Crucifixion

1. Et surgens omnis multitudo eorum duxerunt illum ad Pilatum.
2. Coeperunt autem accusare illum, dicentes: 'Hunc invenimus subver-
    tentem gentem nostram, et prohibentem tributum dare Caesari, et
    dicentem se Christum regem esse.'
3. Pilatus autem interrogavit eum, dicens: 'Tu es rex Iudaeorum?' At ille
    respondens ait: 'Tu dicis.'
4. Ait autem Pilatus ad principes sacerdotum et turbas: 'Nihil invenio
    causae in hoc homine.'
5. At illi invalescebant, dicentes: 'Commovet populum docens per uni-
    versam Iudaeam et incipiens a Galilaea usque huc.'
6. Pilatus autem audiens Galilaeam, interrogavit si homo Galilaeus esset.
7. Et ut cognovit quod de Herodis potestate esset, remisit eum ad
    Herodem, qui et ipse Hierosolymis erat illis diebus.
8. Herodes autem, viso Iesu, gavisus est valde. Erat enim cupiens ex multo
    tempore videre eum, eo quod audiret multa de eo et sperabat signum
    aliquod videre ab eo fieri.
9. Interrogabat autem illum cum multis sermonibus. At ipse nihil illi
    respondebat.
10. Stabant autem principes sacerdotum et scribae constanter accusantes
    eum.
11. Sprevit autem illum Herodes cum exercitu suo, et inlusit indutum veste
    alba, et remisit ad Pilatum.
12. Et facti sunt amici Herodes et Pilatus in ipsa die: nam antea inimici erant
    ad invicem.
13. Pilatus autem, convocatis principibus sacerdotum et magistratibus et
    plebe,
14. dixit ad illos: 'Obtulistis mihi hunc hominem quasi avertentem popu-
    lum: et ecce ego coram vobis interrogans, nullam causam inveni in
    homine isto, ex his in quibus eum accusatis.
15. Sed neque Herodes; nam remisi vos ad illum: et ecce nihil dignum morte
    actum est ei.

16. Emendatum ergo illum dimittam.'
17. Necesse autem habebat dimittere eis per diem festum unum.
18. Exclamavit autem simul universa turba, dicens: 'Tolle hunc, et dimitte nobis Barabbam.'
19. Qui erat propter seditionem quandam factam in civitate et homicidium missus in carcerem.
20. Iterum autem Pilatus locutus est ad illos, volens dimittere Iesum.
21. At illi succlamabant, dicentes: 'Crucifige, crucifige illum.'
22. Ille autem tertio dixit ad illos: 'Quid enim mali fecit iste? Nullam causam mortis invenio in eo: corripiam ergo illum et dimittam.'
23. At illi instabant vocibus magnis postulantes ut crucifigeretur: et invalescebant voces eorum.
24. Et Pilatus adiudicavit fieri petitionem eorum.
25. Dimisit autem illis eum qui propter homicidium et seditionem missus fuerat in carcerem, quem petebant: Iesum vero tradidit voluntati eorum.
26. Et cum ducerent eum, adprehenderunt Simonem quemdam Cyrenensem venientem de villa, et inposuerunt illi crucem portare post Iesum.
27. Sequebatur autem illum multa turba populi et mulierum, quae plangebant, et lamentabant eum.
28. Conversus autem ad illas Iesus dixit: 'Filiae Hierusalem, nolite flere super me; sed super vos ipsas flete, et super filios vestros.
29. Quoniam ecce venient dies, in quibus dicent: "Beatae steriles, et ventres qui non genuerunt, et ubera quae non lactaverunt."
30. Tunc incipient dicere montibus: "Cadite super nos" et collibus: "Operite nos."
31. Quia si in viridi ligno haec faciunt, in arido quid fiet?'
32. Ducebantur autem et alii duo nequam cum eo, ut interficerentur.
33. Et postquam venerunt in locum, qui vocatur Calvariae, ibi crucifixerunt eum, et latrones unum a dextris, et alterum a sinistris.
34. Iesus autem dicebat: 'Pater, dimitte illis; non enim sciunt quid faciunt.' Dividentes vero vestimenta eius, miserunt sortes.
35. Et stabat populus spectans, et deridebant eum principes cum eis, dicentes: 'Alios salvos fecit; se salvum faciat, si hic est Christus Dei electus.'
36. Inludebant autem ei et milites, accedentes et acetum offerentes illi,
37. et dicentes: 'Si tu es rex Iudaeorum, salvum te fac.'
38. Erat autem et superscriptio inscripta super illum litteris graecis et latinis et hebraicis: 'Hic est rex Iudaeorum.'
39. Unus autem de his qui pendebant latronibus blasphemabat eum, dicens: 'Si tu es Christus, salvum fac temet ipsum et nos.'
40. Respondens autem alter increpabat illum, dicens: 'Neque tu times Deum, quod in eadem damnatione es?

41. Et nos quidem iuste; nam digna factis recipimus: hic vero nihil mali gessit.'

42. Et dicebat ad Iesum: 'Domine, memento mei, cum veneris in regnum tuum.'

43. Et dixit Iesus: 'Amen dico tibi: hodie mecum eris in paradiso.'

44. Erat autem fere hora sexta, et tenebrae factae sunt in universa terra usque in nonam horam.

45. Et obscuratus est sol: et velum templi scissum est medium.

46. Et clamans voce magna Iesus ait: 'Pater, in manus tuas commendo spiritum meum.' Et haec dicens, expiravit.

47. Videns autem centurio quod factum fuerat, glorificavit Deum, dicens: 'Vere hic homo iustus erat.'

48. Et omnis turba eorum qui simul aderant ad spectaculum istud, et videbant quae fiebant, percutientes pectora sua revertebantur.

49. Stabant autem omnes noti eius a longe, et mulieres quae secutae erant eum a Galilaea haec videntes.

50. Et ecce vir nomine Ioseph, qui erat decurio, vir bonus et iustus,

51. (Hic non consenserat consilio et actibus eorum) ab Arimathia civitate Iudaeae, qui expectabat et ipse regnum Dei.

52. Hic accessit ad Pilatum, et petiit corpus Iesu.

53. Et depositum involvit sindone, et posuit eum in monumento exciso, in quo nondum quisquam positus fuerat.

54. Et dies erat parasceves et sabbatum illucescebat.

55. Subsecutae autem mulieres, quae cum ipso venerant de Galilaea, viderunt monumentum, et quemadmodum positum erat corpus eius.

56. Et revertentes paraverunt aromata et unguenta, et sabbato quidem siluerunt secundum mandatum.

---

1 **surgens:** 'having arisen' (see G.20(a): other examples are 6 *audiens*, 46 *dicens*, 47 *Videns*.
omnis multitudo...duxerunt: the verb is plural because *multitudo* is taken to mean 'many people'.

2 **Coeperunt... accusare:** 'they began to accuse' or 'they accused' (see G.4(d)).
prohibentem: sc. 'us', 'people'.

4 **Nihil...causae:** 'no fault' (partitive gen.: RLRGr L(d)2).

6 **si:** 'whether' (see G.24(c)).

7 **quod:** 'that' (see G.22(a)).
de...potestate: 'from the jurisdiction...'.
illis diebus: 'during those days'.

8 **Iesu:** abl.
erat cupiens: 'he had wanted' (see G.4(b)).

eo quod: 'because' (see G.30(c)).
sperabat...videre...fieri: 'he hoped to see... being performed' (see G.22(b)).

9 **ipse:** 'he' (i.e. Jesus. See G.11(a)(ii)).

11 **inlusit indutum:** sc. 'him' (contrast *inludo* + acc. here with 36, where dat. is used. Both constructions are CL).

12 **in ipsa die:** 'on that day' (see G.11(a)(ii)).
ad invicem: 'to one another' (see G.11(e)(ii)).

13-14 **convocatis principibus...ad illos:** the abl. abs. and the acc. refer to the same people.

14 **isto:** 'that' (see G.11(c)).
in his: 'in those things' (see G.11(c)).

15 **ei:** 'by him' (dative of agent: see RLRGr L(e)1(iv) and G.16(b)).

17 **eis:** 'for them' (dative of advantage).

per: 'because of'.

unum: 'a person' (see G.10(d)).

19 erat...missus: 'had been sent'.

24 adiudicavit fieri petitionem eorum: 'gave judgement that their petition be granted'.

25 missus fuerat: 'had been sent' (see G.4(a)).

26 portare: 'to carry' (see G.17(a)).

27 populi: i.e. 'of men'.

28 super: 'over', 'on account of' (CL acc. only: see G.15(b)).

29 Beatae steriles: sc. 'are'.

30 incipient dicere: 'they will say' (cf. G.4(d)).

31 in viridi ligno...in arido: 'in the case of...'

33 a dextris...a sinistris: *a* = 'on'.

34 dimitte illis: 'forgive them (sc. their sins)' (CL acc.: see G.15(b)).

non...sciunt quid faciunt: for mood of *faciunt* see G.24(b).

Dividentes: 'those dividing' or 'when dividing' (see G.20(b)).

36 Inludebant: here with dative (cf. 11 above).

39 Unus de his: 'one of those' (see G.15(d)).

temet ipsum: 'yourself'.

40 quod: 'seeing that'.

in eadem damnatione: 'under the same sentence'.

41 et nos quidem iuste: sc. 'are being put to death'.

digna: i.e. 'a recompense which matches...'.

43 Amen: 'verily' (Hebrew: see G.6(c)).

45 medium: lit. 'in the middle'. Tr. 'in two'.

47 factum fuerat: 'had been done' (see G.4(a)).

48 istud: 'that' (see G.11(c)).

49 a longe: 'from afar' (see G.8).

50 ecce: sc. 'there was'.

53 depositum: i.e. *Iesum*.

positus fuerat: 'had been placed' (see G.4(a)).

54 paraceves: Greek gen. 'Preparation (for the sabbath or the Passover)' (see RLRGr H6).

4. 1 Corinthians 13

The Pauline epistles were an important source of readings (*capitula* or *lectiones*) for the Divine Office. In much the same way as the Psalms, then, they made their way into the consciousness of monastic and other clerical writers. This passage, for example, forms a strong background to the twelfth-century Peter the Venerable's attempt to bring to an end the enmity between monks of his own Cluniac order and the rival Cistercians (see section 17.1 for some other parts of this letter).

Faith, hope and charity

1. Si linguis hominum loquar et angelorum, caritatem autem non habeam, factus sum velut aes sonans aut cymbalum tinniens.

2. Et si habuero prophetiam et noverim mysteria omnia et omnem scientiam et habuero omnem fidem ita ut montes transferam, caritatem autem non habuero, nihil sum.

3. Et si distribuero in cibos pauperum omnes facultates meas, et si tradidero corpus meum ut ardeam, caritatem autem non habuero, nihil mihi prodest.

4. Caritas patiens est, benigna est: caritas non aemulatur, non agit perperam, non inflatur.

5. Non est ambitiosa, non quaerit quae sua sunt, non inritatur, non cogitat malum.

6. Non gaudet super iniquitatem, congaudet autem veritati.
7. Omnia suffert, omnia credit, omnia sperat, omnia sustinet.
8. Caritas numquam excidit: sive prophetiae, evacuabuntur, sive linguae, cessabunt, sive scientia, destruetur.
9. Ex parte enim cognoscimus et ex parte prophetamus.
10. Cum autem venerit quod perfectum est, evacuabitur quod ex parte est.
11. Cum essem parvulus, loquebar ut parvulus, sapiebam ut parvulus, cogitabam ut parvulus. Quando factus sum vir evacuavi quae erant parvuli.
12. Videmus nunc per speculum in enigmate, tunc autem facie ad faciem. Nunc cognosco ex parte, tunc autem cognoscam sicut et cognitus sum.
13. Nunc autem manent fides, spes, caritas, tria haec: maior autem his est caritas.

---

1 **si..loquar...non habeam, factus sum:** 'If I were to..., I would become' (see G.28(b)).
2 **si habuero...et noverim:** 'If I possess...and know' (see G.25(b) and 28).
3 **in cibos:** 'upon food', i.e. 'to provide food'.
4 **sive prophetiae:** 'if (sc. there are) prophecies'

(and so also the other *sive* clauses).
10 **quod...quod:** 'that which'.
11 **quae erant parvuli:** 'the things which were (characteristic) of a child' (see RLRGr L(d)1).
12 **facie ad faciem:** 'face to face'.
13 **maior...his:** 'greatest among these' (see G.12(a)).

Section 4
The Church Fathers

The most important group of early Christian Latin writers is that known as the Fathers of the Church. Some, notably St Hilary of Poitiers, St Jerome and St Ambrose, absorbed and transmitted the theology of Eastern Christianity to the West. St Augustine carried the arguments forward in his challenges to schisms and heresies (Donatists, Manichees and Pelagians) and his defence of the faith against the charge that it was responsible for the decline of the Roman Empire (*De civitate Dei* 'The City of God': see section 4.1(b)). Writers such as Pope Leo the Great and Pope Gregory the Great (d. 604) laid the foundations of the central and unifying power of the papacy as well as setting out firm principles for Christian behaviour. The last Latin Father, St Isidore of Seville, epitomized and sanitized for Christian consumption the learning of the ancients. This period and these men had effectively created the Western Church, its theology, its political institutions and its intellectual structure. They had also determined its language – Latin. In the later Middle Ages, they were regarded as authorities (though not on the same level as the biblical writers – see section 16.2) from whom flowed theological insight about the nature of Christ's divinity or of the Trinity, practical wisdom about the nature of man and his duties to the world and to God, knowledge of the world and arguments for what a Christian should know. That is why their names are cited everywhere in the passages which appear in this volume.

The earlier Fathers, such as Jerome, Ambrose and Augustine, had received a classical training and tended to write in a highly sophisticated manner. But it was not possible to receive Christianity in the West in Latin without a sort of linguistic conversion, since the *Vetus Latina* (see section 3 Intro.) and the liturgy were already marked by 'vulgarisms'. It was also necessary to come to terms with the dissonance between style and form, upon which the grammatical and rhetorical education placed great weight, and content. Christian writings, in particular the Bible, held the truth, but expressed it in barbaric Latin. Classical works, such as Cicero's, expressed beautifully what was often the antithesis of the truth.

The psychological problems involved are well illustrated by St Jerome's famous vision. Brought before a heavenly tribunal and asked about his way of life, he replied that he was a Christian. The judge told him that he lied: *Ciceronianus es, non Christianus: ubi enim thesaurus tuus, ibi et cor tuum*: 'You are a Ciceronian, not a Christian; for where your treasure is, there is your heart' (the last part is a quotation from Mt 6.21, cf. Lk 12.34). A chastened Jerome told God that if he ever afterwards possessed or read secular works, he had denied Him. But the anecdote reveals a real tension between the necessity of studying some pagan literature simply in order to achieve the requisite level of linguistic sophistication for biblical commentary and theological investigation, and the dangers thought to be implicit in the material these works contained.

This problem was never fully resolved – there were 'humanists' and 'anti-humanists' throughout the Middle Ages. But the humanist position could be justified because it was validated by St Augustine and St Basil. Augustine said in De doctrina Christiana ('On Christian Education'), 'If the philosophers chanced to utter truths useful to our faith, as the Platonists above all did, not only should we not fear these truths, but we must also remove them from those unlawful usurpers for our own use' (as the Israelites had carried out of Egypt the golden and silver vessels and precious objects with which they were later to construct the Tabernacle). St Basil used a different image: the pagan works were rose-bushes, from which beautiful flowers could be plucked, if one could manage to avoid the thorns which protected them. It was certainly this attitude which saved pagan Latin writing in the West, and pagan Greek in the East, from perishing completely, quite as much as the innate conservatism of the educational systems, which were largely inherited from pagan antiquity (see section 1 Intro.).

The language used by the Fathers is notable in two ways: (1) It introduces special terminology, in theology (e.g. *contritio* 'contrition', *trinitas* 'Trinity', *impeccantia* 'sinlessness'), liturgy (e.g. *palla* 'altar-cloth', *missa* 'Mass') or canon law (e.g. *canonicus* 'canonical'); (2) It uses symbolical language and rich imagery. Hence a word such as *ficus* 'figleaf' can be used by Augustine to mean *peccatum* 'sin', and Babylon is 'the world' as opposed to the City of God; *oleum* 'oil' expresses not only material wealth but also moral wealth. The language is full of such imagistic expressions. Sin (*peccatum, delictum, culpa, uitium, noxa*) is 'the soul's worm' (*tinea animae*), 'mud' (*lutum prauitatis* 'the mire of depravity'), 'abject slavery' (*misera seruitus*) and 'death' (*opera mortis* 'the works of death'). Most noticeable is the wealth of new terms expressive of the warmth of man's affection for Christ and of Christ's for man, of the strength of man's desire for life with God and of human love. For example, the idea of community between God and man is often expressed by new terms produced by the prefix *con-* ('with'), such as *commorior* 'I die with' (e.g. *qui Christo commoritur* 'he who dies with Christ' – Ambrose), and *condescensio* (the 'lowering' or 'condescension' of Jesus in becoming a man). The same prefix is used to reinforce the notion of brotherly unity, as in *commartyr* 'fellow martyr', *commembrum* 'fellow member', *congaudeo* 'rejoice with'.

See further: M. F. Wiles, *The Christian Fathers*, London, 1966; H. A. Wolfson, *The Philosophy of the Church Fathers*, vol. I, 3rd edn, Cambridge, Mass., 1970–.

1. St Augustine of Hippo (354–430)

St Augustine was born in the North African town of Thagaste. He received his education here and in Carthage, where he became a teacher of rhetoric. He was converted to Christianity from Manicheism in 387, in Milan, where he was a teacher of rhetoric and St Ambrose was bishop. In 395 he became bishop of Hippo in Africa, where he died during a siege conducted by the Vandals under Genseric. During this period he wrote constantly – letters, sermons, biblical commentaries, works on aspects of belief, on the sacraments, on the Trinity. Most importantly, he composed the *Confessions* and *The City of God*, the philosophical influence of which upon the medieval mind is all-pervasive and rivalled that of Aristotle.

Augustine's journey towards Christianity was made via the Platonic philosophical tradition known as Neoplatonism. In particular the system of Plotinus influenced his teachings. However, the central aspect of his theology was the priority of faith over understanding. God gives faith as a gift to man. But man is rational and therefore not only can, but must attempt to understand what faith teaches. God is at the centre of everything, at its beginning and at its end. For Augustine, then, there is no separation between theology and philosophy. Moreover, because faith is prior, and that comes from within, understanding will proceed from study of one's inner experience. This location of theological knowledge in internal contemplation is at its most obvious in the *Confessions*, where Augustine traces his own journey to faith. It is this attitude which is central to the influence of Augustine in the Middle Ages and which can be seen at work in thinkers as diverse as John Scottus Eriugena (see section 9.5) and St Anselm (see section 14.2). Only with the conquest of Aristotelian dialectic in the later twelfth and thirteenth centuries did this basic position begin to weaken.

See further: P. Brown, *Augustine of Hippo*, London, 1967; G. J. P. O'Daly, *Augustine's Philosophy of Mind*, London, 1987; M. Haren, *The Western Intellectual Tradition from Antiquity to the Thirteenth Century*, 2nd edn, Toronto, 1993. For a good introduction to Medieval Latin philosophy, with selections and commentaries, see S. J. Tester, *Fides Quaerens Intellectum: Medieval Philosophy from Augustine to Ockham*, Bristol, 1989.

1(a) The Confessions

(i) *Augustine tells how he finally managed to resolve his interior struggle between the world (with its bodily pleasures, including marriage) and Christ (the life of renunciation). The internal storm is now at its height. He goes out into the garden, away from his friend Alypius, to weep.*

Vbi uero a fundo arcano alta consideratio traxit et congessit totam miseriam meam in conspectu cordis mei, oborta est procella ingens, ferens ingentem imbrem lacrimarum. Et ut totum effunderem cum uocibus suis, surrexi ab Alypio – solitudo mihi ad negotium flendi aptior suggerebatur – et secessi remotius, quam ut posset mihi onerosa esse etiam eius praesentia. Sic tunc   5
eram, et ille sensit: nescio quid enim, puto, dixeram, in quo apparebat sonus uocis meae iam fletu grauidus, et sic surrexeram. Mansit ergo ille ubi sedebamus nimie stupens. Ego sub quadam fici arbore straui me nescio quo modo et dimisi habenas lacrimis, et proruperunt flumina oculorum meorum, acceptabile sacrificium tuum, et non quidem his uerbis, sed in hac sententia   10
multa dixi tibi: 'Et tu, Domine, usquequo? Vsquequo, Domine, irasceris in finem? Ne memor fueris iniquitatum nostrarum antiquarum.' Sentiebam enim eis me teneri. Iactabam uoces miserabiles: 'Quandiu, quandiu? Cras et cras? Quare non modo? Quare non hac hora finis turpitudinis meae?'

---

1 **a fundo arcano:** sc. 'of my soul'.
3 **totum:** i.e. *imbrem lacrimarum*.
  cum uocibus suis: lit. with its words, i.e. 'with the words which it (i.e. my pain) prompted'.
4f. **Alypio:** Alypius, a long-standing, slightly younger, friend of Augustine, also born at Tagaste. He attended Augustine's lectures in Carthage, became a Manichee when he did, followed him to Italy and was eventually baptized with him. He was a monk at Tagaste from 391 to

394 and then visited Jerome in Bethlehem. He later became bishop of Tagaste, where he died *c*.430.
  solitudo looks forward to *aptior* (complement) *suggerebatur*. Tr. 'solitude seemed...'.
5 **remotius...posset...praesentia:** 'further away than that his presence could...', i.e. 'too far away for his presence to...'.
8 **nimie stupens:** 'completely dumbstruck' (see G.12(b)).

10 **acceptabile sacrificium tuum:** 'an acceptable sacrifice to you' (the words are in apposition to *flumina oculorum meorum*). The phrase is liturgical and is based on 1 Peter 2.5: *offerre spirituales hostias, acceptabiles Deo per Iesum Christum* ('to offer spiritual victims, acceptable to God through Jesus Christ').

in hac sententia: 'with this meaning' (CL often uses *in* + abl. thus of the meaning of words. Cf. *in eodem sensu* 'with the same meaning').

11 **Et tu, Domine, usquequo?:** cf. Ps. 6.4 *sed tu,*

domine, usquequo. Augustine naturally has recourse to biblical language at emotional high points. CL uses *quousque.*

11f. **Vsquequo, Domine, irasceris in finem?:** Ps. 78.5 *usquequo, Domine irasceris, in finem?* 'How long, O Lord? Will you be angry for ever?'.

12 **Ne...fueris:** 'don't be' (see *RLGVE* 171(a)).

14 **turpitudinis meae:** Augustine is engaged principally at this moment in a struggle against his own sexual desires.

(ii) *As he weeps, he hears a voice saying* 'Take, read'. *He obeys the instruction and is converted.*

Dicebam haec et flebam, amarissima contritione cordis mei. Et ecce audio uocem de uicina domo cum cantu dicentis, et crebro repetentis, quasi pueri an puellae, nescio: 'Tolle, lege, tolle, lege.' Statimque mutato uultu intentissimus cogitare coepi, utrumnam solerent pueri in aliquo genere ludendi cantitare tale aliquid, nec occurrebat omnino audisse me uspiam. Repressoque impetu   5
lacrimarum, surrexi, nihil aliud interpretans diuinitus mihi iuberi, nisi ut aperirem codicem et legerem quod primum caput inuenissem. Audieram enim de Antonio, quod ex euangelica lectione, cui forte superuenerat, admonitus fuerit, tamquam sibi diceretur quod legebatur: 'Vade, uende omnia, quae habes, da pauperibus et habebis thesaurum in caelis; et ueni   10
sequere me,' et tali oraculo confestim ad te esse conuersum.

Itaque concitus redii in eum locum, ubi sedebat Alypius: ibi enim posueram codicem apostoli, cum inde surrexeram. Arripui, aperui et legi in silentio capitulum, quo primum coniecti sunt oculi mei: 'Non in commessationibus et ebrietatibus, non in cubilibus et impudicitiis, non in contentione et aemula-   15
tione, sed induite dominum Iesum Christum, et carnis prouidentiam ne feceritis in concupiscentiis.' Nec ultra uolui legere, nec opus erat. Statim quippe cum fine huiusce sententiae, quasi luce securitatis infusa cordi meo, omnes dubitationis tenebrae diffugerunt.

1 **amarissima contritione:** 'in the most bitter contrition' (accompanying ablative RLRGr L(f)3).

2 **dicentis...repetentis:** 'of a person saying...and repeating' (note that *dicere* in LL often means 'sing').

an: 'or'.

4f. **tale aliquid:** 'any such thing'.

8 **Antonio:** St Antony (*c.*251–356), a Coptic-

speaking Christian from the region of Alexandria in Egypt, the inspiration of the desert hermits. His biography, written by Athanasius, left a deep impression upon both Jerome and Augustine.

quod: 'that' (see G.22(a)) looking forward to *admonitus fuerit* 'he was advised' (see G.4(a)).

9f. **Vade, uende...me:** Mt 19.21.

11 **et...esse conuersum:** 'and...that he (i.e. Ant-

ony) had been converted'. Augustine starts the reported statement with a *quod* clause (*audieram...quod...admonitus fuerit*), but ends with acc.+ inf.

13 **codicem apostoli:** Augustine had been reading St Paul's Epistles, in a codex, not a roll (see section 1.2. (iii), l.1).

14 **Non in commessationibus...:** Paul's verse in

Romans 13.13 begins *sicut in die honeste ambulemus* 'Let us walk honourably, as in the daytime...' and this needs to be supplied to make sense of the quotation.

18 **quasi...meo:** *luce...infusa* is abl. abs: 'light having been...'; *cordi meo* depends on *infusa*: 'into my heart'.

(iii) *He shows the chapter to Alypius, who reads on and finds something which confirms him also. They report back to Augustine's mother.*

Tum interiecto aut digito aut nescio quo alio signo, codicem clausi, et tranquillo iam uultu indicaui Alypio. At ille quid in se ageretur – quod ego nesciebam – sic indicauit. Petit uidere quid legissem: ostendi, et attendit etiam ultra quam ego legeram, et ignorabam quid sequeretur. Sequebatur autem: 'Infirmum autem in fide recipite.' Quod ille ad se rettulit mihique aperuit. Sed   5
tali admonitione firmatus est placitoque ac proposito bono (et congruentissimo suis moribus, quibus a me in melius iam olim ualde longeque distabat), sine ulla turbulenta cunctatione coniunctus est. Inde ad matrem ingredimur, indicamus: gaudet. Narramus, quemadmodum gestum sit: exultat et triumphat, et benedicebat tibi, qui potens es ultra quam petimus aut intelligimus facere,   10
quia tanto amplius sibi a te concessum de me uidebat, quam petere solebat miserabilibus flebilibusque gemitibus. Conuertisti enim me ad te, ut nec uxorem quaererem nec aliquam spem saeculi huius, stans in ea regula fidei, in qua me ante tot annos ei reuelaueras, et conuertisti luctum eius in gaudium, multo uberius, quam uoluerat, et multo carius atque castius, quam de nepotibus   15
carnis meae requirebat.

2 **indicaui:** sc.'what had happened'.
3 **Petit uidere:** 'asked to see' (see G.23(a)).
6f. **placitoque ac proposito bono...coniunctus est:** 'to the good resolution and purpose...he applied himself' (lit. 'he was joined').
8 **indicamus:** sc.'her what had happened'.
10 **tibi:** i.e. 'God'.
potens es...facere: 'you are able to do'.
ultra quam: 'beyond what'.
11 **tanto amplius...uidebat:** 'she saw that so much more had been granted to her by you concerning me'.
13f. **stans in ea regula fidei, in qua...reuelaueras:** See *Confessions* III.xi. Nine years before his

conversion, his mother dreams she is standing on a wooden rule (here interpreted as the 'rule of faith') and is shown by a young interlocutor her wayward son Augustine standing on the same rule.

15f. **multo carius atque castius, quam...requirebat:** 'much more dearly and much more chastely than she used to ask concerning...' Augustine's mother had been attempting for years to stop his philandering by finding him a wife. But for St Paul, chastity was the primary virtue, and marriage acceptable as second best only because it was better than burning with lust (1 Corinthians 7.7–9).

1(b) *Augustine,* City of God

In 410, the armies of Alaric the Goth sacked Rome. Many pagans took the opportunity to blame the Christian God for the disaster. Augustine says in his *Retractions*: 'Fired with a zeal for the house of God, I decided to write my work the *City of God* against their blasphemies and errors.' It was in fact normal for pagans to ascribe disasters to the anger of deities (as Juno is constantly responsible for the obstacles put in Aeneas' path in Virgil's *Aeneid*). Christianity was perceived by them as incompatible with normal political duties. In the work, written between 413 and 425, Augustine used Greek philosophical thinking and Jewish biblical wisdom to demolish this position. His vision speaks of two cities, one built by humans and thus mutable and corruptible, the other heavenly and therefore the opposite. The administration of the temporal city must be carried out under the moral law, or it becomes another Babylon.

In the course of his argument, Augustine has occasion to deal with many central questions of Christian doctrine. In this passage, he argues that the Trinity is simple and unchangeable. His arguments find many echoes in later writers. Note that part is utilized by John Scottus Eriugena in section 9.5. See section 18.3 for Abelard's account of the relationship between the elements of the Trinity.

(i) *The good, i.e. God, is single and changeless. What is engendered from this (Son and Holy Spirit) shares these qualities.*

Est itaque bonum solum simplex et ob hoc solum incommutabile, quod est Deus. Ab hoc bono creata sunt omnia bona, sed non simplicia et ob hoc mutabilia. Creata sane, inquam, id est facta, non genita. Quod enim de simplici bono genitum est, pariter simplex est et hoc est quod illud de quo genitum est; quae duo Patrem et Filium dicimus; et utrumque hoc cum spiritu suo unus   5
Deus est; qui spiritus Patris et Filii spiritus sanctus propria quadam notione huius nominis in sacris litteris nuncupatur.

---

1 **Est:** 'there exists'.
solum simplex: sc. 'which is' (also before the second *solum*).

3 **Quod enim...:** 'for what...' (subject of both *genitum est* and *est* in the main clause).

4 **hoc est quod illud:** 'is the same thing as that...'.

6 **spiritus sanctus** is the complement of *nuncupatur*.

6f. **propria quadam notione:** 'through a certain special meaning...'.

(ii) *But the Holy Spirit is also different from Father and Son. This Trinity is God. It is single because it is what it has.*

Alius est autem quam Pater et Filius, quia nec Pater est nec Filius; sed 'alius' dixi, non 'aliud', quia et hoc pariter simplex pariterque incommutabile bonum est et coaeternum. Et haec trinitas unus est Deus; nec ideo non simplex, quia trinitas. Neque enim propter hoc naturam istam boni simplicem dicimus, quia Pater in ea solus aut solus Filius aut solus spiritus sanctus, aut uero sola est ista   5 nominis trinitas sine subsistentia personarum, sicut Sabelliani haeretici putaue- runt; sed ideo simplex dicitur, quoniam quod habet hoc est, excepto quod relatiue quaeque persona ad alteram dicitur. Nam utique Pater habet Filium, nec tamen ipse est Filius, et Filius habet Patrem nec tamen ipse est Pater. In quo ergo ad semet ipsum dicitur, non ad alterum, hoc est quod habet; sicut ad se   10 ipsum dicitur uiuus habendo utique uitam, et eadem uita ipse est.

1 **Alius est:** 'it' (i.e. the *Spiritus sanctus*).

1f. **sed 'alius' dixi, non 'aliud':** i.e. 'another person' as against 'another thing'.

2 **et hoc:** 'this also', i.e. 'the Holy Spirit'.

4 **naturam...simplicem:** sc. *esse*, acc. + inf. introduced by *dicimus*.
boni: '(of) goodness'.

4f. **quia...sanctus:** sc. *est*.

6 **nominis trinitas:** 'a trinity of name', i.e. 'in name only'.
Sabelliani haeretici: Sabellians (named after Sabellius, *fl.* 220) believed that the persons of the Trinity were only different aspects of a unified God.

7 **quod...est:** 'it is what it has'.
excepto quod: 'except that'.

8 **relatiue** looks forward to *ad alteram* ('in relation to another').

9 **ipse...Filius...ipse...Pater:** *ipse* is in each case the pronoun 'he' and subject of *est* (see G.11(a)(ii)).

9f. **In quo...alterum:** '(sc. in the respect) in which it is spoken of in relation to itself and not to another'.

10f. **ad se ipsum:** 'in relation to himself'.

11 **uiuus:** sc. *esse*.

(iii) *Its nature is single because it cannot lose what it has. Single things show no division between 'quality' and 'substance'.*

Propter hoc itaque natura dicitur simplex, cui non sit aliquid habere quod uel possit amittere; uel aliud sit habens, aliud quod habet; sicut uas aliquem liquorem aut corpus colorem aut aer lucem siue feruorem aut anima sapientiam. Nihil enim horum est id quod habet; nam neque uas liquor est nec corpus color nec aer lux siue feruor neque anima sapientia est. Hinc est   5 quod etiam priuari possunt rebus quas habent et in alios habitus uel qualitates uerti atque mutari, ut et uas euacuetur umore quo plenum est, et corpus decoloretur et aer tenebrescat siue frigescat et anima desipiat... .

Secundum hoc ergo dicuntur illa simplicia quae principaliter uereque diuina sunt, quod non aliud est in eis qualitas, aliud substantia, nec aliorum   10 participatione uel diuina uel sapientia uel beata sunt... .

1f. **cui...amittere:** 'for which it is not possible to have something which it could actually lose'.

2 **uel...habet:** 'or for which "possessing" and "what it possesses" are different from each other' i.e. 'if it is the same as what it has'.

2f. **sicut...sapientiam:** sc. *habet* with each subject and object (e.g. *uas aliquem liquorem habet* etc.).

5f. **Hinc est quod:** 'Hence it comes about that...'.

7 **ut:** 'with the result that...'.

10 **non aliud...aliud:** '(sc. it is) not (the case that) one thing...another...'.

11 **sapientia:** n.pl. adj. (like *diuina* and *beata*, picking up *illa*).

2. St Jerome (c.331–420)

St Jerome was a prolific commentator on the Bible as well as a translator (see section 3 Intro.). Much of this work was done while he was in the East (as a hermit in Syria from 374 for about two years and then a monk in Bethlehem from 385 till his death). In those works the language is plain and often employs neologism. He was also, like Augustine, a prolific letter writer. His letters, by contrast with his other works, are examples of a higher literary genre and show the level of stylistic sophistication that could bring to Christian material. Like their model, the Epistles of St Paul, they always aim to provide material help and guidance to their recipients in the propagation and defence of Christianity and in the task of living the Christian life. In this example, written to one Innocentius *c.*370, Jerome reports a miracle, one of the basic types of proof that the Christian God is at work in the world.

(i) *Jerome finally agrees to Innocentius' request to write about a contemporary miracle.*

Saepe a me, Innocenti carissime, postulasti, ut de eius miraculo rei, quae in nostram aetatem inciderat, non tacerem. Cumque ego id uerecunde et uere, ut nunc experior, negarem meque adsequi posse diffiderem, siue quia omnis humanus sermo inferior esset laude caelesti, siue quia otium quasi quaedam ingenii robigo paruulam licet facultatem pristini siccasset eloquii, tu e contrario   5
adserebas in dei rebus non possibilitatem inspici debere, sed animum, neque eum posse uerba deficere, qui credidisset in uerbo.

So Jerome agrees, likening himself to an unseasoned sailor set adrift on the Black Sea, and begins the story.

1 **postulasti:** = *postulauisti* (see RLRGr A4).

1 **ut** looks forward to *non tacerem*.

1f. **in nostram aetatem:** 'during my lifetime' (*in* follows from *inciderat*).

2f. **Cumque...uerbo:** the basic structure is *cum...negarem* and *diffiderem, siue quia..., siue quia otium...facultatem...siccasset eloquii,* (main

clause) *tu...adserebas...*(2 acc. + inf. clauses) (1) *non possibilitatem...debere, sed animum,* (2) *neque eum...deficere, qui* (antecedent *eum*)...

4 **inferior...laude caelesti:** 'beneath heavenly praise', i.e. 'inadequate to praise heaven', or 'inferior to the hymns of the angels'.

5 **licet:** 'though' (qualifying *paruulam*).

siccasset: *siccauisset* (see RLRGr A5).
6 **debere:** impersonal 'that one should...'.
7 **in uerbo:** 'The Word' (i.e. Christ. Cf. section

2.3, note on 1.11. Note the word play *uerba/ uerbo*).

(ii) *The governor visits Vercellae and has to try a case of adultery. After torture, the man confesses. The woman, a Christian, refuses to confess to a deed she did not do and appeals to Christ.*

Igitur Vercellae Ligurum ciuitas haud procul a radicibus Alpium sita, olim potens, nunc raro habitatore semiruta. Hanc cum ex more consularis inuiseret, oblatam sibi quandam mulierculam una cum adultero – nam id crimen maritus inpegerat – poenali carceris horrore circumdedit. Neque multo post, cum liuidas carnes ungula cruenta pulsaret et sulcatis lateribus dolor quaereret ueritatem,   5
infelicissimus iuuenis uolens conpendio mortis longos uitare cruciatus, dum in suum mentitur sanguinem, accusauit alienum solusque omnium miser merito uisus est percuti, quia non reliquit innoxiae, unde posset negare. At uero mulier sexu fortior suo, cum eculeus corpus extenderet et sordidas paedore carceris manus post tergum uincula cohiberent, oculis quos tantum tortor alligare non   10
poterat, suspexit ad caelum et uolutis per ora lacrimis: 'tu,' inquit, 'testis domine Iesu, cui occultum nihil est, qui es scrutator renis et cordis, non ideo me negare uelle, ne peream, sed ideo mentiri nolle, ne peccem. At tu, miserrime homo, si interire festinas, cur duos interimis innocentes? Equidem et ipsa cupio mori, cupio inuisum hoc corpus exuere, sed non quasi adultera. Praesto iugulum,   15
micantem intrepida excipio mucronem, innocentiam tantum mecum feram. Non moritur quisquis uicturus occiditur.'

1 **Igitur Vercellae:** sc. 'is' (in CL, *igitur* is always 2nd word).
2 **raro habitatore:** 'with few inhabitants' (accompanying ablative, see RLRGr L(f)3).
Hanc: i.e. Vercellae.
consularis: the governors of provinces made a progress round their areas of jurisdiction, dealing with various business, including juridical matters.
3 **oblatam...mulierculam** is the object of *circumdedit.*
4 **inpegerat:** sc. 'upon them'.
5 **sulcatis lateribus:** 'his sides having been furrowed', i.e. 'by (means of) furrowing his sides'.
6f. **dum...mentitur..., accusauit:** 'by lying, he...' (see G.30(b)).
in suum...sanguinem: 'against...'. Tr. *sanguinem* as 'life'.
7 **alienum:** sc. *sanguinem.*

miser: noun, 'wretch'.
8 **non   reliquit...unde:** lit. 'he did not leave...whence'. Tr. 'he left no way for her to'.
9f. **sordidas...manus** is the object of *cohiberent* (subject *uincula*), second verb in the *cum* clause.
11 **uolutis...lacrimis:** 'as the tears fell'.
Tu...testis: sc. *es.* This introduces 2 acc. + inf. clauses: (1) *non...uelle,* (2) *sed...nolle* (*me* is subject of both and in each *ideo* looks forward to *ne*: 'that I am not...so as not to...').
12 **renis:** lit. 'kidney', but with *cordis* it means 'heart and mind' (cf. Ps. 7.10; Rev. 2.23 *ego sum scrutans renes et corda* 'I am he who looks into hearts and minds'). Normally plural in CL.
16 **micantem** looks forward to *mucronem* (obj. of *excipio*).
tantum: 'so long as', 'provided that' (+ subj.).
17 **uicturus:** from *uiuo.* Tr. 'in order to live' (See G. 10(c)), i.e. 'to gain eternal life'.

(iii) *The governor orders further torture, while the woman continues to protest her innocence. Finally, he judges the pair guilty.*

Igitur consularis pastis cruore luminibus, ut fera, quae gustatum semel sanguinem semper sitit, duplicari tormenta iubet et saeuum dentibus frendens similem carnifici minitatus est poenam, nisi confiteretur sexus infirmior, quod non potuerat robur uirile reticere.

'Succurre, domine Iesu: ad unum hominem tuum quam plura sunt inuenta   5
supplicia!' Crines ligantur ad stipitem et toto corpore ad eculeum fortius alligato uicinus pedibus ignis adponitur, utrumque latus carnifex fodit nec papillis dentur indutiae: inmota mulier manet et a dolore corporis spiritu separato, dum conscientiae bono fruitur, uetuit circa se saeuire tormenta. Iudex crudelis quasi superatus adtollitur, illa dominum deprecatur; soluuntur   10
membra conpagibus, illa oculos ad caelum tendit; de communi scelere alius confitetur, illa pro confitente negat et periclitans ipsa alium uindicat periclitantem.

Vna interim uox: 'Caede, ure, lacera; non feci. Si dictis tollitur fides, ueniet dies, quae hoc crimen diligenter excutiat; habebo iudicem meum.' Iam lassus   15
tortor suspirabat in gemitum nec erat nouo uulneri locus, iam uicta saeuitia corpus, quod laniarat, horrebat: extemplo ira concitus consularis: 'Quid miramini,' inquit, 'circumstantes, si torqueri mauult mulier, quam perire? Adulterium certe sine duobus comitti non potest et esse credibilius reor noxiam ream negare de scelere, quam innocentem iuuenem confiteri.'   20

1f. **Igitur...reticere:** the basic structure is *consularis* (subject)...*duplicari tormenta iubet et...minitatus est..., nisi..., quod* ('what...', obj. of *reticere*).
1 **gustatum semel:** 'once he has tasted it' (with *sanguinem*, object of *sitit*).
2 **saeuum:** adv. 'savagely' (a Graecism: see G.10).
5 **quam plura:** 'how many'.
6 **toto corpore** looks forward to *alligato* (abl. abs.).
  fortius: 'very firmly' (see G.12(a)).
9 **dum:** 'while', but it is almost 'because' here (see G.30(a)).
  conscientiae bono: lit. 'the good of conscience'. Tr. 'a good conscience'.
  circa se saeuire: 'to rage upon her'.
10f. **soluuntur membra conpagibus:** 'her limbs are released from their joints', i.e. 'torn from their sockets'.
12 **uindicat:** 'tries to free'.

14 **Vna interim uox:** sc. 'there was' (i.e. 'she kept repeating the same thing').
  dictis: 'from my words', i.e. 'if you don't believe me'.
15 **quae...excutiat:** final: 'to investigate' (she means the Day of Judgement).
16 **suspirabat in gemitum:** lit. 'was sighing into a groan'. Tr. 'was sighing and groaning'.
  uicta saeuitia: probably nom.: 'his savagery, defeated (shuddered at...)' (subj. of *horrebat*, obj. *corpus, quod...*).
17 **laniarat:** *laniauerat* (see RLRGr A5).
18 **consularis** is subj. of *inquit*.
  circumstantes: vocative: 'you who stand round', 'bystanders'.
19f. **esse...reor...negare...quam...confiteri:** 'I think that it is...that...than that...'.
20 **negare de:** 'should deny X' (cf. G.15(b)).

(iv) *The youth is executed, but two blows of the sword barely draw blood from the woman. She tells the executioner he has lost his brooch and Jerome marvels at her lack of fear. A third and fourth blow fail to kill her.*

Pari igitur prolata in utrumque sententia damnatos carnifex trahit. Totus ad spectaculum populus effunditur, et prorsus quasi migrare ciuitas putaretur, stipatis proruens portis turba densatur. Et quidem miserrimi iuuenis ad primum statim ictum amputatur gladio caput truncumque in suo sanguine uolutatur cadauer. Postquam uero ad feminam uentum est et flexis in terram poplitibus   5
super trementem ceruicem micans eleuatus est gladius et exercitatam carnifex dexteram totis uiribus concitauit, ad primum corporis tactum stetit mucro letalis et leuiter perstringens cutem rasurae modicae sanguinem aspersit. Inbellem manum percussor expauit, et uictam dexteram gladio marcescente miratus in secundos impetus torquet. Languidus rursum in feminam mucro   10
delabitur et, quasi ferrum ream timeret adtingere, circa ceruicem torpet innoxium. Itaque furens et anhelus lictor paludamento in ceruicem retorto, dum totas expedit uires, fibulam, quae chlamydis mordebat oras, in humum excussit ignarusque rei ensem librat in uulnus et: 'En tibi,' ait mulier, 'ex umero aurum ruit. Collige multo quaesitum labore, ne pereat.'   15

Rogo, quae est ista securitas? Inpendentem non timet mortem, laetatur percussa, carnifex pallet; oculi gladium non uidentes tantum fibulam uident et, ne parum esset, quod non formidabat interitum, praestabat beneficium saeuienti. Iam igitur et tertius ictus: sacramentum frustrauerat trinitatis. Iam speculator exterritus et non credens ferro mucronem aptabat in iugulum, ut,   20
qui secare non poterat, saltim premente manu corpori conderetur. O omnibus inaudita res saeculis! – ad capulum gladius reflectitur, et uelut dominum suum uictus aspiciens confessus est se ferire non posse.

Jerome now recalls some biblical stories which parallel this divine intervention. Then he tells how the people rose up against the executioner, only to yield to his pleas not to be made to suffer in the woman's place.

1 **Pari...sententia:** abl. abs. (the sentence is death).
2 **prorsus quasi:** 'exactly as if'.
migrare...putaretur: lit. 'might be thought to emigrate'. Tr. 'you would think...was emigrating'.
3 **stipatis...portis:** abl. abs. Take *proruens* with *turba*:'the gates were blocked, and the crowd, rushing forward...'.
miserrimi iuuenis (gen.) depends on *caput* (subj. of *amputatur*).

4 **truncum** looks forward to *cadauer* (subj. of *uolutatur*).
6f. **exercitatam** with **dexteram** (obj. of *concitauit*): tr. 'already exercised...' (i.e. on the youth's neck).
8 **rasurae modicae sanguinem:** 'the blood of...', i.e. 'the amount of blood that a slight scratch would draw'.
9 **uictam dexteram** is the obj. of *miratus* and *torquet*.

gladio marcescente: 'with its sword drooping (i.e. powerless)' (accompanying ablative. See RLRGr L(f)3).

10 **Languidus:** tr. 'feebly' (with *mucro*).

13 **fibulam** is the object of *excussit*.

14 **tibi:** tr. 'your' (dat. of disadvantage: See RLRGr L(e)(ii)).

15 **multo quaesitum labore:** sc. *aurum* 'sought (i.e. obtained) through much labour'.

16 **ista:** 'this' (see G.11(c)).

17 **tantum:** 'only'.

18 **quod:** 'the fact that'.

19 **et tertius ictus:** sc. 'fell' or 'had fallen'.

sacramentum...trinitatis: 'the sacred power/ sacrament of the Trinity' (i.e. the three-in-one God prevented the third blow's effectiveness).

frustrauerat: possibly simple past 'made vain' (see G.9(c)) or a plupf. of instantaneous action.

21 **qui...poterat:** i.e. 'the sword which...'.

(v) A new executioner is brought and the seventh blow appears to kill the woman. As she is being buried, signs of life are seen. An old woman fortuitously dies and is put in her place. The woman recovers, but has to go into hiding.

Nouus igitur ensis, nouus percussor adponitur. Stat uictima Christo tantum fauente munita. Semel percussa concutitur, iterum repetita quassatur, tertio uulnerata prosternitur et – o diuinae potentiae sublimanda maiestas! – quae prius fuerat quarto percussa nec laesa, ideo paululum uisa est mori, ne pro ea periret innoxius. 5

Clerici quibus id officii erat, cruentum linteo cadauer obuoluunt et fossam humum lapidibus construentes ex more tumulum parant. Festinato sol cursu occasum petit, et misericordiam domini celatura nox aduenit. Subito feminae palpitat pectus et oculis quaerentibus lucem corpus animatur ad uitam: iam spirat, iam uidet, iam subleuatur et loquitur, iam in illam potest uocem 10 erumpere: 'Dominus auxiliator meus, non timebo quid faciat mihi homo.'

Anus interim quaedam, quae ecclesiae sustentabatur opibus, debitum caelo spiritum reddidit, et quasi de industria ordine currente rerum uicarium tumulo corpus operitur. Dubia adhuc luce in lictore zabulus occurrit, quaerit cadauer occisae, sepulchrum sibi monstrari petit; uiuere putat, quam mori potuisse 15 miratur. Recens a clericis caespes ostenditur et dudum superiecta humus cum his uocibus ingeritur flagitanti: 'Erue scilicet ossa iam condita, infer nouum sepulchro bellum, et, si hoc parum est, auibus ferisque lanianda membra discerpe; septies percussa debet aliquid morte plus perpeti.'

Tali inuidia carnifice confuso clam domi mulier focilatur et, ne forte creber 20 ad ecclesiam medici commeatus suspicionis panderet uiam, cum quibusdam uirginibus ad secretiorem uillulam secto crine transmittitur. Ibi paulatim uirili habitu ueste mutata in cicatricem uulnus obducitur. Et – 'o uere ius summum summa malitia!' – post tanta miracula adhuc saeuiunt leges.

Eventually, Evagrius, a priest of Antioch (later bishop c.388), appeals to the Emperor and wins freedom for the woman restored to life.

1f. **Christo...fauente munita:** 'defended...by Christ's support'.

3 **sublimanda:** 'to be praised'.

4 **fuerat...percussa:** 'had been...' (see G.4(a)).

6 **officii:** 'part of their duty' (partitive gen.: RLR.Gr. L(d)1).

linteo: with *obuoluunt*.

6f. **fossam humum...construentes:** tr. 'they dug up the ground and by lining it with stones...' (for the use of the present participle see G.20(b)).

8 **celatura:** 'to hide' (Greek usage: see G.10(c)).

11 **meus:** sc. *est*.

non timebo quid faciat mihi homo: Ps. 117.6 (= Ps. 118; the numbering of chapters in the Vulgate differs from that of standard editions).

13 **quasi de industria ordine currente rerum:** 'as though the order of events ran deliberately', i.e. 'as though these events were preordained'.

14 **Dubia adhuc luce:** 'while the light was still doubtful', i.e. 'before dawn'.

in lictore: 'in the person of the lictor'.

15 **monstrari petit:** 'asks for...to be shown' (see G.17(b)).

15f. **uiuere putat, quam...miratur:** 'he thinks she is alive, whom he wonders could have died'.

20 **Tali inuidia** depends on *confuso* ('by...'), part of an abl. abs. with *carnifice*.

20f. **ne...uiam:** the structure is *ne...creber...commeatus* (subj.) *panderet uiam* (obj., upon which *suspicionis* depends).

23f. **o uere ius summum summa malitia:** 'O truly the greatest justice is the greatest evil' (Terence, *The Self-Tormentor* 796).

Section 5
The new Christian genres

From the moment of its official triumph at the end of the fourth century, Christianity began to dictate the types of writing which were done. Roughly speaking, there were three main areas of impetus, which of course interacted. First of all, the Christian life itself, both monastic and secular, necessitated many new forms of literary expression. There was the liturgy itself, with its constant developments (see section 2). There was the sermon (see further on 5.1 below). There was the pilgrimage (see section 2.4 and section 7.4) and with it the handbook describing the routes and the *mirabilia* to which one was headed. There was the need to record the calendar of the sacred year, which eventually brought annotations which grew into chronicles and annals (see sections 10.5, 12.1). There was the constant work of biblical commentary (see section 7.2(b)), education (see sections 1 Intro. and 16) and theological enquiry (see sections 9.5, 14, 18). Secondly, the sacred texts themselves acted as models for literary genres. For example, the saint's life grew out of the account given in the Gospels of Christ's life and martyrdom (see sections 6.3 and 19.1). The Acts of the Apostles provided models for accounts of conversion and collections of miracles (see section 7.3). The Epistles were the basis of the pastoral letter (see section 4.2). The Old Testament was a model for medieval chroniclers and historians, who learned from it how history was the mark of God's will in the world. It is argued by some that the notion of the chosen people was the inspiration for the composition of tribal histories such as those of Gregory of Tours (the Franks, see section 8.3), Paul the Deacon (the Lombards, section 9.3) and Widukind (the Saxons, section 10.3). Thirdly, the pagan classics provided stylistic and formal models for Christian writing, which were naturally refilled with Christian content. The epic survived as one way of retelling the stories of Scripture (as in Iuvencus' reworking of the Gospels in the early fourth century), or could be utilized to relate heroic tales of the present (see sections 9.4(b), 10.1). The pastoral was a favourite with Carolingian poets. The elegiac couplet was still used for

epigrams or dedications (see sections 8.4(b), 7.1(b)), but also for more
serious didactic works (see sections 8.4(b), 12.7). Terence's comedies were
the inspiration for Hrotsvitha's dramas (section 10.4) and for a number of
twelfth-century theatrical pieces.

Two important points arise from the continued influence of pagan
poetry. Firstly, because this was used indiscriminately with prose to teach
grammatica, medieval writers did not distinguish between stylistic and
linguistic devices confined to poetry in antiquity, and so used them in
prose. Hence, for example, hyperbaton (see *RLGVE* p. 316) is very
common in prose (see section 6.3) as is the infinitive of purpose. Secondly,
the loss of the direct tradition of classical teaching in the fifth and sixth
centuries had two consequences: (1) it made the composition of
quantitative poetry difficult and so medieval poets made many errors
(marked in this book as exceptions), (2) the loss of the quantitative system
led (by a process detectable in mid-fifth-century poems by Caelius Sedulius
and Auspicius of Toul) to the increasing use of end-rhyme and stress
rhythm. By the eighth century it is common to find poets writing in both
quantitative and rhythmic verse (see sections 6.1, 12.4, 15.1, 15.3, 20.2, 3,
4). *Rithmus* is notated by scholars in different ways, but the notation used
in this book consists of a number (the syllables in the line or half-line) and
either p (= paroxytone, i.e. penultimate syllable) or pp (= proparoxytone,
i.e. antepenultimate), to show where the final stress of the line or half-line
comes.

See further: R. R. Bolgar, *The Classical Heritage*, Cambridge, 1954; R. P.
H. Green, *Seven Versions of Carolingian Pastoral*, Reading, 1980; D. Norberg,
Introduction à l'étude de la versification latine médiévale, Stockholm, 1958.

1. Caesarius of Arles (*c*.470–542)

Caesarius of Arles was a product of the monastery of Lérins, founded in the
early fifth century on an island off the French Riviera. It was a centre of
learning as well as of ascetic monasticism. He became, reluctantly, bishop of
Arles in 503. He retained his interest in the monastic life and wrote two
Rules which preceded (and possibly influenced) that of St Benedict. His
sermons, like those of other writers of his time, seek to reach more than
just the few literati. As he says elsewhere: 'I humbly beg that the ears of the
educated may be content to bear rustic expressions without complaint, so
that all the Saviour's flock can receive food in a simple and down-to-earth
language. Since the ignorant and the simple cannot raise themselves to the
height of the educated, let the educated deign to lower themselves to their

ignorance. Educated men can understand what has been said to the simple, whereas the simple are not able to profit from what would have been said to the learned.'

The sermon (*homilia*, later *sermo*), strongly encouraged by the model of the ministries of Jesus and St Paul, began as a monastic form, preached daily by the abbot or an ordinary monk, in the morning and at vespers. It normally took its theme from Scripture, often from the daily liturgy. Throughout the Middle Ages, sermons *ad cleros* ('to clerics') were in Latin. They are often marked throughout their history by a very plain and simple style. By the twelfth century, preaching was systematized and taught in the handbooks of the *ars praedicandi* ('art of preaching'), which like many later developments had an early archetype in book IV of St Augustine's *De doctrina Christiana*. Collections of suitable stories then appeared as adjuncts to this practice, such as Petrus Alfonsi's *Disciplina clericalis* or the later *Gesta Romanorum*.

This sermon was delivered during *Quadragesima* ('Lent') and stresses the importance of contemplation of the Psalms, which are central to the *opus Dei* ('Divine Office': see section 2), the main work of the monastery. The concentration upon resisting temptation is explained by the fact that Lent commemorates Jesus' temptation by the Devil (Mt 4).

(i) *Caesarius recommends learning the Psalms and Epistles by heart.*

Admonet me, fratres dilectissimi, amor conversationis vestrae, ut aliqua de sanctis scripturarum libris collecta verba vobis in auribus deo adiuvante insinuem. Sed quid potest mendicus divitibus erogare? Vos ipsi deo auxiliante legendo discitis quod aliis erogare possitis: sed propter illos qui tepidi sunt ad legendum, necesse est aliquid dici. Quid, si legant et forte non intelligant? 5
Adtamen, dilectissimi, si frequentius domino adiuvante voluerimus psalmos recurrere memoriter, lectiones apostolicas cotidie contendamus in cordibus nostris intromittere, bene nostis omnes, quia quod bene molitur nitidius machinatur; sic et quod bene tenetur, nitidius psallitur. Sed ideo dico, ut nulli liceat se excusare, ne accusatorem inveniat, cui resistere non valeat. Unus 10
dicit se parare non posse; alter dicit: 'Volo, sed duram memoriam habeo.' Ecce iamiam pro mendacio reus teneris, ecce in praesenti confunderis: quid te excusas? Noli contra te testimonium falsum proponere. Habes cubiculum, quem dominus fabricavit: aperi eum, reconde ibi pecuniam domini tui. Vult ut recondas modo, dum habes spatium: labora, congrega: pateat cubiculum tuum 15
sapientiae, claudatur stultitiae. Habes, accepisti. Audi testem fidelem, prophetam dicentem: *Dominus dedit mihi linguam eruditam ut sciam reprobare malum et eligere bonum.* Fratres, quod illi dedit, nobis transmisit... .

1 **conversationis vestrae:** 'of intercourse with you', or 'of your way of life'.
aliqua looks forward to *collecta verba* (obj. of *insinuem*).

2 **in auribus:** 'into your ears' (see G.15(c)(ii)).

4 **quod...possitis:** 'what you should be able...' (potential subj.: see *RLGVE* 153.2). ·

5f. **Quid, si legant...intelligant:** 'What if they read...understand'. The subjunctive has no special force (see G.25(b), 28(c)).

6f. **si...voluerimus....contendamus...bene nostis...quia...:** the sentence is not very tightly constructed: 'If we are willing to..., (if) we strive to..., you know... that...' (tr. *voluerimus* fut. pf. as present).

7 **recurrere:** 'to repeat'.
lectiones apostolicas: 'passages from the epistles' (the daily readings from the Epistles of St Paul etc. Cf. Augustine's experience in section 4.1(a)).

7f. **in cordibus nostris:** 'into our hearts' (see G.15(c)(ii)).

8f. **quod...machinatur:** *molitur* is 3rd p.s., pres.indic. pass. of *molo, molere* 'I mill'. *machinatur* is 3rd s. pres. indic. pass. of *machino* (or

macino) *machinare* 'I grind'. Tr. 'What is properly milled is more finely ground.' This must be proverbial.

9 **quod bene tenetur:** 'what is held well', i.e. 'in the memory'.

10 **accusatorem...cui resistere non valeat:** i.e. the Devil (generic subj., RLRGr Q2(a); see G.17(d) for *valeo*).

11 **parare:** 'to learn (it)' (CL 'prepare', 'obtain'; the word is used later in the sermon in this sense).

12 **pro mendacio reus teneris:** 'you are put on trial because of your lying'.

13f. **cubiculum, quem:** 'a chamber (i.e. treasure store), which' (i.e. 'your soul', though *cubiculum* is n., *quem* (m.) refers back to it as antecedent, because it refers metaphorically to something *personal*).

14 **eum:** i.e. *cubiculum* (see preceding note).

17 **dicentem:** 'who says' (see G.20(b)).

17f. **Dominus...bonum:** *Dominus...sciam* Isaiah 50.4, continuing to *bonum* from Isaiah 7.15 (cf. 7.16). Caesarius' memory has let him down here (or the text is wrong).

18 **dedit...transmisit:** the subject of *dedit* is 'God', and of *transmisit* 'the prophet'.

(ii) *The Psalms are weapons against the temptations of the Devil.*

Paret ergo unusquisque vestrum, dilectissimi, quod bonum est; quia et hic inde vivitur, et in futuro inde gaudetur. Fratres, si frequentius psalmos nostros recurrimus, cogitationibus mundanis aditum claudimus; dominatur psalmus spiritalis, fugit cogitatio carnalis. Psalmi vero arma sunt servorum dei: qui tenet psalmos, adversarium non timet; de quo adversario dominus dicit: *Adversarius*   5
vester diabolus est. Ille suggerit adversa, ut si potest occidat: nos cogitamus recta, si psalmos frequentius recitamus. Ille dicit: 'Esto superbus.' Ego cum psalmo decanto quod dominus dicit: *Non habitabit in medio domus meae qui facit superbiam*; et alibi: *Deus superbis resistit*; et in Salomone: *Superbus nihil sciens,*
sed languens circa quaestiones. Ille vero non suaderet superbiam, si sciret eam   10
habere locum inter servos dei in paradiso: et ideo proprie monachis hoc suadet ut superbiant, et postea inde excludantur, unde ille proiectus est; quia, si non superbisset, in caelo principatum tenuisset. Ipse suadet rixas, ipse odia committit, ipse excitat; tu verus psalmista resistis ei dicendo: *Pone domine custodiam ori meo, et non declines cor meum in verba maligna.* Et alibi dicit: *Dixi,*   15
custodiam vias meas, ut non delinquam in lingua mea; posui ori meo custodiam, dum consistit peccator adversus me. Ista talia arma si habet servus dei frequenter in

lingua, omnem telam nequissimi hostis sine mora disrumpit. Nolite mali esse ad invicem, quia dominus detestatur hoc vitium, dicens: *Odivi congregationem malignorum.* Dilectissimi, emendemus ergo vitia carnis propter animae pulchri- 20
tudinem, ubi est imago Christi. Vere dico, fratres, quod, si volumus ista omnia observare, et dicimus temptanti nobis: 'Non me suades, diabole, ut imaginem dei mei te audiendo corrumpam: ille pro me passus est, ille pro me sputis inlitus est, ille pro me alapis caesus est, ille pro me flagellatus est, ille pro me in cruce suspensus est. Dicat hoc servus dei temptanti sibi: 'Vere non mihi suades, ut 25
faciam quod hortaris.'

1 **hic:** i.e. 'in the world'.
  inde: 'from that', 'because of that' (i.e. *quod bonum est*). See G.13.
2 **in futuro:** i.e. 'in heaven'.
3f. **dominatur...fugit:** tr. 'if..., then...'.
5f. **Adversarius...est:** slightly adapted from 1 Peter 5.8. It is God who speaks through the apostles.
6 **adversa...recta:** 'what is wrong...what is right'.
  occidat: sc. 'you'.
8f. **Non habitabit...superbiam:** Ps. 100.7: the subject of *habitabit* is the clause *qui...superbiam* (tr. 'he who acts in pride'; lit. 'he who does pride').
9 **Deus...resistit:** James 4.6.
  in Salomone: i.e. in Proverbs. But actually 1 Timothy 6.4.
9f. **Superbus nihil sciens, sed languens...:** The Vulgate has *est* after *superbus*. Caesarius has omitted the first part of St Paul's sentence: 'If anyone teaches otherwise...' Tr. 'He is proud, though he knows nothing, but has a mania for scholarly disputations' (for this use of the present participle, see G.20(b)).
12 **inde...unde:** 'from the place from which...' (i.e. Paradise).
  ille: i.e. the Devil.
13 **odia:** 'acts of hatred'.
14 **excitat:** 'rouses (people) up'.

14f. **Pone...maligna:** Ps. 140.3–4. Caesarius has left out a clause of v. 3.
15 **non declines:** 'do not turn' (jussive subj.: RLGVE 152; for the negative, see G.23(c)).
15f. **Dixi...mea:** Ps. 38.2 (the Vulgate text is slightly different: *cum consisteret peccator adversum me*).
16 **ut non:** 'so as not to' (for *ut non* for *ne*, see G.27(d)).
18 **omnem telam:** 'every weapon', cf. Ephesians 6.16 *omnia tela nequissimi* 'all the arrows of the evil one' (as though *tela* were 1f. – see G.2: but *tela* 1f. is a 'web' and *disrumpo* suits this image better. Caesarius has got mixed up!).
18f. **ad invicem:** 'to each other' (see G.11(e)(ii)).
19f. **Odivi congregationem malignorum:** Ps. 25.5 (Vlg. has *Odivi ecclesiam malignantium*). *Odivi:* 'I have hated' (for the form see G.2).
21 **ubi:** i.e. in the soul (rather than in the flesh).
21f. **ista omnia observare:** 'to keep all those things' (i.e. to obey God's commandments). For *iste* see G.11(c).
22 **et dicimus:** supply *si* (there is no apodosis – it is forgotten after the riposte to the Devil which follows).
  temptanti nobis: 'to the one tempting us' (i.e the Devil; CL has *tempto* + acc.: see G.16). Cf. *temptanti sibi* below, 'to the one tempting him'.

(iii) *Let us be always at some holy work, especially during Lent.*

Dilectissimi, maxime caritatis dulcedinem teneamus, ut nos non reprobet Christus, sed laudet, et invitet ad praemium aeternum, dicens: *Venite benedicti patris mei, percipite regnum quod vobis paratum est.* O quam felix ille servus, qui a domino invitatur ad regnum suum! Sic tamen, ut frequenter in manibus habeat

unde domini sui voluntatem adimpleat: id est, sit divina lectio, sit sancta   5
cogitatio in corde et iugis oratio; ut quotiens ad temptandos nos accesserit
inimicus, semper nos sanctis operibus inveniat occupatos. Maxime diebus istis
sanctae Quadragesimae nemo se excuset: quia modo non tantum in opere
insistimus, quantum ad opus dei invitamur. Habemus dies istos sanctos, in
quibus quicunque vestrum voluerit fideliter pro animae suae remedio elabo-   10
rare, nulla illi erit excusatio. Quadragesima decima pars anni est: in ipsam
decimam partem multi fructus animae colliguntur. Ergo, dilectissimi, nolo vos
excusetis, quia, quod alieno tempore non occurritis, modo non conpensatur.
Parate quis quod necessarium habetis: qui psalmos, qui lectiones, qui vigilias
amat, vigilet, legat, proficiat, oret, psallat. Habetis omnes, quod agere pro   15
anima potestis. Pauci dies videntur, sed longa in eis beneficia conlata sunt.
Modo plus oras, plus psallis, plus legis, plus vigilas: et si non vis, tamen
conpelleris, aut per sonitum tabularum, aut ad vocem praepositi.

1 **ut...non:** purpose (for negative, see G.27(d)).

2f. **Venite...paratum est:** Mt 25.34 (the text is not the Vulgate: *paratum* means 'prepared').

4f. **Sic...ut...habeat:** 'provided that he has'.

5 **unde:** 'the means to' (lit. 'from whence').

8 **Quadragesimae:** 'Lent' (commemorating the forty days spent by Jesus in the wilderness: Mt 4).

8f. **non tantum...quantum:** 'not so much...as...'.
in opere insistimus: 'press on with our work' (CL uses *in* + acc. or dat.).

9 **Habemus...sanctos:** 'we keep these days sacred'.

9f. **in quibus...excusatio:** '(because) in them who-ever wants...will have no excuse' (i.e. work is suspended during Lent, so that the normal practice of excusing oneself from some offices from pressure of other tasks is also to be set aside).

11f. **in ipsam...partem:** 'in that tithe' (*in* + acc. for *in* + abl. or abl, see G.15(c)(i); *ipsam* 'that' see G.11(a)(ii)). The tithe is an offering made to God. Caesarius argues that Lent is a tithe

which has a spiritual bonus for those who pay it.

12f. **nolo...excusetis:** 'I don't want you to...' (see RLRGr p.426 on ll.57–8).

13 **quia...conpensatur:** 'on the grounds that what you do not achieve at other times is not made up for now' (*occurrere* in CL means 'meet').

14 **Parate quis:** 'learn, each of you'.
necessarium habetis: 'you regard as essential'.

14f. **qui...amat:** 'he who...' (subject of the jussive subjs. *vigilet...psallat* 'let him...').

15 **quod:** 'something which'.

16 **Pauci dies videntur:** 'the days (sc. of Lent) seem few'.

18 **per sonitum tabularum:** 'by the sound of (the) boards'. At Lérins, instead of ringing a bell, the *praepositus* would bang boards to call the monks to the *opus Dei*. This custom is recorded elsewhere. But in other texts *tabulae* means 'castanets', and *tabula* 'gong' – so take your pick!
ad vocem: 'at the voice (of)'.

(iv) *Servant of God, do not wait for someone to tell you to come to the Lord's table. Delight in his service, that you may receive freedom.*

Sed tu, servus dei, qui ut venires huc nemo admonuit: venisti, quid tepescis?
Quid expectas admonitorem? Audis tabulas: quid moraris? Quid tricas? Festina,

curre: ad opus bonum vocaris, quid expectas alium? Non te pigeat, prior intra;
ibi te inveniat, quem expectas. Iam venisti, quid festinas exire? Ad mensam
venisti, non tuam, sed domini tui: sta, imple ministerium tuum. Inde vivis, inde 5
vestiris: servus es, non tibi licet exire. Quid fugis dominum? Quid tibi dicit?
Accipe mercedem officii tui. Delectet te servire tali domino, qui nescit irasci.
Audi te quid iubet. Non sunt amara, non sunt dura; et si dura, servus es. Quid
contemnis? Curre propter libertatem: ut, cum tibi benefecerit, securus
possideas libertatem. Iam inter primos habueris, iam sublimis vocaris, iam 10
laetus exultas in domo domini tui, et dicis: *Beati qui habitant in domo tua Domine,*
in saecula saeculorum laudabunt te. Quod ipse praestare dignetur, qui vivit et
regnat in saecula saeculorum. Amen.

1 **qui...nemo admonuit:** 'whom...no one told
to' (*qui* for *quem*).
2 **tricas:** 'do you delay' (CL *tricor* 'dally', 'make
difficulties'. The reflexive form *se tricare* 'delay'
appears in the Vulgate).
5 **Inde...inde:** 'on that...because of that' (see
G.13).
8 **Audi te quid iubet:** 'Hear what he asks of you'

(*te* is the object of *iubet*). See G.24(b) for the
mood of *iubet*.
et si dura: 'and supposing them to be harsh...'
11f. **Beati qui...te:** Ps. 83.5.
12 **in saecula saeculorum:** 'for ever' (see G.10(a)).
ipse...qui: 'he...who...', i.e. Christ. See G.11
(a)(ii) for *ipse*.

2. Prudentius (348– after 404)

Born in Spain of Christian parents, Aurelius Prudentius Clemens received a
literary and rhetorical education, then became a barrister and an
administrator, and was rewarded with a high honour by the emperor. In his
Contra orationem Symmachi ('Against a speech of Symmachus') he argued that
the imperial mission of Rome was not ended but made nobler by
Christianity. His poetry is the best example of the appropriation of pagan
styles and genres for Christian purposes. He uses the lyric for literary hymns
(in the *Liber Cathemerinon* 'The Daily Round') and tales of the martyrs (in
the *Peristephanon Liber* 'The Book of Martyrs'). Much of his work,
however, is directly in the tradition of classical didactic, which he uses for
imparting Christian theology (e.g. in *Apotheosis* 'The Divinity of Christ' and
Hamartigenia 'The Origins of Sin'). His allegorical epic, *Psychomachia* 'The
Battle for the Soul', was the most influential of his works in the later
Middle Ages. It provides an excellent demonstration of how one type of
biblical interpretation (see section 3 Intro.) could be harnessed for the
propagation of the faith, though it must be said that allegorical writing was
also well established in pagan literature (see e.g. Virgil, *Aeneid* 6.273f., *RL*
6D(ii)). For a later medieval theological allegory, see section 18.4.

Luxury leaves her late-night banquet to fight Sobriety, and threatens to win a runaway victory.

Venerat occiduis mundi de finibus hostis   310
Luxuria, extinctae iamdudum prodiga famae,
delibuta comas, oculis uaga, languida uoce,
perdita deliciis, uitae cui causa uoluptas,
elumbem mollire animum, petulanter amoenas
haurire inlecebras et fractos soluere sensus.   315
at tunc peruigilem ructabat marcida cenam,
sub lucem quia forte iacens ad fercula raucos
audierat lituos, atque inde tepentia linquens
pocula lapsanti per uina et balsama gressu
ebria calcatis ad bellum floribus ibat.   320
non tamen illa pedes, sed curru inuecta uenusto
saucia mirantum capiebat corda uirorum.
o noua pugnandi species! non ales harundo
neruum pulsa fugit, nec stridula lancea torto
emicat amento, frameam nec dextra minatur;   325
sed uiolas lasciua iacit foliisque rosarum
dimicat et calathos inimica per agmina fundit.
inde eblanditis Virtutibus halitus inlex
inspirat tenerum labefacta per ossa uenenum,
et male dulcis odor domat ora et pectora et arma   330
ferratosque toros obliso robore mulcet.
deiciunt animos ceu uicti et spicula ponunt,
turpiter, heu, dextris languentibus obstupefacti
dum currum uaria gemmarum luce micantem
mirantur, dum bratteolis crepitantia lora   335
et solido ex auro pretiosi ponderis axem
defixis inhiant obtutibus et radiorum
argento albentem seriem, quam summa rotarum
flexura electri pallentis continet orbe.
et iam cuncta acies in deditionis amorem   340
sponte sua uersis transibat perfida signis
Luxuriae seruire uolens dominaeque fluentis
iura pati et laxa ganearum lege teneri.

310 **Venerat** will have *hostis Luxuria* as subject. **occiduis** looks forward to *de finibus*; the reference is probably to Rome, widely re- garded as the seat of human self–indulgence. 311 **extinctae** looks forward to *famae*, which depends on *prodiga*.

312 **comas:** 'on her hair' (acc. of respect: see RLRGr L(c)5).

312f. **oculis, uoce** and **deliciis:** tr. 'in...' (ablatives of respect with the accompanying adjectives: see RLRGr L(f)4(vi)).

313 **uitae** depends on *causa*; the phrase is the subject of the *cui* clause (supply *est*).

314f. Sc. 'that is, to..., to....and to....' (the infs. are explaining *uoluptas*); **elumbem** looks forward to *animum*, *amoenas* to *inlecebras* and *fractos* to *sensus*.

316 **peruigilem** looks forward to *cenam*; *marcida* is in apposition to the subject 'she'.

317 **sub lucem** belongs in the *quia* clause. *raucos* looks forward to *lituos*.

318 **tepentia** looks forward to *pocula* (obj. of *linquens*).

319 **lapsanti** looks forward to *gressu* and is qualified by *per...balsama*.

320 **calcatis** looks forward to *floribus* (abl. abs.).

321 **curru** ('upon...', dependent on *inuecta*) is picked up by *uenusto*.

322 **saucia** looks forward to *corda* (governing *mirantum...uirorum*), obj. of *capiebat*.

324f. **torto...amento:** 'from...' (i.e. from a catapult).

328 **inde...Virtutibus:** 'upon...by these things

(*inde*)...' (indir. obj. of *inspirat*).

329 **tenerum** looks forward to *uenenum*.
   labefacta goes with *per ossa*.

333 **turpiter** qualifies *obstupefacti*.

334 **currum** (picked up by *micantem*, which governs *uaria...luce*) is the object of *mirantur*.

335f. **lora** (qualified by *crepitantia*, which governs *bratteolis* 'with...') and **axem** (upon which depend the two phrases *solido...auro* and *pretiosi ponderis* – gen. of description) are the first two objs. of *inhiant*; *defixis* looks forward to *obtutibus* ('with...'); the third is *seriem* (upon which *radiorum* depends), qualified by *albentem* ('which...'), which in turn governs *argento* ('with...').

338f. **quam** picks up *seriem* and is the object of *continet*; the subject is *summa...flexura* (i.e.'the wheel-rim'); **electri pallentis** depends on *orbe* ('by means of...').

340 **in...amorem** looks forward to *transibat*.

341 **uersis** looks forward to *signis* (abl. abs.)
   perfida: 'in its treachery'.

342f. **uolens** picks up *acies* and governs the infinitives (*seruire*, *pati*, *teneri*).

343 **laxa** looks forward to *lege*.

PART TWO
Early Medieval Latin

During the period from the fifth to the tenth century, Western Christianity spread as far as Ireland in the West, Scandinavia in the North and Poland and Hungary in the East. As a mark of the continuing universality of the Church which replaced the 'universal empire', the new creed brought with it the universal language, Latin. A map showing the Church in 1001, with the boundary of the Roman Empire marked reveals at a glance the extent of this linguistic incursion (see map 2). The native tongues of these areas were non-Latin. It can be imagined by any non-Romance speaking modern learner of Latin what additional toil was required for the clergy of such areas to attain the grasp of that language needed for their work.

During most of the period, the central institution for the propagation of Latin learning was the monastery (see section 1 Intro.). Towards the last third of this period, the Carolingian reforms begin the process of establishing schools attached to cathedrals (see section 9 Intro.).

The Latin writing of the period is highly diverse. In some senses, though, some unity can be perceived when works are seen in relation to the local traditions of learning which fostered them. In practice, this is how the Latin of the pre-Carolingian period tends to be studied. The organization of this part reflects this, by setting together the pre-Carolingian writing of Ireland, England and the Romance-speaking lands of Europe separately. The Carolingian Renaissance forces us to take a more international view, because Charlemagne brought in scholars from all these areas to fuel his reforms. But the Ottonian Renaissance is again a much more local phenomenon, centred on Saxon Germany.

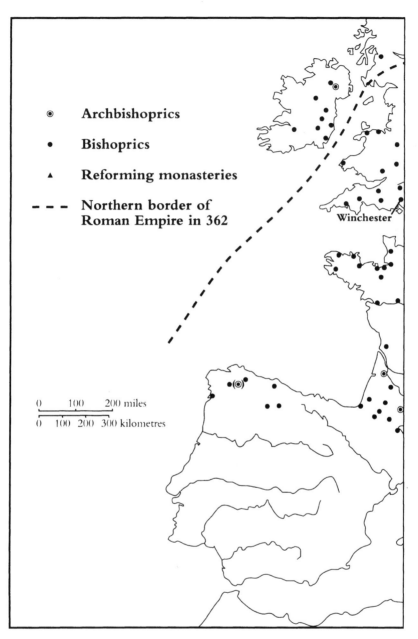

- ◉   **Archbishoprics**

- •   **Bishoprics**

- ▲   **Reforming monasteries**

- – – –   **Northern border of Roman Empire in 362**

Winchester

0   100   200 miles

0   100   200   300 kilometres

2 The Western Church in 1001 and the reforming monasteries (Cluny, 910, Cîteaux, 1098, Clairvaux, 1115, Prémontré, 1120).

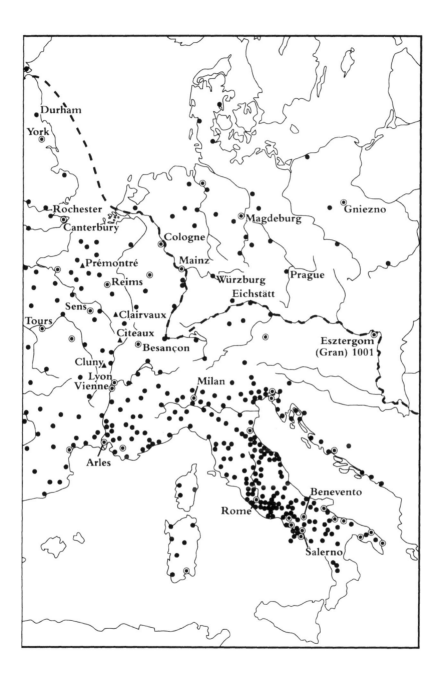

Durham
York
Rochester
Canterbury
Cologne
Prémontré
Mainz
Reims
Würzburg
Eichstätt
Sens
Clairvaux
Tours
Cîteaux
Besançon
Cluny
Lyon
Vienne
Milan
Arles
Magdeburg
Gniezno
Prague
Esztergom
(Gran) 1001
Benevento
Rome
Salerno

Section 6
Hiberno-Latin

The earliest non-Roman area to be converted was Ireland. In 431, Pope
Celestine I sent Palladius as the first bishop 'to the Irish believing in Christ'.
But Irish tradition credited the British St Patrick with the introduction of
Christianity to Ireland. His missionary work also took place during the fifth
century. The Church rapidly changed its form from diocesan – run by
bishops – to monastic – run by abbots (hence *parochia*, which elsewhere
means 'parish', in Ireland means 'a group of monasteries').

The supreme sacrifice for an Irish monk was *peregrinatio pro Christo*
'travelling abroad for Christ' and this activity by men who had studied in
Irish monasteries was of profound importance for Latin learning in Britain
and on the continent. Irish missionaries travelled abroad in the sixth and
seventh centuries and established many important monastic centres (see map
4). For example, in Britain Iona was founded *c.*563 by St Columba (who
had already set up the community at Durrow in Ireland and is credited
with many more, e.g. at Derry, Swords and Kells: see map 3). Lindisfarne
was founded from Iona in 643 by Aidan as a base for the conversion of
Northumbria. St Columbanus went to Gaul in 590 or 591, was given land
by King Guntram of Burgundy in the Vosges, and founded Annegray,
Luxeuil and Fontaines before he was exiled by King Theodoric in 610 (see
section 8.5). Even so, before his death in 615 he had founded another
famous monastery at Bobbio in northern Italy. His travelling companion
Gall, who refused to follow him to Italy, is credited with the foundation of
the Swiss monastery of St Gall.

The Irish (and later the Anglo-Saxons) had to adapt continental grammars
to their own peculiar conditions, focusing most attention on the inflecting
parts of speech and vocabulary, and referring only incidentally to syntax (see
further section 1 Intro.). It seems likely that their Latinity was formed in
contact with the continent, rather than with Britain. But native traditions of
poetic obscurity (the Irish word is *filidecht*) seem to have played an important
part in the development of the almost impenetrable Latin known as

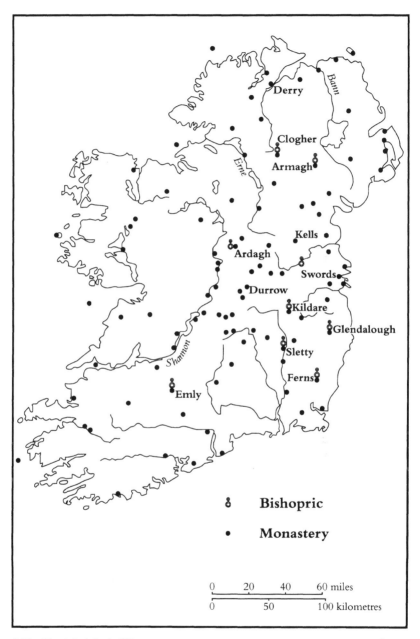

Derry

Bann

Clogher

Armagh

Erne

Kells

Ardagh

Swords

Durrow

Kildare

Glendalough

Shannon

Sletty

Ferns

Emly

⚇ **Bishopric**

• **Monastery**

0	20	40	60 miles
0		50	100 kilometres

3 The Church in Ireland c.800.

'Hisperic', after the *Hisperica Famina*, a collection of writings produced in the sixth and seventh centuries. The style was influential in Ireland until around 700, when the vernacular began to be used for such purposes. Here is an example from a text related to the *Hisperica Famina*, the *Lorica* (lit. 'breastplate' – a type of apotropaic prayer) *of Laidcenn*:

Mei gibrae	pernas omnes libera
tuta pelta	protegente singula,
ut non tetri	daemones in latera
mea uibrent	ut solent iäcula;

Gigram cephale	cum iris et conas,
patham lizanam	sennas atque michinas,
cladum carsum	madianum talias
bathma exugiam	atque binas idumas.

'Deliver all the limbs of me a mortal
with your protective shield guarding every member,
lest the foul demons hurl their shafts
into my sides, as is their wont.

(Deliver) my skull, head with hair, and eyes,
mouth (?), tongue, teeth, and nostrils (?),
neck, breast, side and limbs,
joints, fat, and two hands.'

> (*Hisperica Famina II. Related Poems* ed. and tr. M. W. Herren, Toronto, 1987, pp. 80–1)

Of particular interest is the combination of a correct Latin syntax with a vocabulary largely derived from Hebrew (with the addition of Latin terminations) and Greek. Examples are *gibra* 'mortal', *gigra* 'skull' and *iduma* 'hand' (Hebrew); *cephale* 'head' (3rd declension n.) and *conas* 'eyes' (Greek). These writers occasionally Latinize Irish words too. For example, the word *docca* derives from Old Irish *cloc* 'bell' (and the word *iris* 'hair' in the example *may* be a Celticism).

The vogue for rare vocabulary, which clearly betrays the presence in Ireland of Hebrew and Greek lexical aids, did not entirely die out. It is influential elsewhere, notably in the hymns of St Columba (e.g. *Altus prosator* 'Lofty creator': LL 'ancestor'), the grammarian Virgilius Maro (seventh century) and in Aethicus Ister (eighth century). But not all

Hiberno-Latin is in this style. The examples chosen here represent both this and the more normal Irish tradition of Latin writing.

See further: M. W. Herren, 'Hiberno-Latin Philology', in *Insular Latin Studies*, Toronto, 1981, pp. 1–22.

1. St Columba (521–97)

Columcille (Irish: 'Dove of the Church', hence the Latin *Columba* 'dove') was one of the pioneers of Christian monasticism in Ireland (see Intro.). For anecdotes about his mission among the Picts, see section 6.3 below (from Adomnan's *Vita Sancti Columbae*). An Old Irish poem gives some evidence of his scholarship, and the monastery at Iona became one of the most learned Irish centres in Britain before 800. But very little is certain, and even the ascription of the famous hymn *Altus prosator* is only 'plausible'. The metre is rhythmical rather than quantitative (there are eight syllables to each line) and there is a clear rhyme-scheme. The poem belongs to the 'abecedarial' genre. That is, the opening word of the first verse beings with A, the next with B, and so on through the alphabet.

A. The Holy Trinity

> Altus prosator, vetustus
> dierum et ingenitus
> erat absque origine
> primordii et crepidine,
> est et erit in saecula   5
> saeculorum infinita;
> cuï est unigenitus
> Christus et sanctus spiritus
> coaeternus in gloria
> deitatis perpetuae.   10
> non tres deos depromimus,
> sed unum Deum dicimus,
> salva fide in personis
> tribus gloriosissimis.

1 **prosator** (from *pro-sero* 'sow'): 'creator'.

1f. **vetustus dierum:** 'Ancient of Days' (Daniel 7.9: here and elsewhere, the *Vetus Latina* is used, and not Jerome's Vulgate: Vulgate here has *antiquus dierum*. The construction is a direct translation from the Greek).

2 **ingenitus:** 'not begotten' (CL 'inborn').

4 **crepidine:** 'end' (see Exodus 2.5; Judges 7.23).

5f. **saecula saeculorum:** lit. 'centuries of centuries' (Hebrew: see G.10(a)).

7f. **cuï...unigenitus...et...coaeternus:** 'whose only-begotten son is...and coeternal with whom (is)...'.

10 **deitatis:** 'Godhead' (CL *divinitas*).

11 **non...depromimus:** 'we do not declare (sc. that there are)...' (CL 'draw forth').

13 **salva fide:** abl. abs. 'keeping our belief'.

13f. **in personis tribus:** i.e. the Trinity (see sections 4.1(b) and 18.3).

B. *The creation of the angels*

Bonos creavit angelos   15
ordines et archangelos
principatuum ac sedium
potestatum, virtutium,
uti non esset bonitas
otiosa ac maiestas   20
trinitatis in omnibus
largitatis muneribus,
sed haberet caelestia
in quibus privilegia
ostenderet magnopere   25
possibili fatimine.

16 **ordines:** 'orders' (looking forward to *principatuum...virtutium*)

17f. **principatuum...virtutium** (= *virtutum*): 'Principalities, Thrones, Authorities and Powers' (the list of the nine grades – here *dominationes*, Cherubim and Seraphim are omitted – derives ultimately from the *Celestial Hierarchy* of the Pseudo-Dionysius the Areopagite, which was based on passages such as Ephe-sians 1.21 and Colossians 1.16).

19 **uti non:** CL *ne*: see G.27(d).

20 **otiosa:** goes with both *bonitas* and *maiestas*, on which *trinitatis* depends.

23f. **sed haberet...in quibus ostenderet:** 'but might have (sc. those) in whom...it (the Trinity) might display'.

26 **possibili fatimine:** 'by the powerful utterance' (i.e. 'by the divine voice of power').

C. *The fall of the angels*

Caeli de regni apice
stationis angelicae
claritate, prae fulgoris
venustate speciminis   30
superbiendo ruerat
Lucifer, quem formaverat,
apostataeque angeli
eodem lapsu lugubri
auctoris cenodoxiae   35

pervicacis invidiae,
ceteris remanentibus
in suis principatibus.

27f. The subject of the first clause will be *Lucifer* (v. 32).

Caeli: depends on *regni*.

de goes with *apice*.

28f. **stationis angelicae claritate:** 'in the brilliance of...'.

29 **prae:** 'because of' (with *venustate*); the phrase qualifies *superbiendo*.

30 **speciminis:** 'form' (dependent on *fulgoris*: CL

'sign', 'pattern').

31 **ruerat:** 'fell' (plupf. of instantaneous action, see G.9(c)).

34f. **eodem lapsu lugubri auctoris:** 'in the same...as (that) of...'.

35 **cenodoxiae:** 'of vainglory' (depends on *auctoris* referring to Satan or Lucifer: Greek).

36 **pervicacis invidiae:** sc. 'and of...'.

37 **ceteris:** sc. 'of the angels'.

D. Revelation

Draco magnus taeterrimus
terribilis et antiquus,   40
qui fuit serpens lubricus,
sapientior omnibus
bestiis et animantibus
terrae ferocioribus,
tertiam partem siderum   45
traxit secum in barathrum
locorum infernalium
diversorumque carcerum,
refugas veri luminis
parasito praecipites.   50

39 **Draco:** Rev. 12.9 *draco ille magnus, serpens antiquus* 'that great dragon, the ancient serpent'.

41 **qui fuit...lubricus:** i.e. in the temptation of Adam.

42 **sapientior:** i.e. 'more cunning' (cf. Gen. 3.1 *serpens erat callidior cunctis animantibus terrae*

'the serpent was more cunning than all the creatures of the earth').

49 **refugas:** 'deserters' (in apposition to *tertiam partem siderum*).

50 **parasito praecipites:** 'cast out headlong by the deceiver'.

E. The creation of the earth and of man

Excelsus mundi machinam
praevidens et harmoniam,
caelum et terram fecerat,
mare, aquas condiderat,
herbarum quoque germina,   · 55

virgultorum arbuscula,
solem, lunam ac sidera,
ignem ac necessaria:
aves, pisces et pecora,
bestias, animalia,   60
hominem demum regere
protoplastum praesagmine.

51 **Excelsus:** 'the Most High', i.e. God.
53f. **fecerat...condiderat:** 'made', 'established' (see
    G.9(c)).
56 **arbuscula:** '(small) trees' (n.pl.: CL 1f.: see G.2)
    or 'leaves'.
61 **regere:** 'to rule' (final: see G.17(a)).

62 **protoplastum:** 'first-formed' (Greek): with *ho-
    minem.*
62 **praesagmine:** 'by prophecy' (CL *praesagitio*:
    -men formations are much favoured by Irish
    writers).

F. *The praises of the Heavenly Host*

Factis simul sideribus,
aetheris luminaribus,
collaudaverunt angeli   65
factura pro mirabili
immensae molis Dominum,
opificem caelestium,
praeconio laudabili,
debito et immobili,   70
concentuque egregio
grates egerunt Domino
amore et arbitrio,
non naturae donario.

63 **simul:** tr. the abl. abs. 'as soon as...had been
    made'.
65 **collaudaverunt** looks forward to *Dominum*
    (obj.).
66 **pro:** 'because of' (= *propter.* see G.15(d)), gov-
    erning *factura...mirabili.*
67 **immensae molis** depends on *factura.*

69 **praeconio laudabili:** 'with a paean of praise'
    (*laudabilis* in CL 'praiseworthy').
70 **immobili:** 'unceasing' (CL 'immovable').
73f. **amore et arbitrio...non...donario:** 'from...'
    (abl. of cause, see RLRGr L(f) 4(iii)); i.e.
    they were not *made* by God so as to praise
    him, but do so of their own volition.

G. *The Fall of man*

Grassatis primis duobus   75
seductisque parentibus
secundo ruit zabulus

cum suis satellitibus,
quorum horrore vultuum
sonoque volitantium   80
consternarentur homines
metu territi fragiles,
non valentes carnalibus
haec intueri visibus,
qui nunc ligantur fascibus,   85
ergastulorum nexibus.

75 **Grassatis:** 'having been attacked' (CL deponent: but see RLRGr C4 Note 2).

75f. **primis...parentibus:** i.e. Adam and Eve.

77 **zabulus** = *diabolus* 'the Devil' (the glosses explain that the Devil's first fall was from heaven to earth for tempting God, the second from earth to hell for tempting Adam).

79f. **quorum...consternarentur:** '(at the horror) of whose (with *vultuum*)' and '(by the sound) of whom (with *volitantium*)' men were to be...' (purpose clause).

82 **fragiles** qualifies *homines*.

83 **valentes:** 'able' (see G.17(d)).

83 **carnalibus** looks forward to *visibus*.

84 **haec:** i.e. the Devil and his crew.

85f. **qui...nexibus:** commentators take this to refer to the fallen angels, now confined in the 'bonds of the torture-prisons' i.e. hell, bound in bundles, like the bundles of tares referred to at Mt 13.30: *alligate ea in fasciculos ad comburendum* 'tie them in bundles for burning' (sc. on the last day).

H. *The second fall of the angels*

Hic sublatus e medio
deiectus est a Domino,
cuius aeris spatium
constipatur satellitum   90
globo invisibilium
turbido perduellium,
ne malis exemplaribus
imbuti ac sceleribus
nullis unquam tegentibus   95
saeptis ac parietibus
fornicarentur homines
palam omnium oculis.

87 **Hic:** i.e. the Devil.

e medio: 'from the midst' (but is it of men or of angels?).

89f. **cuius...satellitum globo:** 'with a crowd of whose satellites' (*turbido* qualifies *globo*, and

invisibilium, *perduellium* qualify *satellitum*).

94 **imbuti** looks forward to *homines*, subject. of *fornicarentur*.

95f. **nullis...parietibus:** abl. abs. 'with no...covering (sc. them, viz. men)'.

I. The clouds and the sea

Invehunt nubes pontias
ex fontibus brumalias   100
tribus profundioribus
oceani dodrantibus
maris, caeli climatibus,
caeruleis turbinibus
profuturas segetibus,   105
vineis et germinibus,
agitatae flaminibus
thesauris emergentibus,
quique paludes marinas
evacuant reciprocas.   110

This verse is very obscure in construction and
sense.

99– **invehunt nubes pontias...brumalias...maris:**
103   'the clouds carry the wintry floods from their
       sources'.
101f. **tribus...dodrantibus:** 'that is the three deeper
       floods' (in apposition to *fontibus*). *Dodrans*
       means 'three-quarters', but became synon-
       ymous with 'ocean' because it was thought
       that three-quarters of the world was covered
       by water.
102f. **oceani...maris:** 'of the ocean's sea' (a peculiar
       reduplication of ideas involving the use of a
       noun almost adjectivally).
103   **caeli climatibus:** 'to the regions of the sky' (see
       G.16(a)).

104 **caeruleis turbinibus:** 'with...'.
105 **profuturas** picks up *pontias* (l.99) and governs
      segetibus...germinibus: tr. 'to fructify...' (see
      G.10(c)).
107 **agitatae:** agreeing with *nubes*.
108 **thesauris:** 'from...' (with *emergentibus*).
109 **quique:** *flaminibus* ('winds') seems to be the
      antecedent (although n.).
110 **reciprocas:** 'alternating' (the last clause seems to
      show that the writer thought the winds
      drained the shallow parts of the sea in alter-
      nation, thus creating tides: Isidore – see section
      1 Intro. – mentions some writers who held this
      view).

K. The punishment of sinners

Kaduca ac tyrannica
mundique momentanea
regum praesentis gloria
nutu Dei deposita;
ecce gigantes gemere   115
sub aquis magno ulcere
comprobantur, incendio
aduri ac supplicio
Cocytique Charybdibus

> strangulati turgentibus,   120
> Scyllis obtecti fluctibus
> eliduntur et scrupibus.

111 **Kaduca:** 'tottering' (CL *caduca*: written with K simply to fit the alphabetic stanza scheme): take with *gloria*.

112 **mundique:** *-que* is joining the adjective *tyrannica* to *momentanea. mundi* goes with *praesentis*, and this phrase depends upon *regum*, which depends upon *gloria*.

114 **deposita:** sc. *est* and translate as present.

115f. **gigantes...comprobantur:** 'the giants...are recorded' (CL *comprobo* = 'acknowledge'). Cf. Job 26.5: *ecce gigantes gemunt sub aquis* 'Lo, the giants groan beneath the waters'. But here the poet probably has in mind the giants who perished at the Flood (Wisdom 14.6). They were held to be the descendants of the fallen angels.

116 **magno ulcere:** 'from their great torment' (abl. of cause: see RLRGr L(f) 4(iii); *ulcus* CL 'sore').

118 **aduri:** depends on *comprobantur* — tr. 'to be burned'.

119f. **Cocytique...scrupibus:** *-que* introduces a second main verb *eliduntur*. The phrasing is *Cocyti Charybdibus strangulati* (picking up *gigantes*) *turgentibus* (and) *Scyllis obtecti* (again picking up *gigantes*) *fluctibus eliduntur et scrupibus* (CL *scrupus* 'sharp stone'; perhaps confused with *rupibus*: see G.2). Cocytus is the ancient river of mourning in Hades; Charybdis is the whirlpool which Odysseus struggled with; Scylla was a monster who attacked Odysseus' men.

L. The rain and the rivers

> Ligatas aquas nubibus
> frequenter crebrat Dominus,
> ut ne erumpant protinus   125
> simul ruptis obicibus,
> quarum uberioribus
> venis velut uberibus
> pedetentim natantibus
> telli per tractus istius   130
> gelidis ac ferventibus
> diversis in temporibus
> usquam influunt flumina
> nunquam deficientia.

123 **Ligatas...nubibus:** 'bound to...'. **aquas** is the object of *crebrat*.

124 **crebrat** = *cribrat* 'filters' (see O.11): cf. 2 Samuel 22. 12: *cribrans aquas de nubibus caelorum* 'filtering the waters from the clouds of the heavens'.

125 **ut ne:** i.e. *ne*.

126 **simul:** tr. 'as soon as (the barriers have burst)'.

127f. **quarum...venis:** 'by whose streams'.

128 **velut uberibus:** in apposition to *venis*. Tr. 'as if

they were udders'.

129 **natantibus:** 'flowing'.

130 **telli...istius:** 'of this earth' depends on *tractus* (*telli* = *telluris*: see G.2; for *iste* see G.11(c)).

131 **gelidis ac ferventibus** pick up *venis* again.

132 **diversis in temporibus:** 'at' (see G.15(a)(i)).

133 **usquam influunt:** 'they always flow' (CL *usquam* 'anywhere').

133 **flumina** is direct obj. of *influo* (CL *in* + acc.).

M. The foundations of the earth

Magni Dei virtutibus   135
appenditur dialibus
globus terrae et circulus
abysso magnae inditus
suffultu Dei, iduma
omnipotentis valida,   140
columnis velut vectibus
eundem sustentantibus,
promontoriis et rupibus
solidis fundaminibus
velut quibusdam basibus   145
firmatus immobilibus.

135f. **virtutibus...dialibus:** 'by the divine powers'.

136 **appenditur:** 'is suspended': the subject is *globus terrae* (cf. Job 26. 7: *et adpendit terram super nihili*: 'and he suspended the earth upon nothing').

137f. **circulus abysso magnae inditus:** 'and a circle is set upon the great deep (*abyssus* is f.)' (i.e. 'the sea is held in place on the globe of the earth').

139 **suffultu:** 'by the support' (no such noun exists in CL).

iduma: 'by the hand' (Hebrew).

141f. **columnis...sustentantibus:** abl. abs. Tr. 'since...'.

142 **eundem:** i.e. the *circulus* of the sea.

143f. **promontoriis...immobilibus:** the ablatives depend on *firmatus*, agreeing with *circulus; solidis fundaminibus* is in apposition to *promontoriis et rupibus*, and *velut...immobilibus* describes the whole of *promontoriis... fundaminibus*.

N. Hell

Nulli videtur dubium
in imis esse infernum,
ubi habentur tenebrae,
vermes et dirae bestiae,   150
ubi ignis sulphurius
ardens flammis edacibus,
ubi rugitus hominum,
fletus et stridor dentium,
ubi Gehennae gemitus   155
terribilis et antiquus,
ubi ardor flammaticus,
sitis famisque horridus.

148 **in...infernum:** 'that there is...'
149 **habentur:** 'there are'.
149f. **tenebrae...bestiae:** cf. Ecclesiasticus 10.13: *cum enim moritur homo, hereditabit serpentes et bestias et vermes* 'For when a man shall die, he shall inherit serpents, beasts and worms'.

151 **ubi:** sc 'there is' (so in the other *ubi* clauses below also).
154 **fletus et stridor dentium** = Mt 8.12, 24.51.
158 **sitis famisque:** either genitive dependent on *ardor*, or m. nouns (for CL f.) parallel to *ardor* (cf. vv. 153–4). If the latter, then *famis = fames* (see O.11).

O. *The worship of the underworld*

Orbem infra, ut legimus,
incolas esse novimus,   160
quorum genu precario
frequenter flectit Domino,
quibusque impossibile
librum scriptum revolvere
obsignatum signaculis   165
septem de Christi monitis,
quem idem resignaverat,
postquam victor exstiterat
explens sui praesagmina
adventus prophetalia.   170

159 **infra:** governs *orbem*.
161 **precario:** 'in prayer' (CL 'by request').
162 **flectit:** 'bends' (intrans.: CL trans.).
163 **quibus:** 'for whom...'.
     impossibile: sc. 'it is'.
164 **revolvere:** 'to unroll' (the *Vetus Latina*, where the book was a roll; Vlg. has *aperire*).
164f. **librum...obsignatum signaculis septem:** this is the book seen by John in Rev. 5.1.

166 **de Christi monitis:** 'by the will of Christ' (see G.15(a)(ii)).
168f. **postquam...exstiterat:** 'after he had been' (CL uses perfect: see RLRGr T(a)). This refers to the Resurrection, which in medieval tradition followed the descent into Hell, the occasion on which he is supposed to have unsealed and resealed the book with seven seals.
169 **praesagmina:** 'prophecies'.

P. *The Garden of Eden*

Plantatum a prooemio
paradisum a Domino
legimus in primordio
Genesis nobilissimo,
cuius ex fonte flumina   175
quattuor sunt manantia,
cuius etiam florido
lignum vitae in medio,

cuius non cadunt folia
gentibus salutifera,   180
cuius inenarrabiles
deliciae ac fertiles.

171 **Plantatum:** 'that it was planted' (sc. *esse*, dependent upon *legimus*). The reference is to Gen.
2.8: *plantaverat autem Dominus Deus paradisum
voluptatis a principio* 'The Lord God had planted
a garden of pleasure at the beginning'.
176 **sunt manantia:** 'flow' (see G.4(b)).

177f. **cuius...florido...in medio:** 'in whose flowery
centre...' Sc. 'is'.
179 **cuius non cadunt:** the antecedent is *lignum*.
181f. **cuius...fertiles:** the antecedent is *paradisum*. Sc.
'are'.

Q. The thunders of Sinai

Quis ad condictum Domini
montem ascendit Sinai?
quis audivit tonitrua   185
ultra modum sonantia,
quis clangorem perstrepere
enormitatis buccinae?
quis quoque vidit fulgura
in gyro coruscantia,   190
quis lampades et iacula
saxaque collidentia
praeter Israhelitici
Moysen iudicem populi?

183 **condictum:** 'promised', looks forward to *montem*.
184 **Sinai:** agreeing with *montem* (see G.6(a)).
185f. **quis...perstrepere:** sc. *audivit*.
188 **enormitatis buccinae:** lit. 'of the might of the
trumpet'. Tr. 'of the mighty trumpet'.
190 **in gyro:** lit. 'in a circle'. Tr. 'around' (= *circum*:
cf. It. *in giro*).

191 **lampades:** 'flashes (of lightning)' (usually
'lights': Greek *lampas* means 'torch').
iacula: 'thunderbolts' (CL *iaculum* = 'javelin').
193 **praeter** governs *Moysen*.
Israhelitici: gen. s. looking forward to *populi*.
194 **Moysen:** Greek acc. (see RLRGr H6).

R, S. The Day of Judgement

Regis regum rectissimi   195
prope est dies Domini,
dies irae et vindictae,
tenebrarum et nebulae,
diesque mirabilium
tonitruorum fortium,   200

dies quoque angustiae,
maeroris ac tristitiae,
in quo cessabit mulierum
amor ac desiderium
hominumque contentio 205
mundi huius et cupido.

Stantes erimus pavidi
ante tribunal Domini
reddemusque de omnibus
rationem affectibus, 210
videntes quoque posita
ante obtutus crimina
librosque conscientiae
patefactos in facie;
in fletus amarissimos 215
ac singultus erumpemus
subtracta necessaria
operandi materia.

195 **Regis...rectissimi:** in apposition to *Domini* (for
regis regum see G.10(a)), depending on *dies.*
206 **mundi huius et cupido:** *et* joins *contentio* with
cupido and *mundi huius* depends on *cupido*. Tr.
'desire (sc. of men) for...'.
207 **Stantes erimus:** 'we shall be standing' (see
G.4(b)).
209 **reddemus** with *rationem.*
de: + abl. Tr. 'for...' (CL gen.).

210 **affectibus:** 'desires' (CL *affectus* = 'mood',
'love'). But another text has *effectibus* 'deeds',
'acts'.
213 **libros...conscientiae:** 'the books of conscience'
(a common interpretation of the 'open books'
of Daniel 7.10 and Rev. 20.12).
214 **in facie:** 'in front of us'.
217– **subtracta...materia:** abl. abs. 'now that the
18 opportunity of acting has been withdrawn'.

T. The general Resurrection

Tuba primi archangeli 220
strepente admirabili
erumpent munitissima
claustra ac polyandria,
mundi praesentis frigora
hominum liquescentia, 225
undique conglobantibus
ad compagines ossibus,
animabus aethralibus
eisdem obviantibus

rursumque redeuntibus   230
debitis mansionibus.

220f. **Tuba...admirabili:** abl. abs. 'when the...
trumpet...' (see Rev. 8.7).
220 **primi archangeli:** gen..
223 **claustra ac polyandria** ('tombs': Greek) are
subjects of *erumpent* ('will burst open').
224f. **mundi...liquescentia:** 'thawing (nom. with
claustra and *polyandria*) the cold of men in
the present world'.

227 **ad compagines:** 'to solid structures', i.e. bodies.
228 **animabus** (= CL *animis*)...**redeuntibus:** abl.
abs. '(and) while...'.
229 **eisdem:** 'those' (see G.11(b): presumably the
souls they had when on earth, rather than
the angels).
231 **debitis mansionibus:** 'to their proper...' (dat. of
place to which: see G.16(a)).

V. Types of Christ

Vagatur ex climactere
Orion caeli cardine
derelicto Virgilio,
astrorum splendidissimo;   235
per metas Thetis ignoti
orientalis circuli,
girans certis ambagibus
redit priscis reditibus,
oriens post biennium   240
Vesperugo in vesperum;
sumpta in problematibus
tropicis intellectibus.

232 **ex climactere:** 'from its climacteric' (i.e. highest
point).
233 **caeli cardine:** 'the pivot of heaven', in apposition to *climactere*.
234f. **derelicto...splendidissimo:** abl. abs. 'leaving...'.
234 **Virgilio:** 'the Pleiades'. Orion goes beneath the
waters, though he is one of the brightest stars
in the sky, and returns. So Christ lived a
glorious life, died, and was resurrected.
236 **Thetis:** 'sea' – gen. dependent on *ignoti...circuli*
(CL *Thetidis/Thetidos*).
238 **girans:** the subject will be *Vesperugo* 'Vesper, the

evening star' (= the planet Venus).
238 **certis ambagibus:** 'in fixed windings (i.e. orbits)'.
239 **priscis reditibus:** 'by its ancient return-routes'.
240 **oriens:** 'having risen' (see G. 20(a)).
241 **in vesperum:** 'at eventide' (CL *ad vesperum, sub
vesperum*). Vesper, by a circuitous biennial
orbit, returns to the night-sky. So Christ will
return in glory at the end of time.
242 **sumpta in problematibus:** '(these stars are to
be) taken as puzzles'.
243 **tropicis intellectibus:** 'with figurative meanings'.

X. The Second Coming of Christ

Xristo de caelis Domino
descendente celsissimo   245

praefulgebit clarissimum
signum crucis et vexillum,
tectisque luminaribus
duobus principalibus
cadent in terram sidera   250
ut fructus de ficulnea,
eritque mundi spatium
ut fornacis incendium;
tunc in montium specubus
abscondent se exercitus.   255

244 **Xristo** = *Christo*, X being the Greek letter χ (chi), which is the first letter of 'Christ' in Greek. The construction is abl. abs. 'when...'.

246f. **praefulgebit...vexillum:** the idea that the Second Coming would be marked by a luminous cross in the sky was a commonplace of early biblical commentary.

248f. **tectisque...principalibus:** abl. abs. 'when...'

(the sun and the moon are referred to).

250f. **cadent...ficulnea:** a paraphrase of Rev. 6.13: *et stellae caeli ceciderunt super terram sicut ficus emittit grossos suos*, 'And the stars fell from the sky upon the earth as a fig-tree drops its ripe fruit'.

252f. **eritque...incendium:** the idea that the earth will be consumed by fire is found in 2 Peter 3.10.

255 **exercitus:** 'the hosts' (i.e. 'the people').

Y. The worship of heaven

Ymnorum cantionibus
sedulo tinnientibus,
tripudiis sanctis milibus
angelorum vernantibus,
quattuor plenissimis   260
animalibus oculis
cum viginti felicibus
quattuor senioribus
coronas admittentibus
agni Dei sub pedibus,   265
laudatur tribus vicibus
trinitas aeternalibus.

256f. The stanza is made up of three ablative absolute phrases (*cantionibus...tinnientibus; milibus...vernantibus; quattuor...animalibus...admittentibus*), which lead up to and express the circumstances in which *laudatur...trinitas*. Tr. 'while...'.

258 **tripudiis sanctis:** 'in holy dances'.

259 **vernantibus:** lit. 'verdant', i.e. repeatedly renewing their dance.

260 **plenissimis** goes with *animalibus*, and governs *oculis* (these are the four animals *plena...oculis* of Rev. 4.8 along with the twenty-four elders of Rev. 4.10).

264 **admittentibus:** 'throwing' (for CL *mittebant*: see
    Rev. 4.10: *et mittebant coronas suas ante thronum*
    'and they cast their crowns before the throne').
265 **agni Dei:** i.e. Christ.

266f. **tribus vicibus...aeternalibus:** 'by the eternal
    triple repetition' (this alludes to the cry *Sanctus,*
    Sanctus, Sanctus of Rev. 4.8).

Z. The destruction of the ungodly and the reward of the righteous

Zelus ignis furibundus
consumet adversarios
nolentes Christum credere   270
Deo a patre venisse.
nos vero evolabimus
obviam ei protinus
et sic cum ipso erimus
in diversis ordinibus   275
dignitatum pro meritis
praemiorum perpetuis
permansuri in gloria
a saeculis in saecula.

268 **Zelus:** 'fury' (Greek 'jealousy').
270 **nolentes:** tr. 'who...'.
270f. **Christum...venisse:** 'that Christ came' (possibly
    this reflects the incredulity of pagan Irish when
    confronted by the Christian gospel).

274 **ipso:** 'him' (see G.11(a)(ii)).
276f. **pro...perpetuis:** 'in accordance with the ever-
    lasting deserts of our rewards'.
279 **a saeculis in saecula:** 'for ever and ever'.

2. St Columbanus (d. 615)

St Columbanus was born in Leinster and received his early education in
Ireland, partly at Bangor. Here he must have gained a firm grasp of Latin,
including a thorough knowledge of the Bible, Jerome and Eusebius, and of
the *computus*, the system used for calculating the date of Easter, with which
he was much concerned later. His establishment of monastic centres in
Gaul has been mentioned in the introduction. In keeping with the Irish
style, these were very strict, differing markedly in certain customs from the
Frankish Church, particularly the acceptance of episcopal authority and the
calculation of the date of Easter (see also section 7.2(a)(ii)). In 603
Columbanus was called before the bishops at Chalon-sur-Saône, but refused
to attend. Instead, he sent a letter, one of five now accepted as genuine,
part of which is given here. For an anecdote about Columbanus' troubles
with the Franks, see section 8.5.

Columbanus reveals that his non-attendance is due to religious scruple. He reiterates his position on the date of Easter and calls for peace. Finally, he suggests that he should be allowed to tread the 'narrow way' to Heaven without hindrance.

Ego autem ad vos ire non ausus sum, ne forte contenderem praesens contra apostoli dictum dicentis, *Noli verbis contendere*, et iterum, *Si quis contentiosus est, nos talem consuetudinem non habemus neque ecclesia Dei;* sed confiteor conscientiae meae secreta, quod plus credo traditioni patriae meae iuxta doctrinam et calculum octoginta quattuor annorum et Anatolium ab Eusebio ecclesiasticae historiae 5 auctore episcopo et sancto catalogi scriptore Hieronymo laudatum Pascha celebrare, quam iuxta Victorium nuper dubie scribentem et, ubi necesse erat, nihil definientem, ut ipse in suo testatus prologo, qui post tempora domni Martini et domni Hieronymi et papae Damasi per centum et tres annos sub Hilario scripsit. Vos vero eligite ipsi quem sequi malitis, et cui melius credatis 10 iuxta illud apostoli, *Omnia probate, quod bonum est tenete.* Absit ergo ut ego contra vos contendam congrediendum, ut gaudeant inimici nostri de nostra christianorum contentione, Iudaei scilicet aut heretici sive pagani gentiles – absit sane, absit; alioquin aliter inter nos potest convenire, ut aut *unusquisque in quo vocatus est in eo permaneat apud Deum,* si utraque bona est traditio, aut cum pace et humilitate 15 sine ulla contentione libri legantur utrique, et quae plus Veteri et Novo Testamento concordant, sine ullius invidia serventur. Nam si ex Deo est, ut me hinc de loco deserti, quem pro domino meo Iesu Christo de trans mare expetivi, propellatis, meum erit illud propheticum dicere, *Si propter me haec tempestas est super vos, tollite me et mittite me in mare, ut commotio haec quiescat a vobis;* 20 vestrum tamen prius sit, more illorum nautarum naufragum conari eripere visceribus pietatis et ad terram navem trahere, sicut illi, licet ethnici, fecerunt, scriptura narrante, *Et conabantur viri redire,* inquit, *ad terram et non poterant, quia mare ibat et exurgebat magis fluctus.* Postremo in calce dicti, licet praesumptuose, suggero ut, quia in *via* huius saeculi *spatiosa et lata multi* ambulantes currunt ad 25 compita arcta, si aliqui *pauci* inveniuntur, qui per *angustam portam et arctam, quae ducit ad vitam* iuxta praeceptum Domini, gradiantur, potius a vobis ad vitam transmittantur quam prohibeantur, ne forte et vos cum Pharisaeis sermo Domini sugillet dicentis, *Vae vobis, scribae et Pharisaei, quia clauditis regnum caelorum ante homines, et Nec vos intratis, nec sinitis introeuntes intrare.* 30

2 **Noli...*contendere*:** St Paul in 2 Timothy 2.14.
2f. **Si *quis...Dei*:** St Paul in 1 Corinthians 11.16.
4 **calculum:** the *calculus* (also called *computus*) was the elaborate system of reckoning by which the date of Easter was calculated, and an integral part of the medieval school curriculum.
5f. **Anatolium...laudatum:** also dependent on

iuxta. The Canon of Anatolius was in fact an Irish forgery, which supported the Irish position on the calculation of the date of Easter. Another Anatolius was mentioned with approval in Eusebius' *Ecclesiastical History* vii.32 and in Jerome.

6f. **Pascha celebrare:** 'so as to celebrate Easter', i.e.

'for the celebration of Easter' (see G.17(a)).

7 **quam** 'than' picks up *plus* (1.100).

Victorium nuper...scribentem: in 457.

8 **domni** = *domini*: 'great' (CL 'master'): see O.9.

9 **Martini...Hieronymi...Damasi:** St Martin (*c.* 316–97) was Bishop of Tours from 371 to 397; for St Jerome (Hieronymus) see section 3 Intro and section 4.2 Intro.; St Damasus (*c.*305–84) was Pope from 366 to 384.

9f. **per centum...scripsit:** lit. 'wrote through 103 years under Hilary' i.e. 'calculated the date of Easter for the next 103 years' (Hilary was Pope from 461 to 468).

10 **quem...malitis...cui...credatis:** 'whom to prefer...whom to believe' (purpose: see RLRGr Q2(b)).

melius: 'rather'.

11 **iuxta illud apostoli:** 'in accordance with that saying of the apostle' (i.e. St Paul in 1 Thessalonians 5.21).

Absit...ut: 'far be it that...'.

12 **congrediendum:** 'so as to fight'.

gaudeant...de: 'rejoice in' (see G.15(b)).

12f. **nostra christianorum contentione:** lit. 'our quarrel of Christians', i.e. 'a quarrel between us Christians'.

14f. *unusquisque...Deum:* 1 Corinthians 7.20.

in quo...in eo: 'in the condition in which'.

16 **Veteri** = *Vetere* (see G.7(a)).

17f. **ut me** has as its verb *propellatis*: 'namely, that you...' (picking up *hoc*).

18 **deserti:** 'seclusion' (CL *deserta* n.pl. 'desert places').

de trans mare: 'from over the sea'. The double preposition is not Latin, but it *is* found in Old

Irish, Columbanus' native language. Here, unusually, he has allowed a vernacular structure to influence his Latin.

19 **meum:** sc. 'task' (so below with *vestrum*).

illud propheticum: 'that utterance of the prophet' (the following words paraphrase Jonah 1. 12: Jonah is regularly regarded as a type of the punished sinner who begs for God's pardon – see section 20.4).

21 **vestrum...prius sit:** 'let it be your task...' (jussive subj.: RLGVE 152).

illorum nautarum: i.e. the crew of the ship carrying Jonah (but they were trying to save *themselves*, not Jonah!).

22 **visceribus pietatis:** lit. 'by the bowels of godliness', i.e. out of compassion (abl. of cause: RLRGr L(f)4(iii)).

ethnici: i.e. gentiles (Greek).

24 **in calce dicti:** 'at the end of what I have to say'.

25 **quia:** 'because'.

25f. *via...spatiosa et lata multi* and *pauci... angustam...ad vitam* are adapted from Mt 7. 13–14.

ad compita arcta (= *arta*): 'to the narrow crossroads' (i.e. the secular clergy attempt to get to the narrow road via the broad highway of the world).

26 **qui** looks forward to *gradiantur*.

27 **ad vitam:** i.e. to eternal life in heaven.

28 **transmittantur...prohibeantur:** 'let them...' (jussive subjunctives: RLGVE 152).

29 **sugillet:** 'knock out' (obj. *vos*).

29f. *vae...homines...Nec...intrare:* Mt 23.13.

30 *introeuntes:* 'those who wish to enter'.

3. St Adomnan (*c.*624–704)

Adomnan was the ninth bishop of Iona (679–704). A native of Donegal, he probably received his early training in Ireland. In 688 he was persuaded on a visit to Northumbria to drop the Irish practice concerning the date of Easter (see section 7.2(a)(ii)). He converted the northern Irish shortly before his death, but failed to convince his own monks at Iona. His political and diplomatic involvement can also be seen in the *Lex Innocentium* or Adomnan's Law, enacted at the Synod of Birr (697) to protect women, children and men in orders or monasteries from acts of violence. The *Vita Sancti Columbae* was probably written between 688 and 692, based partly on an earlier life and partly on oral tradition. See *RLGVE* pp. 270–1 for an adapted version of text 3(i).

(i) *St Columba uses the power of the Cross to stop the Loch Ness monster from eating Lugneus mocu-Min.*

DE CUJUSDAM AQUATILIS BESTIAE VIRTUTE ORATIONIS BEATI VIRI REPULSIONE

Alio quoque in tempore, cum vir beatus in Pictorum provincia per aliquot moraretur dies, necesse habuit fluium transire Nesam. Ad cujus cum accessisset ripam alios ex acculis aspicit misellum humantes homunculum, quem ut ipsi sepultores ferebant quaedam paulo ante nantem aquatilis praeripiens bestia mursu momordit sevissimo. Cujus miserum cadaver sero licet quidam in alno   5
subvenientes porrectis praeripuere uncinis. Vir econtra beatus haec audiens praecipit ut aliquis ex comitibus enatans caupallum in altera stantem ripa ad se navigando reducat. Quo sancti audito praedicabilis viri praecepto, Lugneus mocu-Min nihil moratus obsecundans, depositis excepta vestimentis tunica, inmittit se in aquas. Sed bilua, quae, prius non tam satiata quam in praedam   10
accensa, in profundo fluminis latitabat. Sentiens eo nante turbatam supra aquam, subito emergens natatilis ad hominem in medio natantem alveo cum ingenti fremitu aperto cucurrit ore. Vir tum beatus videns, omnibus qui inerant tam barbaris quam etiam fratribus nimio terrore perculsis, cum salutare sancta elevata manu in vacuo aere crucis pincxisset signum invocato dei   15
nomine feroci imperavit bestiae, dicens: 'Noles ultra progredi, nec hominem tangas. Retro citius revertere.' Tum vero bestia hac sancti audita voce retrorsum acsi funibus retraheretur velociore recursu fugit tremefacta, quae prius Lugneo nanti eo usque appropinquavit ut hominem inter et bestiam non amplius esset quam unius contuli longitudo. Fratres tum recessisse videntes   20
bestiam, Lugneumque commilitonem ad eos intactum et incolomem in navicula reversum, cum ingenti ammiratione glorificaverunt deum in beato viro. Sed et gentiles barbari qui ad praesens inerant ejusdem miraculi magnitudine quod et ipsi viderant conpulsi deum magnificarunt christianorum.

Title **DE...REPULSIONE:** *de* goes with *repulsione*; *cuiusdam...bestiae* depends on *repulsione*; *virtute* ('by the power') depends on *repulsione* and governs *beati viri* 'of the saint' (lit. 'blessed man'): for this construction see G.10(b).

1 **Alio...in tempore:** 'at...', see G.15(a)(i).

1f. **per aliquot...dies:** 'for...' (CL uses acc. alone: see RLRGr L(c)3.

2 **necesse habuit:** 'he found it necessary'.
fluium (= *fluvium*)**...Nesam:** tr. 'Loch Ness'.

2f. **Ad cujus...ripam:** *Ad* governs *ripam*; the antecedent of *cujus* is *fluium*.

3 **alios:** tr. 'some' (but it may mean 'others', i.e. besides the dead man).
acculis = CL *incolis* (from *incola*).

misellum...homunculum: 'a wretched fellow' (diminutives of *miser, homo*).

ipsi: 'the' (see G.11(a)(i)).

4 **ferebant:** 'reported'.

quaedam...aquatilis...bestia go together as subject (the word order of the text uses much hyperbaton (see *RLGVE* p. 316)).

paulo ante nantem goes with *homunculum, quem* (obj. of *momordit*).

praeripiens: 'having snatched away' (see G.20 (a)).

5 **mursu** goes with *sevissimo*.

Cujus miserum cadaver: obj. of *praeripuere* (see RLRGr A4 for alternative 3pl. perf. form).

6 **porrectis** goes with *uncinis* (abl. abs.).

econtra: 'in turn' (see G.8).

audiens: 'having heard' (see G.20(a)).

7 **aliquis:** 'someone' (CL 'anyone': for *quidam*).

enatans: 'having swum out' (see G.20(a)).

in altera looks forward to *ripa* (qualifying *caupallum...stantem*).

8 **Quo...audito...praecepto** go together (abl. abs.).

9 **depositis...vestimentis:** abl. abs..

excepta...tunica 'except for...' (abl. abs.).

10 **bilua** = *belua* (see O.11).

in praedam: 'for prey'.

11 **eo nante:** 'by his swimming.'

turbatam: sc. *esse* 'that...'.

12 **natatilis:** '(by) swimming'.

ad hominem looks forward to *natantem*, which is qualified by *in medio...alveo*.

13 **omnibus** looks forward to *perculsis* (abl. abs.).

14 **inerant** = *aderant* (so also in l. 23 below).

fratribus: i.e. 'monks'.

nimio: 'very great'.

15 **salutare...crucis...signum:** (obj. of *pinxisset* = *pinxisset*): here a non-CL construction is used (*pingo X* acc. on *Y in* + abl. : CL *pingo X* acc. with *Y* abl.).

16 **Noles:** 'you will not' (cf. CL *noli* + inf. to express prohibitions).

16f. **nec...tangas:** 'do not touch' (see G.23(c)).

17 **citius:** 'quickly' (see G.12(c)).

18 **acsi** = CL *velut si* 'as if'.

19 **eo usque...ut:** 'so close that'.

inter governs *hominem* and *bestiam*.

20 **recessise** = *recessisse* (see O.7); it depends on *videntes* ('seeing that...'), as also does *reversum* (sc. *esse*).

23 **ad praesens:** 'at the time'.

24 **magnitudine** ('by...') depends on *conpulsi*.

magnificarunt = *magnificaverunt* (see RLRGr A4).

(ii) *St Columba forces the wizard Broichan to release a slave. A stone marked out with God's power is used to cure the illness caused by Broichan's stubbornness.*

DE BROICHANO MAGO OB ANCELLAE RETENTIONEM
INFIRMATO, ET PRO EJUS LIBERATIONE SANATO

Eodem in tempore vir venerandus quandam a Broichano mago scoticam postulavit servam humanitatis miseratione liberandam. Quam cum ille duro valde et stolido retentaret animo, sanctus ad eum loquutus hoc profatur modo: 'Scito Broichane scito quia si mihi hanc perigrinam liberare captivam nolueris priusquam de hac revertar provincia, citius morieris.' Et hoc coram Bruideo   5
rege dicens domum egressus regiam ad Nesam venit fluium. De quo videlicet fluio lapidem attollens candidum, ad comites: 'Signate,' ait, 'hunc candidum lapidem, per quem dominus in hoc gentili populo multas egrotorum perficiet sanitates'. Et hoc effatus verbum consequenter intulit, inquiens: 'Nunc Broichanus fortiter concussus est; nam angelus de caelo misus graviter illum   10
percutiens vitream in manu ejus de qua bibebat confregit in multa biberam fragmenta, ipsum vero anchellantem egra reliquit suspiria morti vicinum. Hoc

in loco paululum exspectemus binos regis nuntios ad nos celeriter misos, ut Broichano morienti citius subveniamus. Nunc Broichanus formidabiliter correptus ancellulam liberare est paratus.' 15

Adhuc sancto haec loquente verba, ecce sicuti praedixit duo a rege misi equites adveniunt; omnia quae in regis munitione de Froichano juxta sancti vaticinium sunt acta enarrantes; et de poculi confractione et de magi correptione et de servulae parata absolutione. Hocque intulerunt dicentes: 'Rex et ejus familiares nos ad te miserunt, ut nutricio ejus Broichano subvenias 20 mox morituro.' Quibus auditis legatorum verbis sanctus binos de comitum numero ad regem cum lapide a se benedicto mittit, dicens: 'Si in primis promiserit se Broichanus famulam liberaturum, tum deinde hic lapillus intinguatur in aqua et sic eo bibat, et continuo salutem recuperabit. Si vero renuerit refragans absolvi servam, statim morietur.' 25

Duo misi verbo sancti obsequentes ad aulam deveniunt regiam, verba viri venerabilis regi enarrantes. Quibus intimatis regi et nutricio ejus Broichano valde expaverunt. Eademque hora liberata famula sancti legatis viri adsignatur; lapis in aqua intingitur, mirumque in modum contra naturam lithus in aquis supernat quasi pomum vel nux, nec potuit sancti benedictio viri submergi. De 30 quo Broichanus natante bibens lapide statim a vicina rediit morte, intigramque carnis recuperavit salutem. Talis vero lapis postea in thesauris regis reconditus multas in populo egritudinum sanitates, similiter in aqua natans intinctus, domino miserante efficit. Mirum dictu, ab his egrotis quorum vitae terminus supervenerat requisitus idem lapis nullo modo reperiri poterat. Sic et in die 35 obitus Brudei regis quaerebatur, nec tamen in eodem loco ubi fuerat prius reconditus inveniebatur.

Title **PRO:** 'because of'.

1 **Eodem in tempore:** 'at...' (see G.15(a)(i)).

1f. **quandam...scoticam...servam** is subject of the acc. + inf. clause (verb *liberandam*, sc. *esse*).

2 **postulavit...liberandam:** 'asked of Broichan that...be freed'.
  humanitatis miseratione: lit. 'through the compassion of humanity', i.e. 'through the proper human feeling of compassion'.

2f. **duro...et stolido** look forward to *animo*.

3 **ad eum loquutus:** CL uses dative.

4 **Scito:** 'know' (see RLRGr A2 Note 1).
  quia: 'that' (see G.22(a)).
  perigrinam goes with *captivam*.

5 **de hac** goes with *provincia*.
  citius: 'quickly' (see G.12(c); also below at l. 14).
  Bruideo: 'Brude'.

6 **domum egresus** (= *egressus*: see O.7) **regiam:** 'leaving the royal house' (CL *egredior ex* + abl.).
  Nesam...fluium (= *fluvium*): tr. 'Loch Ness'.
  videlicet: seems to be used here as an ordinary adverb 'openly' (CL 'clearly', 'it is plain').

7 **fluio** = *fluvio*.
  ad comites...ait: 'said to...' (CL does not have indir. obj. with *aio*).

8 **multas** looks forward to *sanitates*.

9 **consequenter intulit:** 'he said in continuance' (CL *infero* 'bring in', 'produce'; *consequenter* 'suitably', 'consequently').

10 **misus** = *missus* (see O.7).

11 **vitream** looks forward to *biberam*, and **in multa** to *fragmenta*.

12 **ipsum:** 'him' (see G.11(a)(ii)).
  egra goes with *suspiria* (obj. of *anchellantem*).

13 **misos** = *missos* (see O.7).

16 **misi** = *missi* (see O.7); also below at l. 26.

17 **omnia quae** depends on *enarrantes*: 'to tell...' (see G.20(b)).

de Froichano = *de Broichano (Froichan* is the Irish form of the name: in other sources a wizard called Froichan uses magic against Columba at the battle of Cul-drebene, forming a 'druid's fence' for the arms of the High-King Diormit).

19 **parata:** 'prepared' i.e. 'intended'.

intulerunt: 'they said' (see note on l.9 above).

20 **nutricio:** 'foster-father' (translating an Old Irish term).

23 **liberaturum:** sc. *esse.*

24 **intinguatur:** 'let it be...' (jussive subj.: *RLGVE* 152).

eo: 'from it' (i.e. from the stone water).

25 **absolvi servam:** tr. 'the slave's release' (lit. 'that the slave be released').

27 **enarrantes:** 'to tell' (see G.20(b)).

Quibus intimatis...Broichano: abl. abs. 'When this had been disclosed to Broichan'.

28 **expaverunt:** subj. 'they', i.e. the king and Broichan, despite their being in the dative case.

sancti goes with *viri* and depends on *legatis.*

30 **benedictio:** i.e. the stone blessed by the saint.

30f. **De quo...natante...lapide** go together.

31 **bibens:** 'having drunk' (see G.20(a)).

a vicina looks forward to *morte.*

intigram looks forward to *salutem.*

32 **Talis:** 'this' (CL 'such a').

33 **multas...sanitates** is the obj. of *efficit* (= *effecit*: see O.11).

34 **ab his** (= 'those': see G.11(c)); *egrotis* looks forward to *nullo...poterat.*

34f. **vitae terminus...requisitus:** i.e. the destined end of their life.

35 **in die:** 'on...' (see G.15(a)(i)).

36f. **fuerat...reconditus:** 'had been...' (see G.4(a)).

Section 7
Anglo-Latin

Unlike Ireland, Britain had been incorporated into the Roman Empire (by
Claudius in AD 43). From then until the effective detachment from Rome
in the middle of the fifth century, Latin had been the official language of
the province as of other provinces, and a certain amount of written
evidence survives to confirm its use (graffiti, inscriptions and the
Vindolanda writing tablets). However, the native population, the Britons
(*Brettones*), spoke Celtic languages, the ancestors of Welsh and Cornish. As
the Saxon pirate raids of the third century turned into permanent
settlements in the fifth, the native populations were pushed to the
peripheries and the Church and the remnants of Latin learning with them.
There is still British Latin writing in the sixth century. Gildas' *De excidio et
conquaestu Britanniae* ('On the destruction and conquest of Britain') contains
a review of the province's history from the Roman invasion to his own
day and a complaint against abandonment in the face of the Saxon
invasions.

The Church in England, established after the time of Constantine, finally
lost contact with the continent after 455, when it accepted (unlike the
Celtic Church) the new calculation of the date of Easter. But it did not
survive the pagan incursions. It was the Irish foundations – Malmesbury,
Iona, Lindisfarne – which preserved the tradition of ecclesiastical Latin on
the island. The work of conversion in the areas settled by the Germanic
peoples had to be done again. This began with the arrival of St Augustine
in 597 (see map 4). There is no discernible trace of this mission in the later
Latin records. But we know that it was possible to find teachers of Latin in
Canterbury in the 630s and that a native Englishman, Ithamar of
Rochester, was sufficiently learned to be ordained bishop in 644.
Nonetheless, tangible evidence of Latin culture in England does not begin
until after 669, the date when Pope Vitalian sent the Greek Theodore of
Tarsus and Hadrian to Canterbury. The school which they established was
influential, and was a centre for the study of Greek as well as Latin. St

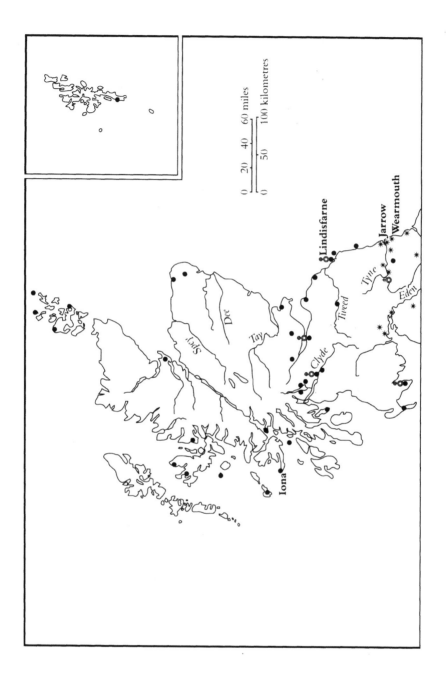

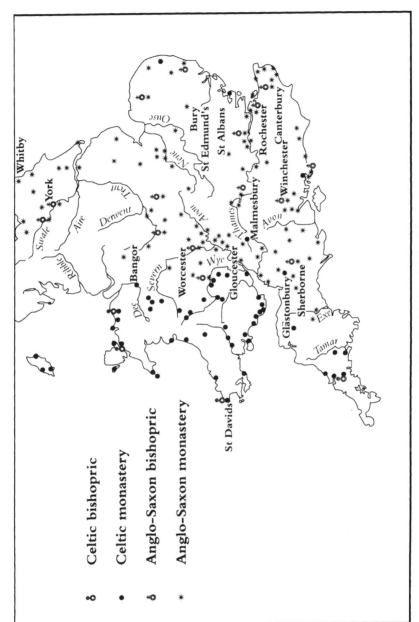

4 The Church in Great Britain c.800.

Celtic bishopric

Celtic monastery

Anglo-Saxon bishopric

Anglo-Saxon monastery

Aldhelm (*c.*640–709) studied there, after his early training under the Irish abbot Maeldubh at Malmesbury, and this may account for the continental influence upon his Latin prose style. His knowledge of classical Latin poetry (including, apparently, the now lost *Orpheus* of Lucan) shows how rich the resources of the libraries at Canterbury and Malmesbury (where he succeeded Maeldubh as abbot in 675) must have been. The prolixity and difficulty of his Latin – we are dealing with one of the first generation of Christian converts in Wessex – are an excellent demonstration of the fact that the history of Medieval Latin is by no means linear.

In 674 and 681 respectively, Benedict Biscop founded the monasteries at Wearmouth and Jarrow, which nurtured the Latinity of Bede (672/3–735). Bede's pupil Egbert, first archbishop of York (732) and founder of the cathedral school and library there, was the tutor of another highly influential Anglo-Saxon Latinist, Alcuin, whom we shall meet in due course (section 9.2) at the court of Charlemagne. Despite the incursions of the Vikings in the ninth century, which produced a situation in which at his accession in 871 King Alfred could find 'not a single literate man south of the Thames', the thread of Latin writing in England continued unbroken through the Middle Ages.

Anglo-Saxon students of Latin were taught, like their Irish counterparts, from grammars adapted somewhat to their special needs. Even so, these grammars were written in Latin and derived from earlier classical models, and were scarcely more than detailed catalogues of definitions and forms.

See further: V. Law, *The Insular Latin Grammarians*, Woodbridge, 1982; M. Lapidge, 'The present state of Anglo-Latin studies', in *Insular Latin Studies: Papers on Latin Texts and Manuscripts of the British Isles 550–1066*, Papers in Medieval Studies 1 (Toronto: Pontifical Institute of Medieval Studies, 1981), pp. 45–82.

1. Aldhelm (before 650–709/710)

Aldhelm was born and educated under Maeldubh at Malmesbury, an Irish foundation in the West Country. His further studies, in law, metre, *computus* and astronomy were done under Hadrian of Canterbury. He returned to Malmesbury as abbot around 673 and remained there until 705, when he became bishop of Sherborne. His works, which were copied, studied and imitated frequently, include letters, poems, a treatise on metre and another on the number seven.

See further: M. Lapidge and M. Herren, *The Prose Works of Aldhelm*, Ipswich, 1979.

(a) The following excerpt comes from the prose part of a work on virginity (*De virginitate*) which was written in both prose and verse (*opus geminatum*), a commonly used form.

(i) *The miracle of the bees portends the future sanctity of the baby Ambrose.*

Ambrosium vero superni nectaris ambrosia redolentem sub taciturnitatis velamento delitescere non patiar, cuius mellifluam dogmatum dulcedinem et purae virginitatis praerogativam pulchra praesagia portendebant, siquidem, infantulus cum in cunis supinus quiesceret, ex improviso examen apium ora labraque sine periculo pausantis complevit, quae ingrediendi et egrediendi per   5 tenera pueruli labella certatim vices frequentabant ac demum genitore Ambrosio eventum rei praestulante et, a berna, quae altrix infantis fuerat, ne abigerentur, imperante supernis caeli climatibus per aethera evolantes catervatim mortalium visus aufugiunt. Qualis autem vel quantus idem patriarcha virtutum gloria et miraculorum signis effulserit, neminem reor   10 expertum, nisi qui gesta conversationis illius a Paulino, viro venerabili, digesta didicerit.

1–9 **Ambrosium...aufugiunt:** the phrasing is *Ambrosium...redolentem* (obj.) *sub...non patiar,* | *cuius* (antecedent *Ambrosium*) *mellifluam...dulcedinem* (obj.) *et purae...praerogativam* (obj.) *pulchra praesagia portendebant* |, *siquidem,*⌐ ('since') | *cum...quiesceret* | ...⌐*examen* (subject) *apium ora labraque* (obj.)...*complevit* |, *quae* (antecedent *apium*) ... *frequentabant ac*⌐ *demum genitore ...praestulante* (abl. abs.) *et a berna,*⌐ ('by' = agent of *abigerentur* and *inside* the *ne* clause which will be governed by *imperante,* second participle in the abl. abs.) | *quae* (antecedent *berna*) ... *fuerat,* | *ne abigerentur,* ⌐*imperante* (second abl. participle with *genitore Ambrosio* governing *a berna...ne abigerentur*) | ⌐*supernis...evolantes* (referring to *apes*)...*visus* (obj.) *aufugiunt* (second verb in *quae... frequentabant* clause). The sentence refers to an anecdote in Paulinus' *Life of St Ambrose.* His father Ambrose, governor of Gaul, saw a swarm of bees flying in and out of his son's mouth as he slept. He stopped little Ambrose's nurse from driving off the bees, to see what end the miracle would have. The bees after a while flew up so high into the sky that they could hardly be seen.

1 **Ambrosium:** St Ambrose – see section 2.3.
2 **mellifluam...dulcedinem:** 'honeyed sweetness of doctrines', i.e. his Christian teaching.
5 **pausantis:** 'of (tr. 'to') the sleeping (child)' (CL *pauso* = 'halt', LL = *requiesco*).
5f. **ingrediendi...vices frequentabant:** lit. 'repeated turns of entering...', i.e. 'kept coming and going'.
7 **Ambrosio:** his father's name was also Ambrose.
praestulante: 'awaiting'.
fuerat = *fuit* (see G.9(c)).
8 **imperante:** 'having...' (see G.20(a)).
supernis...climatibus: 'to...' (see G.16(a)).
9 **qualis...vel quantus:** lit. 'of what sort and how much...he shone'; tr. 'the manner and magnitude with which...he shone'.
11 **expertum:** sc. *esse* 'knows'.
nisi qui...didicerit: 'except (the person) who has learnt of...'.
gesta conversationis illius: 'the deeds of his life' (CL *res gestas:* note the word play with *digesta* 'arranged').
Paulino: i.e. Paulinus of Nola (353/4–431), who wrote the life of St Ambrose in reference to which Aldhelm writes.

(ii) *Before his baptism, a dream of Christ blesses the future St Martin of Tours.*

Nec pudeat, Christi caelibes strictis pudicitiae legibus lascivam naturae
petulantiam coartantes corporeosque titillationum gestus velut indomitos
bigarum subiugales ferratis salivaribus refrenantes, Toronici reminisci pontificis; quem antequam regenerantis gratiae vulva parturiret et sacrosancti
baptismatis rudimenta cognosceret, in catacuminorum gradu et competen-   5
tium statu stipem pauperculis porrigentem agapemque egentibus erogantem,
cum nocturnae membra quieti dedisset, caeleste beavit oraculum, quique pro
adepta integritatis corona et fausta virginitatis infula, quas velut regale diadema
ac gemmatas crepundiorum lunulas indefessis viribus meta tenus servare
satagebat, miris virtutum signis effulsisse memoratur.   10

1–4 **Nec pudeat...pontificis:** The main structure is
*Nec pudeat Christi caelibes...Toronici reminisci
pontificis.* There are two long participle phrases
qualifying *caelibes:* (1) *strictis...coartantes* 'who
strangle *X* (acc.) by means of *Y* (abl.)'; (2)
corporeosque...refrenantes 'who rein in *X* (acc.)
like *Y* by means of *Z* (abl.).'

2 **corporeos...gestus:** lit. 'bodily motions of titil-
lations', i.e. 'titillating bodily movements'.

3 **bigarum subiugales:** lit. 'beasts of chariots', i.e.
'chariot–horses'.

salivaribus: 'bits'.

3f. **Toronici...pontificis:** i.e. St Martin, Bishop of
Tours (d. 397). The rest of the chapter contains reminiscences of a series of events in the
Saint's life as reported in Sulpicius Severus'
biography.

4–10 The rest of this sentence consists of two *qui* clauses
referring back to *Toronici...pontificis:* (1)
quem...oraculum and (2) *quique...memoratur.*

The structure of (1) is: *quem* (obj.)⌐ | *ante-
quam...vulva* (subject) *parturiret* (sc. him) *et* (sc.
he)*...rudimenta* (obj.) *cognosceret,* | ⌐*in...gradu
et...statu stipem* (obj. of)*...porrigentem* (agreeing
with *quem*) *agapemque* (obj. of)*...erogantem,*
(agreeing with *quem*)⌐ | *cum...membra*
(obj.)*...dedisset* (subject 'he')*...*| ⌐*beavit* (gov-

erning *quem*) *oraculum* (subject). This refers to a
vision of Christ vouchsafed in a dream to St
Martin before his conversion because of his
good works (Sulpicius' *Life,* ch. 2).

4 **regenerantis...vulva:** i.e. before he was born
again (see Jo 3.3: *nisi quis renatus fuerit denuo,
non potest videre regnum Dei* 'unless a man be
born again anew, he cannot see the Kingdom
of God').

5 **catacuminorum** = *catechumenorum.*

5f. **competentium:** lit. 'of those who strive together', a technical term for catechumens
who have become candidates for baptism.

agapem: 'charity' (Greek but with 3rd declension ending). The structure of (2) is: *quique*
(subject) *pro...corona et...infula*⌐ *quas* (antecedents
corona, infula) *velut...diadema ac...lunulas...servare*
('he') *satagebat* |...⌐*signis effulsisse memoratur.*

7 **pro:** 'because of' (cf. G.15(d)).

8 **adepta:** 'obtained' (CL, but usually dep.).

9 **gemmatas...lunulas:** lit. 'the gem-encrusted
crescents of toys', i.e. gem-encrusted
crescent-shaped trinkets.

10 **satagebat:** 'tried (to)' (CL *satis ago* 'be in
trouble', 'bustle about').

virtutum: 'of miracles'.

memoratur: 'is said (to)'.

(iii) *The miracles of St Martin.*

Etenim catacumini cadaver, quem dira, ut dicunt, fortunae ferocitas et
parcarum grassatrix nulli parcentum atrocitas, immo gelidae mortis inclemen-

tia regenerantis gratiae sacramento privatum perniciter oppresserat, de porta
mortis redivivum erexit ad lumina vitae. Alios quoque binos crudeli mortis
meta multatos et optatis vitae manubiis spoliatos de latebroso leti barathro et 5
trucis tartari tormento voti compos reduxit ad superos. Procerum frondentis
pini stipitem vetitis paganorum caeremoniis deputatum, quamvis obliqua
reclinem curvatura crebri accolarum bipennes certatim succiderent, intrepidus
nutabundum aspexit et fragore horrisono cassabundum contempsit. Pellaces
Anatolii nebulonis praestigias, quas lividorum fraudulenta aemulorum factio 10
mille nocendi artibus armata ostenso fallacis pepli ludibrio audacter ingerebat,
praepollente meritorum gratia funditus fatescere et procul ut ridiculosum
fantasma evanescere fecit. Priscorum dilubra paganorum a cimentario politis-
simis compacta petris rubrisque tegularum imbricibus tecta mortalium diffidens
amminiculo et angelorum fretus suffragio, qui hastati et scutati famulo Dei 15
praesidium laturi venisse leguntur, solo tenus deruta quassavit, evertit,
destruxit.

1–4 **Etenim...vitae:** The structure is: *catacumini ca-*
daver (obj.)⌐ | *quem* (obj.: antecedent *catacu-*
mini)... *ferocitas* (subject)...*et*...*atrocitas* (subject),
immo (nay rather)...*mortis inclementia* (sub-
ject)...*privatum* (agreeing with *quem*)...
oppresserat (s. verb with last subject), | ⌐...*re-*
divivum (agreeing with *cadaver*) *erexit* (he, St
Martin)...

   This refers to the resuscitation of a convert
who died suddenly, before he could be baptized (Sulpicius' *Life*, ch. 7).

2 **grassatrix:** 'marauding', adj. with *atrocitas*.
   parcentum: agreeing with *parcarum* and governing *nulli*. Note the etymological pun. The fates
(*parcae*) spare (*parcent*) no one.

2f. **mortis inclementia:** a reminiscence of Virgil,
Georgics 3.68: *durae rapit inclementia mortis*
'The mercilessness of harsh death snatched
away'.

3 **sacramento:** 'the mystery/sacrament' – governs
regenerantis gratiae and depends *on privatum*. The
point is that the catechumen had not yet been
baptized.

4 **lumina vitae:** another Virgilian echo (*Aeneid*
6.828).

4–6 **Alios...ad superos:** The structure is *Alios*...*binos*
(obj.) *crudeli*...*multatos et*...*spoliatos* (2 phrases,
the participles agreeing with *alios*) *de*...*tormento*
(2 parallel prepositional phrases dependent on
the verb *reduxit*)...*voti compos* (agreeing with

unstated subject 'he (i.e. St Martin)') *reduxit*
(verb: subject 'he') *ad superos*.

   Sulpicius' *Life* reports only two resuscita-
tions, the one in the previous sentence and a
suicide. But Aldhelm adds a third, taking into
account a passage in a dialogue by Sulpicius.

4 **binos:** 'two' (CL usually 'two each').

6 **voti compos:** 'having obtained his wish'.

6–9 **Procerum...contempsit:** The structure is *Pro-*
cerum...*stipitem* (obj.) *vetitis*...*deputatum*⌐ (participle agreeing with *stipitem* and governing
vetitis...*caeremonis:* tr. 'allotted to...'), | *quamuis*
obliqua reclinem curvatura (*reclinem* obj. agrees
with *stipitem* (tr. 'it bent back') and *obli-*
qua...*curvatura* depends on *reclinem* 'with')
crebri...*bipennes* (subject: tr. 'strokes of the
axe')...*succiderent* (verb) | ⌐*intrepidus* (agrees
with the subject; subject tr. 'he (i.e. St Martin) fearless') *nutabundum* (agrees with *stipitem*
(obj.): tr. 'it, as it tottered') *aspexit* (verb) *et*
fragore...*cassabundum* (phrase: *cassabundum*
agrees with *stipitem* (obj.) and *fragore horrisono*
depends on *cassabundum*: tr. 'it, as it was about
to fall with...') *contempsit* (second verb).

   In this incident (Sulpicius' *Life*, ch. 12), St
Martin wishes to cut down a pine tree revered
by the pagan villagers. They challenge him to
stand beneath the tree as it falls to test the
power of his God. He waits until the direction
of the tree's fall is unequivocal, stands directly

in its path and at the last minute makes the sign of the Cross. The tree falls in a different place.

9–13 **Pellaces...fecit:** the structure is *Pellaces...praestigias* (obj.),⌐ | *quas* (obj.: antecedent *praestigias lividorum*... *factio* (subject) *mille...armata* (participle agrees with *factio: mille...artibus* depends on *armata*) *ostenso...ludibrio* (abl. abs.)...*ingerebat* (verb) | ⌐*praepollente...gratia* (abl. abs. or abl. of means)... *fatescere et...*⌐ | *ut* (like)... *fantasma* | ⌐*evanescere* (infinitives depend on *fecit:* see G.17(c)) *fecit* (sc. '(St Martin) caused').

Sulpicius (ch. 23) reports that a certain Anatolius once claimed that that night God would dress him in a white garment, which he would wear as he went among them, to show that the power of God was in him. Next day, when some companions of Martin's were trying to force him to confront the saint, the robe vanished, proving Martin's power, since the Devil could not hide his pretences from him.

13–17 **Priscorum...destruxit:** the structure is *Priscorum dilubra paganorum* (*dilubra* obj.) *a cimenta-*

rio...tecta (2 participle phrases, agreeing with *dilubra*: (1) *compacta* governing *politissimis...petris* (2) *tecta* governing *rubris ...imbricibus) mortalium...suffragio* (2 participle phrases; the participles *diffidens* and *fretus* agree with unstated subject 'St Martin': *diffidens* governs *mortalium...amminiculo, fretus* governs *angelorum...suffragio)*⌐ | *qui* (subject; antecedent *angelorum) hastati et scutati* (agreeing with *qui) famulo...laturi* (participle phrase agreeing with *qui: laturi* governs *famulo...praesidium)...leguntur* | ⌐*solo...deruta* (participle phrase: *deruta* agrees with *dilubra) quassavit...destruxit* (main verbs in asyndeton: unstated subject 'St Martin').

14 **tegularum imbricibus:** lit. 'pantiles of roof tiles'; tr. roof tiles.

16 **laturi:** 'to bring' (see G.10(c)).

leguntur: lit. 'are read', i.e. 'are said in (Sulpicius') book' (cf. CL *dicuntur:* 'they are said' + inf.).

deruta: 'he cast down...and' (lit. 'having been cast down', but the action is contemporaneous with *quassavit...destruxit*).

(b) Alongside their serious works, many writers, and especially Anglo-Latin writers, produced collections of *aenigmata*. St Boniface (*c.*675–754), also composed such hexameter verse riddles. But in his pieces, the answer is given in acrostic form, reading down from the first letter of each line (e.g. EBRIETAS DICEBAT 'Drunkenness was speaking'). These three examples are from Aldhelm's collection.

(i) *A nettle.*

Torqueŏ torquentes, sed nullum torqueŏ sponte
laedere nec quemquam uolŏ, ni prius ipse reatum
contrahat et uiridem studeat decerpere caulem.
feruida mox hominis turgescunt membra nocentis:
uindicŏ sic noxam stimulisque ulciscor acutis.   5

2 **ni** = *nisi.*

2f. **reatum / contrahat:** lit. 'causes an offence', i.e. 'commits a crime' (see G.28(b) for mood of verb).

4 **feruida:** tr. 'hotly'.

Answer: *Vrtica.*

(ii) *A bookcase.*

Nunc mea diuinis complentur uiscera uerbis
totaque sacratos gestant praecordia biblos;
at tamen ex isdem nequeo cognoscere quicquam:
infelix fato fraudabor munere tali,
dum tollunt dirae librorum lumina Parcae.   5

2 **biblos:** 'books' (Greek).   L(f)1).
4 **fato:** 'in' (abl. of respect: RLRGr L(f)4(vi)).   5 **dum:** 'because' (see G.30(a)).
munere tali: 'of' (abl. of separation: RLRGr   **Answer:** *Arca Libraria.*

(iii) *A woman who has given birth to twins.*

Sunt mihi sex oculi, totidem simul auribus hausi,
sed digitos decies senos in corpore gesto;
ex quibus ecce quater denis de carne reuulsis
quinquiěs at tantum uideo remanere quaternos.

1 **auribus hausi:** lit. 'I drank in with...ears', i.e. 'I   4 **quinquies...quaternos:** 'five times four each'
  hear' (cf. e.g. Virgil, *Georgics* 2.340).   (scansion demands *quīnquǐěs*; CL *quīnquǐěs*).
2 **decies senos:** 'ten times six each'.   **Answer:** *Puerpera geminos enixa.*

2. Bede (672/3–c.735)

What is known of the life of Bede he himself reports at the end of his
Ecclesiastical History of the English Nation (V.24), finished in 731. He was
born in Northumbria, in the territory of the monastery of Wearmouth and
Jarrow (see section 7 Intro.). At seven he was put into the care of Abbot
Benedict (Biscop) and then of Ceolfrith to be educated. From that time on,
he spent his whole life in the monastery, living according to the Rule,
singing in the church, and applying himself to the study of the Scriptures.
He was ordained deacon at nineteen and at thirty priest. Now fifty-nine
years old, he confesses: 'it has always been my delight to learn or to teach
or to write'. This writing he characterizes as making 'brief extracts from the
works of the venerable Fathers on the sacred Scriptures' or adding notes of
his own to clarify their sense and interpretation. The list of works which he
appends to this brief autobiography and his towering fame both in the
Middle Ages and later belie this modest description. They include:
educational treatises covering metre, orthography, cosmology, the
hexameron (the first six days of creation) and the *computus*; works of biblical
exegesis, including commentaries on parts of Genesis, Exodus, 1 Samuel,

1 Kings, Proverbs, the Song of Songs, Ezra and Nehemiah, Habbakuk, Tobit, Mark, Luke, Acts, Paul's Epistles, the seven catholic epistles and Revelation, as well as other aids to biblical study (e.g. *Nomina locorum* etc.); homilies, saints' lives, poems and letters; histories, including, as well as his monumental *Ecclesiastical History*, an account of the abbots of Wearmouth and Jarrow and a chronicle. It is said by one of his pupils, Cuthbert, later abbot of Wearmouth–Jarrow, that Bede died as he had lived, dictating even on his death-bed. His vast contribution was summed up thus by Wordsworth (*The Ecclesiastical Sonnets*, I.23, ll. 10–14):

> The recreant soul, that dares to shun the debt
> Imposed on human kind, must first forget
> Thy diligence, thy unrelaxing use
> Of a long life, and, in the hour of death,
> The last dear service of the passing breath.

See further: G. H. Brown, *Bede the Venerable*, Boston, Mass., 1987; P. H. Blair, *The World of Bede*, Cambridge, Mass., 1990.

(a) Bede, *Ecclesiastical History*

Bede's bibliography describes this work as 'the history of the Church of our island and race, in five books'. Written in the tradition of Eusebius' *Ecclesiastical History* (translated into Latin by Rufinus), it focuses upon the sacred, which provides the framework for explaining the secular. Bede, like Eusebius, uses documents and cites sources. But in uniting Eusebius' methods with local history on the model of Gregory of Tours' *History of the Franks* (see section 8.3), he can be said to be making the English into one of God's chosen peoples. The first three books deal with the conversion of the English. Books four and five describe how the Christian life developed among them.

See further: W. Goffart, *The Narrators of Barbarian History (AD 550–800)*, Princeton, 1988; J. M. Wallace-Hadrill, *Bede's Ecclesiastical History of the English Nation: A Historical Commentary*, Oxford, 1988.

(i) *Pope Gregory the Great (590–604) asks, before his pontificate, for missionaries to be sent to convert the pagan English.*

Nec silentio praetereunda opinio quae de beato Gregorio traditione maiorum ad nos usque perlata est, qua uidelicet ex causa admonitus tam sedulam erga salutem nostrae gentis curam gesserit.

Dicunt quia die quadam, cum, aduenientibus nuper mercatoribus, multa
uenalia in forum fuissent conlata, multique ad emendum confluxissent, et 5
ipsum Gregorium inter alios aduenisse ac uidisse inter alia pueros uenales
positos, candidi corporis ac uenusti uultus, capillorumque forma egregia. Quos
cum aspiceret, interrogauit, ut aiunt, de qua regione uel terra essent adlati.
Dictumque est quia de Brittania insula, cuius incolae talis essent aspectus.
Rursus interrogauit, utrum idem insulani Christiani, an paganis adhuc 10
erroribus essent inplicati. Dictum est quod essent pagani. At ille intimo ex
corde longa trahens suspiria, 'Heu, pro dolor!' inquit 'quod tam lucidi uultus
homines tenebrarum auctor possidet, tantaque gratia frontispicii mentem ab
interna gratia uacuam gestat!' Rursus ergo interrogauit, quod esset uocabulum
gentis illius. Responsum est quod Angli uocarentur. At ille 'Bene,' inquit, 'nam 15
et angelicam habent faciem, et tales angelorum in caelis decet esse coheredes.
Quod habet nomen ipsa prouincia de qua isti sunt adlati?' Responsum est quia
Deiri uocarentur idem prouinciales. At ille 'Bene,' inquit, 'Deiri, de ira eruti, et
ad misericordiam Christi uocati. Rex prouinciae illius quomodo appellatur?'
Responsum est quod Aelle diceretur. At ille adludens ad nomen ait: 'Alleluia, 20
laudem Dei creatoris illis in partibus oportet cantari.' Accedensque ad
pontificem Romanae et apostolicae sedis (nondum enim erat ipse pontifex
factus) rogauit ut genti Anglorum in Brittaniam aliquos uerbi ministros, per
quos ad Christum conuerteretur, mitteret; se ipsum paratum esse in hoc opus
Domino cooperante perficiendum, si tamen apostolico papae, hoc ut fieret, 25
placeret. Quod dum perficere non posset, quia, etsi pontifex concedere illi
quod petierat uoluit, non tamen ciues Romani, ut tam longe ab urbe secederet,
potuere permittere, mox ut ipse pontificatus officio functus est, perfecit opus
diu desideratum, alios quidem praedicatores mittens, sed ipse praedicationem
ut fructificaret, suis exhortationibus ac precibus adiuuans. Haec iuxta opinio- 30
nem quam ab antiquis accepimus, historiae nostrae ecclesiasticae inserere
oportunum duximus.

1–3 **Nec...gesserit:** the basic structure is *Nec...*
  praetereunda (sc. *est*) *opinio* | *quae...perlata est,* |
  qua...ex causa... gesserit.
1 **beato Gregorio:** i.e. St Gregory the Great, Pope
  590–604.
2 **qua...ex causa:** 'why...'.
  uidelicet: 'namely'.
  sedulam looks forward to *curam* (obj. of *gesserit*).
4 **dicunt quia:** 'that' (but the construction is acc. +
  inf.: *ipsum Gregorium...aduenisse ac uidisse*).
5 **fuissent conlata:** 'had been...' (see G.4(a)).
7 **capillorum...forma egregia:** 'and with very
  lovely hair' (*forma egregia* is abl. of description).

9 **quia...insula:** sc. *essent adlati.*
  talis...aspectus: gen. of description.
10 **utrum...Christiani:** sc. 'were'.
12 **longa** looks forward to *suspiria.*
13f. **gratia...ab...gratia:** 'beauty...from...grace' (word
  play with two senses of *gratia*).
14 **gestat:** lit. 'carries', but tr. 'hides'.
16 **tales** goes with *decet* ('it is fitting that such
  people...'); *angelorum* depends on *coheredes*
  (Gregory plays on *Anglus/angelus*: see O.9).
17 **ipsa:** 'the' (see G.11(a)(i)).
18 **Deiri:** inhabitants of Deira, the territory of which
  extended from the Humber to the Tees or

Tyne (Gregory puns on *de ira* 'from anger').

22 **erat** goes with *factus.*

23 **ut genti** ('to...') looks forward to *mitteret.*

23f. **per quos...conuerteretur:** purpose clause (RLRGr Q2(b)).

24 **se ipsum...esse:** sc. 'he said that...'.

24f. **in hoc opus...perficiendum:** 'to do this work'.

25 **si...papae** looks forward to *placeret* (which introduces the *ut* clause).

26 **dum...posset:** 'although...' (= *cum*, cf. G.30(a)).

etsi pontifex looks forward to *uoluit* (which introduces *concedere...petierat*).

27 **ciues Romani** is the subject of *potuere* (= *potuerunt:* RLRGr A4).

ut...secederet: 'that...' (the clause is the obj. of *permittere*).

28 **mox ut:** 'as soon as'.

29 **praedicationem:** obj. of *adiuuans.*

(ii) *Augustine tries to get the bishops of the Britons to abandon practices contrary to Catholic doctrine. The recalcitrant Britons receive their just deserts.*

Interea Augustinus adiutorio usus Aedilbercti regis, conuocauit ad suum colloquium episcopos siue doctores proximae Brettonum prouinciae in loco qui usque hodie lingua Anglorum *Augustinaes Ac,* id est, Robur Augustini, in confinio Huicciorum et Occidentalium Saxonum, appellatur; coepitque eis fraterna admonitione suadere, ut pace catholica secum habita, communem   5
euangelizandi gentibus pro Domino laborem susciperent. Non enim paschae dominicum diem suo tempore, sed a quarta decima usque ad uicesimam lunam obseruabant; quae computatio LXXXIIII annorum circulo continetur; sed et alia plurima unitati ecclesiasticae contraria faciebant. Qui cum longa disputatione habita, neque precibus, neque hortamentis, neque increpationibus Augustini ac   10
sociorum eius adsensum praebere uoluissent, sed suas potius traditiones uniuersis, quae per orbem sibi in Christo concordant, ecclesiis praeferrent, sanctus pater Augustinus hunc laboriosi ac longi certaminis finem fecit, ut diceret: 'Obsecremus Deum, qui habitare facit unianimes in domo Patris sui, ut ipse nobis insinuare caelestibus signis dignetur, quae sequenda traditio, quibus sit   15
uiis ad ingressum regni illius properandum. Adducatur aliquis aeger, et per cuius preces fuerit curatus, huius fides et operatio Deo deuota atque omnibus sequenda credatur.' Quod cum aduersarii, inuiti licet, concederent, adlatus est quidam de genere Anglorum, oculorum luce priuatus. Qui cum oblatus Brettonum sacerdotibus, nil curationis uel sanationis horum ministerio perciperet, tandem   20
Augustinus iusta necessitate conpulsus, flectit genua sua ad Patrem Domini nostri Iesu Christi, deprecans ut uisum caeco, quem amiserat, restitueret, et per inluminationem unius hominis corporalem, in plurimorum corde fidelium spiritalis gratiam lucis accenderet. Nec mora, inluminatur caecus, ac uerus summae lucis praeco ab omnibus praedicatur Augustinus. Tum Brettones   25
confitentur quidem intellexisse se ueram esse uiam iustitiae quam praedicaret Augustinus; sed non se posse absque suorum consensu ac licentia priscis abdicare moribus; unde postulabant ut secundo synodus pluribus aduenientibus fieret.

1 **Interea:** Augustine had sent a series of questions to Pope Gregory in Rome, to which Gregory replied with the book known as *Responsiones* (601). What is reported in this chapter occurs

after Augustine's receipt of these 'Answers'.

Aedilbercti: Ethelbert, King of Kent, *c.* 560–616.

2 **Brettonum:** 'Britons'.

2 **qui** looks forward to *appellatur*.

Augustinaes Ac: 'Augustine's Oak' (possibly modern Aust on the river Severn).

4 **Huicciorum:** 'Hwiccas' (Germanic invaders who occupied territory near the river Avon in Somerset).

5 **ut** looks forward to *susciperent* (obj. *communem...laborem*).

6 **gentibus:** obj. of *euangelizandi:* (lit. 'bringing the good news (sc. of Christ) to...': Greek).

6f. **paschae...diem:** i.e. Easter Day (obj. of *obseruabant*).

7 **suo tempore:** i.e. 'at the correct (viz. Catholic) time' (for *suo* see G.11(e)(iii)). There were two major differences between the Catholic and Celtic *computus* for Easter, which is calculated as the first Sunday after the paschal full moon: (1) Celts used the Jewish cycle of 84 years, while Catholics used a 19-year cycle adopted in 527; (2) if the paschal full moon was itself a Sunday, the Celtic Church celebrated Easter on that day, the Catholic Church on the Sunday following. See section 6.2.

9–14 **Qui cum...diceret:** the structure is *Qui cum ...neque* ('to...')*...neque* ('to...')*...neque* ('to...')

...adsensum praebere uoluissent, sed suas... traditiones uniuersis (looks forward to *ecclesiis*, antecedent of *quae...concordant*)*...praeferrent* (main clause)*...Augustinus... finem fecit, ut diceret.*

12 **sibi:** 'with one another' (see G.11(e)(ii)).

13 **hunc:** looks forward to *finem*.

13f. **ut diceret:** 'by saying'.

14 **Obsecremus** introduces *ut...dignetur.*

habitare facit: 'makes (sc. men) dwell' (see G.17(c)).

15 **sequenda:** sc. *est.*

15f. **sit...properandum:** 'we are to hasten'.

16f. **per cuius preces...huius fides...:** 'through whoever's prayers...this person's faith...'.

17 **fuerit curatus:** 'had been...' (see G.4(a)).

18f. **de genere Anglorum:** 'from...'.

19 **Qui:** 'he' (subject of the *cum* clause, verb *perciperet*).

22 **quem:** antecedent is *uisum* (obj. of *restitueret*).

22f. **et...accenderet** is a second part of the *deprecans ut* clause. The structure is *et per inluminationem...corporalem, in ... corde ... gratiam* (obj.) *...accenderet.*

27 **sed non se posse:** 'but (sc. they said) that...'.

abdicare: 'renounce' (CL *se abdicare* + abl.).

28 **unde:** 'therefore'.

secundo: 'on a second occasion', i.e. 'again' (see G.13).

(iii) *The new synod fails to achieve agreement and Augustine ominously foretells 'if they would not preach to the English nation the way of life, they should through their hands suffer the vengeance of death'. And this, says Bede, was brought to pass, as he had predicted, by the working of divine justice.*

Siquidem post haec ipse de quo diximus, rex Anglorum fortissimus Aedilfrid, collecto grandi exercitu, ad Ciuitatem Legionum, quae a gente Anglorum Legacaestir, a Brettonibus autem rectius Carlegion appellatur, maximam gentis perfidae stragem dedit. Cumque bellum acturus uideret sacerdotes eorum, qui ad exorandum Deum pro milite bellum agente conuenerant, seorsum in tutiore 5 loco consistere, sciscitabatur qui essent hi, quidue acturi illo conuenissent. Erant autem plurimi eorum de monasterio Bancor, in quo tantus fertur fuisse numerus monachorum, ut cum in septem portiones esset cum praepositis sibi rectoribus monasterium diuisum, nulla harum portio minus quam trecentos homines haberet, qui omnes de labore manuum suarum uiuere solebant. 10 Horum ergo plurimi ad memoratam aciem, peracto ieiunio triduano, cum aliis orandi causa conuenerant, habentes defensorem nomine Brocmailum, qui eos

intentos precibus a barbarorum gladiis protegeret. Quorum causam aduentus
cum intellexisset rex Aedilfrid, ait: 'Ergo si aduersum nos ad Deum suum
clamant, profecto et ipsi quamuis arma non ferant, contra nos pugnant qui   15
aduersis nos inprecationibus persequuntur.' Itaque in hos primum arma uerti
iubet, et sic ceteras nefandae militiae copias non sine magno exercitus sui
damno deleuit. Extinctos in ea pugna ferunt, de his qui ad orandum uenerant,
uiros circiter mille ducentos, et solum L fuga esse lapsos. Brocmail ad primum
hostium aduentum cum suis terga uertens, eos quos defendere debuerat,   20
inermes ac nudos ferientibus gladiis reliquit. Sicque completum est presagium
sancti pontificis Augustini, quamuis ipso iam multo ante tempore ad caelestia
regna sublato, ut etiam temporalis interitus ultione sentirent perfidi quod oblata
sibi perpetuae salutis consilia spreuerant.

1 **Siquidem:** 'Now...' (see G.14).
Aedelfrid: 'Ethelfrith'.
2 **Ciuitatem Legionum:** 'The city of the legions',
i.e. Chester.
4 **stragem dedit:** 'performed a massacre'.
qui (antecedent *sacerdotes*) looks forward to *conuenerant*; the construction after *uideret* is acc. +
inf. (*sacerdotes...consistere*).
7 **Bancor:** gen. (cf. G.6(a)): 'Bangor-on-Dee'.
8f. **ut...haberet:** the structure is *ut* ⌐ | *cum...
esset...diuisum* | ⌐ *nulla...portio...haberet.*
13f. **Quorum causam aduentus:** *causam* governs
aduentus, which governs *quorum*.
17f. **ceteras** looks forward to *copias* (obj. of *deleuit*)
and **magno** to *damno*.

18 **Extinctos** (sc. *esse*)...**ferunt:** 'They say that there
were killed' (looking forward to *uiros... ducen-
tos*); a second acc. + inf. follows (*et...esse lapsos*).
de his: 'of those...' (see G.15(d) and G.11(c)).
20 **eos** (antecedent of *quos*) is the obj. of **reliquit.**
21 **ferientibus gladiis:** 'to the striking swords', i.e.
'to the blows of swords'.
Sic looks forward to *ut* (result).
22 **quamuis ipso...sublato:** 'even though he had
been taken up...'.
23 **temporalis interitus ultione:** 'by the vengeance of temporal death', i.e. by losing their
earthly lives (looking forward to the contrast
perpetuae salutis consilia, obj. of *spreuerant*; here
quod means 'that').

(b) Bede, *Commentary on St. Luke's Gospel* 23.13–18 (see section 3.3)

Bede's own view of his work shows that it was his biblical exegesis that he
considered most important. This was also the view of his contemporaries
and of the later Middle Ages. He commented both on books already
heavily annotated by the Fathers (see section 4 Intro.) and on those
untouched by earlier writers. The first type of work was largely one of
digestion and simplification, to provide a handbook of patristic wisdom.
The second type shows us his own deep scholarship and originality. His
method was the standard one of breaking up the texts into short passages
and providing a meditation on each according to the interpretative
procedures of the Fathers, employing allegorical, tropological, anagogical
and literal analyses as seemed appropriate (see section 3 Intro.). He was well
placed for his work on the New Testament in particular, since he knew

Greek (an unusual skill for a Northern European in the Middle Ages). The excerpt comes from his commentary on St Luke's Gospel. Luke had been commented by St Ambrose, but the introductory letter of Bishop Acca shows that this work was too difficult for English students. Bede makes careful use of patristic texts, and also adds remarks of his own. For example, at 23.34: 'Father, forgive them...' (just after this passage), he elucidates the problem of how to reconcile Jesus' prayer for forgiveness of his killers and God's subsequent punishment of the Jews by the destruction of the temple. You will find some minor divergences between the two texts. Some of these are due to orthography (e.g. v for u), others to differences in punctuation. A few are due to a difference between the mss. used by Bede and those used by the editors of the Vulgate.

Pilatus autem conuocatis principibus sacerdotum et magistratibus et plebe dixit ad eos. Quantum dimittendi Iesu studium gerat Pilatus attende. Primo accusantibus sacerdotum principibus nihil se in eo causae dicit inuenisse. Deinde illis in coepto persistentibus mittit ad Herodem ut si uel ille quid in eo sceleris inuenire possit an forte dimittendum decernere uelit exploret. Postremo et 5 huius agnita uoluntate nec inuento in Iesu facinore etiam plebis cui unum dimittere per pascha consueuerat sententiam quaerit. Iterum quoque ac tertio dimittere illum uolens interrogat. Sed quo curiosius auxiliatorem dimittendi Iesum quem non repperit quaerit eo criminosiores eos quos unanimiter eius mortem desiderantes repperit arguit. 10

Obtulistis mihi hominem hunc quasi auertentem populum; ecce ego coram uobis interrogans nullam causam inuenio in homine isto ex his in quibus eum accusatis. Haec dicendo Pilatus absoluit quidem Iesum quem reprobauit insontem sed ut implerentur scripturae quem absoluit iudicio crucifixit mysterio.

Sed neque Herodes, nam remisi uos ad illum, et ecce nihil dignum morte actum est ei. 15 Audi caece Iudaee, audi crudelis pagane. Pilatus ipse fatetur neque se neque Herodem dignum quid morte in Christo repperisse sed tantum in occidendo uel inludendo innoxio alienae crudelitatis obtemperasse clamoribus. Pereant ergo scripta quae tanto post tempore contra Christum composita non illum apud Pilatum magicae artis accusatum sed uos apud dominum perfidiae et 20 falsitatis accusandos esse demonstrant.

Emendatum ergo illum dimittam. Flagris illum et ludibriis quantum ipsi iubetis dummodo innoxium sanguinem non sitiatis afficiam.

Necesse autem habebat dimittere eis per diem festum unum. Necesse habebat non imperiali legis sanctione sed annua gentis cui per talia placere gaudebat 25 consuetudine deuinctus.

Exclamauit autem simul uniuersa turba dicens: Tolle hunc et dimitte nobis Barraban; qui erat propter seditionem quandam factam in ciuitate et homicidium missus in carcerem.

Haeret Iudaeis usque hodie sua petitio quam tanto labore impetrarunt. Quia
enim data sibi optione pro Iesu latronem pro saluatore interfectorem pro datore   30
uitae elegerunt ademptorem, merito salutem uitamque perdiderunt et latrociniis se ac seditionibus in tantum submerserunt ut et patriam regnumque suum
quod plus Christo amauere perdiderint et hactenus eam quam uendidere uel
animae uel corporis libertatem recipere non meruerint.

The commentary is organized into *lemma*, containing the text to be commented upon, and
gloss, the comment. For help with the passages
from the Vulgate, see commentary on the texts
in section 3.3.

2 **Iesu**: gen. (see G.6(b)), with *dimittendi*.

3 **nihil** looks forward to *causae* and is the obj. of
inuenisse.

4 **mittit**: sc. Jesus.

   ut looks forward to *exploret*, which introduces
two indirect questions: (1) *si uel...possit* (2) *an
...uelit* (the construction *si uel...an* replaces CL
utrum...an: see also G.24(c)).

   quid: 'anything' (= *aliquid*; with *sceleris* = 'any
crime', obj. of *inuenire*: partitive gen., see
RLRGr L(d)2).

5 **dimittendum**: sc. *esse eum* 'that he should be let
go'.

6 **huius**: i.e. Herod's.

   plebis looks forward to *sententiam* (obj. of *quaerit*).

   cui ('for whose benefit', antecedent *plebis*) looks
forward to *dimittere...consueuerat*.

7 **per pascha**: 'at the time of passover'.

8f. **quo curiosius...eo criminosiores**: 'the more
assiduously...the more criminal...'.

   auxiliatorem: obj. of *quaerit* and antecedent of
quem.

9 **eos** obj. of *arguit*, and antecedent of *quos*.

14 **quem absoluit iudicio crucifixit mysterio**:
'(the man) whom he acquitted through (human) justice, he crucified because of (divine)
mystery'.

16f. **neque se neque Herodem** are the subjects of
repperisse and *obtemperasse* (= *obtemperauisse*: see
RLRGr A4), acc. + inf. introduced by *fatetur*.

17 **dignum quid**: 'anything worthy (of)'.

18 **alienae crudelitatis** depends on *clamoribus*.

   Pereant: 'may they be damned'.

19f. **scripta** (antecedent) *quae* (subject)...*composita*
(with *quae*)...*illum* ('that he...')...*accusatum*
(with *illum*: sc. *esse*) *sed uos* ('that you...')
...*accusandos* (with *uos*) *esse demonstrant* (verb):
Bede may be thinking of works such as those
of Celsus, against whom Origen wrote in the
late second century.

22 **Flagris illum et ludibriis** look forward to the
verb *afficiam*.

24f. **non...sanctione sed annua...consuetudine**
depends on *deuinctus*.

25 **cui**: antecedent *gentis*.

29 **sua petitio**: 'their (i.e. the Jews') request'.

30f. **pro Iesu latronem pro saluatore interfectorem pro datore uitae...ademptorem**: the
accusatives are all objects of *elegerunt* (the
phrases form an ascending tricolon: see
RLGVE p. 315(f)).

31f. **latrociniis...submerserunt**: *se* is the obj. of
submerserunt; the ablatives mean 'in'.

32 **in tantum...ut**: 'to such an extent...that'.

32f. **ut...meruerint**: the structure is *ut...patriam re-
gnumque...*⌐| *quod...amauere* (= *amauerunt*: see
RLRGr A4) | ⌐*perdiderint et...eam*⌐ (looks
forward to *libertatem*) | *quam uendidere* (=
uendiderunt: see RLRGr A4) | ⌐*...recipere non
meruerint*.

3. The miracles of Bishop Ninian (8th century)

This excerpt is from an eighth-century hexameter poem called *Miracula
Nynie episcopi* ('The miracles of Bishop Ninian'). St Ninian was a fifth-
century missionary to the southern Picts, bishop of Whithorn in Galloway

(Scotland), and founder of the church there dedicated to St Martin of
Tours (see section 7.1(a)). The poem was sent to Alcuin (see section 9.2)
sometime after 782 by his former pupils at York and survives in a later
copy of a *florilegium* put together by him. Its language shows a strong
tendency towards the use of Greek words, e.g. *cephal* 'head', *cleptare* 'to
steal'. Scansion, as often in medieval attempts at classical quantitative metre,
is slightly hit-and-miss. Note for example *lūrĭdā* for CL *lūrĭdā*. Non-classical
quantities are marked.

Ninian proves false accusations of fornication against one of his priests by making the
unborn child name its father.

QUOMODO PRESBYTERUM SUUM A CRIMINE INCESTI PER
INFANTEM NUPER NATUM ET SERMOCINANTEM
LIBERAVERIT.

Presbiter interea baptiste munere functus,	150
quem novŏ incesti pulsabat mānia demens	
sacrilegum patrare nefas cum clamŏre latrans,	
lurīdā sancto medicante infamia cessit.	
splendida dum proceris fluitabant dogmate dicta,	
late per populos provulgans ore loquelas	155
plurima quadrifluis sĕminavit flumina rivis,	
gurgitibus puris populorum corda rigabat.	
ast ubi credentes inrorat dogmate claro,	
ecce inter populos matris profertur ab alvo	
hesterne noctis natus sub tempore parvus	160
atque sacer sancti culpatur crimine prisco	
presbiter, at senior petĭto sīlentiŏ dixit:	
'hunc credo insontem, sed tu quoque famine, pignus,	
dic nunc, adiuro summi per regna tonantis,	
quis tuus est genitor vel quis hoc fecerat auctor.'	165
at tener extimplo cunctis mirantibus infans	
intonuit stolido doctis de pectore verbis –	
hoc unĩus spacium noctis complevit, ut ante	
diximus – et rumpens retinacula tarda loquele	
cepit ab ore pio mysteria pandere sancta:	170
'o sacer et felix Nyniau cognomine dictus,	
insinuans digito genitorem voce fatebor,	
mandăs ut altithroni contestans nomine regis.	
o populi, patris pulsus discernere causam –	
en meus hic genitor, vultūm | huc vertite cuncti,	175

hic nam me genuit matris de corpore nuptis,
at castus membris pura sub mente sacerdos
permanet et nullis zăbuli succŭbuit umbris.'
hec ubi dicta dedit nature iura resolvens,
conticuit stringens sīlenti guttura nodo.   180
quod populus cernens pia Christo verba resultat
et Domino pariter laudes gratesque rependit.

The first four lines give a résumé of the anecdote, which is then told in detail.

150 **Presbiter...functus:** tr. '(There was) meanwhile a priest performing...'.

baptiste = *baptistae* (see O.1).

151–2 **quem...latrans:** the word order here is highly artificial. Construe *quem* (obj.)...*pulsabat mania demens novo cum clamore latrans* (that he) *incesti sacrilegum nefas patrare* (had performed).

153 **lurida** is nom. with *infamia* despite the scansion.

154 **splendida** ('shining') looks forward to *dicta* (subject).

dum: 'when' (see G.29).

proceris: gen. with *dogmate*: 'by the decree of the king'. King Tudvael had opposed Ninian's mission and driven him out of his territory. But he had (as a result, says the poet) been struck blind and then had his sight restored by Ninian. His attitude to Ninian's mission was thus changed and he gave his permission for him to preach the word among his people.

156 **plurima** looks forward to *flumina*.

quadrifluis...rivis: 'by means of the fourfold streams'. The fourfold streams are the four modes of biblical interpretation: (1) literal (2) allegorical (3) moral (4) anagogical (see section 3 Intro.). The image is based originally upon the four streams of the river flowing from Eden in Gen. 2.10, interpreted allegorically. The poet is in fact imitating a poem of Aldhelm which makes the image clearer.

157 **gurgitibus...rigabat:** supply 'and' (asyndeton).

158 **dogmate:** here 'doctrine'.

159 **matris** with *ab alvo*.

profertur: the subject is *natus...parvus*.

160 **hesterne** (= *hesternae*: see O.1) **noctis** depends on *sub tempore* 'at the time'.

161 **sacer** looks forward to *presbiter* and **sancti** depends on *sacer...presbiter*.

crimine prisco: 'of/on the ancient crime/ charge' (i.e. adultery).

162 **senior:** i.e. Ninian.

163 **famine:** 'by speaking'.

164 **tonantis:** 'of the thunderer' i.e. God. The line is an imitation of one from Bede's metrical *Life of St Cuthbert*.

165 **vel:** 'and'.

fecerat: 'did' (see G.9(c)). Note the scansion *quīs hŏc* against CL rules (*quĭs hŏc*).

166 **tener:** goes with *infans*.

167 **stolido** with *de pectore*: 'stupid' (because neonates have not yet learned speech).

168 **hoc** with *spacium*.

complevit: '(the child) had completed' (see G.9(b)).

169 **loquele** = *loquelae* (see O.1).

170 **cepit** = *coepit* (see O.1).

171 **Nyniau:** 'Ninan'. This is a transliteration of British Nynnyaw. Elsewhere the poet uses Bede's form Ninia.

cognomine dictus: 'called' (*dictus* nom. for vocative).

173 **mandas ut:** 'as you command'.

altithroni looks forward to *regis* and the phrase depends on *nomine* ('in the name').

contestans: sc. 'me'.

174 **patris...discernere causam:** 'to settle my father's case' (see Ps. 42.1).

pulsus: 'compelled'.

175 **hic:** 'this (sc. is)'.

vultum huc: scanned *vūltŭm | hūc* against CL rules (*vūlt[um] hūc*). This is a place where in CL an elision would have occurred.

176 **nuptis** = *nuptiis* 'by sexual intercourse (with)'.

177 **castus:** complement of *permanet* ('he remains chaste').

membris: 'in' (abl. of respect).
pura sub mente: 'with a...'.
179 **hec** (= *haec*: see O.1)...**dedit** is a standard Virgilian formula.
nature (= **naturae**: see O.1) **iura resolvens**: 'unloosing the laws of nature', i.e. breaking the

laws of nature (this phrase comes from a poem by Aldhelm).
180 **silenti...nodo:** 'with a silent knot', i.e. 'with the knot of silence'.
181 **pia...verba:** 'words praising Christ'.

4. Hygeburg of Heidenheim (8th century)

Women had a notable role in the English monasteries of the seventh and eighth centuries, being virtually on a par with monks in grammatical and literary studies, scribal activity and the formation of libraries. One such was Hygeburg, a West Saxon, born probably near Winchester, and a relative of the missionary workers, Willibald (d. after 786) and Wynnebald (d. 19 December 761), who after earlier pilgrimages to the Holy Land went to Germany and established communities at Eichstätt and Heidenheim (c.751). It was to Heidenheim that Hygeburg came after Abbot Wynnebald's death in 761, where she composed their biographies sometime after 778. The Life of Willibald was written while he was still alive and probably reports his own version of his journey to the East. Hygeburg's Latin is an interesting mixture, sometimes written in Aldhelmesque style and at other times in a plain style recalling Egeria (section 2.4), but always containing errors of every kind.

See further: P. Dronke, *Women Writers of the Middle Ages*, Cambridge, 1984, pp. 33–5.

The imprisonment and release of Willibald and Wynnebald on their way to the Holy Land in 724.

Et inde ibant ad urbem Constantiam, ubi requiescit sanctus Epiphanius; et ibi morabant usque post natale sancti Iohannis baptiste. Et inde navigantes, venerunt in regionem Sarracinorum in urbem Tharrathas secus mare. Et inde ambulabant super IX aut XII mil. ad castellum que dicitur Arche; et ibi fuit episcopus de gente Grecorum. Et ibi habebant letania secundum con- 5
suetudinem eorum. Et inde pergentes illi, ambulaverunt ad urbem que vocatur Emessa XII mil.; ibi est aecclesia magna, quam fecit sancta Helena in honore sancti Iohannis baptiste; et caput illius fuit ibi diu, hoc est in Syrim. Tunc erant cum Willibaldo VII contribuli illius, et ille ipse fuit octavus. Confestimque illi pagani Sarracini repperientes, quod adveni et ignoti homines illic venti fuerunt, 10
tulerunt eos et captivos habebant; qui nesciebant, de quale fuerant gente, sed

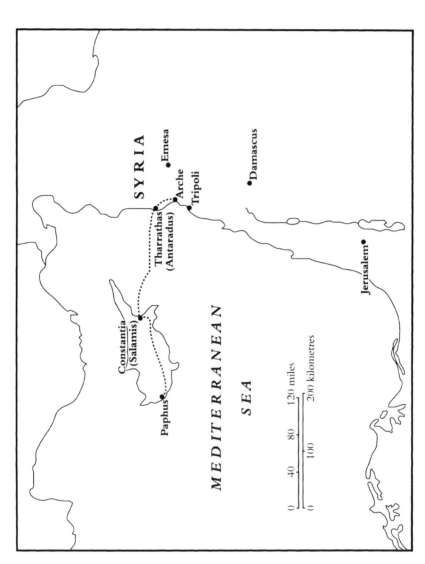

5 The route of Willibald and Wynnebald.

speculatores esse illos estimabant, et captivos eos ducebant ad quendam senem divitem, ut videret et agnosceret, unde essent. Ast ille senex interrogavit illos, unde essent aut quale fungerentur legatione. Tunc illi respondentes, ab exordio totam intimaverunt ei iteneris sui causam. Et ille senex respondens ait: 15 'Frequenter hic venientes vidi homines de illis terre partibus istorum contribulos; non querunt mala, sed legem eorum adimplere cupiunt.' Tum illi inde pergentes, venerunt ad palatium, ut rogarent illis viam transire ad Hierusalem. Cumque illic veniebant, statim ille preses dixit, quod speculatores fuissent, et precepit illos in carcerem trudi usque ad illum tempus, quo repperiret a rege, 20 quid fecisset de illorum causa. Cumque illi fuerant in carcere, confestim miro omnipotentis Dei dispensatione, qui pius ubique suos inter tela et tormenta, inter barbaros et belligeros, inter carceres et contumacium catervas suo protegere parma tutosque conservare dignatus est, unus homo fuit ibi negotiator, qui sibi in elemosinam et animae suae redemptionem volebat 25 illos redemere et de carcere eripere, ut liberi essent pergere in suam voluntatem, et non poterat. Sed econtra cottidie misit illis prandium et cenam, et in quarta feria et in sabbato misit filium suum in carcerem, et eduxit eos ad balneum et iterum introduxit; et dominica die ducebat eos ad aecclesiam per mercimonium, ut de rebus venalibus viderent, quid eorum 30 mente delectaret, et ille tunc suo pretio illis opteneret, quidquid illorum mente aptum foret. Illi cives urbium curiosi iugiter illic venire consueverant illos speculare, qui iuvenes et decori et vestium ornatu induti erant bene. Tunc illis in carcere commorantibus, unus homo de Ispania venit et loquebat cum illis in carcere et diligenter ab illis inquisivit, quid essent aut unde essent. Et illi 35 dixerunt ei omnia secundum ordinem de sua itinere. Ille Ispanius homo habebat fratrem in palatio regis, qui fuit cubicularius regis Sarracinorum. Cumque ille preses, qui eos in carcere mittebat, ad palatium veniebat, et ille Ispanius, qui cum illis in carcere loquebatur, et ille nautor in cuius nave fuerunt, quando pergebant de Cypro, omnes simul venerunt coram rege 40 Sarracinorum cui nomen Myrmumni. Et cum locutio evenerat de illorum causa, ille Ispanius homo omnia que illi dixerunt ei in carcere suo intimavit fratre et illum rogavit, ut regi indicasset et in subsidia illis foret. Post haec itaque cumque omnes isti tres simul coram rege veniebant et omnia iuxta ordinem intimando illo indicabant de eorum causa, ille rex interrogavit, unde essent; et 45 illi dixerunt: 'De occidentale plaga, ubi sol occasum habet, isti homines veniebant, et nos nescimus ruram citra illis et nihil nisi aquam.' Et ille rex respondit eis dicens: 'Quare nos debemus eos punire? Non habent peccatum contra nos. Da eis viam et sine illos abire!'

---

1 **inde:** i.e. from Paphos in Cyprus (see map 5).   **sanctus Epiphanius:** *c.*315–402, bishop of
Constantiam: Salamis (another city in Cyprus).   Constantia 367–402.

2 **morabant** = *morabantur* (see G.3).
usque post: 'until after'.
3 **Sarracinorum:** 'Saracens', i.e. Arabs (the conquerors of the Persians had by this date taken over the whole of North Africa and Spain as well as Palestine, Lebanon, Iraq and Iran).
Tharrathas: Antarados or Tartus (Syria).
4 **super:** 'more than'.
mil. = *milia* (*passuum*) 'miles'.
que has as antecedent *castellum* (incorrectly for *quod*).
Arche: near Tripoli (modern Qlaiaate, Lebanon).
5 **letania** = *letaniam* (see O. 10).
6 **eorum:** this should mean 'of the Greeks', but may be an error for *suam* (see G.11(e)(iii)).
pergentes: 'having...' (see G.20(a)).
7 **sancta Helena:** St Helena (255–330), mother of Constantine the Great.
in honore = *in honorem* (see O.10).
8 **caput illius:** i.e. John the Baptist's severed head (see Mt 14.1–12, Mk 6.14–29).
Syrim: 'Syria' (cf. G.6(a)).
9f. **illi pagani...:** 'the...' (see G.11(d)).
10 **adveni** = *advenae* (2m. ending instead of 1m.: see G.2).
venti fuerunt: 'had come' (see G.9(b), G.4(a)).
11 **qui:** i.e. the Saracens.
de quale: i.e. *de quali* (see G.7(a)).
fuerant: 'were' (see G.9(c) and G.24(b)).
13 **ille:** 'the' (see G.11(d)).
14 **quale:** = *quali* (see G.7(a)) and goes with *legatione*.
15 **iteneris** = *itineris* (see O.11).
ille: 'the' (see G.11(d)).
16 **hic:** i.e. 'to this place'.
terre = *terrae* (see O.1).
istorum: 'of these men' (see G.11(c)).
17 **eorum:** i.e. *suam* (see G.11(e)(iii)).
18 **pergentes:** 'having...' (see G.20(a)).
ut rogarent illis viam transire: 'to ask them to allow passage' (see G.17(a)).
19 **illic:** 'to that place'.
veniebant: 'came' (see G.9(a)).
ille preses: 'the...' (see G.11(d)).
fuissent: 'they were' (plupf. for impf.: see G.9).
20 **precepit...trudi:** 'ordered (them) to be...' (see G.23(a)).
ad illum tempus = *ad illud tempus* (see G.7(b)).

quo: 'at which', 'when'.
21 **fecisset:** 'he should do' (deliberative subj.: *RLGVE* 152 Note 1).
fuerant: 'were' (plupf. for perfect: see G.9(c)).
21f. **miro...dispensatione:** i.e. *mira...dispensatione*.
22f. **qui...dignatus est:** the structure is *qui* (antecedent *Dei*) *pius* (= *pios*; see O.12)...*suos* (obj.) *inter...inter...inter...protegere...conservare dignatus est.*
23f. **suo...parma:** i.e. *sua parma*.
24 **unus:** 'a' (see G.10(d)).
25 **sibi in elemosinam:** 'as alms for himself', i.e. to excite God's pity on him (*elemosina* is derived from the Greek word for 'pity').
26 **pergere:** after *liberi:* 'free to...' (not CL).
26f. **in suam voluntatem:** lit. 'to their wish', i.e. wherever they wanted.
27 **econtra:** 'nonetheless' (see G.8).
28 **in quarta feria et in sabbato:** 'on Wednesdays and Saturdays' (see G.15(a)(i)).
29 **dominica die:** 'on Sundays'.
30 **de rebus venalibus:** '(sc. some) of...' (see G.15(d)).
quid = *quod*.
31 **mente** = *mentem* (see O.10).
mente = *menti* (see O.11).
32 **illi cives...:** 'the...' (see G.11(d)).
illic: i.e. 'to that place'.
consueverant: 'used to' (see G.9(c)).
33 **speculare** (= *speculari:* see O.11 or G.3): 'to...' (purpose: see G.17(a)).
vestium ornatu...induti...bene: 'well dressed in fine clothes'.
34 **unus homo:** 'a...' (see G.10(d)).
de Ispania: 'from Spain' (see O.3(c)). Since 711, the peninsula had been almost wholly in the hands of the Arabs, so this person was a Latin-speaking Arab.
loquebat = *loquebatur* (see G.3).
35 **quid essent:** i.e. 'who they were'.
36 **de sua itinere:** i.e. *de suo itinere*.
Ille: 'the' (see G.11(d)).
38 **ille preses:** 'the...' (see G.11(d)): also *ille Ispanius, ille nautor, ille rex*.
in carcere = *in carcerem* (see O.10).
mittebat: 'had sent'.
veniebat: 'came' (see G.9(a)).
41 **Myrmumni:** this was the Caliph Emir-al-Mummenin.

43 **fratre** = *fratri* (see O.11).

 indicasset (=*indicavisset*: see RLRGr A5): CL *indicaret* (see G.25(a)).

 in subsidia: 'a help (to)' (CL *subsidio*).

44 **isti:** 'these' (see G.11(c)).

 veniebant: i.e. 'had come' (see G.9(a)).

45 **illo** = *illi* (see G.7(a)).

46 **occidentale** = *occidentali* (see O.11 and G.7(a)).

 isti: 'these' (see G.11(c)).

47 **veniebant:** 'came' (see G.9(a)).

 ruram = *rurem*, but meaning 'land' (CL *terram*)

not 'countryside'.

47 **citra illis** (= *illos*): 'beyond them' (but in CL *citra* means 'on the nearer side').

 et nihil...aquam: sc. 'and we know of...'.

48 **Non habent peccatum:** 'they have not sinned' (cf. Fr. *ils ont fait*, It. *hanno fatto* 'they have done', which are composed of the verb 'have' + past participle). No doubt Hygeburg's syntax here reflects the grammar of contemporary Proto-Romance, the predecessor of the Romance languages.

Section 8
Continental Latin (550–768)

The ancient education system survived to different dates in different regions, and was replaced to varying degrees in various places. The strength of the ancient tradition of schooling in North Africa, even in the second half of the seventh century, can be seen from the example of Hadrian, sent to England in 669 with Theodore of Tarsus to take care of education there. The thread was broken by the Arab invasions, which had reached Carthage by 698. The refugee scholars fled in some numbers to Spain, where they organized monastic centres of importance for Visigothic culture. In Spain, the Visigoths encouraged education after their conversion to Catholicism in 589. The centres at Seville, Saragossa and Toledo produced important scholars, of whom Isidore of Seville (c.560–636) is the most celebrated, and the study of grammar and rhetoric flourished. Even the study of ancient poetry continued. Things became more difficult after the Arab invasion of 711. But the tradition was not immediately broken, since it was the Church which organized learning.

In Italy, after the fall of the Roman Empire in the West, the Ostrogoth Theodoric protected the schools and took an interest in literary activities. During the sixth century, the wars between Ostrogoths and Byzantines exhausted the region. The Lombard invasion followed in 568. Continual wars then undermined the structure inherited from the Romans. But the lay schools did not disappear completely, and in Italy alone of the parts of the Roman Empire grammar masters trained on the classical lines kept a slender thread of tradition intact. This unbroken line of lay teaching and scholarship in Italy led eventually to the pre-eminence of the peninsula in the secular studies of law and medicine when the schools blossomed into universities in the twelfth and thirteenth centuries. The seventh century nonetheless contains little enough Latin writing from Italy, and what there is (e.g. Jonas of Bobbio) betrays a less than exact grasp of grammar. The eighth century, by contrast, shows a certain rebirth of interest in Latin studies in Lombardy, especially at Pavia, some of whose products we shall meet at Charlemagne's court in section 9.

In Gaul, the extension of the Frankish domain in the early sixth century to the most fully Romanized parts, Aquitaine, Provence and Burgundy (the latter annexed in 536) effectively brought the end of the publicly funded school system. By the mid-seventh century, there was no trace of it: Latin was learned by clerics and monks only, and this learning was not as rigorous in the sixth century as it had been in the fifth. The effect is visible in the decline of grammatical knowledge in authors from Gregory of Tours (538–94) onwards. It is most marked in the documents, for example the inscriptions (see section 8.1), records of legal judgments (see section 8.2) and the formulae of Angers and Sens.

1. The epitaph of Agapius (601)

The Latin in this inscription is comparable to that of many from the period. Not only has it broken down orthographically (*u* for *o*, *i* for *e* and vice versa, -*ci*-for -*ti*-), but its morphology is insecure. For example, *intuis* is used for the deponent form *intueris*. Two things are clear. First, it was still the done thing to write inscriptions in Latin. Secondly, knowledge of how to write Latin correctly was in short supply and local speech habits were beginning to affect what was put down.

The Christian virtues of Agapius.

> EPYTAFIVM HVNC QVI INTVIS LECTOR
> BONE RECORDACIONIS AGAPI NEGVCIATORIS
> MEMBRA QVIESCVNT. NAM FVIT ISTE STACIO
> MISERIS ET PORTVS EGINIS. OMNEBVS APTVS
> FVIT PRAECIPVAE LOCA SANCTORVM ADSE-   5
> DVE. ET ELEMOSINAM ET ORACIONEM
> STVDVIT. VIXIT IN PACE ANNOS LXXXV OBIIT
> VIII KALENDAS APRILIS LXI POST CONSVLATVM
> IVSTINI INDICTIONE QVARTA

1 **EPYTAFIVM HVNC** is left hanging. There is no connection between it and the next line. Tr. 'In this tomb' (CL *epitaphius* 'funeral speech').
QVI = *quem*, obj. of *intuis* (= *intueris*: see G.3).
2 **BONE** = *bonae* (see O.1).
4 **OMNEBVS** = *omnibus* (see O.11).

5f. **LOCA SANCTORVM...ELEMOSINAM ET ORACIONEM** (= *orationem*: see O.2) are dir. obj. of *studuit* (CL + dat.).
8 **VIII KALENDAS APRILIS:** lit. 'eight days before 1 April', i.e. 25 March. An *indictio* was a period of fifteen years (the date works out at 601).

2. *Cartons des Rois* (September 677 or 678)

Legal documentation also continued to be done in Latin. The Merovingian kings of Francia had control over the appointment of bishops. In this document, judgement is given on just such an ecclesiastical issue. As in 7.1, the orthography is odd (*rigna* for *regna*, *aeclisiae* for *ecclesiae*, *adfuirunt* for *adfuerunt*, etc.). The morphology and syntax are even worse (*de rigna nostra* for *regni nostri*, *per nostra ordenacione* for *per nostram ordinationem*, etc.). Nonetheless, there are also signs of great efforts to write complex sentences (*Dum...adfuirunt*) and it seems clear that we are dealing with a highly formulaic language which is not fully understood by its practitioners. It was Pepin the Short, the first Carolingian, who took this matter in hand (see section 9 Intro.).

Chramlinus, son of Miecio, having obtained the bishopric of Aebredunum (Embrun) improperly, is hereby downgraded. However, he may keep his property (and retire to Saint-Denis).

Dum et episcopos de rigna nostra, tam de Niuster quam et de Burgundia, pro statu aeclisiae vel confirmacione pacis ad nostro palacio Marlaco villa jussemus advenire, et aliqui ex ipsis qui in infidilitate nostra fuerant inventi, per eorum canonis fuirunt judecati, inter quos adfuit Chramlinus, filius Miecio quondam, qui aepiscopatum Aebreduno civitate habuit: inventum est, quod sua prae-   5
sumcione vel per falsa carta, seu per revellacionis audacia, sed non per nostra ordenacione, ipsum aepiscopatum reciperat, eciam nec sicut eorum cannonis contenent ad ipsum benedicendum solemneter episcopi non adfuirunt; unde Genesio, Chadune, Bildramno, Landoberctho et Ternisco, qui matropoli esse videntur, vel reliqui quampluris episcopi ipsus judicantis, in nostri praesencia   10
fuit conscissus adque de suprascripto episcopato aejectus. Ideo nus, una cum consilio suprascriptorum ponteficum vel procerum nostrorum, complacit quatenus, dum secundum cannonis in ipso senodale concilium fuerat degradatus, res suas proprias, pertractavemus, pro mercidis causa, perdere non dibirit; sed quod exinde facere voluerit, una cum suprascriptus patribus nostris, taliter   15
praecipemus ut hoc licenciam habiat faciendi...

† In Christi nomene, Theudericus rex subscripsi. Aghiliberthus recognovit. Datum medio minse September, annum v rigni nostri, Maslaco, in Dei nomene feliciter.

1–11 **Dum...aejectus:** the basic structure is *Dum* ('when': see G.29)... *judecati* (there are two verbs, *jussemus* and *fuirunt judecati*), *inter quos* (antecedent *aliqui*)...*qui...habuit:* (main clause) *inventum est, quod...reciperat, eciam* (= *et*)...*non adfuirunt*

1,3 **et...et** these merely emphasize that there are two distinct actions and do not need to be translated 'both...and'.
  episcopos is the obj. of *jussemus advenire*.
1 **de rigna nostra...de Burgundia:** 'from our kingdom, both Neustria and Burgundy' (the

endings have gone awry on *rigna nostra* (= *regno nostro*: see G.2) and *Niuster*; note *-i-* for *-e-*, *rigna* for *regno*, a common error both ways round in this and other texts of the period: see O.11).

2 **ad nostro palacio:** i.e. *ad nostrum palacium*.
   Marlaco villa: 'at the town of La Morlaye'.
   jussemus = *iussimus* (see O.11).

3 **in infidilitate nostra:** lit. 'in our unfaithfulness', i.e. 'unfaithful to us'.

3f. **per eorum canonis** (= *canones*: see O.11): i.e. by ecclesiastical law.

4 **fuirunt judecati** = *fuerunt iudicati* 'were...' (see O.11 and G.4(a)).
   Miecio: 'of Miecio'.

5 **Aebreduno civitate:** 'in the town of Embrun'.

6 **per falsa carta** = *per falsam cartam* (see O.10).
   per revellacionis audacia = *per rebellationis audaciam* (see O.13, O.10).

6f. **per nostra ordenacione** = *per nostram ordinationem* (see O.10, O.11, O.2).

7 **reciperat** = *receperat* (see O.11).
   cannonis = *canones* (nom.: see O.11, O.7).

8 **adfuirunt** = *adfuerunt* (see O.11).
   unde: 'and so...'.

9f. **Genesio...vel reliqui quampluris** (= *complures*: see O.11)...**judicantis** (=*iudicantes*: see O.11): 'with Genesio...and most of the rest...judging...' (nom. abs.).
   matropoli = *matropolitani*, i.e. archbishops.

10 **ipsus** = *ipsius* 'against him (i.e. Chramlinus)'.
   in nostri praesencia (= *praesentia*: see O.2):

nostri could be gen. of *nos*, or may be an error for *nostra*.

11 **aejectus** = *eiectus* (see O.1).

11f. **nus** (= *nos*: see O.12)...**complacuit:** 'we decided'.

13 **quatenus** ('that') (see e.g. G.23(d)) introduces *res suas proprias...pro mercidis* (= *mercedis*: see O.11) *causa, perdere non dibirit* (= *deberet*: see O.11). But the writer inserts *pertractavemus* (= *pertractavimus*: see O.11) 'we investigated', which might mean 'which we went into', referring back to *res suas proprias*.
   dum: 'although'.
   cannonis = *canones* (acc.: see O.11 and O.7).
   in ipso senodale (= *synodale*) **concilium** = *in ipsum...concilium*, but *in* + acc. is used for *in* + abl. Tr. 'in' (cf. G.15(c)(ii)).

15 **quod:** 'whatever'.
   exinde: 'with them' (i.e. *res proprias*).
   una...praecipemus (= *praecepimus*: see O.11): lit. 'together with...so we', i.e. 'both I and the bishops have given instructions that...'.
   suprascriptus = *suprascriptis*.

16 **hoc** is the obj. of *faciendi*.
   habiat = *habeat* (see O.11).

17 **nomene** = *nomine* (see O.11).
   Theudericus rex: Thierry III.

18 **minse** = *mense* (see O.11).
   annum = *anno*.
   rigni = *regni* (see O.11).
   Maslaco: i.e. 'at La Morlaye'.

3. St Gregory of Tours (538–94)

St Gregory was bishop of Tours from 573 to his death in 594. Among his writings are seven books on miracles, including those of the former bishop of Tours St Martin (d.397: see section 7.1(a)) (ii)–(iii). This passage is taken from the *Libri historiarum decem*, usually known as *The History of the Franks*, a work of which Gregory says: 'I have been moved, in my crude way, to preserve for those who come after a record of what has happened, including the conflicts of the wicked and the lives of those who have lived well.' His Latin, as he himself admits, does not follow the rules of *grammatica*. This makes it sometimes rather difficult.

See further: W. Goffart, *The Narrators of Barbarian History (AD 550–800)*, Princeton, 1988.

(i) *The greed of Bishop Cautinus.*

Denique Cautinus, adsumpto episcopatu, talem se reddidit, ut ab omnibus
execraretur, vino ultra modum deditus. Nam plerumque in tantum infundebatur potu, ut de convivio vix a quattuor portaretur. Unde factum est, ut
epylenticus fieret in sequenti. Quod saepius populis manifestatum est. Erat
enim et avaritiae in tantum incumbens, ut, cuiuscumque possessiones fines eius   5
termino adhaesissent, interitum sibi putaret, si ab eisdem aliquid non minuisset.
Et a maioribus quidem cum rixa et scandalo auferebat, a minoribus autem
violenter diripiebat. Quibus et a quibus, ut Sollius noster ait, nec dabat pretia
contemnens nec accipiebat instrumenta desperans.

The year is 555.
2 **in tantum:** 'to such an extent'.
2f. **infundebatur potu:** lit. 'he was poured into
with drink', i.e. 'he was drunk'.
3 **de:** 'from'.
quattuor: sc. 'men'.
4 **in sequenti:** sc. *tempore*: 'later' (see G.15(a)(i)).
saepius: 'often' (see G.12(c)).
populis: 'the people', 'the public'.
5f. **ut...minuisset:** 'that he thought it death to him,
if whosoever's property (*possessiones* = *posses-
sionis*: see O.11) boundaries were adjacent to
his boundary, from those he did not make
some diminution', i.e. 'that he was mortified if
he didn't get at least some of the land adjacent

to his own' (for *idem* see G.11(b)).
7 **maioribus:** 'from the great' (dat. of disadvantage
with *auferebat*: see RLRGr L(e)(ii)); cf. *minoribus* 'the unimportant'.
8 **quibus et a quibus:** 'to whom and from whom'.
Quibus refers forward to *dabat pretia* and *a
quibus* to *accipiebat instrumenta*.
Sollius = Gaius Sollius, known as Apollinaris
Sidonius (431/2–487/9), bishop of Clermont.
The words come from a letter addressed to
Ecdicius on the malice of Seronatus, an Au-
vergnese official: 'All he desires he more or less
gets, and he neither pays the price in his
arrogance, nor does he receive title-deeds
because he has no hope (sc. of getting them).'

(ii) *Anastasius resists Cautinus' demands, is buried alive and has a narrow escape.*

Erat enim tunc temporis Anastasius presbiter, ingenuus genere, qui per chartas
gloriosae memoriae Chrodichildis reginae proprietatem aliquam possidebat.
Quem plerumque conventum episcopus rogat suppliciter, ut ei chartas
supradictae reginae daret sibique possessionem hanc subderet. Sed ille cum
voluntatem sacerdotis sui implere differret eumque episcopus nunc blanditiis   5
provocaret, nunc minis terreret, ad ultimum invitum urbi exhiberi praecepit
ibique impudenter teneri et, nisi instrumenta daret, iniuriis adfici et fame negari
iussit. Sed ille virili repugnans spiritu, numquam praebuit instrumenta, dicens,
satius sibi esse ad tempus inedia tabescere quam sobolem in posterum miseram
derelinqui. Tunc ex iussu episcopi traditur custodibus, ut, nisi has cartulas   10
proderet, fame necaretur. Erat enim ad basilicam sancti Cassii martyris cripta
antiquissima abditissimaque, ubi erat sepulcrum magnum ex marmore Phario,
in quo grandaevi cuiusdam hominis corpus positum videbatur. In hoc sepulcro

super sepultum vivens presbiter sepelitur operiturque lapide, quo prius
sarcofagum fuit obtectum, datis ante ostium custodibus. Sed custodes fidi,   15
quod lapide premeretur, cum esset hiemps, accenso igne, vino sopiti calido,
obdormierunt. At presbiter, tamquam novus Ionas, velut *de ventre inferi*, ita de
conclusione tumuli Domini misericordiam flagitabat. Et quia spatiosum, ut
diximus, erat sarcofagum, etsi se integrum vertere non poterat, manus tamen in
parte qua voluisset libere extendebat. Manabat enim ex ossibus mortui, ut ipse   20
referre erat solitus, foetor letalis, qui non solum externa, verum etiam interna
viscerum quatiebat. Cumque pallium aditus narium obseraret, quamdiu flatum
continere poterat, nihil pessimum sentiebat; ubi autem se quasi suffocari
potabat, remoto paululum ab ore pallio, non modo per os aut nares, verum
etiam per ipsas, ut ita dicam, aures odorem pestiferum hauriebat. Quid plura?   25
Quando Divinitati, ut credo, condoluit, manum dexteram ad spondam
sarcofagi tendit, reperitque vectem, qui, decedente opertorio, inter ipsum ac
labium sepulcri remanserat. Quem paulatim commovens, sensit, cooperante
Dei adiutorio, lapidem amoveri. Verum ubi ita remotum fuit, ut presbiter
caput foris educeret, maiorem quo totus egreditur aditum liberius patefecit.   30
Interea operientibus nocturnis tenebris diem nec adhuc usquequaque diffusis,
ad alium criptae ostium petit. Erat enim seris fortissimis clavisque firmissimis
obseratum, verumtamen non erat ita levigatum, ut inter tabulas aspicere homo
non possit. Ad hos aditus presbiter caput reclinat advertitque hominem viam
praetereuntem. Hunc, licet voce tenui, vocat. Exaudit ille; nec mora, securem   35
manu tenens, sudes ligneos, quibus serae continebantur, incidit aditumque
presbitero patefecit. At ille de nocte praeteriens, ad domum pergit, satis virum
obsecrans, ne de hoc cuiquam aliqua enarraret.

---

1 **tunc temporis:** 'at that time'.

gloriosae memoriae depends on *Chrodichildis
reginae*, which qualifies *chartas*. Queen Chrodi-
child (= St Clotilda) was the wife of Clovis.
She is praised because of her conversion to
Christianity.

3 **Quem...conventum:** 'whom...having been
visited' (obj. of *rogat*), i.e. the priest.

3 **ei:** i.e. 'to the bishop' (CL *sibi* as in the next part
of the clause: see G.11(e)(i)).

5 **sacerdotis sui:** i.e. the bishop.

6 **ad ultimum:** 'finally'.

invitum: sc. *eum*.

urbi exhiberi: 'to be brought to the city' (see
G.16(a) and 17(b)).

7 **negari** = *necari* (see O.17).

8 **virili** looks forward to *spiritu*.

9f. **satius sibi esse...derelinqui:** 'that it was preferable to him to...than that...'.

9 **ad tempus:** 'now' (CL 'in time', 'for the
moment').

sobolem: celibacy for secular priests was not an
absolute rule until the Lateran Council decrees
of 1123 and 1139.

10 **ex iussu:** 'by the order of' (CL *iussu*).

11 **sancti Cassii martyris:** the story of St Cassius of
Arvernum and his conversion of his persecutor
Victorinus is told by Gregory in Book I.33.

12 **ex marmore:** 'made of...'.

13 **positum videbatur:** 'had been laid' (lit. 'seemed
(to) have been laid') (see G.4(d)).

14 **sepultum:** 'the man already entombed there'.

15 **fuit obtectum:** 'had been...' (see G.4(a)).
15f. **fidi, quod:** 'believing that'.
16 **premeretur:** sc. the priest.
17 **novus Ionas:** the prophet Jonah was swallowed by a whale (Jonah 1.17).

    de ventre inferi: a quotation from Jonah's prayer to God from inside the whale (*de ventre inferi clamavi et exaudisti vocem meam* (Jonah 2.3): 'from the mouth of hell I shouted and you heard my cry').

19f. **in parte qua:** 'to whatever part' (see G.15(c)(ii)).
20 **voluisset:** subj. for ind. (see G.25(c)).
    extendebat: 'he was able to stretch out'.
    enim: simple connective (see G.14).
21 **externa:** 'his external organs'.
22 **pallium:** subj. of *obseraret.*
23 **poterat...sentiebat:** subj. 'he (i.e. the priest)'.
24 **potabat** = *putabat* (see O.12).
26 **Divinitati...condoluit:** 'God had compassion on him' (CL *condoleo/condolesco* = 'feel pain with', but here the verb is impersonal ('it pained God': = CL *dolet*) – LL often uses compounds without intensive force).
27 **ipsum:** 'it' (see G.11(a)(ii)).
29 **remotum fuit:** 'had been...' (see G.4(a)).
30 **foris:** 'out' (CL *foras*).
    maiorem: with *aditum.*
    quo: 'through which'.
32 **ad alium...ostium petit:** 'he made for another door' (*alium* for *aliud*, see G.7(b)).
    enim: 'well...' (see G.14).
33 **levigatum:** 'well-fitted'.
34 **reclinat:** 'bent' (CL 'bend back').
36 **Sudes ligneos:** in CL *sudis* is f. (see G.2).
37 **de nocte:** 'at night' (CL *nocte, noctu*).
    ad domum: CL *domum.*
    satis: 'very much'.
38 **aliqua:** 'anything' (see G.11(f)).

(iii) *Anastasius secures his property by appeal to the king.*

Domum igitur suam ingressus, inquisitis chartis, quas ei memorata regina tradiderat, ad Chlotharium regem defert, indicans, qualiter ab episcopo suo vivens sepulturae fuerat mancipatus, stupescentibus autem omnibus et dicentibus, numquam vel Neronem vel Herodem tale facinus perpetrasse, ut homo vivens sepulcro reconderetur. Advenit autem ad Chlotharium regem Cautinus episco-   5
pus, sed accusante presbitero, victus confususque discessit. Presbiter autem, acceptis a rege praeceptionibus, res suas ut libuit defensavit posseditque ac suis posteris dereliquit. In Cautino autem nihil sancti, nihil pensi fuit. De omnibus enim scripturis, tam ecclesiasticis quam saecularibus, adplene immunis fuit. Iudaeis valde carus ac subditus erat, non pro salute, ut pastoris cura debet esse sollicita, sed   10
pro comparandis speciebus, quas, cum hic blandiretur et illi se adulatores manifestissime declararent, maiori quam constabant pretio venundabant.

2 **qualiter:** 'that' (see G.22(a)).
4f. **ut...reconderetur:** 'that...' (consecutive).
8f. **De...immunis:** 'devoid of knowledge of...' (CL with gen., or *a* + abl.: see generally G.15(b)).
10 **salute:** sc. 'their', 'of them'.

11 **quas** (antecedent *speciebus*) is the obj. of *venundabant.*
12 **maiori** (= *maiore:* see O.11 or G.7) looks forward to *pretio* and introduces *quam* ('than').

---

4. Venantius Fortunatus (530–609)

Venantius Fortunatus, a native of northern Italy, was educated in Milan and Ravenna. He emigrated to Francia, where in 565 he was at the court of

King Sigibert, winning favour for his encomiastic verses. Later he moved to Poitiers, where he formed a friendship with Radegunda, a princess who had founded a convent there after escaping from a forced marriage with King Clothair. Eventually, in 599, he became bishop of Poitiers. His attempts to write verses in classical metres and his fairly correct Latin show that the classical tradition of education was still alive in mid-sixth century Ostrogothic Italy. The contrast with the Frankish and later Italian and Spanish material is instructive.

These poems are written in quantitative metre (elegiac couplets, see *RLGVE* 185).

See further: J. W. George, *Venantius Fortunatus: A Latin Poet in Merovingian Gaul*, Oxford, 1992.

(a) These extracts come from a long poem in which Fortunatus treats the theme of female virginity and its heavenly reward. After an exhaustive catalogue of the saints, the poet envisages their assembly in heaven, called by Christ to consider the case of a virgin who has devoted her life to Him.

(i) *Christ speaks to the assembly of the saints.*

> Maiestas arcana dei tum pondere fixo
>   alloquitur proceres quos sua dextra regit:
> 'haec mihi pollicitum servavit virgŏ pudorem
>   nec voluit placitam dilacerare fidem: 190
> sollicitis animis sponsi vestigia sectans
>   et mea vota petens inviolata venit.
> per tribulos gradiens spinae cavefecit acumen.
>   sentibus in mediis nescia ferre vepres.
> vipera serps iaculus basiliscus ĕmorrois aspis   195
>   faucibus horrificis sibila torsit iners.
> inde sagitta volans, hinc terruit arcus euntem:
>   doctast insidiis cautius ire suis.
> inter tŏt hostes nulli se subdidit insons;
>   vulnera suscepit, sed tolerandŏ fugit.'   200

---

187 **pondere fixo:** 'with immovable authority'.
189 **haec** looks forward to *virgo*.
   pollicitum: 'promised' (see RLRGr C4 Note 2).
190 **placitam:** 'plighted'.
191 **sponsi:** Christ is regularly described as a bride-

groom and the virgins who commit themselves to Him are his brides (see Mt 9.15: *Et ait illis Iesus: Numquid possunt filii sponsi lugere quamdiu cum illis est sponsus?* 'And Jesus said to them "Can the sons of the groom mourn while the groom is with them?"'; Jo 3.29 (John the

Baptist speaking): *Qui habet sponsum, sponsus est: amicus autem sponsi, qui stat et audit eum* 'He who has a spouse is a bridegroom; but the one who stands and listens to him is a friend of the groom'; Mt 25.1f. (the parable of the wise and foolish virgins); cf. Ps. 19.5 (Vlg. 18.6): *tamquam sponsus procedens de thalamo suo* 'like a bridegroom coming out of his chamber'.

191f. **sectans...petens:** 'having...' (see G.20(a)).

194 **nescia ferre:** '(sc. she was) unable to endure'.

195 **serps** = *serpens.*

196 **faucibus horrificis:** 'from...'.
    iners: 'to no purpose'.

197 **euntem:** '(her) as she...'.
    doctast = *docta est.*

198 **insidiis...suis:** 'by the attacks made upon her'.

199 **tot hostes:** Fortunatus counts *tot* heavy (*tŏt:* though in CL the following h is not a consonant and the word should be scanned with a light syllable. Cf. Ovid, *Amores* 2.12(13).3.).

200 **tolerando:** 'by enduring (them)'.

(ii) *Christ repeats the virgin's lament.*

' "Strata solo recubo lacrimans neque cernŏ quod opto,
    tristis in amplexu pectore saxa premo.
  sponso absente manens tam dura cubilia servo,
    nec mea quem cupiunt membra tenere queunt.   230
  dic ubi sis quem exspectŏ gemens, qua te urbe requiram
    quave sequar, nullis femina nota locis.
  ipsa venire velim, properans si possit in astris
    pendula sideream planta tenere viam.
  nunc sine te fuscis graviter nox occupat alis,   235
    ipsaque sole micans est mihi caeca dies.
  lilia narcissus violae rosa nardus amomum,
    oblectant animos germina nulla meos.
  ut te conspiciam, per singula nubila pendo
    et vaga per nebulas lumina ducit amor.   240
  ecce procellosos suspecta interrogŏ ventos,
    quid mihi de domino nuntiet aura meo.
  proque tuis pedibus cupio caementa lavare,
    et tua templa mihi tergere crine libet.
  quidquid erit tolerem, sunt omnia dulcia dura: 245
    donec te videam, haec mihi poena placet.
  tu tamen estŏ memor, quoniam tua vota requiro;
    est mihi cura tui, sit tibi cura mei" '.

228 **tristis:** 'sadly'.

229 **manens:** sc. 'behind'.

231 **quem:** '(sc. you) whom'.

231f. **requiram...sequar:** 'I am to...' (deliberative subjunctives: *RLGVE* 152 Note 1). The lines are based loosely on the Song of Songs 1.6 (see section 3.2).

232 **nullis...locis:** 'a woman known to no places', i.e. 'a stranger to this place'.

233 **properans si:** 'hurrying (sc. to see) if' (see n. on l.250).

234 **pendula:** 'hanging in mid-air'.

235 **occupat:** sc. *me.*

236 **caeca:** 'dark'.

237 **lilia...amomum:** loosely constructed in apposition to *gemina nulla* Tr. 'No plants, whether *X* or *Y* or *Z*...'.

239 **per...pendo:** the obj. is *vaga...lumina* in l.240 (also the obj. of *ducit*); tr. 'I hang my wandering eyes upon...' (or else *per...pendo* belong together (tmesis) and the direct obj. is *singula nubila*: 'I consider every single cloud').

239f. The virgin watches clouds because of Christ's prophecy of the Second Coming at Lk 21.27: *et tunc videbunt Filium hominis venientem in nube* 'and they shall see the Son of man coming in a

cloud' (cf. Daniel 7.13).

241 **suspecta:** 'uncertain'.

244 **templa:** 'shrines' (ll. 243–4 recall the actions of the unnamed prostitute at Lk 37–8, who washed Christ's feet with her tears and wiped them with her hair).

tolerem: 'let me endure'.

245 **omnia...dura:** 'all hardships' (*dulcia* is the complement of *sunt*).

247 **esto:** 'be'.

tua vota requiro: 'I am searching for what you want (of me)' (i.e. 'I am fulfilling your wishes').

(iii) *The virgin's reward.*

'Haec referens avidis iactabat brachia palmis,
    si posset plantas forte tenere meas;   250
cum decepta sibi sine me sua dextra rediret,
    luminis instillans ora lavabat aquis.
Cum recubaret humo neque victa sopore quievit,
    consiliturus ei saepe simul iacui,
condolui pariter, lacrimarum flumina tersi,   255
    oscula dans rutilis mellificata favis.
Nunc igitur regnet placitoque fruatur amore,
    quae mihi iam pridem pectore iuncta fuit.'
Adsensu fremit aula poli residente senatu.
    Nomen perpetuo scribitur inde libro.   260
Traditur aeternum mansura in saecula censum,
    virginis in thalamos fundit Olympus opes.'

249 **iactabat brachia:** 'she flung out her arms'.

250 **si:** '(sc. to see) if' (see n. on l. 233: this action recalls Aeneas' attempt to embrace the ghosts of his wife and his father Anchises in Virgil, *Aeneid* 2.792–4, 6.700–2).

251 **sibi:** 'to her' (dat. of place to which after *rediret*: see G.16(a)).

252 **luminis...aquis:** 'with the waters of her eye', i.e. tears.

instillans: 'dripping (sc. tears) on (it, i.e. her face)'.

254 **consiliturus:** 'to take care of' (see G.10(c)).

256 **mellificata:** 'made honey-sweet' (CL 'make honey'). The sense is 'as sweet as the yellow

honeycombs', but literally the line means 'giving kisses made sweet as honey by the yellow honeycombs'.

257 **placito:** 'plighted'.

258 **iuncta fuit:** 'was...' (see G.4(a)).

259 **residente senatu:** 'from the senate in session'.

260 **perpetuo...libro:** This is the *liber vitae* referred to in Rev. 3.5, etc.

261 **aeternum...mansura...censum:** 'to await (see G.10(c)) the eternal census', i.e. the Day of Judgement, when the final citizen-roll of heaven will be drawn up.

262 **Olympus:** i.e. heaven.

(b) Fortunatus' attachment to Radegunda kept him at Poitiers. This is one of a large number of poems addressed to her in a spirit of close friendship.

Fortunatus and Agnes beg you to drink wine to keep up your strength.

> Si pietas et sanctus amor dat vota petenti,
>   exaudi famulos munere larga tuos.
> fortunatus agens, Agnes quoque versibus orant,
>   ut lassata nimis vina benigna bibas.
> sic tibi det dominus quaecumque poposceris ipsum,   5
>   et tibi, sicut amas, vivat uterque rogans:
> suppliciter petimus, si non offendimus, ambo,
>   ut releves natos, mater opima, duos.
> non gula vos, sed causa trahat modo sumere vina,
>   talis enim potus viscera lassa iuvat.   10
> sic quoque Timotheum Paulus, tuba gentibus una,
>   ne stomachum infirmet sumere vina iubet.

2 **munere larga:** 'beneficent in your gifts' (many poems testify to the thoughtfulness of Radegunda in sending gifts of e.g. plums, eggs and milk).

3 **agens:** perhaps 'earnestly' (= *instanter*), or 'the speaker' (Fortunatus is writing the poem, but Agnes, Radegund's sister and abbess of another priory in Poitiers, joins in his plea. Note the anagrammatic word play in *agens/Agnes*, and the play with *fortunatus* when treated as an adj. with *agens* as noun).

5 **ipsum:** 'of him' (see G.11(a)(ii)).

6 **et tibi...vivat:** 'live for you'.
sicut amas: 'just as you love (them)'.
uterque rogans: 'each of your two petitioners' (i.e. Fortunatus and Agnes: cf. *agens* in 1.3).

9 **vos:** i.e. *te.*
trahat: 'let it draw...'.
sumere: 'to take' (purpose: see G.17(a)).

11 **Timotheum Paulus:** St Paul in 1 Timothy 5.23: *modico vino utere propter stomachum tuum* 'use a little wine for the sake of your stomach'.
tuba gentibus una: 'the only trumpet for the pagans'.

5. Jonas of Bobbio (*fl.* 650)

Jonas was a monk of Bobbio, the monastery founded by St Columbanus between 612 and 615 after his expulsion from Francia (see section 6 Intro.). This passage, used later by Fredegar in his chronicle, is from the *Vita Columbani*, written in 643. The problems of writing in Latin seem to be the same for Jonas as for his Frankish near-contemporaries.

(i) *Columbanus' strictures against Brunhilda's children cause a battle of wits between the saint and King Theodoric.*

Evenit ergo, ut quadam die beatus Columbanus ad Brunichildem veniret. Erat

enim tunc apud Brocariacum villam. Cumque illa eum in aulam venisse
cerniret, filios Theuderici, quos de adulterinis permixtionibus habebat, ad
virum Dei adducit; quos cum vidisset, sciscitatur, quid sibi vellint. Cui
Brunichildis ait: 'Regis sunt filii; tu eos tua benedictione robora.' At ille: 5
'Nequaquam,' inquid, 'istos regalia sceptra suscepturus scias, quia de lupanaribus emerserunt.' Illa furens parvolus abire iubet. Egrediens vir Dei regiam
aulam, dum limitem transiliret, fragor exorta totam domum quatiens omnibus
terrorem incussit nec tamen misere feminae furorem conpescuit. Paratque
deinde insidias molire: vicinus monastirii per nuntius imperat, ut nulli eorum   10
extra monasterii terminos iter pandatur, neque receptacula monachis eius vel
quaelibet subsidia tribuantur. Cernens beatus Columbanus regios animos
adversum se permotus, ad eos properat, ut suis monitis misere pertinaciae
intentu frangat; erat enim tunc temporis apud Spissiam villam publicam. Quo
cum iam sol occumbente venisset, regi nuntiant, virum Dei inibi esse nec in   15
regis domibus metare velle. Tunc Theudericus ait, melius esse virum Dei
oportunis subsidiis honorare, quam Dominum ex servorum eius offensam ad
iracundiam provocare. Iubet ergo regio cultu oportuna parare Deique famolo
dirigi. Itaque venerunt et iuxta imperium regis oblata offerunt. Quae cum
vidisset dapes et pocula cultu regio administrata, inquiret, quid sibi de ista   20
vellint. Aient ille, tibi a rege fore directa. Abominatus ea, ait: 'Scriptum est:
Munera impiorum reprobat altissimus; non enim dignum est, ut famolorum Dei ora
cibis eius polluantur, qui non solum suis, verum etiam aliorum habitaculis
famulis Dei aditum deneget.' His dictis, vascula omnia in frustra disrupta sunt,
vinaque ac sicera solo diffusa ceteraque separatim dispersa. Pavifacti ministri rei   25
gestae causam regi nuntiant. Ille pavore perculsus, cum avia delucolo ad virum
Dei properant, precantur de commisso veniam; se inpostmodum emendare
pollicentur. His pacatus promissis, ad monasterium rediit.

1 **Brunichildem:** Brunhilda, Theodoric's concubine.

2 **apud:** 'at'.
   Brocariacum villam: 'the town of Bruyères-le-
   Châtel'.

3 **cerniret** = *cemeret* (see O.11).
   Theuderici: Theodoric.
   de adulterinis permixtionibus: 'from adulterous liaisons'. The Frankish kings practised
   polygamy, which was tolerated by the Frankish Church.

4 **quid sibi vellint** (= *velint* – see O.7): strictly
   'what their intentions were', but probably
   'what they wanted of him'.

6 **Nequaquam...istos** (see G.11(c)) **suscepturus**

(= *suscepturos*: see O.12): '(that) they will
never...'.

6f. **de lupanaribus emerserunt:** 'they came out of
   brothels', i.e. 'they were born in adultery'
   (Columbanus, because an Irish-born and
   Irish-trained monk, was very strict in his
   moral regulations, as in his ascetic lifestyle,
   and regarded polygamy as a sin, the additional
   wives as whores and their children as bas-
   tards).

7 **parvolus** = *parvulos* (see O.12): i.e. his sons.

7f. **Egrediens vir Dei regiam aulam:** 'as the...was
   going out of...' (nom. abs.: *egredior* is intrans. in
   CL; the subject of the sentence (verbs *incussit*
   and *conpescuit*) is actually *fragor exorta*).

8 **dum...transiliret:** 'while...' (for *dum* + subj. see G.29).

9 **misere** = *miserae* (see O.1).

10 **molire** = *moliri* (see O.11 or G.3).
   vicinus = *vicinos* (see O.12).
   monastirii = *monasterii* (see O.11).
   nuntius = *nuntios* (see O.12).

10f. **ut nulli...iter pandatur:** 'that to none of them should a way be made open' (*pandatur, tribuantur* instead of *panderetur, tribuerentur*).

12 **quaelibet:** 'any'.

13 **permotus** = *permotos* (see O.12).
   misere = *miserae* (see O.1).

14 **intentu** = *intentum* (see O.10).
   Spissiam: 'at Époisses'.

15 **sol occumbente** = *sole occumbente*: 'at sunset'.
   nuntiant: sc. 'the king's servants'.

16 **metare** = *metari* (see O.11 and G.3): 'to stay' (probably because of his adherence to a different church from that of the king).

17 **ex...offensam** = *ex...offensa*: 'by offending'.

18 **parare** = *parari* (see O.11).

20 **inquiret** = *inquirit* (see O.11 and G.3).

20f. **quid sibi de ista vellint:** 'what they wanted of him in relation to them' (see above note on l.4 *quid sibi vellint*: *vellint* = *velint*; for *ista* see G.11(c); for *de* + acc. cf. G.15(c)(i)).

21 **Aient ille** = *Aiunt illi:* (see G.2)
   fore = *esse:* (see G.5).

22 **Munera...altissimus:** Ecclesiasticus 34.23 (but the Vlg. has *dona iniquorum non probat Altissimus*).

23 **suis...aliorum habitaculis:** '(not only) to their own ... (but also) to the homes of others' (dat. after *aditus* 'entrance' for CL *ad* + acc.).

24 **frustra** = *frusta*.

25f. **rei gestae causam** = *rem gestam*: 'what had happened' (*causa* 'matter': CL 'cause', cf. It. *cosa*, Fr. *chose*).

26 **delucolo:** 'at daybreak'.

27f. **properant, precantur...pollicentur:** the subjects are *ille* (the king) and his grandmother (*avia*).

28 **pacatus:** i.e. Columbanus.

(ii) *Theodoric reneges on his agreement and, incited by Brunhilda, visits Columbanus at Luxeuil, where a furious argument takes place.*

Sed polliciti vademonii iura non diu servata violantur; exercentur miseriarum incrementa, solitoque a rege adulteria patrantur. Quae audita, beatus Columbanus litteras ad eum verberibus plenas direxit comminaturque excommunicationem, si emendare dilatando non vellit. Ad haec rursum permota Brunichildis, regis animum adversum Columbanum excitat omnique conatu 5 perturbare intendit oraturque proceris, auligas, obtimatis omnis, ut regis animum contra verum Dei perturbarent, episcopusque sollicitare adgressa, et de eius religione detrahendo et statum regulae, quam suis custodiendam monachis indederat, macularet. Obtemperantis igitur auligae persuasionibus miserae reginae, regis animum contra verum Dei perturbant, cogentes, ut 10 accederet hac relegionem probaret. Abactus itaque rex ad virum Dei Luxovium venit; conquestusque cum eo, cur ab conprovincialibus moribus disciscere, et intra septa secretiora omnibus christianis aditus non pateret. Beatus itaque Columbanus, ut erat audax atque animo vigens, talibus obicienti regi respondit, se consuetudinem non habere, ut saecularium hominum et 15 relegioni alienis famulorum Dei habitationes pandant introitum; se et oportuna aptaque loca ad hoc habere parata, quo omnium hospitum adventus suscipiatur. Ad haec rex: 'Si' inquid 'largitatis nostrae munera et solaminis suppli-

mentum capere cupis, omnibus in locis omnium patebit introitus.' Vir Dei
respondit: 'Si, quod nunc usque sub regularis disciplinae abenis constrictum 20
fuit, violare conaris, nec tuis muneribus nec quibuscumque subsidiis me fore a
te sustentaturum. Et si hanc ob causam tu hoc in loco venisti, ut servorum Dei
caenubia distruas et regularem disciplinam macules, cito tuum regnum funditus
ruiturum et cum omni propagine regia dimersurum.' Quod postea rei probavit
eventus. Iam enim temerario conatu rex refecturium ingressus fuerat. His ergo 25
territus dictis, foris celer repetat. Duris post haec vir Dei increpationibus rex
urguetur. Contra quae Theudericus ait: 'Martyrii coronam a me tibi inlaturam
speras'; non esse tantae dementiae, ut hoc tantum patraret scelus, sed potiores
consilii se ageret utilia paraturum, ut qui ab omnium saecularium mores
disciscat, quo venerit, ea via repetare studeat. Auligum simul consona voce 30
vota prorumpunt, se habere non velle his in locis, qui omnibus non societur.
Ad haec beatus Columbanus se dicit de caenubii septa non egressurum, nisi
violenter abstrahatur.

1 **polliciti:** passive 'promised' (see RLRGr C4 Note 2).

1f. **exercentur...incrementa:** 'additions to their crimes were practised' (i.e. they slipped back into their old ways).

2 **solitoque a rege:** lit. 'by the accustomed king', but tr. as though *solito* agreed with *adulteria*.
Quae audita: 'when he had heard this' (acc. abs.).

4 **emendare** = *se emendare*.
dilatando: 'by delaying'.
vellit = *vellet* (see O.11).

4f. **Ad haec...macularet:** the structure is *Brunichildis* (subject)...*excitat*...(and) *intendit oraturque...ut...perturbarent,* (and) *sollicitare adgressa, et...detrahendo et statum regulae,⌐ | quam... indederat | ⌐...macularet* (probably an error for *maculando,* parallel with *detrahendo*).

6 **proceris** = *proceres* (see O.11).
obtimatis omnis = *optimates omnes* (see O.18 and 0.11).

7 **verum** = *virum* (see O.11).
episcopus = *episcopos* (see O.12: the Frankish bishops, whose own practices were very different from those of Columbanus' Celtic Church; there was a major dispute over the date of Easter – see section 6.2 – but it is not mentioned here).
adgressa: sc. *est* 'set about' (+ inf.).

8 **statum regulae** = *regulam:* lit. 'the character of

the rule'.

9 **indederat** = *indiderat* (see O.11).
Obtemperantis = *Obtemperantes* (see O.11).

10 **verum** = *virum* (see O.11).

11 **hac relegionem probaret:** sc. *ut* 'to test the religious practice in this place' (i.e. at Luxeuil).

11f. **Luxovium:** 'to Luxeuil' (the monastery founded by Columbanus some time after 591).

12 **conquestusque cum eo:** 'asking him in complaint' (CL *apud* + acc.).

13 **intra septa:** it was normal Frankish, but not Irish, practice to allow everyone (except sometimes women) into all monastic buildings.

14 **vigens:** 'confident'.

14f. **talibus obicienti regi:** 'to the king throwing at him such words' (CL uses acc. after *obicio;* alternatively, *talibus* might refer to Columbanus' words: 'with such words to the king opposing (sc. him) he replied').

15f. **respondit...suscipiatur:** *respondit* introduces two acc. + inf. clauses, *se...non habere (consuetudinem* looks forward to *ut* ('the custom that...'), whose verb is *pandant,* (obj.) *introitum,* subject *famulorum...habitationes)* and *se...habere (loca* looks forward to *quo* ('where...')... *suscipiatur).*
saecularium hominum: 'to laymen' (this should be in the dative, as is the parallel phrase *religioni* (i.e. *religioni) alienis* 'to those hostile to his rule').

18f. **solaminis supplimentum:** lit. 'the aid of relief',
i.e. protection from me.

19 **omnium:** i.e. *omnibus* (see note on *saecularium
hominum* above).

20 **Si** looks forward to *violare conaris* (obj. *quod*
('what...')...*constrictum fuit* ('has been...') – see
G.4(a).

nunc usque: 'up to now'.

21 **quibuscumque:** 'any'.

21f. **fore...sustentaturum:** '(sc. do not expect that I)
will be sustained' (CL *fore ut...sustenter* or
sustentatum iri).

22 **hoc in loco:** 'to this place' (see G.15(c)(ii)).

23f. **cito...dimersurum:** sc. 'I predict that...'.

25 **enim:** 'Now...' (simple connective: see G.14).

ingressus fuerat: 'had...' (see G.4(a)).

26 **foris:** 'the outside' (CL = 'outside').

repetat = *repetit* (see G.3).

Duris looks forward to *increpationibus* 'by...' (on
which depends *vir Dei* = *viri Dei*).

27 **urguetur** = *urgetur*.

inlaturam: 'will be given' (see note on *sustentaturum* 1.21f. above).

28 **non esse:** sc. '(but he) was not...'.

28f. **sed potiores** (= *potioris:* see O.11) **consilii se
ageret:** 'but he (i.e. Columbanus) should act
to learn the uses of better counsel'.

29f. **ut qui ab omnium saecularium mores disciscat, quo venerit, ea via** (i.e. *eam viam:*
see O.10) **repetare** (= *repetere:* see G.2)
studeat: '(sc. saying) that a man who differed
from the customs of all the world (i.e. the
Frankish world) should seek again that road
whence he had come.' (*ab...mores:* cf.
G.15(c)(i)).

30f. **Auligum** (= *aulicorum*)...**vota prorumpunt:** lit.
'the wishes of the courtiers burst forth', i.e.
'the courtiers expressed vigorously their
view... (that)'.

qui: sc. *eum.*

32 **de...septa:** 'from the precincts' (for *de* + acc. cf.
G.15(c)(i)).

6. The Mozarabic Chronicle (*c*.754)

In Spain, the writing of Latin survived even under the Muslim Umayyad
Caliphate, which took over most of the Iberian peninsula in 711, after
defeating the Visigoths. Not until the recapture of Toledo in 1085 was the
tide turned for Christendom, though the Emirate of Granada in the
extreme south was to remain Islamic throughout the Middle Ages. The
Mozarabic Chronicle is probably the product of a cleric or clerics from
Toledo (Mozarabic is the name given to Christians under Islamic rule in
what would later become Spain and Portugal). The Latin is often almost as
hard to follow as Fredegar, with its misuse of formulae (e.g. *huius temporibus*
'during this period') and a flowery language without a very firm syntactical
foundation.

*Taio, bishop of Saragossa, was sent to Rome by King Chindaswinth (Visigoth king
642–53) to find a copy of Gregory the Great's Moralia. When the archivists failed
to locate it, Taio found it by appealing for divine assistance. This is the account he
gave to the Pope of the miraculous book search.*

Requisitus uero et coniuratus Taio episcopus a papa Romano quomodo ei tam
ueridicus fuisset librorum illorum locus ostensus, hoc illi post nimiam
deprecationem cum nimia alacritate est fassus, quod quadam nocte se ab

hostiariis eclesie beati Petri apostoli expetit esse excubium. At ubi hoc repperit inpetratum, subito in noctis medium cum se nimiis lamentis ante beati Petri 5
apostoli loculum deprecando faceret cernuum, lux celitus emissa ita ab inenarrabili lumine tota eclesia extitit perlustrata, ut nec modicum relucerent eclesie candelabra, simulque cum ipso lumine una cum uoces psallentium et lampades relampantium introire sanctorum agmina. Denique ubi orrore nimio extitit territus, oratione ab eis conpleta paulatim ex illa sanctorum curia duo 10
dealbati senes gressum in ea parte, qua episcopus orationi degebatur, ceperunt dare prependulum. At ubi eum reppererunt pene iam mortuum, dulciter salutatum reduxerunt ad proprium sensum. Quumque ab eis interrogaretur quam ob causam tam grande extaret fatigium uel cur ab Occidente properans tam longum peteret nauigerium, hoc et hoc ab eo quasi inscii relatum 15
auscultant opere pretium. Tum illi multis eloquiis consolatum ei oportunum, ubi ipsi libri latebant, ostenderunt loculum. Igitur sancti illi requisiti que esset sanctorum illa caterua eis tam claro cum lumine comitantium, responderunt dicentes Petrum Xpi esse apostolum simulque et Paulum inuicem se manu tenentes cum omnibus successoribus eclesie in loco illo requiescentibus. 20
Porro ubi et ipsi requisiti fuerunt qui domini essent qui cum eo tam mirabile habebant conloquium, unus ex illis respondit se esse Gregorium, cuius et ipse desiderabat cernere librum, et ideo aduenire ut eius remunerarent tam uastum fatigium et auctum redderent longissimum desiderium.

Tunc interrogatus si tandem in illa sancta multitudine adesset sapiens 25
Agustinus, eo quod ita libros eius sicut et ipsius sancti Gregorii semper ab ipsis cunabulis amaret legere satis perauidus, hoc solummodo respondisse fertur: 'Uir ille clarissimus et omnium expectatione gratissimus Agustinum quem queris, altior a nobis eum continet locus.' Certe ubi ad eorum pedes cepit proruere uncus, ab oculis eius ostiariis et ipsis territis simul cum luce euanuit uir 30
ille sanctissimus. Unde et ab eo die a cunctis in eadem apostolorum sede uenerabilis Taio extitit gloriosus, qui ante despicabatur ut ignabus.

---

2 **ueridicus:** 'truthfully'.
  fuisset with **ostensus** ('had been...': see G.4(a)).
  hoc is the obj. of *est fassus* and looks forward to *quod* ('that...').
2f. **nimiam...nimia:** 'very great' (cf. *nimis:* G.12(b)).
3f. **se...expetit esse excubium:** lit. 'he asked that he be on vigil', i.e. he asked to be allowed to keep vigil in the church: *excubium* appears to be a noun meaning 'sentinel', 'guard' (CL *excubiae* 1f.pl. 'keeping watch').
4 **eclesie** = *ecclesiae* (see O.7, O.1).
5 **inpetratum** = *impetratum* (see O.21): lit. 'when

he discovered this had been granted', but it is meant to mean 'when this request had been granted'.
  in noctis medium = *media nocte* (cf G.15(c)(i)).
  cum se looks forward to *faceret cernuum* ('threw himself face down').
6 **lux celitus emissa:** 'a light came forth from heaven and' (nom. abs.).
7 **extitit** (= *exstitit*) **perlustrata** = *perlustrata est* (see G.4(d)).
  nec modicum: 'not even a small amount' (i.e. the light completely eclipsed the ordinary candlelight of the church).

8f. simulque...introire: 'and there entered along with...' (acc. + inf. co-ordinated with the *ut* clause, instead of a second subjunctive).

8 ipso: 'that' or 'the' (see G.11(a)(i)–(ii)).

cum uoces...et lampades = *cum uocibus...et lampadibus* (see G.15(c)(i)).

9 relampantium: '(with the lights) of glittering people' (probably a misquotation of a liturgical phrase: we find *lampadibus relampantibus* in another eighth-century Spanish writer).

10 extitit (= *exstitit*) **territus** = *territus est* (see G.4(d)).

11f. gressum...ceperunt dare prependulum: 'began to take hanging steps' (i.e. to float in the air); perhaps 'began to move eagerly'.

11 degebatur: 'was spending his time in' (CL active).

14 extaret = *exstaret* 'there was' (cf. Sp. *estar*).

15 hoc et hoc: 'this and that', picked up by *relatum* (*inscii* agrees with the subject of *auscultant*).

16 opere (= *operae*: see O.1) **pretium:** 'to repay their concern'.

consolatum ei: 'after soothing him they showed him' (for *consolatum* used as a passive, see G.3, but also RLRGr C4 Note 2).

16f. oportunum: 'right' looks forward to *loculum* ('bookcase'), obj. of *ostenderunt*.

17 ipsi: 'the/those' (see G.11(a)(i)–(ii)).

Igitur: 'and then' (simple connective: see G.14).

17f. que esset has *illa caterua* as subject (on which depends *sanctorum... eis* (= the old men, dependent on)...*comitantium*).

19 Xpi = *Christi* (an abbreviation based on the Greek letters χρ, which stand for *Khristos*).

19f. inuicem se manu tenentes: 'holding each other's hands' (see G.11(e)(ii)).

20 eclesie = *ecclesiae* (O.7, O 1).

21 requisiti fuerunt: 'were...' (see G.4(a)).

22 Gregorium: i.e. Pope Gregory the Great (*c*.540–604), the author of the *Moralia*, a copy of which Taio was seeking.

cuius looks forward to *librum*, obj. of *desiderabat*.

24 auctum redderent: 'render accomplished' (CL *augeo* 'augment', 'endow').

25 interrogatus si: 'asked whether...' (see G.24(c)).

26 Agustinus = *Augustinus*: St Augustine (see section 4.1).

eo quod ita looks forward to *amaret legere*, obj. *libros eius*; *ita...sicut et* means 'just as much...as...'.

27 satis perauidus: 'very eagerly' (see G.12(b)).

28 omnium expectatione (= *exspectatione*) **gratissimus:** 'most beloved in the contemplation of all' (*exspectatio* CL 'expectation').

Agustinum: acc. because attracted by *quem*.

30 uncus: 'bent double', i.e. 'prostrate'.

ostiariis et ipsis territis: probably abl. abs. 'with the doorkeepers also terrified'.

31 Unde: 'because of which'.

eadem: 'that' (see G.11(b)) or 'the aforesaid'.

32 extitit = *exstitit*, i.e. 'became'.

despicabatur: 'was despised' (CL deponent: see G.3).

ignabus: tr. 'as an idler'.

Section 9
The Carolingian Renaissance

The circumstances described in the introduction to section 8, obtaining in the Frankish kingdom in particular, led to orthographic reforms. These were already in train in the reign of Pippin the Short (750–68). His son, Charlemagne (768–814) extended the scope of these changes. In his capitulary *De litteris colendis* ('On the pursuit of learning'), written sometime between 780 and 800, he tells of his receipt of letters from his clergy, in which he noted *sensus rectos et sermones incultos* 'correct views and uncouth words'. He feared that this lack of skill in expression might be symptomatic of an inability correctly to understand the sacred texts. He consequently enjoined that in his kingdoms schools should be set up in every see and at every abbey. The effect of these changes was to ensure the continuity of more or less classical standards of spelling and grammar. More or less, since, for instance, *ae* never fully replaced *e* as the spelling of the diphthong and *quod/quia* for acc. + inf. remained standard until the Renaissance. On the organizational level, Charlemagne had here sown the seeds of the universities of the thirteenth century.

Elsewhere, for instance in England, Ireland, Italy and Spain, the situation had not perhaps been so bad (though it is interesting to contrast insular Latin with continental Latin during this period: see sections 6, 7 and 8). It is no accident that Charlemagne turned to scholars from these countries to help him, bringing Peter of Pisa and Paul the Deacon from the Lombard centre of learning Pavia in the 770s, Alcuin from York in 782, Theodulf from Spain a little later, and from Ireland scholars such as Cadac-Andreas and the poet Hibernicus Exul ('Irish exile'), identified as Dungal or Dicuil. This confluence of talent is a potent instance of the way Latin facilitated intellectual contact in Europe during the Middle Ages.

The new school curriculum was developed by Alcuin. It was based upon study of Christian writers. But Charlemagne's ambitions in the realm of Latin were much greater than simply to provide a literate clergy. He was concerned to imitate antiquity, both biblical and Roman, in gathering round him at court a circle of poets who would celebrate his achievements in Latin poetry. He was called David by his poets. The success of this enterprise is visible not only in the amount and quality of the surviving verse, but in the very image of his reign which persisted in later ages.

The classical aspect of his image-making perhaps explains that feature of the 'Carolingian Renaissance' which has attracted most attention, the revival of interest in classical literature, which led to the careful copying of many pagan texts in the beautiful hand known as 'Caroline minuscule', and to the eventual survival of much which would otherwise have been lost. It is worth noting here as an example the interest of Lupus of Ferrières in a work such as Cicero's *De oratore*, which he is the first medieval writer to mention. Lupus moreover anticipates by several centuries the fifteenth-century Renaissance practice of establishing texts by collating mss.

As far as the use of classical material goes, of particular note is the way in which Einhard, Charlemagne's biographer, utilizes Suetonius' portraits of Roman emperors to describe his king, and the way in which (possibly) the same writer assimilates Charlemagne to Aeneas, as he describes the foundation of Aachen.

Charlemagne was followed in his literary interests by his immediate successors, Louis the Pious (d. 840) and Charles the Bald (d. 877). But there was no centre, as Aachen had been after 794 for Charlemagne's poets. Writers worked in their separate monastic institutions – Fulda, Reichenau, Corbie, Tours, St Gall, St Amand, Auxerre, Rheims, Metz and Liège – and sent their pieces to the ruler. The only exception to this is the patronage given to the Irish philosopher and Greek scholar John Scottus Eriugena by Charles the Bald.

See further P. Godman, *Poetry of the Carolingian Renaissance*, London, 1985 and *Poets and Emperors*, Oxford, 1987; L. D. Reynolds and N. G. Wilson, *Scribes and Scholars*, 3rd edn, Oxford, 1991; R. McKitterick, *The Carolingians and the Written Word*, Cambridge, 1989; D. A. Bullough, *Carolingian Renewal: Sources and Heritage*, Manchester, 1991.

1. Charlemagne's *Capitulare episcoporum* (780?)

Charlemagne governed his vast kingdom by means of edicts (*capitularia*) drawn up primarily as a record of an *oral* statement made by the king. Their authority was based on the royal power of the *bannum* ('ban'), which gave him the right to order, forbid and exact punishment. The capitularies (so called because they were divided into *capita*, 'articles') were usually promulgated through *missi dominici* ('the king's messengers'), who read them before various assemblies, which then gave consent. Sometimes they were published by the bishops or counts instead. Like his Merovingian predecessors (see section 8.2), his concerns covered both secular and sacred matters.

The Latin is greatly improved since the Merovingian period, especially in orthography. But there are still syntactical oddities, such as for example *de* + acc. instead of abl. (*de pauperes famelicos*).

A crisis (perhaps a famine, perhaps a military difficulty) draws forth an edict for the saying of masses and psalteries for the king, the army and the present troubles, the giving of alms to the poor by both ecclesiastical and secular dignitaries, and the observance of fasts.

Capitulare qualiter institutum est in hoc episcoporum consensu: id est ut unusquisque episcopus tres missas et psalteria tria cantet, unam pro domno rege, alteram pro exercitu Francorum, tertiam pro presenti tribulatione; presbiteri vero unusquisque missas tres, monachi et monachae et canonici unusquisque psalteria tria. Et biduanas omnes faciant, tam episcopi, monachi et   5 monachae atque canonici, atque eorum infra casatum homines, vel qui potentes sunt. Et unusquisque episcopus aut abbas vel abbatissa, qui hoc facere potest, libram de argento in elemosinam donet, mediocres vero mediam libram, minores solidos quinque. Episcopi et abbates atque abbatissae pauperes famelicos quatuor pro isto inter se instituto nutrire debent usque   10 tempore messium: et qui tantum non possunt, iuxta quod possibilitas est, aut tres aut duos aut unum. Comites vero fortiores libram unam de argento aut valentem, mediocres mediam libram; vassus dominicus de casatis ducentis mediam libram, de casatis centum solidos quinque, de casatis quinquaginta aut triginta unciam unam. Et faciant biduanas atque eorum homines in eorum   15 casatis, vel qui hoc facere possunt; et qui redimere voluerit, fortiores comites uncias tres, mediocres unciam et dimidiam, minores solidum unum. Et de pauperes famelicos, sicut supra scriptum est, et ipsi faciant. Haec omnia, si Deo placuerit, pro domno rege et pro exercitu Francorum et praesente tribulatione missa sancti Iohannis sit completum.   20

4f. **presbiteri...tria:** sc. *cantent.*

5 **faciant:** 'let...' (jussive subj.: *RLGVE* 152: so also *donet,* 1.8).

6f. **eorum...sunt:** 'men of those within..., at least those who were capable' (sc. 'of sustaining a two-day fast').

10 **pro...instituto:** 'in accordance with their mutual decision'.

10f. **usque tempore messium:** 'up to the time of...'.

11 **iuxta quod:** 'according to what...'.

11f. **aut...unum:** sc. *nutrire debent.*

13 **valentem:** i.e. 'of the same value'; supply *donent* as the verb for this sentence.

   de casatis ducentis...: 'with...'.

15 **atque:** 'also'.

   homines is subject of *faciant.*

16 **qui...possunt:** 'those who...'.
qui...voluerit: 'he who...'.
redimere: i.e. to make a payment instead of actually undertaking the fast.

16f. **fortiores comites...unum:** Sc. 'let them pay...'.

17f. **de pauperes famelicos** for *de pauperibus famelicis* (see G.15(c)).

18f. **Haec omnia...sit completum:** 'Let all this be

completed...' (the syntax has gone wrong – s. verb for pl. subject).

19 **praesente:** abl. (= *praesenti*: see G.7(a); note the correct -i- form stem is used above at l.3).

20 **missa...Iohannis:** 'by...' (perhaps 24 June, the feast of St John the Baptist, since the capitulary speaks of relief being given up to harvest-time).

2. Alcuin of York (*c.*730–804)

Alcuin (Ealhwine), generally known as Albinus and in the court circle at Aachen as Flaccus (after Horace) was born in Northumbria and educated at York. There he began to teach in 768, taking over as head of the school in 778. He met Charlemagne for the second time at Parma while returning from a trip to Rome to collect the *pallium* of the new archbishop Eanbald I. He was invited to take over the palace school at Aachen, which he ran until 796. In that year he became abbot of St Martin at Tours, where he remained until his death on 19 May 804.

He produced a number of educational works on the subjects of the *trivium* and was involved in some way in the provision of correct and readable texts of Scripture and the liturgy. He was used by Charlemagne as spokesman in theological debates. Yet his most enduring and attractive monument lies in his poetic and epistolary works. He composed a long poem on the church at York, and many occasional poems for the court circle at Aachen. His surviving letters run to more than 300.

(a) This letter was written in 796, probably from Tours to Charlemagne at Aachen On its central request, Alcuin's appeal hit its mark, as appears from a later letter to Pippin.

Alcuin appeals for mercy to be shown to the captives taken in Pippin's successful campaign against the Huns.

Domine mi dilectissime, et dulcissime, et omnium desiderantissime, mi David, tristis est Flaccus vester propter infirmitatem vestram. Opto, et toto corde Deum deprecor ut cito convaleatis, ut gaudium nostrum sit plenum in vobis, et sanitas vestra sit plena, anima et corpore.

   Domine mi, memor sit pietas vestra captivorum, dum est Pippinus tuus   5
tecum, propter gratiarum actiones mirabilis beneficii quod vobiscum de Hunis divina fecit clementia, et propter prosperitatem inminentium rerum; ut clementissima illius potentia omnes adversarios sui sancti nominis vestris

velociter subiciat pedibus: sed et de peccantibus in vos – si fieri possit, et vestrae
videatur providentiae – aliqua de aliquibus fiat indulgentia et remissio. Tamen   10
propter incognitas illorum causas cautius de his loquor. Vos enim ipsi optime
scitis quod utile est regno vobis a Deo dato, et paci sanctae Dei ecclesiae.
Proficuum facientes faciatis in omnibus voluntatem Dei, quatenus illius
sanctissima gratia vos proficientes ubique protegat, regat et custodiat, domine
et dulcissime et desiderantissime.   15

1 **David:** Charlemagne (see Intro. to this section).

2 **Flaccus:** Alcuin (see Intro. to this section).

propter infirmitatem vestram: presumably a
minor ailment. His biographer Einhard (see
section 9.4 below) reports serious health
problems only in his last four years (*Vita Karoli*
22).

4 **anima et corpore:** 'in...'.

5 **memor** governs *captivorum*.

pietas vestra: this could refer to Charlemagne
himself ('your piousness'; cf. *affectio uestra* 'your
kindness' in section 2.4) or might mean
'religious conscience'.

Pippinus tuus: 773–810, son of Charlemagne
and Hildegard (see section 9.3(b), known as
Karlman (Carolomannus) before his christen-
ing by Pope Hadrian I in 781 and anointment
as King of Italy. Leader of the expedition
against the Huns. He presumably came to
Aachen (Aquisgranum) after the success of
the campaign in 796.

6 **propter...beneficii:** 'because of the actions of
(divine) grace (involved in) the amazing service...'.

de Hunis: 'in relation to...'.

7 **propter prosperitatem:** 'because of...', here in
the sense of 'to safeguard'.

8 **illius:** i.e. God's.

vestris looks forward to *pedibus* (indir. obj. of
subiciat).

9 **sed et...:** understand *ut* 'but in addition...that
there be some...'.

9f. **si...providentiae:** 'if... it seems right to Your
Providence' (see note on *pietas vestra* above).

12 **quod utile est...:** 'what is useful for...' (*regno* is
picked up by *dato*; *quod* is used for *quid*; for
mood of *est* see G.24(b)).

13 **Proficuum facientes:** 'in doing the advantageous thing' (see G.20(b)).

quatenus: 'in order that...' (see G.27(b)).

14 **vos proficientes:** 'you as you advance...' (see
G.20(b)).

(b) Alcuin's most famous poems are his address to his cell (*O mea cella*),
written after he left Aachen for Tours, and his praise of the nightingale.
But his poetic production has far greater range than these elegies testify,
running from the verse epistle and eclogue, through historical poetry to
religious acrostic and *aenigmata*. This short set of elegiac verses served as a
preface to Alcuin's *Rhetoric*, and takes for its opening idea a conceit from
Ovid's *Ars Amatoria* about the shortness of life and the need to use time
well. For Ovid, of course, one's youth should be used for amorous play.
Alcuin sees it as the time to study and gain knowledge of morality which
will bring honour to one's old age. For a wider selection (with English
translation), see Godman, *Poetry*, pp. 118–49. This poem is in elegiac
couplets (see *RLGVE* 185).

Youth's the time for study.

> O vos, est aetas, iuvenes, quibus apta legendo,
>   discite: eunt anni more fluentis aquae.
> atque dies dociles vacuis ne perdite rebus:
>   nec redit unda fluens, nec redit hora ruens.
> floreat in studiis virtutum prima iuventus,   5
>   fulgeat ut magno laudis honore senex,
> utere, quisque legas librum, felicibus annis.
>   auctorisque memor dic: 'miserere deus.'
> si nostram, lector, festucam tollere quaeris,
>   robora de proprio lumine tolle prius: 10
> disce tuas, iuvenīs, ut agat facundia causas,
>   ut sis defensor, cura, salusque tuis.
> disce, precor, iuvenis, motus moresque venustos,
>   laudetur toto ut nomen in orbe tuum.

1 **O vos, est aetas...quibus:** 'You who have...' (*quibus* is the conjunction of this clause, *vos* is its antecedent: the tangled word order reflects the difficulty of writing in classical metres).

2 **discite...aquae:** this line is the same as Ovid, *Ars Amatoria* 3.62, except that the first word in Ovid is *Ludite* ('make sport').

3 **vacuis...rebus:** 'in...'.
ne...: 'don't'.

4 **nec...ruens:** a paraphrase of the next two lines of *Ars Amatoria* (*Nec quae praeteriit iterum revocabitur unda, / nec quae praeteriit hora redire potest* 'Neither will the water which has passed by be recalled, nor can the hour which has passed return'). The rhyme in the pentameter (*fluens/ ruens*) is called *leonine*.
fluens...ruens: these are used as simple adjectives.

5 **floreat:** 'let...' (jussive subj.: *RLGVE* 152).

6 **fulgeat ut:** 'so that...' (*ut* is postponed).
senex: lit. 'old man'; tr. 'your old age'.

7 **quisque** (= *quisquis*) **legas librum:** 'whoever (sc. you are who) read (this) book' (i.e. the primer of rhetoric to which the poem is a preface).

8 **miserere deus:** the Latin translation of *Kyrie eleison* 'Lord have mercy'. This is the opening of the Latin mass, and Alcuin may imply seriously that his students should say mass for his soul, rather than humorously suggest that the author of such a work needs praying for!

9f. **festucam...robora:** 'mote...beam' (the allusion to Christ's words reported in Mt 7.3 and Lk 6.41: *quid autem vides festucam in oculo fratris tui et trabem in oculo tuo non vides?* 'Why do you see the mote in your brother's eye, and you do not see the beam in your own?').

11 **disce, tuas...causas:** construe *disce...ut* ('so that...'); *tuas...causas* is the obj. of *agat*.
facundia: 'eloquence', because the book is a rhetoric primer.

13 **motus moresque venustos:** 'elegant tropes and manners' (rhetorical training must go hand in hand with Christian values; *motus* stands for all the technical content of the rhetorical textbook).

14 **laudetur...tuum:** the conjunction is *ut* ('so that...'); *toto* looks forward to *in orbe*, and *nomen* to *tuum*.

3. Paul the Deacon (*c.*720–*c.*799)

A Lombard noble by birth, Paul studied at Pavia, and later, around 770, became tutor to Adelperga, daughter of King Desiderius. He became a monk of Monte Cassino probably in 773 or 774, the time of Charlemagne's annexation of Lombardy. His first contact with Charlemagne appears to have been in 782/3, when he went to Aachen to intervene on behalf of his imprisoned brother Arichis. The appeal is encapsulated in a moving poem. He remained at Aachen for two or three years, then returned to Monte Cassino. Paul contributed to the poetic milieu at Aachen in various ways, including epitaphs and a verse exchange with his fellow Lombard Peter of Pisa. His collection of homilies from the Fathers of the Church was recommended for use throughout the Empire. He also wrote on grammar. But his best known writings are historical, the most important being his *Historia Langobardorum* ('History of the Lombards') (to 774 – leaving out the events of Paul's lifetime, including Charlemagne's conquest of Lombardy).

See further: W. Goffart, *The Narrators of Barbarian History (AD 550–800)*, Princeton, 1988.

(a) This extract from book five of the *Historia Langobardorum* deals with the end of Duke Alahis of Trent, who had instituted a major rebellion against King Cunincpert (680–700). The historical significance of Alahis' defeat is that it forced the northern bishops to accept the papal position in the theological dispute over the 'Three Chapters'. In this, parts of the writings of Theodore of Mopsuestia, Theodoret of Cyr and Ibas of Edessa had been anathematized in an edict of Justinian of 544. As the text begins, the rival leaders' armies have encamped at Cornata, near Como.

(i) *Cunincpert challenges Alahis to single combat. Seno, a deacon from Pavia, takes his place and is killed.*

Ad quem Cunincpert nuntium misit, mandans ei, ut cum eo singulare certamen iniret, nec opus esset utrorumque exercitum fatigare. Ad quae verba Alahis minime consensit. Cui cum unus e suis, genere Tuscus, ei persuaderet, virum bellicosum fortemque eum appellans, ut contra Cunincpertum audenter exiret, Alahis ad haec verba respondit: 'Cunincpert, quamvis 5 ebriosus sit et stupidi cordis, tamen satis est audax et mirae fortitudinis. Nam tempore patris eius quando nos erabamus iuvenculi, habebantur in palatio berbices mirae magnitudinis, quos ille supra dorsum eorum lanam adprehendens, extenso eos brachio a terra levabat; quod quidem ego facere non poteram.' Haec ille Tuscus audiens, dixit ad eum: 'Si tu cum Cunincperto 10 pugnam inire singulari certamine non audes, me iam in tuo adiutorio socium non habebis.' Et haec dicens, proripuit se et statim ad Cunincpertum confugiit

et haec ipsa illi nuntiavit. Convenerunt itaque, ut diximus, utraeque acies in
campo Coronate. Cumque iam prope essent, ut se coniungere deberent, Seno
diaconus Ticinensis ecclesiae, qui custus erat basilicae beati Iohannis baptistae,   15
quae intra eadem sita est civitatem, quam quondam Gundiperga regina
construxerat, cum nimium diligeret regem et metueret, ne rex in bello
periret, ait ad regem: 'Domine rex, omnis vita nostra in tua salute consistit;
si tu in bello perieris, omnes nos iste tyrannus Alahis per diversa supplicia
extinguet. Placeat itaque tibi consilium meum. Da mihi apparatum armorum   20
tuorum, et ego vadam et pugnabo cum isto tyranno. Si ego obiero, tu
recuperabis causam tuam; si vero vicero, maior tibi, quia per servum viceris,
gloria adscribetur.' Cumque rex hoc se facturum esse denegaret, coeperunt
eum pauci qui aderant eius fideles cum lacrimis deposcere, ut ad ea quae
diaconus dixerat adsensum praeberet. Victus tandem, ut erat pii cordis, eorum   25
precibus et lacrimis, loricam suam, galeam atque ocreas et cetera arma diacono
praebuit in suaque persona eum ad proelium direxit. Erat enim ipse diaconus
eiusdem staturae et habitus, ita ut, cum fuisset de tentorio armatus egressus, rex
Cunincpert ab omnibus esse putaretur. Commissum itaque est proelium et totis
viribus decertatum. Cumque Alahis ibi magis intenderet, ubi regem esse   30
putaret, Cunincpertum se extinxisse putans, Senonem diaconem interfecit.
Cumque caput eius amputari praecepisset, ut, levato eo in conto, 'Deo gratias'
adclamarent, sublata casside, clericum se occidisse cognovit. Tunc furibundus
exclamans: 'Heu me!' inquit, 'nihil egimus, quando ad hoc proelium gessimus,
ut clericum occiderimus. Tale itaque nunc facio votum, ut, si mihi Deus   35
victoriam iterum dederit, quodunum puteum de testiculis impleam clericorum.'

1 **Ad quem:** i.e. Alahis.
   cum eo: i.e. with Cunincpert (see G.11(e)(i)).
2 **nec opus esset:** sc. 'and saying that'.
3 **unus e suis:** 'one of his own men' (CL *propriis*:
   see G.11(e)(iii)).
   Tuscus: 'Tuscan'.
6 **satis...audax:** 'very bold' (see G.12(b)).
7 **erabamus:** 'we were' (the normal form is *eramus*;
   cf. It. *eravamo* and see G.2).
   habebantur: 'there were (kept)'.
8f. **berbices...levabat:** the basic structure is *berbices*
   (antecedent) *quos ille...a terra levabat.*
8 **supra...lanam:** 'the wool (which was) on...' (see
   G.10(b)).
9 **extenso...brachio:** abl. abs. 'by extending...'
   (note the hyperbaton of *eos*: see *RLGVE* p.
   316).
10 **ille:** 'the' (cf. G.11(d)).

audiens: 'having heard' (see G.20(a)).
12 **dicens:** see previous note.
   confugiit = *confugit*.
14 **Coronate:** Cornata d'Adda, in the territory of
   Milan (the name is 1f. gen.: see O.1).
   prope...ut...deberent: 'close (sc. enough)...
   to...' (CL *coniungerent*: see G.25(c); in the next
   chapter Paul uses the CL form).
15 **Ticinensis:** 'of Pavia'.
16 **eadem** = *eandem* (with *civitatem*).
   Gundiperga: Gundeberga. Her first husband
   was Arioald, duke of Turin, who deposed
   her brother, King Adaloald in 626 and
   reigned 626–36. Later she married Rothari,
   duke of Brescia.
19 **iste:** 'that' (see G.11(c): so also *isto* below).
22 **maior** looks forward to *gloria*.
23f. **Cumque...praeberet:** the structure is *Cum rex*⌐ |

hoc...esse (acc. + inf. introduced by denegaret)
| ⌐denegaret, coeperunt...pauci⌐ |qui... fideles|⌐...
deposcere, ut⌐ |ad ea quae...dixerat| ⌐adsensum
praeberet.

28 **fuisset...egressus:** 'had emerged' (see G.4(a)).

31 **extinxisse:** tr. 'was killing' (lit. 'had killed').

32 **caput...amputari:** 'his head to be...' (inf. is
sometimes found after *praecipio* in CL).

34f. **ad hoc...ut...occiderimus:** 'to this end...that

we should have killed'.

35f. **Tale...clericorum:** the structure is *Tale... facio
votum, ut,*⌐ | *si...Deus...victoriam... dederit* |,
⌐*quodunum puteum...impleam.*

36 **quodunum:** 'every single' (CL *unum quidque*; cf.
Fr. *chacun*, It. *ciascuno*).

36f. **de testiculis...clericorum:** 'with...' (see
G.15(a)(ii)).

(ii) *The two armies join battle after Alahis has refused another challenge. Alahis is
killed and Cunincpert returns to Pavia triumphant.*

Igitur Cunincpert perdidisse suos conspiciens, statim se eis ostendit
omniumque corda, sublato pavore, ad sperandam victoriam confortavit.
Instruuntur iterum acies, et hinc Cunincpert, inde Alahis ad belli certamina
praeparantur. Cumque iam prope essent, ut se utraeque acies ad pugnandum coniungerent, Cunincpert ad Alahis iterato in haec verba mandavit: 5
'Ecce, quantus populus ex utraque parte consistit! Quid opus est, ut tanta
multitudo pereat? Coniungamus nos ego et ille singulari certamine, et cui
voluerit Dominus de nobis donare victoriam, omnem hunc populum
salvum et incolomem ipse possideat.' Cumque Alahis sui hortarentur, ut
faceret quod Cunincpert illi mandavit, ipse respondit: 'Hoc facere ego non 10
possum, quia inter contos suos sancti archangeli Michahelis, ubi ego illi
iuravi, imaginem conspicio.' Tunc unus ex illis: 'Prae pavore,' inquit,
'cernis quod non est; et tibi iam tarde est modo ista meditari.' Conseruntur
itaque acies perstrepentibus bucinis, et neutra parte locum dante, maxima
populorum facta est strages. Tandem crudelis tyrannus Alahis interiit, et 15
Cunincpert, adiuvante se Domino, victoriam cepit. Exercitus quoque
Alahis, conperta eius morte, fugae subsidium arripuit. E quibus quem
mucro non perculit, Addua fluvius interemit. Caput quoque Alahis
detruncatum cruraque eius succisa sunt, informeque tantum truncumque
cadaver remansit. In hoc bello Foroiulanorum exercitus minime fuit, quia, 20
cum invitus Alahis iurasset, propter hoc nec regi Cunincperto nec Alahis
auxilium tulit, sed cum illi bellum commississent, ipsi ad propria sunt reversi.
Igitur Alahis hoc modo defuncto, rex Cunincpert corpus Senoni diaconi
ante fores basilicae beati Iohannis, quam ipse rexerat, mirifice sepelire
mandavit; ipse vero regnator cum omnium exultatione et triumpho 25
victoriae Ticinum reversus est.

1 **Cunincpert...conspiciens:** 'Cunincpert seeing
that his men had lost' (*perdere* is used intransi-
tively here).

2 **corda** is the obj. of *confortavit*.

4 **prope...ut:** 'close (enough) to...' (compare the
construction with *deberent* in (i) l.14 above).

5 **in haec verba:** '(sc. a message) in the following
words'.

8 **de nobis:** 'of us' (see G.15(d)).

9 **ipse:** '(let) him' (see G.11(a)(ii)).

Cumque Alahis sui hortarentur: Alahis is the object of *hortarentur* and *sui* the subject ('his men').

11 **Michahelis:** '(St) Michael' (the archangel, venerated as head of the heavenly armies and the patron of soldiers).

11f. **ubi...iuravi:** 'when...I had sworn'.

13 **tarde est:** 'it is too late' (lit.: 'it is lately').

ista: 'these things' (see G.11(c)).

16f. **Exercitus...Alahis:** '...of Alahis' (as also in *Caput...Alahis* below: see. G.6(a)).

20 **Foroiulanorum:** 'of the people of Friuli'.

minime fuit: 'played a very small part'.

21f. **cum...Alahis iurasset...nec Alahis...tulit:** 'since it had sworn to Alahis...it brought...to Alahis' (see. G.6(a)).

22 **illi...ipsi:** 'they (sc. the belligerents)...they (sc. the soldiers of Friuli)' (see G.11(a)(ii)).

ad propria: 'to their own lands'.

23 **Alahis...defuncto:** 'when Alahis (abl.)...'.

Senoni: i.e. *Senonis* 'of Seno'.

24 **rexerat** = *erexerat* (procope; cf. O.10).

sepelire = *sepeliri* (see O.11: acc. + inf. is sometimes used with *mando* in CL).

(b) This moving epitaph (in elegiac couplets: see *RLGVE* 185) was written for a daughter of Charlemagne called Hildegard. She was the daughter of Charlemagne's second wife Hildegard, whom Charlemagne married after renouncing his bond with the Lombard princess Desiderata in 770. Hildegard was the last of her nine children, who included the future king, Louis the Pious (d. 840).

> Hildegard, rapuit subito te funus acerbum,
>   ceu raptat Boreas vere ligustra novo.
> explevit necdum vitae tibi circulus annum,
>   annua nec venit lux geminata tibi.
> parvula, non parvum linquis, virguncula, luctum,   5
>   confodiens iaculo regia corda patris;
> matris habens nomen renovas de matre dolorem,
>   post quam vixisti vix quădrăgintă dies.
> pectore nos mesto lacrimarum fundimus amnes,
>   tu nimium felix gaudia longa petis.   10

2 **vere:** with *novo*.

3 **explevit:** 'had...completed' (see G.9(b)).

vitae...circulus is the subject of *explevit*.

4 **annua...tibi:** 'nor did the yearly light come (back) to you twinned' (i.e. 'you did not live to see your second year'; as often, the pentameter repeats the idea of the hexameter).

5 **parvum** looks forward to *luctum*.

6 **confodiens:** 'having pierced' (see G.20(a)).

7 **habens:** 'because you had' (see G.20(b)).

de matre dolorem: 'grief for your mother' (cf. G.10(b)), i.e. Hildegard (did she die in childbirth?).

8 **quădrăgintă:** this could not fit into this position in CL metre, being scanned *quădrāgīntā*.

9 **pectore** with *mesto; lacrimarum* depends on *amnes*.

10 **tu...petis:** i.e. the baby Hildegard is in heaven, where the baptized innocents go directly.

nimium felix: 'very happy' (see G.12(b)).

4. Einhard (*c.*770–840)

Einhard, educated at the monastery of Fulda, came to Charlemagne's school at Aachen early in the 790s. He probably took over the headship when Alcuin went to Tours in 796. He was a poet and an expert in the practical arts (he supervised the building of the basilica at Aachen: see section 10.3). Later in Charlemagne's reign, he played an important political role as an ambassador. On Louis the Pious' succession, he became secretary to the new emperor whose accession he had successfully argued for in 813. Despite many preferments (including abbeys and land-grants), he gradually drew away from his close ties with Louis and in 830, when an open quarrel broke out between Louis and his sons, Einhard retired to the monastery he had founded at Seligenstadt in 828, where his wife Imma became abbess, and spent the rest of his life there as a monk. His extant works include a treatise on the Cross and some sixty letters. But most important are his biography of Charlemagne, which owes much to classical influences (especially Suetonius' *Lives of the Caesars*), and (if it is really by him) his epic generally known as *Karolus Magnus et Leo Papa*.

(a) The *Vita Karoli Magni* is the first secular biography of the Middle Ages. Einhard composed it probably in the early 830s at Seligenstadt. In this section, which follows one on Charlemagne's care in educating his children and precedes one stressing his magnanimity towards foreigners, the historian records two conspiracies against the emperor.

Erat ei filius nomine Pippinus ex concubina editus, cuius inter ceteros mentionem facere distuli, facie quidem pulcher, sed gibbo deformis. Is, cum pater bello contra Hunos suscepto in Baioaria hiemaret, aegritudine simulata, cum quibusdam e primoribus Francorum, qui eum vana regni promissione inlexerant, adversus patrem coniuravit. Quem post fraudem detectam et 5 damnationem coniuratorum detonsum in coenobio Prumia religiosae vitae iamque volentem vacare permisit. Facta est et alia prius contra eum in Germania valida coniuratio. Cuius auctores partim luminibus orbati, partim membris incolomes, omnes tamen exilio deportati sunt; neque ullus ex eis est interfectus nisi tres tantum; qui cum se, ne conprehenderentur, strictis gladiis 10 defenderent, aliquos etiam occidissent, quia aliter coerceri non poterant, interempti sunt. Harum tamen coniurationum Fastradae reginae crudelitas causa et origo extitisse creditur. Et idcirco in ambabus contra regem coniuratum est, quia uxoris crudelitati consentiens a suae naturae benignitate ac solita mansuetudine inmaniter exorbitasse videbatur. Ceterum per omne 15 vitae suae tempus ita cum summo omnium amore atque favore et domi et foris conversatus est, ut numquam ei vel minima iniustae crudelitatis nota a quoquam fuisset obiecta.

1 **ex concubina editus:** Paul the Deacon and other sources say that she was called Himmel-trud. Charlemagne was legally married four times, but also had five or six concubines, by whom he had children. According to Walah-frid Strabo's account of the vision of a monk called Wetti (*c.*826), Charlemagne was being punished for his lust in purgatory by having an animal tearing at his genitals.

cuius depends on *mentionem*, obj. of *facere* (which depends on *distuli*).

2 **gibbo deformis:** 'deformed by a hump', i.e. 'hunch-backed'.

2–5 **Is...coniuravit:** the structure is *Is*⌐ | *cum pater ...hiemaret*|⌐...*cum quibusdam...*⌐|*qui...inlexerant*|⌐ ...*coniuravit.*

3 **bello...suscepto:** abl. abs. The war against the Huns (or Avars) began in 791 and lasted for eight years, resulting in the complete destruc-tion of the Avar nobility.

in Baioaria: 'in Bavaria'. Charlemagne fought only one campaign in this war, in Pannonia. The rest he left to his son Pippin (see section 9.2(a) commentary) and other commanders. The conspiracy took place in 792.

5–7 **Quem...detonsum...permisit:** 'Whom...shorn of his hair (his father Charlemagne) allowed...' Pippin was given the monk's tonsure.

5 **in coenobio Prumia:** 'in the monastery at Prüm' (*Prumia* is in apposition to *coenobio*: cf. *urbs Roma*).

6 **religiosae vitae** depends on *vacare*: 'to devote himself to...'.

7 **iamque volentem:** 'and in fact of his own free will' (*iamque* is usually *et iam* in CL). Pippin died in 811.

alia looks forward to *valida coniuratio*. This was the conspiracy of Hartrat, in 785/6.

9 **membris incolomes:** 'safe in respect of their limbs', i.e. 'physically intact'.

exilio: 'to exile' (see G.16(a)).

10f. **qui...interempti sunt:** the structure is *qui*⌐ | *cum* *se*⌐*ne* *comprehenderentur*⌐*...defenderent*, (supply *et*) *aliquos...occidissent,* | ⌐*quia...poterant,* | ⌐*interempti sunt.*

10 **ne...:** 'in order not...'.

11 **aliquos etiam occidissent:** 'and had actually...' (a second part of the *cum* clause, the first verb of which is *defenderent*).

12 **Harum...coniurationum** depends on *causa et origo*.

Fastradae reginae: Fastrada was Charlemagne's third queen, daughter of the Frankish Count Rudolf. She died in 794.

13 **extitisse** = *exstitisse:* 'to have been'.

idcirco looks forward to *quia* 'for this rea-son...because...'.

in ambabus (sc. *coniurationibus*).

14 **conspiratum est:** lit. 'it was conspired', i.e. 'people conspired' (see *RLGVE* 155).

consentiens: '(sc. the king) falling in with...' (+ dat. *crudelitati*).

16 **ita** looks forward to *ut* 'so...that...' (i.e. 'with such...that...').

17 **ei:** 'against him'.

vel minima looks forward to *nota*.

iniustae crudelitatis nota: lit. 'sign/reproach of...', tr. 'charge of...'.

18 **fuisset obiecta:** 'was put forward' (see G.4(a)).

(b) The hexameter poem known as *Karolus Magnus et Leo Papa* is now thought to be the third book of an otherwise lost work composed in the very early 800s by a writer who may have been Einhard. It owes much to Virgil's *Aeneid*, which 'he set out to recall, to imitate – and to surpass' (Godman, *Poetry*, p.24). Here the poet uses the famous dream in *Aeneid* 2.271ff. (where the ghost of Hector appears to Aeneas) to shape his account of Charlemagne's protection of Pope Leo III. The pope was attacked in

Rome on 25 April 799 and fled to Charlemagne at Paderborn. The aid given by him to the pope was not unrelated to his coronation as Holy Roman Emperor in Rome on Christmas Day 800 (an event which surprised and annoyed him possibly because he saw the papal initiative as a bad precedent for the terms of the power relationship between empire and papacy: see further sections 12 and 19.3).

> Portentum rex triste videt monstrumque nefandum
> in somnis, summum Romanae adstare Leonem
> urbis pontificem mestosque effundere fletus,
> squalentes oculos, maculatum sanguine vultum,
> truncatam linguam horrendaque multa gerentem   330
> vulnera. Sollicitos gelidus pavor occupat artus
> Augusti. rapidos Romana ad moenia missos
> tres iubet ire, foret si sanus pastor opimus
> explorare gregis; quid tristia somnia signent
> miraturque; piam curam gerit ille fidelem.   335
> festinant rapidis legati passibus; ipse
> Saxoniam repetit cum multis milibus heros.
> agmina conveniunt diversis partibus orbis,
> cognataeque acies properant super ardua Rheni
> litora, Saxonum populum domitare rebellem   340
> et saevam gelido gentem rescindere ferro.
> culmina iam cernunt urbis procul ardua Romae
> optatumque vident legati a monte theatrum;
> tristior occurrit vulgataque fama repente,
> lumen apostolicum crudeli funere plagis   345
> occubuisse feris; nam serpens saevus et atrox,
> qui solet unanimes bello committere fratres,
> semina pestiferi iactare nocenda veneni,
> suasit in innocuum caecatis mentibus omnes
> saevire, et famulos dominum trucidare potentem.   350
> dira animis inlapsa lues et sensibus haesit;
> virus pestiferum concepit pectus anhelum.
> insidias posuere viro mortemque parabant
> insonti tristemque necem; plebs impia telis
> pastorem in proprium seseque armavit iniquis.   355
> dum solitum transisset iter Leo papa benignus,
> et sacra Laurenti peteret pede limina sancti,
> plebs demens populusque vĕcors, male sana iuventus,
> fustibus et gladiis, nudatis ensibus, omnis

inruit in summum pastorem turba tumultu,   360
caeca furens, subito diris commota procellis.
sacra sacerdotis torquebat membra flagellis,
unĭus in casum multorum saevit hiatus;
carnifices geminas traxerunt fronte fenestras,
et celerem abscidunt lacerato corpore linguam.   365
pontificem tantum sese extinxisse putabat
plebs pietate carens atrisque infecta venenis;
sed manus alma patrĭs oculis medicamina ademptis
obtulit atque novo reparavit lumine vultum.
ora peregrinos stupuerunt pallida visus,   370
explicat et celerem truncataque lingua loquellam.
cum sociis magnus paucis fugit inde sacerdos;
clam petere auxilium Spulitinam tendit ad urbem.

---

326 in somnis: cf. Virgil, *Aeneid* 2.270: *In somnis, ecce....*

326f. summum...fletus: '(namely) the chief priest (i.e. pope)...Leo...standing near and...' (the acc. + inf. clause is in apposition to *Portentum* and *monstrum*: note the classical periphrasis *summus pontifex* for ML *papa*).

328 mestosque effundere fletus: cf. *Aeneid* 2.271: *largosque effundere fletus* 'and pouring forth copious tears' (of the ghost of Hector).

329f. squalentes...vulnera: the accusatives all depend on *gerentem*, which agrees with *summum...Leonem...pontificem*; tr. 'with his eyes...'. The passage is closely based on *Aeneid* 2.276–7: *squalentem barbam et concreto sanguine crinis / uulneraque illa gerens...* 'with his beard filthy and his hair thick with blood and those wounds...' The poet believed (as also did Einhard) that the pope's eyes had been put out (see v. 364), so by *squalentes* he means 'gory', 'bloody'.

331 sollicitos looks towards *artus*, the two forming the object of *occupat*. The sentence recalls Lucan, *Bellum Ciuile* 1.246: *gelidus pauor adligat artus* 'cold panic bound their limbs', but the context of that remark is not relevant (the inhabitants of Ariminum see Caesar's army approaching after it has crossed the Rubicon).

332 Augusti: i.e. Charlemagne (but he was not crowned emperor until the next year, 800).

332–3 rapidos...missos...tres: 'three swift messengers'

(cf. *Aeneid* 7.153–4, where Aeneas sends 100 speakers to Latinus' city: *centum oratores...ad moenia regis / ire iubet* 'one hundred orators he orders to go to the king's city...').

333f. foret...gregis: '(and) to find out whether... was...' (see G.24(c)).

334f. quid...miraturque: 'and he wonders what...' (*-que* has been postponed along with the introductory verb).

335 fidelem: sc. 'and...' (second adjective with *curam*).

336 festinant...passibus: cf. *Aeneid* 7.156–7 (see note on vv. 332–3 above): *festinant iussi rapidisque feruntur passibus* 'those detailed hurried and were borne along by rapid steps'.

ipse looks forward to *heros* (another Virgilian borrowing: Aeneas is often called *heros*, and the implication that Charlemagne is the new Aeneas is clear).

337 Saxoniam: the protracted war with the Saxons began in 772 and did not end until 804.

338 diversis partibus: 'from...'.

339 cognataeque acies: the phrase is borrowed from Lucan's *Bellum Ciuile* (1.4), where it expresses the horror of Rome's Civil War (brother fights brother). That resonance is absent here: these are the various tribes of Francia joining to suppress the rebel Saxons (see Einhard's *Vita Karoli* 7 for justification of the war).

342 cernunt: subject *legati* in the next line. This line recalls *Aeneid* 7.160–1 *tecta Latinorum/ardua cernebant* 'they saw the high roofs of the Latini' (for the context, see note on vv. 332–3 above).

343 **optatum** looks forward to *theatrum* (metaphorical = Rome, where the drama is taking place).

344 **tristior:** sc. 'than they would wish to hear' (tr. 'rather grim'): it looks forward to *fama*.
occurrit: sc. 'them'.
vulgataque...repente: 'and (rumour) which has been noised abroad suddenly' (i.e. as soon as the event has occurred: the writer may expect his readers to recall Virgil's portrait of Fama in *Aeneid* 4.173f.).

345–6 **lumen...feris:** '(the rumour) that...'.
lumen apostolicum: i.e. the Pope.
crudeli funere...occubuisse: a variation on the CL *morte occumbere* 'to die'.

346–7 **serpens...qui...fratres:** the poet has adapted Virgil's fury Allecto, who incites Turnus to fight the Trojans of Aeneas at Juno's instigation, to the Christian picture of the Devil, who works evil of his own accord (cf. *Aeneid* 7.335 *tu potes unanimos armare in proelia fratres* 'You can arm brothers of one mind for battle (sc. against each other)': Allecto also has snakes about her person, ibid. 329).

347 **bello committere:** 'to join to war', i.e. to make fight with one another (cf. CL *bellum committere* 'to begin a war').

348 **semina...veneni:** sc. 'and...'(continuing the *qui* clause).
nocenda: 'harmful' (CL *nocens, nociuus, nociturus: noceo* takes dat. in CL and has no personal gerundive usages).
pestiferi...veneni: i.e. civil war or rioting.

349–50 **suasit...omnes...saevire et...trucidare:** 'persuaded everyone to...and to...' (*suadeo* usually takes dat. of person and *ut* + subj. in CL prose).

351 **dira** with *lues*: i.e. the devil's incitement to riot.
inlapsa: sc. *est.*

352 **virus pestiferum:** signifying the same as *dira lues* (and subject of *concepit*).
pectus anhelum: 'their breathless hearts' (the oddness of this expression is due to the fact that it is borrowed from *Aeneid* 6.48, where the physical signs of the Sibyl's inspiration are described – her chest actually is heaving.

The reminiscence images the devil's influence on him).

353 **posuere** = *posuerunt* (see RLRGr A4).

354f. **plebs impia...iniquis:** *telis* looks forward to *iniquis*; the *-que* on *seseque* is redundant (or postponed, if it links this to the preceding sentence) – ignore it in translation (the construction is *plebs...telis...in pastorem...sese... armavit*).

356 **dum...transisset** (= *transiret:* see G.9): 'while... was passing along' (see G.29).

357 **Laurenti...sancti:** i.e. the Church of St Laurence (built over the martyr's tomb, one of the seven principal churches of Rome and a favourite place for pilgrimages).

358f. **plebs...omnis...turba:** the relationship between all these nominatives is rather vague; best take *plebs...populusque* as subject, *iuventus* in apposition and tr. *omnis...turba* 'the whole mob' (embracing *plebs...populusque*).
male sana: 'hardly in their right minds' (another Virgilian reminiscence, this time of the love-crazed Dido in *Aeneid* 4.8).

361 **caeca furens:** 'in a blind madness' (lit. 'raging mad things').
diris...procellis: i.e. the storms of the Devil's inspiration.

362 **sacra** looks forward to *membra*.
torquebat: subject is the mob (*plebs...populusque ...turba*).

363 **in casum:** 'to promote the fall...' (in CL *saevire in* means 'rage against').

364 **geminas** looks forward to *fenestras* (i.e. his eyes).
fronte: 'from...'.

365 **celerem** looks forward to *linguam*.

366 **pontificem...plebs:** 'so great a...did the people...think it had...'.

367 **atris...venenis:** i.e. the Devil's inspiration.

368 **patris:** i.e. God.
oculis...ademptis: (dat. after *medicamina*) 'medicine for...'.

369 **novo...lumine:** s. for pl..

370 **ora...pallida:** sc. of the mob, who thought he had been blinded.
peregrinos looks forward to *visus*: 'foreign eyesight' because it has been restored miraculously by God.

371 **explicat et:** *et* is postponed – 'and (his tongue) unfolded...'.

truncataque: if -*que* means anything, it should
be translated 'even though...'.

373 petere auxilium: 'to...' (purpose: see G.17(a)).

Spulitanam...ad urbem: i.e. Spoleto (in Um-
bria).

5. John Scottus Eriugena (d. *c*.877–9)

The *peregrinatio* of the Irish to the continent is a feature of the ninth
century, as well as of the eighth and earlier centuries (see section 6 Intro.).
John Scottus ('the Irishman'), who calls himself Eriugena ('born in Ireland'),
must have been for some years away from home when he first appears in
the record, debating on predestination with Gottschalk of Orbais around
851. At that time he was working at the court of Charles the Bald.
Unusually for a northern European before the sixteenth century, he was a
notable Greek scholar, and his translations of Pseudo-Dionysius and others
were highly influential. This direct access to Greek patristic and philosophical thought inspired him to create his own theological synthesis, the
Periphyseon ('On the division of nature'). His poems also show strong marks
of Greek learning, both in language and content.

This extract comes from John's earliest work, *De praedestinatione*, written
at the request of Archbishop Hincmar of Rheims and Bishop Pardulus of
Laon against the monk Gotescalc (Gottschalk) of Orbais. The issue is
'double predestination', that is the idea that mankind is divided into good
and bad, and that the good are predestined to gain eternal life, the bad
hell-fire. John uses Aristotelian dialectic, rhetoric and a large dash of St
Augustine in his tart refutation of a doctrine he claims is heretical. The
tone may be gathered from his appropriation in the prologue of a Greek
word from Augustine to describe his opponent – *saprophilus* 'a lover of
deformity'. Here John argues that *voluntas* is central to God's being and
cannot coexist with *necessitas*, without which Gottschalk's notion of
praedestinatio cannot stand.

See further: D. Moran, *The Philosophy of John Scottus Eriugena: A Study of
Idealism in the Middle Ages*, Cambridge, 1989.

ARGVMENTO NECESSITATIS COLLIGITVR DVAS
PRAEDESTINATIONES FIERI NON POSSE.

Vbi sunt ergo, Gotescalce, duarum praedestinationum tuarum necessitudines?
Tuarum dico, non diuinarum; tua etenim eas peruersitas finxit, et ideo non
sunt nec fieri possunt. Quomodo enim potest esse quod conatur auferre quod
est? Vbi autem est necessitas, ibi non est uoluntas; atqui in deo est uoluntas; in
eo igitur non est necessitas. Deus quidem omnia quae fecit sua propria   5

uoluntate nulla uero necessitate fecit. Quid enim cogeret deum ut aliquid faceret? Quod si aliqua eum causa compelleret ad faciendum, ea merito maior meliorque eo crederetur; ac per hoc ipsa, non ipse, summa omnium causa deusque coleretur. Si uero una et principalis totius uniuersitatis causa uoluntas dei et pie creditur et recte intelligitur, frustra in ipsa uel ante ipsam necessitas   10 fingitur.

Age iam; si omne quod in deo est deus est, uoluntas autem dei in deo est, deus est igitur dei uoluntas. Non enim aliud est ei esse et uelle; sed quod est ei esse, hoc est et uelle.

Proinde si uoluntas dei libera est – aliter enim credere impium est – libera   15 uero uoluntas omni caret necessitate, igitur nulla necessitas uoluntatem dei possidet; atqui quicquid de diuina uoluntate sane intelligitur, de eius quoque praedestinatione necesse est similiter intelligatur; expulsa est autem omnis necessitas a diuina uoluntate; igitur expulsa est et ab eius praedestinatione.

Title **ARGVMENTO NECESSITATIS**: 'from the evidence of...'.

COLLIGITVR: 'it is deduced'.

1 **necessitudines**: 'grounds of necessity (for)...'.

2 **tua**: note the emphasis 'it is your (*peruersitas*) that...'.

3f. **esse...est**: in both cases the verb means 'exist', as it does also throughout the next sentence.

4 **atqui**: 'and yet.'

5f. **sua...uoluntate nulla...necessitate**: 'from...' (abl. of cause: see RLRGr L(f)4(iii)).

6 **Quid...cogeret**: 'what could have forced...?' (potential subj.: see *RLGVE* 153.2).

7 **Quod si...compelleret**: 'But if...had compelled...', or 'But if...were to compel...'.

8 **eo**: 'than Him' (i.e. God).

ipsa, non ipse: 'it...not He...' (for *ipse*, see G.11(a)(ii)).

9f. **uoluntas dei...creditur et intelligitur**: 'is believed and understood (sc. to be) the will of God'.

10 **in ipsa...ante ipsam**: 'it', i.e. the will of God (see G.11(a)(ii) for *ipse*). The argument is taken from St Augustine: 'Why did God wish to make the world? He who enquires why God wished to make the world is asking the cause of God's will. But every cause is an efficient cause. But everything which effects is greater than what is effected. But nothing is greater than the will of God. So its cause is not a matter for investigation' (*De diuersis quaestioni-*

bus 83, q. 28); 'The Manichees enquire into the causes of God's will, though God's will is itself the cause of everything which exists. For if God's will has a cause, there is something which precedes the will of God, which it is heretical to believe. When someone asks why God made the world, the proper response is "because he willed it". For God's will is the cause of heaven and earth, and so is greater than heaven and earth. When someone asks why he made the heaven and the earth, he is seeking something greater than God's will. Yet nothing greater can be found' (*De Genesi contra Manichaeos* I.2.4).

12f. **si...uoluntas**: all examples of *est* in this sentence mean 'is'.

13 **aliud**: 'one thing (sc. being) and another (will)'

esse et uelle: 'being and willing', 'existence and will' (nouns). The ideas are again Augustinian: 'Whatever can be understood in him (God) is substance' (*De fide et symbolo* 9.20); 'so God is called "single" because he is what he possesses' (*De ciuitate Dei* XI.10.1 = section 4.1(b)). Compare Alcuin: *Nec deo aliud est esse, aliud uelle, sed unum atque idem* 'Nor for God is being one thing and will another, but they are one and the same thing' (*De fide sanctae et indiuiduae trinitatis* II.13).

15 **Proinde**: 'likewise' (the argument moves on to another consideration).

15f. **si...uero...igitur**: note the progression of the

arguments from proposition (premiss), through necessary inference (*uero*), to conclusion (*igitur*). This structure is a syllogism.

17 **atqui:** 'and yet': the argument has yet to make the connection between will and predestination. To refute the premiss of Gottschalk's case the argument proceeds as the one before.

18 **necesse est...intelligatur:** 'must be understood' (for *uelle* + subj. see *RLGVE* p. 426 Notes on ll. 57–8). This argument is also traditional, appearing in Florus and Prudentius.

Section 10
The Ottonian Renaissance

The death of Charles the Bald in 877 signalled the final break-up of the
Carolingian Empire, which had been fragmented in 843 by division among
Charlemagne's grandsons and temporarily reunited in 875. The main heirs
were the kingdoms of France, Italy and Germany. But it was to Saxon
Germany that the major political and missionary developments of the tenth
century were due. Under Otto I ('The Great': reigned 936–73) Italy was
annexed (951–61), the Empire re-established (Otto was crowned Emperor
in 962), and Poland and Hungary prepared for integration into Western
Christendom. Under Otto III (980–1002) and his teacher Gerbert of
Aurillac (Pope Sylvester II, 999–1003), the latter task was completed. In
1000 the see of Gniezno in Poland was established, and that of Esztergom
in Hungary in 1001 Otto III undertook in 998 a *renovatio imperii
Romanorum*, 'renewal of the Roman Empire', an attempt to set up a
permanent imperial government in Rome.

In the later ninth and early tenth centuries, the Viking depredations
caused havoc in West Francia (Paris was besieged in 885–6) and the British
Isles. But by the end of the tenth century, the Norsemen had been pushed
to the periphery in Britain and temporarily contained in Francia by the
concession of Normandy (911). Moreover, Scandinavia began to accept
Catholic Christianity (and Latin) from around 960 onwards. The efforts of
King Alfred (848–903) in England were not just military, but intellectual
also. It was he who created propitious circumstances for the educational
work of St Dunstan (*c.*924–88), abbot of Glastonbury, Ethelwald (*c.*908–
84), bishop of Worcester, and later of Aelfric (*c.*955– *c.*1030), abbot of
Eynsham (see section 1 Intro. for an extract from his *Colloquies*).

In the continental literature of the first part of this period, the figure of
Charlemagne and the output of the first generation of Carolingian writers
were still potent influences. The anonymous Saxon poet who wrote an
account of Charlemagne's deeds between 888 and 891 amply demonstrates
the first point, when he visualizes Charlemagne on the Day of Judgement

as the apostle of the Saxons (whom he had in fact converted by force). The second is illustrated by the epic poem of Abbo of St Germain on the siege of Paris, which stands directly in the line of political historical writing begun two generations before by the writer of *Karolus Magnus et Leo Papa* (see section 9.4(b)) and continued by Ermoldus Nigellus in the reign of Louis the Pious.

The reinvigorated intellectual climate in Germany during the period of the three Ottos (936–1002) has given the period the name 'the Ottonian Renaissance'. The achievement of Otto the Great in unifying a loose confederation into an imperial state owed much to his alliance with the German bishops. These in turn used their new-found prestige and wealth to foster learning in the monasteries of the empire. A good example is Bruno, archbishop of Cologne (925–65), brother of Otto I, who gave extensive patronage to the Benedictine abbey of Gandersheim, where the nun Hrotsvitha wrote the first medieval dramas. The emperor Otto III was himself involved in literary activity, taking part, for example, in the composition of a poetic life of his martyred friend Bishop Adalbert of Prague.

It is generally admitted that this 'Renaissance' produced no writers as distinguished as those of the Carolingian period. Nonetheless, it has also been pointed out that the tenth century was the seedbed of a great religious movement which would later spawn distinguished literature. For 910 saw the foundation of Cluny, and here and at Monte Cassino the timid beginnings of the monastic reform movement. And in the accelerating literacy of the Italian laity are disclosed 'the germs of a greater renaissance than the efforts of any isolated scholar or artist could possibly promote' (R. S. Lopez, 'Still another Renaissance?', *American Historical Review*, 57 (1951), p. 19).

1. Abbo of St Germain (d. after 921)

1. Abbo, a Neustrian (that is from the territory between the Seine and Loire) was educated at St Germain-des-Prés in Paris. His hexameter epic *De bellis Parisiacae urbis* ('On the battles for the city of Paris') was composed with a West Frankish perspective during the reign of King Odo (882–98). It is written in the so-called 'hermeneutic' style, a Latin which is involved and uses obscure vocabulary, often Greek in origin (compare Aldhelm in section 7.1(a)).

(i) *The Normans attack: the help of St Geneviève.*

denique, cum medius Titane incenditur orbis
cumque sitit tellus pecorique libet magis umbra,
sibilat et gratus silvas zephyrus per amenas,
Pergama loetiferis stipantur ab hostibus urbis,   230
quae passim patiebatur certamen; et unum
bellabant muri, speculae, pontes quoque cuncti,
pugnabat pelagus, contra tellus magis ampla.
classica valdĕ tonant, mensis discedere cives;
'eûs!' clamant litui 'convivia temnite cuncti!'   235
urbs terrore, simul cives, invaditur omnis;
nullus in urbe locus fuerat, qui bella lateret.
pila falas lacereque tegunt nimium catapulte,
arva velut pluvie, plumbi necnon onerosi
poma dabant peltis gemitus et grandia saxa.   240
haec nobis illi tribuebant premia semper;
at contra lapides rapidos pariterque balistas
direxere feris nostri celeresque sagittas.
his aër seritūr hinc inde volantibus amplum;
non inter caelos aliud tranabat et arva;   245
Mars magis atque magis regnat tumidusque superbit.
Virgo dei Genovefa caput defertur ad urbis,
quo stātim meritis eius nostri superarunt;
inde fugaverunt etiam pinnis procul illos.

227 **cum...orbis:** lit. 'when the middle circle (sc. of the day) is lit', i.e. at midday (*medius orbis = meridies*).
    Titane: 'by the sun' (the first two lines are a variation on Virgil, *Georgics* 4.401–2: *medios cum sol accenderit aestus / cum sitiunt herbae et pecori iam gratior umbra est* 'when the sun has kindled its middle heat and when the grass is thirsty and to the herd the shade is now more pleasing').
229 **sibilat et:** 'and (the...zephyr) whistles' (postponed *et*: we are still in the *cum* clause).
230 **Pergama...urbis:** 'the citadel' (Pergama was originally the citadel of Troy, as often in the *Aeneid*).
    loetiferis looks forward to *hostibus.*
231 **quae:** antecedent *urbis.*
    unum: 'as one', 'all together'.
233 **pelagus:** lit. 'the sea', but it means the River Seine.

contra: 'but'.
    magis: 'more' (with *pugnabat*, not with *ampla*, which goes with *tellus*).
234 **mensis:** 'from their...' (i.e. midday meals).
    discedere: 'departed' (historic inf.: RLRGr M(d)).
235 **eus** = *heus* (see O.3(c)).
236 **urbs** looks forward to *omnis.*
    terrore: 'by...'.
    simul cives: sc. *invaduntur terrore.*
237 **fuerat:** 'was' (see G.9(c)).
    qui...lateret: 'which was hidden from...' (generic subj., see RLRGr Q2(a)).
    bella: pl. for s. (or, as in his title, 'battles').
238f. **pila...saxa:** the enemy's actions are being described.
238 **falas:** usually the protective structure used by an enemy attacking a city, but here the towers along the wall.

lacere (= *lacerae*: see O.1)...**catapulte** (= *cata-pultae*: see O.1): 'wounding missiles' (from catapults).

239 **arva...pluvie** (= *pluviae*: see O.1): 'just as showers (sc. *tegunt*) the fields' (they are probably snow-showers).

239f. **plumbi...onerosi/poma:** 'balls of heavy lead' (CL *pomum* = 'fruit': *grandia saxa* is also a subject of *dabant*).

dabant peltis gemitus: lit. 'gave groans to the shields', i.e. 'made our shields resound when they hit them'.

243 **feris:** 'against the wild men' (i.e. the enemy).

244 **his:** 'with these...' (i.e. missiles).

amplum: 'a lot' (CL *ampliter, ample*): but it might be a n. adj. attached to *aer* by false analogy with

the plural *aera*, for which see v.261 below).

245 **inter caelos...et arva:** 'between heaven and earth'.

246 **Mars:** i.e. War.

247 **Virgo...Genovefa:** St Geneviève (*c.*422–*c.*500), patroness of Paris. In 451 when Attila's troops were near Paris she is reputed to have urged the Parisians not to leave the city. The invading army left Paris alone. It was frequently claimed that she protected Paris after her death.

caput...ad urbis: 'to the top of the city' (to protect the defenders).

248 **quo:** sc. *facto* (or it might mean 'in which place', sc. *loco*).

meritis: 'by...'.

249 **pinnis procul:** 'far from our turrets'.

(ii) *The desperation of the people in the city.*

partibus ex aliis longe surgunt ăcriora
prelia; plangores clipeique cient galeeque   255
stridores; nostri bellant, sed fortius illi;
defecere fatigati bello quoque dextri.
pro dolor! alta nimis flentes lamenta trahebant:
cana senecta gemit multum florensque iuventa;
plorabant monachi, lacrimatur clericus omnis,   260
aëra voce tonant, luctus sed et ethra facessit.
hi tristes animos urbem metuendŏ revelant
hoste capi; caelo laeti torquere cachinnos
moenia vocisonos rentes lucrare severi.
femineusque iubas sexus lugens lacerando   265
verrebat terras proprio de crine soluto.
eheu! nuda suis quatiebant pectora pugnis
un-que-gulis facies secuerunt, tristia ac ora.
voce rogant lacrimosa omnes: 'Germane beate,
auxiliare tuis; alioquin nunc moriemur!   270
o pie, nunc succurre citus, succurre! perimus.'
Germanum reboat tellus, necnon fluviusque.
littora et omne nemus pariter circum resonabat:
'o Germane sacer, nobis miserere, rogamus!'
templorum campana boant merentia, clamant   275
vocibus his et humus tremuit flumenque remugit;
urbs extrema verens instantis carpere lucis
omnia lamentis lacrimans spargebat amaris.

254 **longe...acriora:** 'far more fierce...'.

255 **plangores clipeique cient:** 'the shields cause clangings' (*-que* is redundant; *plangor* usually in CL refers to the sound of lamentation).

galee = *galeae* (see O.1).

257 **bello quoque dextri:** 'even those skilled in war' (*bello* is abl. of respect with *dextri*).

258 **pro dolor:** 'Alas the grief!'.

nimis: probably take with *alta* 'very deep...' (see G.12(b)).

lamenta trahebant: 'they (i.e. the defenders, the ordinary citizens of Paris) lengthened out laments', i.e. they lamented constantly.

259 **multum:** 'much' (adv. with *gemit*).

261 **aëra...tonant:** 'the heavens thunder...' (*aër* is m. in CL and uses Greek forms: but in LL it is sometimes used as a n. – cf. v. 244 – here it is probably n.pl. subject though it is impossible to be quite certain, since *tono* is also used transitively in LL, and the phrase might mean 'they (i.e. the people) make the air thunder...': see G.2).

sed et: 'but also...' (postponed: the contrast suggests that *voce* is the noise of battle).

ethra = *aethera* (see O.1 and O.9) 'the sky' (acc., Greek form: see RLRGr H6).

facessit: 'departs' (*ethra* must be taken as acc. of place: 'to the sky'; an alternative is to construe *facessit* as something like 'fills').

262f. **hi...severi:** 'These (i.e. the citizens of Paris)...the harsh ones (i.e. the attacking Norsemen)'.

262 **tristes animos** is the object of *revelant*.

262f. **urbem metuendo...hoste capi:** 'fearing that the city would be...' (see G.18).

263f. **caelo laeti torquere cachinnos...vocisonos ...severi:** 'to the heaven happily did the enemy turn their vociferous cackles' (for *caelo* see G.16(a); *torquere* is historic inf., see RLRGr M(d)).

264 **moenia...rentes lucrare:** 'thinking that they

would capture the walls' (*rentes* is pres. part. of *reor*, CL *lucrari*, see G.3).

265 **femineus** looks forward to *sexus*.

iubas is the object of *lacerando*: tr. 'and tearing...' (perhaps dependent on *lugens* 'mourning by tearing...').

266 **proprio de crine soluto:** 'with...' (see G.15(a)(ii)).

267 **nuda** looks forward to *pectora* (obj. of *quatiebant*: the subject is 'the women').

suis looks forward to *pugnis*.

267f. **quatiebant...secuerunt:** translate both verbs as '...were...ing' or '...ed' (cf. G.9(a)).

268 **un-que-gulis:** 'and with their claws' (tmesis, 'cutting', rare in Latin poetry, normally splits a compound word; but this type of tmesis is a feature of Abbo's 'learned' style).

tristia ac ora: 'and their...' (second obj. of *secuerunt*; *ac* is postponed).

269 **lacrimosa:** abl. f.s. with *voce*.

Germane: St Germain (*c*.496–576), bishop of Paris from 555 and founder of St Germain-des-Prés.

272 **Germanum:** i.e. 'the name "Germanus"'.

fluviusque: *-que* is redundant (unless it means 'also').

273 **resonabat:** s. with the nearer subject (*nemus*), but *littora* is also its subject.

275 **campana:** 'the bells' (in LL the noun is f., here n.pl.: see G.2).

merentia: 'mournfully'.

276 **vocibus his:** 'with this message' (i.e. v. 274).

277 **urbs...lucis:** 'the city fearing that it was enjoying the last parts of the present light (i.e. life)', i.e. fearing that this was the city's last day: as at v. 264, the Greek construction nom. + inf. is used, as sometimes in CL poetry).

278 **omnia:** obj. of *spargebat*.

lamentis is completed by *amaris* 'with...'.

2. Notker Balbulus ('The Stammerer': *c*.840–912)

Notker was a monk in the Benedictine abbey of St Gall, from 870 in East Francia. In his prose work *Gesta Karoli* ('The deeds of Charlemagne'), inspired by the visit of Charles III ('the Fat') to St Gall, the image of Charlemagne is already the popular one of the strong but pious king who stands as an example to the world. Notker's main claim to fame, however, is his contribution to the new form of hymn, the sequence. This was a chant which followed the Allelluia of the Mass (see section 2 Intro.). In the preface to his collection (the *Liber Ymnorum*), compiled *c.*880, he tells the story of a monk who arrived at the abbey, fleeing from the Viking sack of the monastery of Jumièges in West Francia. He had with him his antiphonary, which contained some *versus* and *sequentiae*. Notker liked the idea, but hated the texts. He began to compose his own.

The sequence probably originated in West Francia around 830. By the time Notker began to write, *c.*860, the form had probably developed into the sophisticated combination of melisma (*sequentia*) and text (*prosa*) which we see in his work. There are two main features of these *prosae*: (1) correspondence between syllable and note, (2) repetition (the text is constructed in pairs of blocks, with the same melody for each pair: aa bb cc, etc.). The sequence had developed by the eleventh century into regular rhymed verse (cf. *Stabat mater*), and it remained an integral element in the liturgy until it was almost completely removed by the Council of Trent (1545–63).

See further: P. Dronke, 'The beginnings of the sequence', in *The Medieval Poet and his World*, Rome, 1984, pp. 115–44.

This day celebrates the martyrs, whose contempt for the world has earned them a place with God, whence they lend support to Christ's flock. Intercede for us with Him.

IN NATALE MARTYRUM

VOX EXULTATIONIS

A Agone triumphali
militum regis summi
Dies iste celebris
est populis
ipsi regi credulis.

1	Hi delectamentum respuerant mundanorum	Et crucem tunc turpem cottidie baiolarunt.	2
3	Hos nullius feritas a Christo separat,	Quin ad eum mortibus millenis properent.	4
5	Non carcer ullus aut catena molliunt fortia in Christo pectora:	Sed nec ferarum morsus diri martyrum solidum excavant animum.	6
7	Non imminens capiti gladius territat	Fortissimos milites optimi domini.	8

9 Nunc manu dei   Et plebi Christi   10
  complexi persequentum   solamen suppeditant
  insultant furoribus   in cunctis laboribus
  quondam crudelibus   lubrici saeculi.

11 Vos Christi martyres   Nos valde fragiles   12

Z precibus nos iusto iudici
  sinceris iugiter
  commendare curate.

Title **IN NATALE MARTYRUM:** 'on the anniversary (birthday into heaven) of martyrs' (*natale* =
natali: see G.7(a), or is acc., in which case tr.
'for...').
VOX EXULTATIONIS: this is the name of
the melisma or tune to which the *prosa* is set
(Notker wrote another *prosa* for this tune).
A **Agone triumphali:** 'because of...'.
iste: 'this' (see G.11(c)).
celebris = *celeber* (f. for m.) 'famous'.
ipsi regi credulis: 'who believe in the ...' (for
ipse see G.11(a)(i)).
1 **respuerant:** possibly simple past (see G.9(c)).
2 **baiolarunt** = *baiulauerunt* (see O.12 and RLR.Gr
A4).
4 **Quin...properent:** 'so that they don't...'.

5 **fortia in Christo:** 'which are strong in Christ'
(with *pectora*).
6 **solidum excavant animum:** lit. 'hollow out
the solid intent...' (i.e. undermine).
7 **capiti** with *imminens*: 'hanging over...'.
9 **complexi:** 'embraced' (see RLR.Gr C4 Note 2).
persequentum ('of those who persecute
(them)') depends on *furoribus...crudelibus*
(which is dat. obj. of *insultant* 'mock').
10 **lubrici saeculi:** 'of (this) dangerous world'.
11f. **Vos...Nos:** sc. *estis, sumus*.
12 **valde fragiles:** 'very weak' (see G.12(b)).
Z **precibus...sinceris:** 'by...'.
nos: obj. of *commendare*.
curate: 'take the trouble to...', i.e. 'please!'.

3. Widukind of Corvey (d. after 973)

Nothing is known of Widukind except that he was Saxon and a monk at
Corvey, the oldest monastery of Saxony (established in 822). He perhaps
entered the cloister in the later part of the abbacy of Folcmar (917–42). His
three books of *Res gestae Saxonicae* deal with the origins of the race, the
deeds of Henry I ('The Fowler'), duke of Saxony and later king (919–36),
and the deeds of Otto I (reigned 936–73). They were dedicated to Matilda,
daughter of Otto, a nun in the abbey of Quedlinburg.

Otto I is crowned king at Aachen, 7 or 8 August 936.

Defuncto itaque patre patriae et regum maximo optimo Heinrico omnis
populus Francorum atque Saxonum iam olim designatum regem a patre,
filium eius Oddonem elegit sibi in principem. Universalisque electionis
notantes locum iusserunt esse ad Aquasgrani palatii. Est autem locus ille

proximus Iulo, a conditore Iulio Caesare cognominato. Cumque illo ventum   5
esset, duces ac prefectorum principes cum caetera principum militum manu
congregati in sixto basilicae Magni Karoli cohaerenti collocarunt novum
ducem in solio ibidem constructo, manus ei dantes ac fidem pollicentes
operamque suam contra omnes inimicos spondentes, more suo fecerunt
eum regem. Dum ea geruntur a ducibus ac caetero magistratu, pontifex   10
maximus cum universo sacerdotali ordine et omni plebe infra in basilica
prestolabatur processionem novi regis. Quo procedente pontifex obvius laeva
sua dexteram tangit regis, suaque dextera lituum gestans, linea indutus, stola
planetaque infulatus, progressusque in medium usque fani subsistit; et reversus
ad populum, qui circumstabat – nam erant deambulatoria infra supraque in illa   15
basilica in rotundum facta –, quo ab omni populo cerni posset: 'En,' inquit,
'adduco vobis a Deo electum et a domino rerum Heinrico olim designatum,
nunc vero a cunctis principibus regem factum Oddonem; si vobis ista electio
placeat, dextris in caelum levatis significate.' Ad haec omnis populus dextras in
excelsum levans cum clamore valido inprecati sunt prospera novo duci.   20
Proinde procedit pontifex cum rege tunica stricta more Francorum induto
pone altare, super quod insignia regalia posita erant, gladius cum balteo, clamis
cum armillis, baculus cum sceptro ac diadema. Eo quippe tempore erat summus
pontifex nomine Hildiberhtus, Franco genere, monachus professione, nutritus
vel doctus in Vuldo monasterio, et ad id honoris merito progrediens, ut pater   25
eiusdem loci constitueretur, deinde summi pontificatus Mogontiacae sedis
fastigium promeruisset. Hic erat vir mirae sanctitatis et preter naturalem animi
sapientiam litterarum studiis satis clarus. Qui inter caetera gratiarum dona
spiritum prophetiae accepisse predicatur. Et cum quaestio esset pontificum in
consecrando rege, Treverensis videlicet et Coloniae Agrippinae – illius, quia   30
antiquior sedes esset et tamquam a beato Petro apostolo fundata; istius vero,
quia eius ad diocesim pertineret locus: et ob id sibi convenire arbitrati sunt
huius consecrationis honorem – cessit tamen uterque eorum Hildiberhti
cunctis notae almitati. Ipse autem accedens ad altare et sumpto inde gladio
cum balteo, conversus ad regem ait: 'Accipe,' inquit, 'hunc gladium, quo eicias   35
omnes Christi adversarios, barbaros et malos Christianos, auctoritate divina tibi
tradita omni potestate totius imperii Francorum, ad firmissimam pacem
omnium Christianorum.' Deinde sumptis armillis ac clamide induit eum:
'His cornibus', inquit, 'humitenus demissis monearis, quo zelo fidei ferveas,
et in pace tuenda perdurare usque in finem debere.' Exinde sumpto sceptro   40
baculoque: 'His signis,' inquit, 'monitus paterna castigatione subiectos corripias, primumque Dei ministris, viduis ac pupillis manum misericordiae
porrigas; numquamque de capite tuo oleum miserationis deficiat, ut in
presenti et in futuro sempiterno premio coroneris.' Perfususque ilico oleo
sancto et coronatus diademate aureo ab ipsis pontificibus Hildiberhto et   45

Wichfrido, ac omni legitima consecratione completa, ab eisdem pontificibus ducitur ad solium, ad quod per cocleas adscendebatur, et erat inter duas marmoreas mirae pulchritudinis columpnas constructum, unde ipse omnes videre et ab omnibus ipse videri posset.

Divina deinde laude dicta sacrificioque sollempniter celebrato descendebat   50
rex ad palatium, et accedens ad mensam marmoream regio apparatu ornatam resedit cum pontificibus et omni populo; duces vero ministrabant.

1 **Defuncto...Heinrico:** abl. abs. (the date is 936).

2 **iam...patre:** this phrase goes with *filium eius Oddonem* ('Otto'), obj. of *elegit*.

3f. **Universalis...palatii:** the sentence is not very clear. Perhaps 'The officials (*notantes*) ordered the place of the universal election to be at (the site) of the palace of Aachen'.

5 **Iulo:** *Iulus* = Jülich.

   a conditore: 'after...' (depending on *cognominato*: the derivation is bogus, but reflects a desire to connect the ancient Roman Empire with the Holy Roman Empire of Charlemagne, whose capital was at Aachen).

   illo: 'thither'.

6 **duces:** 'dukes' (the peers of the duke of Saxony whom they are about to crown king).

   prefectorum principes: lit. 'leaders of the prefects'; but in Germany *praefecti* are counts (elsewhere *comites*).

   cum caetera principum militum manu: 'with the rest of the group of military leaders'.

7 **in sixto:** phonetic confusion for *in xysto* 'in the colonnade/cloisters'.

   cohaerenti agrees with *sixto* and governs *basilicae*.

   basilicae Magni Karoli: the basilica of the Virgin Mary, built by Charlemagne at Aachen.

7f **novum ducem:** 'the new duke', sc. of Saxony.

8f. **dantes...pollicentes...spondentes:** 'by...ing' (see G.20(a). This ceremony marks the duke's new position at the head of the feudal hierarchy.

10f. **pontifex maximus:** 'archbishop' (on this occasion Hildebert, archbishop of Mainz from 927 to 937).

12 **Quo procedente...regis:** 'as he (the king)...' (note the lack of concord).

   obvius: 'coming to meet him'.

13 **lituum gestans:** 'holding the bishop's crozier'

(the *-que* on *suaque* is redundant: the sentence is rather loosely constructed, but is clear enough: all these participles, *gestans, indutus, infulatus*, and then *progressus* and *reversus* describe Hildebert).

   linea: 'in a linen garment'.

14f. **stola planetaque infulatus:** 'adorned with the stole and chasuble'.

14 **in medium** with *fani*.

16 **in rotundum facta:** 'made into a circle' (with *deambulatoria*). The basilica was an octagonal building, based on the design of S. Vitale in Ravenna, which has an open gallery on the second floor.

   quo...posset: 'from where he could...' (purpose clause).

17 **electum:** sc. 'the person (chosen)'.

18 **ista:** 'this' (see G.11(c)).

19 **placeat:** for *placet* (see G.28(c)).

   dextris...levatis: 'by raising...'.

20 **inprecati:** the verb is plural by sense with the grammatically singular *populus*.

   prospera: 'prosperity'.

21 **cum rege** looks forward to *induto*, which governs *tunica stricta* ('in...').

23 **diadema:** abl. (as though 1f., but the usual CL form is *diadema, diadematis* n.: see G.2).

25 **vel:** 'and'.

   in Vuldo monasterio: 'in the monastery of Fulda' (Vuldo is in apposition to *monasterio*; cf. *urbs Roma*).

   ad id...ut: 'to such a pitch of... that...'.

   pater: i.e. abbot (of Fulda).

26f. **summi...fastigium:** *summi pontificatus* ('archbishopric') depends on *fastigium*, and *Mogontiacae sedis* (= 'the see of Mainz') upon *summi pontificatus*.

28 **satis clarus:** 'very distinguished' (see G.12(b)).

   gratiarum: 'of divine grace'.

29 **predicatur:** 'is reported'.

29f. **cum quaestio...rege:** 'though there was a debate between the bishops on the matter of...', i.e. as to which one should preside at the coronation.

30 **Treverensis:** 'of Trier' (Rotbert, brother of Queen Matilda, bishop 931–56).

Coloniae Agrippinae: 'of Cologne' (but Wich-frid, archbishop of Cologne 924–53, is mentioned as a participant below).

30f. **illius...istius:** 'the former...the latter...' (the genitives are in apposition to *pontificum*).

32 **sibi convenire:** 'that...was fitting for them...' (i.e. that they should have the honour).

32f. **Hildeberhti...almitati:** 'to the kindness of Hildebert, known to all', i.e. 'to Hildebert, known to everyone for his kindness'.

34 **Ipse:** 'he', i.e. Hildebert (see G.11(a)(ii)).

35 **quo eicias:** 'with which to...' (purpose) or 'with which you must...' (jussive).

36f. **auctoritate...potestate:** *tradita...potestate* is abl. abs. 'now that...', and *auctoritate divina* means '(*tibi tradita*) by...'.

39 **His cornibus:** the *armillae* were made in the form of horns, pointing to the ground, symbolizing the king's humility.

monearis: 'be warned' (jussive subj., *RLGVE* 152).

quo...ferveas: 'with what zeal for the faith you are to boil' (jussive subjunctive, *RLGVE* 152).

40 **et...debere:** 'and (sc. be warned) that you must...' (see G.17(b)).

41 **His signis** goes with *monitus* ('by...').

paterna castigatione depends on *subiectos* ('those subjected by...').

41f. **corripias...porrigas:** 'you must...and must...' (jussive subjunctives: *RLGVE* 152).

43 **oleum miserationis:** 'the oil of compassion' (cf. *oleum exultationis* 'the oil of exultation' in Vlg. Hebrews 1.9).

44 **sempiterno premio:** 'with...' (after *coroneris*: the prize is eternal life).

45f. **ab...Wichfrido:** the ceremony was performed by Archbishop Hildebert of Mainz and Archbishop Wichfrid of Cologne.

46 **omni...completa:** 'when...' (abl. abs.).

47 **solium:** this time in the basilica (the feudal ceremony with the dukes etc. took place in the nearby colonnade or cloister).

per cocleas; 'by a spiral staircase' (lit. 'by snails'; cf. modern It. *chiocciola* 'snail' and 'spiral staircase').

adscendebatur: 'one climbed' (impersonal passive).

47f. **erat** looks forward to *constructum* (subject *solium*), and **marmoreas** to *columpnas*.

50 **Divina...celebrato:** 'when...' (two abl. abs.).

51 **accedens:** 'having...' (see G.20(a)).

ad...ornatam is one phrase (*regio apparatu* depends on *ornatam*).

4. Hrotsvitha of Gandersheim (*c.*935–*c.*1001/3)

Hrotsvitha was a nun in the Saxon abbey of Gandersheim, established by Duke Liudolf of Saxony in 852. She was of noble birth and entered the monastery around 855, shortly before the arrival of Gerberga II (a niece of Bruno of Cologne: see section 10 Intro.) as abbess (*c.*959). Hrotsvitha's early education was directed by the nun Rikkardis, but she owed to the younger but more knowledgeable Gerberga an acquaintance with authors encountered by the abbess before her arrival at Gandersheim. Hrotsvitha's reading in both pagan and Christian writers was wide. She certainly knew Virgil's *Aeneid* and *Eclogues*, Ovid's *Metamorphoses* and the comedies of Terence, and modelled herself on Prudentius. Her works are in three books, two of which are dedicated to Gerberga. The first contains eight sacred legends in leonine hexameters (i.e. with internal rhyme between the words at the strong caesura and the end) and elegiacs, the second six dramas and a poem, the third two historical poems in hexameters on the reign of Otto I and the foundation of the abbey of Gandersheim. The quality of Hrotsvitha's Latin underlines once more the strength of the Saxon tradition of women's education in the monasteries (see section 7.4).

These excerpts come from the second, and most innovative, of Hrotsvitha's books. In this she attempts to undermine the argument usually put forward for reading the lascivious dramas of Terence, namely that though his subject matter is harmful, his style is delightful. Her intention, she tells her readers in the preface, is to use Terentian style and form to celebrate the deeds of the holy virgins. She does not use strict metre, but articulates the dialogue by constant use of rhymed (leonine – see above) prose. There is no evidence that her plays were performed, and for that reason they stand rather outside the development of the medieval theatre, both liturgical and secular.

See further: M. M. Butler, *Hrotsvitha: The Theatricality of her Plays*, New York, 1960; A. L. Haight, *Hroswitha of Gandersheim; her Life, Times and Works...*, New York, 1965; P. Dronke, *Women Writers of the Middle Ages*, Cambridge, 1984, pp. 55–83.

(i) *Scene I: Calimachus asks his friends for a private word.*

CALIMACHUS.	Paucis vos, amici, volo. |
AMICI.	Utere, quantum libet, nostro colloquio. |
CALIMACHUS.	Si aegre non accipitis, malo, | vos interim sequestrari aliorum a collegio. |
AMICI.	Quod tibi videtur commodum, | nobis est sequendum. | 5
CALIMACHUS.	Accedamus in secretiora loca, | ne aliquis superveniens interrumpat dicenda. |
AMICI.	Ut libet.

1 **Paucis...volo:** 'I want a few words with you...' (cf. Terence, *Andria* 1.1.2: *paucis te volo*).

2 **quantum:** 'as much as'.
libet: sc. 'you'.

3 **sequestrari:** 'to be separated' (or it could be 'I prefer to separate...', with deponent form for active: see G.3).

6 **ne aliquis:** 'in case someone' (CL *ne quis*: see *RLGVE* 145 Note 2).

7 **dicenda:** 'the things I have to say'.

8 **Ut:** 'As...' (i.e. 'OK': cf. Terence, *Self-Tormentor* 4.4.16 etc.).

Note the use of rhyme in this (and later) scenes, e.g. *volo/colloquio, malo/collegio, commodum/sequendum, loca/dicenda*. These are marked by bar-lines (\|).

(ii) *Scene II: Calimachus reveals his love for Andronicus' wife Drusiana, a Christian, and is warned off by his friends.*

CALIMACHUS. Anxie diuque gravem | sustinui dolorem, | quem vestro consilio | relevari posse spero. |

AMICI. Aequum est, ut communicata invicem compassione patiamur, | quicquid unicuique nostrum utriusque eventu fortunae ingeratur. |

CALIMACHUS. O utinam voluissetis meam compassionem compatiendo mecum partiri!

AMICI. Enuclea, quid patiaris, et, si res exigit, compatiemur; | sin autem, animum tuum a nequam intentione revocari nitimur. |

CALIMACHUS. Amo.

AMICI. Quid?

CALIMACHUS. Rem pulchram, | rem venustam. |

AMICI. Nec in solo, nec in omni; | ideo atomum, quod amas, per hoc nequit intellegi. |

CALIMACHUS. Mulierem.

AMICI. Cum mulierem dixeris, | omnes comprehendis. |

CALIMACHUS. Non omnes aequaliter, | sed unam specialiter. |

AMICI. Quod de subiecto dicitur, | non nisi de subiecto aliquo cognoscitur. | Unde, si velis nos enarithmum agnoscere, dic primam usyam. |

CALIMACHUS. Drusianam. |

AMICI. Andronici huius principis coniugem?

CALIMACHUS. Ipsam.

AMICI. Erras, socie; | est lota baptismate. |

CALIMACHUS. Inde non curo, | si ipsam ad mei amorem attrahere potero. |

AMICI. Non poteris. |

CALIMACHUS. Cur diffiditis? |

AMICI. Quia rem difficilem petis. |

CALIMACHUS. Num ego primus huiusmodi rem peto, | et non multorum ad audendum provocatus sum exemplo? |

AMICI. Intende, frater: ea ipsa, quam ardes, sancti Iohannis apostoli doctrinam secuta, totam se devovit deo, in tantum, ut nec ad thorum Andronici | christianissimi viri | iam dudum potuit revocari, | quo minus tuae consentiet vanitati. |

CALIMACHUS. Quaesivi a vobis consolationem, | sed incutitis mihi desperationem. |

AMICI.	Qui simulat, fallit; et qui profert adulationem, | vendit
	veritatem. | 40
CALIMACHUS.	Quia mihi vestrum auxilium subtrahitis, ipsam adibo |
	eiusque animo | mei amorem blandimentis persuadebo. |
AMICI.	Haut persuadebis. |
CALIMACHUS.	Quippe vetar fatis. |
AMICI.	Experiemur. | 45

1f. **quem...relevari...spero:** 'which I hope can be...' (see 22(b)).

3 **communicata invicem compassione:** 'by sharing our experience with one another' (see G.11(e)(ii)).

4f. **quicquid...ingeratur:** 'whatever is inflicted upon each of us by the outcome of...'.
utriusque...fortunae: i.e. good or bad (cf. Petrarch's *Remedium utriusque fortunae*).

6 **O...voluissetis:** 'Would that you wished...'.
compatiendo: lit. 'by suffering (it) with', but tr. 'sympathetically'.

8f. **sin autem:** 'but if not'.

9 **nitimur:** i.e. *nitemur*.

13 **Nec in solo, nec in omni:** 'Not in one thing only nor in everything (sc. is this quality)' (in this passage the *amici* use the language of medieval logic to make Calimachus specify the object of his passion: this tag is explained in the Pseudo-Augustinian *Categories*: 'as if a person defining a man were to say a man was what was white: not in one thing only, nor in everything').

13f. **per hoc:** 'by this (sc. definition)'.

18f. **Quod...cognoscitur:** 'What is said of a proposition, is not understood except about a particular proposition'; that is, e.g. the category 'animal' signifies 'man' or 'horse', that of 'man' all men. Unless you specify the particular 'man', you are not understood.

19 **Unde:** 'And so...'.
si velis: 'if you would like...'.
enarithmum: 'the individual' (Greek *hen* 'one'

and *arithmos* 'number': with this and *atomum* above Hrotsvitha borrows and Latinizes Greek words from the Pseudo-Augustinian work *Categories*).

20 **primam usyam:** 'first substance' (*usyam* is Greek for 'existence': the Latin term is *prima substantia*; cf. Martianus Capella: 'A *subiectum* is *prima substantia*, that which attaches inseparably to nothing else'; with bookish humour, the *amici* extract the woman's name).

23 **Ipsam:** tr. 'Yes' (lit. 'her' see G.11(a)(ii)).

24 **est lota** (from *lavo*): 'she has been washed', i.e. 'she is a Christian'.

25 **Inde:** 'About that' (see G.13).
ipsam: 'her' (also below l. 000: see G.11(a)(ii)).

30 **non multorum** with *exemplo*.

32 **ardes:** 'you love' (trans.).

35f. **quo minus...vanitati:** lit. 'by how much less will she consent to your deception', i.e. 'so she won't...'.

42 **eiusque...persuadebo:** take *eius...animo* with *persuadebo*; *mei amorem* 'to love of me' (the construction *persuadeo* x dat. to y acc. is CL).

44 **Quippe vetar fatis:** 'To be sure, I shall be forbidden by the fates' (ironical: as its source, Virgil, *Aeneid* 1.39 *quippe vetor fatis*, where the enraged Juno, having spotted Aeneas' fleet heading for Italy, soliloquizes and plots further trouble for Aeneas, despite the will of Jupiter and the Fates).

45 **Experiemur:** 'We shall see' (lit. 'We shall find out from experience').

(iii) *Scene III: Calimachus declares his love to Drusiana and is rejected.*

CALIMACHUS.	Sermo meus ad te, Drusiana, praecordialis amor. |
DRUSIANA.	Quid mecum velis, Calimache, sermonibus agere,
	vehementer admiror. |

CALIMACHUS.	Miraris? |	5
DRUSIANA.	Satis. |	
CALIMACHUS.	Primum de amore. |	
DRUSIANA.	Quid de amore? |	
CALIMACHUS.	Id scilicet, quod te prae omnibus diligo.	
DRUSIANA.	Quod ius consanguinitatis, | quaeve legalis conditio	
	institutionis | compellit te ad mei amorem?	10
CALIMACHUS.	Tui pulchritudo. |	
DRUSIANA.	Mea pulchritudo? |	
CALIMACHUS.	Immo. |	
DRUSIANA.	Quid ad te? |	
CALIMACHUS.	Pro dolor! hactenus parum, | sed spero, quod attineat	15
	postmodum. |	
DRUSIANA.	Discede, discede, | leno nefande; | confundor enim	
	diutius tecum verba commiscere, | quem sentio plenum	
	diabolica deceptione. |	
CALIMACHUS.	Mea Drusiana, ne repellas te amantem | tuoque amore	20
	cordetenus inhaerentem, | sed impende amori vicem. |	
DRUSIANA.	Lenocinia tua parvi pendo | tuique lasciviam fastidio, |	
	sed te ipsum penitus sperno. |	
CALIMACHUS.	Adhuc non repperi occasionem irascendi, | quia, quid	
	mea in te agat dilectio, forte erubescis fateri. |	25
DRUSIANA.	Nihil aliud, nisi indignationem.	
CALIMACHUS.	Credo, te hanc sententiam mutatum ire. |	
DRUSIANA.	Non mutabo, percerte! |	
CALIMACHUS.	Forte!	
DRUSIANA.	O insensate et amens, cur falleris? | cur te vacua spe	30
	illudis? | quo pacto, qua dementia reris me tuae cedere	
	nugacitati, | quae per multum temporis a legalis thoro viri	
	me abstinui? |	
CALIMACHUS.	Pro deum atque hominum fidem! si non cesseris, | non	
	quiescam, | non desistam, | donec te captuosis |	35
	circumveniam insidiis. |	

1 **Sermo...amor:** lit. 'My conversation with you, Drusiana, heartfelt love', which seems from what follows to mean: 'I would like a word with you, my beloved Drusiana'.

2 **sermonibus agere:** 'to discuss'.

5 **Satis:** 'Yes'.

9f. **quaeve legalis conditio institutionis:** 'or what condition of lawful arrangement' (the two questions refer respectively to the propriety of the address (1) of a relative (2) of a husband).

13 **Immo:** 'Yes'.

14 **Quid ad te:** 'What business is it of yours?'.

15 **Pro dolor!:** 'Alas!'.
quod attineat...: 'that it will be my business...'.

17 **confundor:** lit. 'I am ashamed to...'.

20 **te amantem:** 'one who loves you'.

21 **impende...vicem:** lit. 'pay the return to my love' (i.e. 'return my love').

24f. **quid...dilectio:** 'the effect on you of my love' (the clause is introduced by the following *erubescis*).

26 **Nihil aliud...:** sc. 'its effect is to produce'.

27 **te...mutatum ire:** 'that you will change' (CL *mutaturam esse; mutatum iri* would be a future passive – see RLRGr B2).

28 **percerte:** 'for sure'.

31 **quo pacto:** 'in what manner?', 'how?'.
cedere: 'will give in' (for CL *cessuram esse*).

32 **per multum temporis:** 'for a long time'.

34 **Pro deum atque hominum fidem:** '(sc. I invoke) the help of the gods and men', i.e. 'by all that's holy...'.

In scene IV Drusiana prays to Christ for death and dies. Andronicus rushes off to find St John. In scene V St. John and Andronicus prepare to go to Drusiana's tomb, which is being guarded by one Fortunatus.

(iv) *Scene VI: Calimachus bribes Fortunatus to allow him access to Drusiana's corpse.*

CALIMACHUS. Quid fiet, Fortunate? | quia nec morte Drusianae | revocari possum ab amore. |
FORTUNATUS. Miserabile. |
CALIMACHUS. Pereo, nisi me adiuvet tua industria.
FORTUNATUS. In quo possum adiuvare? |
CALIMACHUS. In eo, ut vel mortuam me facias videre. |
FORTUNATUS. Corpus adhuc integrum manet, ut reor, quia non languore exesum, | sed levi, ut experiebare, febre est solutum. |
CALIMACHUS. O me felicem, si numquam experirer!
FORTUNATUS. Si placabis muneribus, | dedam illud tuis usibus.|
CALIMACHUS. Quae in praesenti ad manus habeo, interim accipe; | nec diffidas, te multo maiora accepturum fore. |
FORTUNATUS. Eamus cito.
CALIMACHUS. In me non erit mora.

1 **nec:** 'not even'.

4 **nisi...adiuvet:** 'unless...comes to the aid of...' (for mood of verb, see G.28(c)).

6 **in eo, ut:** 'in this, that...', i.e. 'by...ing'.
vel mortuam: '(sc. her) even though (she is) dead'.
facias videre: 'allow...to...' (see G.17(c)).

8 **experiebare** (= *experiebaris*: see RLRGr C3): 'you know' (lit. 'you found out by experience': but Drusiana seems to be alone in the scene where she begs for death, and is discovered by Andronicus).

9 **O me felicem:** 'O happy me!' (acc. of exclamation: see RLRGr L (c)7).
si...experirer: 'if I had...' (see RLRGr S2(c)2 Note 2).

10 **Si...muneribus:** sc. *me*.
illud: viz. *corpus*.

11f. **nec diffidas:** 'and do not...' (jussive subj.: *RLGVE* 152).

12 **accepturum fore** = *accepturum esse* (cf. G.5).

(v) *Scene VII: As Calimachus is about to molest Drusiana's corpse, Fortunatus is mortally wounded by a snake, and Calimachus dies of fear.*

FORTUNATUS.	Ecce corpus: nec facies cadaverosa, │ nec membra sunt tabida. │ Abutere, ut libet.
CALIMACHUS.	O Drusiana, Drusiana, quo affectu cordis te colui, │ qua sinceritate dilectionis te visceratenus amplexatus fui, │ et tu semper abiecisti, │ meis votis contradixisti! │ Nunc in 5 mea situm est potestate, │ quantislibet iniuriis te velim lacessere. │
FORTUNATUS.	Atat! horribilis serpens invadit nos.
CALIMACHUS.	Ei mihi, Fortunate, cur me decepisti? │ cur detestabile scelus persuasisti? │ En, tu moriaris serpentis vulnere, │ et 10 ego commorior prae timore. │

---

1 **nec...cadaverosa:** sc. 'is' (the phrase *cadaverosa facie* is from Terence, *Hecyra* 3.4. 27).

4 **amplexatus fui:** 'I embraced' (see G.4(a)): the form *amplexor* is favoured in comedy and other low-style writing, *amplector* elsewhere).

5 **abiecisti:** sc. *me*.
meis votis: obj. of *contradixisti* 'you opposed...'.

5f. **in mea** with *potestate* (the whole phrase = *possum*).

6 **quantislibet...velim:** 'with whatever...I like'.
te obj. of *lacessere* (which depends on *situm est*).

8 **Atat!:** 'Alas!' (an exclamation often used in comedy: e.g. Terence, *Andria* 1.1.98).

9 **Ei mihi:** 'Woe is me'.

In scene VIII, Jesus appears to Andronicus and St John, and explains that he intends to resuscitate Drusiana and 'the one who lies near her tomb'. In scene IX.1–8 John and Andronicus arrive at the tomb, discover Drusiana's body outside the tomb and the two men Calimachus and Fortunatus entangled in the embrace of the serpent. St John bids the snake depart and it obeys.

(vi) *Scene IX.9–20: the resuscitation and conversion of Calimachus.*

IOHANNES.	Deus incircumscriptus et incomprehensibilis, │ simplex et inaestimabilis, │ qui solus es id, quod es │ qui, diversa duo socians, │ ex hoc et hoc hominem fingis, │ eademque dissocians, │ unum, quod constabat, resolvis, │ iube, ut, reducto halitu disiunctaque compagine rursus conliminata, 5 Calimachus resurgat plenus, ut fuit, homo, quo ab omnibus magnificeris, │ qui solus miranda operaris. │
ANDRONICHUS.	Amen. – Ecce vitales auras carpit, │ sed prae stupore adhuc quiescit. │
IOHANNES.	Calimache, surge in Christi nomine, │ et, utcumque se res 10 habeat, confitere; │ quantislibet obnoxius sis vitiis, proferas, │ ne nos vel in modico lateat veritas. │
CALIMACHUS.	Negare nequeo, quin patrandi causa facinoris accesserim, quia infelici languore tabescebam │ nec inliciti aestum

	amoris compescere poteram.	15
IOHANNES.	Quae dementia, quae insania te decepit, | ut castis praesumeres fragmentis | alicuius iniuriam conferre dehonestatis?|	
CALIMACHUS.	Propria stultitia huiusque Fortunati fraudolenta deceptio.	
IOHANNES.	Num triplici infortunio adeo infelix effectus es, | ut nefas, quod voluisti, perficere posses? |	20
CALIMACHUS.	Nullatenus. Licet non defuisset velle, | possibilitas tamen omnino defuit posse. |	
IOHANNES.	Quo pacto impediebaris?	
CALIMACHUS.	Ut primum, distracto tegmine, | conviciis temptavi lacessere corpus exanime, | iste Fortunatus, qui fomes mali et incensor extitit, | serpentinis perfusus venenis, periit.|	25
ANDRONICHUS.	O factum bene!	
CALIMACHUS.	Mihi autem apparuit iuvenis, | aspectu terribilis, | qui detectum corpus honorifice texit; | ex cuius flammea facie candentes in bustum scintillae transiliebant, quarum una resiliens mihi in faciem ferebatur, simulque vox facta est, dicens: 'Calimache, morere, ut vivas!' His dictis, expiravi.	30
IOHANNES.	Opus caelestis gratiae, | qui non delectatur in impiorum perditione. |	35
CALIMACHUS.	Audisti miseriam meae perditionis: | noli elongare medelam tuae miserationis. |	
IOHANNES.	Non elongabo.	
CALIMACHUS.	Nam nimium confundor, | cordetenus contristor, | anxio, gemo, doleo super gravi impietate mea.	40
IOHANNES.	Nec inmerito; quippe grave delictum | haut leve poenitudinis expectat remedium. |	
CALIMACHUS.	O utinam reserarentur secreta | meorum viscerum latibula, | quo interni amaritudinem, quam patior, doloris perspiceres | et dolenti condoleres! |	45
IOHANNES.	Congaudeo huiusmodi dolori, | quia sentio, te salubriter contristari. |	
CALIMACHUS.	Taedet me prioris vitae, | taedet delectationis iniquae. |	
IOHANNES.	Nec iniuria.	
CALIMACHUS.	Poenitet me; deliqui.	50
IOHANNES.	Et merito.	
CALIMACHUS.	Displicet omne, quod feci, | in tantum, ut nullus amor, nulla voluptas est vivendi, | nisi renatus in Christo merear in melius transmutari. |	
IOHANNES.	Non dubito, quin superna gratia in te appareat.	55

CALIMACHUS.   Ideo ne moreris, | ne pigriteris | lapsum erigere, |
maerentem consolationibus attollere, | quo tuo monitu,
tuo magisterio a gentili in christianum, | a nugace in
castum | transmutatus virum, | tuoque ducatu semitam
arripiens veritatis, | vivam iuxta divinae praeconium   60
promissionis. |

IOHANNES.   Benedicta sit unica progenies divinitatis | idemque
particeps nostrae fragilitatis, | qui te, fili Calimache,
parcendo occidit | et occidendo vivificavit, | quo suum
plasma mortis specie | ab interitu liberaret animae. | 65

ANDRONICHUS.   Res insolita | omnique admiratione digna. |

IOHANNES.   O Christe, mundi redemptio | et peccatorum propitiatio, |
qualibus laudum praeconiis te talem celebrem, ignoro. |
Expaveo tui benignam clementiam | et clementem
patientiam, | qui peccantes nunc paterno more tolerando   70
blandiris, | nunc iusta severitate castigando ad
poenitentiam cogis. |

ANDRONICHUS.   Laus eius divinae pietati.

IOHANNES.   Quis auderet credere, | quisve praesumeret sperare, | ut
hunc, quem criminosis | intentum vitiis | mors invenit | 75
et inventum abstulit, | tui miseratio ad vitam excitare, |
ad veniam dignaretur reparare? | Sit nomen tuum
sanctum benedictum in saecula, | qui solus facis stupenda
mirabilia! |

2f. **diversa duo socians:** 'joining together two different things' (viz. body and spirit).
3 **ex hoc et hoc:** 'from this and this' (i.e. body and spirit).
4 **unum...resolvis:** 'you destroy one (of the two things) which was there' (viz. the body: though it could mean 'you release', in which case the reference is to the soul).
5 **disiuncta...conliminata:** 'the disjoined union (sc. of body and soul) having been once more restored to its threshold' (i.e. his body having been revived).
6f. **quo...magnificeris:** 'in order that...' (see G.27(c)).
8 **vitales auras carpit:** 'he grasps the breezes of life' (based on Virgil, *Aeneid* 1.387–8 *auras / uitales carpis*).
10f. **utcumque...habeat:** 'however things stand'.
12 **proferas:** 'reveal' (jussive subj.: see *RLGVE* 152).

13 **quin:** 'that...'.
16f. **ut...dehonestatis:** 'so that you dared to bring against the chaste remains an injury involving some dishonour' (CL uses *iniuriam inferre*: *dehonestas* is LL).
19 **Propria:** 'My own'.
20 **triplici infortunio:** i.e. by Drusiana's death, his unfulfilled passion and Fortunatus' acquiescence.
22 **defuisset** = *deesset*.
velle: 'the will' (noun).
22f. **possibilitas...posse:** lit. 'there was lacking the possibility to be able', i.e. 'there was no possibility at all of being able'
24 **Quo pacto:** 'How?'
25 **tegmine:** viz. the shroud.
conviciis: 'with reproaches' (we are left to guess precisely what he intended to do).
26 **iste:** 'that' (see G.11(c)).

27 **extitit** = *exstitit*: 'was' (*exsisto*).

32 **resiliens mihi in faciem ferebatur:** 'rebounding was carried against my face', i.e. 'ricocheted and hit me in the face'.

34f. **qui...perditione:** '(since) he (i.e. God) does not delight in...'.

40 **doleo super:** 'I grieve over' (CL *de* or *ex*: cf. G.15(b)).

41f. **leve** with *remedium*.

42 **expectat** = *exspectat*: 'requires'.

43 **secreta** looks forward to *latibula* (and *meorum viscerum* depends on it).

44f. **quo...perspiceres:** 'in order that you might...' (see G.27(c)).

44 **interni** with *doloris* (dependent on *amaritudinem*, obj. of *perspiceres*).

45 **dolenti:** sc. 'with me...'.

52f. **ut...vivendi:** both *nullus amor* and *nulla voluptas* govern *vivendi* (tr. 'love of...pleasure in...': for the mood of *est*, see G.26(a)).

56f. **lapsum...maerentem:** 'one who has fallen...one who grieves...'.

57f. **quo...promissionis:** the verb is *vivam* 'in order that I may...' (see G.27(c)); *tuo monitu, tuo magisterio* (note the asyndeton: tr. 'by...and') depend upon *transmutatus*; *a...in* 'from...into' (note asyndeton between *christianum* and *a nugace*: tr. 'from...into...and from...into...'): *iuxta...praeconium* 'according to the...' (governing *divinae...promissionis*).

62f. **unica progenies...fragilitatis:** i.e. Christ.

64 **parcendo...occidendo:** 'in...'.

64f. **quo...liberaret:** 'in order to...' (see G.27(c)).

65 **plasma:** 'creation' (Greek: man was created by God, Gen. 1.27). **ab interitu** governs *animae*.

68 **qualibus...celebrem:** 'with what...I am to...' (deliberative subj.: see *RLGVE* 152 Note 1); *talem* 'as such', i.e. as *mundi redemptio* etc.

70 **peccantes:** 'sinners'. **paterno more:** 'in the manner of a father'.

73 **Laus...pietati:** 'Praise (be) to his (Christ's) divine love'.

74 **auderet:** 'would have dared' (see *RLGVE* 153;.2). **praesumeret:** 'would have presumed...' (see *RLGVE* 153.2).

74f. **ut...reparare:** the structure is *ut* ('that') *hunc,⌐ | quem...mors invenit et...abstulit, | ⌐...miseratio...excitare...dignaretur* (and) *reparare*.

75 **quem...vitiis:** 'whom as he was bent upon criminal acts...'. **inventum:** 'him, when come upon (by death)'.

76 **tui miseratio:** 'your...' (Hrotsvitha is fond of using *mei, tui*, genitives of *ego, tu*, instead of the adjectives *meus, tuus*).

76f. **ad vitam...reparare;** 'would have thought fit to...and to...'.

78f. **stupenda mirabilia:** 'amazing miracles'.

In scene IX.21–5 Drusiana is resuscitated and asks for the resuscitation of Fortunatus. Calimachus resists, but St John argues that no one should be begrudged the grace of God. Drusiana is given the task. In scene IX.26–30 Fortunatus is resuscitated, but chooses to die again rather than look on such examples of grace. In the remaining sections (IX.31–3), St John discourses on the link between pride and hatred and the disposition of Fortunatus. The piece ends with a prayer of thanks to God for the resuscitation of Drusiana and Calimachus and the conversion of the latter.

5. Chronicon Salernitanum (c.978)

The chronicle of Salerno was written by an anonymous monk of the monastery of St Benedict at Salerno. It gives an account of the history of the Lombard leaders from 758 to 974. Salerno, later famous for its *Studium Generale*, specializing in medicine – one of the earliest universities in

Europe – was part of the duchy of Benevento during much of the Lombard period, and for a time the residence of its *principes*. The work is of greatest interest for its language, which in vocabulary, morphology and syntax reflects the difficulty which a tenth-century Italian had in writing correct Latin. One factor was no doubt the closeness of Italian to Latin (as another Italian writer of the period notes). Another was an altered phonology, which made spelling a difficult task. But a third was surely, as in the case of Hygeburg of Heidenheim (section 7.4), a limited education.

See further: U. Westerburgh, *Chronicon Salernitanum*, Lund, 1956.

A cautionary tale: Duke Arichis (d.787) leaves to Christ's judgement the case of a man accused of murder and adultery, with surprising results.

Quedam mulier virum proprium abebat et cum alio viro se commiscebat. Factum est, ut una nocte una cum alieno in dolo suum virum proprium stranguillaret, et idipsum ingenti voce emitteret, inquid ad suos: 'Surgite, quia meus vir apoplexia est nimirum extinctus.' Dum ex more vicini et consanguinei circumquaque altrinsecus flerent, cum magno obsequio ad sepulcrum   5
usque perducitur, eumque humarunt. Dum ad aures principis pervenissent, ut non propria morte fuisset extinctus, statim comprehendi virum illum qui mulierem defuncti fedaverat iussit, et in verbis talia promit: 'Nisi extimplo quod clam iessisti nobis enodaveris, ilico nimirum morieris!' At ille quod nequiter gessit, omnia propalavit. Princeps idem alta trahens suspiria, tandem in   10
voce erupit, inquid ad suos: 'Virum histum comprehendite, eumque super mortuum facie ad faciem dixtriccius colligate; et quid exinde Redemptor humani generis iudicaverit, intimate.' Quo peracto, tercia die indagare iussit, quid exinde fuisset factum. Tunc reppererunt virum illum qui fuerat stranguillatus desuper stratum et ore naresque sui perentori corrosas. Proinde huic   15
istorie conscripscimus, ut fideles mulierem halienam omnimodis caveant et ulcio divina cautissime metuant.

---

1 **abebat** = *habebat* (see O.3(c)).
2 **una nocte:** 'one night' (see G.10(d)).
   una cum: 'together with'.
   in dolo: 'by means of a trick' (see G.15(a)(ii)).
3 **idipsum:** 'the fact (sc. of his death)'.
   inquid: supply 'and then...'.
4f. **Dum...flerent:** 'while...were...' (see G.29).
5 **altrinsecus:** 'on each side' (if it means something different from *circumquaque*, it perhaps implies a division of position between neighbours and relatives at the funeral).

6 **perducitur...humarunt** (= *humaverunt*: RLRGr A4): 'he was...and they...'.
   dum...pervenissent: 'when it reached...' (see G.29; *pervenissent* = *pervenisset*).
7 **fuisset extinctus:** 'had been...' (see G.4(a)).
   propria morte: 'by a natural death'.
   comprehendi depends on *iussit*.
9 **iessisti** = *gessisti* (the spelling was probably caused by a sound-change which made the sounds earlier associated with *ge-* and *ie-* indistinguishable from each other: see O.0).

At: 'and' (CL 'but').

10f. **in voce** = *in vocem* (see O.10).

11 **inquid:** supply 'and...'.

  histum = *istum* (see O.3(c)) 'this' (see G.11(c)).

12 **facie ad faciem:** 'face to face'.

  dixtriccius = *districtius* (see O.16 and O.2): 'very tightly' (see G.12(a)).

14 **exinde:** 'about it' (see G.13); tr. so also in the next sentence.

fuisset factum: 'had been...' (see G.4(a): so also for *fuerat stranguillatus*).

15 **ore** (= *os*: acc.) **naresque** (acc.) **sui perentori** (= *peremptoris*: gen.) **corrosas** (acc. with *nares*): the morphology has gone badly wrong here (see also below l. 17).

16 **istorie** = *historiae* (see O.3(c) and O.1).

  conscripscimus = *conscripsimus*.

17 **ulcio** (= *ultionem*) **divina** (= *divinam*: see O.10): nom. has been written for acc.

PART THREE
From the end of the Ottonian Renaissance (1002) to the Concordat of Worms (1122)

By the turn of the millennium, the boundaries of Western Christendom were largely established. There would still be some temporary expansion in the East, due to the Crusades: the Norman Conquest of Sicily and South Italy would reclaim the one from Islam and the other from the Eastern Church; and there would be modest expansions in Scandinavia, the Baltic and the Balkans, due to the movement eastwards of the Christian states Denmark, Poland/Lithuania and of the Teutonic Knights. Within Christendom three major themes dominate the history and the Latin writing of the eleventh and early twelfth centuries. First is the expansion of the Normans, into South Italy and Sicily (1091) in one branch (Robert Guiscard) and from Normandy into England (1066) in another (William of Normandy). Second is the struggle for power between the German Emperor and the Papacy fuelled by the strengthened Church reform movement and usually called the 'Investiture Contest', which reached a temporary conclusion with the Concordat of Worms (1122). Third is the First Crusade, preached by Pope Urban II at the Council of Clermont in 1095 and crowned by the capture of Jerusalem on 15 July 1099.

During this period, Latin learning was beginning to progress more strongly in the cathedral schools. The most famous of them was founded at Chartres in 990 by Fulbert (a pupil of Otto III's teacher Gerbert of Aurillac, Pope Sylvester II). These schools concentrated on the education of the secular clergy and, as monasteries gradually stopped training non-monks, they became crucial places for the free development of learning. At the same time, there are clear advances in specialist professional learning, and the growth of centres at Salerno (medicine), Bologna (law) and Paris (theology) is a sign of things to come. Another harbinger of future trends is the *Elementarium doctrinae rudimentum* ('Elementary introduction to learning') of Papias the Lombard, the first dictionary of the Middle Ages. But the systematization of knowledge in this way was to take several more centuries to achieve. The most important educational movement, with the most far-reaching intellectual impact, was undoubtedly the increasing reliance upon logic in theological and philosophical discussion.

Section 11
The Norman Conquest

The eleventh century marks the rise of the Normans. From their involvement with the anti-Byzantine 'resistance movement' of Melo of Bari (1016) to the final acquisition by Robert Guiscard of the Kingdom of Sicily (1091) they played an increasingly important part in the power-politics centred on the Italian peninsula. More than once during the struggle with the German Emperor the Pope was forced to rely on their aid (only to regret it). The energy, forcefulness and ruthlessness of the conquerors of South Italy and Sicily was seen also in the bastard son of Robert I of Normandy, who succeeded as a minor when his father died on pilgrimage to Jerusalem in 1035. William survived attempts to oust him when, with the help of the French king he defeated the rebel barons at Val-des-Dunes in 1047 and took a firm grip on his duchy. In 1051 he visited England, and returned with what he later claimed was a promise from his kinsman King Edward that he would be named to succeed him. He defied a papal ban to marry Matilda of Flanders (1053) and strengthened his position in the ensuing attacks by Henry I of France by defeating the aggressors in 1054 and 1058. By 1062 he was in a position to lay claim to the French county of Maine.

On 5 January 1066, King Edward of England died. He was buried somewhat hastily on the following day at Westminster and the earl of the West Saxons, Harold Godwinson, was elected to succeed him, claiming that this had been Edward's dying wish. When William heard the news, he at once sent messengers to Harold to demand his allegiance, sent envoys to the Pope (he had been reconciled with his predecessor in 1059) denouncing Harold as a perjurer and usurper and asking for a blessing on his planned invasion, and summoned his barons to Lillebonne to persuade them to support him in this enterprise. Harold determined to resist, the pope sent William a consecrated banner and the barons agreed to help. On Thursday 28 September 1066, William's fleet sailed from Saint-Valéry and landed next morning at Pevensey. From there the army marched to

Hastings, where the building of a castle was at once ordered. Harold, who had just defeated his exiled brother Tostig and Harold Hardrada, king of Norway, near York on 25 September, received the news and prepared to march south directly to face the challenge. His forces reached the vicinity of Hastings on 13 October. The place was called Senlac (= Anglo-Saxon *Sandlacu* 'Sandstream', now Battle). The next day they were attacked and routed, with the loss of Harold and his two brothers, by William's army. The rest (as they say) is (English) history.

See further: D. Bates, *William the Conqueror*, London, 1989; M. Chibnall, *Anglo-Norman England 1066–1166*, Oxford, 1986.

THE BATTLE OF HASTINGS (14 OCTOBER 1066)

1. William of Poitiers (*fl.* 1066)

Little is known of the author of *Guillelmi ducis Normannorum gesta* ('The deeds of Duke William of Normandy'). He was probably a noble, who had been a knight before taking religious orders. Later, he was an archdeacon at Lisieux, and clearly remained a fervent supporter of William. His history, which ends with the events of 1067, is highly eulogistic. It is composed in a vigorous style, which borrows much from Caesar, Cicero, Sallust and Virgil, and is marked by a penchant for classical *exempla* and comparisons (e.g. Marius or Pompey would not have engaged in reconnaissance themselves, as did Duke William). His account of the battle of Hastings is given here in an edited form, the eulogy cut down in favour of the events.

(i) *Following a speech of encouragement, the Normans march against the Saxons, who have taken up a strong defensive position on a ridge.*

Hac autem commodissima ordinatione progreditur, vexillo praevio quod apostolicus transmiserat. Pedites in fronte locavit, sagittis armatos et balistis, item pedites in ordine secundo firmiores et loricatos, ultimo turmas equitum, quorum ipse fuit in medio cum firmissimo robore, unde in omnem partem consuleret manu et voce. Scribens Heraldi agmen illud veterum aliquis in ejus   5
transitu flumina epotata, silvas in planum reductas fuisse memoraret. Maximae enim ex omnibus undique regionibus copiae Anglorum convenerant. Studium pars Heraldo, cuncti patriae praestabant, quam contra extraneos, tametsi non juste, defensare volebant. Copiosa quoque auxilia miserat eis cognata terra

Danorum. Non tamen audentes cum Guillelmo ex aequo confligere, plus eum   10
quam regem Noricorum extimentes, locum editiorem praeoccupavere,
montem silvae per quam advenere vicinum. Protinus equorum ope relicta,
cuncti pedites constitere densius conglobati. Dux cum suis neque loci territus
asperitate ardua clivi sensim ascendit. Terribilis clangor lituorum pugnae signa
cecinit utrinque. Normannorum alacris audacia pugnae principium dedit.   15
Taliter cum oratores in judicio litem agunt de rapina, prior ferit dictione
qui crimen intendit. Pedites itaque Normanni propius accedentes provocant
Anglos, missilibus in eos vulnera dirigunt atque necem. Illi contra fortiter quo
quisque valet ingenio resistunt. Jactant cuspides ac diversorum generum tela,
saevissimas quasque secures et lignis imposita saxa. Iis veluti mole letifera statim   20
nostros obrui putares. Subveniunt equites et qui posteriores fuere fiunt primi.
Pudet eminus pugnare, gladiis rem gerere audent. Altissimus clamor hinc
Normannicus, illinc barbaricus armorum sonitu et gemitu morientium super-
atur. Sic aliquandiu summa vi certatur ab utrisque. Angli nimium adjuvantur
superioris loci opportunitate, quem sine procursu tenent et maxime conferti,   25
ingenti quoque numerositate sua atque validissima corpulentia, praeterea
pugnae instrumentis, quae facile per scuta vel alia tegmina viam inveniunt.
Fortissime itaque sustinent vel propellunt ausos in se districtum ensibus
impetum facere. Vulnerant et eos qui eminus in se jacula conjiciunt. Ecce
igitur hac saevitia perterriti avertuntur pedites pariter atque equites Britanni et   30
quotquot auxiliares erant in sinistro cornu; cedit fere cuncta ducis acies, quod
cum pace dictum sit Normannorum invictissimae nationis. Romanae majestatis
exercitus copias regum continens vincere solitus terra marique fugit aliquando,
cum ducem suum sciret aut crederet occisum. Credidere Normanni ducem ac
dominum suum cecidisse. Non ergo nimis pudenda fuga cessere, minime vero   35
dolenda, cum plurimum juverit.

Princeps namque prospiciens multam partem adversae stationis prosiluisse et
insequi terga suorum fugientibus occurrit et obstitit, verberans aut minans
hasta. Nudato insuper capite detractaque galea exclamans. 'Me,' inquit,
'circumspicite. Vivo et vincam, opitulante Deo. Quae vobis dementia fugam   40
suadet? Quae via patebit ad effugiendum? Quos ut pecora mactare potestis,
depellunt vos et occidunt. Victoriam deseritis ac perpetuum honorem; in
exitium curritis ac perpetuum opprobrium. Abeundo, mortem nullus vestrum
evadet.' His dictis, receperunt animos. Primus ipse procurrit, fulminans ense,
stravit adversam gentem quae sibi – regi suo – rebellans commeruit mortem.   45
Exardentes Normanni et circumvenientes aliquot millia insecuta se, momento
deleverunt ea, ut ne quidem unus superesset. Ita confirmati, vehementius
immanitatem exercitus invaserunt, qui maximum detrimentum passus non
videbatur minor. Angli confidenter totis viribus oppugnabant, id maxime
laborantes, ne quem aditum irrumpere volentibus aperirent. Ob nimiam   50

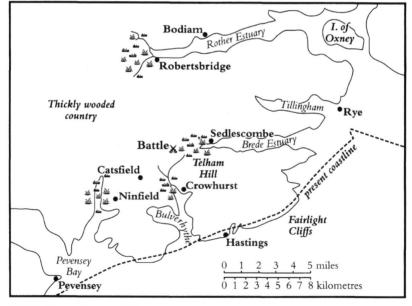

6.1 The Hastings district in 1066.

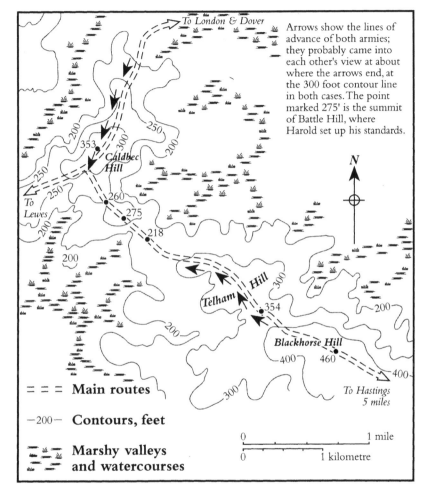

To London & Dover

Arrows show the lines of
advance of both armies;
they probably came into
each other's view at about
where the arrows end, at
the 300 foot contour line
in both cases. The point
marked 275' is the summit
of Battle Hill, where
Harold set up his standards.

N

353

Caldbec
Hill

To
Lewes

260

275

218

200

Telham Hill

354

Blackhorse Hill

400   460

400

To Hastings
5 miles

= = = **Main routes**

−200− **Contours, feet**

**Marshy valleys
and watercourses**

0   1 mile

0   1 kilometre

Blackhorse Hill
460

500

Caldbec
400 Hill

350

Telham
Hill
360

300

275

218

200

6.2 The isthmus of the Hastings peninsula and battleground.

densitatem eorum labi vix potuerunt interempti. Patuerunt tamen in eos viae incisae per diversas partes fortissimorum militum ferro. Institerunt eis Cenomanici, Francigenae, Britanni, Aquitani, sed cum praecipua virtute Normanni.

1 **Hac...ordinatione:** 'with this...arrangement (sc. of his forces)' (the description follows).
progreditur: the subject is William.
1f. **vexillo...transmiserat:** 'with the banner in front which...' See section 11 Intro. for Pope Alexander II's (= *apostolicus*) support for William: in the view of the *Curia*, the English Church might be stimulated towards reform by William's victory. The banner is shown on the Bayeux Tapestry and was preserved in Battle Abbey until its destruction by fire in 1931.
pedites...firmiores et loricatos: i.e. the hand-to-hand fighting troops, clad in chain-mail: the verb is *locavit*, carried over from the first colon).
4 **quorum** with *in medio*.
ipse: 'he', i.e. William (see G.11(a)(ii)).
4f. **unde...consuleret:** 'so that he might give advice from there' (purpose clause: *RLGVE* 145 Note 3).
5 **scribens:** 'in describing...' (with *veterum aliquis*, i.e. 'an ancient writer').
Heraldi: 'of Harold'.
5f. **in ejus transitu...fuisse:** 'that...rivers had been...and forests had been...' (acc. + inf. dependent on *memoraret*; for the forms *epotata fuisse* and *reductas fuisse* see G.4(a): *flumina epotata* is a reminiscence of Juvenal 10.177 (*epotaque flumina*)).
6 **in planum:** 'to open spaces' (because the army will have cut a path through the densely wooded terrain of England). These hyperboles may have been borrowed from Guy of Amiens (see section 11.2).
memoraret: 'would have...' (see *RLGVE* 153.2).
Maximae looks forward to *copiae*. But Harold did not wait to receive the help of the earls of Mercia and Northumbria, relying instead on troops hastily levied around London.
8 **pars...cuncti:** 'some...but everyone...'.
9f. **cognata terra Danorum:** the Godwin family was semi-Danish, and had been raised from obscurity by the Danish conqueror of England

Knut (or Canute). In fact, his cousin Svein Estrithson, king of Denmark 1047–75, would have been more likely to oppose Harold because of his own claims to the English throne. However, it seems he did not intervene against the Normans until 1069.
10 **audentes:** the subject is 'the English'.
Guillelmo: 'William' (cf. Fr. *Guillaume*).
ex aequo: 'on equal terms'.
10f. **plus...extimentes:** 'because they...' (see G.20(b)).
11 **regem Noricorum:** 'the king of the Norwegians' (i.e. Harold Hardrada, whom they had just defeated: see section 11 Intro.).
praeoccupavere = *praeoccupaverunt* (see RLRGr A4).
12 **montem silvae...vicinum:** in apposition to *locum editiorem*. The reference is to Battle Hill (see map 6.2).
per quam advenere (= *advenerunt*: see RLRGr A4): *silvae* is antecedent of *quam*.
13 **constitere** = *constiterunt* (RLRGr A4).
neque: 'not even'.
loci depends on *asperitate* (which is governed by *territus*).
18 **vulnera...atque necem:** 'they aim wounds and death', i.e. 'they try to wound or kill' (a CL poetic expression).
18f. **quo...ingenio:** 'with whatever ability each could'.
20 **saevissimas quasque:** 'all the most savage' (modelled on CL: see *RLGVE* 176); the reference is to the battleaxe, wielded with two hands, which had been borrowed from the Danes.
lignis imposita saxa: 'rocks mounted on sticks', i.e. 'maces'.
20f. **Iis...obrui:** acc. + inf. dependent on *putares*.
mole letifera: 'by a...siege engine'.
21 **putares:** 'you would have...' (see *RLGVE* 153.2).
qui...primi: this relates to the actual arrangement of the battle (see the opening lines), but is reminiscent of Lk 13.30: *et ecce sunt novissimi qui*

erunt primi 'And lo! it is the last who shall be first'.

22 **Pudet:** sc. 'the knights'.

24 **certatur:** 'fighting was being done...' (see *RLGVE* 155: note the vivid historic present employed throughout the description of the battle: see *RLGVE* 112).

nimium: 'very much'.

26 **quoque:** 'and also' (serves to add another colon to the *quem...tenent* clause)

praeterea: 'and also...' (adds a further means by which they held their position).

28 **ausos:** 'those who had dared'.

28f. **districtum ensibus impetum:** lit. 'an attack engaged with swords', but this looks like a confused way of saying *strictis ensibus* 'with drawn swords'.

30 **Britanni:** 'Breton' (on the Norman side). The Norman army advanced in three columns. On the left wing were Bretons, men of Anjou, Le Mans and Poitiers; on the right, Franks and Flemish; in the centre, the Normans.

31 **cedit:** 'and...' (asyndeton is used extensively in this passage: see *RLGVE* pp. 314–15 (c)).

31f. **quod...dictum sit:** 'and let this have been said...'.

32 **cum pace:** 'with the peace...', i.e. 'without objections from...'.

Romanae majestatis: i.e. of the Roman people.

33 **continens:** 'which held in check...'.

34 **occisum:** sc. *esse.*

Credidere = *Crediderunt* (see RLRGr A4).

35 **nimis pudenda:** 'in a very...' (see G.12(b)).

cessere = *cesserunt* (see RLRGr A4).

35f. **minime vero... juverit:** 'and it was indeed not..., since it...' (this was the model of the pretended retreat which later changed the whole face of the battle).

37 **prospiciens:** 'having seen (that)...' (see G.20(a)).

39 **insuper:** 'moreover'. William's dramatic gesture is featured on the Bayeux Tapestry.

41 **Quos...potestis:** 'those whom...' (these people become the subjects of *depellunt, occidunt*).

45 **stravit:** 'and...' (asyndeton).

sibi – regi suo – rebellans: 'by rebelling against him their king' (see G.11(e)(i)).

46 **exardentes...et circumvenientes:** 'having...' (see G.20(a)).

aliquot millia (= *milia*: see O.7) **insecuta se:** 'the several thousand who had...' (obj. of *circumvenientes*).

47 **ne quidem unus:** 'not even one man' (CL *ne unus quidem*).

48 **immanitatem exercitus:** lit. 'the immensity of the army', i.e. 'the huge army'.

50 **irrumpere volentibus:** 'to those who wished to break in'.

51 **labi...interempti:** 'the dead were scarcely able to fall down'.

52f. **Cenomanici:** 'men from Le Mans'.

53 **Francigenae:** 'Franks' (these were the knights of the Île-de-France).

Aquitani: 'men from Aquitaine'.

(ii) *A Norman retreat draws the Saxon line forward. The Normans wheel and the tide of battle turns in their favour.*

Animadvertentes Normanni sociaque turba non absque nimio sui incommodo hostem tantum simul resistentem superari posse terga dederunt, fugam ex industria simulantes. Meminerunt quam optatae rei paulo ante fuga dederit occasionem. Barbaris cum spe victoriae ingens laetitia exorta est. Sese cohortantes exultante clamore nostros maledictis increpabant et minabantur   5
cunctos illico ruituros esse. Ausa sunt ut superius aliquot millia quasi volante cursu quos fugere putabant urgere. Normanni repente regiratis equis interceptos et inclusos undique mactaverunt, nullum relinquentes. Bis eo dolo simili eventu usi, reliquos majori cum alacritate aggressi sunt, aciem adhuc horren-

dam et quam difficillimum erat circumvenire. Fit deinde insoliti generis pugna,   10
quam altera pars incursibus et diversis motibus agit, altera velut humo affixa
tolerat. Languent Angli et quasi reatum ipso defectu confitentes vindictam
patiuntur. Sagittant, feriunt, perfodiunt Normanni, mortui plus dum cadunt
quam vivi moveri videntur. Leviter sauciatos non permittit evadere sed
comprimendo necat sociorum densitas. Ita felicitas pro Guillelmo triumpho   15
maturando cucurrit.

1 **Animadvertentes:** 'having noticed...' (see G.20(a)).	7f. **interceptos et inclusos:** 'those they had intercepted and cut off'.
absque nimio sui incommodo: 'without very great inconvenience to themselves'.	8f. **eo...usi:** *usi* governs *eo dolo*.
	simili eventu 'with...' (accompanying abl.).
3f. **Meminerunt quam...occasionem:** 'they recalled what achievement (or the achievement of) their desired objective the flight a little earlier gave' (see the narrative in section 11.1(i)).	9f. **aciem...circumvenire:** *aciem...horrendam* is in apposition to *reliquos*; *et...circumvenire* is an awkward appendix to *aciem...horrendam*: 'and it was terribly difficult to surround (sc. it)'.
4 **Barbaris:** 'among the barbarians' (i.e. the English).	11 **altera pars...altera:** i.e. 'the Normans etc.' and 'the English' respectively.
6 **ut superius:** 'as earlier'.	13 **mortui plus** looks forward to *moveri videntur*.
7 **quos...urgere:** *urgere* depends on *ausa sunt* and *quos...putabant* on *urgere* ('those whom they thought...').	14f. **Leviter...densitas:** *Leviter sauciatos* 'the walking wounded' is the object of *permittit* and *necat*, which share the same subject, *sociorum densitas*.
	15f. **triumpho maturando:** 'to hasten his triumph'.

(iii) *After a page of description and eulogy of William's valour, the narrative of the battle resumes. The Saxons, disheartened by their losses, especially that of Harold and his brothers, flee and are pursued and cut to pieces by the Normans.*

Jam inclinato die, haud dubie intellexit exercitus Anglorum se stare contra
Normannos diutius non valere. Noverunt se diminutos interitu multarum
legionum, regem ipsum et fratres ejus regnique primates nonnullos occubuisse,
quotquot reliqui sunt prope viribus exhaustos, subsidium quod exspectent
nullum relictum. Viderunt Normannos non multum decrevisse peremptorum   5
casu et, quasi virium incrementa pugnando sumerent, acrius quam in principio
imminere, ducis eam saevitiam quae nulli contra stanti parceret, eam fortitudinem quae nisi victrix non quiesceret. In fugam itaque conversi quantotius
abierunt, alii raptis equis, nonnulli pedites, pars per vias, plerique per avia.
Jacuerunt in sanguine qui niterentur aut surgerent non valentes profugere.   10
Valentes fecit aliquos salutem valde cupiens animus. Multa silvestribus in abditis
remanserunt cadavera, plures obfuerunt sequentibus per itinera collapsi.
Normanni, licet ignari regionis, avide insequebantur, caedentes rea terga,
imponentes manum ultimam secundo negotio. A mortuis etiam equorum
ungulae supplicia sumpsere, dum cursus fieret saper jacentes. Rediit tamen   15

fugientibus confidentia, nactis ad renovandum certamen maximam opportunitatem praerupti valli et frequentium fossarum. Gens equidem illa natura
semper in ferrum prompta fuit, descendens ab antiqua Saxonum origine,
ferocissimorum hominum. Propulsi non fuissent, nisi fortissima vi urgente.
Regem Noricorum, magno exercitu fretum et bellicoso, quam facile nuper   20
vicerunt.

1 **Jam inclinato die:** lit. 'when the day had already
turned', i.e. 'in the afternoon'.
stare looks forward to *valere*, upon which it
depends ('that they could...').

2f. **Noverunt...relictum:** there are four acc. + inf.
phrases following *Noverunt*, all in asyndeton:
(1) *se...legionum*; (2) *regem...occubuisse*; (3) *quotquot ...exhaustos* (sc. *esse*); (4) *subsidium...relictum*
(sc. *esse*).

3 **fratres ejus:** Gyrth, earl of East Anglia and
Leofwine, earl of Kent and Essex had been
killed early in the battle.

4 **quod exspectent:** 'for them to...' (purpose
clause).

6 **et** introduces the second acc. + inf. clause; its
verb is *imminere*.
virium incrementa: 'an increase in...' (object of
sumerent).

7f. **ducis...quiesceret:** two further acc. + inf.
clauses dependent on *viderunt*; supply *esse* with
each *eam*.
**eam saevitiam quae...eam fortitudinem
quae...:** 'such (was)...that...(and) such his...
that...' (in each case *quae* introduces a consecutive clause: RLRGr S 2(a)3(ii)).

10 **Jacuerunt in sanguine:** 'They lay dead in (a
pool of) blood...'.
qui...non valentes...: 'men who were in diffi-

culties or trying to get up, unable...'.

11 **Valentes...animus:** *Valentes* and *aliquos* are
complement and obj. of *fecit* ('made *aliquos
valentes*'); the subject is the phrase *salutem...animus* (*salutem* is obj. of *cupiens* 'which
desired...').
Multa looks forward to *cadavera* (subject of
remanserunt).

12 **plures** is expanded by *per itinera collapsi* (tr. 'by
collapsing...').

13 **licet ignari:** 'albeit ignorant of...'.
rea: used as an adjective 'guilty'.

14 **manum ultimam:** 'the final touch'.
A mortuis looks forward to *supplicia sumpsere* (=
sumpserunt: RLRGr A4); tr. 'from...'.

15 **dum:** 'since' (see G.30(a)).

16 **nactis:** agreeing with *fugientibus* and governing
opportunitatem ('when they took the opportunity to...(presented by) (lit. 'of')...'.

18 **descendens:** 'because it descends...' (see
G.20(b)).

19 **Propulsi...fuissent:** 'they would...have been...'
(for the form see G.4(a)).
nisi...urgente: 'had not...been besetting (sc.
them)'.

20 **regem Noricorum:** Harold Hardrada (see section 11 Intro.).
quam facile (CL *quam facillime*): 'very easily'.

(iv) *After the victory is secured, William returns to the battlefield. Harold is
identified and buried on the shore. A brief homily is addressed to the presumption of
the fallen usurper.*

Sic victoria consummata ad aream belli regressus reperit stragem quam non
absque miseratione conspexit, tametsi factam in impios, tametsi tyrannum
occidere sit pulchrum, fama gloriosum, beneficio gratum. Late solum operuit
sordidatus in cruore flos Anglicae nobilitatis atque juventutis. Propius regem
fratres ejus duo reperti sunt. Ipse carens omni decore quibusdam signis,   5

nequaquam facie, recognitus est et in castra ducis delatus, qui tumulandum
eum Guillelmo agnomine Maletto concessit, non matri pro corpore dilectae
prolis auri par pondus offerenti. Scivit enim non decere tali commercio aurum
accipi. Aestimavit indignum fore ad matris libitum sepeliri, cujus ob nimiam
cupiditatem insepulti remanerent innumerabiles. Dictum est illudendo, opor-   10
tere situm esse custodem littoris et pelagi, quae cum armis ante vesanus insedit.
Nos tibi, Heralde, non insultamus, sed cum pio victore tuam ruinam lacrymato
miseramur et plangimus te. Vicisti digno te proventu ad meritum tuum et in
cruore jacuisti et in littoreo tumulo jaces, et posthumae generationi tam
Anglorum quam Normannorum abominabilis eris. Corruere solent qui   15
summam in mundo potestatem summam beatitudinem putant, et, ut maxime
beati sint, rapiunt eam, raptam vi bellica retinere nituntur. Atqui tu fraterno
sanguine maduisti, ne fratris magnitudo te faceret minus potentem. Ruisti dein
furiosus in alterum conflictum, ut adjutus patriae parricidio regale decus non
amitteres. Traxit igitur te clades contracta per te. Ecce non fulges in corona   20
quam perfide invasisti, non resides in solio quod superbe ascendisti. Arguunt
extrema tua quam recte sublimatus fueris Edwardi dono in ipsius fine. Regum
terror cometa post initium altitudinis tuae coruscans exitium tibi vaticinatus
fuit.

1 **regressus:** the subject is William.

2 **tametsi...tametsi:** the first *tametsi* goes with *factam* (agreeing with *stragem*); the second introduces a clause with the verb *sit* (subject *tyrannum occidere* complements *pulchrum, gloriosum* and *gratum*).

3 **fama...beneficio:** 'in...' abl. of respect (see RLRGr L(f)4(vi)).

4 **Propius:** 'quite near' (+ acc.).

5 **fratres ejus duo:** the Earls Gyrth and Leofwine.
Ipse: 'he' (i.e. Harold: see G.11(a)(ii)).
quibusdam signis: 'by...' (abl. of means).

6f. **qui tumulandum eum...concessit:** 'who entrusted his burial to...'.

7 **Maletto:** i.e. Mallett.
matri looks forward to *offerenti*. Her name was Gytha, sister of Ulf, widow of Earl Godwin.

8 **Scivit:** the subject is now William.
non decere: 'that it was not right that...'.

9f. **indignum...cupiditatem:** 'that it would not be right (sc. for a man) to be buried...whose excessive greed was responsible for the fact that...' (lit. 'because of whose...greed...').

10 **Dictum est illudendo:** lit. 'It was said in joking', tr. 'William jested that...'.

10f. **oportere:** subject 'Harold'.

11 **quae...insedit:** Harold had a fleet patrolling the south coast and a strong armed force stationed on the shore.

12 **lacrymato** agreeing with *victore* 'who has wept over...' (deponent for active: see G.3).

13 **digno te proventu:** 'in...worthy of you'.

15 **Corruere solent qui...:** 'Those who...usually fall'.

17 **eam:** i.e. *summam potestatem.*
raptam: 'and when they have seized it (i.e. *summam potestatem*)...', obj. of *retinere.*

17f. **fraterno sanguine:** by killing Tostig (see section 11 Intro.).

19 **adjutus patriae parricidio:** 'helped by the murder of your fatherland'; i.e. by the deaths of English soldiers.

22 **quam recte sublimatus fueris** (for the form see G.4(a)): 'how justifiably you were elevated'(ironic: i.e. 'how unjustifiable was your presumption that you were elevated').

22f. **Regum terror:** in apposition to *cometa* (m.). The comet was thought of as a portent of disaster. This was the April 1066 appearance of Halley's comet, represented on the Bayeux

Tapestry with the inscription *Isti mirant stel-* 23f. **vaticinatus fuit** (for the form see G.4(a)):
lam.   'prophesied'.

2. Guy (Wido), bishop of Amiens (1058–75)

Guy, a scholar and later patron of the abbey of Saint-Riquier, seems to
have written this account of the battle of Hastings very soon after the
event, possibly within six months. It is composed in elegiac couplets (see
RLGVE 185). It is almost certainly one of the sources used by William of
Poitiers in his prose work. It is also fuller than the account by William of
Jumièges in *Gesta Normannorum ducum* and more explicit than the Bayeux
Tapestry. There is scarcely any doubt that its purpose was in some sense
political: it occasionally errs in tact towards William, while mentioning
some of the deeds of Eustace of Boulogne, who soon after Hastings
quarrelled with the duke and then began a rebellion.

It is notable that neither William of Jumièges nor William of Poitiers
gives a description of Harold's death. The passage excerpted here is
probably the source of William of Poitiers' account of Harold's funeral
(section 11.1(iv)). However, whereas William chose to interpret the ritual
as a jest against Harold, it seems likely that the burial upon the headland
ultimately reflects a pagan Viking ceremony. William raises a howe (burial-
mound) over him, mourns him, erects an inscription which enjoins him to
rest and watch, and takes the name of king at this spot. They are linked by
a power greater than their enmity, the magic which will prevent further
invasions.

See further: C. Morton and H. Muntz, *The Carmen de Hastingae Proelio of
Guy Bishop of Amiens*, Oxford, 1972.

(i) *The field is almost won by the Normans, but William sees Harold still
slaughtering his men from an elevated position. He calls for help and kills him.*

> iam ferme campum uictrix effecta regebat,
> iam spolium belli Gallia leta petit,
> cum dux prospexit regem super ardua montis
> acriter instantes dilacerare suos.
> aduocat Eustachium; linquens ibi prelia Francis,   535
> oppressis ualidum contulit auxilium.
> alter ut Hectorides, Pontiui nobilis heres
> hos comitatur Hugo, promtus in officio;
> quartus Gilfardus, patris a cognomine dictus:

regis ad exicium quatuor arma ferunt.   540
ast alii plures. aliis sunt hi meliores.
  si quis in hoc dubitat, actiŏ uera probat:
per nimias cedes nam, bellica iura tenentes
Hēraldus cogit pergere carnis iter.
per clipeum primus dissoluens cuspide pectus,   545
  effuso madidat sanguinis imbre solum;
tegmine sub galee caput amputat ense secundus;
  et telo uentris tertius exta rigat;
abscidit coxam quartus; procul egit ademptam:
  taliter occisum terra cadauer habet.   550

531f. The subject of both verbs is *Gallia leta; uictrix effecta* is in apposition to it. Tr. 'Already *Gallia leta*, made *uictrix* was..., already...(she) was...'.

533f. **regem** (i.e. Harold) is subject of *dilacerare* (tr. '...ing'); its object is *suos*, qualified by *acriter instantes* ('who were...').

535 **Eustachium:** Eustace II, count of Boulogne; he is then the subject of *linquens...contulit.*

536 **ualidum** looks forward to *auxilium.*

537 **Hectorides** ('son of Hector') refers to Eustace of Boulogne (the name has the same rhythm as Eustachius and the Franks claimed descent from Troy, so this is a flattering poetic invention).

Pontiui...heres: his name (Hugo) is given (in apposition to *nobilis heres*) in 538 (he is the heir of Guy I, count of Ponthieu, who seems to have outlived him).

539 **patris** depends on *a cognomine* (this probably means that he had his father's surname, Giffard – which means 'chubby-cheeks' – and not his forename; William of Malmesbury says that this act caused William to expel the culprit from his army).

540 **regis** depends on *ad exicium.*

quatuor: 'four men' (William, Eustace, Hugo of Ponthieu, and Giffard; *aduocat* in 535 shows that William took the lead himself, but required help).

541 **ast alii plures:** sc. 'there were'.

542 **probat:** sc. 'it'.

543 **nam** is postponed; tr. as first word.

bellica iura tenentes: object of *cogit*; tr. 'those who held the rights of war' (i.e. the Normans who were winning the battle).

544 **pergere carnis iter:** i.e. 'to die'.

545 **primus:** sc. 'knight' (probably William).

546 **effuso** looks forward to *imbre* (governing *sanguinis*).

547 **tegmine** is governed by *sub* and governs *galee* (= *galeae*: see O.1).

secundus: sc. 'knight' (probably Eustace).

548 **uentris** is governed by *exta* (obj. of *rigat*).

tertius: sc. 'knight' (probably Hugo).

549 **quartus:** sc. 'knight' (almost certainly Giffard).

ademptam: 'it having been...' (the *coxa*).

550 **taliter occisum** looks forward to *cadauer.*

(ii) Harold's death sparks a rout. William slaughters many English. Eustace (Hectorides) continues the pursuit through the night. At daybreak, William collects his own dead.

fama uolans 'Hēraldus obit!' per prelia sparsit;
  mitigat extimplo corda superba timor.
bella negant Angli. ueniam poscunt superati.
  uiuere diffisi, terga dedere neci.

dux ibi per numerum duo milia misit ad orcum,   555
  exceptis aliis milibus innumeris.
uesper erat; iam cardŏ diem uoluebat ad umbras,
  uictorem fecit cum Deus esse ducem.
solum deuictis nox et fuga profuit Anglis
  densi per latebras et tegimen nemoris.   560
inter defunctos noctem pausandŏ peregit
  uictor, et exspectat lucifer ut redeat.
peruigil Hectorides sequitur cedendŏ fugaces;
  Mars sibi tela gerit; mors sociata furit.
duxit ad usque diem uario certamine noctem;   565
  nec somno premitur; somnia nec patitur.
illuxit postquam Phebi clarissima lampas
  et mundum furuis expiat a tenebris,
lustrauit campum, tollens et cesa suorum
  corpora, dux terre condidit in gremio.   570
uermibus atque lupis, auibus canibusque uoranda
  deserit Anglorum corpora strata solo.

551 **'Heraldus obit!'** is the object of *sparsit*; sc. 'the cry...'.
  mitigat will have as subject *timor*.
  corda superba are those of the English troops.
554 **uiuere** depends on *diffisi* (tr. 'despairing of life').
  dedere = *dederunt* (RLRGr A4).
555 **per numerum:** 'in number'.
556 **exceptis...innumeris:** i.e. the soldiers killed in the battle up to this point.
558 The whole line is a clause introduced by *cum*.
  fecit has *ducem* as direct object and is completed by *uictorem...esse*.
559 **deuictis** looks forward to *Anglis* (dependent upon *profuit*).
560 **densi** looks forward to *nemoris* (dependent on *per latebras et tegimen*).
561 **pausando:** 'resting' (see G.18).
562 **lucifer** is the subject of the *ut* clause.

563 **Hectorides:** see n. on 537.
  cedendo: 'killing (sc. them)' (see G.18).
564 **sibi:** i.e. for Eustace (the phrase implies the job of squire, who attended the heavily armoured knight in battle to assist him).
  sociata: 'associated (sc. with him)'.
565 **duxit** (tr. 'spent') will have *noctem* as object.
567f. These lines are a clause introduced by *postquam* (*illuxit* will have *lampas* as subject); *furuis* looks forward to *a tenebris*.
569 The subject of *lustrauit* will be *dux* (= William).
  tollens et: the order is reversed because of the metre; *et* joins *lustrauit* and *condidit*.
570 **terre** (= *terrae*: see O.1) depends on *in gremio*.
571 **uoranda** (n.pl. acc.) looks forward to *corpora* (obj. of *deserit*).
  solo: 'on the ground'.

(iii) *William takes up the body of Harold and gives it a Viking burial on the cliff-tops, refusing to yield it up to his mother.*

Hēraldi corpus collegit dilaceratum,
  collectum texit sindone purpurea;
detulit et secum, repetens sua castra marina,   575

expleat ut solitas funeris exequias.
Hēraldi mater, nimio constricta dolore,
    misit ad usque ducem, postulat et precibus,
orbate misere natis tribus, et uiduate,
    pro tribus, unius reddat ut ossa sibi,   580
si placet aut corpus puro preponderet auro.
sed dux iratus prorsus utrumque negat,
iurans quod pocius presentis littora portus
    illi committet aggere sub lapidum.
ergŏ uelut fuerat testatus, rupis in alto   585
    precepit claudi uertice corpus humi.
extimplo quidam, partim Normannus et Anglus,
    compater Hēraldi, iussa libenter agit.
corpus enim regis cito sustulit et sepeliuit;
    imponens lapidem, scripsit et in titulo: 590
'per mandata ducis rex hic Hēralde quiescis,
    ut custos maneas littoris et pelagi.'
dux, cum gente sua, plangens super ossa sepulta,
    pauperibus Christi munera distribuit.
nomine postposito ducis, et sic rege locato,   595
    hinc regale sibi nomen adeptus abit.

573f. The subject of *collegit* and *texit* is William.

574 **collectum:** sc. 'it' (picking up *corpus*).
   sindone: made of linen, like altar-cloths.

575 **et** is postponed and joins *detulit* to what precedes.

576 **expleat** is the verb in the *ut* clause.

577 **Heraldi mater:** her name was Gytha.
   nimio looks forward to *dolore*.

578 **postulat et:** the order is reversed; *et* joins *postulat*
   to *misit*.

579f. Contains the substance of Harold's mother's
   entreaty: *orbate misere* (= *orbatae miserae*: see
   O.1) and *uiduate* (= *uiduatae*: see O.1) both
   look forward to *sibi* (indirect object of *reddat*) –
   'to her bereft...' (*natis tribus* 'of...' depends on
   orbate). They are thus part of an *ut* clause
   introduced by *postulat* which has two verbs –
   reddat (subject William, object *unius...ossa*) and
   preponderet, which is joined to *reddat* by the
   postponed *aut*; the subject of *preponderet* is 'she'
   (tr. 'she should...'); *puro* looks forward to *auro*
   'with...' (the idea is that she will give William
   more than Harold's weight in gold). William

of Poitiers mentions Harold's brothers' death
(see above section 11.1.(iii)).

582 **utrumque:** i.e. both the deals offered by Harold's mother.

583 **presentis** looks forward to *portus* (Pevensey,
   where William landed); the phrase depends
   on *littora*, object of *committet*.

584 **committet:** tr. 'he would...'.
   aggere is governed by *sub*.

585 **fuerat testatus:** 'had...' (see G.4(a)).
   in alto looks forward to *uertice*.

586 **humi** qualifies *claudi*.

587 **quidam:** William of Poitiers names him as
   William Mallett (on his father's side he was
   descended from a Scandinavian prince established in Normandy; his mother was daughter
   of Leofric, earl of Mercia; he was a first cousin
   of Harold's wife).

590 **et** is postponed and joins *scripsit* to what precedes.

592 **custos** governs *littoris et pelagi*.

594 **Christi munera:** 'alms' (the only specifically
   Christian aspect of the funeral, though it

may also reflect the gifts given to the dead at pagan burials).

595 **rege:** i.e. Harold.
596 **hinc** looks forward to *abit.*
regale...adeptus: it looks as though this quasi-pagan ceremony was more important to William than the Christian coronation which took place in Westminster Abbey (founded by Edward and the resting-place of his body) on Christmas Day 1066.

THE NORMAN OCCUPATION

3. The Book of Winchester (*Liber de Wintonia*) or Domesday Book (1086)

By the end of 1071, William was in control of all the English shires. His original claim to be Edward's lawful heir allowed him at first to act through Englishmen, even making use of local English levies in military operations. But there was prolonged resistance in many places, and this led to a change of policy. Almost all the greater lay lords of England now came under suspicion of rebellion and their lands were confiscated. The best were retained by the crown, others went to reward his leading fighters. Church and monastery holdings were left alone. In 1086, the situation was calm enough for the conqueror to order a land survey, which we call 'Domesday Book', covering all but the four northern counties and a few towns (such as London and Winchester). Bands of commissioners were sent through the shires. They convened the 'moots' and set questionnaires before juries drawn from each hundred. The information required was: (1) how many 'manors' were there in each hundred; (2) who had owned them in King Edward's time and to whom had they afterwards been allotted; (3) what stocks of peasants and plough-oxen did they possess; (4) what was their annual value, before and after the Conquest; (5) the categories of peasant, details of woods, meadows and pasture, and the amount of tax for which each manor would be responsible in the event of a Danegeld being levied by the king.

Like most medieval documents, the original is written in abbreviated form. For example, lines 2–3 of the ms. shorten *tempore Regis Edwardi* to *T.R.E.*, and *Terra est VIII. carrucis* to *Tra. e. VIII. car. IIII*[or] stands for *quattuor.* The vocabulary is highly vernacular (e.g. *hundredum*). There is a useful introduction to English documentary Latin by E. Gooder, *Latin for Local History*, London, 1975, which contains many examples and some plates.

TERRA COMITISSAE GODEVAE. IN COLESHELLE HUNDREDO. COMITISSA GOD-
EVA tenuit tempore Regis Edwardi AILSPEDE. Ibi sunt IIII^{or} hide. Terra est
VIII carrucis.Ibi sunt VIII uillani et I bordarius cum II carrucis et dimidia.
Silua habet I leuugam et dimidiam longitudine et unam leuugam
latitudine. Tempore Regis Edwardi ualebat XL solidos et post et modo   5
XXX solidos.

Ipsa comitissa tenuit in ADERESTONE III hidas. Terra est V carrucis. Ibi
sunt XI uillani et II bordarii et I seruus cum IIII carrucis. Ibi VI acrae
prati. Silua II leuugas longitudine et II leuugas latitudine. Valuit XL libras,
modo LX solidos.   10

Ipsa comitissa tenuit in ARDRESHILLE et HANSLEI II hidas. Terra est VII
carrucis. Ibi sunt XIII uillani cum V carrucis. Ibi VI acrae prati. Valuit IIII
libras. Modo C solidos.

Ipsa comitissa tenuit CHINESBERIE. Ibi sunt VI hidae. Terra est VII
carrucis. In dominio sunt II carrucae et I seruus et XXXIII uillani et III   15
bordarii cum II presbiteris habentes XVI carrucas. Ibi molendinum de IX
solidis et IIII denariis et XII acrae prati. Silua I leuuga longitudine et
tantundem latitudine. Tempore Edwardi Regis ualebat VI libras et post VII
libras. Modo XIII libras ad pondus.

Ipsa comitissa tenuit ANESTIE et FOCHESHELLE. IN BOMELAV HUNDREDO.   20
Ibi sunt IX hidae. Terra est VII carrucis. In dominio sunt II et II serui et
XXX uillani et VI bordarii cum XI carrucis. Tempore Edwardi Regis et
post ualuit X libras. Modo XII libras.

Ipsa comitissa tenuit COVENTREV. Ibi sunt V hidae. Terra est XX
carrucis. In dominio sunt III carrucae et VII serui et L uillani et XII   25
bordarii cum XX carrucis. Ibi molendinum de III solidis. Silua II leuugas
longitudine et tantundem latitudine. Tempore Edwardi Regis et post ualuit
XII libras. Modo X libras ad pondus.

HAS TERRAS GŌDĪVAE tenet NICOLAVS ad firmam de rege.

1 **IN COLESHELLE HUNDREDO**: Coleshill hundred (an
administrative district within a shire, with an
assembly which usually met each month).

2 **AILSPEDE**: Alspath.

hida *hidae* (hide: a unit of land measurement,
usually 80–120 acres).

3 **carrucis**: *carruca* plough (calculated together with
its oxen, usually 8; that is why there can be
'half- ploughs').

uillanus: villager (member of a *uilla* = Old
English *tun*).

bordarius: smallholder (a cultivator with less
land than a *uillanus* and of lower status).

5 **solidos**: shillings (cf. £.s.d. *libra, solidus, denarius*).

7 **ADERESTONE**: Atherstone.

8 **seruus**: serf (one tied to his land and his
master).

11 **ARDRESHILLE ET HANSLEI**: Hartshill and Ansley.

14 **CHINESBERIE**: Kingsbury.

16 **habentes** picks up *uillani* and *bordarii*.

16f. **de IX solidis et IIII denariis**: 'of...', i.e. its
value is 9s 4d.

19 **ad pondus** as opposed to a *libra* of money (£).

20 **ANESTIE et FOCHESHELLE IN BOMELAV HUNDREDO**:
Ansty and Foleshill in Brinklow hundred.

24 **COVENTREV**: Coventry (in Stoneleigh hundred).

29 **GODIVAE**: the superscript word was written to
clarify the word below. Note the different

orthography of the genitive (*-e* for *-ae*: see O.1).

ad firmam de rege: 'for the revenue of...' (*firma* = Old English *feorm*, provisions due to the king or the lord, or a fixed sum paid in the place of these and other miscellaneous duties). Countess Godiva, widow of Earl Leofric, grandmother of Earl Edwin, died between 1066 and 1086. Her lands had not yet been granted to others.

Section 12
The 'investiture contest'

By the tenth and eleventh centuries benefices such as bishoprics and abbacies were associated everywhere with landed wealth and so also with political power. It was commonplace to find such positions bought and sold by the lay rulers who thus effectively controlled the political make-up of their kingdoms. As the Church gradually became an arm of the secular ruler, other abuses within it also increased. Clerical marriage, for example, was commonplace. The need for a return to good order and Christian teaching was felt by many and underlay the reform movement which grew in strength at monasteries such as Cluny and Monte Cassino and eventually spilled over into the Church at large. Selling and buying benefices was condemned as simony. Clerical marriage was branded 'concubinage'.

By the early eleventh century the Papacy itself had become the battleground for secular interests. The major influence in election of the pontiff was that of the German Emperor. Henry II, for example, by giving military support to Cardinal Theophylact against Gregory in 1013 was instrumental in his succession as Benedict VIII. Under Henry III (1039–56) the German Church pressed reform onwards. But it was the same Henry who, it seems, removed Pope Gregory VI from his throne in 1046.

The so-called 'investiture contest' is really the story of two issues. One is the struggle of the Church to defeat simony and concubinage by asserting its own control over ecclesiastical affairs and the other is its claim for the Pope, as its head, to exert authority over secular rulers. Henry III's vigorous support of reform (he named four reforming popes) was not attended by an appreciation of a possible conflict of interests between Empire and Papacy. But his death in 1056 and the accession of the minor Henry IV (six years old) left control in the hands of less powerful secular individuals and gave the initiative to the increasingly radical ecclesiastical reformers. They revised procedures for papal election in 1059, excluding the Emperor, and in the same year and in 1063 forbade the ceremonial investment of clerics with churches by laymen. With the election of the radical Hildebrand as Pope Gregory VII (1073–85) and the arrival of Henry IV's majority conflict broke out. The Pope aimed to extirpate lay control and to establish the obedience of secular rulers to papal authority. Henry IV, whose power in Germany and Italy largely rested on his ability to appoint and so control the major ecclesiastical positions in his kingdom, clearly was not going to accept this. The question of control of the appointment of archbishops to Milan sparked off a savage contest in 1075. Henry and his bishops decreed Gregory's deposition. In 1076 Gregory announced Henry's excommunication and deposition as Emperor. For pragmatic reasons (see section 12.I–II Intro.) Henry was forced to beg Gregory's pardon at Canossa in 1077. The eventual result was a thirty-year schism, in which Henry supported anti-Popes and the Papacy anti-Emperors, neither side quite gaining success.

On the accession of Henry V (1106), the schism was ended and the question of which power was superior was tacitly laid aside. It was now that the question of lay investiture came to the forefront, for Henry V was no less vigorous than his father in claiming royal rights. Eventually (see section 12.III–IV Intro.) Henry forced Paschal to concede investiture and crown him. But the Pope was in turn forced by his radical cardinals and archbishops publicly to renounce this concession, which he did in 1112 and 1116 at the Lenten synods. Meanwhile, in 1112 Henry had to face the backlash in Germany from his treatment of Paschal, a nine-year struggle against the Saxons and sundry allies, including many leading ecclesiastics. In 1118 the breach once more became a schism when on the death of Paschal II, Henry set up an excommunicated archbishop as anti-Pope (Gregory VIII). The new Pope, Gelasius II, excommunicated them both. Peace was sought under Gelasius' successor, Calixtus II, in 1119, but terms could not be agreed. Finally, in 1122, after the capture of the anti-Pope and the settlement between Henry and his enemies at the Diet of Würzburg in 1121, the Concordat of Worms brought the conflict to a (temporary) close. The Emperor guaranteed the security of Church property and freedom in elections, and gave up irrevocably investiture with ring and staff (symbols of sacred power). The Pope granted for Henry's lifetime the concession of royal presence at elections in Germany, but not in Italy or Burgundy. In Germany the abbot/bishop-elect would receive the symbols of temporal power (*regalia* = the sceptre) from the king (also the Emperor), and was to do homage and take the oath of fealty before consecration. In Italy and Burgundy, a free election was followed by consecration. Within six months the king (also the Emperor) would give the *regalia* and receive homage. This settlement largely recognized existing facts, leaving the Emperor in control of the Church in Germany. And it resolved only the minor issue of investiture. The question of papal or imperial supremacy was laid aside. Yet the Papacy made two major gains from the dispute. First it had established its independence from secular authority. Secondly, it had established its authority over the Church as an international organization. This was bound to lead, as it did, to an eventual renewal of the major issue of supremacy (see section 19.III).

See further: *The Cambridge Medieval History*, vol. V, Cambridge, 1926.

12. I–IV THE EVENTS

12. I–II CANOSSA (1077)

The early years of Henry IV's majority were fraught with alarms. In 1071, a revolt by Duke Otto of Bavaria was easily crushed. But Henry's policy of establishing royal control by the building of castles in Saxony aroused fierce resentment and fear among the Saxon nobles. At the same time, he abandoned his former meek submission to the Pope's claims, and challenged Alexander II's right to interfere in the appointment of the archbishop of Milan in 1072. The Pope's reply was to excommunicate his counsellors. In 1073 the Saxons revolted and Henry was shown clearly his dependence upon the German nobles when they refused to allow the immediate use of an army gathered against Poland to quell the rebellion. Henry decided to concentrate his attention on the home front and wrote to the new Pope, Gregory VII, humbly begging absolution for his faults. Gregory acceded. But as soon as Henry had settled affairs in Saxony in 1075, he reneged on his settlement and sent ambassadors, including probably men under papal ban, to establish an imperial archbishop in Milan against the Pope's nominee. The Pope sent an embassy to Henry early in 1076 threatening excommunication. Henry replied in a letter rejecting Gregory's claim of authority over him, and then, after obtaining the support of the bishops of northern Italy, he sent Roland of Parma to Rome to tell the Pope he had been deposed. The Pope's response was to sentence Henry in return. He was declared excommunicated and deposed. But Henry had again miscalculated his strength at home, and the Pope's ban had the effect of allowing the German and the Saxon nobles to join forces to impose a settlement on Henry which placed their own particular interests above those of the kingdom. This they did at the Diet of Tribur (16 October 1076). The decisions reached were (a) that Henry would be deposed if he did not gain absolution from the Pope within a year and a day, and (b) that the Pope be invited to a council at Augsburg on 2 February 1077 to preside over the debate on the future of Germany. Henry's only way out was to obtain papal absolution. He escaped from Germany and made his way over the Mont Cenis pass to the castle at Canossa, where the Pope was awaiting an escort from the German nobles to see him safely to Augsburg. After three days of waiting (days which reflect the difficulty of Gregory's situation), the Emperor was admitted and given absolution. Henry's apparent change of heart was tested over the next three years by the Pope, who refused finally to decide the question of whether Henry or the king elected by the nobles (Rudolf of Swabia) was to be recognized. By 1080, Henry's power had once more grown enough for him to be less dependent upon papal favour, and his threatening message to the Lenten synod in that year led at once to a decision in favour of Rudolf. Henry was to prevail in the battle for control of Germany, but the excommunication he endured caused a schism which was deeply damaging to the kingdom and led ultimately to his betrayal by his son, Henry V, shortly before his death in 1106.

1. Lampert (or Lambert) of Hersfeld (*c*.1025–84/5)

Lambert was educated at Bamberg, became a Benedictine monk and around 1081 abbot of Hasungen. He was a strong supporter of the reform movement (Hasungen joined the Cluniac group of monasteries in 1081). It is not surprising, therefore, to find his *Annales Hersfeldenses* tinged with partisanship in their treatment of the events of 1072 and following. His vivid style is highly reminiscent of Sallust.

(i) *Henry crosses the Alps.*

Difficulter assecuto transeundi licentiam protinus alia successit difficultas. Hyemps erat asperrima, et montes, per quos transitus erat, in inmensum porrecti et pene nubibus cacumen ingerentes ita mole nivium et glaciali frigore obriguerant, ut per lubricum precipitemque decessum nec equitis nec peditis gressum sine periculo admitterent. Sed dies anniversarius, quo   5
rex in excommunicationem devenerat, e vicino imminens nullas accelerandi itineris moras patiebatur, quia, nisi ante eam diem anathemate absolveretur, decretum noverat communi principum sententia, ut et causa in perpetuum cecidisset et regnum sine ullo deinceps restitutionis remedio amisisset. Igitur quosdam ex indigenis locorum peritos et preruptis Alpium iugis assuetos   10
mercede conduxit, qui comitatum eius per abruptum montem et moles

nivium precederent et subsequentibus quaqua possent arte itineris asperitatem
levigarent. His ductoribus cum in verticem montis magna cum difficultate
evasissent, nulla ulterius progrediendi copia erat, eo quod preceps montis latus
et, ut dictum est, glaciali frigore lubricum omnem penitus decessum negare   15
videretur. Ibi viri periculum omne viribus evincere conantes, nunc manibus et
pedibus reptando, nunc ductorum suorum humeris innitendo, interdum
quoque titubante per lubricum gressu cadendo et longius volutando, vix
tandem aliquando cum gravi salutis suae periculo ad campestria pervene-
runt. Reginam et alias, quae in obsequio eius erant, mulieres boum coriis   20
impositas duces itineris conductu preeuntes deorsum trahebant. Equorum alios
per machinas quasdam summittebant, alios colligatis pedibus trahebant, ex
quibus multi, dum traherentur, mortui, plures debilitati, pauci admodum
integri incolumesque periculum evadere potuerunt.

1 **assecuto:** 'to him (sc. Henry) having obtained...'
   (the participle governs *licentiam*).
   transeundi licentiam: via the Mont Cenis pass,
   which was in the control of his wife's family,
   the counts of Savoy.
2 **in inmensum:** 'boundlessly'.
4 **per lubricum precipitemque decessum:** 'all
   along their...point of descent' (*decessus* 'departure' appears to be used here for *descensus*
   'descent').
5 **quo:** 'on which...' Henry had been excommunicated and deposed by the Pope on 21
   February 1076 and had until 22 February
   1077 to gain absolution, otherwise he stood
   to lose both his kingdom and his soul.
6 **e vicino:** 'nearly'.
6f. **nullas...moras:** 'no delays in...'.
8 **decretum:** 'that it had been decided...' (sc. *esse*:
   acc. + inf. after *noverat*, looking forward to *ut*
   'that...').
9 **et regnum...amisisset:** the subject is 'he
   (Henry)'.
9f. **Igitur...conduxit:** once more the unstated

subject is 'Henry'.
11f. **qui comitatum eius...precederent:** 'to go
   ahead of his' (i.e. Henry's: see G.11(e)(iii)).
12 **subsequentibus:** 'for those...' (dative of advantage).
13 **His ductoribus:** this abl. abs. phrase is within
   the *cum* clause.
14 **eo quod:** 'because' (see G.30(c)).
   preceps: 'being...'.
15 **decessum** = *descensum* (see earlier note).
17f. **reptando...innitendo...cadendo...voluta-
   do:** 'crawling...leaning...falling...rolling' (as
   though agreeing with *viri*: see G.18).
21 **conductu preeuntes:** 'leading the way so as to
   conduct (sc. them)' (an irregular use of abl. of
   the supine, which usually occurs with adjectives, e.g. *mirabile dictu* 'amazing to say').
23 **multi...plures...pauci:** 'many...more...and...'
   (note asyndeton).
   dum traherentur: 'while...' (for the mood of
   the verb, see G.29).
   mortui: sc. *sunt*.
   debilitati: sc. *sunt*.

(ii) *His arrival in Italy is greeted with enthusiasm by opponents of the Pope.*

Postquam per Italiam fama percrebruit venisse regem et superatis asperrimis
rupibus iam intra Italiae fines consistere, certatim ad eum omnes Italiae episcopi
et comites confluebant, eumque, ut regia magnificentia dignum erat, summo
cum honore suscipiebant, atque intra paucos dies infinitae multitudinis ad eum

congregatus est exercitus. Erant enim iam ab exordio regni eius semper   5
desiderantes adventum eius in Italiam, eo quod regnum illud bellis, sedicio-
nibus et latrociniis ac variis privatorum infestationibus assidue infestaretur, et
omnia quae preter leges et iura maiorum ab improbis hominibus presume-
bantur regiae auctoritatis censura corrigi sperarent. Preterea, quia fama
vulgaverat ad deponendum papam ferocibus eum animis properare, admo-   10
dum gratulabantur oblatam sibi occasionem esse, qua in eum, qui se iam
pridem ab ecclesiastica communione suspenderat, iniuriam suam idonee
vindicarent.

1–2 **fama...venisse...consistere:** 'the news that...
and...'.

2 **intra Italiae fines consistere:** the king made his
way through the bishopric of Turin to Pavia.

4 **infinitae multitudinis** depends on *exercitus*
(gen. of description).

5f. **Erant...desiderantes:** 'they had always longed
for...' (see G.4(b)).

6 **eo quod:** 'because' (see G.30(c): the subjunctive
verbs suggest that the reason is that of the
Italians, not the writer – see RLRGr U).

9 **corrigi sperarent:** 'they hoped would be put
right' (see G.22(b)).

9f. **fama vulgaverat...eum...properare:** 'rumour
had spread the news that...'.

10 **ferocibus** looks forward to *animis*.

11f. **qua...vindicarent:** 'by which to...' (purpose).
eum, qui...suspenderat: i.e. the Pope, Gregory
VII, who at the Lenten synod of 1076 deposed
and excommunicated the Lombard bishops,
for their complicity with Henry's disobedience
over the matter of papal authority and investiture (in CL, the verb would have been
subjunctive, within indirect speech: see
RLRGr R4(a)).

(iii) *The Pope sets out for Augsburg and, hearing of Henry's arrival, is diverted by
Countess Matilda, who is with him, to her fortress at Canossa.*

Interea papa rogatus per litteras a principibus Teutonicis, qui in Oppenheim
convenerant, ut in purificatione sanctae Mariae ad discuciendam causam regis
Augustae occurreret, invitis Romanis principibus et propter incertum rei
eventum iter illud dissuadentibus, Roma egressus est, et quantum poterat
profectionem accelerans, statuto die presto esse satagebat, ducatum ei prebente   5
Mathilda derelicta ducis Lutheringorum Gozelonis, filia Bonifacii marchionis
et Beatricis comitissae ... Igitur papa, dum in Gallias properaret, ex insperato
audiens regem iam esse intra Italiam, hortante Mathilda in castellum quoddam
munitissimum, quod Cannusium dicitur, divertit, expectare volens, donec
consilium adventus eius diligentius exploraret, utrum scilicet veniam admissi   10
postulare an iniuriam excommunicationis suae militari manu persequi plenus
animorum adveniret.

2 **in purificatione sanctae Mariae:** 'on (sc. the
feast of the)...', i.e. 2 February 1077.

3 **Augustae:** 'at Augsburg', in Bavaria.

3f. **invitis...et...dissuadentibus:** 'with...unwilling
...and...advising against...' (abl. abs.).

5f. **prebente Mathilda:** abl. abs. (obj. *ducatum*).

6 **derelicta...filia:** abl. in apposition to *Mathilda.*
Lutheringorum: lit. 'of the people of Lorraine',
tr. 'of Lorraine'.

6f. **Gozelonis....Bonifacii....Beatricis:**   Gozelo,
Boniface and Beatrice.

7 The passage left out gives details of Countess
Matilda's marriage, her close relationship with
Pope Gregory after her husband's death, and
after detailing the charges made against her by
the Emperor's supporters – especially the
clerics – of an improper relationship with
the Pope, refutes them by an appeal to
circumstances and the Pope's saintly life.

dum...properaret: 'while...' (see G.29 for the
mood of the verb).

in Gallias: 'to the Gauls', i.e. Cisalpine (North
Italy), Transalpine and Comata, from where he
would make his way to Augsburg.

8 **audiens:** 'having heard...' (see G.20(a)).

10f. **utrum...an...adveniret:** the subject is Henry.

10 **veniam admissi:** 'forgiveness for the crime he
had committed'.

11 **postulare:** 'to...' (purpose: see G.17(a)).
iniuriam excommunicationis suae: 'the injury of (i.e. caused by) his...' (for misuse of *suus*
see G.11(e)(iii)).
persequi: 'to...' (purpose: see G.17(a).

2. Bruno of Magdeburg (*fl.* 1084)

Bruno was a cleric at the court of Archbishop Werner of Magdeburg. He
wrote his *De bello Saxonico* in 1082 (it covers the years 1073–81). Since his
lord was one of the principal leaders of the Saxon revolt, it is understandable that Bruno's account of events should place on them an interpretation favourable to the rebels. The notable feature of his version of
Canossa is the assertion that the Pope imposed conditions on Henry which
he at once broke. His chronology of events, especially the documents he
cites, has been seriously questioned.

*Henry, in Italy and in a quandary, decides to humble himself before the Pope at
Canossa. He accepts the Pope's conditions for absolution, but soon afterwards breaks
them, and, according to Bruno, returns to the status of an excommunicate.*

Heinricus autem per Italiam vagans loco, sed magis animo, quid ageret
nesciebat, quia quicquid ageret regnum perdere timebat. Nisi enim supplex
ad apostolicum veniret et per eum solutus a banno fuisset, regnum se non
recepturum pro certo sciebat. Si vero supplex ad satisfactionem veniret,
timebat, ne sibi pro magnitudine criminum regnum pontifex auferret, vel   5
sibi inobedienti vincula potestatis apostolicae duplicaret. Ergo in multis curis in
diversa dividitur. Quamvis autem utroque modo se perditum et periturum non
dubitaret, tamen illam partem, in qua aliquid spei esse putabat, elegit; et laneis
indutus nudis pedibus ad apostolicum venit, dicens se plus amare regnum
coeleste quam terrenum, et ideo poenitentiam quamcunque sibi vellet   10
imponere se humiliter suscepturum. Apostolicus vero de tanti viri tanta
humilitate laetatus, praecepit ei ut regalem ornatum, donec ipse permitteret,
sibi non imponeret, quatenus omnipotenti Deo acceptior esset cordis eius

contritio, quo eam et foris ostenderet vilis habitus testimonio, et ut eos qui
erant excommunicati, convivio vel colloquio vitaret, ne quod in se propria   15
conversione fuisset Dei gratia mundatum, aliorum contagio fieret magis quam
fuerat inmundum. Quod utrumque cum se facturum polliceretur, absolutus
hac lege dimittitur, multum monitus ne Deo mentiatur, quia si promissa non
impleverit, non solum priora vincula non auferantur, sed etiam alia strictiora
superaddantur. Itaque reversus ad suos, cum coepisset eos a suo convivio   20
separare, magnum coeperunt tumultum facere, dicentes ei, quia si eos, quorum
sapientia et virtute obtinuisset hactenus regnum, nunc a se repelleret,
apostolicus ei nec illud reddere nec aliud acquirere potuisset. His et aliis
talibus verbis animus eius immutatur, et ad consueta pravo pravorumque
consilio revertitur. Imponit capiti aureum diadema, et in corde retinet ferro   25
fortius anathema. Excommunicatorum communioni miscetur, et a sanctorum
communione miser ille repellitur. Nunc fecit omnibus manifestum, quia non
verum esset quod dixit, plus se amare regnum coeleste quam terrenum. Quod
si parumper in obedientia permansisset, et regnum nunc terrenum cum pace
teneret, et quandoque coeleste sine fine possessurus acciperet. Nunc vero factus   30
inobediens, et hoc quod amat non habebit, nisi cum magno labore, et illud non
accipiet, nisi magna totius vitae mutatione.

1 **vagans...animo:** the two ablatives of respect are
inserted for rhetorical effect. Tr. as adverbs:
'geographically', 'mentally'.
   quid ageret: 'what to do' (deliberative subjunctive: see *RLGVE* 152 Note 1: the clause
depends on *nesciebat*).
2 **quicquid...timebat:** i.e. he was afraid that he
would lose (not 'he was afraid to lose...': CL
would have used a *ne* clause, not inf. here).
3 **solutus...fuisset:** 'were to have been released...'
(for the form see G.4(a)).
4 **recepturum:** sc. *esse*.
5 **sibi:** 'from him' (dat. of disadvantage with
auferret).
6 **sibi inobedienti:** 'upon him for his disobedience' (dat. of disadvantage with *vincula*).
6f. **in diversa dividitur:** lit. 'he was divided into
different directions', i.e. he was in two minds.
7 **se perditum et periturum:** sc. *esse* (the verb is
dubitaret).
10 **poenitentiam** is the object of *suscepturum* (sc.
esse), and is expanded by the clause *quamcunque
...imponere* ('whatever (one) he (the Pope)...').
12 **donec ipse...:** 'until he (i.e. the Pope)...' (see
G.11(b)).

13 **sibi non imponeret:** i.e. upon himself, Henry
(though in CL the reflexive refers back to the
subject of the introductory verb: see
G.11(e)(i)).
   quatenus...: 'in order that...' (see G.27(b)).
   eius: i.e. Henry's.
14 **quo:** 'in order that...' (see G.27(c)).
   eam: his *contritio*.
   et foris: 'on the outside too' (as well as in his
heart).
   testimonio: 'as evidence' (predicative dative).
   et ut: the clause depends on *praecepit* and the
subject is Henry.
15 **convivio vel colloquio:** 'at...or in...'.
   ne: 'in case...' (the verb is *fieret*).
   quod: 'that which...', 'what...'.
   in se: i.e. 'in Henry' (see G.11(e)(i)).
16 **fuisset...mundatum:** 'had been...' (for the form
see G.4(a)).
   magis looks forward to *inmundum* and forms a
comparative.
17 **Quod utrumque:** 'both things (i.e. conditions)'
(object of *facturum* sc. *esse*, acc. + inf. depending on *polliceretur*, verb of the *cum* clause).
18 **quia:** 'since...'.

18f. **si...impleverit...auferantur...superaddantur:** 'if he did not...would be...would be'.

20 **reversus ad suos:** this belongs within the *cum* clause (but *suos* and *eos* suggest that the writer changes his mind about the ultimate subject).

21 **dicentes ei, quia...:** 'saying...that...'.
    si: the verb is *repelleret* 'were to drive away...'.

23 **potuisset:** 'would be able' (the condition should mean 'if he had driven away...the Pope would not have been able...' (see G.28).

24f. **pravo pravorumque consilio:** lit. 'with wickedness and the advice of wicked men'.

27 **manifestum, quia:** 'clear that'.

29f. **et...et...:** the two apodoses to the *si...permansisset* clause.

30 **coeleste:** sc. *regnum*, obj. of *acciperet* and also of *possessurus* (tr. 'which he would possess...').

31 **hoc quod amat:** i.e. his earthly kingdom.
    illud: i.e. the kingdom of heaven.

32 **magna...mutatione:** 'through...'.

12. III–IV THE IMPRISONMENT OF POPE PASCHAL II (1111)

Henry IV had managed to reimpose his will on his recalcitrant nobles. But he had never managed to mend the breach with Rome. Under both Urban II (1088–99) and then Paschal II (1099–1118) the ban remained in force. Henry's son and heir recognized the damage this was doing to the strength of the imperial position and took the opportunity of discontent among the nobles following the murder of a Bavarian count by one of his underlings to set himself at the head of a rebellion in December 1104. The Pope welcomed this new ally with alacrity. Henry V was received back into the Church with the ceremony of laying on of hands in early 1106. But Paschal continued adamant in the policy of opposition to lay investiture, and when the death of Henry IV in August 1106 absolved Henry V of the need to appease the Papacy he too returned to his father's posture. The climax to several more years of manoeuvring and negotiation came with an agreement made by the plenipotentiaries of the two sides at Turri on 4 February 1111, which was to be ratified in Rome by Henry and the Pope. Imperial coronation (probably Henry's reason for continuing to negotiate) was to follow. On 12 February Henry entered St Peter's in Rome. The terms of the pact were that the Emperor was to renounce lay investiture, the Pope the *regalia* (i.e. the temporal privileges and possessions which went with the high ecclesiastical positions). But acceptance of the agreement was prevented by both ecclesiastics and lay nobles present, and the coronation could not take place either. Henry's response was to take the Pope and cardinals prisoner. After two months of captivity, Paschal was forced to concede lay investiture as an essential preliminary to consecration, to retract the ban on absolution and Christian burial for Henry IV, and to carry out the imperial coronation (13 April). Henry and the Empire did not get any real long-term benefit from this action.

3. Ekkehard of Aura (d. *c.*1126)

Ekkehard was abbot of Aura from 1108, having previously participated in the crusade of 1101 (see section 13). His *Chronicon* was a continuation of the work of Frutolf of Michelsberg. It is hard to reconcile the standard view that he supported the Papacy in the investiture contest with the fulsome treatment of Henry V's actions in the following account of Paschal's imprisonment.

(i) *Henry reduces Aricia, makes a provisional deal with the Church authorities at Sutri, and then heads for Rome.*

Postquam rex Heinricus rebus prospere per Longobardiam atque Tusciam dispositis apud Florentiam dominicae nativitatis gaudia cum ingenti suorum tripudio et mirando ac eatenus illius patriae civibus nunquam viso decore et honore percelebravit, moto inde versus Ariciam exercitu illoque perveniens a clericis benivole, a civibus subdole recipitur. Quorum etiam insolentiam satis   5
habundeque perdomuit, scilicet civitate illorum cum turribus, quas ad repugnandum regi preparaverant, funditus eversa. Aecclesiae tamen omni sua iusticia, quam idem cives violenter abstulerant, iuxta clericorum petitionem restituta. Inde ad Aquam-pendentem progressus legatos suos dudum ab Aricia missos ab apostolico boni nuncii baiulos reperit, remissisque aliis nunciis cum   10
Romanorum, qui supplices illic sibi occurrerant, paulatim Sutriam processit. Ibi legati apostolici cum missis regiis advenientes promptum esse papam ad consecrationem et omnem regis honorem et voluntatem, si tamen ipse sibimet annueret libertatem aecclesiarum, laicam ab illis prohibens investituram, recipiendo nichilominus ab aecclesiis ducatus, marchias, comitatus, advoca-   15
tias, monetas, thelonea, caeterorumque regalium quae possident summam. Prebuit rex assensum, sed eo pacto, quatinus haec transmutatio firma et autentica ratione, consilio quoque vel concordia totius aecclesiae ac regni principum assensu stabiliretur; quod etiam vix aut nullo modo fieri posse credebatur. Qua conventione facta, dimissis legatis et obsidibus utrimque rex   20
hilariter ad Urbem properat. Domnus apostolicus cum omni clero immo tota Roma se in eius occursum adornat.

1 **Postquam** introduces everything up to *percelebravit*.

2 **dominicae nativitatis gaudia:** i.e. Christmas.
   cum governs *ingenti...tripudio* and *mirando ac...nunquam viso decore et honore*.

3 **civibus:** 'by...' (dat. of agent with *viso*: see G.16(b)).

4 **perveniens:** 'having arrived' (see G.20(a)).

5 **Quorum:** 'their...' i.e. *civium* (connecting relative).
   etiam: 'however'.

6 **scilicet civitate...eversa:** 'that is by razing to the ground...'.

7f. **sua iusticia:** 'its own rights' (see G.11(e)(iii)).

9   **restituta:** sc. *est.*
9f. **Aquam-pendentem...Aricia...Sutriam:** Aquapendente, Ariccia and Sutri (all in the Lazio region).
10f. **cum Romanorum, qui...:** i.e. 'with (those of) the Romans who...'.
12 **apostolici:** gen. s.
    promptum esse: sc. 'said (that)...'.
13 **consecrationem:** i.e. anointing Henry Holy Roman Emperor.
    si tamen ipse sibimet...: 'if only he (the king) were to ...to him (the Pope)...' (see G.11(a)(ii) and G.11(e)(i)).

15 **recipiendo nichilominus:** 'nevertheless receiving...' (as though *recipiendo* agreed with the subject, 'he (the king)': see G.18).
16 **caeterorumque regalium** depends on *summam.*
17 **eo pacto, quatinus...:** 'on this condition, that...' (see G.26(b)).
17f. **firma...ratione:** 'in a...way'.
    vel: 'and'.
19 **quod etiam:** 'but this...' (i.e. the achievement of the preceding condition).
21 **Urbem:** i.e. Rome.

(ii) *Ekkehard lists briefly the momentous events in Rome, culminating in the agreement of the Pope to Henry's demands and Henry's victory over the Romans.*

Post haec quae gesta sunt, longissimum est enarrare; utpote quam immensa honorificentia sit receptus et per Argenteam portam usque ad mediam rotam antiquo Romanorum instituto deductus, ibique lectis publice privilegiis, tumultuantibus in infinitum principibus pre aecclesiarum spoliatione ac per hoc beneficiorum suorum ablatione, quam ingenti periculo, quam varia   5
disceptatione tota dies illa consumpta sit, et postremo pater apostolicus ab episcopis et aliis fidelibus regis sit custoditus, usque ad pacatam et aecclesiasticam consecrationem imperatoris, in exemplum patriarchae Iacob dicentis ad angelum: *Non dimittam te, nisi benedixeris michi.* His ita in dominica quadragesimae transactis, Romani tota nocte congregati summo mane impetum   10
undique fecerunt in exercitum regis adeo ut commissa aliquandiu pugna regem per se ipsum necesse esset exercitui succurrere; quod et impigre fecit et usque ad inclinatam iam diem fortissimi militis et optimi ducis opus agens Dei gratia suis victoriam, hostibus post multam stragem fugam incussit.

1   **utpote quam:** 'that is to say with what...'.
2   **per...rotam:** the *Argentea porta* was one of the doors of St Peter's; *rota* (CL 'wheel') probably means 'court', as in the later 'Rota Romana'. Where is meant, however, is unclear.
3   **antiquo...instituto:** 'in ancient tradition...'.
3f. **ibique...consumpta sit:** the second colon of the narrative begins with two abl. abs. phrases (*lectis...privilegiis* and *tumultuantibus...ablatione*) and continues with another *quam* clause: 'with how great...how varied...'.
4   **principibus:** in this account these must be the

bishops and archbishops, since the emphasis is upon the removal from the churches of the worldly trappings which went with them (lands, taxes, etc.). But other accounts show that the lay nobles were just as anxious about the loss of prestige they would suffer with the freeing of their control over Church appointments.
6f. **et postremo...michi:** the final colon of the narrative does not have a conjunction: tr. 'and finally (sc. the way in which)...'.
7f. **usque ad...consecrationem:** 'until...(sc. took place)'.

8 **in exemplum…michi:** 'following the example (of)…'; *dicentis* (agreeing with *patriarchae Iacob*) 'who said…'. The reference is to Gen. 32.26, where Jacob wrestles with God at the place he later calls Phanuel ('I saw God face to face') and refuses to release him until he gives him his blessing. The biblical parallel gives a powerful justification for the action of Henry in holding the Pope.

9f. **in dominica quadragesimae:** 'on the Sunday of Lent'; but the date intended is 12 February,

the Sunday of *quinquagesima*.

10 **summo mane:** 'at first light'.

11f. **regem per se ipsum necesse esset…:** '(that) it was necessary for the king in person…'.

12 **quod et…et…:** 'this he both…and…'.

12f. **usque ad inclinatam iam diem:** 'right up to midday'.

14 **suis victoriam, hostibus…fugam incussit:** 'he produced victory for his men, but flight for the enemy'.

(iii) *Henry takes Paschal to his camp, where the Pope performs the imperial coronation and grants Henry the privilege of investiture.*

Post triduum Roma secedens domnum apostolicum secum duxit et eo quo potuit honore tenuit donec, compositis quae res poscebat per regiones negociis, pacatis omnibus adversariis, instans pascha non longe ab Urbe in castris celebravit ibique, sedatis inter ipsum et apostolicum inter regnum et sacerdotium dissensionibus inveteratis, post octavas paschae cum nimio populi Romani   5
immo totius aecclesiae ac inestimabilis exercitus tripudio ante confessionem sancti Petri augusti nomen et imperium a Christo ipse crismate rite perunctus et sacratus et sub augustissima pompa coronatus suscepit, dato sibi in presenti per manum apostolici sub testimonio astantis aecclesiae privilegio investiturae aecclesiasticae, iuxta quod utriusque predecessoribus placuerat et permanere   10
consueverat. Cuius inconvulsibilem stabilitatem domnus papa mox sub anathemate confirmabat. Sic denique ea die *gloria in excelsis Deo et in terra pax hominibus bonae voluntatis*, ut ita dicam, est recuperata, dum tam inveterata et eatenus incorrigibilia de regno Christi scismatum ablata sunt scandala.

1f. **eo** with *honore*.

2 **donec** looks forward to *instans…celebravit*: the Pope was held from 16 February to 12 April.
compositis looks forward to *negociis*, which is the antecedent of *quae* (the object of *poscebat*).

4 **sedatis** looks forward to *dissensionibus inveteratis* (abl. abs.).
ipsum = *se*.

5 **post octavas paschae:** 13 April.
nimio looks forward to *tripudio* and the genitives between depend on this phrase.

6 **confessionem:** here, the place where Peter died confessing his belief in Christ, i.e. tomb, shrine, catafalque.

7 **a Christo** looks forward to *suscepit*.

8 **dato** looks forward to *privilegio* (abl. abs.).

9f. **investiturae aecclesiasticae:** i.e. lay investiture, just what Popes from Gregory VII to Paschal had always striven to remove from the kings of the Catholic West.

10f. **iuxta quod…placuerat:** 'according to (sc. the terms) which had been agreed by…' (see below section 12.V–VI for the arguments used by the two sides).

11 **Cuius:** 'Its…' (i.e. of the privilege allowing lay investiture).

11f. **sub anathemate:** 'under an anathema': the reference is to the oath sworn by Paschal and sixteen cardinals that he would take no further action over investiture and never pronounce an anathema against the king (he was forced to recant at the Lenten synod of 1112 on investiture and later in the year meekly confirmed the anathema decreed against the king by Archbishop Guy of Vienne).

12f. *gloria...voluntatis:* Lk 2.14 (another biblical reference – the words of the angel to the shepherds – which implicitly justifies the actions of the king).

13 **dum:** 'when' (see G.29).

13f. **inveterata** and **incorrigibilia** look forward to *scismatum.*

14 **de regno Christi:** depends on *scismatum* ('dissensions about...': see G.10(b)).

scandala: subject of *ablata sunt.*

4. *Rhythmus de captivitate Paschalis papae*

The author of this poem seems to have been an Italian supporter of the Papacy at Rome. It appears to have been composed while Pope Paschal was being detained (i.e. between 12 February and 12 April 1111), since it ends with an appeal to the Normans (*principes Apuliae*) to rescue him from the Germans. The metre is 8pp with an AA BB CC rhyme scheme. See section 5 Intro., p. 58.

(i) *The scorpion's arrival.*

> Dum floret verno tempore
> Auster quieto equore,
> ex aquilonis partibus
> currens equis velocibus
> natus ex adulterio   5
> surrexit quidam scorpio.
>
> Subiugavit Liguriam
> peragravitque Tusciam,
> Romam ingressus fraudibus
> et fedavit sanguinibus   10
> ac sanctissimum presulem
> a Roma fecit exulem.

1f. **Dum floret...Auster:** lit. 'while the South Wind was in flower', i.e. early in the New Year (*verno tempore* 'in spring' is surprising; but in Ireland the start of spring is marked by St Brigid's Day, 1 February!).

2 **quieto equore:** abl. abs. 'when...'.

3 **ex...partibus:** i.e. from Germany.

4f. **currens** and **natus** look forward to *quidam scorpio* (i.e. Henry V).

5 **natus ex adulterio:** a calumny – Henry V was the son of Henry IV and Bertha of Turin. But since Henry IV had been excommunicated by 1080, it was possible to speak as though he had not received the proper sacraments of marriage.

9 **ingressus:** sc. *est.*

fraudibus: 'deceitfully'.

11 **presulem:** i.e. the Pope.

12 **a...exulem:** Paschal was held at Henry's camp outside the city walls.

(ii) *The agreement at Sutri.*

Stanzas 3–4 suggest that history contains no instance of so vile a deed. In comparison, the deeds of Herod and Nero appear saintly!

Cum pervenisset Sutrium	25
Urbis Rome confinium,	
papa premisit nuncios	
illi presules obvios,	
qui sacram pacem quererent	
nec non illi assererent.	30

Tunc iurat ille scorpio	
cor adnectens periurio	
supra sacras reliquias,	
quod linqueret ecclesias,	
nec pastoralem baculum	35
ultra daret vel anulum.	

Promittit pacem regiam,	
sacra firmans inperia,	
defendere catholicos,	
dampnare simoniachos.	40
iurat pape obsequium	
iuxta morem fidelium.	

Devovit coram omnibus	
qui aderant presulibus,	
quod pauperes defenderet	45
ac raptores obprimeret,	
dampnaret sacrilegia,	
pugnaret pro ecclesia.	

25 **pervenisset:** the subject is Henry, but changes to *papa* in the main clause.

26 **Urbis Rome** (= *Romae*: see O.1) **confinium:** in apposition to *Sutrium* – 'a place near to...'.

27 **nuncios:** 'as...' in apposition to *presules*.

28 **illi** looks forward to *obvios*: 'to meet...'.

29 **qui...:** purpose clause.

30 **nec...assererent:** 'and to make sure of claiming (sc. it, i.e. *pacem*) for him (the Pope)'.

31 **iurat** looks forward to *quod* ('that...').

34 **linqueret:** 'he would leave (sc. free)'.

36 **ultra:** 'in future'.

38 **sacra...inperia:** sc. 'thus' with *firmans*, i.e. accepting the priority of ecclesiastical power.

39f. **defendere...dampnare:** sc. 'he promises...'; there is asyndeton between the lines, so sc. 'and...' (for inf. with *promitto* see G.22(b)).

40 **simoniachos:** in practice clerics who had paid

for their offices were much more likely to take the king's line, since extreme ecclesiastics claimed that the sacraments administered by such priests were null.

41 **pape** = *papae* (see O.1).

43 **Devovit** looks forward to *quod* ('that...').

45 **defenderet** (and the other verbs in the *quod* clause): 'he would...'.

47f. **dampnaret...pugnaret:** in asyndeton within *quod* clause: sc. 'and that...' with each.

(iii) *Henry's arrival in Rome and his capture of Pope Paschal.*

> Tunc Romam his blandiciis
> perrexit, sed insidiis.   50
> pueri ei cum avibus
> occurrunt atque laudibus,
> tribuni atque proceres
> et post iuvenes veteres.

Stanzas 10 and 11 describe the reactions of the clergy (monks, cardinal-priests and priests) and the procession to St Peter's, conducted amid hymns and general rejoicing.

> Cum vidit papam obvium,
> falsum offert obsequium.
> os osculum dat pedibus,
> sed cor manet in cedibus.   70
> papa suscepit dulciter,
> osculatur fideliter.
>
> Post hec intrat ecclesiam
> beati Petri agiam.
> caudam sue perfidie   75
> valvis levat ecclesie.
> sanctissimum pontificem
> invasit ut carnificem.
>
> Manu cepit sacrilega,
> se christianum abnegat   80
> et ad Christi iniurias
> has paravit insidias,
> quas nec Herodes inpius
> paravit neque Claudius.

50 **insidiis:** 'with plots (sc. in mind)'.

51 **cum avibus:** there seems no good reason why the king should be met by boys carrying birds, so *avibus* may be a plural of *ave*, and mean 'greetings', 'cries of *ave*'.

53 **tribuni...:** more subjects with *occurrunt*.

67 **vidit:** the subject is Henry.

68 **offert:** sc. to the Pope.

70 **in cedibus** = *in caedibus* (see O.1): '(sc. intent) on...'.

71 **suscepit:** sc. Henry.

72 **osculatur:** sc. 'and...' (asyndeton).

75 **caudam sue perfidie** (= *suae perfidiae*: see O.1)...*ecclesie* (= *ecclesiae*: see O.1): lit. 'he lifted the tail of his treachery at the doors of the church', i.e. he revealed finally what he was really about.

78 **carnificem:** grammatically this agrees with *pontificem*, but since it is Henry who is the aggressor, it looks as though it should refer to him (this error may reflect the Italian *camefice*, the ordinary word for what the writer is trying to say).

79 **sacrilega:** n.pl. 'a sacrilegious course of action'.

83 **Herodes inpius:** see for example Mt 2.16 for the massacre of the innocents.

84 **Claudius:** presumably the Roman emperor Claudius (10 BC–AD 54).

(iv) *A valediction to Paschal and an appeal to the Normans.*

Stanzas 15–18 describe the German attack on the people and clergy, their mutilation of children, the plight of the nobles, the Pope's misfortune and the reactions of onlookers. Stanzas 19–24 describe the lamentations of the pious women of Rome, ask Germany why it has turned to sacrilege from piety, appeal for vengeance and describe Henry as the standard-bearer of Antichrist. Stanzas 25–6 are a prayer to St Peter for help.

Salve, papa catholice, 145
vir Paschalis pacifice!
letare nunc in carcere,
coronandus in ethere.
flagicium hoc punies,
cum martirium finies. 150

Utinam simus miseri
digni consortes fieri
tue laudande glorie,
vir celebris memorie.
ora pro nobis miseris, 155
dignus coniungi superis.

Vos principes Apulie,
orti stirpe Neustrie
bellica arma capite,
Romam ire satagite. 160
vestro sternenda gladio
Teutonicorum concio.

147 **letare:** 'be glad...'.

148 **coronandus in ethere:** 'because you will be...' (see G.19).

151f. **Utinam...digni:** *miseri* '(we) poor creatures' is an apposition to the subject of *simus*; *digni* governs *fieri*.

153 **tue laudande glorie** (= *tuae laudandae gloriae*: see O.1): depends on *consortes* 'sharers in...'; *laudande* 'praiseworthy'.

154 **memorie** = *memoriae* (see O.1).

156 **dignus...superis:** sc. 'you who are (worthy to...)'.

157 **principes Apulie** (= *Apuliae*: see O.1): the

Normans, who had often supported papal policy during the eleventh century with their armed might.

158 **Neustrie** = *Neustriae* (see O.1): Normandy.

161 **sternenda:** sc. *est* ('must be laid low (by)...') looking forward to *concio*.

12. V–VII THE ARGUMENTS

The vast literature generated by this conflict covers almost every conceivable genre – chronicle, history, biography, dialogue, Scriptural commentary, epistle, sermon, verse (both classical and rhythmic metres). Much of the argumentative material can be found gathered together in the three volumes of *Monumenta Germaniae Historica* entitled *De lite* ('On the (investiture) contest'). The central questions are always: (a) who has power over whom; (b) has the king authority to invest ecclesiastics with the ring and staff, symbols of spiritual power. But the first is usually treated as part of the debate over the Emperor's place in papal election, which was the practical point at issue when the dispute began. The election in 1061 during Henry's minority of Pope Alexander II without the consent of the German regency and against its wishes, following on from procedures newly agreed by the Church in 1059, called forth the first pamphlets. This is the context of St Peter Damian's *Disceptatio synodalis* (see further below). The second question was also part of the discussion from the earliest stages, as the Church had outlawed lay investiture in 1063, but became more important in the later stages (after the accession of Henry V), when it became clear that no final answer was possible on the bigger issue. The very strong feelings aroused by these seemingly trivial questions are understandable since upon their resolution depended real power, whether for the Empire or for the reform movement in the Church. The style of discussion is of great interest. Each side adduces authorities, biblical, historical and legal, to bolster its case. Argument is then built upon these. This is the standard medieval method of conducting disputations, but one which is already under threat from the increased use and prestige of dialectic (see below, section 14, on Anselm and Berengar).

12. V–VI PAPAL ELECTION

On the papal side it could be argued on the basis of the forged decretal known as 'The donation of Constantine' that the Emperor Constantine had given temporal power in Italy to the Pope and that this excluded the Emperor from any necessary part in papal election. The imperial camp could cite papal decrees which made the involvement of the temporal ruler essential. Both could use biblical texts to good effect. The following extracts, which belong to different moments in the conflict, give some idea of the style of the debate.

5. St Peter Damian (1007–72)

Peter Damiani, born in Ravenna and educated at Faenza and Parma, became a monk at the Apennine hermitage of Fonte Avellana in about 1035. A formidable and gifted speaker, he was active in his promotion of the ascetic life and of Church reform. He interested himself especially in the question of simony, on which he took the position that while simony was wrong, the sacraments offered by simoniacal priests were still valid. In 1057 he was appointed cardinal-bishop of Ostia and from then on was a leading figure in the events surrounding papal elections. The following extract comes from his *Disceptatio synodalis* ('Debate in synod'), a dialogue between 'a defender of the Roman Church' and 'the king's advocate'. It reflects a desire on Peter's part to influence discussion at the council called at Augsburg on 27 October 1062 to settle the question of which Pope was the legitimate one, the cardinals' candidate, Alexander II, or the imperial choice, Cadalus, bishop of Parma (Honorius II). His arguments do not present an extreme papal position, since he accepted that the king's privilege should in some way be defended. But the *Regius advocatus* concedes far more than the *Defensor Romanae aecclesiae* and the work ends with a virulent condemnation (in verse) of the anti-Pope Cadalus.

(i) *The donation of Constantine and the behaviour of later Emperors towards Rome argues that the Church is pre-eminent, not the Emperor.*

Defensor Romanae aecclesiae: Ut autem id ipsum adhuc manifestius pateat et te super hac dimicandi materia perdidisse tibimet ipsi clarius innotescat, lege Constantini imperatoris edictum, ubi sedis apostolicae constituit super omnes in orbe terrarum aecclesias principatum. Nam postquam supra corpus beati Petri basilicam fundator erexit, postquam patriarchium Lateranense in beati Salvatoris honore construxit, mox per imperialis rescripti seriem Romanae   5

aecclesiae constituit dignitatem. Ubi nimirum beato Silvestro suisque successoribus obtulit, ut regali more et aurea corona plecterentur in capite et ceteras
regii cultus infulas usurparent. Verum beatus Silvester ornamenta quae
sacerdotali congruere iudicabat officio in proprios usus assumpsit, coronam   10
vero vel cetera, quae magis ambiciosa quam mistica videbantur, omisit. Cui
etiam Constantinus Lateranense palatium, quod eotenus aula regalis extiterat,
perpetuo iure concessit, regnum Italiae iudicandum tradidit. Ipse vero
Constantinopolim velut in secunda Roma perpetuo regnaturus abscessit.
Longe vero post Theodosius imperator beati Pauli basilicam coepit. Quo   15
defuncto, filius eius Honorius eandem basilicam ad calcem usque perduxit. Hi
quoque Romanae aecclesiae privilegium nichilominus firmaverunt. Quomodo
ergo prerogativam sibi in Romani pontificis electione relinquerent, qui
Romanam aecclesiam nequaquam sibi studuerunt subdere, sed preferre, non
precipere, sed parere, non precellere, sed subesse?   20

1 **id ipsum:** viz. that it is the Pope who has precedence over the Emperor.

1f. **et...innotescat:** 'and so that it will become more clearly known to you yourself that you have lost over this topic of contention'.

3 **edictum:** sc. *est* 'it (i.e. the primacy of the Pope) was...'.

sedis apostolicae depends on *principatum* (obj. of *constituit*).

5 **fundator:** '(sc. as)...'.

patriarchium Lateranense: 'the Lateran papal palace'.

6 **per...seriem:** 'in the course of...'. The rescript is the forged document known as the 'Donation of Constantine'.

6f. **Romanae aecclesiae** depends on *dignitatem* (obj. of *constituit*).

7 **Ubi:** 'in this document' (connecting relative).

beato Silvestro: St Silvester (Pope 314–35).

10 **sacerdotali** looks forward to *officio* and the phrase depends on *congruere (quae...congruere* is acc. + inf. depending on *iudicabat*).

11 **vel cetera:** 'and...'.

Cui: 'to him (i.e. Silvester)' (connecting relative).

12 **extiterat:** 'had been'.

13 **regnum...:** 'and...' (asyndeton).

iudicandum: 'to rule'.

Ipse: 'he' (the Emperor Constantine: see G.11(a)(ii)).

14 **Constantinopolim:** 'to', acc. of place (looks forward to *abscessit*).

velut looks forward to *regnaturus* ('intending to...' see G.10(c)).

15 **post:** 'afterwards'.

Theodosius: the Emperor Theodosius I (d. 395).

beati Pauli basilicam: the church of San Paolo fuori le Mura, built on the supposed site of St Paul's decapitation.

16 **Honorius:** son of Theodosius I and western Emperor from 393 at Rome.

ad calcem usque: i.e. *usque ad calcem* 'right to...'.

17f. **Quomodo...relinquerent:** 'How can they have...'.

18 **prerogativam sibi:** 'the prerogative for themselves...' (obj. of *relinquerent*).

qui...: lit. 'who...'; tr. 'when they...'.

19 **Romanam aecclesiam** looks forward to *subdere*, of which it is the object.

19f. **nequaquam...subdere, sed...non...sed...non ...sed...:** 'by no means to...but to... not to...but to...not to...but to'.

(ii) *That is true, but Nicholas II gave Henry III a privilege in papal elections and this privilege remains in force.*

Regius advocatus: Adsentior plane et ratum duco, quod loqueris. Sed esto, quod nunc regia celsitudo ex antiquorum consuetudine principum hoc sibimet allegare non possit. Verumtamen tu hoc negare non potes, quod pater domini mei regis piae memoriae Heinricus imperator factus est patricius Romanorum, a quibus etiam accepit in electione semper ordinandi pontificis principatum. 5 Huc accedit, quod prestantius est, quia Nicolaus papa hoc domino meo regi privilegium quod ex paterno iam iure successerat prebuit et per sinodalis insuper decreti paginam confirmavit. Cum ergo privatus quisque a suo decidere iure non debeat, donec ventilato negotio iudicialis in eum sententia promulgetur, quo pacto maiestas regia prerogativam hanc suae dignitatis amisit, 10 quam et ex apostolicae sedis liberalitate percepit et ex paterno imperialis fastigii iure successit? Quo, inquam, modo in Romana aecclesia dignitatis adeptae locum sine iudicio perdidit, qui Romanam aecclesiam non offendit?

1 **ratum duco:** 'I consider valid...'.
quod: 'what...'.
esto: 'let it be (that)...' (imper. of *sum*: see RLRGr E1). This sentence and the next work in tandem, and could be expressed in English as one, constructed thus: 'But even granting that..., nevertheless...').
2 **regia celsitudo:** i.e. 'the king'.
3f. **domini mei regis:** i.e. Henry IV.
4 **Heinricus:** Henry III, made Holy Roman Emperor at the Roman synod of 1046. **imperator** looks forward to *patricius* and governs *Romanorum*.
5 **ordinandi pontificis principatum:** 'the leading role in...' (obj. of *accepit*).
6 **Huc accedit, quod...quia:** 'add to this what...(namely) that ...'.
Nicolaus: Pope Nicholas II, 1058–61 (formerly Gerard, bishop of Florence).
7 **privilegium** looks forward to *prebuit* and *confirmavit*, of which it is the object.
6 **quod...successerat:** 'which he had received...' (CL uses dat. or *in* + acc.).
7f. **per...paginam:** 'in a page of a synod decree as well' (one of a number of rather inflated and slightly unclear expressions used by the writer). This has not survived, but was granted before

the famous Roman synod decree on papal election of 1059, in which the cardinal-bishops have the principal role and the Emperor eventually takes the oath from the elected Pope before he is consecrated. But this right of assent was not inalienable and had to be renewed for each successive Emperor.

8 **privatus quisque:** 'all private individuals' (see RLRGr I5(c)(i)).
a suo looks forward to *iure*.
9 **iudicialis** looks forward to *sententia* (subject of *promulgetur*).
10 **quo pacto:** 'how..?'.
maiestas regia: i.e. 'the king' (cf. *regia celsitudo*).
prerogativam governs *suae dignitatis* (and is obj. of *amisit*).
11 **ex** looks forward to *liberalitate* (which governs *apostolicae sedis*).
ex paterno looks forward to *iure* (which governs *imperialis fastigii*).
12 **successit:** as above, so here, with acc. (*quam*).
Quo looks forward to *modo*: 'how...?'.
12f. **in...locum:** *in...aecclesia* depends on *locum* ('the position...in...': see G.10(b)), *dignitatis adeptae* depends on *locum* ('the position of...') and *adeptae* is passive (see RLRGr C4 Note 2).
13 **qui:** '(sc. he) who...'.

(iii) *Yes, but circumstances (the minority of Henry IV and riots at Rome) demanded an immediate papal election, which had to go ahead without consultation.*

Defensor Romanae aecclesiae: Privilegium invictissimo regi nostro ipsi quoque defendimus et ut semper plenum illibatumque possideat vehementer optamus. Porro autem Romana aecclesia multo nobilius atque sublimius quam mater carnis mater est regis. Illa siquidem peperit ut per eius traducem revertatur in pulverem, ista genuit ut Christi sine fine regnantis efficiat coheredem. Et cuncti 5 liquido novimus, quia rex, licet egregiae indolis, tamen adhuc puer est. Quid ergo mali Romana fecit aecclesia, si filio suo, cum adhuc impubes esset, cum adhuc tutoris egeret, ipsa tutoris officium subiit et ius quod illi competebat implevit? Sepe mater iudicis tribunal irrumpit, testes adsciscit, notarios convocat, sicque per adstipulationes et rata, insuper et apicum monimenta 10 omnia bonorum suorum filio iura delegat. Interim tamen, usque dum ille ad iuvenilis aetatis incrementa perveniat et rationis capax fiat, illa cuncta dispensat, omnia ordinat, sicque quod iam alieni iuris est patrimonium ad propriae disponit provisionis arbitrium. Nunquid ob hoc dicenda est mulier illa filio suo concessa subtrahere? Immo verius perhibetur, ut puto, pietatis studio deservire, 15 quia, quae rudis adhuc filius dilapidare ac prodigere poterat, haec illa sibimet apte disposita, caute retenta et rationabiliter ordinata conservat. Carnalis ergo mater adiuvat filium in rebus terrenis, et mater aecclesia filio suo regi prebere non debet auxilium in spiritalibus donis? Obmutescat ergo plectenda versutia, quae scilicet hoc damnat, quod predicare debuerat, illi crimen imponere 20 nititur, quae pro benefactis gloriae titulum promeretur.

Huc accedit, quia nonnumquam ob varietatem temporum sepe mutandus est ordo causarum. Tunc enim, quando pontificem Romana sibi prefecit aecclesia, tantae simultatis fomes in seditionem cives accenderat, tantus livor et odium tumultuantis populi corda turbaverat, ut de tam longinquis terrarum 25 spatiis nequaquam regiae clementiae prestolari possemus oraculum. Nisi enim quantocius ordinaretur antistes, perniciosus in populo gladius mutuis vulneribus deseviret et non parva Romanorum civium strages fieret.

---

1 **Privilegium...nostro:** sc. *datum.*
ipsi: agreeing with the subject of *defendimus.*
2 **ut...possideat** depends on *optamus.*
semper...illibatumque: sc. *privilegium* (the phrase is the object of *possideat*).
3f. **Romana aecclesia...mater est regis** is the core of this sentence.
4f. **Illa...ista:** 'she (the *mater carnis*)...(but) she (the *Romana ecclesia*)...' (see G.11(a)(ii)).
4 **siquidem:** here simply emphatic 'indeed' (see G.14).
ut...revertatur: the subject is 'he', i.e. 'her child'.
5f. **ut...efficiat coheredem:** the subject is *ista*; sc.

'him' (i.e. 'her son') before *coheredem* (which governs *Christi...regnantis*).
6 **adhuc puer est:** on the death of Henry III in 1056 his son Henry IV was not quite six and a troubled regency lasted until March 1065; at the date of the *Disceptatio* (1062) Henry was about twelve.
6f. **Quid...mali:** 'What wrong...?'.
7 **Romana** goes with *aecclesia.*
filio suo: 'for...' (dat. of advantage) looking forward to *subiit* and *implevit.*
8 **ipsa:** 'she' (i.e. the *Romana aecclesia*): see G.11 (a)(ii)).

ius looks forward to *implevit* (of which it is the object).

9 **iudicis** depends on tribunal (obj. of *irrumpit*).

10 **insuper...monimenta:** 'and in addition (through) written records' (lit. 'the memorials of writings'): *monimenta* depends on *per*.

11 **omnia...iura:** obj. of *delegat* (*bonorum suorum* depends on it); *filio* is indirect object of *delegat*.

usque dum: 'until'.

11f. **ad...incrementa:** i.e. to the end of his minority.

12 **illa:** i.e. his mother (subject).

13 **sicque** looks forward to *disponit*.

quod...patrimonium: 'the patrimony (obj. of *disponit*) which is now in someone else's jurisdiction'.

ad looks forward to *arbitrium*, which governs *propriae provisionis* (a compressed phrase which means 'the way she thinks it should best be managed with an eye to the future').

14f. **dicenda...subtrahere:** 'should that woman be said to be...' (*concessa* 'things handed over to' is the object of *subtrahere* and governs *filio suo*).

15 **perhibetur...deservire:** 'she should be said to...' (lit. 'she is said...').

16 **quia:** 'because...' (looks forward to *conservat*).

quae: 'the things which...' (obj. of *dilapidare* and *prodigere*, and picked up by *haec*, obj. of *conservat*).

poterat: 'would have been able...' (see RLRGr S2(c)2 Note 6).

illa: 'she' (subject of *conservat*).

sibimet: 'by herself' (dat. of agent – see G.16(6) – depending on *disposita*, *retenta* and *ordinata*, n.pl. accusatives agreeing with *haec*).

18 **prebere** looks forward to *auxilium* (which is the direct object; **filio...regi** is the indirect object).

19 **plectenda:** 'wicked' (lit. 'to be punished').

20 **hoc...quod:** 'that which...' (see G.11(c)).

predicare debuerat: 'it (i.e. *versutia*) ought to have...'.

20f. **illi...quae:** '(sc. and) upon her (indir. obj. of *imponere*)...who...' (i.e. upon the Church).

21 **promeretur** is from *promereor*.

22 **Huc accedit quia:** 'add to this that...'.

23 **ordo causarum:** 'the way things are arranged'.

Tunc enim: i.e. 30th September 1061, when the cardinal-bishops of the Roman Church had met near Rome and elected Anselm of Baggio, the Patarine bishop of Lucca, as Pope Alexander II. The Roman nobility and the bishops of Lombardy elected Cadalus, bishop of Parma, as Pope Honorius II, a choice confirmed on 28 October by Henry IV at Basle. The bloody struggle which ensued between the supporters of the two sides was settled practically, if not finally, in favour of Alexander II by the Synod of Augsburg, 27 October 1062.

Romana looks forward to *aecclesia*.

24 **tantae simultatis** depends on *fomes* (subject of *accenderat*).

25 **tumultuantis populi** depends on *corda* (obj. of *turbaverat*).

25f. **de** looks forward to *spatiis* (i.e. 'from so far away').

26 **regiae clementiae** looks forward to *oraculum* (obj. of *prestolari*) on which it depends; the phrase really means 'the merciful king'.

26f. **nisi...ordinaretur...deseviret et...fieret:** 'Had not...would have...and...would have...'.

27 **perniciosus** looks forward to *gladius* and **parva** to *strages*.

in populo is probably better understood with *deseviret* than with *gladius*.

27f. **mutuis vulneribus:** 'with (the result of)...'; i.e. there would have been civil war (and in fact there was: Cadalus/Honorius II won a bloody battle on 14 April 1062 in the Neronian field, but Rome was divided between the rival popes until the arrival of Duke Godfrey of Lorraine with an army).

6. Gregory of Catina (*fl.* 1111)

Gregory of Catina was a monk of the Italian monastery of Farfa, in the province of Rieti, and probably the author of a chronicle composed there. The *Orthodoxa defensio imperialis* ('Orthodox defence of the Emperor') belongs to the year 1111, probably to the summer – the period of Paschal

II's imprisonment (see above section 12.III–IV Intro.). The author brings together a battery of authorities, including the 'Donation of Constantine' and Mt 22.21 (*quae sunt Cesaris reddendum Cesari* 'Render unto Caesar the things that are Caesar's'), to establish the case for imperial election of the Pope, imperial authority over the Pope and the right of lay investiture.

De investitura ergo baculi vel anuli, quam rex vel imperator quilibet eclesiae prelatis faciunt, exemplo Constantini contenti imperatoris, adhuc perscrute-mur, si quid inrationabile aut infidele in ipsa invenire valeamus, et per quam non sacri honoris gradum, non munus praelacionis sanctae, non ministerium spirituale, non eclesiarum vel clericorum consecrationes, nec aliquod divinum   5
sacramentum, sed potius sui defensionem tribuunt officii, secularium rerum seu temporalium atque corporalium possessionum omniumque eclesiae eiusdem bonorum iuris confirmationem; in qua eciam cernitur concordia principis, oblatio obsequii eiusdem potestatis et ministerium ipsius principis benigne professionis. Ergo eiusdem ratio investiturae sanum sapienti non videtur contra   10
fidem, quia regibus et imperatoribus quoquo modo fuit concessum antiquitus, dum omnimodis venalitas caveatur. Nec unquam legitur a quoquam sancto-rum catholicorum fuisse interdictum. Magis vero per multa annorum curricula idcirco inolitum credimus, quoniam fideliter ab orthodoxis et in nomine Domini gestum dignoscitur. Apostolus nempe docet, quod quicquid extra   15
fidem agitur peccatum omnino censeatur et quodcunque vera fide operatur divino iudicio minime condempnatur. Desinant itaque pseudoloqui sive rudiloqui imperii vigorem dissipare et eclesias Dei quibusdam scissionibus dilacerare et variis surreptionibus belligerare, et quia inimici sunt non querant in sirpo nodum et imperii decus nunquam amplius calumnientur.   20

1f. The structure of the first sentence is *De investi-tura...quam... faciunt...perscrutemur, si...valeamus, et per quam...tribuunt...in qua...cernitur.*

1 **De investitura** looks forward to *baculi vel anuli.*

1f. **eclesiae prelatis:** 'for the...of...'.

2 **exemplo** depends on *contenti* (agreeing with subject of *perscrutemur*); *Constantini...imperatoris* depends on *exemplo.*

3 **si quid:** 'whether anything...' (CL *num quid*: see G.24(c)).

et per quam...: second of three relative clauses relating back to *investitura*; the nouns *gradum, munus, ministerium, consecrationes, sacramentum, defensionem* and *confirmationem* are all objects of *tribuunt* (subject *rex vel imperator*).

6 **sui** looks forward to *officii*, but seems to mean 'their', i.e. 'the prelates'', rather than 'the king's' (see G.11(e)(iii)).

6f. **secularium...confirmationem:** the phrase is in apposition to *defensionem*, with *iuris* dependent upon *confirmationem* and *secularium...bonorum* upon *iuris* (tr. '(that is) a confirmation of the right to...').

8 **in qua eciam...:** last relative clause describing *investitura*; the verb *cernitur* has three subjects: *concordia (principis), oblatio (...potestatis)* and *ministerium (...professionis).*

9 **obsequii** depends on *oblatio* and *eiusdem* ('afore-mentioned') *potestatis* (= *principis*) upon *obse-quii.*

9f. **benigne** (= *benignae*: see O.1) **professionis**

depends on *ministerium* and *ipsius principis* upon *benigne professionis*.

10 **eiusdem** ('aforementioned') looks forward to *investiturae*.

sanum goes with *sapienti:* 'to a person in his right mind'.

11 **quoquo modo:** lit. 'in whatever way', sc. 'they wanted to use it'.

12 **dum:** 'provided that...'.

Nec...legitur: introduces acc. + inf. 'that it was...by...'.

13 **fuisse inderdictum:** 'that it was...' (for form see G.4(a)).

14 **idcirco** looks forward to *quoniam*.

inolitum: '(sc. that it, i.e. the procedure of lay investiture) has been ingrained...'.

14f. **fideliter** with *gestum:* 'because it is recognized that (it) was performed...'.

15 **Apostolus:** i.e. St Paul, Epistle to the Romans 14.23: *Omne autem quod non est ex fide, peccatum est* 'Everything not based on faith is a sin'.

quod...: 'that...' (the verb is *censeatur*, the subject of which is the clause *quicquid...agitur*; *peccatum* is the complement).

16 **quodcunque...operatur** is the subject of *condempnatur*.

19f. **non querant in sirpo** (= *in scirpo*) **nodum:** an ancient proverb (e.g. Plautus, *Menaechmi* 2.1, 22; Terence, *Andria* 5.4.38) meaning 'to seek what doesn't exist'.

20 **nunquam...calumnientur:** 'let them no more...' (cf. G.23(c): CL *ne...umquam*).

12. VII LAY INVESTITURE

The practice of investiture with the ring and staff by kings went back a long way, and since the power of precedent counted for much in the Middle Ages, the imperial side had a strong case. They sought to bolster it by claiming that these items were not a divine sacrament but only a confirmation of the temporal and corporal possessions of the Church (Gregory of Catina's argument). They did so precisely because these emblems were given sacred significance by the papal party, as can be seen from the excerpts from Rangerius of Lucca's poem.

7. Rangerius of Lucca (*fl.* 1097)

Rangerius was a monk and bishop of Lucca from 1097 to 1112. His two works – both completions of works by Donizo, the first a life of St Anselm of Lucca, and the long poem *De anulo et baculo* ('On the ring and staff') – were produced for Matilda, countess of Tuscany. As we have seen (above section 12.1(iii)), she was a strong proponent of the Papacy. The poem is written in elegiac couplets, generally without the characteristic medieval ornaments of internal (leonine) or end-rhyme (see section 10.4 Intro.).

(i) *Ring and staff are sacred symbols, signifying marriage and pastoral care.*

> Anulus et baculus duo sunt sacra signa, nec ullo
> de laici manibus suscipienda modo.

anulus est sponsi, sponsae datur anulus, ut se
noverit unius non alium cupere.
gemma notat sponsam, sponsus signatur ab auro,   5
haec duo conveniunt, sicut et illa duo.
atque ideo clamat primi vox illa parentis
propterea matrem cum patre linquit homo
et sic haerebīt uxori, quatenus ultra
non sunt carne duo, sed magis una caro.   10
at baculus prefert signum pastoris opusque,
ut relevet lapsos, cogat et ire pigros.
Christus utrunque sibi nomen tenet officiumque.
Christus habet sponsam, Christus ovile regit.

1 **nec ullo** looks forward to *modo*.

3f. **ut se/noverit unius...cupere:** 'so that she
knows that she (belongs to) one man (and
should) not...'.

6 **sicut et illa duo:** 'just like those two' (i.e. *anulus
et baculus*).

7 **primi...parentis:** 'that saying of...' (the reference is to the words of Adam – *primus parens* –
at Gen. 2.24, uttered when he woke up to find
Eve beside him: *quamobrem relinquet homo
patrem suum et matrem et adhaerebit uxori suae,
et erunt duo in carne una* 'Therefore shall a man
leave his mother and his father and cleave to
his wife and the two shall be one flesh'; cf. Mt
19.5).

8 **propterea:** 'that...'.

9 **haerebit:** scanned with a heavy final syllable,
against CL rules.
quatenus: 'that...' (result clause: see G.26(b)).

12 **lapsos:** 'those who have fallen'.
cogat et: *et* is postponed; tr. 'and should...'.

13 **sibi:** 'as his own'.

14 **sponsam:** i.e. the Church.
ovile: the laity.

(ii) *The arguments advanced by temporal rulers on lay investiture simply subordinate
Christ and the Church to lay control.*

praesule sacrato sollemniter atque peruncto
anulus et baculūs in sacra signa datur.   860
anulus, ut sponsum se noverit et sibi iunctam
(non sibi, sed Christo) diligat ecclěsiam.
at vero baculūs, ut Christi servet ovile
et caveat sevos terrificetque lupos.
si sic est, imo quoniam sic esse negari   865
nequaquam sobria de ratione potest,
quae ratio vel quae magis est insania contra
aecclěsiae ritus quemlibet arripere
quod sibi concessum numquam fuit? et pietatem
solvit et errorem suscitat aecclěsiae.   870
contendunt reges haec signa dedisse priores:

ostendant, vel quos vel quibus et faciant.
quod si non possunt ostendere, cesset abusus
nec iam sub gladio serviat hic baculus.
an quia ditavit pia munificentia regum 875
aecclĕsias, debet posteritas rapere,
vel quid deteriūs, et libertatis honorem
et quae non tribuīt omnia deprimere?
an non eripitur libertas pontificalis,
quandō iuratur regibus et dominis? 880
quandŏ manus dantur et per sacra iura ligantur,
et ius et ratio subditur imperio.
subditur et Christūs, et Christi iure soluto
curia curetur, curia diligitur.

859 **praesule...peruncto:** abl. abs. 'when...'.
860 **in sacra signa:** 'as...'.
datur: tr. 'are...'.
861 **anulus:** sc. 'is given'.
se...noverit...: 'should know that he (is)...and that...'.
sibi iunctam looks forward to *ecclesiam* (scanned with second syllable light).
862 **non...Christo:** although the priest is joined to the Church, in fact the Church is *married* to Christ; the author cannot forbear making this clear and so obfuscating the neat picture he has drawn.
863 **baculus:** sc. 'is given'.
Christi depends on *ovile*.
864 **sevos** looks forward to *lupos* and the phrase is the object of both verbs, despite the intervention of *-que*.
865f. **imo quoniam...potest:** 'nay, since it is in no way possible for it to be denied that it is so...'.
866 **sobria de ratione:** 'by...' (see G.15(a)(ii)).
867 **quae...quae:** tr. 'what...or what..,?'.
magis: 'rather'.
contra looks forward to *ritus* (governing *aecclesiae* – scanned with second syllable light).
868 **quemlibet arripere...:** 'for a person to...' (in the text adopted here, the object of *arripere* is *quod... fuit* 'what...'; for *concessum fuit* see G.4(a)).

869f. **et...et...:** the subject is 'This...(i.e. grabbing what isn't yours)', the main idea of the preceding sentence.
871 **contendunt reges...:** sc. *se* 'that they first...', or 'that their predecessors...'.
872 **vel...faciant:** '(let them show) whom and to whom, and (sc. then) let them do (it)', i.e. if they can prove their claim, then lay investiture can continue.
873 **quod si...:** 'and if...this (obj. of *ostendere*)'.
876 **rapere:** sc. what the *pia munificentia regum* gave to the churches.
877 **vel...deterius:** 'Or what is worse...'.
877f. **et...et...deprimere:** the infinitive depends on *debet*.
878 **quae...omnia...:** 'all the things which it...' (obj. of *deprimere*).
879 **libertas:** a watchword of the Church reform movement.
880 **iuratur:** 'an oath is made...'.
manus dantur: lit. 'hands are given', i.e. an oath of feudal fealty is made.
884 **curia...diligitur:** *curetur* is an error for *curatur* and *diligitur* for *deligatur* (cf. *ligantur*, l. 881 above); the *curia* is the papal court, so here 'the Papacy' or 'the Pope', and so 'the Church'. Tr. 'the Church is taken into (sc. the Emperor's) care, the Church is bound to a liege-lord'.

Section 13
The First Crusade

On 27 November 1095 at Clermont Pope Urban II delivered his call for Christians to take up the crusade against the Muslims. The immediate reason for the announcement was an appeal in 1094 by the hard-pressed Byzantine emperor Alexius (1081–1118). He asked the Pope as head of Western Christendom for help against the advance of the Turks. The defeat at Manzikert (1071) had left Asia Minor open to the enemy, and they duly overran the territory. They were now established not far from Constantinople itself. But the emotive issue for Christians was rather the grip of the infidel upon the holy places of Palestine, which were established in the tradition as objects of veneration and in practice by the institution of pilgrimage (see above sections 2.4 and 7.4). There was a third factor. The northern Italian trading cities (Genoa, Pisa and Venice) and the Normans under Robert Guiscard had by the early 1090s pushed back substantially the sphere of Muslim influence in the Mediterranean. It was certainly in their interests to push it back further. Moreover, the possibility of carving out Latin kingdoms in the East, despite the ostensible purpose of aiding the Byzantines, was a very real inducement to impoverished nobles. This coincidence of religious zeal, economic interest and political opportunity accounts for the success of Urban's call.

From France especially and from the Norman kingdoms (but not from imperial Germany, which was embroiled in its own battles, not least with the Papacy) armies travelled to Constantinople between the springs of 1096 and 1097. Their journeys were fraught with problems and there were many military encounters even with the troops of Alexius. From Constantinople, the route towards the crusaders' ultimate goal, Jerusalem, lay through the Muslim capital at Nicaea and through Antioch, once a principal outpost of the Eastern empire (see map 7). Nicaea fell on 19 June 1097. To the next stage of the journey, the success of the crusaders at Dorylaeum (1 July) against the army of Qilij-Arslan opened the way. Armenia Minor was quickly won, not least because it had a Christian population. But Antioch, gateway to Syria and Jerusalem, was a tougher nut. The siege lasted from 21 October 1097 until the city's betrayal on 3 June 1098 (see further section 13.II Intro.). Despite the claims of Alexius, Bohemond (son of Robert Guiscard, the Norman conqueror of south Italy and Sicily) established himself as prince of Antioch. The rest of the army began its march towards Jerusalem on 13 January 1099 and arrived outside the walls on 7 June. The city submitted to assault on 15 July. On 22 July Godfrey of Bouillon became the first ruler of the Latin kingdom of Jerusalem. This success was consolidated by the victory over an Egyptian army near Ascalon on 12 August. In one form or another, the kingdom of Jerusalem was to last until 1291.

See further: Steven Runciman, *A History of the Crusades*, vol. I, *The First Crusade*, Cambridge, 1968.

I THE COUNCIL OF CLERMONT (27 NOVEMBER 1095)

Four independent accounts of the Pope's speech at Clermont survive by people who were present. They agree in substance about the aims for the Crusade expressed there. Christendom is shamed by Muslim supremacy in the East. The Church there has often asked for help. The Holy Land belongs by right to Christendom but is in the hands of the infidel. The Christian princes should turn their weapons away from each other against these foes and, in a Holy War, oust the usurpers from the holy places. The soldiers who lose their lives in this enterprise will go to heaven and be absolved of their sins.

1. Baudri (Baldricus) of Bourgueil (1046–1130)

Baudri was a Benedictine monk, abbot of Bourgueil from 1089 and archbishop of Dol from 1107. He was a notable poet, with important contacts. His *Historia Hierosolymitana*, written in 1108, is mostly a second-hand account of the First Crusade, composed for stylistic reasons on the basis of another history (see below 13.II Intro.). But he *was* at Clermont and his clear, if effusive, style captures something of the vigour and excitement of Urban's address.

7 The route of the crusaders from Durazzo to the Holy Land.

BLACK SEA

MINOR
Dorylaeum

ANIA)

ARMENIA

Antioch
St Simeon's
Port

CYPRUS

Tripoli

Damascus

Jerusalem
Ascalon Bethlehem

Urban addresses the princes and urges them to turn from their internecine conflicts to the true military service – that of Christ.

Quid dicimus, fratres? Audite et intelligite. Vos accincti cingulo militiae magno superbitis supercilio, fratres vestros laniatis, atque inter vos dissecamini. Non est haec militia Christi, quae discerpit ovile Redemptoris. Sancta Ecclesia ad suorum opitulationem sibi reservavit militiam, sed vos eam male depravastis in malitiam. Ut veritatem fateamur cujus praecones esse debemus, vere non tenetis viam per   5
quam eatis ad vitam,vos pupillorum oppressores, vos viduarum praedones, vos homicidae, vos sacrilegi, vos alieni juris direptores. Vos pro effundendo sanguine Christiano expectatis latrocinantium stipendia, et sicut vultures odorantur cadavera, sic longinquarum partium auspicamini et sectamini bella. Certe via ista pessima est, quoniam omnino a Deo remota est. Porro si vultis animabus vestris   10
consuli, aut istiusmodi militiae cingulum quantocius deponite aut Christi milites audacter procedite et ad defendendam Orientalem Ecclesiam velocius concurrite. Haec est enim de qua totius vestrae salutis emanaverunt gaudia, quae distillavit in os vestrum divini lactis verba, quae vobis propinavit Evangeliorum sacrosancta dogmata. Haec ideo, fratres, dicimus ut et manus homicidas a fraterna nece   15
contineatis et pro fidei domesticis vos exteris nationibus opponatis. Et sub Jesu Christo duce nostro acies Christiana, acies invictissima melius quam ipsi veteres Jacobitae, pro vestra Jerusalem decertetis, et Turcos qui in ea sunt nefandiores quam Jebusaeos impugnetis et expugnetis. Pulchrum sit vobis mori in illa civitate pro Christo in qua Christus pro vobis mortuus est. Ceterum si vos citra mori   20
contigerit, id ipsum autumate mori in via si tamen in sua Christus vos invenerit militia. Deus ejusdem denarii est retributor, prima et hora undecima. Horrendum est, fratres, horrendum est vos in Christianos rapacem manum extendere. Minus malum est in Sarracenos gladium vibrare. Singulare bonum est, quia et caritas est pro fratribus animas ponere. Ne vero de crastinis evectionibus solliciti sitis: sciatis   25
quia timentibus Deum nihil deest nec his qui eum diligunt in veritate. Facultates etiam inimicorum vestrae erunt, quoniam et illorum thesauros expoliabitis et vel victoriosi ad propria remeabitis vel sanguine vestro purpurati perenne bravium adipiscemini. Tali imperatori militare debetis cui omnis non deest potentia, cui quae rependat nulla desunt stipendia. Via brevis est, labor permodicus est qui tam   30
immarcescibilem vobis rependet *coronam*. Jam nunc igitur auctoritate loquamur prophetica. '*Accingere,*' o homo unusquisque, '*gladio tuo super femur tuum, potentissime*': 'Accingimini,' inquam, 'et estote filii potentes, quoniam melius est vobis mori in bello quam videre mala gentis vestrae et sanctorum. Non vos demulceant illecebrosa blandimenta mulierum rerum vestrarum quin eatis, nec   35
vos deterreant perferendi labores quatenus remaneatis.'

---

1 **magno** looks forward to *supercilio*: 'with...'.

2 **inter vos dissecamini**: 'you are cutting one

another to pieces'.

4 **depravastis** = *depravavistis* (see RLRGr A4).

5 **Ut...fateamur:** 'to...'.

5f. **per quam eatis:** 'on which to...' (purpose clause).

7f. **pro...sanguine Christiano:** 'in return for...'.

9 **longinquarum partium** looks forward to and depends on *bella*: tr. 'wars in...'.

10 **animabus** = *animis*.

11 **consuli:** 'that consideration should be given to...' (impersonal passive).

Christi milites: sc. 'as...'.

12 **velocius:** 'quickly' or 'very quickly' (see G.12(a),(c)).

13 **Haec:** i.e. the eastern Church, the seedbed of Christianity.

de qua: 'from...'.

totius...salutis looks forward to and depends on *gaudia* (subject of *emanaverunt*).

13f. **quae...verba:** the image likens the Christian message to the milk given to babies.

16 **pro...domesticis:** 'for the sake of your family-members in faith', i.e. the eastern Christians.

17 **acies...acies...:** These nominatives are in apposition to the subject of *decertetis*. Tr. 'you should...as..., as...'.

18 **Jacobitae:** the descendants of Jacob, who won the promised land back, but were unable to evict the Jebusites (Joshua 15.63).

Jerusalem: abl. (see G.6(a)).

decertetis: 'you should...' (jussive subj.:*RLGVE* 152)).

Turcos looks forward to and is the object of *impugnetis* and *expugnetis* (jussive subjunctives like *decertetis*).

19 **Jebusaeos:** see note above on *Jacobitae*; the Christian crusaders will make a better job of their capture of Jerusalem than the sons of Jacob because they will evict the Muslims (who are much worse than the Jebusites were).

Pulchrum sit: 'let it be...', i.e. 'consider it...'.

20 **in qua Christus...mortuus est:** at Golgotha, see e.g. Lk 23.33 (section 3.3).

citra: i.e. before you get there (as would be the case for many).

21 **id...in via:** 'think of this as dying on the journey (sc. to free Jerusalem)'.

si tamen: 'if only...'.

21f. **in sua** looks forward to *militia*.

22 **prima:** sc. *hora*. The reference is to the parable of the workers in the vineyard (Mt 20.1–16), who are paid by the master (= God) the same amount, whether they have laboured all day or only for the last hour.

23 **vos...extendere:** 'for you to...'.

24f. **caritas est...ponere:** 'it is actually *charity* (sc. for Christians)'.

25 **Ne...sitis:** 'lest...'; a clear reminiscence of Christ's words to the disciples at Mt 6.28–34 and Lk 12.22f., exhorting them not to worry about food and clothing, which God provides for his followers (such as the Crusaders will be).

sciatis: 'you should...' (jussive subj.: *RLGVE* 152).

26 **timentibus:** 'to those who...'.

his qui: 'to those who...' (see G.11(c)).

28 **ad propria:** 'to your own (sc. estates, possessions)'.

perenne bravium (= *brabium* – Greek): i.e. eternal life.

29 **Tali...cui...cui:** i.e. Christ. *Tali...imperatori* is governed by the infinitive *militare*. Tr. 'to serve such a...'.

30 **quae rependat:** 'for him to...' (looks forward to *nulla...stipendia*).

30f. **tam immarcescibilem** looks forward to *coronam* (obj. of *rependat*).

32f. *Accingere...gladio tuo super femur tuum, potentissime:* a quotation from Ps. 44.4 (hence *auctoritate...prophetica*). *Accingere* is imperative passive 2s. and *Accingimini* below is the 2pl. form ('be girded').

33 **estote:** 'be' (imperative of *sum*: see RLRGr E1).

34f. **Non...demulceant:** 'Let...not...' (see G.23(c)).

35 **quin:** 'not to...' (see RLRGr S2(e)).

35f. **nec...deterreant:** 'and let...not...' (see G.23(c)).

36 **quatenus:** 'so that...' (see G.26(b)).

II THE SIEGE OF ANTIOCH (21 OCTOBER 1097 – 28 JUNE 1098)

The crusade's success hinged very largely upon the army's ability in siege warfare. This tactic might be successful in one of two main ways. As at

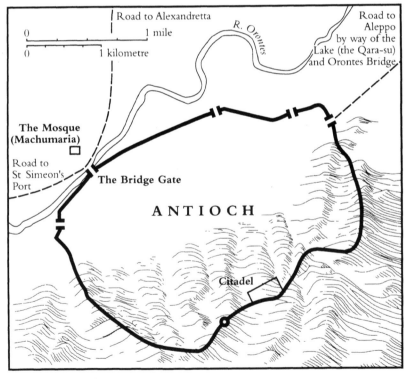

The Mosque
(Machumaria)

Road to
St Simeon's
Port

The Bridge Gate

A N T I O C H

Road to Alexandretta

0 _____ 1 mile

0 _____ 1 kilometre

R. Orontes

Road to
Aleppo
by way of the
Lake (the Qara-su)
and Orontes Bridge

Citadel

8 The siege of Antioch.

Nicaea, for example, engineering operations (undermining, use of catapults, etc.) might produce a breach in the defences. Or the privations caused by the break in the food and water supply might induce treachery or surrender. Antioch was a strongly fortified city, sited on the south bank of the Orontes river (see map 8). Possibly through lack of resources, the crusaders made no serious attempt to invest it fully until the spring of 1098. During the winter, the defenders were able to use the city's northern gate freely. This gave access onto a bridge over the Orontes, leading to plains which they could use for pasturing horses on the other side. Cutting off this point of egress was a vital strategic objective. The gate was used for harrying the crusaders' line of supply. Their camp was on the city side of the river, to the east, reached across a bridge of boats from the northern plain. The obvious thing was to capture and fortify a low hill in front of the bridge. On 1 March, two of the leaders – Raymond of St Gilles, count of Toulouse, and Bohemond of Taranto – set off in force to the port of St Simeon to the west, to bring back workmen and materials for this task. As they marched back on 5 March, they were attacked by Muslim defenders and routed. But, as will be seen from the following extracts, the Muslims mismanaged their success and ended by conceding the hill. Once this was fortified, the city could no longer bring in supplies, and eventually on 3 June, the crusaders gained easy access from the west thanks to collusion between a defender and Bohemond. The citadel, however, remained in enemy hands. The capture of the city was opportune. A strong Muslim force was by then approaching, commanded by Karbuqa, amir of Mosul, with the objective of relieving the siege. On 5 June they camped only eight miles away and sent an advance party of cavalry to the city. The crusaders were besieged in their turn under appalling conditions from 8 to 28 June. Encouraged by the finding of the Holy Lance by Peter Bartholomew on 14 June, they decided to risk battle. They appointed Bohemond as commander-in-chief. On 28 June they crossed the bridge, were allowed to establish strong positions and routed the army of Karbuqa. The citadel now surrendered to the crusaders. Despite the claim on Antioch of the emperor Alexius, Bohemond argued that he had broken the terms of the treaty, which had assigned it to him. Under this he was to have brought material assistance to the crusaders at Antioch, and he had not done so. Raymond of Toulouse argued for Alexius' rights. But by January 1099, the struggle for power had been decided in favour of Bohemond, who now became prince of Antioch. It remained a Christian Latin kingdom until its capture by the Mameluke sultan Baibars Bunduqdari in 1268.

RAYMOND OF AGUILERS AND THE *GESTA FRANCORUM ET ALIORUM HIEROSOLIMITARUM*

The story of the battle for control of access from the Orontes bridge is given here in two contrasting accounts. Both are by men who accompanied the crusade, but they differ very widely in style, and their authors had entirely different backgrounds and perspectives. The first passage, which recounts the battle in which the crusaders snatched victory from the jaws of defeat and captured the hill, is from the *Historia Francorum* of Raymond of Aguilers. Raymond was a canon at Le Puy, the chaplain of his lord, the bishop of Le Puy, Raymond of St Gilles, count of Toulouse, whom he followed on crusade. His style is not overly polished, but nonetheless is strongly marked by rhetorical devices such as anaphora. The second passage, which contains the same story from where the first passage ends, is taken from the *Gesta Francorum*, an anonymous work completed by the beginning of 1101. It is very likely the main source for almost all later histories of the First Crusade, including that of Baudri of Bourgueil (see section 13.1 above), who tells us in his preface that he was impelled to write his account from 'a little book' which was rustic and unpolished in style. The author was, unusually, a layman and a knight. He was most probably a Norman from Apulia, since he was a vassal of Bohemond. But he left Bohemond's service after it became clear that his lord was not interested in the liberation of Jerusalem, and joined Raymond of Toulouse. The style of the *Gesta* is simple, with few complex sentences and limited vocabulary, which includes loan-words such as *ammiralius* 'amir', *soldanus* 'sultan' and *machumaria* 'mosque', which make up in clarity what they lack in elegance. It is accessible in an excellent edition with translation (R. Hill, London, 1962).

2. Raymond of Aguilers (*fl.* 1095)

Raymond of Aguilers, who was in the camp, tells how the battle was turned and describes the joyful return of many poor soldiers with wondrous spoils. Stories of the vast losses of the enemy are discounted by the hearers.

Videns igitur Gracianus, qui civitatis rector erat, et nostrorum spolia et suorum victoriam et adhuc quorumdam nostrorum audaciam milites et pedites suos omnes emisit atque in spem victoriae adductus portas civitatis post suos recludi jussit, denuntians militibus suis vincere vel mori. Interea nostri paulatim et pro imperio procedere, Turci autem discurrere, sagittare, nimis audacter nostris   5
incurrere. At nostri interdum patiebantur, dum densatis incurrere possent, nec

ad impetum eorum retardabantur. Tantus vero luctus et clamor in castris ad Deum erat ut affluentia lacrymarum Dei pietatem descendendam putares. Quumque cominus res gerenda foret, quidam Hisnardus miles de Gagia, provincialis nobilissimus, cum centum quinquaginta peditibus invocato Deo 10 genibus flexis socios hortatus est, dicens: 'Eia, milites Christi!', atque hostibus incurrit. Similiter et aliae acies nostrae incurrunt. Hostium itaque superbia turbatur. Porta clausa est et pons strictus, fluvius vere maximus. Quid igitur? Hostes turbati prosternuntur et caeduntur ac saxis in flumine obruuntur, fuga autem nulla patet. Quod nisi Gracianus pontis portam aperuisset, illa die de 15 Antiochia pacem habuissemus. Audivi ego a multis qui ibi fuerunt quod viginti Turcos et amplius de ponte sumptis spondalibus in flumine obruissent. Claruit ibi multum dux Lotharingiae. Hic namque hostes ad pontem praevenit atque ascenso gradu venientes per medium dividebat. Celebrata itaque victoria cum ingenti exsultatione et multis spoliis et equis multis nostri ad castra redeunt. 20 Contigit ibi quoddam memorabile, quod utinam qui nos suis prosequuntur votis videre potuissent! Quidam enim eorum eques timore mortis dum praeceps profundum fluminis ingrederetur, a multis de sua gente comprehensus et ab equo suo dejectus in medio fluminis obrutus est cum illa multitudine quae eum apprehenderat. 25

Operae pretium est vidisse quosdam pauperes a victoria revertentes. Alii namque intra tentoria in equis fariis discurrentes relevationem suae paupertatis sociis ostendebant. Alii autem duobus vel tribus induti sericis vestimentis largitorem victoriae et muneris Deum magnificabant. Alii vero tribus vel quattuor muniti clypeis victoriae suae triumphum alacriter praetendebant. 30 Dumque his atque aliis ostentamentis fidem magnificae victoriae nobis persuasissent, de multitudine interfectorum suadere non potuerunt. Quoniam victoria sub nocte habita est, caesorum capita ad castra delata non sunt.

---

1 **Videns:** 'having...' (see G.20(a)) looks forward to three objects, *nostrorum spolia, suorum victoriam* and *adhuc...audaciam* (*adhuc* qualifies *audaciam*: tr. 'continuing').
Gracianus: the name of this person was Bagi Seian (or Bagui-Sian).
4 **denuntians...mori:** 'telling...to...' (see G.23(a)).
5f. **procedere, discurrere, sagittare, incurrere:** tr. 'were...ing' (historic infinitives: see *RLGVE* 146).
5 **nimis audacter:** 'very...' (see G.12(b)).
6 **dum...possent:** 'until...'.
densatis: '(sc. them) when they were...'.
8 **affluentia:** 'from...' (abl. of cause: RLRGr L(f)4(iii)).

Dei...putares: 'you would have thought that...would come down...' (sc. *esse* with *descendendam:* see G.19).
9 **gerenda foret:** 'was going to have to be...'.
de Gagia: 'from Gayac'.
10 **provincialis nobilissimus:** i.e. a *comes provincialis,* 'landgrave'.
11 **genibus flexis:** i.e. 'having genuflected'.
Eia!: 'Come on!'.
15 **quod nisi...:** 'And if...had not...'.
17 **de...spondalibus:** 'since the...had been taken from...'.
18 **dux Lotharingiae:** Godfrey of Bouillon, duke of Lower Lorraine, the only important German noble involved in the First Crusade.

19 **venientes:** 'those who came against him' (obj. of *dividebat*).
  per medium dividebat: 'he cut in half'.
20 **et multis spoliis et equis multis** ('with...') both qualify *redeunt*. Note the chiasmus (see *RLGVE* p. 315(d)).
21 **quod** looks forward to *videre potuissent* (of which it is the object); **utinam** looks forward to *potuissent*: 'and I wish that...it'.
  qui: 'those who...'.
  suis looks forward to *votis*: 'with their...'.
22 **timore mortis** is within the *dum* clause: tr. 'in...' (*dum* = *cum*: see G.29).

23 **de sua gente:** 'of...' (see G.15(d)).
26 **Operae pretium est vidisse:** 'It would have been worthwhile to see'.
29 **largitorem:** sc. 'as...' in apposition to *Deum* (obj. of *magnificabant*).
31 **Dumque:** 'And when...' (see G.29).
  fidem...nobis persuasissent: 'they had persuaded us of the truth...'.
33 **habita est:** 'had occurred...'.
  caesorum...sunt: this gruesome form of gloating was regularly practised during the crusade.

3. *Gesta Francorum et aliorum Hierosolimitarum*

The author of the Gesta *tells how the Turks buried the bodies and the crusaders exhumed them, removing their heads to prove the truth of their accounts of the enemy losses. They build the new fortification.*

Crastina uero die summo diluculo exierunt alii Turci de ciuitate et colligerunt omnia cadauera foetentia Turcorum mortuorum quae reperire potuerunt super ripam fluminis, exceptis illis quae in alueo latebant eiusdem fluminis; et sepelierunt ad machumariam quae est ultra pontem ante portam urbis; simulque illis consepelierunt pallia, bisanteos aureos, arcus, sagittas, et alia   5
plurima instrumenta, quae nominare nequimus. Audientes itaque nostri quod humassent mortuos suos Turci, omnes sese preparauerunt et uenerunt festinantes ad diabolicum atrium et iusserunt desepeliri et frangi tumbas eorum, et trahi eos extra sepulchra. Et eiecerunt omnia cadauera eorum in quandam foueam et deportauerunt cesa capita ad tentoria nostra quatinus   10
perfecte sciretur eorum numerus, excepto quod onerauerant quatuor equos de nuntiis ammiralii Babiloniae et miserant ad mare. Quod uidentes Turci doluerunt nimis fueruntque tristes usque ad necem. Nam cotidie dolentes nichil aliud agebant nisi flere et ululare. Tertia uero die coepimus simul iuncti cum gaudio magno aedificare castrum supradictum, de lapidibus scilicet quos   15
abstraximus de tumulis Turcorum. Peracto itaque castro, mox coepimus ex omni parte coangustare inimicos nostros, quorum superbia ad nichilum iam erat redacta. Nos autem secure ambulabamus huc et illuc, ad portam et ad montaneas, laudantes et glorificantes Dominum Deum nostrum, cui est honor et gloria per omnia seculorum secula. Amen.   20

1 **summo diluculo:** 'at earliest...'.
3 **eiusdem fluminis:** 'of the aforementioned...'.
4 **sepelierunt:** sc. 'them'.

6 **Audientes:** 'having... ' (see G.20(a)).
7 **humassent** = *humauissent* (see RLRGr A5).
8 **desepeliri:** sc. 'the bodies'.

10 **cesa:** 'severed'.

quatinus: 'in order that...' (see G.27(b)): cf. the end of the passage from Raymond of Agulers (section 13.2).

11 **excepto quod:** 'except that...'.

quatuor equos de: 'four horses of (i.e. belonging to)...' (see G.15(d)): no doubt the heads were themselves a defiant and threatening message for the amir.

12 **Babiloniae:** 'of Cairo'.

Quod uidentes: 'Having seen this' (see G.20(a)).

13 **tristes usque ad...:** 'sad right up to the point of (i.e. almost to)...'.

14 **simul iuncti:** 'having joined forces'.

15 **de lapidibus:** 'with...' (see G.15(a)(ii)).

20 **per...secula:** 'for all the centuries of centuries', i.e. 'for ever and ever' (see G.10(a)).

Section 14
Philosophy and theology

A distinction between the realms of philosophy and theology, of reason and faith, was as foreign to the eleventh century as it had been to St Augustine in the fourth. During the period covered in this section there is, however, a debate about the place of dialectic in theology. Some writers supported the view that theology should be conducted by textual commentary and paraphrase of Scripture. Others saw the need for analysis of what God had revealed. Peter Damiani (see above section 12.5) argues on the anti-dialectical side: 'Conclusions drawn from the arguments of dialecticians or rhetoricians ought not to be lightly applied to the mysteries of divine power; and as for the rules which perfect the use of the syllogism and the art of speech, let them cease to be obstinately opposed to the laws of God and to claim to impose the so-called necessities of their inferences on the divine power' (M. J. Charlesworth, *St Anselm's Proslogion*, Notre Dame and London, 1979, p. 24). The opposing school of thought, exemplified by Anselm of Besate, inclined towards the view that all truth was approachable through dialectic. Berengar of Tours was to show the force of this in his examination of the Eucharist (see below, 14.1). St Anselm of Canterbury leads the discussion onto a middle path: 'since it is by the rational mind that man is most like God, it is by the mind that man knows God' (*Monologion* 66) shows his acceptance of dialectic. This view mirrors that of Augustine, who supported its use as a tool for undermining heresies (*De doctrina Christiana* 2.31). On the other hand, his use of the maxim *credo ut intelligam* ('I believe so that I may understand') suggests the priority of faith over reason in theology, as does his famous formulation *fides quaerens intellectum* ('faith seeking understanding') (see further below).

The main philosophical question raised at this time was that of 'universals', and the controversy divided its students into two groups, known respectively as 'nominalists' and 'realists'. The issue, which arose from Porphyry's and Boethius' discussions of Aristotle's *Categories*, is this: are general terms (e.g. 'man') merely words, or do they relate to things which really exist? Nominalists (from *nomen* 'word') argued that only individuals truly existed and that *genus* and *species* did not have analogues in the real world. Realists (from *res* 'truth') regarded the *genera* and *species* as having true existence, whether they regarded the individual as simply a variant of the universal category (extreme realism), or argued for the presence of the *genera* and *species* in individuals and for the existence of individuals as separate things (moderate realism). The debate began with the theological work of Roscelin (*c*.1050– 1125), whose view of the Trinity was condemned by the Council of Soissons in 1092. St Anselm traced his errors to his refusal to accept the reality of universals: Roscelin was the first nominalist. It was his pupil Abelard who was to give the debate a new twist.

The general situation at the beginning of the twelfth century may be summed up as follows. The main streams of thought flowed in two traditional courses, the theological and the dialectical. The first still focused on explaining Scripture. The second centred on classification, not on enquiry.

1. Berengar of Tours (*c*.1000–88)

Berengar, born at Tours, was educated at the cathedral school of Chartres (a pupil of the founder, Fulbert). Later he became head of the school at Tours and archdeacon of Angers. His contemporaries mention him as a grammarian, but his main claim to fame is his unorthodox teaching on the Eucharist. He argued that transubstantiation (alteration of the bread and wine of the Mass to the body and blood of Christ) did not take place. Instead, Christ's presence in the sacrament was figurative. His views were condemned (along with those of John Scottus Eriugena) at the Council of Vercelli, and often thereafter. He suffered two personal condemnations at papal councils held in Rome in 1059 and 1079. His views were combated by Lanfranc, then prior at the abbey of Bec and later archbishop of Canterbury (1070–89), among others, whose responses are the chief sources for Berengar's teachings. His only surviving work, known as *De sacra coena* ('On the holy meal'), survives in one manuscript and consists of two replies (*rescripta*) to Lanfranc's *Liber de corpore et sanguine Domini*, written *c*.1063. It was composed *c*.1065–73, when he was probably in Tours again. It is more concerned with refutation than with setting out his teaching. But its hostile flavour and its quotations from Lanfranc make it a fascinating, if unclear, document of an important controversy.

See further: M. Gibson, *Lanfranc of Bec*, Oxford, 1978, ch. IV, pp. 63–97.

(i) *Berengar rejects Lanfranc's allegations that his views on the Eucharist are crazy*
and deserving punishment, and are not supported, as he claims, by St Ambrose.
He will show that Ambrose does support his view that the bread and wine when
consecrated both stay the same and are changed to something else.

Ubi ego scripsi: 'Per consecrationem altaris fiunt panis et vinum sacramenta
religionis, non ut desinant esse quae erant, sed ut sint quae erant et in aliud
commutentur, quod dicit beatus Ambrosius in libro *De sacramentis*,' o mentem,
inquis tu, amentem, o hominem impudenter mentientem, o puniendam
temeritatem! Ambrosium testem accire presumis quod panis et vinum altaris   5
non desinant esse quod erant sed commutentur in aliud quod non erant; et
quidem si de sacramentis vel ceteris, de quibus Ambrosius scripsit, omnes
revolvas libros quos nunc ecclesia in usu habet, tale aliquid ab Ambrosio dictum
taliterque expositum reperire non poteris. Quod si dixisset preclarissimae famae
suae plurimum detraxisset, sibi ipsi contrarius extitisset, rem incredibilem   10
credibilem esse constituisset: quis enim compos sui credat rem aliquam
converti in aliam, nec tamen in ea parte desinere esse quod erat?

Ad haec ego, sicut dicit beatus Augustinus ad quendam, si venalia, inquio,
invenisti convitia, bona illa mercatione videris accepisse, quae tanta in me
profundis facilitate. Mentem michi amentem tribuis atque impudentiam   15
mentiendi, plectendae me adiudicas temeritatis. Ego contra convitia tua nichil
modicum, sed beatitudinem expecto ab illo, cui datum esse iudicium omne
non nescio, qui dicit: *beati eritis cum dixerint homines omne malum adversum vos*
mentientes propter me, ego propicio ipso, qui haec dilectoribus spopondit suis, qui
Veritas est, omnibus veritatis amatoribus, qui haec forte legerint, manifestum   20
faciam non potuisse mentiri spiritum veritatis ubi dicit: *tu es sacerdos secundum*
ordinem Melchisedhec, quod, id est sacerdos esse secundum ordinem Melchisedhec, qui panem et vinum revera optulit, eo momento dubio procul
desisteret esse Christus dominus, quo sacrificium altaris panis et vini subiecta
amitteret, vereque illud me constat scripsisse per consecrationem – quod nullus   25
interpretari potest: per subiecti corruptionem – fieri panem et vinum in
sacrificio ecclesiae sacramenta religionis, non ut desinant esse quae fuerant,
sed ut sint quae erant (alioquin consecrari non possent) et in aliud commutentur, beatumque me Ambrosium minime de amentia, minime de mentiendi
impudentia, minime de temeritate plectenda huius rei testem summo iure,   30
nulla iniuria citavisse: ego quod dicis in omnibus quae scripsit Ambrosius, quae
ad manum nunc ecclesia habeat, non posse inveniri, manifestum propicia
divinitate facturus sum omnibus fumo contentionis non cecis diligenterque
legentibus, in uno illo qui *De sacramentis* inscribitur libro, quem in manu
habebas, suficientissime inveniri.   35

1 **Ubi ego scripsi:** in the work attacked by Lanfranc in his *Liber de corpore et sanguine Domini.*

3–12 **o mentem...quod erat:** this is a quotation from Lanfranc's attack.

3f. **o...temeritatem:** accusatives of exclamation (RLRGr L(c)7.

5 **testem...quod:** 'as a witness that...'.

6 **quod erant:** 'what they were'.

7f. **et quidem si...revolvas...non poteris:** 'if you unroll...you will not be able...' (irregular condition: see G.28(b)).

9 **preclarissimae famae suae:** dative with *detraxisset.* Tr. 'from his...'.

11 **quis...credat:** 'who would believe...' (*RLGVE* 153.2).

13 **beatus Augustinus:** the passage cannot be found in the extant works.

14 **bona...mercatione:** 'at a good price'.
   quae: 'since...them...' (obj. of *profundis*).

16 **plectendae...temeritatis:** gen. with *adiudicas* ('guilty of...').
   contra...tua: 'in recompense for...'.

18f. **beati eritis...propter me:** slightly misquoted from Mt 5.11, the Sermon on the Mount.

19 **propicio ipso:** 'with the blessing of him' (abl. abs.: for *ipso* see G.11(a)(ii)).

19f. **qui...est:** tr. 'and who...'.

20 **omnibus...amatoribus:** dative looking forward to *manifestum* ('clear to...').

21f. **tu...Melchisedhec:** Ps. 109.4, cited in Hebrews 5.6.

22 **quod:** this introduces the clauses *eo momento... dominus* and *vere...constat.* Tr. 'meaning that...'.

22f. **id...optulit:** this appears to be in parentheses. Tr. 'by the way, being a priest according to the order of Melchisedhec means obtaining real bread and wine'. The reference is to Gen. 14.18–19: 'And verily Melchisedhec, King of

Salem, bringing forth bread and wine (for he was a priest of God most high) blessed it and said...'.

23 **dubio procul:** lit. 'far from doubt', i.e. 'without doubt'.

24 **quo:** 'at which' (picking up *eo momento*).
   panis et vini subiecta: 'the subjects of bread and wine'. *Subiectum* in medieval philosophy means 'primary substance', that which actually makes a thing what it is and not something else (as opposed to *accidentia*, 'secondary characteristics').

25 **vereque illud me constat scripsisse:** 'and that it is agreed that that was the truth I wrote (that...)' (*vereque illud me scripsisse* is indirect statement dependent on *constat*).

25f. **per consecrationem...fieri panem et vinum...sacramenta religionis:** 'that through ...' (indirect statement dependent upon *illud me scripsisse*).
   quod...corruptionem: 'a statement which...'.

27 **quae fuerant:** 'what they were' (*fuerant* = *erant*).

28 **non possent:** 'they could not...' (potential subjunctive: *RLGVE* 153.2).

29f. **beatumque...citavisse:** 'and that I cited...' (a second indirect statement dependent on *illud me scripsisse*).

29 **de amentia:** 'from...' (i.e. 'out of', 'because of').

31 **ego:** looks forward to *facturus sum.*

31f. **quod dicis...inveniri:** 'what you claim cannot be found...'.

32 **manifestum:** picking up *quod...inveniri* and introducing a further indirect statement. Tr. 'clear that it is sufficiently discovered...'.

33 **omnibus** looks forward to *cecis...legentibus.*

34 **in uno...libro:** 'that...' (the beginning of the indirect statement, introduced by *manifestum*, whose verb is *inveniri*).

(ii) *Ambrose, in his* De sacramentis, *distinguishes between the visible and the invisible in a passage which clearly relates to the Eucharist. What communicants see is clearly bread. Its spiritual essence is not seen. But Lanfranc argues that after communion Christ's flesh is on the altar sensibly, although he says it is invisible. But it is visible, if it has colour, as Lanfranc asserts. Therefore what is seen is not Christ's flesh but bread.*

Et primum illud insistendum, quam vere beatus Ambrosius in eo libello sentiat non deesse secundum sua subiecta mensae dominicae non panem qui de celo descendit, quod dicitur tropice corpus Christi, quo tu sophistice contendis elabi – sophisticorum est enim illa perversitas ut non intensa depellant, cum sit contradictio eiusdem de eodem sicut et consensio – sed panem qui de pistrino   5
venit ad communem aut dominicam mensam, qui propria locutione dicitur panis, non tropica, et non vinum quod letificat cor, quod dicitur Christi sanguis similiter locutione tropica, sed vinum quod non tropica locutione dicitur vinum, quod de torculari ad communem paratur vel ad dominicum calicem.
Quod si beato Ambrosio auctore constiterit, constabit etiam de conversione   10
alius in aliud, ut sit quod erat et in aliud commutetur: non enim sine competenti conversione panis in altari consecratus factus dicitur Christi corpus. Primo ergo deposita superbiae pervicatia, attende quam manifeste panem et vinum beatus Ambrosius secundum proprietatem speciei suae –
'speciei' autem dico secundum subiecta ipsa panem et vinum, non secundum   15
colorem vel quae in subiectis eis sunt accidentia – in altari post consecrationem constituat superesse ubi ait, premissa de Naaman, cui contemptui fuerunt aquae Iordanis, similitudine: *nunc illud consideremus, ne quis forte visibilia videns – quoniam quae sunt invisibilia non possunt humanis oculis comprehendi – dicat forte,*
parvi scilicet faciens quae videt sicut Naaman Iordanis aquas: '*Haec sunt quae*   20
preparavit deus unicae suae, aecclesiae suae?' Haec dicens beatus Ambrosius negari non potest cum his qui mensae communicarent dominicae sermonem habuisse, qui autem mensae dominicae communicant quid videant cogimur necessario dicere. In hoc te ipse deicis, nec attendis: dicis portiunculam carnis post consecrationem esse sensualiter in altari, eam esse invisibilem asseris, quod   25
tibi tamen nulla ratione licebat. Dicebas enim portiunculam illam carnis Christi panis esse colore adopertam, quod dicens asserere eam invisibilem non poteras, quia si supervestiatur facies tua colore Ethiopis, necesse est faciem tuam videri si colorem illum videri constiterit. Non ergo tibi licet dicere, videre accedentes ad communicandum mensae dominicae portiunculam carnis Christi, quam tu   30
sensualiter confingis esse in altari, quia tu eam invisibilem asseris.

---

1 **illud insistendum:** sc. *est* ('we must...'); *illud*   2 **non deesse...mensae dominicae:** 'that there
refers forward to the clause *quam vere...sentiat.*   are present at...' (lit. 'that there are not lacking

to...'). The subjects of *deesse* are *panem* and *vinum*. The rest of the sentence is made up of two pairs of statements about *panem* (*non panem...consensio* and *sed panem...tropica*) and another two about *vinum* (*et non vinum...tropica* and *sed vinum...calicem*).

3 **quod...Christi:** 'which...' (i.e. the bread, though the relative pronoun ought to be *qui*, but is 'attracted' by the n. *corpus*).

3f. **quo...elabi:** 'the way you...' (in Lanfranc's attack on his doctrine).

4 **illa...ut:** 'such...that' (result clause: see RLRGr S2(a)).

non intensa: 'things which were not intended' (i.e. they set up a straw man which misrepresents what their adversary said).

4f. **cum...consensio:** 'whether there is a self-contradiction or an agreement'.

6 **propria locutione:** 'literally'.

9 **ad communem** looks forward to *calicem* (*communis* 'ordinary' contrasts with *dominica* 'the Lord's': so also above, l.6).

10 **Quod si...constiterit:** 'if this (i.e. the fact that bread and wine with their primary characteristics are on the altar at the Eucharist)...'.

auctore: 'on the authority of...'.

11 **alius** (gen.) **in aliud:** i.e. *alterius in alterum* 'of one thing into another'.

ut sit...commutetur: 'that it is what...and is changed...'.

12 **competenti:** 'corresponding'.

panis is nom. with *consecratus* and is the subject of *dicitur*.

factus dicitur: 'is said (to be) made (into)...'.

13 **deposita...pervicatia:** 'laying aside...' (abl. abs.).

13f. **quam...superesse:** the construction of the clause is *quam manifeste...beatus Ambrosius...constituat* (subject and verb), ('that...') *panem et vinum...secundum...suae...in altari post consecrationem...superesse* (indirect statement introduced by *constituat*); '*speciei*'...*accidentia* (parenthesis explaining what he means by *speciei*).

14f. **speciei suae – 'speciei'...accidentia:** Berengar explains that he means 'species' by this word and not 'appearance'. He is speaking of the *subiecta*, the essential characteristics, and not the *accidentia*, the non-essential or secondary characteristics, such as colour.

17 **premissa** looks forward to *similitudine*: 'setting down first...' (abl. abs.).

17f. **de Naaman...Iordanis:** the reference is to the commander of the army of the king of Aram, who was told by the prophet Elisha that he could cure his leprosy by bathing seven times in the Jordan. The story is told in 2 Kings 5.1ff. Naaman's first response was anger: 'Are not Albana and Pharpar, the rivers of Damascus, better than any of the waters of Israel?' (v. 12).

cui...fuerunt: tr. 'who disdained...' (lit. 'to whom the waters...were a source of contempt': *contemptui* is predicative dative: RLRGr. L(e)(2)).

18 **ne quis...videns** is completed by *dicat forte*.

20 **parvi...faciens:** 'making light of', 'thinking worthless' (*parvi* is gen. of value: see RLRGr L(d)5).

sicut...aquas: sc. *parvi fecit*.

Haec: 'Is *this* what...', i.e. 'bread and wine' (the point of the comparison is that Naaman could not see the spiritual power invested in what was manifestly water, so the onlooker at the Eucharist must not think that there is no spiritual aspect to the blessed bread and wine, even if they are still manifestly bread and wine).

22 **cum his** looks forward to *sermonem habuisse*.

mensae...dominicae: i.e. 'take communion' (the imperfect tense is in the wrong sequence: see G.25(a)).

23f. **qui...dicere:** *qui...communicant* 'those who...' is the subject of the clause *quid videant*. This in turn is the object of *cogimur...dicere* (so begin tr. with this). Berengar means that what the communicant actually sees is bread and wine.

24 **te...deicis:** i.e. 'you refute yourself'.

25 **eam...asseris:** 'but you assert that...'.

25f. **quod...tamen:** 'and yet this...'.

26 **carnis Christi** depends on *portiunculam*.

27 **panis** (gen.) looks forward to *colore* (dependent on *adopertam*).

quod dicens: 'but in saying this...'.

eam invisibilem: sc. *esse*.

28 **si supervestiatur...necesse est:** 'if...were clothed in...it would be necessary...' (irregular condition: see G.28(b)).

28f. **si...constiterit:** 'if it is agreed that...'.

29f. **videre accedentes...Christi:** 'that those who come forward to see...'.

30f. **quam...altari:** *quam...sensualiter...esse in altari* is indirect statement, introduced by *tu...confingis*.

31 **eam invisibilem:** sc. *esse*.

2. St Anselm of Canterbury (1033–1109)

Born in Aosta of a noble family, Anselm left home in 1056. Eventually he settled at the Norman abbey of Bec, where Lanfranc of Pavia led the teaching. He took monastic vows in 1060 and when Lanfranc moved to the new abbey at Caen, became prior of Bec. In 1078 he succeeded Herluin as abbot. In 1093, he unwillingly accepted the archbishopric of Canterbury, and spent the next four years in conflict with the king, William Rufus, over the question of lay investiture (see section 12.7). In 1097, when he insisted on visiting Rome without the king's consent, his see was forfeited. He returned to Canterbury after William Rufus' death in 1100. However, the quarrel over investiture broke out again with Henry I and from 1103 to 1107 Anselm was once more in exile. An agreement was reached in 1107, when the king surrendered the right of lay investiture. Anselm died at Canterbury on 21 April 1109, surrounded by his students, including his biographer Eadmer, who reports that on his deathbed he was still contemplating the problem of the origin of the soul. The intellectual vitality revealed by this anecdote is amply attested by Anselm's writings, which cover a wide range of philosophical and theological topics. These include the *Monologion* ('Soliloquy'), which attempts to prove the existence of a single supreme nature and demonstrate the rational foundation of the doctrine of creation from nothing, and the *Cur Deus homo* ('Why God became a man'), in which he attempts to explain the rationale of the Incarnation and Redemption.

His most famous work is the *Proslogion* ('Address'), in which he attempts to prove by one argument and by reason alone (*sola ratione*) the existence and nature of God. This argument was later labelled 'the ontological argument', and it is now generally known by this title. Modern scholars have disagreed over whether Anselm did or did not begin from faith. At any rate the reply of the monk Gaunilo, posing as the fool in Ps. 13.1 and 52.1, who says in his heart 'there is no God', suggests that Anselm did intend to produce an argument which would convince a person without faith. The following excerpts represent the 'ontological argument' from the *Proslogion* and Gaunilo's criticism on behalf of the fool, to which Anselm produced a reply. All these texts can be most conveniently followed up in the edition of M. J. Charlesworth, Oxford, 1965 (reprinted Notre Dame and London 1979).

See further: J. Hopkins, H. Richardson, *Anselm of Canterbury*, London, 1974.

(i) *The 'something-than-which-a-greater-cannot-be-thought' cannot exist only in the mind, because it can also be thought to exist in reality, which is greater. In that case 'that-than-which-a-greater-cannot-be-thought' is 'that-than-which-a-greater-can-be-thought'. This is impossible.*

QUOD VERE SIT DEUS

Ergo, domine, qui das fidei intellectum, da mihi, ut quantum scis expedire intelligam, quia es sicut credimus, et hoc es quod credimus. Et quidem credimus te esse aliquid quo nihil maius cogitari possit. An ergo non est aliqua talis natura, quia 'dixit insipiens in corde suo: non est deus'? Sed certe ipse idem insipiens, cum audit hoc ipsum quod dico: 'aliquid quo maius nihil   5
cogitari potest', intelligit quod audit; et quod intelligit in intellectu eius est, etiam si non intelligat illud esse. Aliud enim est rem esse in intellectu, aliud intelligere rem esse. Nam cum pictor praecogitat quae facturus est, habet quidem in intellectu, sed nondum intelligit esse quod nondum fecit. Cum vero iam pinxit, et habet in intellectu et intelligit esse quod iam fecit. Convincitur   10
ergo etiam insipiens esse vel in intellectu aliquid quo nihil maius cogitari potest, quia hoc cum audit intelligit, et quidquid intelligitur in intellectu est. Et certe id quo maius cogitari nequit, non potest esse in solo intellectu. Si enim vel in solo intellectu est, potest cogitari esse et in re, quod maius est. Si ergo id quo maius cogitari non potest, est in solo intellectu, id ipsum quo maius cogitari non   15
potest, est quo maius cogitari potest. Sed certe hoc esse non potest. Existit ergo procul dubio aliquid quo maius cogitari non valet, et in intellectu et in re.

Title **QUOD...SIT**: 'that...exists'.

1 **da...ut**: 'grant that...' (the verb in the *ut* clause is *intelligam*).

quantum scis expedire: 'as much as you know (it) to be fitting' (the clause depends on *intelligam*).

2 **quia**: 'that...' (dependent on *intelligam*).

quod credimus: sc. 'that you are'.

Et quidem: 'And indeed...'.

3 **quo**: '(greater) than which...' (abl. of comparison with *maius*).

4 **quia**: 'because...' (picking up *ergo*).

'dixit...deus': Ps. 13.1, 52.1 (the posture of the atheistic fool is the one taken up by Gaunilo in his reply).

5 **ipse...ipsum**: 'this...actual' (for the first meaning see G.11(a)(ii)).

quod dico: 'which...'.

6 **quod audit...quod intelligit**: 'what...that which...'.

7 **etiam si non intelligat**: tr. 'even if he does not...'.

illud esse: 'that it exists'.

Aliud...aliud: 'it is one thing for...another to...that' (the first *rem esse* depends on *Aliud...est* and the

second on *intelligere*, which depends on *aliud*; the first *esse* means 'is', the second 'exists').

8 **quae**: 'the things which...'.

habet: sc. 'them'.

9 **sed...fecit**: *esse* means 'that it (i.e. the picture) exists' and *quod* 'because'.

10 **et habet...et...**: 'he both...(sc. the picture)...and...'.

esse quod: 'that it exists because...'.

Convincitur...esse: 'is convinced...that...exists...' (*convinco* CL 'refute', 'prove').

11 **vel**: 'at least'.

12 **quia...intelligit**: 'because...' (the verb is *intelligit*).

13f. **vel...est**: 'even...exists' (the subject is *id quo maius cogitari nequit*).

14 **potest...esse**: 'it can be thought to exist'.

quod: 'and this...' (i.e. existing in reality).

15f. **id ipsum...est quo...**: 'the very thing than which ...is equivalent to (sc. the thing) than which'.

17 **non valet**: 'cannot' (= *non potest* and *nequit*: see G.17(d); these variations are the only concessions to style which the writer allows himself, since his aim is absolute lucidity of argument).

(ii) *Proof that God ('that-than-which-a-greater-cannot-be-thought') cannot be thought not to exist.*

QUOD NON POSSIT COGITARI NON ESSE

Quod utique sic vere est, ut nec cogitari possit non esse. Nam potest cogitari esse aliquid, quod non possit cogitari non esse; quod maius est quam quod non esse cogitari potest. Quare si id quo maius nequit cogitari, potest cogitari non esse, id ipsum quo maius cogitari nequit, non est id quo maius cogitari nequit; quod convenire non potest. Sic ergo vere est aliquid quo maius cogitari non   5
potest, ut nec cogitari possit non esse.

Title **QUOD...NON ESSE:** 'That (sc. God)...to exist'.

1 **Quod...sic...ut...non esse:** 'And this (i.e. that-than-which-a-greater-cannot-be-thought)...so ...that...not to exist'.

potest: subject *aliquid* (antecedent of *quod*).

2 **esse:** all occurrences in this section mean 'to exist'.

quod maius est quam quod...: 'and this...than what...' (the first *quod* is the subject of *est*, the

second of *potest*).

3f. **si...non esse:** 'if that than which...can...' (the protasis of the condition).

4 **id ipsum quo...non est id quo...:** '(sc. then it follows that) that very thing than which...is not that than which...'.

5 **quod convenire...:** 'and this...be agreed'.

Sic...vere est...: 'So truly does there exist' (looking forward to *ut*, result).

6 **nec:** 'not even'.

(iii) *Gaunilo's reply on behalf of the fool begins with a résumé of Anselm's argument.*

QUID AD HAEC RESPONDEAT QUIDAM PRO INSIPIENTE

Dubitanti utrum sit vel neganti quod sit aliqua talis natura, qua nihil maius cogitari possit, cum esse illam hinc dicitur primo probari, quod ipse negans vel ambigens de illa iam habeat eam in intellectu, cum audiens illam dici id quod dicitur intelligit; deinde quia quod intelligit, necesse est ut non in solo intellectu sed etiam in re sit, et hoc ita probatur quia maius est esse et in re   5
quam in solo intellectu, et si illud in solo est intellectu, maius illo erit quidquid etiam in re fuerit, ac sic maius omnibus minus erit aliquo et non erit maius omnibus, quod utique repugnat; et ideo necesse est ut maius omnibus, quod esse iam probatum est in intellectu, non in solo intellectu sed et in re sit, quoniam aliter maius omnibus esse non poterit: respondere forsan potest.   10

Title **QUID...RESPONDEAT QUIDAM...:** 'What someone replies [*or* might reply]...' (the someone's name is Gaunilo, but he is playing the devil's advocate here).

The first chapter is a complex résumé of the 'ontological' argument of the *Proslogion*, consisting of a single sentence. Its basic structure is: *cum...hinc dicitur...probari* 'whereas it is said here (i.e. in the Proslogion) that...is proved...(by the following arguments: *primo...deinde...et ideo...)'...respondere forsan potest* 'he (i.e. the fool) can perhaps reply...' (leading on to the second section).

1 **Dubitanti...vel neganti...**: 'to one who... (whether)...or who...(that)...' (these participles are inside the *cum* clause and are indirect objects of *dicitur*).

utrum sit...quod sit...: the subject of both verbs is *aliqua ...possit* (*qua* is f. because its antecedent is *natura*: tr. *natura* as 'substance').

2 **esse illam:** 'that it (referring to *natura*) exists' (this phrase is the subject of dicitur).

2f. **primo...quod...intelligit:** 'first because...:' (summing up Anselm's first argument).

ipse negans vel ambigens de illa...: 'the very person who... (it) or...it (i.e. the *natura, qua nihil maius cogitari possit*)': the use of *de* + abl. with *ambigo* = 'I doubt' is not CL: see generally G.15(b)).

3 **cum:** 'since' (despite the indicative verb – *intelligit*, which introduces *id quod dicitur*).

illam dici: 'it (sc. *naturam* etc.) being spoken (of)' (acc. + inf. depending on *audiens*).

4f. **deinde...repugnat:** 'next (sc. it is proved) because...' (summing up Anselm's second argument).

4 **quod intelligit:** 'what he...' (the subject of *sit* in

the *ut* clause).

5 **et hoc ita probatur quia...:** 'and this (i.e. that it exists not only in the mind but also in reality) is proved thus since... (i.e. 'as follows...')'.

esse et in re: 'to exist also in reality' (subject of *est*).

quam: sc. *esse*.

illud: i.e. 'that-than-which-a-greater-cannot-be-thought'.

illo: 'than...' (abl. of comparison; see *RLGVE* 100B1).

6f. **quidquid...fuerit:** 'whatever existed also...' (subject of *erit*).

7 **maius...aliquo:** '(sc. that which is) greater than...will be smaller than...'.

8 **quod:** 'and this (sc. conclusion)'.

8f. **et ideo...poterit:** 'and therefore...' (summing up the concluding part of Anselm's argument).

ut: the verb is *sit* (subject *maius omnibus* 'that which is greater than...').

quod...intellectu: 'which (antecedent *maius omnibus*)...' (*esse* 'to exist' is to be taken with *in intellectu*: the whole phrase depends on *iam probatum est*).

9 **non...sed et:** 'not...but also...'.

10 **poterit:** the subject is 'it' (i.e. *maius omnibus*, l.8) and here *maius omnibus* (l.10) is the complement.

(iv) *The fool's reply. Why should he not assert that many unreal things may be thought, and are not therefore necessarily real?*

Quod hoc iam esse dicitur in intellectu meo, non ob aliud nisi quia id quod dicitur intelligo. Nonne et quaecumque falsa ac nullo prorsus modo in seipsis existentia intellectu habere similiter dici possem, cum ea dicente aliquo, quaecumque ille diceret, ego intelligerem? Nisi forte tale illud constat esse ut non eo modo quo etiam falsa quaeque vel dubia haberi possit in cogitatione, et ideo non dicor illud auditum cogitare vel in cogitatione habere, sed intelligere et in intellectu habere, quia scilicet non possim hoc aliter cogitare, nisi intelligendo id est scientia comprehendendo re ipsa illud existere. Sed si hoc est, primo quidem non hic erit iam aliud idemque tempore praecedens habere rem in intellectu, et aliud idque tempore sequens intelligere rem esse, ut fit de pictura quae prius est in animo pictoris, deinde in opere. Deinde vix umquam poterit esse credibile, cum dictum et auditum fuerit istud, non eo modo posse cogitari non esse, quo etiam potest non esse deus. Nam si non potest, cur contra

negantem aut dubitantem quod sit aliqua talis natura, tota ista disputatio est
assumpta? Postremo quod tale sit illud ut non possit nisi mox cogitatum   15
indubitabilis existentiae suae certo percipi intellectu, indubio aliquo probandum mihi est argumento, non autem isto quod iam sit hoc in intellectu meo
cum auditum intelligo, in quo similiter esse posse quaecumque alia incerta vel
etiam falsa ab aliquo cuius verba intelligerem dicta adhuc puto; et insuper
magis, si illa deceptus ut saepe fit crederem, qui istud nondum credo.   20

1 **quod:** 'That...' (introduced by *respondere* in the previous section).

hoc: i.e. 'that-than-which-a-greater-cannot-be-thought', subject of *dicitur*.

esse: 'to exist'.

quia: '(sc. the fact) that' (the verb is *intelligo*, obj. *id quod dicitur*)

2f. **Nonne et...possem:** 'Could I not also...' (potential subjunctive, see *RLGVE* 153.2: CL would use present tense; *possem* governs the infinitive. *dici*, which introduces *habere*).

quaecumque...existentia: 'all sorts of... which...' (this phrase is the object of *in intellectu habere*).

3 **cum...:** the verb is *intelligerem* (tr. both this and *diceret* as though present).

ea...aliquo: *ea* is the object of *dicente*, which forms abl. abs. with *aliquo*.

3f. **quaecumque...diceret:** this clause is the object of *intelligerem*.

4 **tale** looks forward to *ut* 'of such a kind that...'.

illud: i.e. 'that-than-which-a-greater-cannot-be-thought' (subject of *constat*).

4f. **ut non...in cogitatione:** the main idea here is *ut non haberi possit* (subject still *illud*).

eo...dubia: 'in the way in which...(sc. can *haberi in cogitatione*)'.

5f. **et ideo...dicor:** this is co-ordinate with the *constat* clause.

6 **illud auditum:** 'it (i.e. that-than-which-a-greater-cannot-be-thought) when I have heard it' (obj. of *cogitare, habere, intelligere, habere*).

7 **quia:** 'because...'.

possim: 'I could...' (potential subjunctive: *RLGVE* 153.2).

8 **id est:** 'that is...' (explaining *intelligendo*).

re ipsa: 'in actual fact' (*re...existere* is acc. + inf. dependent on *comprehendendo*).

hoc est: sc. 'the case' (a number of things follow

logically: these are introduced by *primo, deinde, postremo*).

9 **non hic erit iam:** lit. 'here (it) will not be any more...' (tr. 'it will no longer be...').

9f. **aliud...habere..., et aliud...intelligere...:** the basic structure here means 'one thing to...and another to...'; the phrases *idemque tempore praecedens* and *idque tempore sequens* agree with *aliud* in each case: tr. '(one) and the same thing preceding in time' and '(another) and that following in time' (i.e. there will no longer be a difference such as can currently be established by temporal relationship between what is merely *planned* and what actually *exists*).

10 **de pictura:** 'in the case of...'.

11 **vix umquam:** 'scarcely at all...'.

12 **credibile** looks forward to the acc. + inf. phrase *eo...esse*.

dictum et auditum fuerit: 'has been...' (for the form see G.4(a)).

istud: 'this' (see G.11(c)), i.e. whatever one has in mind which does not yet exist.

12f. **non eo modo...quo...:** '(that) in the same way...as...' (the subject of this phrase is *istud* and the verbs are in logical order).

13 **potest non esse:** sc. *cogitari non esse* (subject *deus*).

cur: the verb is *est assumpta*.

14 **negantem aut dubitantem:** 'a person who...'.

quod: 'that...'.

15 **Postremo quod...:** 'Finally that...' (this clause is the subject of *probandum...est*).

tale looks forward to *ut non*: 'of such a kind that...' (*illud* is again 'that-than-which-a-greater-cannot-be-thought').

15f. **non possit...intellectu:** the phrasing is *non possit nisi...percipi* ('cannot but be...'), *mox cogitatum* (agreeing with *illud*) 'as soon as...', *indubitabilis existentiae suae certo...intellectu* 'by means of a...of its' (*indubitabilis...suae* depends on *certo...intellectu*).

16 **indubio aliquo** looks forward to *argumento* ('by means of...').

17 **mihi:** 'to me' (not 'by me').

isto: sc. *argumento* (the one used by Anselm).

quod: 'that...'.

hoc: i.e. 'that-than-which-a-greater-cannot-be-thought'.

18 **auditum:** 'when I have heard it'.

in quo similiter: 'according to which (sc. argument) similarly...'.

18f. **esse posse...puto:** 'that there could exist *quaecumque...falsa* spoken of *[dicta]* ab *aliquo* whose *verba...intelligerem* I still think'

19f. **et insuper...crederem:** 'and even more (sc. I think that according to this argument such things could exist) if I were to believe (sc. that) they (*illa*) (sc. existed), deceived, as...'.

20 **qui...credo:** 'I who do not yet believe in that (sc. argument)' (i.e. 'even though I...').

(v) *For example, they say there exists a 'Lost Island', rich beyond all other places. I can understand what this is when I am told. But if someone argued it was real, by asserting that it is more excellent to exist in reality than in the mind alone, and that if it did not exist then any land which does exist would be more excellent than that-than-which-no-land-is-more-excellent, I should not believe him. He would first have to show that its excellence exists in my mind as a reality.*

Exempli gratia: Aiunt quidam alicubi oceani esse insulam, quam, ex difficultate vel potius impossibilitate inveniendi quod non est, cognominant aliqui 'perditam', quamque fabulantur multo amplius quam de fortunatis insulis fertur, divitiarum deliciarumque omnium inaestimabili ubertate pollere, nulloque possessore aut habitatore universis aliis quas incolunt homines terris possidendorum redundantia usquequaque praestare. Hoc ita esse dicat mihi quispiam, et ego facile dictum in quo nihil est difficultatis intelligam. At si tunc velut consequenter adiungat ac dicat: non potes ultra dubitare insulam illam terris omnibus praestantiorem vere esse alicubi in re, quam et in intellectu tuo non ambigis esse; et quia praestantius est, non in intellectu solo sed etiam esse in re; ideo sic eam necesse est esse, quia, nisi fuerit, quaecumque alia in re est terra praestantior illa erit, ac sic ipsa iam a te praestantior intellecta praestantior non erit; si inquam per haec ille mihi velit astruere de insula illa quod vere sit ambigendum ultra non esse: aut iocari illum credam, aut nescio quem stultiorem debeam reputare, utrum me si ei concedam, an illum si se putet aliqua certitudine insulae illius essentiam astruxisse, nisi prius ipsam praestantiam eius solummodo sicut rem vere atque indubie existentem nec ullatenus sicut falsum aut incertum aliquid in intellectu meo esse docuerit.

5

10

15

[Anselm's reply is to appeal to Gaunilo's 'faith and conscience' for proof that 'that-than-which-a-greater-cannot-be-thought' is truly understood and thought, and is in the mind and in thought. This might well be considered as a concession that *sola ratio* cannot prove God's existence, since it presupposes faith. But in fact it is an *ad hominem* argument to the believer

Gaunilo. Anselm goes on to produce a different rational argument, namely that 'that-than-which-a-greater-cannot-be-thought' can have no beginning, and that 'that-which-has-no-beginning' exists necessarily. For evaluation of this counter-argument, see Charlesworth, op. cit., pp. 91f.]

1 **alicubi oceani:** 'somewhere in...'.
quam: obj. of *cognominant*.

2 **quod non est:** 'that which does not exist'.

3 **fabulantur:** 'they say...' (CL 'I converse'); introduces two acc. + inf. phrases: (1) *quam... divitiarum...pollere*; (2) *nulloque...praestare*.

3f. **quam...fertur:** 'than is reported...' (the *fortunatae insulae* are named first in Hesiod's *Works and Days* as the place where the heroes continue their existence after their 'death', but Gaunilo attaches the classical name to a motif from folk-tale).

5 **nullo...habitatore:** tr. 'because it has...' (abl. abs.).

universis aliis looks forward to *terris* (the antecedent of *quas*); its case (dat.) and that of *redundantia* (abl.) are explained by *praestare* ('be superior to *X* dat. in *Y* abl.').

6 **possidendorum:** lit. 'of things to be possessed', i.e. 'of possessions'.

6f. **Hoc...quispiam:** lit. 'Let someone...that...', but since it introduces a hypothesis, tr. 'Now suppose that...' (and ignore *et*).

7 **dictum:** object of *intelligam* and antecedent of *in quo*.

nihil governs *difficultatis*: 'no...' (see RLRGr L(d)2).

8 **ultra** looks forward to *quam*: 'any more...than...'.

8f. **insulam illam...in re:** *insulam illam* is subject of *esse* ('exists') and is amplified by *terris...praestantiorem* ('more...than...').

9f. **et...esse:** 'that (it) is in...' (the phrase is introduced by *non ambigis*, which does not need the negative in English).

10f. **non...esse in re:** sc. 'you cannot doubt that...' (*esse* '(it) exists').

11 **ideo sic...esse:** 'so thus...' (i.e. because of the premises already accepted; the acc. + inf. *eam...esse* 'that it exists' is introduced by *necesse est*).

quia: 'because...' (explaining why the island *must* exist).

11f. **nisi fuerit...erit:** 'if it (i.e. the island) did not exist, *quaecumque...terra* ('whatever...land... exists'; subject of *erit*) would be...than...' (*fuerit* may be perfect subjunctive; the condition is irregular, see G.29).

12f. **ac...non erit:** *ipsa* ('the very (sc. land)')...*praestantior intellecta* ('understood (sc. as) more...') would not...' (a second apodosis of the *nisi* clause).

13f. **si...non esse:** 'if, I say, *per haec* (sc. arguments) *ille* (the *quispiam* of earlier in the passage) were to...that (the acc. + inf. after *astruere* is ambigendum...non esse* 'that one should not...')...that it (the island...)...exists (*quod...sit* is introduced by *ambigendum...esse*)'.

14f. **aut nescio quem...:** 'or I would not know whom I should...more...' (strictly speaking, *nescio* should be subjunctive).

16 **insulae illius essentiam:** 'the existence of...' (obj. of *astruxisse*).

16f. **nisi...docuerit:** 'unless he has...(sc. me) that...' (the acc. + inf. is in outline *ipsam praestantiam...in intellectu meo esse* 'that its (i.e. the island's)...exists...'; this is amplified by the contrast *solummodo sicut...nec ullatenus sicut...* 'only as...and not in any way as...').

Section 15
Poetry

It will be clear from the texts presented in sections 11–14 that during the period under scrutiny literature, including verse, was at the service of politics, both ecclesiastical and secular, as well as of theology. Poetic composition is used to celebrate the deeds of the great (for example William of Apulia's long account of the Norman Robert Guiscard's conquest of Sicily, commissioned by Pope Urban, whom Guiscard supported). The papal position on investiture is argued for in verse, as for example in Rangerius' poem *De anulo et baculo* (see section 12.7). Poetry continues to eulogize kings, as for instance do Baudri of Bourgeuil's verses to William the Conqueror's daughter Adela. But during this period we see also the emergence of a more hedonistic poetry, which appears to have functioned rather as entertainment, albeit for the same Latinate élite and not without didactic elements. In Germany the *Ruodlieb* and the *Cambridge Songs* (so called from their survival in a Cambridge University Library ms.) give us almost our first taste of Latin in contact with vernacular culture. In Normandy and Norman England the institution of the *rotulus mortuorum*, a roll sent round the Benedictine foundations in the care of a messenger (the *rolliger*) to gather prayers and commemorative verses upon the death of a notable individual, gives us many glimpses of the poetic activity in the monastic schools and provides yet another context in which the writing of verse had a religious, eulogistic or otherwise political function.

Verse continues to be written in both quantitative (classical) and rhythmic metres, and the sequence, the melodies of which are now well established and diffused, begins to be used as the basis for secular poetry. Style as always reflects the study of earlier poetry. This would include both Christian writers (such as Prudentius) and pagan ones. Scholars sometimes attempt to characterize the epochs of ML verse by general labels according to the main classical influence. The eighth and ninth centuries would be the *aetas Vergiliana*, the tenth and eleventh the *aetas Horatiana*, the twelfth and thirteenth the *aetas Ovidiana*. Though it is clearly too simplistic a picture, there is some truth in the changing availability and use of pagan books as evidenced by library catalogues and the detailed study of vocabulary. It is for example the case that 'the library catalogues of the eleventh and twelfth centuries record a striking increase in the copies of Ovid, Horace, Persius and Juvenal' (R. R. Bolgar, *The Classical Heritage*, New York, 1964, p. 189 p. 189).

See further: F. J. E. Raby, *A History of Secular Latin Poetry*, 2 vols., Oxford, 1957.

1. *Carmina Cantabrigiensia* ('The Cambridge Songs')

The *Cambridge Songs* form part of an eleventh century manuscript written in England, but the original collection was put together in Germany, perhaps in the Rhineland. There are forty-nine pieces in the anthology, some of them extracts from classical poetry, others Merovingian and Carolingian poems and yet others occasional verses belonging to the tenth and eleventh centuries. Religious and secular poems stand together, emphasizing the limited value of such a distinction. Among the non-sacred and non-occasional material, perhaps the most interesting pieces are the love lyrics which appear in strength here for the first time and the examples of the *ridiculum*, a humorous story, many of which are in sequence form. The purpose of the collection is not clear, but it was perhaps the repertoire of an entertainer who catered for the imperial court.

The two poems given here are both in stress-based metre (see section 5 Intro., p. 58 for notation) and represent the two new genres, love lyric and *ridiculum*, mentioned above. The love poem is on a homosexual theme (very rare) and perhaps comes from tenth-century Verona. It is written in a learned style, with much Greek vocabulary and classical ornament. The *ridiculum* is a German poem, set in Homburg on the Unstrut. By contrast, its style is totally unpretentious.

(a) *O admirabile Veneris idolum*

Metre: 6pp + 6pp. Rhyme scheme: 6A.

The author bids farewell to the young boy who has rejected his advances, with a prayer for the protection of God, the Fates and the sea deities in his journey across the river Tesis.

O admirabile Veneris idolum,
cuius materie nihil est frivolum,
archos te protegat, qui stellas et polum
fecit et maria condidit et solum.
furis ingenio non sentias dolum,　　　　　　　5
Cloto te diligat, que baiolat colum.

'Salvato puerum' non per ipotesim,
sed firmo pectore deprecor Lachesim,
sororem Atropos, ne curet heresim.
Neptunum comitem habeas et Tetim,　　　　10
cum vectus fueris per fluvium Tesim.
quo fugis, amabo, cum te dilexerim?
miser quid faciam, cum te non viderim?

Dura materies ex matris ossibus
creavit homines iactis lapidibus,　　　　　　15
ex quibus unus est iste puerulus,
qui lacrimabiles non curat gemitus.
cum tristis fuero, gaudebit emulus.
ut cerva rugio, cum fugit hinnulus.

1 **idolum:** 'image' (Greek).

2 **cuius materie:** 'in whose make-up'.
frivolum: adj. used as a noun, tr. 'fault', 'defect'.

3 **protegat:** 'may...' (so also *sentias* l. 5, *diligat* l.6).
archos: 'the chief' (i.e. God: Greek).

5 **furis ingenio:** 'through a (sc. love-)thief's cunning...'.
non sentias: 'I pray you may not...' (CL *ne* + subj.: see G.23(c)).

6 **Cloto:** i.e. Clotho, one of the three Fates. The other two, Lachesis and Atropos, are mentioned in the next stanza. Clotho holds the spindle, Lachesis pulls the thread (of life) and Atropos cuts it. The lines play on a well-known verse (of the ninth or tenth century): *Clotho colum baiulat, Lachesis trahit, Atropos occat* 'Clotho holds the distaff, Lachesis pulls the thread, Atropos breaks it.'

7 **salvato puerum:** 'save...' (= CL *salveto*, future imperative: see RLRGr A2 Note 1). This is the substance of the plea to Lachesis in *deprecor*.
per ipotesim: 'hypothetically' (*hypothesis*: Greek).

8 **firmo pectore:** i.e. 'in earnest'.

9 **sororem Atropos:** '(and) Lachesis' sister Atropos...' (*Atropos* must be treated here as indeclinable: cf. G.6(a)); (Lachesis pulls the thread, so the prayer for safety is addressed to her in l. 7, while *ne...heresim* brings in Atropos, asking her not to cut it).
ne...heresim: 'not to pay attention to a heresy', i.e. to make sure the boy does not choose to follow some other lover than himself, the true lover (the imagery mixes the idea of Atropos' breaking the thread of life with that of a heretic leaving the true church for a sect).

10 **Tetim:** i.e. Thetis (sea nymph mother of Achilles).

11 **vectus fueris:** 'you travel...' (see G.4(a)).
Tesim: 'Tesis' (some editors alter the text to read *Athesim*, which is recorded as an Italian river name; this would be a scholarly joke, because Greek *thesis* means 'position' (see O.3(a)) and the *a-* in Greek would signify 'not' - so the name *Athesis* would be a paradox, since a river is never in the same position from one moment to the next). For technical reasons, however, this

reading is unacceptable and Petrarch mentions a river called *Tesin* which can be reasonably identified with *Tesis*.

12 **amabo:** 'please (sc. tell me)'.

cum...dilexerim: 'although I love...' (the perfect subjunctive is used merely for the rhyme; cf. also *viderim* in l.13).

14 **ex matris ossibus:** i.e. from stones (the poet alludes to the story of Deucalion and Pyrrha in Ovid, *Metamorphoses* 1.318f. After the flood, in reply to a prayer to repopulate the world, they receive an oracle from Themis instructing them to throw behind their backs the bones of their great mother (1.383: *ossaque post tergum magnae iactate parentis*). From these stones a new race is born, but one 'hard...and inured to hardships'(1.414: *inde genus durum sumus experiensque laborum*).)

15 **iactis lapidibus:** 'when...' (abl. abs.).

16 **iste:** 'this' (see G.11(c)).

17 **lacrimabiles** looks forward to *gemitus* (obj. of *curat*).

19 **rugio:** 'I roar' (usually of lions or asses).

(b) *Est unus locus Homburh dictus*

Metre: 5p + 5p, with leonine rhyme (see section 10.4 Intro.), mostly one syllable only, each stanza of three lines, no end-rhymes.

The nun Alfrad loses a pregnant ass to a wolf. Her sensible sisters Adela and Fritherun comfort her with the thought that God will replace the beast.

Est unus locus	Homburh dictus,	
in quo pascebat	asinam Alfrad,	
viribus fortem	atque fidelem.	
Que dum in amplum	exiret campum,	
vidit currentem	lupum voracem.	5
caput abscondit,	caudam ostendit.	
Lupus accurrit,	caudam momordit:	
asina bina	levavit crura	
fecitque longum	cum lupo bellum.	
Cum defecisse	vires sensisset,	10
protulit grandem	plangendo vocem	
vocansque suam	moritur domnam.	
Audiens grandem	asine vocem	
Alfrad cucurrit:	'sorores,' dixit,	
'cito venite,	me adiuvate!	15
Asinam caram	misi ad erbam;	
illius magnum	audio planctum;	
spero, cum sevo	ut pugnet lupo.'	

Clamor sororum   venit in claustrum,
turbe virorum   ac mulierum   20
assunt, cruentum   ut captent lupum.

Adela namque,   soror Alfrade,
Rikilam querit,   Agatham invenit,
ibant, ut fortem   sternerent hostem.

At ille ruptis   asine costis   25
sanguinis undam   carnemque totam
simul voravit,   silvam intravit.

Illud videntes   cuncte sorores
crines scindebant,   pectus tundebant,
flentes insontem   asine mortem.   30

Denique parvum   portabat pullum;
illum plorabat   maxime Alfrad,
sperans exinde   prolem crevisse.

Adela mitis,   Fritherun dulcis
venerunt ambe,   ut Alverade   35
cor confirmarent   atque sanarent:

'Delinque mestas,   soror, querelas!
Lupus amarum   non curat fletum:
Dominus aliam   dabit tibi asinam.'

1 **unus locus:** 'a...' (see G.10(d)).
  Homburh: Homburg an der Unstrut.
4 **Que:** i.e. *asina*.
  dum...exiret: 'while...' (for subjunctive verb, see G.29).
5 **currentem:** sc. 'towards her'.
6 **caudam ostendit:** sc. 'and' (asyndeton; also in the next line).
7 The ass is the subject of all the verbs in this stanza.
11 **plangendo:** 'in lamentation' (used as a present participle: see G.18).
13 **Audiens:** 'having heard' (see G.20(a)).
  asine = *asinae* (see O.1).
14 **sorores:** their names are Adela and Fritherun.
18 **spero:** 'I believe...'.

  cum with *sevo...lupo*.
19 **in claustrum:** i.e. 'to the monastery'.
20 **turbe** (= *turbae*: see O.1) **virorum:** were the men monks, or is this a jest at the expense of the nuns, that they are harbouring males in their cloister?
21 **assunt** = *adsunt* (assimilation: cf. O.21).
  cruentum looks forward to *lupum*.
22 **namque:** 'for' (postponed; if it does mean 'for', rather than being an otiose connective, then it implies that Adela sought Rikila and Agatha in the monastery).
  Alfrade = *Alfradae* (see O.1).
25 **At ille:** i.e. the *lupus*.
  ruptis with *costis* (abl. abs.): tr. 'when he had...'.

asine = *asinae* (see O.1).

27 **silvam intravit:** sc. 'and...' (asyndeton).

28 **cuncte** = *cunctae* (see O.1).

29 **pectus tundebant:** sc. 'and...' (asyndeton).

30 **insontem asine** (= *asinae*: see O.1) **mortem:** i.e. 'the death of the innocent...' (transferred epithet).

31 **Denique:** 'finally', i.e. 'the final misery was that...'.

portabat: subject *asina*.

33 **sperans...crevisse:** 'because she had hoped that offspring would have grown from it' (see G.22(b) for irregular acc. + inf. – CL would

have used future inf. *creturum esse* – and G.13 for *exinde* = 'from it').

34 **Fritherun** (nom.) **dulcis:** sc. 'and...' (asyndeton).

35 **ambe** = *ambae* (see O.1).

Alverade: probably *Alfrade* (gen.: *-e* = *-ae*, see O.1).

37 **Delinque** = *linque:*'leave off...' (in CL *delinquo* = 'fail', 'do wrong': such errors in the use of verb prefixes are common in ML).

39 **Dominus:** i.e.'God' (the point of the whole *ridiculum* seems to be that one should not cry over spilt milk: only God can help and he will do so).

2. Ruodlieb

Ruodlieb is a fragmentary narrative poem composed by a monk of Tegernsee (South Germany) perhaps around 1050. It tells the story of a knight errant, Ruodlieb, exiled from his own country. He impresses a foreign king with his unusual skills in hunting and enters his service. Later he acts as commander-in-chief against a foreign invader and, after victory, as the magnanimous king's peace negotiator. After ten years, he is called home, and chooses as his parting gift wisdom rather than wealth. This consists of twelve moral precepts, which are explored during the narrative of his journey home. The king also gives him two loaves, filled – unknown to Ruodlieb – with gold, to be opened at home. Eventually after Ruodlieb's arrival at home and the wedding of his nephew, Ruodlieb's mother decides that he too should marry. He has little success until a dwarf prophesies that he will marry a king's daughter, if he can defeat her father and brother. The poem ends abruptly before this comes about. But the plan would probably have been accomplished happily.

The narrative blends together elements from folklore, literature and everyday life in a fresh and lively manner. The verse is composed in leonine hexameters (see section 10.4 Intro.). The vocabulary is highly unusual, with many Greek words being used alongside both normal classical terms and words from a lower register. Some examples of the last category are: *gamba* 'leg' (as in Italian); *lahs* 'salmon' (German *Lachs*); *scachi* 'chess' (Italian *scacchi*). Word order is often highly convoluted.

Ruodlieb uses pills made from the herb bugloss to catch fish. Once they have eaten the herb, they can no longer swim under water. The king is impressed.

illĭus herbae vim medici dicunt fore talem,
torridula trita cum parvo polline mixta,
hinc pilulae factae si fient more fabellae
et iaciantur aquis, quicunque comēderet ex his
piscis, quod nequeat subtus supra sed aquam net.   5
inter tres digitos pilulas tornandŏ rotundas
dilapidat stagno, quo pisces agmine magno
conveniunt avide capiendŏ pilam sibi quisque,
quam qui gustabant, sub aqua plus nare nequibant
sed quasi ludendo saltus altos faciendo   10
undique diffugiunt nec mergere se potuerunt.
ille sed in cimba percurrit remige stagna,
post pisces virga cogens ad littora sicca, ·
quos duo cum funda circumcinxere sub unda,
cum terram peterent ad aquam resalire nequirent.   15
sic piscandŏ sibi ludum fecitque sodali.
tunc iussere cocos prunis assare minores,
maiores scuto regi portant ioculando:
'venari meliūs hodie nos non poteramus.'
Rex: 'retibus aut hamis hos cepistis ve sagenis?'   20
Ven.:   'non sic piscamur,' ait incola, 'sed dominamur
piscibus, e fundo veniant ad nos sine grato,
et sūper stagnum saliendŏ iocum dare magnum:
dum sub aquam nequeunt satis et saltandŏ fatiscunt,
hos tandem virga facimus requiescere terra.'   25
'hoc volŏ,' rex dixit, 'speculari, copia dum fit.'

---

1 **Illius herbae vim:** i.e. of bugloss (*bugloss-a ae* 1f.); the phrase is part of an acc. + inf. phrase (*vim...fore*) dependent on *dicunt* (note CL scansion *illĭus* (in this position); cf. l. 19 *mĕlĭūs hŏdĭē* – CL *mĕlĭūs hŏdĭē*).
fore = *esse* (see G.5).
talem looks forward to *quod nequeat* in l. 5, but tr. as though 'that' follows immediately.
2 **torridula...mixta:** abl. abs. 'when (sc. 'it,' the bugloss) is *torridula*, having been *trita* and has been *parvo polline mixta*'.
3 **hinc:** 'from this...'.
3f. **factae si fient...et iaciantur:** 'if...are made... and thrown...' (irregular condition, see G.28; *factae fient* – CL *factae erint* or *fient*).

4 **aquis:** 'into...' (see G.16(a)).
quicunque with *piscis*.
comederet ex his: 'eats (some) of...' (the sequence of tenses is irregular – see G.25(a) – and so is the use of *ex* after *comedere*).
5 **quod...net:** 'that...' (consecutive; see G.26(b)); the meaning is compressed from *nequeat* (*nare*) *subtus* (*aquam*) and *sed* is postponed and so divides *supra...aquam*.
6 **pilulas tornando rotundas:** 'having made...' (the gerund is used as a past active participle).
7 **dilapidat stagno:** 'he (i.e. Ruodlieb)...into...' (cf. *aquis* in l. 4).
quo: 'to where...'.
agmine magno: 'in...'.

8 **capiendo:** 'catching' (as if agreeing with *pisces*: see G.18).

9 **quam qui gustabant:** 'those who...it (lit. 'which': connecting relative)...' (*qui gustabant* is the subject of *nequibant* and of *diffugiunt* and *potuerunt* in l.11).

10 **ludendo, faciendo:** '...ing' (as if agreeing with *pisces...qui...*: see G.18).

12 **Ille sed:** i.e. Ruodlieb; *sed* is postponed.

remige: 'oared' (adj. agreeing with *cimba*: CL 'rower', 'crew').

13 **post:** 'behind' (adv.; or construe with *pisces* and understand 'them' as obj. of *cogens*).

14 **duo:** 'two men' (subject of *circumcinxere*).

15 **ad aquam...nequirent:** sc. 'so that' (*ut* is omitted).

16 **piscando:** '...ing' (as if agreeing with *ille*: see G.18).

fecitque: -*que* is misplaced – tr. as though the line read *sibi ludum fecit sodalique*.

17 **cocos** = *coquos*.

prunis: 'on...'.

minores: sc. *pisces*.

18 **regi:** i.e. *ad regem* (see G. 16(a)).

ioculando: '...ing' (as if agreeing with the subject of *portant*: see G.18).

19 **poteramus:** 'we could...have...'.

20 **ve:** 'and' (joining *hamis* and *sagenis*; CL 'or', always attached to the end of a word, like -*que*).

21f. **dominamur/piscibus...veniant:** 'we induce... to...' (*ut* is omitted; *pisces* is unstated subject of *veniant*).

22 **sine grato:** 'against their will'.

23 **saliendo:** '...ing' (as though agreeing with *pisces*: see G.18).

24 **dum:** 'since...' (see G.30(a)).

nequeunt: sc. *nare*.

satis: 'much'.

saltando: '...ing' (as though agreeing with *pisces*: see G.18).

25 **hos...facimus requiescere:** 'we make them...' (see G.17(c)).

terra: 'on...'.

26 **dum:** 'when...' (see G.29).

3. The *rotulus mortuorum* of Matilda (1113)

Matilda was the daughter of William the Conqueror, and the first abbess of the female monastery established by her father at Caen in Normandy and dedicated to the Trinity in 1066. On her death, probably in 1113, a *rotulus* prefaced by an encyclical eulogizing her was sent with a *rolliger* ('roll-bearer') around all the sister foundations in Normandy and Norman England. The aim was to collect prayers for the soul of the deceased and verse tributes. This particular roll is one of the longest known, at around 20½ metres (unfortunately the original was destroyed during the French Revolution). The *rolliger* visited some 253 institutions, from Caen itself to York. At some places he obtained only a brief prayer with a request for prayers in return. At others he procured verses from the scholars, sometimes, as at York, substantial pieces. The vast majority are serious treatments of Christian notions of death and forgiveness of sins, with particular emphasis upon prayers for Matilda's soul. But there are some pieces which are not at all suitable for such a collection and in a good number of poems anti-feminism rears its head in very ugly guise. One scholar even produces a *praeteritio* ('I shall not speak about...'), mentioning that he has obeyed the *rolliger*'s injunction not to say anything untoward about women, as he normally would. Here are two surprising poems, the first written at the abbey of

Noyers in the diocese of Tours, the second at the nunnery of Saint Mary
and Saint Julian at Auxerre. Both are rhythmic (see section 5 Intro. for
notation). The first contains an insulting address to the *rolliger*. The second
bitterly attacks abbesses who punish their nuns for falling in love. It is, of
course, difficult to know with what degree of seriousness these pieces should
be taken, or whether the second was actually written by a nun.

(i) *You are a fool, roll-bearer, to die of cold waiting for additions to your roll. It is
psalms and masses which will save her soul, not the verses you demand.*

The metre is 8p + 7pp, with end-rhyme AA, BB, CC and leonine rhyme
in the first half of each line (*inepta/cepta, vilane/mane, vade/trade* etc).

TITULUS SANCTAE MARIAE NUCARIENSIS

Res inepta, male cepta, importuno tempore,
fol vilane, sero, mane, morieris frigore;
ergo vade, ne te trade morti pro pecunia.
abbatissae psalmi, missae, conferent suffragia,
non scriptura vel pictura rotuli, quem bajulas,   5
in quo versus tu perversus supplex scribi postulas.

---

1 **Res:** 'You...' (addressing the *rolliger*).
  importuno tempore: sc. 'arriving at...'.
2 **fol:** 'fool' (OFr).
  vilane = *villane* (see O.7: OFr).
  frigore: 'of...' (abl. of cause: RLRGr L(f)4(iii)).

3 **ne...trade:** 'do not...' (CL *ne* + subj.).
4 **abbatissae:** 'To...' (dat.).
  psalmi, missae: sc. 'and' (asyndeton).
6 **versus...scribi postulas:** 'you ask for...to be...'.

(ii) *Death to abbesses who punish nuns for falling in love, as I have been punished.*

The metre is 8p, with end-rhymes AA, BB, CC, DD.

TITULUS SANCTI JULIANI MONACHARUM

Abbatissae debent mori,
quae subjectas nos amori
claudi jubent culpa gravi.
quod tormentum jam temptavi.
loco clausa sub obscuro,   5
diu vixi pane duro.
hujus poenae fuit causa
quod amare dicor ausa.

2 **subjectas nos:** 'us when...' (*subiectas* governs *amori*).

3 **culpa gravi:** 'because of...' (abl. of cause: RLRGr L(f)4(iii)).

4 **quod tormentum:** 'This...' (connecting relative, obj. of *temptavi*).

5 **loco** looks forward to *sub obscuro*.

6 **pane duro:** 'on...'.

7f. **hujus...causa / quod...:** 'The reason for... that...'.

8 **ausa:** sc. *esse* 'to have...'.

PART FOUR
The twelfth-century Renaissance

The extraordinary explosion of Latin literary activity in the later twelfth century was a consequence of many factors, chief among them perhaps being the more settled political conditions, which allowed population growth, the rise of the towns and sustained economic development. This was a period of new movements, especially in religious life, which is marked by a proliferation of new monastic orders such as the Cistercians. Heresies, such as that of the Cathars, also abound. The advance in the status of the cathedral schools already noticeable in the eleventh century, continues, and is especially marked in France at Chartres, Orléans, Rheims, Laon and Paris. The growing idea of nationhood brought with it the desire for centralization and hence an expansion in the courts of monarchs. A steady supply of clerics educated to the highest level in Latin learning became essential to the sustaining of this new system. Such men formed with their peers in religious houses an intellectual élite which could take and give pleasure by the production of sophisticated works in the traditional language. Production of such material could in this climate be valuable in attaining positions of considerable emolument, so that literary patronage became important once more, as it had been in Charlemagne's day (see section 9), except that now it was far more widely spread.

An essential element in the progress of learning during this time was the access gained through Spain and Sicily to hitherto unknown works of Greek mathematics, science and philosophy through translations from Arabic. Important commentaries by Arab writers also became part of the tumultuous intellectual climate of the day. In other areas refining of analytical techniques (as in the *ars dictaminis* used to teach letter-writing) and the compilation of encyclopaedic *summae* of various fields (e.g. canon law and theology) were the central concerns. The continuing application and development of dialectic in theology is especially noteworthy, leading as it eventually did to the domination of the university curriculum by scholastic philosophy from the thirteenth century until the Renaissance of the later fourteenth century.

See further: C. H. Haskins, *The Renaissance of the Twelfth Century*, Cambridge, Mass., 1927; C. Brooke, *The Twelfth-century Renaissance*, London, 1969.

Section 16
The schools and the scholastic method

The schools are at the centre of the intellectual life of the period. There was as yet no fully formal organization of institutions of higher education, such as would come about with the organization of *universitates* ('guilds of students/masters') in the thirteenth century. But by the later part of the century, Paris at least, with its three schools, the cathedral school of Notre-Dame, those of the canons regular at St Victor and on the Montagne Ste-Geneviève, was moving towards faculties and the grouping of students by *nationes* (countries of origin). Even at this date, Paris is of European importance, drawing students from far afield and producing an old-boy network as well as an intellectual diaspora. *Magistri* ('masters') seem to have been free to set up schools, set their own fees, and to move on when they encountered problems or were not earning enough. Students would attach themselves to *magistri* according to their reputation and what they wished to study. The teaching method was the lecture, by which was meant *lectura*, reading a text with the *magister* supplying a commentary. Around 1200, Alexander of Neckam lists some of the texts so studied: for grammar and rhetoric, Priscian and Donatus; for dialectic, the *Logica nova* of Aristotle (*Prior and Posterior Analytics, Topics* and *Elenchi*, which began to be known from about 1128 onwards); for arithmetic and music, Boethius; for geometry, Euclid (known from the early twelfth century); for astronomy, Ptolemy's *Almagest* (known from around 1160); for law, the *Corpus iuris civilis* of Justinian (rediscovered in the eleventh century) and Gratian's *Decretum* (see section 16.3 below); for Medicine, Galen and Hippocrates (recovered by Spanish translators); for theology, the Vulgate and Peter Lombard's *Sententiae*.

1. John of Salisbury (c.1115–80)

Born in Old Sarum into a family of no great wealth, John studied in the schools of Paris between 1136 and 1148. He was not cut out for a teaching career, however, despite his extraordinary learning (particularly his knowledge of the classical writers). He returned to England with a reference from Bernard of Clairvaux (see section 17.2) to serve with Theobald, archbishop of Canterbury. From then until 1176, he was connected with that see and its incumbents, Theobald, Thomas Becket and Richard of Dover. During the 1150s he spent much time in Rome and was charged with gaining for Henry II from the English Pope, his friend Hadrian IV (1154–9), a permission to take over Ireland (see section 19.II Intro.). When Becket clashed with Henry and was exiled to Paris (1164–70: see section 19.I), John went to Rheims. In 1176, King Louis VII of France appointed him bishop of Chartres, which John administered until his death in 1180.

The cathedral obituary record (*Necrologium*) calls him 'a deeply religious man, lit up by the rays of all learning, a shepherd loved by all for his words, his life and his character, cruel only to himself, at all times mortifying his flesh with a hair shirt from neck to feet'. It also preserves a list of the books he left to its library, which includes a number of patristic texts, Seneca's *Quaestiones naturales*, Cicero's *De officiis* and *De oratore*, and his own *Policraticus* ('The Statesman': see section 18.1). John's voluminous writings include, beside the *Policraticus*, a large collection of letters, a fragmentary Memoir of the papal court (containing an account of Bernard of Clairvaux's attempts at the Council of Rheims to have Gilbert de la Porrée condemned for heresy – see section 17.2), a biography of Thomas Becket (at whose martyrdom he was – almost – present: see section 19.I) and a life of St Anselm. His *Metalogicon* ('After logic'; the title is modelled on Aristotle's *Metaphysics*) is a reflection upon the teaching of logic and its place on the broader canvas of education, written during his exile at Rheims. In this passage, ultimately critical of dialectic *per se* (that is, when taught and investigated without the other two parts of the *trivium*, grammar and rhetoric), he recalls memorably the teachers of his youth.

See further: K. S. B. Keats-Rohan, 'John of Salisbury and education in twelfth-century Paris, from the account of his *Metalogicon*', *History of Universities*, 6 (1986), pp. 1–45.

(i) *John recalls his days as a student in Paris, where he studied the rudiments of logic. He gives his opinion of his teachers.*

Cum primum adulescens admodum studiorum causa migrassem in Gallias, anno altero postquam illustris rex Anglorum Henricus leo iustitiae rebus excessit humanis, contuli me ad Peripateticum Palatinum, qui tunc in Monte Sanctae Genouefae, clarus doctor et admirabilis omnibus, praesidebat. Ibi ad pedes eius prima artis huius rudimenta accepi et pro modulo ingenioli mei   5
quicquid excidebat ab ore eius tota mentis auiditate excipiebam. Deinde post discessum eius qui mihi praeproperus uisus est, adhaesi magistro Alberico, qui inter ceteros opinatissimus dialecticus enitebat, et erat reuera nominalis sectae acerrimus impugnator. Sic ferme toto biennio conuersatus in Monte, artis huius praeceptoribus usus sum Alberico et magistro Roberto Meludensi (ut   10
cognomine designetur quod meruit in scholarum regimine, natione siquidem Angligena est); quorum alter ad omnia scrupulosus locum quaestionis inue- niebat ubique, ut quamuis polita planities offendiculo non careret et, ut aiunt, ei scirpus non esset enodis. Nam et ibi monstrabat quod oporteat enodari. Alter autem in responsione promptissimus subterfugii causa propositum nunquam   15
declinauit articulum quin alteram contradictionis partem eligeret aut, deter- minata multiplicitate sermonis, doceret unam non esse responsionem. Ille ergo in quaestionibus subtilis et multus, iste in responsis perspicax breuis et commodus. Quae duo si pariter eis alicui omnium contigissent, parem utique disputatorem nostra aetate non esset inuenire. Ambo enim acuti erant ingenii et   20
studii peruicacis et (ut reor) magni praeclarique uiri in philosophicis studiis enituissent, si de magno litterarum niterentur fundamento, si tantum institissent uestigiis maiorum quantum suis applaudebant inuentis. Haec pro tempore quo illis adhaesi. Nam postea unus eorum profectus Bononiam dedidicit quod docuerat. Siquidem et reuersus dedocuit. An melius, iudicent qui eum ante et   25
postea audierunt. Porro alter in diuinis proficiens litteris, etiam eminentioris philosophiae et celebrioris nominis assecutus est gloriam.

1 **anno altero postquam:** i.e. 1137.
  Henricus: Henry I of England (ruled 1100–1 December 1135).
  rebus looks forward to *humanis*; both are gov- erned by the *ex-* in *excessit*.
3 **Peripateticum Palatinum:** 'the peripatetic (i.e. teacher in the Aristotelian tradition) from le Pallet', i.e. Peter Abelard (see section 16.2 Intro.).
3f. **Monte Sanctae Genouefae:** Montagne Ste- Geneviève in Paris (the high ground across the Seine from Notre-Dame).
4 **omnibus** (dat.) qualifies *admirabilis*.
5 **prima...rudimenta:** that is of *dialectice*, logic.

pro...ingenioli: 'in line with...' (the diminutives are John's attempt at humility).
  quidquid...eius is the object of *excipiebam*.
7 **discessum...qui:** *discessum* not *eius*, is the ante- cedent of *qui*.
  magistro Alberico: Alberic de Monte, perhaps identical with the Alberic who was at this time chancellor of Ste Geneviève; *magister* was the title taken by masters in the schools.
8 **nominalis sectae:** Alberic was a 'realist' (for 'nominalists' and 'realists', see section 14 Intro.).
10 **Roberto Meludensi:** Robert of Melun (d. 1167); see next note.

10f. **ut...est:** 'to call him by...' (Robert was an Englishman, but ran a school at Melun from 1142 to 1148; he took over Abelard's chair of theology at Paris and eventually became bishop of Hereford, 1163–7).

11f. **natione...Angligena:** 'of...' (abl. of origin: RLRGr L(f)1).

12 **alter:** i.e. Alberic.
    ad omnia: 'in...' (with *scrupulosus*).

13 **quamuis...planities:** 'however smooth the surface (sc. on which you were walking), it...'.

14 **scirpus...enodis:** with dry humour John elegantly reworks the proverb *nodum in scirpo quaerere* 'to look for a knot in a bulrush', i.e. to find a problem where there is none (see above section 12.6).
    et ibi: i.e. 'even where there was no problem'.

15 **propositum** looks forward to *articulum*.

16 **quin...eligeret:** introduced by *declinauit*; lit. 'never avoided a point...so as not to...', i.e. 'never failed to take up a point so as to....'.

17f. **Ille...iste:** 'Alberic...Robert' (see G.11(c)); *multus* 'diligent' (the implication may be that he is

'over the top', 'a bit much').

19 **Quae duo:** i.e. the major strengths of Alberic and Robert (one in questions, the other in answers).
    pariter eis: 'in equal measure as they had fallen to them (Alberic and Robert)'.

20 **non esset:** 'it would not have been possible'.
    acuti looks forward to *ingenii*. This phrase and *studii peruicacis* are genitives of description: RLRGr L(d)4).

21 **magni praeclarique:** tr. 'as...'.

22 **enituissent:** 'would have...'.
    de magno looks forward to *fundamento* (tr. 'on...').

23 **Haec:** sc. 'holds good (for...)'.

24 **unus:** i.e. Alberic.

25f. **An melius...audierunt:** 'Or better, let those... who...' (*audierunt* = audiuerunt: RLRGr A4).

26 **alter:** Robert.
    in diuinis proficiens litteris: 'having...(see G.20(a)) in theology'.

26f. **etiam...nominis** all depends on *gloriam*.

(ii) *In the section omitted, John tells how he reviewed his studies and decided to go back to basics. He then moved on to other teachers and even took pupils. He refutes a theory of one of them. In this excerpt, John relates how his studies were interrupted by the need to earn money. On his return to Paris he heard more theological lectures. He found his peers unchanged. He concludes that dialectic is a tool and not a discipline in its own right.*

Extraxerunt me hinc rei familiaris angustia, sociorum petitio, et consilium amicorum, ut officium docentis aggrederer. Parui. Reuersus itaque in fine triennii repperi magistrum Gillebertum, ipsumque audiui in logicis et in diuinis. Sed nimis cito subtractus est. Successit Rodbertus Pullus, quem uita pariter et scientia commendabant. Deinde me excepit Simon Pexiacensis, fidus   5
lector, sed obtusior disputator. Sed hos duos in solis theologicis habui praeceptores.

Sic fere duodennium mihi elapsum est, diuersis studiis occupato. Iucundum itaque uisum est ueteres quos reliqueram et quos adhuc dialectica detinebat in Monte reuisere socios, conferre cum eis super ambiguitatibus pristinis ut   10
nostrum inuicem ex collatione mutua commetiremur profectum. Inuenti sunt qui fuerant et ubi. Neque enim ad palmam uisi sunt processisse. Ad quaestiones pristinas dirimendas, neque propositiunculam unam adiecerant. Quibus urgebant stimulis, eisdem et ipsi urgebantur. Profecerant in uno

dumtaxat; dedidicerant modum, modestiam nesciebant. Adeo quidem ut de   15
reparatione eorum posset desperari. Expertus itaque sum quod liquido colligi
potest, quia sicut dialectica alias expedit disciplinas, sic si sola fuerit iacet
exanguis et sterilis, nec ad fructum philosophiae fecundat animam, si aliunde
non concipit.

3 **magistrum Gillebertum:** Gilbert of Poitiers (1076–1154) or de la Porrée, bishop of Poitiers (1142–54) and famed for his lectures on the Bible and Boethius. He was tried at Rheims in 1148 for heretical views on the Trinity thought to be expressed in his commentaries. He was not condemned, but the mud stuck.

4 **Rodbertus Pullus:** Robert Pullen, a theologian, archdeacon of Rochester 1138–43. He left Paris in 1144 when he was made cardinal. He had been recommended as a teacher at Paris by Bernard of Clairvaux (see sections 17.2 Intro. and 18.2)

5 **Simon Pexiacensis:** Simon of Poissy or of Paris,

of whom nothing else is known. One might infer from *Metalogicon* I.5 that he was also an 'orthodox' theologian.

6 **obtusior:** 'rather...'.

8 **mihi** looks forward to *occupato*.

9 **uisum est** looks forward to *reuisere* (then to *conferre*) and **ueteres** to *socios*.

11 **nostrum** looks forward to *profectum* (obj. of *commetiremur*).

inuicem: 'with each other' (G.11(e)(ii)).

12 **ad palmam:** i.e. 'their final goal'.

12f. **Ad...dirimendas:** '(That is) to...'.

14 **Quibus...stimulis, eisdem:** 'by the very same goads with which they drove (sc. others)'.

17 **fuerit:** tr. 'is'.

2. Peter Abelard (*c*.1079–21 April 1142)

The most celebrated teacher of his day, as John of Salisbury notes (above, section 16.1 (i)), Abelard lived a stormy life full of controversy. His own studies in dialectic took him between 1095 and 1102 to Loches, Tours and Paris, and brought him into contact with the teachers Roscelin of Compiègne (see section 14 Intro.) and William of Champeaux. From 1102 to 1105 he taught at Corbeil and then Melun. Between around 1105 and 1108 he returned to Brittany, where he continued to study dialectic. In 1108–9 he returned to Paris to study rhetoric. It was during this period that his acrimonious debate on the nature of universals took place with his former teacher William of Champeaux. From 1109 to 1112 he taught at Melun and then on the Montagne Ste-Geneviève in Paris. In 1113 he took time out to study divinity with Anselm at Laon. The years of his greatest triumph as a teacher at Notre-Dame in Paris (1114–16) were also the period of his disastrous love-affair with Heloise, his secret marriage and his castration (see section 17.4). After the debacle, he entered the abbey of St-Denis and subsequently taught from a church dependent upon it (1116/17–21). A further problem was caused him in 1121, when his *Theologia 'Summi Boni'* was condemned and burnt at the Council of Soissons. Eventually, he obtained release from his monastic obligation at St-Denis and permission to establish an oratory near Quincy. From 1122 to 1127 he taught at this place, now dedicated to the Paraclete. During this period the *Sic et Non* was written. In 1127 he became abbot of St-Gildas-de-Ruys, but by 1132 was back in Paris attached to the school of Ste-Geneviève. Here he remained until late 1137 (see 16.1 above). At a date unknown he returned to St-Hilaire in Paris. Work was meanwhile progressing on a later version of the *Theology*. To defend his views against Bernard of Clairvaux among others he came to the Council of Sens on 2 June 1140 (see below sections 17.2 and 18.3). He appealed to Rome against the decision to condemn him. Within a month he had taken refuge at Cluny. On 16 July Innocent II issued a letter of condemnation, but Abelard had already revised the anathematized passages of the *Theology* and made a settlement with Bernard before it reached France. By 1141 his excommunication had been rescinded. He was transferred in ill health to St-Marcel-sur-Saône, where he died in 1142 or 1143.

The *Sic et Non* was a teaching text. Behind it lay the idea of collecting the authorities for canon law, which Ivo of Chartres (d. 1116) had enshrined in his *Panormia*. Ivo had pointed out that authorities might seem to conflict and laid down some rules for resolving such problems. Abelard transferred the idea to theological questions, setting forth principles for the resolution of cruces and then a series of conflicting texts. Like Ivo, he gave no answers. But his reason was not Ivo's (lack of self-confidence). He wished thus to sharpen the minds of his students. The method they would be asked to apply was dialectic. The introduction to the work, from which this passage is taken, outlines its principles.

See further: D. E. Luscombe, *The School of Peter Abelard*, Cambridge, 1969.

(i) *Abelard has just quoted Augustine extensively to show that he made a distinction between the canonical authority of the Old and New Testaments and other books. He now shows what views Jerome held on the interpretation of the 'doctors of the Church', whose discordant views form the substance of the* Sic et Non.

Beatus quoque Hieronymus cum inter ecclesiasticos doctores quosdam ceteris anteferret, ita nobis legendos esse consuluit ut eos magis diiudicemus quam sequamur. Unde est illud eius consilium ad Laetam *De Institutione Filiae*: 'Cypriani,' inquit, 'opuscula semper in manu teneat; Athanasii opuscula et Hilarii librum inoffenso currat pede; illorum tractatibus, illorum ingeniis   5 delectetur in quorum libris pietas fidei non vacillat; ceteros sic legat ut magis diiudicet quam sequatur.' Idem in psalmo LXXXVI, quasi auctoritatem his omnibus penitus auferens, ait: '*Dominus narrabit in scriptura populorum et*

principum, horum qui fuerunt in ea. Non dixit qui sunt in ea sed *qui fuerunt.*
Populorum non sufficit sed etiam principum dicit, et quorum principum? *Qui*   10
fuerunt. Videte ergo quomodo scriptura sancta sacramentis plena est. Legimus
apostolum dicentem: *An experimentum eius quaeritis qui in me loquitur Christus?*
Quod Paulus loquitur, Christus loquitur (*qui enim vos recipit, me recipit*) in
scripturis principum, *in scriptura populorum,* quae est scriptura populis omnibus.
Videte quid dicat: *qui fuerunt,* non qui sunt; ut exceptis apostolis quodcumque   15
aliud postea dicatur, abscidatur, non habeat postea auctoritatem. Quamvis ergo
sanctus sit aliquis post apostolos, quamvis dissertus sit, non habeat auctoritatem.' Idem ad Vigilantium: 'Quisquis multorum tractatorum opuscula legit,
debet esse sicut probatus nummularius, ut, si quis nummus adulter est et
figuram Caesaris non habet nec signatus moneta publica, reprobetur; qui autem   20
Christi faciem claro praefert lumine in cordis marsupio recondatur. Non enim
praeiudicata doctoris opinio sed doctrinae ratio ponderanda est, sicut scriptum
est: '*Omnia probate, quod bonum est tenete.*' Hoc tamen de commentatoribus
dictum est, non de canonicis scripturis quibus indubitatam fidem convenit
adhibere. Idem ad Paulinum de sanctis doctoribus in ea *Bonus homo de bono*   25
cordis thesauro: 'Taceo de ceteris vel defunctis vel adhuc viventibus, super quibus
in utramque partem post nos iudicabunt alii.'

2 **nobis:** 'by us' (with *legendos esse*).

3 **ad Laetam:** Jerome, Epistle 107.

4f. **teneat...currat...delectetur...legat:** 'let her...' (the subject is Laeta's daughter); *librum* is the object of *currat* 'traverse' (usually intransitive 'run'); *inoffenso* looks forward to *pede*.

7 **in psalmo LXXXVI:** the text is Ps. 86.6 (Vlg.) and the comment from Jerome's Tractate on Ps. 86: *horum qui fuerunt in ea* '(of) those (kings) who were in it'.

9 **Non dixit qui sunt in ea sed *qui fuerunt*:** Jerome's point becomes slightly clearer later, when he interprets the past tense here as an indication that no *princeps* outside the Bible is necessarily expressing the will of God.

12 **apostolum dicentem:** St Paul in 2 Corinthians 13.3: *an experimentum quaeritis eius qui in me loquitur Christi...?* 'Do you seek proof of him who speaks in me, Christ?'.

13 **qui...recipit:** 'he who...' (Mt. 10.40).

15 **ut:** 'so that...' (result).

16 **abscidatur, non habeat:** 'let it...(*quodcumque ...dicatur*)'.

16f. **Quamvis...quamvis:** 'However...someone may be...'.

18 **ad Vigilantium:** actually, this is from Jerome's letter to the monks Minervius and Alexander (*Epistle* 129), but is like what he says at the start of his letter to Vigilantius (*Epistle* 61).

19 **ut** ('so that...': result) looks forward to *reprobetur.*

20 **signatus:** sc. *est.*

20f. **qui...recondatur:** 'but let the (writer) who....' (Jerome keeps the image of the coin going in this sentence).

23 **Omnia...tenete:** 1 Thessalonians 5.21.

24f. **quibus...adhibere:** 'to which it is right to apply...'.

25 **ad Paulinum:** Jerome, *Epistle* 58 on the text (*in ea*) Luke 6.45: *Bonus homo de bono thesauro cordis sui profert bonum* 'The good man brings forth good from the good treasure-store of his heart'.

27 **in utramque partem:** 'on one side or the other' (i.e. that they are right or wrong).

(ii) *Abelard concludes his introductory remarks by claiming dominical authority for the dialectical approach to theological education which the following work is designed to foster.*

His autem praelibatis placet, ut instituimus, diversa sanctorum patrum dicta colligere, quae nostrae occurrerint memoriae aliquam ex dissonantia quam habere videntur quaestionem contrahentia, quae teneros lectores ad maximum inquirendae veritatis exercitium provocent et acutiores ex inquisitione reddant. Haec quippe prima sapientiae clavis definitur assidua scilicet seu   5
frequens interrogatio; ad quam quidem toto desiderio arripiendam philosophus ille omnium perspicacissimus Aristoteles in praedicamento *Ad Aliquid* studiosos adhortatur dicens, 'Fortasse autem difficile est de huiusmodi rebus confidenter declarare nisi saepe pertractata sint. Dubitare autem de singulis non erit inutile.' Dubitando quippe ad inquisitionem venimus; inquirendo   10
veritatem percipimus. Iuxta quod et Veritas ipsa *Quaerite*, inquit, *et invenietis, pulsate et aperietur vobis.* Quae nos etiam proprio exemplo moraliter instruens, circa duodecimum aetatis suae annum sedens et interrogans in medio doctorum inveniri voluit, primum discipuli nobis formam per interrogationem exhibens quam magistri per praedicationem, cum sit tamen ipsa Dei   15
plena ac perfecta sapientia.

1 **His...praelibatis:** i.e. 'After these preliminary remarks'.
   diversa looks forward to *dicta*.
2 **quae...occurrerint:** 'such as have...' (generic subjunctive: *RLGVE* 140.1).
   nostrae looks forward to *memoriae* (dependent on *occurrerint*).
2f. **aliquam...contrahentia:** the construction is *contrahentia* ('as bringing along') *aliquam quaestionem* (obj. of *contrahentia*) *ex dissonantia quam habere videntur.*
3f. **quae...provocent:** 'so that they may...' (purpose clause: see RLRGr S2(6) Note 1).
   ad maximum looks forward to *exercitium* (and *inquirendae veritatis* depends on it).
4f. **acutiores...reddant:** sc. 'them'.
5 **prima...clavis:** sc. 'as'.
6 **ad quam** looks back to *interrogatio* and forward to *arripiendam*; the phrase depends on *adhortatur*.
7 **in praedicamento *Ad Aliquid*:** 'in the category "To Something"' (Aristotle's *Categories* and

Boethius' *Commentary* are the points of reference).
11 **Veritas ipsa:** i.e. the Bible or Christ; the quotation is Mt 7.7.
12 **Quae** and **nos** depend on *instruens* ('Teaching us this...', or 'To teach...': see G.20(b)); the unstated subject is 'he, Christ'.
   moraliter: i.e. the level of biblical meaning on which actions are interpreted as giving ethical lessons (see section 3 Intro.).
13 **sedens et interrogans** need to be understood as complements of *inveniri* ('he..to be...ing and ...ing').
14f. **primum...quam:** for *prius...quam.*
14 **discipuli** depends on *formam* (obj. of *exhibens*), which then is to be understood also with *magistri.*
15f. **cum...sapientia:** 'even though he (Christ) is...'; take *Dei* with *sapientia*, and *ipsa...plena ac perfecta* purely as adjectives. In Abelard's *Theology*, the second person of the Trinity, the Son, has the property of *sapientia* (see section 18.3).

3. Gratian (*fl.* 1140)

We know very little about the man who revolutionized canon law by the publication in *c.*1140 of the *Concord of Discordant Canons*, otherwise known as the *Decretum* ('Decree', 'Precept'). He may have been a monk in the enclosed order of Camaldoli in Bologna. His work built on a tradition begun by Burchard of Worms (*c.*965–1025) in his *Decretum*, a collection of canons, and Ivo of Chartres (d. 1116) in his *Panormia*, a collection of conflicting authorities presented without any resolutions. Gratian's work in turn seems, in its recognition of the concept of a 'legal system', to have been strongly influenced by the Bolognese lawyer Irnerius' rediscovery of the *Corpus iuris civilis*, Justinian's code of Roman law, in the late eleventh century. But Gratian rejected the authority and the practice of Roman law, probably because it represented the interests of the Empire whereas canon law represented those of the Papacy (see sections 12 and 19.III). The work was timely, in that it appeared when there was rapid growth of appeals to Rome in cases we would regard as in the secular province (such as suits relating to inheritances). Though it was not at first an officially recognized authority, it was soon accepted as the basic text. The position was changed when Pope Gregory IX issued the *Decretals* in 1234, the first official collection of papal documents, as a supplement to Gratian's *Decretum*.

Gratian's method – using dialectic – is similar to that of Abelard's *Sic et Non*. The principle is to discover the answers to problematic issues by arguing from conflicting authorities. The *Decretum* is in three parts, the largest of which is the *Causae*, imaginary cases which are the basis for *quaestiones* on legal points, which are answered in various ways both by citation of authorities and Gratian's own comments. The following excerpt from one of the *causae* on marriage shows how fascinating this dry legal material can be in its own right, and how important as a source for understanding medieval society.

See further: S. Kuttner, *Gratian and the Schools of Law, 1140–1234*, London, 1983.

(i) *The case. A noblewoman's marital problems and the questions raised by them.*

Cuidam nobili mulieri nunciatum est quod a filio cuiusdam nobilis petebatur in coniugem. Prebuit illa assensum. Alius uero quidam, ignobilis atque seruilis condicionis, nomine illius se ipsum obtulit atque eam in coniugem accepit. Ille

qui sibi prius placuerat tandem uenit eamque sibi in coniugem petit. Illa se
delusam conqueritur et ad prioris copulam aspirat.   5

Questio I: Hic primum queritur, an sit coniugium inter eos?

Questio II: Secundo, si prius putabat hunc esse liberum et postea depre-
hendit illum esse seruum, an liceat ei statim ab illo discedere?

1 **in coniugem:** 'as his wife'.

2f. **seruilis condicionis:** gen. of description
(RLRGr L(d)4).

3f. **Ille qui sibi...eamque sibi:** the first *sibi* is '(to)
her' (= *ei*: see G.11(e)(i)) and the second is
'(for) himself'.

4f. **se delusam:** sc. *esse.*

5 **prioris:** 'with the first one'.

6 **queritur:** 'it is asked' (impersonal passive:
RLGVE 155) = *quaeritur* (see O.1 and contrast *conqueritur*, from *conqueror*).

(ii) *The answer to question I consists of five sections, which follow from the proof
that they are married: (1) consent cannot be based on error; (2) but not every error
negates consent, only an error of person; (3) a biblical example seems to refute this,
but there is a distinction between consent prior to and consent after consummation;
(4) proof of the excuse provided to some by error of person based on three examples;
(5) but an error of fortune or kind does not negate consent.*

Quod autem coniugium sit inter eos probatur hoc modo. Coniugium siue
matrimonium est uiri et mulieris coniunctio, indiuiduam uitae consuetudinem
retinens. Item consensus utriusque matrimonium facit. Quia ergo isti coniuncti
sunt, ut indiuiduam uitae consuetudinem conseruarent, quia uterque consensit
in alterum, coniuges sunt appellandi.   5

1. His ita respondetur:

Consensus est duorum uel plurium sensus in idem. Qui autem errat non sentit,
non ergo consentit, id est simul cum aliis sentit. Hec autem errauit; non ergo
consensit: non itaque coniux est appellanda, quia non fuit ibi consensus
utriusque, sine quo nullum matrimonium esse potest. Sicut enim qui   10
ordinatur ab eo, quem putat esse episcopum et adhuc est laicus, errat nec
uocatur ordinatus, immo adhuc ab episcopo est ordinandus: sic ista errans nulli
est copulata coniugio, immo adhuc est copulanda.

2. Ad hec:

Non omnis error consensum euacuat. Qui enim accipit in uxorem quam putat   15
uirginem, uel qui accipit meretricem quam putat esse castam, uterque errat,
quia ille corruptam existimat esse uirginem, et iste meretricem reputat castam.
Numquid ergo dicendi sunt non consensisse in eas? Aut dabitur utrique facultas
dimittendi utramque et ducendi aliam? Verum est quod non omnis error
consensum excludit. Sed error alius est personae, alius fortunae, alius con-   20

dicionis, alius qualitatis. Error personae est quando hic putatur esse Virgilius et
ipse est Plato. Error fortunae quando putatur esse dives qui pauper est, uel e
conuerso. Error condicionis quando putatur esse liber qui seruus est. Error
qualitatis quando putatur esse bonus qui malus est. Error fortunae et qualitatis
coniugii consensum non excludit. Error uero personae et condicionis coniugii   25
consensum non admittit. Si quis enim pacisceretur se uenditurum agrum
Marcello et postea ueniret Paulus dicens se esse Marcellum et emeret agrum ab
illo, numquid cum Paulo conuenit iste de precio, aut dicendus est agrum sibi
uendidisse? Item si quis promitteret se uenditurum michi aurum et pro auro
offerret michi auricalcum et ita me deciperet, numquid dicerer consensisse in   30
auricalcum? Numquam uolui emere auricalcum, nec ergo aliquando in illud
consensi, quia consensus non nisi uoluntatis est. Sicut ergo hic error materiae
excludit consensum, sic et in coniugio error personae. Non enim consensit in
hunc, sed in eum quem hunc putabat esse.

3. Sed obicitur: 35
Iacob non consenserat in Liam, sed in Rachel. Septem quidem annis pro
Rachel seruierat. Cum ergo eo ignorante Lia esset sibi subposita, non fuit
coniugium inter eos, si error personae consensum excludit, quia, ut dictum est,
non in eam consenserat, sed in Rachel.

His ita respondetur: 40
Consensus est alius precedens, alius subsequens. Precedit consensus, quando
ante carnalem copulam in indiuiduam uitae consuetudinem uterque consentit.
Subsequitur quando post concubinalem siue fornicarium coitum consentiant in
idem. Iacob ergo et Liam non fecit coniuges precedens consensus, sed
subsequens. Nec tamen ex primo concubitu fornicarii iudicantur, cum ille   45
maritali affectu eam cognouerat et illa uxorio affectu sibi debitum persoluerit,
putans lege primogenitarum et paternis inperiis se sibi iure copulatam.

4. Quod autem error personae nonnullos excuset, illa auctoritate probatur, qua
soror uxoris utroque inscio, sorore uidelicet et marito, in lectulum eius iisse et a
uiro suae sororis cognita perhibetur, que cum sine spe coniugii perpetuo   50
manere censeatur, ille tamen qui cognouit eam per ignorantiam excusatur.
    Aliter etiam hoc probatur. Diabolus nonnumquam se in angelum lucis
transformat, nec est periculosus error si tunc creditur esse bonus, cum se
bonum simulat. Si ergo tunc ab aliquo simplici quereret an suae beatitudinis
uellet esse particeps et ille responderet se in eius consortium uelle transire,   55
numquid dicendus esset consensisse in consortium diabolicae dampnationis, an
non pocius in participationem eternae claritatis?

Item si quis hereticorum nomine Augustini uel Ambrosii uel Ieronimi alicui catholicorum se ipsum offerret atque eum ad suae fidei imitationem prouocaret, si ille preberet assensum, in cuius fidei sentenciam diceretur consensisse?   60 Non in hereticorum sectam, sed in integritatem catholicae fidei, quam ille hereticus se mentiebatur habere.

Quia ergo hec persona decepta errore non in hunc, sed in eum quem iste se mentiebatur esse consensit, patet quod eius coniux non fuerit.

5. Error fortunae et qualitatis non excludit consensum, ueluti si quis consentiret   65 in prelaturam alicuius ecclesiae, quam putaret esse diuitem, et illa esset minus copiosa, quamuis hic deciperetur errore fortunae, non tamen posset renunciare prelaturae acceptae. Similiter, que nubit pauperi, putans illum esse diuitem, non potest renunciare priori condicioni, quamuis errauerit.

Error qualitatis similiter non excludit consensum, utpote si quis emerit   70 agrum uel uineam quam putaret esse uberrimam, quamuis iste erraret qualitate rerum, rem minus fertilem emendo, non potest tamen uenditionem rescindere.

Similiter qui ducit meretricem in uxorem uel corruptam quam putat esse castam uel uirginem, non potest eam dimittere et aliam ducere.

Question II is answered more succinctly, in two parts which are each supported by authorities. Part I argues that a woman may not leave a husband because he is a slave. Part II replies that she is free to leave him if she did not know his true condition when she married him.

2 **indiuiduam uitae consuetudinem:** 'a single habit of life', i.e. lifelong cohabitation.

3f. **Quia...quia:** in both instances the conjunction means 'because'.

coniuncti...coniuges: Gratian draws attention to the etymology of *coniunx* 'spouse' by using the verb *coniungere* 'to join together'.

6 **respondetur:** 'it is replied', 'one might reply' (impersonal passive: *RLGVE* 155).

7 **Consensus...sensus:** the first is subject, the second complement; *sensus* governs *duorum vel plurium*.

Qui: 'He who...'.

8 **Hec:** 'She' (the noble woman in the case).

10 **Sicut...qui:** 'Just as the man who...'.

12 **ordinandus:** 'waiting to be...' (cf. *copulanda*: see G.19).

ista: 'she', i.e. the noblewoman again (see G.11(c)).

errans: 'because she was misled'.

14 **Ad hec:** sc. *respondetur*.

15f. **Qui...uel qui:** 'The man who...or who...'.

15 **quam:** '(a woman) whom...'.

17 **ille...iste:** 'the former...the latter' (see G.11(c)).

corruptam: sc. *mulierem*.

20 **Sed error alius...alius...:** construe *error* with each of the genitives and tr. *alius...alius...* 'one thing...another...' etc.

22 **qui pauper est:** 'the man who...' (subject of *putatur*: the same pattern is found in the next two sentences with *qui seruus est/qui malus est*).

22f. **e conuerso:** 'vice versa'.

26 **Si...:** 'Just suppose...' (notice that the apodosis is a question with indicative verbs: 'did... or must...?').

uenditurum: sc. *esse*.

27f. **ab illo:** i.e. the vendor.

28 **iste:** i.e. the vendor.

sibi: i.e. 'to Paulus' (for *ei*: see G.11(e)(i)).

29 **Item si quis...:** 'Likewise suppose...' (this time the apodosis also has subjunctive verbs: 'would I...?').

32 **nisi uoluntatis:** 'except of will', i.e. 'except a voluntary one'.

33 **consensit:** sc. 'she' (the noblewoman in the *causa*).

35 **obicitur:** 'it might be objected' (see note above on *respondetur*).

36 **Iacob...in Rachel:** the biblical example comes from Gen. 29.16–30. Jacob serves Laban for seven years for his daughter Rachel's hand. But she is the younger daughter, so at the wedding Laban substitutes Leah, and Jacob, thinking she is Rachel, sleeps with her.
Septem...annis: 'For...' (abl. for acc.: see G.16(c)).

37 **seruierat** = *seruiuerat* (see RLRGr A5).
Cum ergo: 'So since...'.
sibi: 'to him' (for *ei*: see G.11(e)(i)).

41 **Consensus est alius...alius...:** 'There are two kinds of consensus, one...the other...'.

46f. **sibi...persoluerit...sibi...copulatam** (sc. *esse*): 'to him' (for *ei*: see G.11(e)(i)).

48 **Quod...excuset:** 'That...should excuse...' (the clause is subject of *probatur*).
qua: 'according to which...' (the basic structure is: *soror...iisse et cognita* (sc. *esse*) *perhibetur* ('is said')).

49 **uxoris:** this is the wife of the man the *soror* goes to bed with.
eius: i.e. of her sister's husband.

50f. **que cum...ille tamen:** 'and although she... nevertheless he...' (the old story: medieval ideology, based on the Bible, regarded virginity in the woman as a precondition for marriage and sexual promiscuity in men as venial).

53f. **se bonum:** sc. *esse*.

54 **Si...quereret:** 'Just suppose...'; the subject is still *diabolus*, but the subject of *an...uellet* is 'the simpleton' (he is *ille* also).

56 **dicendus esset:** 'would he be said...'.

56f. **diabolicae dampnationis....eternae** and **claritatis:** tr. 'participation in' in both cases.

58 **si quis...:** the structure is 'If someone...*offerret atque...prouocaret* ', then another condition – *si ille* (i.e. the *alicui catholicorum* of the first *si* clause), then the apodosis *in...consensisse* 'into...would he be...'.
hereticorum: there were several contemporary heretical sects; the Cathars of Provence were the most prominent.
nomine: 'using the name...' (the names are those of the three great Fathers, St Augustine, St Ambrose and St Jerome: see sections 2 and 4).

60 **in...sentenciam...consensisse:** 'to have agreed to the views of which faith...' (then *Non in...sed in...* mean 'Not to...but to...', understanding *consensisse*).

62 **se** goes with *habere* (acc. + inf. introduced by *mentiebatur*: see also in the next sentence *quem iste se mentiebatur esse*).

63 **hec persona:** the noblewoman of the *causa*.
non in hunc looks forward (as does *sed in eum*) to *consensit*.

67 **quamuis...deciperetur:** 'even though he had been...'.
non...posset: apodosis 'he would not...'.

68 **que...:** 'the woman who...' (subject also of *non potest*).

71f. **qualitate rerum:** 'in respect of...'.

73 **qui ducit...:** 'the man who...' (subject of *non potest*).
corruptam: sc. *mulierem*.

Section 17
The religious life

It would be perfectly reasonable to characterize the twelfth century as an age of religious fervour and theological controversy. New monastic orders sprang up regularly, in response to the ideal of the truly simple Christian life of prayer and poverty as opposed to the wealth and worldliness of older foundations. Female visionaries were encouraged to let the world hear the voice of God directly from their lips. New crusades were preached and instituted. But ever present was the danger of straying beyond the bounds of orthodoxy. Sects such as the Cathars and the Waldensians were branded as heretics. Even within the Church, the zeal of reformers could corner a great teacher and force him to rewrite what he had thought out. The crusades brought home for almost the first time the relationship of Islam to Christianity, so that this too was now fought as a heresy. In both these tendencies we can see the seeds of important innovations of the next century, the inauguration of the mendicant orders on the one side and the Inquisition on the other.

On the practical side, the liturgy was invigorated by new musical advances and by the increasing use of drama. Church building received a boost from the more prosperous economic conditions and the self-aggrandizement of prelates. For the great dignitaries of the Church were also great landlords and, as such, men with considerable political power and often the will to use it. At a lower level, the monasteries, abbeys and cathedrals all needed to be administered. We have during this period good inside accounts of how the system worked and of the human frailties at play even where the Lord's work was central. Elsewhere too, we begin to see more markedly the individuality of the great figures through the proficiency and delicacy of their writing.

1. Peter of Cluny ('The Venerable': 1092 or 1094–1156)

Peter, born of a noble family, became a monk before 1109 and abbot of Cluny in 1122, after the disastrous administration of Pontius (elected in

1109 and forced to resign in 1122). Cluny, founded in 910 (see map 2), had been at the head of the reform movement in the tenth and early eleventh centuries, but its growing power as the central authority over a large number of houses all over Europe had made people like St Bernard (see section 17.2) think that its central concerns were the magnificence of its feasts, its furniture and its buildings. Hence already before Peter became abbot the reaction had begun which led inexorably to the decline of the Cluniac order.

Like Bernard, his contemporary and friend, Peter had connections all over Christendom. His letters (collected and edited on Peter's orders by his secretary Pierre le Poitevin) are addressed to Popes, the kings of France, Sicily, Jerusalem, Castile, Aragon and Norway, and the Byzantine Emperor, as well as to cardinals and bishops in France, England and Italy. They deal with contemporary events, the history of the Cluniac order, and matters of the order's administration. They also reveal his relationship with other famous literary figures, such as Abelard, Heloise and St Bernard. More than this, though, like other collections of the period, their existence in this form reflects a clear desire on the author's part to produce a careful image of himself and his concerns. His style is usually clear, but his sentences are often quite complex. He was not influenced by the increasingly important conventions of the *ars dictaminis* and its prescription of the *cursus* (see further below, section 17.4 Intro.). As one might expect given Cluny's collection of some 100 classical texts, he often quotes from pagan writers such as Virgil, Horace and Persius. Yet his chief concerns are religious and his orientation, like St Bernard's, is towards mysticism rather than philosophy.

He travelled extensively, to Rome (six times), to England (in 1155) and to Spain (in 1127 and 1142), where he commissioned a translation of the Koran. The Spanish visits also caused him to write his own attack on Islam, *Adversus nefandam sectam Saracenorum* (*c*.1143). He had earlier composed a *De miraculis* (*c*.1138) and a tract against the Jews (*Adversus Iudaeorum inveteratam duritiem*; *c*.1140). Like many another abbot and abbess, he also composed liturgical poetry.

The following extracts are taken from Letter 111, which was written to Bernard of Clairvaux in the late spring or early summer of 1144. It has two main themes, the first of which, the quarrel between Cluny and Cîteaux, goes back to the foundation of Cîteaux in 1098. Peter himself had earlier written a letter (28) to Bernard, possibly in the 1130s, in which the standard Cistercian charges were answered point by point. Bernard had also written an *Apologia* for the Cistercian order. Despite their differences, in their correspondence they display friendly relations. The second theme,

Islam, comes at the end of the letter, and this part seems to have been composed after and on the basis of a letter dealing with his translations of Islamic texts and a work called the *Summa totius haeresis Saracenorum* ('Compendium of the whole Saracen heresy'). It is the second theme which is excerpted here.

See further: G. Constable, *Letters of Peter the Venerable*, Cambridge, Mass., 1967, 2 vols. (especially no. 115 to Heloise on Abelard's death); J. Kritzeck, *Peter the Venerable and Islam*, Princeton, 1964 (= Princeton Oriental Studies 23), esp. pp. 56–8.

(i) *Peter tells Bernard that he has also enclosed a translation of a work attacking the heresy of Muhammed, and has in addition had made a complete Latin version of the Koran.*

Misi et nouam translationem nostram contra pessimam nequam Mahumet heresim disputantem quae dum nuper in Hyspaniis morarer meo studio de lingua Arabica uersa est in Latinam. Feci autem eam transferri a perito utriusque linguae uiro, magistro Petro Toletano. Sed quia lingua Latina non adeo ei familiaris uel nota erat ut Arabica, dedi ei coadiutorem doctum uirum dilectum   5
filium et fratrem Petrum notarium nostrum, reuerentiae uestrae (ut aestimo) bene cognitum. Qui uerba Latina impolite uel confuse plerumque ab eo prolata poliens et ordinans epistolam, immo libellum, multis (ut credo) propter ignotarum rerum notitiam perutilem futurum perfecit.

Fuit autem in transferendo haec mea intentio ut morem illum patrum   10
sequerer, quo nullam unquam suorum temporum uel leuissimam (ut sic dicam) heresim silendo preterirent, quin ei totis fidei uiribus resisterent et scriptis ac disputationibus esse detestandam ac dampnabilem demonstrarent. Hoc ego de hoc praecipuo errore errorum, de hac fece uniuersarum heresum, in quam omnium diabolicarum sectarum quae ab ipso saluatoris aduentu ortae sunt   15
reliquiae confluxerunt, facere uolui ut, sicut laetali eius peste dimidius pene orbis infectus agnoscitur, ita quam sit execrandus et conculcandus, detecta eius stultitia et turpitudine, a nescientibus agnoscatur.

Agnoscetis ipse legendo et (sicut arbitror), ut dignum est, deflebitis per tam nefarias et abiectissimas sordes tantam humani generis partem decaeptam et a   20
conditore suo per spurcissimi hominis sectam etiam post redemptoris gratiam tam leuiter auersam. Nec ignoro equidem quoniam scriptura ista quae perditis illis in propria lingua prodesse non potuit, in Latinam uersa minus proderit. Sed proderit fortasse aliquibus Latinis, quos et de ignotis instruet et quam dampnabilis sit heresis quae ad aures eorum peruenerat impugnando et   25
expugnando ostendet.

Et ut nihil dampnabilis sectae nostros lateret, totam illam illorum legem, quam in propria lingua Alkoran uel Alkyren uocant, ex integro et per ordinem feci transferri. Interpretatur autem Alkoran uel Alkyren, si e uerbo uerbi expressa translatio fiat, collectaneus praecaeptorum quae sibi per partes de caelo 30 missa nequam ille confinxit.

1 **nouam...nostram** is picked up by *disputantem* ('which...'), governing *contra...heresim (nequam Mahumet* is genitive: cf. G.6(a)), then by *quae...Latinam.* Christians had faced the threat of Islam since the seventh century in the East and Africa, and since the eighth and ninth in Spain and Sicily, but Peter's are the first efforts to look directly at its central texts and belief system. The text in question is the *Risala* ('Apology') of Al-Kindi, a Christian Arab. It is a defence of Christianity against Islam.

3 **Feci...transferri:** 'I had it translated' (see G.17(c)).
perito looks forward to *uiro* (which in English would come first).

4 **Petro Toletano:** Peter of Toledo, which, having been reconquered from the Muslims only in 1085, was one of the main centres for the transfer of Arab learning in the twelfth century.

6 **Petrum notarium nostrum:** Pierre le Poitevin (i.e. of Poitiers: see Intro.).
reuerentiae uestrae looks forward to and depends on *cognitum.*

7 **uerba Latina** is picked up by *prolata* (which governs the intervening words) and is the object of *poliens et ordinans* (like other translators, Peter of Toledo seems to have used the 'word for word' technique which you have learned to avoid).

8 **epistolam** looks forward to *perfecit* (of which it is the object).
multis ('to...') depends on *perutilem,* while *futurum* picks up *libellum* ('a...destined to be...').

10 **Fuit** looks forward to *mea intentio* (subject); *haec* is the complement looking forward to *ut...sequerer.*

11 **quo:** 'according to which...'.
nullam looks forward to *heresim (uel leuissimam* 'even the least serious').

12 **silendo:** 'in silence'.

12f. **quin...demonstrarent:** 'without...ing...and...ing...' (*ei* refers back to *heresim; totis* looks

forward to *uiribus;* the subject of *esse... dampnabilem* is *heresim).*

13 **Hoc** looks forward to *facere uolui.*
de: 'with...' (see G.15(a)(ii)); *errore errorum*: tr. literally (see G.10(a)).

14 **heresum** = *haeresium* (cf. G.7(a)).

14f. **in quam...confluxerunt:** the structure is *in quam omnium...sectarum...reliquiae confluxerunt* with *quae...sunt* describing *sectarum.*

16 **ut** ('so that...') looks forward to *agnoscatur* (subject 'it'), which introduces *quam...conculcandus* (take *detecta...stultitia* with *ut...agnoscatur*); the clause is complicated by the substructure *sicut* ('just as')...*agnoscitur,* whose subject is *dimidius...orbis* and which is constructed with infinitive (*infectus* (sc. *esse*) governing *laetali...peste* 'by...'), *ita* ('so')...(*agnoscatur*).

19 **Agnoscetis ipse:** Peter uses the polite second-person verb, but is speaking to Bernard alone (hence the singular *ipse*).
deflebitis: the construction is acc. + inf. (subject *tantam...partem,* infinitives *decaeptam* and *auersam,* sc. *esse* with each; the means is expressed by the phrases *per...sordes* and *per...sectam*).

21 **post redemptoris gratiam:** i.e. the life, death and Resurrection of Christ.

22 **quoniam** ('that') looks forward to *proderit* (sc. 'them' i.e. *perditis illis,* which is governed within the *quae* clause by *prodesse*); *scriptura ista* refers to the Arabic anti-Islamic tract which the two Peters have translated at the behest of the third.

24f. **quam...peruenerat** depends on *ostendet* (tr. *peruenerat* 'has come': see G.9(c)).

27 **ut...lateret:** the subject is *nihil...sectae (nostros* i.e. 'Christians').
totam...legem looks forward to *feci transferri* ('I have had translated': see G.17(c)).

28 **Alkoran, Alkyren:** 'the Koran'. The translator was the Englishman Robert of Ketton, who came to study in Barcelona in 1136, and soon after 1143 became archdeacon of Pamplona. In

1145 he translated the algebra of Al-Khwārizmi, which began European algebra.

29 **Interpretatur:** the subject is *Alkoran uel Alkyren* and the complement *collectaneus*.

29f. **e uerbo uerbi...translatio:** 'a word-for-word translation'.

30 **quae** is picked up by *missa* (sc. *esse*: acc. + inf. introduced by *confinxit*; 'which that...*confinxit* had been...').

per partes: 'in...'.

(ii) *After outlining the way Muhammed appropriated certain aspects of the Jewish and Christian faiths in the Koran, Peter describes with horror the prophet's perversions of Christian doctrine and his vision of paradise.*

Sic ab optimis doctoribus Iudaeis et hereticis Mahumet institutus Alkoran suum condidit et tam ex fabulis Iudaicis quam ex hereticorum naeniis confectam nefariam scripturam barbaro illo suo modo contexuit. Quod paulatim per Thomos a Gabriele, cuius iam nomen ex sacra scriptura cognouerat, sibi allatum mentitus gentem Deum ignorantem laetali haustu infecit et more 5
talium oram calicis melle liniens, subsequente mortifero ueneno, animas et corpora gentis miserae, proh dolor, interemit. Sic plane impius ille fecit quando et legem Iudaicam et Christianam collaudans nec tamen esse tenendam confirmans, probando reprobus reprobauit.

Inde est quod Moysem optimum prophetam fuisse, Christum dominum 10
maiorem omnibus extitisse confirmat, natum de uirgine praedicat, nuntium Dei, uerbum dei fatetur, nec nuntium, uerbum et spiritum ut nos aut intelligit aut confitetur. Filium dei dici aut credi prorsus deridet. Et de humanae generationis similitudine uaccinus homo filii dei aeternam natiuitatem metiens uel gignere uel generari deum potuisse quanto potest nisu denegat 15
et subsannat. Resurrectionem carnis sepe replicando astruit, iudicium commune in fine saeculi non a Christo, sed a deo exercendum esse non negat. Illi tamen iudicio Christum ut omnium dominum ac se ipsum ad gentis suae praesidium affuturum uaesanit. Inferni tormenta qualia sibi libuit et qualia adinuenire magnum pseudo prophetam decuit describit. Paradysum non 20
societatis angelicae, nec uisionis diuinae, nec summi illius boni *quod nec oculus uidit, nec auris audiuit, nec in cor hominis ascendit,* sed uere talem qualem caro et sanguis, immo fex carnis et sanguinis concupiscebat, qualemque sibi parari optabat, depinxit. Ibi carnium et omnigenorum fructuum esum, ibi lactis et mellis riuulos et aquarum splendentium, ibi pulcherrimarum mulierum et 25
uirginum amplexus et luxus, in quibus tota eius paradysus finitur, sectatoribus suis promittit. Inter ista omnium pene antiquarum heresum feces quas diabolo imbuente sorbuerat reuomens, cum Sabellio trinitatem abnegat, cum suo Nestorio Christi deitatem abiicit, cum Manichaeo mortem domini diffitetur, licet regressum eius non neget ad caelos. 30

1 **ab...hereticis** depends on *institutus*.
Alkoran: treated as a neuter noun (obj.).

2 **tam...confectam** looks forward to *nefariam scripturam* (obj. of *contexuit*: tr. 'weaving his...from...').

3 **Quod** looks forward to *allatum* (sc. *esse*) *mentitus* ('saying falsely that this had been...').

3f. **per Thomos** (= *tomos*: see O.3(a)): 'in...'.

4 **Gabriele...cognouerat:** from Daniel 8.16 and 9.21, Lk 1.19 and 26.

5 **Deum** is obj. of *ignorantem.*

6 **oram...liniens:** 'having...the...' (see G.20(a)).

6f. **animas** and **corpora** look forward to *interemit* (they are objects).

8 **legem...Christianam** are objects of *reprobauit* (subject *reprobus* 'the false one', i.e. Muhammed); the basic idea is expanded by *collaudans...confirmans* '...ing (sc. them) but not...ing that (they) ought...' (*tenendam* refers back to *legem*, but means both the Jewish and the Christian law).

10f. **Moysem...exstitisse** is introduced by *confirmat.*

11 **natum:** sc. *esse Christum.*

12 **nec...spiritum:** sc. 'that Christ is...' (introduced by *aut...confitetur*).

13 **Filium...credi:** 'That (sc. Christ)...'.

13f. **de...metiens:** 'the *uaccinus homo* measuring about the eternal...by analogy with...'. Does he call Muhammed 'cow-like' from *Koran,* Sura 2, the 'Sura of the Cow'?

15f. **uel...subsannat:** 'he denies and ridicules (the notion) that God could have either...or...with as much effort as he can'.

16 **iudicium** looks forward to *exercendum esse,* which depends on *non negat.*

17f. **Illi...iudicio** depends on *affuturum* (introduced by *uaesanit*: '(that)...will be present at...').

18f. **ad...praesidium:** 'to act as...'.

19 **Inferni tormenta** is the object of *describit.*

19f. **qualia...decuit:** 'such as it pleased him (sc. to invent) and such as it befitted a....to...'.

20 **Paradysum** is the object of *depinxit (non...boni:* 'not as...').

21f. **quod...ascendit:** 1 Corinthians 2.9, ending *quae praeparavit Deus iis qui diligunt illum* 'which God has prepared for those who love him' (cf. Isaiah 64.4).

23 **qualemque:** 'and (sc. such) as...'.

24f. **Ibi...promittit:** the basic structure is *Ibi...esum, ibi...riuulos..., ibi...amplexus et luxus...promittit (in quibus...finitur* ('by which...') describes *luxus*). Koran, Sura 47.15 contains some elements of this description: 'there will be streams of pure water, and streams of milk...and streams of wine...and streams of purest honey' (cf. Sura 2.25).

27 **Inter ista:** i.e. 'his doctrines' (in the Koran).

omnium...heresum depends on *feces* (picked up by *quas...sorbuerat*).

28f. **Sabellio...Nestorio...Manichaeo:** Sabellius *(fl.* 220) denied that the Son had an existence distinct from that of the Father; Nestorius (*c.* 381–451), Patriarch of Constantinople, taught that Mary should be called 'Mother of Christ', not 'Mother of God'. Manichaeus, a Persian prophet, Mani or Manes, who taught that existence was a battle between good and evil; matter, the corporeal world, was the source of evil. Cf. Cathar beliefs, which derived from Manichaeanism.

2. St Bernard of Clairvaux (1090–1153)

Born of a noble Burgundian family, Bernard joined the struggling community at Cîteaux in 1113 (see map 2). This had been set up by Robert, abbot of Molesme, in 1098, as a reaction against the wealth, pomp and worldliness of other Benedictine foundations (see above, section 17.1 on Cluny and below, section 17.6 on St-Denis). Bernard had brought with him four of his five brothers and other kinsmen and friends, drawn along by the magnetic personality who was to have such influence on the spiritual and secular affairs of his day. In 1115, Bernard set out to found a new offshoot of Cîteaux, Clairvaux (see map 2), of which he remained abbot until his death. The Cistercian houses were bound together by a *Carta Caritatis* ('Charter of love'), confirmed by Pope Calixtus II on 23 December 1119. By Bernard's death, there were 343 Cistercian foundations, situated from Italy and Spain in the south, to England and Ireland in the west, Germany, Hungary and Bohemia in the east, and Scotland, Denmark, Norway and Poland in the north.

Bernard was a fervent supporter of the rights of the Church, strictly orthodox and a powerful influence in political and religious affairs. His action in both supporting Innocent II in 1130 against the rival Pope Anacletus II and persuading the kings of France and England to do so prevented another schism. In 1144, Edessa was taken by the Muslims. The new Pope, a Cistercian, Eugenius III, gave Bernard the task of preaching the Second Crusade. This he did at Vézelay in March 1146 and at Speyer in December. His efforts were instrumental in persuading Louis VII of France and Conrad III of Germany to take the cross. In the pursuit of orthodoxy, he was himself a crusader, securing the condemnation of Peter Abelard for heresy in July 1140, and attacking Gilbert de la Porrée at the Council of Rheims in 1148 for his views on the Trinity. On the other hand, his support for the mystic Hildegard of Bingen (see section 17.5) reflects his greater ease with symbolism and vision than with dialectic.

His voluminous writings (see also section 18.2) include 547 letters, many of them associated with other groups and their causes. The following belongs to a block relating to the attacks on Peter Abelard. On the basis of a document sent to him by William of St Thierry, noting thirteen heretical views propagated by Abelard, and a meeting with him, Bernard met Abelard in person. A negative result, presumably, led to Bernard's formal appeal to the Pope (Letter 190). Abelard responded with a *Confessio fidei* and other apologetic material, and a challenge to Bernard to debate the matter publicly. Bernard was forced to accept. The discussion was held at Sens on 2 June 1140. The following extract gives Bernard's account of that meeting. The letter is addressed to Pope Innocent, because at the end of the proceedings Abelard had appealed to him and thus forestalled the inevitable condemnation. The end of this story is told in the introduction to section 16.2. Bernard's style has been justly characterized as 'talking Bible'. He is lucid, forceful and simple, larding his sentences with biblical phrases which simply spring into his mind while dictating. Yet elsewhere (see section 18.2) he can be highly rhetorical.

See further: G. R. Evans, *The Mind of St Bernard of Clairvaux*, Oxford, 1983.

(i) *In the first part of the letter, addressed to Pope Innocent, Bernard has expressed his weariness of the world and his folly at thinking that once peace had been re-established in the Church after the Anacletan schism of 1130 he could have rest.*

But having escaped the lion, they have fallen in with a dragon, in the form of heretical books. In this section he inveighs against these.

Volant libri et qui oderant lucem, quoniam mali sunt, impegerunt in lucem, putantes lucem tenebras. Urbibus et castellis ingeruntur pro luce tenebrae, pro melle vel potius in melle venenum passim omnibus propinatur. *Transierunt de gente in gentem et de regno ad populum alterum.* Novum cuditur populis et gentibus Evangelium, nova proponitur fides, fundamentum aliud ponitur praeter id 5 quod positum est. De virtutibus et vitiis non moraliter, de sacramentis Ecclesiae non fideliter, de arcano sanctae Trinitatis non simpliciter nec sobrie disputatur; sed cuncta nobis in perversum, cuncta praeter solitum et praeterquam accepimus, ministrantur.

1 **Volant libri:** the image is of weapons rather than of birds.
  qui…: 'those who…'.
2 **putantes…tenebras:** *tenebras* is the object of *putantes.*
  Urbibus et castellis: 'Into…' (dependent on *ingeruntur*, whose subject is *tenebrae:* see G.16(a)).
3f. **Transierunt…alterum:** Ps. 104.13.
4f. **Novum** looks forward to the subject *Evangelium,*

and **nova** to *fides*. Bernard's view can be contrasted with what Abelard says about the canonical texts as against other theological commentary in the introduction to the *Sic et Non* (see section 16.2).

6 **non moraliter:** the first of three similarly structured sections, which all look forward to *disputatur* ('Discussion goes on…').

8 **cuncta** looks forward to (and is the subject of) *ministrantur; nobis* 'to us'.

(ii) *He pictures Abelard coming forward against the Church as Goliath against the Israelites, calling the tiny David (Bernard) to single combat (at Sens) against him, when all the rest have fled.*

Procedit Golias procero corpore, nobili illo bellico apparatu circummunitus, antecedente quoque ipsum armigero eius Arnaldo de Brixia. Squama squamae *coniungitur, et nec spiraculum incedit per eas.* Siquidem sibilavit apis quae erat in Francia api de Italia, et *convenerunt in unum adversus Dominum et adversus Christum eius. Intenderunt arcum, paraverunt sagittas suas in pharetra, ut sagittent* 5 *in obscuro rectos corde.* In victu autem et habitu *habentes formam pietatis, sed virtutem eius abnegantes,* eo decipiunt plures, quo transfigurant se in angelos lucis, cum sint Satanae. Stans ergo Golias una cum armigero suo inter utrasque acies, clamat adversus phalangas Israel exprobratque agminibus sanctorum, eo nimirum audacius quo sentit David non adesse. Denique in sugillationem 10 Doctorum Ecclesiae, magnis effert laudibus philosophos, adinventiones illorum et suas novitates catholicorum Patrum doctrinae et fidei praefert, et, cum omnes fugiant a facie eius, me omnium minimum expetit ad singulare certamen.

1 **Golias:** i.e. Abelard; Goliath in biblical exegesis is a figure of the scoffer against God. The story is in 1 Kings (1 Samuel) 17 = section 3.1.
procero corpore: 'with...'.
nobili...apparatu depends on *circummunitus* and refers to Abelard's dialectic.

2 **Arnaldo de Brixia:** Arnold of Brescia, an Italian pupil of Abelard, but more zealous than his master in the cause of radical Church reform. A man of pious life, he attacked the right of clerics to own property, and of bishops to the *regalia* (temporal possessions). He was silenced by Innocent II in 1139. Even after Abelard's defeat he continued his struggle in Paris, then in Zurich. He gained the protection of Cardinal Guido, legate in Germany. He was absolved by Eugenius III and sent for penance to Rome, where he was welcomed by and strengthened the republic which had been set up there and which prevented Eugenius from taking full control of the city. When the new Pope, Hadrian IV, was about to make a deal with Frederick Barbarossa in 1155, as a sign of good faith Frederick had Arnold arrested and executed.

3 **coniungitur...per eas:** Job 41.7 (= NIV 41.16); in Job God is describing the monstrous behemoth. Bernard begins his sentence with military vocabulary (because he is thinking of Goliath; *squama* means 'scale-armour' in Virgil), but the word *squama* reminds him of the preceding verse in Job (*corpus illius quasi scuta fusilia, compactum squamis se prementibus* 'his body is like cast shields, made up from scales pressing upon each other') so that he ends with the Job quotation. A similar process of association seems to govern his other biblical citations, but elsewhere only the references to Vlg. will be given.
sibilavit...Italia: the bees are Abelard and Ar-

nold respectively; the image comes from Isaiah 7.18.

4f. **convenerunt...eius:** Ps. 2.2 (the original subject was *principes*).

5f. **Intenderunt...corde:** Ps. 10.3 (= NIV 11.3: the original subject was *peccatores* 'sinners'); *rectos corde* 'the upright in...'.

6f. **habentes...abnegantes:** Paul's epistle 2 Timothy 3.5, a prophecy of what men would be like in the future. Elsewhere St Bernard admits that at least Arnold of Brescia is 'austere in life'. But St Paul's remark in v. 4 about *voluptatum amatores* would apply well to Abelard (see below sections 17.3 and 17.4).

7 **eo...quo:** 'by this means...because...' (*plures* 'quite a few people').

7f. **transfigurant...Satanae:** *Satanae*, genitive, balances *lucis* (based on 2 Corinthians 11.14: *ipse enim Satanas transfigurat se in angelum lucis*).

8f. **Stans...Israel:** based on 1 Kings (= 1 Samuel) 17.8–10 (*Israel* genitive: see G.6(a)).

9f. **eo...quo:** 'the more...because...'.

10 **David:** accusative (see G.6(a)); i.e. a champion on the other side.
in: 'as...', 'in order to...'.

11 **magnis** looks forward to *laudibus* (for Abelard's actual view of the *Doctores Ecclesiae* or 'Church Fathers', see section 16.2; for one of his heretical arguments borrowed from the philosophers, Plato and Aristotle among others, see section 18.3).

11f. **adinventiones...novitates** look forward to *praefert* (of which they are the objects); *catholicorum...fidei* completes the construction ('prefer *X* acc. to *Y* dat.').

12f. **cum...eius:** based on 1 Kings (= 1 Samuel) 17.24.

13 **me...minimum:** Bernard likens himself to the little David.

(iii) *Bernard describes how, despite his own reluctance to debate issues of faith, he was persuaded to go to Sens. There parts of Abelard's works were read out and found to be contrary to the faith and the truth.*

Denique scripsit mihi, sollicitante quidem ipso, archiepiscopus Senonensis, diem statuens congressionis, quo ille in praesentia eius et coepiscoporum

suorum deberet, si posset, statuere prava dogmata sua, contra quae ego ausus
mutire fuissem. Abnui, tum quia puer sum et ille vir bellator ab adulescentia,
tum quia iudicarem indignum rationem fidei humanis committi ratiunculis 5
agitandam, quam tam certa ac stabili veritate constet esse subnixam. Dicebam
sufficere scripta eius ad accusandum eum, nec mea referre, sed episcoporum,
quorum esset ministerii de dogmatibus iudicare. Ille nihilominus, immo eo
amplius levavit vocem, vocavit multos, congregavit complices. Quae de me ad
discipulos suos scripserit, dicere non curo. Disseminavit ubique se mihi die 10
statuto apud Senonas responsurum. Exiit sermo ad omnes, et non potuit me
latere. Dissimulavi primum, nec enim satis rumore populari movebar. Cedens
tamen, licet vix, ita ut flerem, consilio amicorum, qui videntes quomodo se
quasi ad spectaculum omnes pararent timebant ne de nostra absentia et
scandalum populo et cornua crescerent adversario et, quia error magis 15
confirmaretur, cum non esset qui responderet aut contradiceret, occurri ad
locum et diem, imparatus quidem et immunitus, nisi quod mente illud
volvebam: *Nolite praemeditari qualiter respondeatis; dabitur enim vobis in illa hora*
quid loquamini, et illud: *Dominus mihi adiutor, non timebo quid faciat mihi homo.*
Convenerant autem praeter episcopos et abbates plurimi viri religiosi et de 20
civitatibus magistri scholarum et clerici litterati multi, et Rex praesens erat.
Itaque in praesentia omnium, adversario stante ex adverso, producta sunt
quaedam capitula de libris eius excerpta. Quae cum coepissent legi, nolens
audire exivit, appellans ab electis iudicibus, quod non putamus licere. Porro
capitula, iudicio omnium examinata, inventa sunt fidei adversantia, contraria 25
veritati. Haec pro me, ne levitate aut certe temeritate usus in tanto negotio
putarer.

The end of the letter appeals to the Pope not to give Abelard refuge but to crush his
heresy. He sends Nicolas of Montieramy, his notarius *('amanuensis'), to plead the*
case viva voce, *which he appears to have done with success.*

1 **ipso:** i.e. Abelard.
Senonensis: 'of Sens'.
2 **ille:** i.e. Abelard.
eius...suorum: i.e. of the archbishop and his
bishops (see G.11(e)(iii)).
3 **ausus** with *fuissem*: 'had...' (see G.4(a)).
4 **quia...adulescentia:** based on 1 Kings (= 1
Samuel) 17.33.
5 **quia iudicarem:** the subjunctive has no particular force here (we would expect indicative,
as in the parallel clause *quia puer sum*: see
RLRGr U).
5f. **indignum...agitandam:** 'that it was intolerable

that...be (*committi*)...to...to be (*agitandum*)...'
(*humanis* looks forward to *ratiunculis*).
6 **quam...subnixam:** 'when it is agreed that it (i.e.
fides)...' (*tam...veritate* depends on *esse subnixam*).
7 **nec mea...sed episcoporum:** 'it is not my
business but the bishops''.
8 **quorum esset ministerii:** 'whose job it was'.
11 **responsurum:** sc. *esse*.
Exiit sermo: cf. Jo 21.23.
12 **Cedens** looks forward to *consilio* ('to...').
13 **qui** looks forward to *timebant*.
se looks forward to *pararent* (subject *omnes*).

15 **scandalum populo** ('for the people') looks forward to *crescerent*, but the verb has been chosen rather to go with *cornua*.

cornua...adversario: 'my adversary's horns might grow (sc. longer)' (so that in future he would be more difficult to defeat).

quia: 'because...'.

16 **qui...contradiceret:** 'anyone to...'.

18f. **Nolite...loquamini:** *dabitur* has as subject *quid loquamini* 'what to say'. Bernard has fused together Mt 10.19 and Lk 21.14, changing the latter slightly in the process. These are Jesus' words to the Apostles telling them how to approach the tasks of (a) evangelization and (b) defence against accusations.

19 **Dominus...homo:** sc. *est* with *Dominus...adiutor*.

Ps. 117.6.

21 **Rex:** Louis VII (reigned 1137–80).

23 **capitula** is picked up by *excerpta* (these are the thirteen chapters located by William of Champeaux: see section 18.3 for Abelard's version of one of them).

nolens: i.e. Abelard.

24 **appellans ab...iudicibus:** 'appealing against...' (Bernard's point is that it was Abelard who had selected this forum and these judges).

quod: 'a thing which...'.

26 **Haec pro me:** 'That's all I have to say for my part...'.

26f. **ne...putarer:** 'in case I am...to have employed...' (sc. *esse* with *usus*, which governs *levitate... temeritate*).

3. Peter Abelard (*c.*1079–1142)

Details of Abelard's life and of some of his writings are given above (section 16.2; see also section 18.3). The *Historia calamitatum* ('Story of my troubles') was written by Abelard some time between 1132 and 1137 in the form of a letter of consolation to a friend, 'so that you may recognize that your trials are nothing or only modest compared with mine and bear them better'. It tells his story with great emphasis upon the persecutions he suffered at the hands of others jealous of his mighty talents, starting with his teacher William of Champeaux. But the part which continues to draw our attention is the account of his relationship with Heloise (see further section 17.4 Intro.). He writes in a very polished style, with great attention to the rhythmic balance of his sentences and their endings (the *cursus*: for this, see section 17.4 Intro.).

See further: Peter Abelard, *The Story of his Misfortunes*, tr. B. Radice, London, 1977.

(i) *Abelard relates how, relying on his reputation and his good looks, he harbours designs on the niece of canon Fulbert, a young woman of beauty and literary (i.e. Latin) education.*

Erat quippe in ipsa civitate Parisius adolescentula quedam nomine Heloysa, neptis canonici cujusdam qui Fulbertus vocabatur, qui eam quanto amplius diligebat tanto diligentius in omnem qua poterat scientiam litterarum promoveri studuerat. Que cum per faciem non esset infima, per habundantiam

litterarum erat suprema. Nam quo bonum hoc litteratorie scilicet scientie in 5
mulieribus est rarius, eo amplius puellam commendabat et in toto regno
nominatissimam fecerat. Hanc igitur, omnibus circunspectis que amantes
allicere solent, commodiorem censui in amorem mihi copulare et me id
facillime credidi posse. Tanti quippe tunc nominis eram et juventutis et forme
gratia preminebam, ut quamcunque feminarum nostro dignarer amore nullam 10
vererer repulsam. Tanto autem facilius hanc mihi puellam consensuram credidi
quanto amplius eam litterarum scientiam et habere et diligere noveram; nosque
etiam absentes scriptis internuntiis invicem liceret presentare et pleraque
audacius scribere quam colloqui et sic semper jocundis interesse colloquiis.

1 **Parisius:** in apposition to *civitate* (the name is normally regarded as indeclinable).

2 **eam** looks forward to *diligebat*, of which it is the object, and *promoveri studuerat* where it is the subject of the infinitive clause (see below on *in...studuerat*).

2f. **quanto amplius...tanto diligentius:** 'the more ...the more diligently...'.

3f. **in...studuerat:** 'had eagerly sought that she be...to all the knowledge...in which she was capable' or 'to all knowledge in so far as he was able'.

4 **Que cum:** 'Although she...'.
   per faciem: lit. 'for her face', i.e. 'to look at'.

5f. **quo...rarius, eo amplius:** 'the rarer...the more...' (the subject of all the verbs is *bonum hoc (litteratorie...scientie = litteratoriae scientiae*: see O.1).

7 **nominatissimam fecerat:** sc. 'her'.

7f. **Hanc...commodiorem censui...copulare:** lit. 'I thought her rather suitable (or more suitable (sc. than others)) to join to myself in love', i.e.

'I reckoned she was the best choice for an affair'.

8f. **et me...posse:** 'and I...that I could...(sc. achieve) that (goal)'.

9 **Tanti** looks forward to *nominis* (genitive of description qualifying 'I' in *eram*).

9f. **juventutis...gratia:** 'in...of...and...' (*forme = formae*: see O.1).

10 **preminebam:** sc. 'so much'.
   nostro looks forward to *amore* (dependent on *dignarer*), **nullam** looks forward to *repulsam* (obj. of *vererer*).

11f. **tanto...quanto...:** 'the more easily...the more...' (which amounts to: 'I believed. that...because I knew that...').

11 **consensuram:** sc. *esse* ('that (she) would...').

12 **eam:** 'that she...' (*litterarum scientiam* is the object of *habere et diligere*).
   nosque...presentare: 'and (sc. I believed that) it would be possible for us to show ourselves to one another...' (for *invicem*, see G.11(e)(ii)).

14 **jocundis** looks forward to *colloquiis* (dependent on *interesse*).

(ii) *He persuades Fulbert to give him lodgings in his house and care for the education of Heloise.*

In hujus itaque adolescentule amorem totus inflammatus, occasionem quesivi
qua eam mihi domestica et cotidiana conversatione familiarem efficerem et
facilius ad consensum traherem. Quod quidem ut fieret, egi cum predicto
puelle avunculo, quibusdam ipsius amicis intervenientibus, quatinus me in
domum suam, que scolis nostris proxima erat, sub quocumque procurationis 5
precio susciperet, hanc videlicet occasionem pretendens, quod studium

nostrum domestica nostre familie cura plurimum prepediret, et impensa nimia
nimium me gravaret. Erat autem cupidus ille valde atque erga neptim suam, ut
amplius semper in doctrinam proficeret litteratoriam, plurimum studiosus.
Quibus quidem duobus facile ejus assensum assecutus sum et quod obtabam   10
obtinui, cum ille videlicet et ad pecuniam totus inhiaret et neptim suam ex
doctrina nostra aliquid percepturam crederet. Super quo vehementer me
deprecatus, supra quam sperare presumerem votis meis accessit, et amori
consuluit, eam videlicet totam nostro magisterio committens, ut quotiens
mihi a scolis reverso vaccaret, tam in die quam in nocte ei docende operam   15
darem, et eam si neglegentem sentirem vehementer constringerem. In qua re
quidem, quanta ejus simplicitas esset vehementer ammiratus, non minus apud
me obstupui quam si agnam teneram famelico lupo committeret. Qui cum eam
mihi non solum docendam, verum etiam vehementer constringendam
traderet, quid aliud agebat quam ut votis meis licentiam penitus daret et   20
occasionem (etiam si nollemus) offerret ut quam videlicet blanditiis non
possem, minis et verberibus facilius flecterem. Sed duo erant que eum maxime
a turpi suspicione revocabant, amor videlicet neptis et continentie mee fama
preterita.

1 **In** looks forward to *amorem* (dependent on *inflammatus*).
   adolescentule = *adulescentulae* (see O.1).
2f. **qua...efficerem et...traherem:** 'by which to...and to...'.
2 **mihi** looks forward to and depends on *familiarem*.
   domestica...conversatione: 'through...'.
3 **Quod:** 'This', i.e. his getting to know Heloise.
4 **puelle** (= *puellae*: see O.1) **avunculo:** canon Fulbert.
   quatinus ('so that...': see G.27(b)) looks forward to *susciperet* (of which *me* is the object).
5f. **sub...precio:** 'at whatsoever price for the trouble', i.e. Abelard would pay whatever he asked.
6 **hanc** 'the following' looks forward to *occasionem* (obj. of *pretendens*), and is picked up by *quod...prepediret, et...gravaret*.
7 **domestica** looks forward to *cura* (governing *nostre familie* = *nostrae familiae*: see O.1).
8 **atque...ut** ('that (she) should...') looks forward to *plurimum studiosus* (a second complement to *Erat...ille*).
10 **Quibus...duobus:** 'By means of these...' (i.e. the reasons he had given to Fulbert for wanting to stay at his house).

11f. **neptim...percepturam:** 'that his...would' (acc. + inf. dependent on *crederet*).
12 **super quo:** i.e. his niece's education.
13 **supra...presumerem:** 'further than I would have...'.
14 **ut** looks forward to *operam darem* and *constringerem*.
14f. **quotiens...vaccaret:** lit. 'whenever there was spare time to me...'(*mihi* agrees with *reverso*).
15 **ei docende** (= *docendae*: see O.1): depends on *operam darem* 'to teaching...'.
16 **eam** is the object both of *sentirem* and *constringerem*.
17 **quanta...esset** depends on *ammiratus*.
17f. **apud me:** 'in myself'.
18 **committeret:** 'he had been entrusting'.
   Qui cum looks forward to *traderet*.
20 **quam ut** ('than...ing and...ing') looks forward to *licentiam...daret* and *occasionem...offerret* (this then introduces *ut* 'so that I might...' *flecterem*; *quam...possem* depends on *flecterem* 'her whom I...').
22 **duo:** 'two things'.
23 **continentie mee** (= *continentiae meae*: see O.1) depends on *fama preterita*.

(iii) *Master and pupil spend lesson times making love.*

Quid plura? Primum domo una conjungimur, postmodum animo. Sub occasione itaque discipline, amori penitus vaccabamus et secretos recessus quos amor optabat studium lectionis offerebat. Apertis itaque libris, plura de amore quam de lectione verba se ingerebant, plura erant oscula quam sententie; sepius ad sinus quam ad libros reducebantur manus, crebrius oculos amor in se 5 reflectebat quam lectio in scripturam dirigebat. Quoque minus suspicionis haberemus, verbera quandoque dabat amor, non furor, gratia, non ira, que omnium unguentorum suavitatem transcenderent. Quid denique? Nullus a cupidis intermissus est gradus amoris, et si quid insolitum amor excogitare potuit, est additum; et quo minus ista fueramus experti gaudia, ardentius illis 10 insistebamus et minus in fastidium vertebantur.

Abelard's teaching duties (but not his study or his lovemaking) suffer. His creative impulses are used only for writing love-songs. His pupils are aggrieved. Eventually, the story breaks and Fulbert, the last to know, is mortified. Heloise announces her pregnancy to Abelard and he whisks her off to his home town, where she has a son, Astrolabius ('Astrolabe'). Abelard promises Fulbert amends and seems to have won him over when he promises marriage to Heloise, so long as it remains secret. Abelard goes to bring back Heloise, who tries to dissuade him from marriage mainly because it would ruin his career.

1 **Quid plura?:** sc. *dicam* 'What more need I say?'.
2 **discipline** = *disciplinae* (see O.1).
  secretos recessus looks forward to *offerebat* (of which it is the object).
3 **plura** looks forward to *verba* (subject of *se ingerebant*).
4 **sententie** (= *sententiae*: see O.1): tr. 'interpretations', 'expositions'.
5 **in se**: 'upon each other'.
6 **quam...dirigebat:** sc. *oculos* as object of *dirigebat*.
  Quoque minus: 'And so that...less....'.

7 **verbera** is the object of *dabat* and is picked up by *que...transcenderent.*
8 **Nullus** looks forward to *gradus*, subject of *intermissus est.*
9 **et si quid insolitum:** 'and anything...that...' (obj. of *excogitare*).
10 **et quo minus...ardentius...et minus...:** 'and the less...the more ardently...and the less...'.
  ista looks forward to *gaudia* (object of *fueramus experti*, 'we had...': see G.4(a)).
11 **in fastidium vertebantur:** lit. 'they turned to disgust', i.e. 'they tended to disgust us'.

(iv) *Abelard insists, and they wed on their return to Paris. But Fulbert does not keep his promise and quarrels with Heloise.*

Nato itaque parvulo nostro, sorori mee commendato, Parisius occulte revertimur, et, post paucos dies, nocte secretis orationum vigiliis in quadam ecclesia celebratis, ibidem, summo mane, avunculo ejus atque quibusdam nostris vel ipsius amicis assistentibus, nuptiali benedictione confederamur moxque occulte divisim abscessimus, nec nos ulterius nisi raro latenterque 5 vidimus, dissimulantes plurimum quod egeramus. Avunculus autem ipsius

atque domestici ejus, ignominie sue solatium querentes, initum matrimonium
divulgare et fidem mihi super hoc datam violare ceperunt; illa autem e contra
anathematizare et jurare quia falsissimum esset. Unde vehementer ille commotus crebris eam contumeliis afficiebat.   10

1 **Nato...commendato:** 'When...and...' (ablative
  absolutes in asyndeton; *mee* = *meae*: see O.1).
  Parisius: 'to Paris'.
2f. **secretis...celebratis:** 'after...'. It was customary
  to hold a prayer vigil the night before a
  wedding.
3 **summo mane:** 'at dawn'.
5f. **nec nos...vidimus:** 'nor did we...one another...'.
6 **dissimulantes:** 'because we were...' (see
  G.20(b)).

quod: 'what...'.
6f. **Avunculus...atque domestici** look forward to
  ceperunt (= *coeperunt*: see O.1), upon which
  depend the phrases *initum...divulgare* and *fidem...datam violare*.
7 **ignominie sue** (= *ignominiae suae*: see O.1):
  dependent on *solatium* ('for...').
8 **illa autem:** i.e. Heloise (sc. 'began').
9 **vehementer** qualifies *commotus*.
10 **crebris** looks forward to *contumeliis*.

(v) *Abelard reacts by moving her to the abbey of Argenteuil near Paris. Her uncle,
thinking that he has forced her to take the veil, procures entry to Abelard's lodgings
and exacts a dreadful revenge.*

Quod cum ego cognovissem, transmisi eam ad abbatiam quandam sancti-
monialium prope Parisius, que Argenteolum appellatur, ubi ipsa olim
puellula educata fuerat atque erudita, vestesque ei religionis que conversationi monastice convenirent, excepto velo, aptari feci et his eam indui.
Quo audito, avunculus et consanguinei seu affines ejus opinati sunt me   5
nunc sibi plurimum illusisse, et ab ea moniali facta me sic facile velle
expedire. Unde vehementer indignati et adversum me conjurati, nocte
quadam quiescentem me atque dormientem in secreta hospicii mei camera,
quodam mihi serviente per pecuniam corrupto, crudelissima et pudentissima
ultione punierunt, et quam summa ammiratione mundus excepit, eis   10
videlicet corporis mei partibus amputatis quibus id quod plangebant
commiseram. Quibus mox in fugam conversis, duo qui comprehendi
potuerunt oculis et genitalibus privati sunt, quorum alter ille fuit supra-
dictus serviens qui, cum in obsequio meo mecum maneret, cupiditate ad
proditionem ductus est.   15

3 **educata fuerat atque erudita:** 'had been...' (see
  G.4(a)).
  vestes (governing *religionis*) looks forward to
  aptari feci 'I caused...to be...on her (*ei*)' (see
  G.17(c)).
4 **monastice** (= *monasticae*: see O.1) qualifies
  conversationi.

6f. **et ab ea...expedire:** 'and that I...to...myself
  from...' (introduced by *opinati sunt*).
7 **conjurati:** 'conspiring' (the object will be *quiescentem me atque dormientem* and the verb
  punierunt).
8 **in secreta** looks forward to *camera* (governing
  hospicii mei).

10 **et quam:** 'and one (i.e. an *ultio*) which...'.
10f. **eis ... amputatis quibus ... commiseram:**
'namely by...ing...those...with which I...' (*quod
plangebant* is introduced by *commiseram*).

13 **oculis et genitalibus:** 'of...' (dependent on
privati sunt). A standard punishment was 'an
eye for an eye' (but here a little extra is taken).

4. Heloise (*c*.1100–63)

Heloise was the niece of one Fulbert, a canon of Notre-Dame cathedral in
Paris, in whose house in the cathedral close she lived. She had received an
excellent education and Fulbert boasted of her extraordinary literary talents.
She met Abelard when he was teaching at Notre-Dame and became his
lover when Fulbert agreed to give Abelard lodgings. She bore their son,
Astrolabe, in 1116. Soon afterwards, she and Abelard married secretly,
despite her attempt to dissuade him because of the effect it would have on
his career. After his castration (see section 16.2 Intro. and section 17.3 (v)
above), on his instructions she entered the nunnery of Argenteuil, near Paris.
There she remained until the expulsion of the sisters in 1129. Abelard then
invited her to establish a monastic community at Quincy, in the diocese of
Troyes, where he had earlier led a monastery dedicated to the Paraclete.
From this date until her death Heloise led the new community as abbess.

Relations between them from 1117 to the mid 1130s are not a matter of
record. It was not until Heloise read Abelard's *Historia calamitatum*, probably
not by chance but because he had sent her a copy, that the brief but
famous correspondence began. She wrote him three letters, the first two
dealing with her feelings over the incidents related in Abelard's book, the
third promising silence and obedience, and containing a request for a new
Rule. From this time on, Abelard set willingly about the task of supplying
the needs of his new foundation. His gifts to the nunnery included a new
hymnary and sermons. But he also answered a set of *Problemata* sent to him
by Heloise, to which she wrote a prefatory letter. Her last known work is a
brief letter to Peter of Cluny (see above section 17.1), who had sheltered
Abelard in his troubled final years.

Heloise was already an accomplished Latinist when Abelard took over
her tuition. Among the many marks of this high level of education is the
use of the *cursus*, which gives rhythmical shape to the ends of sentences. A
particular favourite of hers, perhaps derived from the influence of an Italian
teacher of the *ars dictaminis*, is the *cursus tardus*, in which the stress falls on
the third and sixth syllables from the end: e.g. *possessórem osténderem*.

See further: P. Dronke, *Women Writers of the Middle Ages*, Cambridge,
1984, pp. 107–43.

(i) *Heloise, having read Abelard's story written to console another man, asks him to write to console her for her loss of him. She points out that she has obeyed him even to the point of cutting herself off from him forever, so as to show that he owns her.*

Nosti, karissime, noverunt omnes quanta in te amiserim et quam miserabili casu summa et ubique nota proditio me ipsam quoque mihi tecum abstulerit, ut incomparabiliter major sit dolor ex amissionis modo quam ex dampno. Quo vero major est dolendi causa, majora sunt consolationis adhibenda remedia, non utique ab alio, sed a te ipso, ut, qui solus es in causa dolendi, solus sis in   5
gratia consolandi. Solus quippe es qui me contristare, qui me letifi-
care seu consolari valeas, et solus es qui plurimum id mihi debeas et nunc maxime cum universa que jusseris in tantum impleverim ut cum te in aliquo offendere non possem, me ipsam pro jussu tuo perdere sustinerem. Et quod majus est dictuque mirabile, in tantam versus est amor insaniam ut quod solum   10
appetebat, hoc ipse sibi sine spe recuperationis auferret, cum ad tuam statim jussionem tam habitum ipsa quam animum immutarem, ut te tam corporis mei quam animi unicum possessorem ostenderem.

2 **summa...proditio:** the act of Fulbert and his henchmen, viz. castrating Abelard; see 17.3 (v), from *Historia calamitatum*, for the reason why the deed was *ubique nota*.

   mihi: 'from myself' (dative of disadvantage); she explains this in the *ut* clause which follows (what they did took away the possibility of a continued sexual relationship).

3f. **Quo...major...majora...:** 'The greater the... the greater...'.

4 **consolationis** depends on *remedia*.

5 **qui:** '(you) who...'.

6 **qui...contristare:** the verb governing the infinitive is *valeas* (generic subjunctive, irregularly, as is *debeas* in the next clause: see G.25(b);

Solus... es is to be understood also with *qui...valeas.*

8 **universa:** obj. of *impleverim*.

   in tantum: 'to such an extent...'; it looks forward to *ut*, whose verb is *sustinerem*.

10 **dictu:** 'to relate' (with *mirabile*: supine ablative form, see RLRGr A7 Note 2(iii)).

   in tantam looks forward to *insaniam*.

   ut looks forward to *auferret*.

11 **appetebat:** the subject is *amor* (which is what *ipse* also refers to).

   sibi: 'from itself' (dative of disadvantage).

   ad tuam looks forward to *jussionem*.

12 **ipsa:** 'I myself'.

(ii) *She tells Abelard that she only wanted him. She never wanted marriage, argued with him against it (as he wrote in* Historia calamitatum, *and would prefer to be called his whore than the Roman Empress.*

Nichil umquam (Deus scit) in te nisi te requisivi, te pure, non tua con-
cupiscens. Non matrimonii federa, non dotes aliquas expectavi, non denique meas voluptates aut voluntates, sed tuas, sicut ipse nosti, adimplere studui. Et si uxoris nomen sanctius ac validius videretur, dulcius mihi semper extitit amice vocabulum aut, si non indigneris, concubine vel scorti, ut, quo me videlicet   5

pro te amplius humiliarem, ampliorem apud te consequerer gratiam et sic etiam excellentie tue gloriam minus lederem. Quod et tu ipse tui gratia oblitus penitus non fuisti in ea quam supra memini ad amicum epistola pro consolatione directa, ubi et rationes nonnullas, quibus te a conjugio nostro et infaustis thalamis revocare conabar exponere non es dedignatus, sed   10 plerisque tacitis quibus amorem conjugio, libertatem vinculo preferebam. Deum testem invoco, si me Augustus universo presidens mundo matrimonii honore dignaretur, totumque mihi orbem confirmaret in perpetuo possidendum, karius mihi et dignius videretur tua dici meretrix quam illius imperatrix.

1 **te...tua:** objects of *concupiscens*.
2f. **federa...dotes...voluptates...voluntates:** all objects of *adimplere*.
3f. **Et si...videretur:** 'And (even) if...appeared'.
4f. **amice, concubine:** gen. s. (see O.1).
5 **si non indigneris:** tr. as though indicative (G.28(b)).
5f. **quo...amplius...:** 'the more I...'.
6 **ampliorem** looks forward to *gratiam*.
7 **excellentie tue:** gen. s. (see O.1).
  tui gratia: 'for your own purposes'.
  oblitus with *non fuisti*: '(you) did...' (see G.4(a)).
8 **in ea** looks forward to *epistola...directa* (the reference is to *Historia calamitatum*).
9 **et:** tr. 'actually'.
  rationes nonnullas is the object of *exponere*.

9f. **sed plerisque tacitis quibus:** 'but keeping quiet about those by which...'.
11 **amorem conjugio:** the verb will be *preferebam* (as for the next phrase).
12f. **si...dignaretur...confirmaret...videretur:** 'If ...were to...and were to...would...' (irregular condition: G.28(a) – CL rule is present subjunctive).
12 **Augustus:** the German Emperor.
  universo looks forward to *mundo* and depends on *presidens*.
13f. **totumque...possidendum:** 'that the whole... would be owned by...'.
14 **tua** looks forward to *meretrix* (complement of *dici*).

5. Hildegard of Bingen (1098–1179)

Born in Bermersheim in the diocese of Mainz, the tenth child of the noble Hildebert and Mechtild, Hildegard was given to God as a tithe. In 1106 she was made the companion of an anchoress called Jutta, who taught the girl reading (i.e. Latin) and singing. Around Jutta grew up a community, eventually placed under the care of the abbot of St Disibod. Hildegard became a nun and in 1136, at Jutta's death, abbess. In 1141, she began to respond to what she perceived as the command of God to write what she saw in her visions. These she tells us in the prologue of this work, the *Sciuias* ('Know the ways (sc. of the Lord)'), had been with her since childhood. She appears to have experienced a kind of radiance, always in her view but not blocking her normal vision, and to have perceived in it both 'the living light' and symbols. These she interpreted via a voice which dictated her books and letters – in Latin. This *visio* never left her and sometimes produced painful physical experiences. She was given human assistance by a nun called Richardis von Stade and Volmar, a monk of St Disibod, the latter often acting as a corrector of her Latin.

In 1147/8, while she was working on the *Sciuias*, with its three books of twenty-six visions, at the instigation of Bernard of Clairvaux (see section 17.2 Intro.) and of Heinrich, archbishop of Mainz, her gift was brought to the attention of Pope Eugenius III, who was attending a synod at nearby Trier. Eugenius procured a copy of her work, read from it before the synod and then sent Hildegard a letter of blessing and protection. Such a gift could so easily have been seen, as Hildegard was aware, as the work of Satan. She became immediately famous, both for her visions and for her extraordinary songs, composed for liturgical use. These were later to form the *Symphonia armonie celestium revelationum* ('The Symphony of the harmony of celestial revelations'). This fame brought pressure on the meagre space available at St Disibod, and after some difficulty Hildegard established a new community at Rupertsberg in 1150. From 1158 to 1163 she was at work on her second record of visions, the *Liber vitae meritorum* ('Book of life's merits'). By 1173/4 she had completed a third, the *Liber divinorum operum* ('Book of divine works'). In 1178 she suffered excommunication along with her nuns in a conflict with the Mainz authorities over the burial of a nobleman said to have died excommunicate. Hildegard had refused to have the body dug up and cast out. The interdict laid upon her community forbade them not only to celebrate Mass and the Eucharist, but also to sing the Divine Office. In an extraordinary letter to the prelates, Hildegard explains that to stop such music is the Devil's work. In March 1179, just before her death, the ban was lifted.

On top of her visionary writings and her settings of her own poetic texts, Hildegard wrote two books on medicine, the *Physica* and the *Causae et curae*, the first an encyclopaedia of the medicinal properties of herbs, trees, gems, etc., the second a manual of physical and mental diseases. The extracts here are taken from *Sciuias* and the *Symphonia*.

As might be expected from a writer whose formal education (in medieval terms) was non-existent, Hildegard's Latin was formed by the Bible and exegetical literature. Its ideas, images, vocabulary and syntax constantly recall Scripture. For instance, the opening three lines of this extract from the *Sciuias* are reminiscent of Ezekiel 1.1 and 7.1: *et factum est in trigesimo anno...cum essem in medio captivorum...aperti sunt coeli et vidi visionem* 'It happened in my thirtieth year...when I was in the midst of prisoners...the heavens were opened and I saw a vision'; *et factus est sermo Domini ad me dicens* 'And there was the word of the Lord, saying...'. Note the contrast with St Bernard (section 17.2), whose Latin is full of quotation rather than reminiscence.

See further: P. Dronke, *Women Writers of the Middle Ages*, Cambridge, 1984, pp. 144–201; B. Newman, *Symphonia armonie celestium revelationum*, Ithaca and London, 1988 (for discography, see pp. 329–30). Recent CDs of some of Hildegard's music are available on Hyperion CDA 66039 and Christophorus Musica Practica CHR 74584.

(a) *Sciuias*

(i) *Hildegard explains that she is writing an account of her visions at the command of a voice from heaven.*

Et ecce quadragesimo tertio temporalis cursus mei anno, cum caelesti uisioni magno timore et tremula intentione inhaererem, uidi maximum splendorem in quo facta est uox de caelo ad me dicens: 'O homo fragilis et cinis cineris et putredo putredinis, dic et scribe quae uides et audis. Sed quia timida es ad loquendum et simplex ad exponendum et indocta ad scribendum ea, dic et   5 scribe illa non secundum os hominis nec secundum intellectum humanae adinuentionis nec secundum uoluntatem humanae compositionis, sed secundum id quod ea in caelestibus desuper in mirabilibus Dei uides et audis, ea sic edisserendo proferens quemadmodum et auditor uerba praeceptoris sui percipiens, ea secundum tenorem locutionis illius, ipso uolente, ostendente   10 et praecipiente propalat. Sic ergo et tu, o homo, dic ea quae uides et audis et scribe ea non secundum te nec secundum alium hominem, sed secundum uoluntatem scientis, uidentis et disponentis omnia in secretis mysteriorum suorum.' Et iterum audiui uocem de caelo mihi dicentem: 'Dic ergo mirabilia haec et scribe ea, hoc modo edocta, et dic.'   15

1 **quadragesimo tertio** look forward to *anno* (on which the intervening words depend). **temporalis...mei:** i.e. 'my earthly life'. **caelesti uisioni** depends on *inhaererem*.

3f. **cinis cineris et putredo putredinis:** tr. literally: the genitive is of a type found in the Vulgate imitating a Hebrew construction, which intensifies the noun almost into a superlative, e.g. King of Kings (see G.10(a)). For the ideas, cf. Gen. 3.19, Job 30.19.

4f. **ad:** tr. 'in...'.

7f. **secundum id quod:** 'according to the fact that...' (*ea* is the object of *uides* and *audis* and

refers to *illa*, i.e. her visions).

8 **sic** looks forward to *quemadmodum*: 'in the way....that...'.

9 **uerba** is the object of *percipiens*, which picks up *auditor* (the verb will be *propalat*).

10 **illius:** i.e. of the teacher (who is also referred to in *ipso...praecipiente*).

13 **scientis...disponentis:** 'of the one who...' (i.e. God).

14 **Et iterum...dicentem:** cf. Rev. 14.13: *Et audivi vocem de coelo dicentem mihi: 'Scribe...'.*

15 **edocta:** f. s. nom., agreeing with the subject 'you (Hildegard)'.

(ii) *She describes the vision which revealed to her the meanings of the sacred texts and the manner in which since childhood she had seen and suppressed her experiences.*

Factum est in millesimo centesimo quadragesimo primo Filii Dei Iesu Christi incarnationis anno, cum quadraginta duorum annorum septemque mensium essem, maximae coruscationis igneum lumen aperto caelo ueniens totum cerebrum meum transfudit et totum cor totumque pectus meum uelut flamma non tamen ardens sed calens ita inflammauit, ut sol rem aliquam calefecit super   5
quam radios suos ponit. Et repente intellectum expositionis librorum, uidelicet psalterii, euangelii et aliorum catholicorum tam ueteris quam noui Testamenti uoluminum sapiebam, non autem interpretationem uerborum textus eorum nec diuisionem syllabarum nec cognitionem casuum aut temporum habebam. Virtutem autem et mysterium secretarum et admirandarum uisionum a puellari   10
aetate, scilicet a tempore illo cum quinquennis essem usque ad praesens tempus mirabili modo in me senseram sicut et adhuc; quod tamen nulli hominum exceptis quibusdam paucis et religiosis qui in eadem conuersatione uiuebant, qua et ego eram, manifestaui, sed interim usque ad id temporis cum illud Deus sua gratia manifestari uoluit, sub quieto silentio depressi. Visiones uero quas   15
uidi, non eas in somnis, nec dormiens, nec in phrenesi, nec corporeis oculis aut auribus exterioris hominis, nec in abditis locis percepi, sed eas uigilans et cirumspecta in pura mente, oculis et auribus interioris hominis, in apertis locis, secundum uoluntatem Dei accepi. Quod quomodo sit, carnali homini perquirere difficile est.   20

1 **in** looks forward to *anno* (this opening is again reminiscent of Ezekiel (8.1)).

2 **quadraginta...mensium:** '(sc. at the age) of...'.

3 **maximae coruscationis:** genitive of description depending on *igneum lumen* (subject, picked up by *ueniens*).
   aperto caelo: 'from...'.

4 **totum cor...meum:** obj. of *inflammauit* (subject is still *lumen*).

6 **intellectum** is the object of *sapiebam*.

8f. **non autem...habebam:** Hildegard expresses her ignorance of the analytical tools of *grammatica* (*eorum* 'of them', not with *uerborum*).

10 **Virtutem...mysterium:** objects of *senseram*.

12 **nulli hominum** depends on *manifestaui*.

14 **id temporis:** 'that time'.
   illud looks forward to *manifestari uoluit*.

17 **sed eas:** the verb is *accepi*.

18 **cirumspecta...mente:** 'aware in purity of mind' (i.e. she knew what was happening and her conscience was clear).

19f. **Quod...est:** for the idea cf. 1 Corinthians 2.14.

(iii) *She explains how she still resisted the divine injunction, but eventually, forced by the illness sent by God and with the support of two confidants, set to. It has taken her ten years to complete.*

Sed ego quamuis haec uiderem et audirem, tamen propter dubietatem et malam opinionem et propter diuersitatem uerborum hominum, tamdiu non in pertinacia sed in humilitatis officio scribere recusaui quousque in lectum aegritudinis flagello Dei depressa caderem, ita quod tandem multis infirmatibus compulsa, testimonio cuiusdam nobilis et bonorum morum puellae et   5 hominis illius quem occulte (ut praefatum est) quaesieram et inueneram, manus ad scribendum apposui. Quod dum facerem, altam profunditatem expositionis librorum, ut praedixi, sentiens uiribusque receptis de aegritudine me erigens, uix opus istud decem annis consummans ad finem perduxi.

2 **malam opinionem:** probably the fear of what others might say (that she was mad, for example, which some did think).
tamdiu looks forward to *quousque*: 'for so long...until...'.

4 **ita quod:** 'with the result that...' (the verb, indicative, not subjunctive, is *apposui*: see G.26(a)–(b)).

5 **cuiusdam...puellae:** the nun Richardis.

6 **hominis illius....inueneram:** the Disibodenberg monk, Volmar, to whom she had secretly revealed her experiences (as she says in a previous section not printed here).

7 **dum:** 'when' (= *cum*: see G.29).
altam profunditatem is the object of *sentiens*.

8 **erigens:** 'having...' (see G.20(a)).

9 **consummans:** 'having...' (see G. 20(a): sc. 'it', i.e. *opus istud* is the object).

(iv) In the first vision, Hildegard describes a great mountain, atop which sits a bright figure. The picture on the book cover illustrates this passage (see Note on cover illustration, pp. vii–viii, for further details).

Vidi quasi montem magnum, ferreum colorem habentem, et super ipsum quendam tantae claritatis sedentem ut claritas ipsius uisum meum reuerberaret, de quo ab utraque parte sui lenis umbra uelut ala mirae latitudinis et longitudinis extendebatur. Et ante ipsum ad radicem eiusdem montis quaedam imago undique plena oculis stabat, cuius nullam humanam formam prae 5
ipsis oculis discernere ualebam, et ante istam imago alia puerilis aetatis, pallida tunica sed albis calceamentis induta, super cuius caput tanta claritas de eodem super montem ipsum sedente descendit ut faciem eius intueri non possem. Sed ab eodem qui super montem illum sedebat multae uiuentes scintillae exierunt, quae easdem imagines magna suauitate circumuolabant. In ipso autem monte 10
quasi plurimae fenestellae uidebantur, in quibus uelut capita hominum quaedam pallida et quaedam alba apparuerunt.

2 **tantae** looks forward to *ut* (result).
3 **de quo:** i.e. the *quendam...sedentem*.
sui: 'of him'.
5 **undique** qualifies *plena*.
cuius: tr. 'in which'.

6 **imago alia** is picked up by *induta* (governing *pallida...calceamentis*).
puerilis qualifies *aetatis* (genitive of description).
7 **de eodem** looks forward to *sedente* ('from the aforementioned...').

Hildegard explains that the mountain symbolizes the stability of the kingdom of God. The figure on it in its splendour shows God's incomprehensibility to human minds. At the foot of the mountain 'Fear of the Lord', full of eyes, makes forgetting God impossible. The other figure, illuminated by God, is 'Poverty of Spirit'. The sparks flying around these figures are virtues (or miracles?), which comfort the fearful and poor in spirit. The windows in the mountain with their pale faces represent the impossibility of men hiding the basis of their deeds from God.

(b)   *Symphonia armonie celestium revelationum*

(i)   *A responsory for virgins, in praise of virginity.*

O nobilissima viriditas,
que radicas in sole
et que in candida serenitate
luces in rota
quam nulla terrena excellentia   5
comprehendit:

Tu circumdata es
amplexibus divinorum
ministeriorum.
tu rubes ut aurora   10
et ardes ut solis flamma.

1 **viriditas:** in this image, Hildegard addresses in the second person the notion of virginity (see sections 7.1(a) and 8.4(a)).

4 **rota:** i.e. in the wheel of heaven (the highest of the spheres).

7 **Tu...ministeriorum:** this is a refrain, repeated in the music after ll. 10–11.

Barbara Newman says that the imagery is suggestive of 'the burning bush, a figure of Mary', but also of the 'tree of life'. She quotes a letter of Hildegard: 'What a marvellous thing you are (sc. Virginity), who laid a foundation in the sun and transcended the earth!...The virgin stands in the beautiful simplicity and integrity of a paradise which will never grow dry, but will remain for ever verdant...' (PL 197, 337b–d).

(ii)   *An antiphon for St Ursula, in which the blood of her martyrdom is imaged as an everlasting flower.*

O rubor sanguinis
qui de excelso illo fluxisti
quod divinitas tetigit:
tu flos es
quem hyems de flatu serpentis   5
numquam lesit.

2 **qui:** '(you) that...'.
3 **quod:** antecedent *excelso*.
5 **hyems...serpentis:** tr. literally; *de...serpentis* depends on *hyems* (G.10(b)); the serpent is Satan, whose influence on Adam and Eve deprived man of everlasting spring in Paradise. St Ursula was a British princess. So the story goes, to delay her marriage to a pagan prince she went on pilgrimage to Rome with 11,000 virgin companions. On their return, they were met at Cologne by Attila the Hun and all were martyred. Her cult became popular in the wake of the discovery in Cologne of a Roman cemetery, which was claimed to contain the relics of the martyrs. Hildegard's interest in Ursula may have been stimulated by the visions of her protegée Elisabeth of Schoenau in 1156–7, which replied to doubts about the authenticity of the finds. She devotes a whole section of the *Symphonia* to this saint (60–5, Newman).

6. Abbot Suger of St-Denis (1081–13 January 1151)

Suger was a child of poor parents and was given as an oblate to the abbey of St-Denis near Paris when he was nine or ten years old. He was educated at the school of St-Denis-de-l'Estrée. By 1122 he was abbot, having served in a number of subordinate capacities in other establishments in the possession of St-Denis, such as Berneval-le-Grand in Normandy and Toury-en-Beauce near Chartres. St-Denis, founded by King Dagobert, had for centuries had close connections with the royal household. The Frankish kings Charles the Bald and Hugh Capet had been titular abbots and many kings were buried there. Even before his appointment as abbot, Suger had been used as a royal envoy to Rome and his diplomatic skills were instrumental in producing a firm alliance between the French king and the papal *Curia*. He also often acted as intermediary between Louis VI and Henry I of England. Suger's diplomatic talent was matched by his administrative and creative flair in all matters to do with his abbey. Threatened and bullied by Bernard of Clairvaux (see section 17.2 above) for running an 'unreformed' abbey, Suger made his peace in 1127 in such a way as to receive Bernard's congratulations and blessing, without actually altering his main course. For his most famous achievement, recorded in his two books *De rebus in administratione sua gestis* and *Libellus alter de consecratione Ecclesiae Sancti Dionysii*, was the rebuilding of the abbey church in the Gothic style which was to dominate cathedral-building for centuries, the richness of decoration and ornament in which ran directly counter to the puritanical aesthetic of the Cistercians. Suger received intellectual sustenance for his position in what he thought (but Abelard did not) were the works of St Denis, Dionysius the Areopagite, which John Scottus Eriugena (see section 9.5) had translated. Here material beauty was seen as leading upwards towards the truth. The new building was consecrated with great ceremony on 11 June 1144. Suger's part in the project had been central and emotional. One night he went to bed worrying about new roof-beams and in the morning set out with his carpenters to find trees of the right size himself. The following episode is typical of his writing, in which rhetorical flourish is uppermost, but covers deep concern with the project and a desire to be remembered for it.

See further: E. Panofsky, *Abbot Suger on the Abbey Church of St-Denis and its Art Treasures*, 2nd edn, Princeton, 1979.

Among several other instances of the aid of God and the Saints to the work of rebuilding the church, Suger mentions the survival of the nearly finished building from the onslaught of a violent storm, which caused widespread damage elsewhere in the region.

Nec illud etiam silere dignum duximus, quod, dum praefatum novi augmenti opus capitellis et arcubus superioribus ad altitudinis cacumen produceretur, cum necdum principales arcus singulariter voluti voltarum cumulo cohaer-erent, terribilis et pene intolerabilis obnubilatione nubium, inundatione imbrium, impetu validissimo ventorum subito tempestatis exorta est procel- 5
la, quae usque adeo invaluit ut non solum validas domos, sed etiam lapideas turres et ligneas tristegas concusserit. Ea tempestate, quadam die, anniversario gloriosi Dagoberti regis, cum venerabilis Carnotensis episcopus Gaufredus missas gratiarum pro anima ejusdem in conventu ad altare principale festive celebraret, tantus oppositorum ventorum impetus praefatos arcus nullo 10
suffultos podio, nullis renitentes suffragiis impingebat, ut miserabiliter tremuli et quasi hinc et inde fluctuantes subito pestiferam minarentur ruinam. Quorum quidem operturarumque impulsionem cum episcopus expavesceret, saepe manum benedictionis in ea parte extendebat et brachium sancti senis Simeonis signando instanter opponebat, ut manifeste nulla sui constantia, sed sola Dei 15
pietate et Sanctorum merito ruinam evadere appareret. Sicque cum multis in locis firmissimis, ut putabatur, aedificiis multa ruinarum incommoda intulisset, virtute repulsa divina titubantibus in alto solis et recentibus arcubus nihil proferre praevaluit incommodi.

1 **Nec...duximus:** 'Nor did we think it right to keep quiet about the following...'.
praefatum looks forward to *opus*, which governs *novi augmenti* (the reference is to the new building of Suger, which extensively remo-delled the existing church).
2 **capitellis...superioribus:** tr. 'with...' qualifying *opus*.
3 **cum necdum...cohaererent:** 'when the main arches independently vaulted were not yet held together by the mass of the webs' (Panofsky explains that *principales...voluti* re-fers to the skeleton of the arch-and-rib system

of the central nave, which had not yet been made firm by the filling in of the compart-ments of the vaults. It would still have been possible at this stage to see the roof from the floor of the church).
4 **terribilis** and **intolerabilis** look forward to *tempestatis...procella* ('a violent storm'); but take *obnubilatione, inundatione, impetu validissi-mo* as ablatives of respect with *intolerabilis* ('a storm...intolerable for...').
7 **Ea tempestate:** 'At this time' (not 'During this storm').
7f. **anniversario...regis:** i.e. 19 January (1143).

The foundations were laid on 14 July 1140 and the work was completed in three years and three months, i.e. by September 1143. King Dagobert ruled 629–639.

8 **Gaufredus:** Geoffroy II de Lèves, bishop of Chartres 1116–49.

9 **missas gratiarum...in conventu:** 'a conventual mass of gratitude for...' (either for Dagobert's many benefactions or because Dagobert might be one of those saved through his own merits).

10 **tantus** looks forward to *impetus* (governing *oppositorum ventorum*); the verb will be *impingebat.*

10f. **nullo** looks forward to *podio,* dependent on *suffultos* (with *arcus*); **nullis** looks forward to *suffragiis,* dependent on *renitentes* (with *arcus*). At this stage both scaffolding and props had been removed to allow the completed skeleton to settle and the mortar to harden before work began on infilling the ribs.

12 **pestiferam** looks forward to *ruinam.*
Quorum (sc. 'arches') looks forward to *impulsionem,* which governs it and *operturarum.*

13 **operturarumque:** the roof had been erected before the vaulting work began, so as to protect the workers and to avoid interruptions to the building-schedule. The presence of the roof probably increased the risk of collapse.

14 **in ea parte:** 'towards...'.
sancti...Simeonis: see Lk 2.25. An arm-bone, supposedly his, was one of the prized relics of St-Denis. It was kept in a golden reliquary shaped like an arm. On its open palm rested a tiny figure. There is a drawing in M. Félibien, *Histoire de l'Abbaye Royale de Saint-Denys en France,* Paris, 1706, p. 536, pl. I,G.

15 **signando:** 'while making the sign (sc. of the Cross)' (see G.18).

15f. **ut...appareret:** 'so that he appeared to...not by...but through...and...' (i.e. 'he obviously...').

16f. **cum...intulisset:** 'although (it)...' (i.e. the storm).
multis looks forward to in *locis*; **firmissimis...aedificiis** (dat.: tr. 'upon') is dependent on *intulisset*; **ut putabatur** qualifies *firmissimis* (i.e. people thought the buildings were stable, until this storm).

17 **multa...incommoda:** lit. 'many inconveniences of collapses', i.e. 'complete collapse'.

18 **virtute** looks forward to *divina,* dependent on *repulsa* (which agrees with the unstated subject *tempestas*).
titubantibus...arcubus: dat. 'to...' (*solis* because they were not yet fully connected together: see above).
nihil looks forward to *incommodi* 'no damage' (object of *proferre*).

7. Jocelin of Brakelond (*c.*1155–after 1209)

Jocelin of Brakelond (a street in Bury St Edmund's) entered the monastery of St Edmund's Bury in 1173. He filled a number of important positions in the abbey during his subsequent career, including those of prior's chaplain, abbot's chaplain, guestmaster (*hospiciarius*) and almoner (*elemosinarius*). A contemporary described him as *vir religionis eximie, potens in sermone et opere* ('an outstandingly religious man, powerful in word and deed'). His only surviving work is the *Cronica,* which gives a detailed and lively account of events within the abbey in the period from 1173 to 1201. Chief among them is a detailed portrait of Abbot Samson, elected in 1182 and served closely by Jocelin for six years from that date.

Jocelin was not a writer whose style was formed through close contact with the classics. It is plain and unadorned, though he sometimes has recourse to quotation from both the Bible and the pagan writers. Because he deals with many matters of abbey administration, he often uses vocabulary of the sort found otherwise chiefly in Latin documents from England, based on vernacular terms. Some examples are: *gilda* 'guild'; *bailivus* 'bailiff'; *plegiare* 'to stand surety for'; *froggum* 'frock'; *warda* 'castleward'; *manerium* 'manor'; *haneparium* 'hamper'; *torneare* 'to tourney'; *saisiare* 'to seize'; *sochagium* 'sokage'; *hustengium* 'hustings court'; *sopa* 'shop'; *lardearium* 'larder'.

Like other religious institutions of the period, the abbey of St Edmund's Bury had a crucial role in the everyday life of the people in its immediate area. This was known as the Liberty of St Edmund and had been granted to the abbey by Edward the Confessor in 1044. The abbot was a tenant-in-chief of the crown and held a jurisdiction equivalent to that of a sheriff in other shires. Hence the abbot owed service to the crown (forty knights), held a court of justice and was the chief administrator of a large feudal estate of eight and a half hundreds. To save revenue for the abbey in times between the tenures of abbots (when his holding reverted to the crown), the holdings were divided between abbot and convent. The town of Bury St Edmund's was a separate unit within the control of the sacrist, its borders marked outside the walls by the *bannaleuca* (Fr. *banlieue*). It had its own council and court (the 'portman-moot'), subordinate to that of the abbot. The following story illustrates the hard-nosed business end of religious life in the twelfth century.

See further: Jocelin of Brakelond, *Cronica*, ed. H. E. Butler, London, 1949.

Jocelin relates an infringement of the rights of the abbot and convent of St Edmund. Herbert sets up a windmill and Abbot Samson orders him to pull it down.

Herbertus decanus leuauit molendinum ad uentum super Hauberdun: quod cum audisset abbas, tanta ira excanduit, quod uix uoluit comedere uel aliquod uerbum proferre. In crastino, post missam auditam, precepit sacriste ut sine dilacione faceret carpentarios suos illuc ire et omnia subuertere et materiam lignorum in saluam custodiam reponere. Audiens hoc decanus uenit dicens se   5
hoc de iure posse facere super liberum feudum suum, nec beneficium uenti alicui homini debere denegari, et dixit se uelle suum proprium bladum ibi molere, non alienum, ne forte putaretur hoc facere in uicinorum molendinorum detrimentum. Et respondit abbas adhuc iratus: 'Gratias tibi reddo ac si ambos pedes meos amputasses; per os Dei, nunquam panem manducabo donec   10
fabrica illa subuertatur. Senex es et scire debuisti quod nec regi nec iustitiario licet aliquid immutare uel constituere infra bannam leucam sine abbate et conuentu; et tu tale quid presumsisti? Nec hoc sine detrimento meorum

molendinorum est, sicut asseris, quia ad tuum molendinum burgenses concurrent et bladum suum molerent pro beneplacito suo, nec eos possem de iure   15
aduertere, quia liberi homines sunt. Nec etiam molendinum celerarii nouiter
leuatum stare sustinerem, nisi quia leuatum fuit antequam fui abbas. Recede,'
inquit, 'recede; antequam tuam domum ueneris, audies quod fiet de molendino tuo.' Decanus autem timens a facie abbatis consilio filii sui magistri
Stephani famulos sacriste preueniens molendinum illud eleuatum a propriis   20
famulis suis sine omni mora erui fecit; ita quod, uenientibus seruientibus
sacriste, nichil subuertendum inuenerunt.

1 **decanus:** either 'rural dean' or *decanus Christianitatis*, the sacrist's deputy in the administration
of the town.
Haberdun: a place within the *bannaleuca*, where
the dean had no right to erect a mill without
the permission of abbot and convent.

2 **tanta** looks forward to *quod...uoluit* (result clause:
see G.26 (a)–(b)).

4 **faceret...ire:** 'make...go...' (see G.17(c)).

5 **Audiens:** 'Having...' (see G.20(a)).

6 **super...suum:** 'on his free fief', i.e. without
having to submit to anyone else's judgement, because the decision fell within the
feudum ('fief') he received through his office
(he was wrong).

6f. **nec...denegari:** 'and that...ought not...'.

8 **ne...putaretur:** 'in case he might be...'.
in looks forward to *detrimentum* (governing
uicinorum molendinorum: tr. 'to...').

9 **ac si:** 'as (sc. I would) if...'.

10 **amputasses** = *amputauisses* (see RLRGr A5).

11 **debuisti:** 'ought to have...'.
iustitiario: i.e. a judge holding court (such as a
justice in eyre, who would move round from
place to place).

13 **quid:** 'why?'.

15 **molerent, possem:** tr. 'would...' (notice the

irregular change from future indicative to
imperfect subjunctive).

16 **celerarii:** the cellarer had certain tenements and
privileges within the town walls, held a court
there and controlled a large slice of the lands
within the *bannaleuca*. The revenues from these
helped him to fulfil his main duty, the maintenance of the abbey and those who lived
there.

17 **sustinerem:** 'would I have allowed...'.
nisi quia leuatum fuit: 'except that it was...'.

18 **de:** tr. 'with'.

19 **timens a facie abbatis:** 'in fear before the face
of the abbot' (a biblical expression: cf. Jeremiah
42.11: *nolite timere a facie regis Babylonis* 'Do not
fear before the face of the king of Babylon').

20 **famulos sacriste** (= *sacristae:* see O.1): obj. of
preueniens.

20f. **a propriis famulis** looks forward to *erui fecit*
('made to be...': see G.17(c)); it does not go
with *eleuatum* (tr. 'which had been...').

21f. **ita quod...inuenerunt:** 'so that...' (result: see
G.26(a)–(b)) despite the ablative absolute, the
subject of *inuenerunt* is *seruientibus sacriste* (=
sacristae: see O.1); tr. *uenientibus* 'having...' (see
G.20(a)).

Section 18
Theology and philosophy

The pattern set by Anselm of the use of dialectic in the elucidation of the problems of faith continued through the twelfth century with Abelard's theological writings. But the century is more diverse philosophically than the eleventh. The study of dialectic was based primarily on Aristotle. But there was a group centred on Bernard of Chartres which addressed rather the connections between the existence of the world and that of God. Their inspiration was drawn from Plato, through the *Timaeus* (at this time his only known work) and Chalcidius' commentary, Augustine and the Neoplatonic Plotinus, known from Macrobius and Pseudo-Dionysius. They were important in the development of an interest in natural phenomena *per se*, which would eventually be bolstered by the thorough analysis of the structure and elements of being provided by the *Logica nova* of Aristotle (see section 16 Intro.) and the Arabian philosophers, whose works began to be known later in the century. This combination produced the natural theology of the thirteenth century. A third group of theologians, whose inspiration was biblical and inward, were the mystics. For them the inner experience of God, which transcends all human understanding, is central and they are, not surprisingly, utterly at odds with the rational approach of Abelard. Political philosophy, which hitherto had hidden under the guise of partisan ideology (for example during the investiture contest – see section 12), emerges isolatedly in John of Salisbury's *Policraticus*. It was not to develop further until the availability of Aristotle's *Politics* (*c.*1260).

1. John of Salisbury (*c.*1115–80)

Details of John's life are given above (section 16.1 Intro.). Political philosophy was not a concern of the earlier Middle Ages. But when it begins, with John of Salisbury's *Policraticus*, like other aspects of medieval thought, it has clear roots in the Christian tradition, specifically in St Augustine's *De civitate Dei* (see section 4.1(b)). John began the *Policraticus*

('Man of great power') as a response to his exile (on the orders of Henry
II) from the court of Theobald, archbishop of Canterbury, in 1156–7.
Books 7 and 8 preserve this meditation on how men may achieve the good
life. The rest of the work, which was completed in mid-1159, contains an
outline political philosophy beginning from a critique of the behaviour one
may observe in courts (books 1–3). In books 4–6, John develops a theory
of government whose goal is to produce a just earthly society in which
there is a proper balance between the personal liberty required for private
pursuit of knowledge and virtue, and the requirements of society as a
whole. The image which John uses to articulate this notion is of the state
as a body (the 'body politic'), whose head is the ruler, whose soul is the
Church and so on. He ascribes this daring notion to the Greek writer
Plutarch's *Instruction of Trajan*, though it is fairly clear that John was
protecting himself behind a bogus authority (there is no such work). As
other types of philosophical enquiry in the Middle Ages were considered of
paramount importance in real life (note Peter the Venerable's attacks on
heresy, or St Bernard's campaign against Abelard: section 17.1–2), so the
Policraticus represents an aid towards the achievement both for individual
and community of the good life.

See further: John of Salisbury, *Policraticus*, ed. C. C. J. Webb, Oxford,
1919; C. J. Nederman, *Policraticus: Of the Frivolities of Courtiers and the
Footprints of Philosophers*, Cambridge, 1990.

*John describes the 'body politic', in an account purporting to come from the works of
the Greek writer Plutarch.*

Est autem res publica, sicut Plutarco placet, corpus quoddam quod diuini
muneris beneficio animatur et summae aequitatis agitur nutu et regitur quodam
moderamine rationis. Ea uero quae cultum religionis in nobis instituunt et
informant et Dei (ne secundum Plutarcum deorum dicam) cerimonias tradunt,
uicem animae in corpore rei publicae obtinent. Illos uero qui religionis cultui   5
praesunt, quasi animam corporis suspicere et uenerari oportet. Quis enim
sanctitatis ministros Dei ipsius uicarios esse ambigit? Porro, sicut anima totius
habet corporis principatum, ita et hii, quos ille religionis praefectos uocat, toti
corpori praesunt. Augustus Cesar eo usque sacrorum pontificibus subiectus fuit
donec et ipse, ne cui omnino subesset, Vestalis creatus est pontifex et paulo post   10
ad deos relatus est uiuus.
  Princeps uero capitis in re publica optinet locum uni subiectus Deo et his qui
uices illius agunt in terris, quoniam et in corpore humano ab anima uegetatur
caput et regitur. Cordis locum senatus optinet, a quo bonorum operum et

malorum procedunt initia. Oculorum, aurium et linguae officia sibi uendicant   15
iudices et praesides prouinciarum. Officiales et milites manibus coaptantur. Qui
semper adsistunt principi, lateribus assimilantur. Quaestores et commentarienses (non illos dico qui carceribus praesunt, sed comites rerum priuatarum)
ad uentris et intestinorum refert imaginem. Quae, si immensa auiditate congesserint et congesta tenacius reseruauerint, innumerabiles et incurabiles generant   20
morbos, ut uitio eorum totius corporis ruina immineat. Pedibus uero solo
iugiter inherentibus agricolae coaptantur, quibus capitis prouidentia tanto
magis necessaria est, quo plura inueniunt offendicula, dum in obsequio
corporis in terra gradiuntur, eisque iustius tegumentorum debetur suffragium, qui totius corporis erigunt, sustinent et promouent molem. Pedum   25
adminicula robustissimo corpori tolle, suis uiribus non procedet sed aut turpiter
inutiliter et moleste manibus repet aut brutorum animalium ope mouebitur.

1f. **diuini muneris** depends on *beneficio* ('by...') and
summae aequitatis depends on *nutu* ('at...',
'by...').

3 **Ea** is the subject of *obtinent* (obj. *uicem animae*).
cultum religionis is the object of *instituunt* and
informant, and **Dei** looks forward to and
depends on *cerimonias* (obj. of *tradunt*).

4 **ne...dicam:** the significant word is *deorum*,
which is the object of *dicam* because it
picks up *Dei*; imagine *deorum* in inverted
commas.

5 **Illos** is the object of *suspicere* and *uenerari*; tr.
oportet 'it is right (to)...'.

6f. **Quis...ambigit:** the structure is 'Who is in
doubt that *sanctitatis ministros* are *Dei ipsius
uicarios*?'.

7 **totius** looks forward to *corporis* and the phrase
depends on *principatum*.

8 **hii:** i.e. the priests (subject of *praesunt*).
ille: i.e. Plutarch.

9f. **eo...donec:** 'to that moment...when'.

9 **sacrorum pontificibus:** 'to the priests (in
charge) of the rites'.

10 **Vestalis** looks forward to *pontifex* (it means
pontifex maximus, the chief priest of Rome,
one of whose duties was to officiate at
sacrifices at the temple of Vesta; Augustus
was chosen for this position on 6 March 12
BC).

11 **ad deos...uiuus:** Horace, *Odes* 1.2.44f. represents Augustus as a living god, but he was not
actually deified until his death in AD 14.

12 **capitis** looks forward to and depends on *locum*
(obj. of *optinet*).
uni looks forward to *Deo* (depending on *subiectus*,
picking up *Princeps*).

12f. **et his...in terris:** *his* picks up and depends on
subiectus; *qui...terris* refers to God's agents, the
priests. This opinion, which John pretends
(*quoniam...regitur*, subject *caput*) is forced on
him by his analogy, can be recognized as
taking the papal side in the long-running
dispute between Empire and Papacy (see
sections 12 and 19.III). John supported Becket against Henry II in 1163 and had already
incurred Henry's displeasure in 1156–7.

14f. **bonorum...malorum** depends on *initia* (subject
of *procedunt*).

15 **Oculorum...linguae** depend on *officia* (obj. of
sibi uendicant; subject *iudices et praesides...*).

16 **coaptantur:** lit. 'are fitted to', i.e. 'are compared
to'.

16f. **Qui...principi:** 'Those who...'.

17f. **Quaestores et commentarienses:** objects of
refert (unstated subject 'he', i.e. Plutarch); *ad*
(completing the structure of *refert*) looks forward to *imaginem* (which governs *uentris et
intestinorum*).

18 **comites...priuatarum:** 'counts of the exche-
quer' (lit. '...of private matters').

19 **Quae, si:** 'If these (sc. organs of state)...'.

19f. **congesserint:** sc. 'wealth' as unstated object.

20 **congesta:** 'what they have accumulated' (obj. of
reseruauerint).

innumerabiles et incurabiles look forward to *morbos* (obj. of *generant*).

21 **ut:** 'with the result that...'.

totius corporis depends on *ruina* (subject of *immineat*).

Pedibus ('to...'), picked up by *inherentibus* (governing *solo*), depends on *coaptantur* (see note on l. 16 above).

22 **quibus:** 'for whom...'.

22f. **tanto magis** 'the more' is picked up by *quo plura* 'the more' (*plura* looks forward to *offendicula*, obj. of *inueniunt*, whose subject is *agricolae*).

24 **eisque:** 'and to them', i.e. 'the peasants' (looking forward to *debetur*).

iustius: 'justly' ('more justly (sc. than to other groups)').

tegumentorum depends on *suffragium* (subject of *debetur*).

25 **qui:** 'since they...'.

totius corporis depends on *molem* (object of *erigunt...promouent*).

25f. **Pedum...tolle...procedet...:**'Take...from...and it (i.e. 'the body')' (but the clause is really a protasis: tr. 'if you take...').

27 **brutorum...ope:** *ope* governs the genitives and depends on *mouebitur* (i.e. on horseback).

2. St Bernard of Clairvaux (1090–1153)

Details of St Bernard's life are given in the introduction to section 17.2. For the Song of Songs see section 3.2. An anonymous commentator clearly under the influence of Peter Abelard (see sections 16.2, 17.3, below, section 18.3) wrote of St Bernard during his lifetime: 'he has pursued that amazing gift of speaking and teaching others through the spirit of God rather than subtlety of intellect'. Yet Bernard was *au fait* with scholastic method and had quite a reputation as a problem-solving theologian. For example, he did not scruple to attempt an answer to the difficult question of the relationship between free will in men and God's foreknowledge, predestination and grace (in the *De gratia et libero arbitrio* of 1127). This had been tackled by Anselm of Canterbury and taken up by Abelard in his commentary on Aristotle's *De interpretatione*. But while Abelard relied very much upon dialectic, Bernard's approach stresses rather the traditional reliance upon authority before logic, and he had a gift for making difficult matters clear.

The *Sermons* on the Song of Songs, on the eighty-sixth of which Bernard was working when he died, were begun around 1135. The inspiration of this series can be set much earlier, however, probably during conversations *c.*1118 with William of St Thierry (who later induced Bernard to attack Abelard's 'heresy'). Bernard found the Song a key to the life of faith. It was a dialogue between God and the human soul, a *theoricus sermo*, which looks upwards in contemplation of God. Though many passages in the *Sermons* deal with recognizably theological problems, Bernard's emphasis is upon spirituality rather than theory. It was this spiritual aspect which Bernard thought was lacking in Abelard's theoretical approach. Nonetheless, it has been observed that Bernard's view of will, for instance, expressed in the following extract from Sermon 40, is not dissimilar from that of Abelard in the *Scito teipsum*, which was among the *capitula* discussed at Sens in 1140.

See further: G. R. Evans, *The Mind of St Bernard of Clairvaux*, Oxford, 1983.

(i) *Bernard takes his text from the Song of Songs 1.9, 'Beautiful are thy cheeks like those of a turtle-dove.' In the opening section (omitted), he explains the literal meaning, but warns against taking this as the true sense. The 'cheeks' are to be understood as 'the intention', 'the mind's face'. But why is the plural 'cheeks' written rather than the singular 'face'?*

There are two aspects of intention, the matter and the cause, from which the beauty or ugliness of one's soul can be gauged. Hence the image of beautiful cheeks in the Song. Some examples show how the intentions can be judged.

Duo quaedam in intentione, quam animae faciem esse diximus, necessarie requiruntur: res et causa, id est quid intendas et propter quid. Et ex his sane duobus animae vel decor vel deformitas iudicatur, ut, verbi causa, anima quae ambo ista recta et pudica habuerit, illi merito veraciterque dicatur: PULCHRAE SUNT GENAE TUAE SICUT TURTURIS. Quae vero altero   5
horum caruerit, non poterit dici de ea, quod pulchrae sint genae tuae sicut turturis, propter eam, quae adhuc ex parte erit, deformitatem. Multo autem minus illi hoc poterit convenire, quae neutrum horum habere laudabile invenitur. At id totum fiet planius in exemplis.

Si, verbi causa, intendat quis animum inquirendae veritati, atque id solo   10
veritatis amore, nonne is tibi videtur et rem et causam habere honestam, meritoque sibi vindicare quod dicitur: PULCHRAE SUNT GENAE TUAE SICUT TURTURIS, quippe cui in neutra genarum naevus reprehensionis appareat? Quod si minime quidem veritatis desiderio, sed aut inanis gloriae aut alterius qualiscumque commodi temporalis obtentu in veritatem intenderit,   15
iam etsi unam genarum videatur habere formosam, non tamen (ut arbitror) dubitabis iudicare vel ex parte deformem, cuius alteram faciem causae turpitudo foedaverit. Si autem videris hominem nullis honestis studiis intendentem, sed carnis irretitum illecebris, ventri et luxuriae deditum, quales sunt illi quorum Deus venter est et gloria in confusione eorum qui terrena sapiunt: 20
quid istum? Nonne ex utraque parte foedissimum iudicabis, in cuius utique intentione et res et causa reproba invenitur?

---

1 **Duo quaedam** (tr. 'Two things') is the subject of *requiruntur*.
animae is governed by *decor* and *deformitas* (subjects of *iudicatur*).

3 **ut** 'so that' looks forward to *dicatur*, of which the subject is 'it...', not *anima; illi* refers back to *anima*, which is best translated 'in respect of the...'. This kind of syntax is typical of the Vulgate.

verbi causa: 'so to speak'.
4 **ambo ista** (see G.11(c)): object of *habuerit* (tr.
'has': *recta et pudica* are adjuncts to *ambo ista*,
which refers to *res* and *causa*).
5 **Quae:** sc. 'the soul'.
6 **non poterit:** subject 'it...'.
7 **propter eam** looks forward to *deformitatem*
(antecedent of *quae...erit*).
ex parte: 'in part'.
8 **illi** (sc. 'soul') depends on *convenire* and **hoc** refers
to the quotation from the Song.
quae is the subject of *invenitur* (completed by
habere; laudabile is an adjunct to *neutrum horum*,
viz. *res* and *causa*: tr. 'in a...state').
10 **Si** looks forward to *quis* (subject of *intendat*; the
object is *animum*).
inquirendae veritati: 'towards...ing...'.
solo looks forward to *amore* ('through...').
11 **videtur** is completed by *habere*.
13 **quippe cui:** lit. 'in as much as for him...' (see
RLGVE 140.2).
14 **Quod si** looks forward to *intenderit* (subject 'he');
the structure of the rest is governed by
minime...sed..., each part being expressed by
an ablative of cause (*desiderio...obtutu*), which in
turn govern the genitives attached to them
(*veritatis...inanis...commodi*).

inanis gloriae: the phrase is a reminiscence of
Galatians 5.26 or Philippians 2.3.
16 **etsi...formosam:** that is, the *res* (because his
objective is the truth).
17 **iudicare:** sc. 'him'.
cuius alteram faciem: tr. 'one of whose two
cheeks'.
17f. **causae turpitudo:** i.e. because though his *res* is
good, his *causa* is not.
18 **hominem** is picked up by *intendentem* (governing *nullis...studiis*), *irretitum* (governing *illecebris*,
on which *carnis* depends) and *deditum* (governing *ventri et luxuriae*).
19 **quales:** 'as'.
20 **gloria...confusione:** understand as a second
part of the *quorum* clause ('and whose...',
supplying *est*); *eorum...sapiunt*: take *eorum* to
mean 'their own', and tr. *qui...sapiunt* in
apposition 'these people who...'. The whole
phrase from *quorum...sapiunt* is adapted slightly
from Philippians 3.19, which in the Greek
means: 'Their end is destruction, whose God
is the belly and whose glory is in their shame.
They are concentrating on wordly things.'
21 **quid istum** (see G.11(c)): sc. 'will you think of'.
iudicabis: sc. 'him'.
in looks forward to *intentione*.

(ii) *Bernard distinguishes the acceptability of various objects of intention; i.e. concentrating not on God but on the world; on God but not for God's sake; on God for
the sake of worldly necessities; on something other than God for God's sake. The
last of these is marred by the world, but is forgiven. The verse of the Song only
applies to the person whose intention is towards God for God's sake.*

Ergo intendere non in Deum, sed in saeculum, saecularis animae est, nec ullam
prorsus genarum speciosam habentis. Intendere autem quasi in Deum, sed non
propter Deum, hypocritae plane animae est, cuius etsi una facies decora
videtur, quod ad Deum qualicumque intentione respiciat, ipsa tamen simu-
latio omne in ea decorum exterminat, magis per totum ingerit foeditatem. Si   5
autem vel solum vel maxime ob vitae praesentis necessaria ad Deum
converterit intentionem, non quidem faece hypocrisis putidam, pusillanimitatis tamen vitio dicimus subobscuram et minus acceptam. Porro, e contrario,
intendere in aliud quam in Deum, tamen propter Deum, non otium Mariae,
sed Marthae negotium est. Absit autem ut quae huiusmodi est quidquam illam   10
dixerim habere deforme. Nec tamen ad perfectum affirmaverim pervenisse

decoris: quippe quae adhuc sollicita est et turbatur erga plurima, et non potest terrenorum actuum vel tenui pulvere non respergi. Quem tamen cito facileque deterget, vel in hora sanctae dormitionis, casta intentio et bonae conscientiae interrogatio in Deum. Ergo solum inquirere Deum propter ipsum solum, hoc   15 plane est utramque bipertitae intentionis faciem habere pulcherrimam; atque id proprium ac speciale sponsae, cui merito singulari praerogativa audire conveniat: PULCHRAE SUNT GENAE TUAE SICUT TURTURIS.

1 **intendere** is the subject of *est*.
saecularis animae: sc. 'the mark (of)...' (picked up by *habentis* 'which...', obj. *ullam...genarum*, adjunct *speciosam*).

2f. **Intendere autem...est:** the structure is the same as in the preceding sentence (*hypocritae...animae*, tr. 'the mark (of)...').

5 **omne** looks forward to *decorum* (obj. of *exterminat*).
magis: sc. 'and' (asyndeton).
per totum: sc. 'man'.

5f. **Si...acceptam:** the structure is *Si...converterit intentionem, non...tamen...dicimus* (*dicimus* introduces two hidden acc. + inf. phrases: their subject is *intentionem* from the preceding clause, their verb *esse* understood, and complements *putidam* (governing *faece hypocrisis*: 'in...'), *subobscuram* (governing *pusillanimitatis...vitio*: 'with...') and *acceptam*.

6 **ob** looks forward to *necessaria* (governing *vitae praesentis*).

9 **intendere** is once more the subject, this time with noun complements (*non otium..., sed...negotium est*: note the chiasmus in this clause, *RLGVE* p. 315(d)). The story of the sisters Martha and Maria is told by Lk 10.38–42. Maria listened to Jesus, while Martha served. When Martha asked Jesus to reproach Maria, he said that Maria had chosen the better path. Symbolically, this was interpreted as meaning that attention to the call of heaven

was more praiseworthy than attention to the affairs of this world.

10 **Absit...ut:** lit. 'Let it be absent that...', i.e. 'Don't think I mean that...'.
quae ('she who...') is picked up by *illam* (subject of acc. + inf. introduced by *dixerim*; the object is *quidquam...deforme*).

11 **ad perfectum** looks forward to and governs *decoris*; *affirmaverim* 'would I...' (*RLGVE* 171(b)); *pervenisse* 'that (sc. 'she')...'.

12 **quippe quae:** 'in as much as she...'.
sollicita...plurima: slightly adapted from Lk 10.41 (see note on l.9 above).
non potest is completed by *non respergi* (on which *vel tenui pulvere* depends: 'by even a small amount of the...(of terrenorum actuum)').

13 **Quem:** i.e. *terrenorum actuum...pulvere*.

14 **deterget:** subjects *casta intentio et...interrogatio* (take *in Deum* 'towards...' with *bonae conscientiae*).
vel...dormitionis: i.e. on one's deathbed.

15 **inquirere** is the subject, picked up by *hoc... est...habere* (obj. *utramque...faciem*, adjunct *pulcherrimam*).

16 **id:** sc. *est*.

17 **sponsae:** here Bernard seems to equate the bride specifically with the Church, the intention of which towards Christ the bridegroom is correct in both *res* and *causa*.
cui depends on *conveniat* (completed by *audire*, which has as object *pulchrae* etc.).

3. Peter Abelard (*c.*1079–1142)

Details of Abelard's life and relationship with Heloise are given above at sections 16.2, 17.3 and 17.4. Details of his conflict with St Bernard of Clairvaux are given above at section 17.2.

The furious conflict between Abelard and St Bernard was the result of the logical development of two separate lines of theological analysis and thought. On St Bernard's side was the patristic appeal to authority and orthodoxy, on Abelard's the desire to use dialectic to find correct language for discussing the articles of faith, a trend already visible in late eleventh-century writers such as Anselm of Canterbury (see section 14.2). To a degree, Abelard was misrepresented by his critics as wishing to change the content of the faith.

The *Theologia* of Abelard developed in stages. It was the *Theologia 'Summi Boni'* which was burnt at Soissons in 1121. A later version, itself extant in three separate versions, the *Theologia 'Scholarium'*, was the basis of the attack at Sens in 1140. The main intention of the work was to put forward rational analogies and arguments to clarify the doctrine of the Trinity. Abelard assumed that since God reveals himself through reason, reason can be used to obtain some understanding of God.

The condemnation articulated by Innocent II in July 1140 mentions nineteen *capitula*, which Bernard had put together on the basis of the *Disputatio* of William of St Thierry. This had in turn been based not only on the *Theologia 'Scholarium'* of Abelard, but also on a work called *Liber sententiarum magistri Petri*, which is not by Abelard at all. Abelard replied in his *Apologia*, which was in turn answered by another monk, Thomas of Morigny. All three attacks on Abelard pay attention to his attribution of power, wisdom and benignity to Father, Son and Holy Spirit respectively. The first of the condemned *capitula* was: 'That the Father is complete power, the Son a certain power, the Holy Spirit no power.' Abelard challenged Bernard to find this explicitly stated anywhere, saying that his view was that each of the persons is equally powerful, wise and benign; the wisdom and love of God are all-powerful, but one cannot suitably say that they are also the same as omnipotence. This linguistic and logical defence presupposes orthodox faith. But William, Bernard and Thomas were all deeply concerned by the imagery Abelard used to describe the relationship between the persons of the Trinity. The following passage, where Abelard likens the relationship to a bronze seal, is specifically mentioned by William and Thomas, and a later chapter, which is mentioned by Bernard, takes up the same image. The analogy owes something to Boethius' *De Trinitate*, Remigius of Auxerre and a gloss on Psalm 4.7, possibly written by Roscelin of Compiègne.

See further: CCCM xiii, pp. 15–21, 203–10, 277–92; D. E. Luscombe, *The School of Peter Abelard*, Cambridge, 1969, pp. 103–142.

(i) *'A strong analogy taken from the philosophers'*. Abelard uses the analogy of a
bronze seal to explain the way in which the Trinity is of the same substance yet has
different functions and different relations between its parts.

Verbi causa, es quoddam est inter creaturas, in quo artifex operans et imaginis
regie formam exprimens regium facit sigillum, quod scilicet ad sigillandas litteras,
cum opus fuerit, cere imprimatur. Est igitur in sigillo illo ipsum es materia ex quo
factum est, figura vero illa imaginis regie forma eius, ipsum vero sigillum ex his
duobus materiatum atque formatum dicitur, quibus videlicet sibi convenientibus   5
ipsum est compositum atque perfectum. Nichil quippe est aliud sigillum ipsum
quam es ita formatum. Idem itaque essentialiter est ipsum es quod est materia erei
sigilli et sigillum ipsum cuius est materia, cum tamen in suis proprietatibus ita sint
disiuncta ut aliud sit proprium eris, aliud erei sigilli. Et quamvis idem sint
essentialiter, sigillum tamen ereum est ex ere, non es ex ereo sigillo, et es est   10
materia sigilli, non sigillum eris. Nec ullo modo es materia sui ipsius esse potest,
quamvis sit materia sigilli quod est ipsum es. Non enim es ex ere fit sicut sigillum
ex ere est constitutum. Et quamvis idem sit materia ipsa quod est materiatum,
nequaquam tamen in sigillo illo materiatum est materia vel materia est
materiatum. Facto autem ex ere sigillo, iam sigillabile est, hoc est aptum ad   15
sigillandum, etsi nondum sit actualiter sigillans. Cum autem per ipsum sigillari
ceram contingit, iam in una eris substantia tria sunt proprietate diversa, es
videlicet ipsum, et sigillabile et sigillans. Que quidem ad invicem sic se habent
ut ex ere sit factum sigillabile, hoc est sigillum, et ex ere simul et sigillabili
contingat fieri sigillans. Ex ere quippe quod primitus erat, ad hoc productum est   20
ipsum es ut sigillabile esset, deinde ut, quod es sigillabile iam erat, sigillans fieret.
Sic igitur cum sit eadem essentia eris et sigillabilis et sigillantis que tria proprietate
diversa sunt, ita hec tria invicem sunt sibi coniuncta, ut ex ere sigillabile et ex ere
simul et sigillabili sigillans habeat suum esse.

1 **Verbi causa:** 'To illustrate'.
   es...est: 'there exists a kind of...' (*es, eris = aes,
   aeris* and *ereus = aereus* throughout this passage:
   see O.1).
1f. **operans et...exprimens:** 'by...' (*regie = regiae*
   with *imagines*: see O.1)
2 **regium** looks forward to *sigillum* (obj. of *facit*).
3 **fuerit:** tr. 'is'.
   cere (= *cerae*, dative: see O.1) depends on
   imprimatur 'upon...'
3f. **Est...factum est:** the subject is *materia*, the
   complement *ipsum es* (picked up by *ex
   quo...est,* subject *sigillum*).
4 **figura...eius:** subject *forma eius*, complement
   figura...regie.

ipsum...sigillum is the subject of *dicitur* (completed by *materiatum atque formatum,* sc. *esse*).
6 **quibus...convenientibus:** 'from which...'.
   ipsum: i.e. the *sigillum.*
6f. **Nichil...quam:** 'Nothing (sc. other) than...'.
7f. **Idem...et...:** 'The same as...'.
8 **cuius...materia:** subject *ipsum es.*
   cum tamen: 'even though...'.
9 **proprium:** 'proper to' (governing *eris* and *erei
   sigilli*).
11 **non...eris:** sc. *materia.*
   Nec...potest: subject *es*, complement *materia.*
12 **quamvis...sit:** subject *es.*
13 **idem...quod:** 'the same...as' (subject of *sit* is
   materia).

materiatum: 'what has been made' (the point seems to be that the material and the manufactured object might be thought the same in that both can be called 'bronze'; but the object is a 'bronze seal', distinct from the bronze of which it is made).

16 **sit...sigillans:** 'it is...ing' (see G.4(b)).
per...sigillari: 'in the process of...' (*sigillari* is a noun); *cum* = 'when' (subject is *sigillum*).

17 **tria sunt...diversa:** 'there are three things different in...'.

18 **sigillabile et sigillans:** the adjectives are now nouns, 'the potential seal' and 'the actual seal'.

Que...habent: 'These (sc. three things) relate to each other...'.

20 **contingat...sigillans:** 'it happens to become (actually) sealing'.
ad hoc ('for this purpose') looks forward to *ut.*

21 **quod...erat:** 'since...'.

22 **cum...sigillantis:** 'even though the *essentia* of....is eadem'.

22f. **que...diversa sunt:** 'and these...'.

23 **invicem...coniuncta:** 'connected with each other'.

23f. **ut...esse:** the two subjects of *habeat* are *sigillabile* and *sigillans* (*esse* is a noun here).

(ii) *If this analogy is applied to the Trinity, it provides a neat refutation of the pseudophilosophers who attack me.*

Que quidem omnia, si ad divine trinitatis doctrinam congruis proportionibus reducantur, facile est nobis ex ipsis philosophorum documentis pseudophilosophos qui nos infestant refellere. Sicut enim ex ere sigillum est ereum et ex ipso quodammodo generatur, ita ex ipsa dei patris substantia filius habet esse, et secundum hoc ex ipso genitus dicitur.   5

1 **Que...omnia:** this belongs within the *si...reducantur* clause (note the irregular construction: *si* + subjunctive, indicative but meaning 'if...were to..., it would be...' (see G.28(b)).
ad looks forward to *doctrinam.*

2 **facile est nobis** is completed by *refellere* (obj. *pseudophilosophos...infestant*).

3 **ex:** sc. 'made'.
sigillum...ereum is the subject.

3f. **ex ipso:** i.e. *es.*

4 **ex ipsa** looks forward to *substantia.*
esse is a noun here.

5 **ex ipso:** i.e. 'the Father'.
genitus: sc. *esse.*

4. Alan of Lille (d. 1202 or 1203; b. *c.*1115–20?)

Alan served his intellectual apprenticeship in the schools of Paris and Chartres, possibly in the 1130s and 1140s, at the same time and under some of the same masters as John of Salisbury (see Section 16.1). Unlike John, Alan became a master, first at Paris, later in the South of France, almost certainly at Montpellier. Here he was an active campaigner against heretics such as the Cathars and wrote a four book treatise *De fide catholica: contra haereticos, Valdenses, Iudaeos et paganos* (*c.*1185–1200). In his old age he entered the Cistercian order, and died at Cîteaux.

Alan's interests are attested by the vast output of his theological writings, such as *Summa quoniam homines* (*c.*1155–65), *Regulae theologicae* (same period) and *Distinctiones dictionum theologicalium* (1179–95). These covered the whole range of the subject in its theoretical and practical aspects. Alan was a teacher, so that much of his work had a pedagogic aim. He was one of the first to compose an 'art of preaching' (*ars praedicandi*), a confessional handbook, a *summa theologica* and a dictionary of theological terms. His great intellectual achievement was the devising of a scheme to encompass all theological studies and thus all the branches of the liberal arts, which he regarded as 'handmaids of theology'. For him, as for others, poetry was therefore a servant of theology, another language in which the mysteries of God's revelation could be explored and the soul be made fit for heaven. It is no surprise, then, to find him writing a nine-book allegorical poem, the *Anticlaudianus* (1181–4).

The poem's form and subject-matter owe much to earlier and near-contemporary writing, especially to Martianus Capella's *De nuptiis Mercurii et Philologiae* ('Marriage of Philology and Mercury'), Prudentius' *Psychomachia* (see section 5.2) and Bernardus Silvestris' *Cosmographia* (c.1147). Alan shared Bernardus' interest in Platonism (as mediated mostly through Boethius and other commentators, since the only text available was *Timaeus*). Bernardus' work tells the story of Nature's first fashioning of man. It is an allegory of creation. Alan's poem is entitled the 'Counter-Claudian' partly in answer to the *In Rufinum* of the fourth/fifth-century pagan poet Claudian, partly by confusion with Claudianus Mamertus, who had written on the creation of the soul. It tells the story of Nature's scheme to make a perfect man, to replace the imperfect creature of her earlier attempt. This involves a journey to heaven by Ratio (Reason) and Phronesis (Prudence) to ask God to create a perfect soul. Eventually Phronesis, guided first by Theology, then by Faith, reaches God, who grants the request. Nous (Mind) makes the soul, it is taken back to earth and fitted to the perfect body made by Nature, the Virtues endow the creature with all their gifts, the perfect man fights a battle against the Vices and upon victory becomes the ruler of a restored earth.

In his prologue, Alan explains that the work has three levels of meaning, literal, moral and allegorical, of which the last is the highest. His ideas are all easily located within the Christian theological framework. Yet there is a startling originality in the notion of a perfect man who is not Christ ruling a perfect earth. Alan's language is deliberately rich and recherché, overflowing with rhetorical flourishes. In this passage from the final battle, he seems to have been inspired both by Claudian's phrase (*In Rufinum* I.31) *Leto vicina Senectus*, 'Old Age, Death's neighbour', and by the portrait of Sleep in Ovid *Metamorphoses* XI.593f. The metre is hexameter (*RLGVE* pp. 319–20), traditionally used for didactic poetry as well as epic.

Further reading: G. R. Evans, *Alan of Lille: The Frontiers of Theology in the Later Twelfth Century*, Cambridge, 1983; C. S. Lewis, *The Allegory of Love*, repr., Oxford, 1977, ch. 2, pp. 44–111.

(i) *Old Age enters the fray. But its first attack on the horse of the divine man fails.*

quamuis pigra foret, quamuis longeua Senectus,	
quamuis delirans, quamuis torpore fatiscens,	150
prona tamen calet in bello, iuuenescit in armis,	
nec baculi iam quaerit opem, suffulta furore,	
nec regimen poscit que substentatur ab ira,	
debilitate potens, morbo robusta, dolore	
diues, segnicie fortis, pigredine prompta.	155
ergŏ propinqua neci, morti uicina propinque,	
florida canicie, rugis sulcata Senectus	
oppositum ruit in iuuenem, nec primitus instat	
ense, nec aggreditur telo, nec cuspide pulsat,	
sed quadam specie lucte cognatur ut illum	160
in terram demittat, equm subducat et armis	
exutum liber gladius grassetur in hostem.	
sed monitu calcaris equs succensus in illam	
irruit et terre miseram deponit, at illa	
exurgens uires pariter cum mente resumit.	165

149 **foret** = *esset (RLGVE* 130 Note 2); the adjectives are f. because *Senectus* is f. (though pictured as a warrior).

151 **prona**: 'easily' (RLRGr J Intro. (c)).

152 **baculi** looks forward to (and depends on) *opem.*

153 **nec...que**: 'Nor does (Old Age) who...'.

154f. **debilitate potens...prompta**: sc. 'being'; note the series of oxymorons, expressed by ablatives of respect 'in...' (RLRGr L(f)4(vi); *diues* must here mean 'happy').

156 **morti** depends on *uicina* and is picked up by *propinque* (= *propinquae*: see O.1).

157 **canicie**: 'in...' (abl. of respect, see RLRGr L(f)4(vi); Old Age has white hair (notice the

chiasmus in *florida...sulcata*, see *RLGVE* p. 315(d)).

158 **oppositum** looks forward to *in iuuenem.*

159f. **ense...telo...cuspide...quadam specie**: 'with...'.

160 **lucte** = *luctae* (gen. s.): see O.1.

cognatur = *conatur* (*ut* 'to...'; not CL; the verbs are *demittat, subducat, grassetur* – the subject of the last is *gladius*).

161 **equm** = *equum.*

161f. **armis exutum** ('stripped of...') looks forward to *in hostem.*

163 **monitu** depends on *succensus* ('fired by...').

164 **terre** = *terrae* (dat.: see O.1): 'upon the ground' (see G.16(a)).

(ii) *Old Age decides to use its weapons. But they are worn out. In particular, the sword cannot be pulled from its sheath. Eventually, however, the aged blade emerges. But it is unable to cause a wound.*

uertit in arma manus et spem deponit in armis,
sed cassis torpore iacet, scalore senescit,
atque situ scabre morsum rubiginis horret.
parma suum multa rubigine computat euum
nec uetat ingressum nudata crate sagitis.   170
lorice fragiles mordens rubigŏ cathenas
dissuit et iunctis addit diuorcia squamis.
pigritat affixus uagine mucrŏ nec extra
de facili prodit, longo tempŏre quiescens,
quem Senium nudare parat; sed degener ensis   175
respuit egressus istos dextreque monenti
denegat officium, malens torpore quietis
uti quam uarios belli sentire tumultus.
sed tamen a loculo tandem producitur ensis
segnis, hebes, scalore iacens nec iam memor ire   180
bellorum, pacemque magis quam bella requirit
hic mucro, si mucrŏ tamen de iure uocari
debeat hic gladius et non mucronis ymago.
impetit ergŏ uirum gladio munita Senectus,
uulnus ab ense petit, sed uulneris immemor ensis,   185
in cassum pulsans, aditus ad uulnera nescit,
sed stupet ad galeam, uario delirus in ictu.

166 **deponit** = *ponit.*
167 **torpore iacet:** 'lies inactive' (lit. 'in inactivity').
168 **situ:** 'in neglect' ('neglected') or 'where it lies'.
   scabre = *scabrae* (gen. s: see O.1) looks forward to *rubiginis*; both depend on *morsum.*
169 **suum** looks forward to *euum.*
170 **nudata crate:** abl. abs. 'now that its ribs (i.e. its frame) have been...'.
171 **lorice** = *loricae* (gen. s.: see O.1) ('chain mail') depends on *fragiles...cathenas*, obj. of *mordens*, which qualifies *rubigo*, and *dissuit.*
172 **iunctis** looks forward to *squamis* (dat.).
173 **uagine** = *uaginae* (dat.: see O.1) depends on *affixus* (with *mucro*).

174 **de facili:** 'easily'.
   quiescens: 'Having...' (see G.20(a)).
175 **Senium** = *Senectus.*
176 **dextre** = *dextrae* (dat. s.: see O.1) with *monenti:* 'which...'.
177 **torpore** depends on *uti* (prolative inf. with *malens*).
178 **uarios** looks forward to *tumultus* (obj. of *sentire*).
179 **loculo:** perhaps a joke, since one meaning of *loculus* is 'coffin'.
180 **ire** = *irae* (see O.1: gen. s. after *memor* and governing *bellorum*).
186 **in cassum** = *incassum* 'in vain'.
187 **uario** looks forward to *in ictu* (i.e. the sword waggles all over the place).

(iii) *Old Age, defeated, urges the youth to kill him. But he refuses. Senility throws away its weapons and retreats leaning on its stick.*

> ergŏ Senecta, uidens proprium nil posse furorem,
> miratur seseque dolet sine uulnere uinci;
> sed quamuis esset morti uicina, propinquam 190
> maturare uolens, hostis sibi prouocat ensem.
> sed iuuenis, miseratus eam nec digna rependens
> hosti pro meritis, nolenti uiuere uitam
> concedit fatumque negat sua fata uolenti.
> sistit equm, frenum retinens, sermone Senectam 195
> aggrediens animosque truces et uota retardans,
> prodit in hec: 'cur fata paras, cui proxima fatur
> mors finem, cui uita mori, cui uiuere fatum?
> cur queris tibi concessum? cur poscis inepte
> quod Natura parat, quod mors uicina minatur? 200
> utere que restat uita nec quere propinquos
> anticipare dies; uite compendia mortem
> solentur, mortis dispendia uita repenset.'
> ergo uicta fugit belloque renunciat, ensem
> deicit, expellit clipeum galeamque Senectus 205
> exuit, et solo baculo contenta recedit.

188 **proprium** looks forward to *furorem*.
190 **propinquam:** sc. *mortem*.
191 **hostis:** gen. s. dependent upon *ensem*.
   sibi: 'against...'.
193f. **nolenti, uolenti:** '(sc. to Old Age)...'.
195 **equm** = *equum*.
   frenum retinens: 'and...' (asyndeton).
197 **prodit in hec:** 'he comes forward to these (sc. words)', i.e. 'he begins as follows'.
   fata: pl. for s.
   cui: 'you to whom...'.

197f. **proxima** looks forward to *mors*, subject of *fatur* (obj. *finem*).
198 **uita mori...uiuere fatum:** sc. *est* with each clause (note the chiasmus); the infinitives *mori, uiuere* are nouns ('death', 'life').
201 **utere** governs *uita* (antecedent of *que*).
   quere governs *anticipare* ('to...').
202f. **uite** = *uitae* (gen. s.: see O.1); note the word play in *compendia/dispendia* 'profit'/'loss'; the verbs are jussive subjunctives 'let...' (*RLGVE* 152).

Section 19
Historical writing

The main types of historical work already evident in earlier periods, that is the chronicle, the annal and the saint's life, all continued to be composed during the twelfth century. But the increasing importance of education is manifest in the strong development of deliberate ideological manipulation of personalities and events. More and more in the wake of the investiture contest, rulers and churchmen alike needed to win battles with the word and so to have writers in their circle who could perform the task persuasively. The large number of biographies of Thomas Becket shows what a golden opportunity for the proponents of the Church was his murder. Secular rulers were also interested in how images of themselves and the past of their nation could help them in the task of retaining and increasing power. Otto of Freising's *Gesta Friderici* (completed by Rahewin) is a good example of the selective use of data to produce such an effect. The growing activity and diversity of life in Europe is reflected in the greatly increased numbers of narratives dealing with brief episodes or particular events. Often, as for example with Giraldus Cambrensis' account of the conquest of Ireland, an ideological purpose is also clearly visible. Increasingly, especially in the Italian communes, the Norman kingdoms and the papal *Curia*, records began to be kept. From this point on, then, we are less at the mercy than in earlier periods of the particular circumstances, interests and biases of the historiographers. Often, though, the writers insert such documents into their narrative. When this occurs, it is often, without external corroboration, difficult to tell whether we are reading the original, a forgery, or an adaptation made to suit the tale the author wishes or needs to tell.

I THE MURDER OF THOMAS BECKET, 29 DECEMBER 1170

Henry II succeeded in 1154 to a kingdom which stretched from the north of England to the Pyrenees. On the advice of the archbishop of

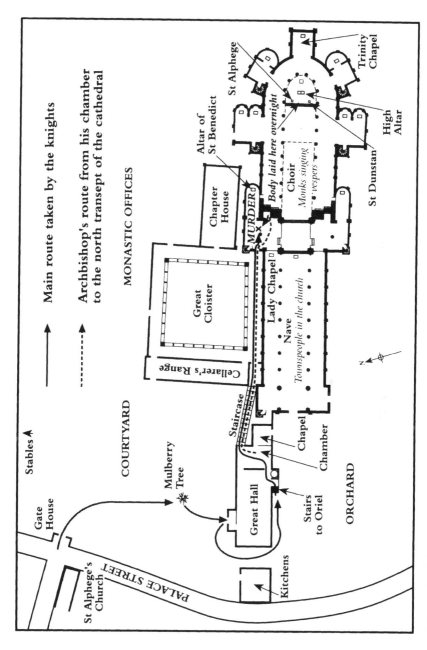

Main route taken by the knights

Archbishop's route from his chamber to the north transept of the cathedral

Gate House

St Alphege's Church

PALACE STREET

Stables

COURTYARD

MONASTIC OFFICES

Mulberry Tree

Kitchens

Great Hall

Stairs to Oriel

Chapel Chamber

ORCHARD

Staircase

Cellarer's Range

Great Cloister

Chapter House

Lady Chapel

Nave

Townspeople in the church

MURDER
X

Body laid here overnight

Choir
Monks singing vespers

Altar of St Benedict

St Alphege

High Altar

Trinity Chapel

St Dunstan

N

9 The murder of Thomas Becket.

Canterbury, Theobald, he entrusted the post of chancellor to a Canterbury clerk named Thomas Becket. Becket profited greatly from this position, during his tenure of which he neglected his duties as an archdeacon, but was able to offer direct access to the king for ambitious clerics like Arnulf of Lisieux and John of Salisbury. In 1162, a year after Theobald's death, Henry appointed Becket to the vacant see. He immediately resigned the chancellorship and began a belligerent campaign to restore lands and rights to Canterbury. In July 1163 he came into direct conflict with the king over a proposal to pay sheriff's aid into the royal treasury. Henry backed down. But in October, at the Council of Westminster, Henry would not withdraw a demand that accused clerks should answer in a lay court. Becket refused to accept this, despite the support of canon law. Henry's next move was to insist that the bishops accept the customs of the kingdom. Becket resisted, but was eventually bullied into agreeing at the Council of Clarendon in 1164. However, he refused to add his seal to the document. When a series of misjudgements brought Becket later that year to Northampton to answer for contempt of the king's court, he was adjudged guilty. The king insisted on his accounting for various sums for which he had been responsible and forbade his leaving until satisfaction had been made. Becket instructed the bishops not to be party to judgements against him in matters relating to his chancellorship, appealed to the Pope and ordered anyone who gave effect to a lay court's judgement upon him to be excommunicated. This was a direct contravention of the Constitutions of Clarendon. The bishops appealed to the Pope to depose Becket for perjury. The judgement of the king's court was sent to Becket. But by then, 2 November 1164, he had fled to France.

Becket remained in France for six years. From Easter 1166 he gained the support of Pope Alexander III. This made things harder for Henry, who was obliged eventually to agree to a reconciliation. This was made at Fréteval on 22 July 1170, but it was done in a way which left all the issues to be resolved later. In fact, a short while before, on 14 June, Henry had had his eldest surviving son and namesake crowned king of England at York. This provoked Becket's anger because coronation was Canterbury's prerogative, and before his return to England on 1 December, he had obtained from the Pope letters suspending the three prelates who had performed this ceremony.

Becket's return solved nothing, because he was adamant that he would not or could not revoke the sentences. In fact he confirmed the excommunications on Christmas Day in Canterbury Cathedral. During the weeks intervening between these two events, the young king and Becket had played a cat and mouse game, with the king ordering Becket to stop visiting royal cities and manors and to go back to Canterbury, and with Becket taking his time to obey. Eventually, Henry lost patience and uttered words which appeared to some of his vassals to suggest that Becket must be brought to book. Four of his knights set out for Canterbury with their retinue, possibly with the intention merely of arresting Becket. On arrival, they left their men outside the gate, entered with a single archer, dismounted, disarmed and went to seek an interview with the archbishop. It did not go well, ending with their arrest of the two knights guarding Becket. They returned to their armour, leaving two knights on horseback to secure the palace door for their return. The palace had already been secured from the city by their collaborators. However, the palace servants managed to shut the inner door and the knights were forced to break in by way of an upper gallery (an oriel). The noise prompted the archbishop's companions to urge him to escape into the cathedral, where Vespers were being sung. This they did by way of the cellarer's range. Becket insisted that the cross be borne before him. The extract tells the story from this point. See the plan (map 9) for the geography of these events.

The murder was hailed almost at once as a martyrdom. Miracles were recorded among others by John of Salisbury. Soon Canterbury was the centre of a vast pilgrimage industry, with people coming 'from every shires ende/of Engelonde.../the hooly blisful martir for to seke/that hem hath holpen whan that they were seeke' (Chaucer, General Prologue to the *Canterbury Tales*, ll. 15–18).

1. William FitzStephen (*fl.* 1170)

William FitzStephen was a clerk and friend of Thomas Becket, and a fellow Londoner. He was present at the murder and later produced one of the major biographies. He worked as a *dictator* ('drafter') in Becket's chancery and was his chaplain, subdeacon and judicial assistant. He was banished with Becket's household in 1164, but gained pardon from the king by presenting him with a rhyming prayer he had composed for his use. He rejoined Becket on his return in December 1170. It is probable that he went over again to the king's side after the murder, though the identification of him with the William FitzStephen who was sheriff of Gloucester from 1171 to 1179 and itinerant justice from 1175 to 1191 is unsubstantiated.

FitzStephen wrote his *Vita* in 1173–4. It is independent of the other contemporary accounts. His style is generally quite elevated, with occasional classical citation and a tendency towards biblical syntax.

See further: F. Barlow, *Thomas Becket*, London, 1986.

(i) *Becket enters the cathedral, followed by the conspirators and others.*

Intratum est in ecclesiam ipsam. Monachi ecclesiae pro tali et tanto tumultu tam pavidi quam attoniti, relictis et non percantatis vesperis, Domino archiepiscopo in ecclesiam intrante, a choro exeunt ei obviam, gaudentes et Deo gratiam habentes quod eum vivum cernunt et recipiunt, quem jam detruncatum audierant. Et cum alii prae gaudio vel timore flerent, alii hoc, alii   5 aliud suaderent, ut Petrus Domino dicens, 'Propitius esto tibi,' ille pro ecclesiae Dei libertate et causa non timidus mori jussit eos abire et a se recedere, utique ne impedirent passionem ejus, quam futuram praedixerat et imminere videbat. Iturus ad aram superius, ubi missas familiares et horas solebat audire, jam quatuor gradus ascenderat cum ecce ad ostium claustri,   10 quo veneramus, primus adest Raginaldus Ursonis loricatus, ense evaginato, et vociferans, 'Nunc huc ad me, homines regis!' Nec multo post adduntur ei tres praedicti socii ejus, similiter loricis contecti corpora et capita, praeterquam oculos solos, et ensibus nudatis. Plurimi etiam alii sine loricis, armati, de sequela et sociis suis, et aliqui de urbe Cantuariae, quos coactos secum illi   15 venire compulerant.

---

1 **Intratum est:** i.e. 'he, Becket...' (impersonal passive: see *RLGVE* 155). Becket had come from the adjoining palace, closely pursued by the knights.

pro...tumultu ('in the face of...') qualifies *pavidi* and *attoniti*; the verb is *exeunt* (picked up by *gaudentes* and *habentes*). The *tumultus* was caused by the knights, their followers and others who had forced their way into the monastery by a back entrance (see plan, map 9)

2f. **relictis...intrante:** two ablative absolutes, but translate the first as though a main clause with subject *monachi*, the second 'when...'.

3 **ei obviam:** 'to meet him'.

4 **eum** is picked up by *quem* (subject of the acc. + inf. *jam detruncatum*, sc. *esse*, introduced by *audierant* = *audiverant*: RLRGr A5).

5 **alii hoc** looks forward to *suaderent* (tr. 'and' before *alii*, which is part of the preceding *cum* clause).

6 **ut...tibi:** FitzStephen is a little mixed up here. He appears to be thinking of Lk 18.13, where the publican prays: *Deus propitius esto mihi peccatori* 'God be merciful unto me, a sinner'. Peter appears speaking to Jesus only at v. 28.

6f. **pro...causa** depends on *non timidus mori*. *Libertas* is a watchword of the cause of the Church in the dispute with the Empire and secular authority in general (see section 12 and 19.3 below).

8 **quam...praedixerat:** sc. *esse*. The biographers interpret many remarks made by Becket in his final hours as prophetic, but it is very doubtful that he conducted himself in such a way as deliberately to seek martyrdom, until he was left with no choice.

9 **superius:** i.e. the high altar (see map 9).

missas...horas: private Masses and the canonical hours (prime, terce, etc.: see section 2 Intro.).

10 **ad ostium** is picked up by *quo*.

11 **Raginaldus Ursonis:** Reginald FitzUrse, son of Richard, lord of Bulwick in Northamptonshire, the leader of the knights, though not the highest in rank. It was through Becket that he had obtained his place in the royal court.

12f. **tres...socii:** William de Tracy, baron of Bradninch in Devon, the oldest of the knights, Hugh de Morville, a younger man, but the highest in rank of the four, baron of Burgh-by-

Sands in Cumbria, and Richard le Bret (see below), the youngest of the group.

13 **contecti...capita:** tr. 'their bodies...covered by...'

(*capita* is acc. of respect: see RLRGr L(c)5).

14f. **Plurimi...alii...et aliqui...:** sc. 'entered'.

15 **coactos:** tr. 'under duress'.

(ii) *Becket refuses to allow the monks to bar the cloister door and all but three of the clerks run for cover.*

Visis, inquam, illis armatis, voluerunt monachi ostium ecclesiae obfirmare, sed bonus homo, fiduciam habens in Domino et non expavescens repentino terrore irruentes potentias impiorum, e gradibus descendit regressus, prohibens ne ostium ecclesiae clauderetur et dicens, 'Absit ut de ecclesia Dei castellum faciamus. Permittite intrare omnes ecclesiam Dei intrare volentes. 5
Fiat voluntas Dei.' Eo tunc a gradibus descendente versus ostium ne clauderetur, Johannes Saresberiensis et alii ejus clerici omnes, praeter Robertum canonicum et Willelmum filium Stephani et Edwardum Grim, qui novus ad eum venerat, praesidia captantes et se in tuto collocare curantes, relicto ipso, petiverunt alii altaria, alii latibula. 10

Though Becket had time and opportunity to run and hide, he preferred to await the hour of his martyrdom with patience, courage and constancy.

1 **inquam:** William means 'to return to what I was saying' (he has just mentioned that the coasts were being guarded against an attempt by Becket to flee the country).

2 **expavescens** (qualified by *repentino terrore* 'in...') looks forward to *potentias impiorum* (qualified by *irruentes* 'which...').

4 **ne:** 'that...'.
Absit ut: 'Let it not happen that...'.

5 **omnes** is picked up by *volentes* (completed by *ecclesiam...intrare*).

7 **Johannes Saresberiensis:** John of Salisbury (see sections 16.1 and 18.1); *et...omnes* is picked up by *captantes* and *se...collocare curantes* (the main

verb is *petiverunt*).

6f. **Robertum canonicum:** canon of Merton, Becket's chaplain and constant companion.

8 **Willelmum filium Stephani:** William FitzStephen, the author of this text.
Edwardum Grim: a stranger to Canterbury, who had arrived recently on the recommendation of Arnulf of Lisieux. He had lost the church at Saltwood during Becket's exile and could now hope to profit by Becket's return. His heroic attempt to save Becket's life is described below. He later wrote his own account of the murder.

(iii) *The murderers enter the cathedral church.*

Ecce jam illi spiculatores, furia invecti, praeter spem apertum cernentes cursim ostium intrant ecclesiae. 'Quo, quo scelesti ruitis?' 'Quis furor, o miseri? quae tanta licentia ferri?' Quidam autem illorum monachis dixit, qui cum eo astabant, 'Ne vos moveatis.' Et quidem quasi confusi et attoniti, a reverentia vultus ejus illi grassatores primo retulerunt pedem, viso archiepiscopo. Postea 5

clamavit aliquis, 'Ubi est ille proditor?' Archiepiscopus, suam in patientia animam possidens, ad verbum illud non respondit. Aliquis item: 'Ubi est archiepiscopus?' Ille: 'Ecce ego, non proditor, sed presbyter Dei, et miror quod in tali habitu ecclesiam Dei ingressi estis. Quid placet vobis?' Unus grassator: 'Ut moriaris. Impossibile est ut vivas ulterius.' At ille: 'Et ego in nomine   10
Domini mortem suscipio et animam meam et ecclesiae causam Deo et beatae Mariae et sanctis hujus ecclesiae patronis commendo. Absit ut propter gladios vestros fugiam: sed auctoritate Dei interdico ne quempiam meorum tangatis.' Aliquis eorum bisacutam et gladium simul habuit, ut in securi et bisacuta, si eis obfirmaretur, ostium dejicerent ecclesiae. Sed retento gladio, bisacutam, quae   15
adhuc ibi est, deposuit.

1   **apertum** looks forward to *ostium* (obj. of *cementes* and governing *ecclesiae*; *cursim* goes with *intrant*).

2   **Quo…ruitis:** Horace, *Epodes* 7.1.

2f. **Quis…ferri:** Lucan, *Bellum Ciuile* I.8; sc. 'is this' with *Quis furor*; sc. 'is' with *quae…ferri* (tr. *ferri* 'with…', depending on *licentia*).

4   **Ne…moveatis:** 'Don't…' (*RLGVE* 152.2).

4f. **a…ejus:** 'from…' (because he looked so holy).

6f. **suam** looks forward to *animam* (obj. of *possidens*).

11 **animam meam** (obj.) looks forward to *commendo*.

12 **sanctis** (noun 'saints' or adj. 'holy') looks for-

ward to *patronis* (governing *hujus ecclesiae*: if *sanctis* is a noun, *patronis* is in apposition). These were St Dunstan (910–88) and St Aelfege (*c.*954–1012), both buried near the high altar.

Absit ut: 'Let it not be that…'.

14 **ut** looks forward to *dejicerent* (obj. *ostium …ecclesiae*).

  in securi et bisacuta: 'with…' (see G.15(a)(ii)).

14f. **si…obfirmaretur:** 'if it (the door) were to have been shut against them'.

15 **bisacutam** (obj.) looks forward to *deposuit*.

(iv) Becket stands his ground and despite the intervention of Edward Grim is seriously wounded in the head.

Quidam eum cum plano ense caedebat inter scapulas dicens, 'Fuge, mortuus es.' Ille immotus perstitit et cervicem praebens se Domino commendabat, et sanctos archiepiscopos martyres in ore habebat, beatum Dionysium et sanctum Aelfegum Cantuariensem. Aliqui dicentes, 'Captus es, venies nobiscum,' injectis manibus eum ab ecclesia extrahere volebant, nisi timerent quod   5
populus eum esset erepturus de manibus eorum. Ille respondens, 'Nusquam ibo. Hic facietis quod facere vultis et quod vobis praeceptum est,' quod poterat, renitebatur. Et monachi eum retinebant, cum quibus et magister Edwardus Grim, qui et primum a Willelmo de Traci in caput ejus vibratum gladii ictum brachio objecto excepit, eodemque ictu et archiepiscopus in capite inclinato et   10
ipse in brachio graviter est vulneratus.

1   **cum…ense:** i.e. 'with the flat of…'.

3f. **beatum Dionysium et Aelfegum Cantua-**

riensem: St Denis (d. Paris 250) and St Aelfege, Archbishop of Canterbury 1005–12, martyred on 9 April. He refused to allow himself to be ransomed from the Danes and was executed with a battleaxe.

5 **volebant, nisi timerent:** 'would have wanted, had they not...'.

7 **quod poterat:** 'as far as he could'.

8f. **Edwardus Grim:** see above on (ii) l. 8; the clause *qui...excepit* describes him (*ejus*, i.e. Becket's; *ictum* is the object of *excepit*, further qualified by *vibratum*, which is constructed with *a* and *in*; for *Willelmo de Traci*, see above on (i) l. 12f.)

11 **ipse:** Edward Grim.

(v) *Becket prepares himself for death and falls after a second blow. As he lies there he receives two more blows.*

Archiepiscopus a capite defluum cum brachio detergens et videns cruorem gratias Deo agebat, dicens: 'In manus tuas, Domine, commendo spiritum meum.' Datur in caput ejus ictus secundus, quo et ille in faciem concidit, positis primo genibus, conjunctis et extensis ad Deum manibus, secus aram quae ibi erat sancti Benedicti, et curam habuit vel gratiam ut honeste caderet, pallio suo cooperfus usque ad talos, quasi adoraturus et oraturus. Super dextram cecidit, ad dextram Dei iturus. 5

Eum procumbentem Ricardus Brito percussit tanta vi ut et gladius ad caput ejus et ad ecclesiae pavimentum frangeretur, et ait, 'Hoc habeas pro amore domini mei Willelmi, fratris regis.' Hic siquidem Willelmus appetiverat 10 conjugium comitissae de Warenna, sed archiepiscopus contradixerat, quo- niam hic Willelmus ex matre imperatrice Mahalt, ille comes Warennae Willelmus ex patre rege Stephano, consobrinorum fuerant filii. Unde Wil- lelmus, frater regis Henrici, inconsolabiliter doluit et omnes sui archiepiscopo inimici facti sunt. 15

Quatuor omnino habuit ictus sanctus archiepiscopus, omnes in capite, et corona capitis tota ei amputata est. Tunc videre erat quomodo artus spiritui famulabantur. Nam sicut nec mente, ita nec membrorum objectu vel dejectu morti visus est depugnare, quia mortem excepit magis ex Dei desiderio voluntariam, quam de gladiis militum violentam. Quidam Hugo de Horsea, 20 cognomento Malus Clericus, sancti martyris procumbentis collum pede comprimens, a concavitate coronae amputatae cum mucrone cruorem et cerebrum extrahebat.

1 **defluum:** here a noun, obj. of *detergens* ('having...': see G.20(a)).
videns: 'having...' (see G.20(a)).

2f. **In...meum:** Jesus' last words, according to Lk 23.46 (but in the Vulgate they are *Pater, in...meum*).

3 **Datur:** subject is *ictus secundus* (the tense is historic present: see *RLGVE* 112 Note).
quo: 'at...', 'because of...'.

et: 'also...' (Edward Grim had been felled by the first blow).

3f. **positis...manibus:** tr. 'having...' (*positis* sc. 'on the ground'). Becket adopted (or is piously represented as having adopted) an attitde of prayer and acceptance of God's will (not supplication of God to save him from death).

4f. **aram...Benedicti:** see plan (the murder took

place in the north transept, on Becket's route to the high altar).

5 **curam...vel gratiam:** i.e. either he deliberately did this or God's grace caused the action (viz. falling so that no part of his flesh was exposed). FitzStephen may have in mind Suetonius' description of Caesar's death (*Diuus Iulius* 82).

6 **quasi...oraturus:** he had already adopted the position of prayer. He fell forward on his face, a position often seen adopted by clergy, e.g. on stained glass windows, and probably to be interpeted as adoration.

7 **ad dextram...iturus:** Mk 16.19 says this is where Jesus sits. He is joined there by the holy martyrs.

8 **Ricardus Brito:** Richard le Bret, younger son of Simon, a military tenant of the lords of Dunster in north Somerset.

8f. **ad...ad...:** tr. 'on...on...'.

9 **Hoc habeas:** 'Take that' (jussive subjunctive: see *RLGVE* 152).

10 **Willelmi...regis:** the youngest of the three brothers, Henry II and Geoffrey being the others. He had died on 30 January 1170.

11 **comitissae de Warenna:** *de* 'of' (see G.15(d)). She was the countess of Surrey, widow of King Stephen's younger son, William of Boulogne, earl of Surrey.

12 **ex...imperatrice Mahalt** looks forward to *con-sobrinorum...filii* (first of two subjects); Matilda was the daughter of Henry I, and had been the wife of the German Emperor Henry V until his

death in 1125. Stephen was Henry I's nephew, so a first cousin of Matilda. Matilda had asked permission for the marriage in 1159, but it was banned by Becket in 1163 on the grounds of consanguinity (the pair were distant cousins). William's early death was put down by some of his friends to Becket's ban on the match. **ille** looks forward to *Willelmus*.

13 **ex...rege Stephano:** second subject of *fuerant*. Stephen reigned from 1135 to 1154, but Matilda pressed the claim – imposed by her father Henry I – of her husband Geoffrey Plantagenet, count of Anjou, and much of his reign was disrupted by civil war. In 1154, Henry II, grandson of Henry I and son of Matilda by Geoffrey, succeeded to the throne.

14 **archiepiscopo** ('to...') depends on *inimici*.

16 **Quatuor** looks forward to *ictus* (obj. of *habuit*), which is picked up by *omnes*.

17 **ei:** 'from him', tr. 'his'.
erat: 'it was possible'.

18 **mente...objectu...dejectu:** 'in...' (each of the last two governs *membrorum*).

19 **morti** depends on *depugnare*.
mortem is picked up by *magis...voluntariam*, *quam...violentam* (tr. 'a death which was...').

20f. **Hugo de Horsea...Clericus:** Hugo Mauclerk, a subdeacon with the party of knights.

21 **sancti...procumbentis** depends on *collum* (obj. of *comprimens*, which picks up *Hugo*).

23 **extrahebat:** tr. '...ed' (see G.9(a)).

(vi) *The writer expostulates on the cruelty of the deed and the constancy of Thomas. He reports the disturbance caused at his death, as at Christ's crucifixion, upon the elements.*

O triste spectaculum! O crudelitas inaudita eorum qui Christiani esse debuerant! Sed pejores sunt qui sub nomine Christiano opera agunt paganorum, quam qui aperte et ex errore paternarum traditionum sunt infideles. O vere felicem et constantem sanctum Dei martyrem Thomam! Occidi potuit, sed flecti non potuit.   5

Et quidem, sicut quondam Christo patiente in proprio corpore, ita et eodem nunc patiente in milite suo Thoma, avertit sol oculos, abscondit radios, obtenebravit diem, ne videret scelus hoc, et horrida tempestas caelum contraxit, subiti ruerunt imbres, intonuit de caelo. Postea rubor aeris magnus

emicuit in effusi sanguinis signum, in flagitii horrorem, in ultionis celeritatem   10
superventurae his qui ita immane se efferarunt et hoc piaculari se depravaverunt
et qui mortis hujus causa exstiterunt, exesa et exuta omni naturae humanae
mansuetudine.

2 **debuerant:** 'ought to have...'.
Sed...qui: '(those) who...'.
opera looks forward to and governs *paganorum*.
3 **quam qui:** 'than (those) who...'.
ex...infideles: such as Muslims, whose cruelty towards Christians is expected.
6 **Christo patiente:** 'when...'.
6f. **et...patiente:** 'when also the same person (i.e. Christ)...'.
8 **horrida...contraxit:** Horace, *Epodes* 13.1.
aeris is from *aër* (not *aes*).
9 **subiti** looks forward to *imbres*.

10 **in** looks forward to *signum* (tr. 'as...').
in...horrorem: tr. 'in...at...'.
10f. **in...superventurae:** tr. 'to mark...' (*ultionis...superventurae* depends on *celeritatem*).
11 **his:** 'to those...'.
efferarunt = *efferaverunt* (RLRGr A4).
12 **mortis...causa:** complement of *exstiterunt* (*hujus* = Becket).
exesa et exuta omni look forward to *mansuetudine* (governing *naturae humanae*); it is abl. abs. (tr. 'having...all...').

II. HENRY II AND IRELAND

One of Henry's main problems upon succession was his own family. To
bolster himself against the claims of his second brother Geoffrey to Anjou
and Touraine by providing a kingdom for another brother William, Henry
proposed at the Council of Winchester in September 1155 a plan to
conquer Ireland. John of Salisbury was sent to Rome to use his influence
with Hadrian IV. It seems that in the bull *Laudabiliter* Hadrian did make a
grant of permission for the conquest, but apparently in such a way as to
suggest that Ireland was in the papal gift. Henry solved the problem with
Geoffrey by an expedition in 1156. The Irish plan was shelved.

In 1166, Dermot MacMurrough (Diarmait Mac Murchada), king of
Leinster, was driven into exile. He appealed to Henry for help and did
homage to him. Henry as a result issued letters patent allowing his subjects
to give aid to Dermot. With the help of Norman colonists in Wales,
Dermot regained his kingdom by 1169. He had also made a bargain with
Richard FitzGilbert, son of the earl of Pembroke, for his daughter's hand
and the kingdom on his death in exchange for help. FitzGerald (known as
Strongbow) landed in August 1170, married Dermot's daughter and
inherited Leinster in 1171, despite Henry's withdrawal of support. For by
this time, Henry had revived his own plan of conquest. He stopped
reinforcements from reaching Strongbow and laid plans for his own
expeditionary force. Strongbow met him in Wales and did homage for

Leinster, but surrendered the seaports. Henry stayed in Ireland from
October 1171 to April 1172. He received the homage of many Irish chiefs,
held a Church council at Cashel and authorized ecclesiastical reforms. He
left Hugh de Lacy as Justiciar, but after his departure conquest was largely
left to adventurers, to balance whom Henry made pacts with local chiefs.
Another expedition, sent in 1185, was prompted by the refusal of Henry's
son Richard to surrender Aquitaine to his brother John. This expedition,
under John's leadership, was a complete failure.

2. Giraldus Cambrensis (1146–1223)

Giraldus Cambrensis, otherwise known as Gerald of Wales or Girault du
Barri, came from a Cambro-Norman family with strong royal connections.
He was a student first at St Peter's Abbey in Gloucester, then in Paris,
where in three visits he studied the *trivium*, canon law and theology.
Periods between visits were taken up with collecting benefices in Wales
and England, which gave him a sound financial base for the rest of his
career. In later life he obtained the see of St David's, but his election was
disputed and finally quashed, after vigorous campaigning by Giraldus
himself at Rome (1199–1203). He was a prolific writer. Among his many
works are the *Itinerarium Kambriae* ('Journey through Wales', 1191), the
Descriptio Kambriae ('Description of Wales', 1194) and the *Gemma
Ecclesiastica* ('Jewel of the Church', *c*.1197).

In 1184, after a trip to Ireland, he took a position as a royal clerk in
Henry II's court. One of his duties was to accompany Prince John to
Ireland on his unsuccessful campaign in 1185. The literary fruits of his two
visits were the *Topographia Hibernica*, completed around 1188, a description
of Ireland, its customs and its early history, and the *Expugnatio Hibernica*,
finished probably around 1189, an account of Anglo-Norman attempts to
subdue Ireland. The following extract is taken from the *Expugnatio*, which
was clearly written with a bias in favour of Giraldus' relatives the
FitzGeralds, who had formed the vanguard of the colonizing movement,
but were during the 1180s being pushed aside by more recent arrivals. One
of the remarkable features of the work is its quite critical view of Henry
II's relationship with the Church.

Giraldus was a keen Latin stylist, with a penchant for classical quotation.
Though he tells us that this work is written plainly, we should not be too
quick to believe him. He was fond of rhetorical embellishment and word
play, features which make his Latin at times quite difficult, and followed
classical precedent (notably Sallust) in composing pairs of speeches for
appropriate moments in the narrative.

See further: A. B. Scott, F. X. Martin, *Giraldus Cambrensis, Expugnatio Hibernica*, Dublin, 1978.

A portrait of Henry II.

Erat igitur Anglorum rex Henricus secundus vir subrufus, cesius, amplo capite
et rotundo, oculis glaucis, ad iram torvis et rubore suffusis, facie ignea, voce
quassa, collo ab humeris aliquantulum demisso, pectore quadrato, brachiis
validis, corpore carnoso et, nature magis quam gule vicio, citra tumorem
enormem et torporem omnem moderata quadam immoderancia ventre   5
preamplo. Erat enim cibo potuque modestus ac sobrius, et parsimonie, quoad
principi licuit, per omnia datus. Et ut hanc nature iniuriam industria reprimeret
ac mitigaret, carnisque vicium animi virtute levaret, bello plus quam intestino
tamquam in se coniurans, immoderata corpus vexacione torquebat. Nam
preter bellorum tempora que frequenter imminebant, quibus, quod rebus   10
agendis supererat, vix id tantillum quieti dabat, pacis quoque tempore sibi nec
pacem ullam nec requiem indulgebat. Venacioni namque trans modestiam
deditus, summo diluculo equo cursore transvectus, nunc saltus lustrans, nunc
silvas penetrans, nunc montium iuga transcendens, dies ducebat inquietos:
vespere vero domi receptum, vel ante cenam vel post rarissime sedentem   15
conspexeris. Post tantas namque fatigaciones, totam stacione continua curiam
lassare consueverat. Sed quoniam hoc *adprime in vita utile, ut nequid nimis,*
nullumque remedium simpliciter bonum, cum tibiarum pedumque tumore
frequenti, recalcitrancium ad hec iumentorum ictibus aucta lesione, ceteras id
ipsum corporis incommoditates accelerabat, et si non aliam, matrem malorum   20
omnium ac ministram certe vel senectutem.

1 **amplo capite...**: 'with...' (the rest of the sentence continues with a string of ablatives of
description).
2 **ad iram**: 'when he was angry'.
4 **et, nature...vicio**: 'and through the fault of...'
(*nature, gule* are gen. s.; see O.1); *et* joins *corpore
carnoso* with *ventre preamplo*, which is explained
by *nature....immoderancia.*
  citra: tr. 'stopping short of...' (+ acc.).
5 **moderata...immoderancia**: 'through...' (note
the oxymoron; Giraldus is fond of verbal
games).
6 **cibo potuque**: 'in...' (ablatives of respect with
modestus ac sobrius).
  parsimonie: dat. – see O.1 (looking forward to
datus; cf. English 'given to...').

7 **nature**: gen. s. (see O.1).
  industria: abl. 'by means of...' (the subject of the
verbs is Henry).
8 **bello...intestino**: 'in...' (depending on *in se
coniurans*); this is a joke, depending on two
senses of *intestinus*, 'civil' and 'intestinal'.
9 **immoderata** looks forward to *vexacione*
('with...').
10 **quibus**: 'during which...'.
10f. **quod...supererat**: 'what (sc. time) was left
from...' (*quod* is picked up by *id tantillum*,
obj. of *dabat*).
12 **Venacioni** looks forward to *deditus.*
13 **equo cursore**: i.e. 'on a swift horse'.
15 **receptum**: sc. 'him when...'.
16 **conspexeris**: 'you would have...'.

totam looks forward to *curiam; stacione continua* 'by...' depends on *lassare*.

17 **adprime...nimis**: 'is especially useful in life, viz. "nothing in excess"'; a classical quotation, from Terence, *Andria* I.i.34 (v. 61).

18 **nullumque...bonum**: sc. *est* (still in the *quoniam* clause).

   cum looks forward to *tumore*: tr. 'what with...'.

19 **recalcitrancium** (= *recalcitrantium*: see O.2)

   ...lesione: the phrase contains an abl. abs.

aucta lesione 'the injury being increased', which is amplified by *ictibus* 'by...', further defined by *recalcitrancium...iumentorum*; *ad hec* refers ungrammatically back to *tibiarum pedumque*.

ceteras looks forward to *incommoditates*.

19f. **id ipsum**: subject of *accelerabat*, i.e. 'his excessive physical activity'.

21 **vel**: 'in other words'.

III. FREDERICK BARBAROSSA AND THE PAPACY

Frederick was the elected king of Germany from 1152 to 1190, and in 1155 was crowned Holy Roman Emperor by the recently elevated Pope Hadrian IV. This coronation had taken place after negotiations with his predecessor Pope Eugenius III, leading to the Treaty of Constance in March 1153. This marked the continuance of the policy of Conrad III, Frederick's predecessor, of close co-operation between Empire and Papacy, and alliance against Norman Sicily and the citizens of Rome. But the Italian expedition undertaken to secure the imperial crown which began in late 1154 was not a success, and Barbarossa's plan for a campaign against Sicily had been brought to an abrupt end by the withdrawal of the German princes whose power was the basis of Frederick's. By 1156, Frederick had begun to change tack. The curtailment of the Sicilian war, the retreat of Frederick and successes by William of Sicily had also forced Hadrian to make peace with the enemy in the Treaty of Benevento. Frederick regarded this as a definite contravention of the Treaty of Constance. From this point on until July 1177, when he made his peace with Alexander III, Frederick and the Papacy were at war, and a new schism had come about in which anti-Popes reigned alongside Popes.

Frederick's new plan was based on the establishment for himself of a secure power base, virtually a new and tightly organized state in a geographically defined area, Alsace and Swabia in the north, Burgundy to the west, Lombardy to the south. The change was marked by the appointment of a new chancellor, Rainald von Dassel, archbishop of Cologne, in May 1156. Above all he was a man, albeit a cleric, who nurtured a deep hostility to the Papacy and was committed to the superiority of the Empire as a sacred institution. Hence, whenever Frederick's new policy required attacks on the Papacy, Rainald was always in the forefront.

The first move, however, was made by Pope Hadrian and his closest adviser, Cardinal Roland. They were finding it difficult to keep to the political pattern established by the Treaty of Benevento because of opposition in the *Curia*. But an incident in Frederick's territory gave them an opening. Eskil, bishop of Lund in Sweden, was seized by robbers in 1156 on his way back through Germany after paying his respects to Hadrian in Rome. Frederick did not lift a finger to help, probably because Eskil had been responsible for the withdrawal from the see of Hamburg of the northern churches, which Frederick saw as 'imperial' property. Hadrian and Roland took this opportunity to send a legation in September to Frederick's court, which was being held at Besançon. Its purpose was to use a protest at Eskil's continued captivity to raise publicly the sensitive issue of the superiority of Papacy over Empire and so to provoke a response which would send danger signals to the anti-Benevento party in Rome. The extracts tell the story of this opening skirmish in the long battle between Barbarossa and the Papacy.

3. Rahewin (d. after 1170)

Rahewin was secretary and chaplain to Otto of Freising, who had completed two books of the *Gesta Friderici* by the time of his death (1158). On his deathbed, Otto charged Rahewin with the continuation of his work. Barbarossa endorsed this request, and Rahewin wrote books 3 and 4, continuing Otto's work from August 1157 to February 1160, the Synod of Pavia. Though he lived another ten years after this, Rahewin left off writing about June 1160. It seems that he was writing to a prearranged design, intended to promote the idea that Frederick's new plan had been implicit from the start of his reign. This is evidenced in particular by the omission by Otto of the Treaties of Constance and Benevento (see above). The decision to end with the triumph of the anti-Pope Victor IV at Pavia seems very much in line with this ideological structure.

Rahewin was also a poet. He was well-read and purports to objectivity through presenting original documents. His style is elegant and at times complex. The papal letters which form much of this section make use of the system of rhythmical sentence construction and especially sentence ending known as the *cursus* (see further section 17.4 Intro.).

See further: P. Munz, *Frederick Barbarossa*, London, 1969.

(i) *Frederick comes to Besançon in Burgundy in mid-October 1157 to hold court, which is attended by both subjects and foreigners eager to pay him honour as the new*

Emperor (crowned by Pope Hadrian IV in 1155). Rahewin postpones narration of the proceedings at Besançon until after he has dealt with the incident involving the messengers from Pope Hadrian, which had important consequences. These were important men, both cardinals, and one was Roland Bandinelli, Hadrian IV's chief adviser, later as Pope Alexander III (1159–81) a supporter of the Sicilian party and a fierce opponent of Barbarossa. In this extract, he describes their reception by Frederick and their greeting. The writer gives his reasons for including the documents relating to this and other issues.

Principe ergo die quodam a strepitu et populi tumultu declinante, in cuiusdam oratorii privatiore recessu predicti nuncii in conspectum eius deducti ab eoque (ut oportebat, sicut qui boni se nuncii baiolos assererent), benigne et honeste recepti sunt. Exordium autem sermonis illorum in fronte ipsa notabile comparuit, quod tale fuisse dicitur: 'Salutat vos beatissimus pater noster papa   5
Adrianus et universitas cardinalium sanctae Romanae aecclesiae, ille ut pater, illi ut fratres.' Paucisque interpositis, litteras quas ferebant protulere. Quas et aliarum quae in hac turbulentia hinc inde discurrebant rescripta litterarum idcirco huic operi interserere curavi, ut quivis lector qui in partem declinare voluerit, non meis verbis vel assertionibus, sed ipsarum partium propriis scriptis   10
tractus et vocatus libere eligat utri parti suum velit accommodare favorem.

1 **Principe** looks forward to *declinante* (abl. abs.).
   in governs *privatiore recessu* (governing *cuiusdam oratorii*).
2 **nuncii:** subject (picked up by *deducti*, sc. *sunt*).
   ab eoque: *-que* includes *ab*, introducing the second verb *recepti sunt*.
3 **ut...qui...assererent:** 'as...in the case of people who...' (*boni* looks forward to *nuncii*, which depends on *baiolos*; sc. *esse* with *se...baiolos*, acc. + inf. depending on *assererent*).
4 **notabile:** complement of *comparuit*.
6 **Adrianus:** Pope Hadrian IV (1154–9), born Nicholas Breakspear near St Alban's in England. His earlier career had seen him abbot of Saint-Ruf in Provence, then cardinal-bishop of Albano and head of the Norwegian missions.

ille ut pater: the implication could be thought to be that the Pope claimed not only spiritual but also temporal priority over the Emperor.
7 **protulere** = *protulerunt* (RLRGr A4); subject is 'the messengers'.
   Quas ('This' sc. *litterae*), obj. of *interserere*; a second obj. is *rescripta* governing *aliarum... litterarum* and picked up by *quae...discurrebant*.
9 **idcirco** looks forward to *ut* (verb *eligat*).
   quivis lector is picked up by *qui...voluerit* (tr. 'wishes') and then by *tractus et vocatus* (on which the ablatives *non meis...scriptis* depend).
11 **utri parti:** 'to which side...' (dependent on *accommodare*; *suum* looks forward to *favorem*, direct object of *accommodare*).

(ii) *In his letter, Pope Hadrian reprimands Frederick for not taking steps to release from the hands of German brigands Eskil, archbishop of Lund, despite a previous letter from Hadrian.*

Adrianus episcopus, servus servorum Dei, dilecto filio Friderico, illustri Romanorum imperatori, salutem et apostolicam benedictionem.

Imperatoriae maiestati paucis retroactis diebus recolimus nos scripsisse, illud horrendum et execrabile facinus et piaculare flagitium tempore nostro commissum in Teutonicis partibus, sicut credimus aliquando intemptatum, 5 excellentiae tuae ad memoriam revocantes, nec sine grandi ammiratione ferentes quod absque digna severitate vindictae usque nunc transire passus sis tam perniciosi sceleris feritatem. Qualiter enim venerabilis frater noster E. Lundenensis archiepiscopus, dum a sede apostolica remearet, a quibusdam impiis et scelestis (quod sine grandi animi merore non dicimus) in partibus illis 10 captus fuerit et adhuc in custodia teneatur, qualiter etiam in ipsa captione predicta viri impietatis, semen nequam, filii scelerati in eum et in suos evaginatis gladiis violenter exarserint et eos, ablatis omnibus, quam turpiter atque inhoneste tractaverint et tua serenissima celsitudo cognoscit atque ad longinquas et remotissimas regiones fama tanti sceleris iam pervenit. Ad cuius 15 utique vehementissimi facinoris ultionem, sicut his cui bona placere, mala vero displicere credimus, constantius exurgere debuisti et gladium qui tibi ad vindictam malefactorum, laudem vero bonorum est ex divina provisione concessus, in cervicem desevire oportuit impiorum et gravissime conterere presumptores. Tu vero id ipsum ita dissimulasse diceris, seviciam neglexisse, 20 quod eosdem non est quare peniteat commisisse reatum, quia se inpunitatem sacrilegii quod gesserunt iamiam sentiunt invenisse.

Hadrian adds that the reason for this inaction is unknown to him, since he has not knowingly offended the Emperor or his office. In the next extract, he reminds Frederick of the attitude of the Church, proven by the action of his coronation in 1155. He has no regrets about this coronation, and would even have been glad had the Emperor received even greater beneficia from him. But his current attitude to Eskil's capture makes Hadrian fear that Frederick has some cause for annoyance with the Church.

Debes enim, gloriosissime fili, ante oculos mentis reducere quam gratanter et quam iocunde alio anno mater tua sacrosancta Romana aecclesia te susceperit, quanta cordis affectione tractaverit, quantam tibi dignitatis plenitudinem 25 contulerit et honoris et qualiter imperialis insigne coronae libentissime conferens benignissimo gremio suo tuae sublimitatis apicem studuerit confovere, nichil prorsus efficiens quod regiae voluntati vel in minimo cognosceret obviare. Neque tamen penitet nos tuae desideria voluntatis in omnibus

implevisse, sed si maiora beneficia excellentia tua de manu nostra suscepisset, si   30
fieri posset, considerantes quanta aecclesiae Dei et nobis per te incrementa
possint et commoda provenire, non inmerito gauderemus. Nunc autem, quia
tam inmensum facinus, quod in contumeliam universalis aecclesiae et imperii
tui noscitur etiam commissum, negligere ac dissimulare videris, suspicamur
utique ac veremur ne forte in hanc dissimulationem et negligentiam propter   35
hoc tuus animus sit inductus, quod suggestione perversi hominis zizania
seminantis adversus clementissimam matrem tuam sacrosanctam Romanam
aecclesiam et nos ipsos indignationem, quod absit, aliquam conceperis vel
rancorem.

To deal with this and other matters, Hadrian has sent Cardinals Bernhard and
Roland with full powers to represent his view and asks Frederick to treat them well.

2 **salutem...benedictionem:** sc. 'sends'.

3 **Imperatoriae maiestati:** 'To (sc. your)...' (indir. obj. of *nos scripsisse*, which is acc. + inf. introduced by *recolimus*).

retroactis: tr. 'ago'.

3f. **illud...commissum** (picked up by *sicut...intemptatum*) is obj. of *revocantes* (agreeing with the subject of *recolimus; excellentiae tuae* depends on *ad memoriam*).

7 **ferentes quod:** 'putting up with the fact that...' (the verb is *passus sis* and the object *feritatem*, qualified by *tam...sceleris*).

8-15 **Qualiter..pervenit:** the basic structure is *Qualiter...teneatur, qualiter...exarserint et...quam turpiter...tractaverint* 'How...how, and how ...ly...' which are introduced by *et... cognoscit atque...fama...pervenit*.

8 **E.:** Eskil, bishop of Lund in Sweden. See Intro.

10 **quod...dicimus:** 'a thing which we...'.

12 **viri...scelerati:** subject of *exarserint* (the phrase is based on Isaiah 1.4: *Vae...semini nequam, filiis sceleratis* 'Woe to the evil seed, criminal sons'); *viri impietatis = viri impii*.

13 **eos:** obj. of *tractaverint*, inside the *quam* clause.

15 **Ad** governs *ultionem* (on which *cuius...facinoris* depends) and is completed by *exurgere debuisti*.

16 **his cui** = *is qui* (see O.3(c)), 'the sort of man to whom we...' (*bona...displicere* are acc. + inf. depending on *credimus*).

17 **gladium** (picked up by *qui...est...concessus*; note that *ad* governs both *vindictam* and *laudem*, before which supply *et*) goes with *oportuit* 'your sword ought to have...' (governing

desevire and *conterere*).

19 **in cervicem** looks forward to *impiorum*.

20 **id ipsum:** i.e. the capture of Eskil.

ita goes with *dissimulasse* and *seviciam neglexisse* (asyndeton; supply *et*) and looks forward to *quod* 'that...' (result: see G.26(b)).

21 **non est quare:** 'there is no reason why...'; *eosdem* goes with *peniteat* ('these same men ought to...'), which governs *commisisse* (tr. 'having... ed...').

se is the subject of *invenisse* (introduced by *sentiunt* and having as object *inpunitatem*, which governs *sacrilegii* 'for the...').

23f. **Debes...obviare:** the main structure is *Debes...reducere quam...et quam...susceperit, quanta...tractaverit, quantam...contulerit et...qualiter... studuerit confovere, nichil...efficiens quod... cognosceret obviare.* The subject of all the subordinate clauses, picked up by *efficiens*, is *mater tua...aecclesia.*

25 **quanta** looks forward to *affectione*; sc. *te* with *tractaverit.*

quantam looks forward to *plenitudinem* (which governs *dignitatis* and *honoris*).

26 **imperialis** looks forward to *coronae* and both depend on *insigne* (obj. of *conferens* 'by...ing').

27 **tuae sublimitatis** depends on *apicem* (obj. of *confovere*); the phrase means 'your supreme highness' (cf. *affectio uestra* in section 2.4(i)).

28f. **quod...obviare:** 'which it (i.e. the Church) knew would...' (*obviare* governs *regiae voluntati*).

28 **in minimo:** sc. 'degree'.

29 **penitet** governs *implevisse* (obj. *desideria*, governing *tuae...voluntatis*).

30 **maiora beneficia** is obj. of *suscepisset*; the apodosis of the *si...suscepisset* clause is *non...gauderemus*.

31 **considerantes** agrees with the subject of *gauderemus*.

quanta looks forward to *incrementa...et commoda* (subjects of *possint...provenire*, which governs *aecclesiae...et nobis*).

33 **tam...facinus** (picked up by *quod...commissum* (sc. *esse*)) is the object of *negligere ac dissimulare videris*.

35 **in...negligentiam** depends on *sit inductus*.

35f. **propter hoc** looks forward to *quod* ('because...').

36f. **zizania seminantis:** based on Mt 13.25 (*venit inimicus eius et superseminavit zizania in medio tritici* 'an enemy of his came along and sowed tares in the middle of his wheat'). The reference is to Rainald von Dassel (see section 19.III Intro.).

37f. **adversus...rancorem:** the basic structure is *adversus...ipsos indignationem...aliquam conceperis vel rancorem*.

38 **quod absit:** lit. 'which may it be absent', i.e. 'Heaven forfend!'.

(iii) *The letter is interpreted for the court by the anti-papal chancellor, Rainald von Dassel, who focuses attention on the apparent claim that the Empire is a fief awarded to the Emperor by the Pope. This interpretation is accepted by them because of their knowledge of a painting at Rome depicting the Emperor Lothair as a papal vassal, with an inscription claiming papal superiority. Frederick had earlier asked the Pope to remove this inflammatory article and the Pope had agreed.*

Talibus litteris lectis et per Reinaldum cancellarium fida satis interpretatione diligenter expositis, magna principes qui aderant indignatione commoti sunt, quia tota litterarum continentia non parum acredinis habere et occasionem futuri mali iamiam fronte sua preferre videbatur. Precipue tamen universos accenderat quod in premissis litteris inter caetera dictum fuisse acceperant 5 dignitatis et honoris plenitudinem sibi a Romano pontifice collatam et insigne imperialis coronae de manu eius imperatorem suscepisse, nec ipsum penitere, si maiora beneficia de manu eius suscepisset, habita consideratione, quanta aecclesiae Romanae per ipsum possent incrementa et commoda provenire. Atque ad horum verborum strictam expositionem ac prefatae interpretationis 10 fidem auditores induxerat quod a nonnullis Romanorum temere affirmari noverant imperium Urbis et regnum Italicum donatione pontificum reges nostros hactenus possedisse, idque non solum dictis, sed et scriptis atque picturis representare et ad posteros transmittere. Unde de imperatore Lothario in palatio Lateranensi super eiusmodi picturam scriptum est: 15

Rex venit ante fores, iurans prius Urbis honores,
Post homo fit papae, sumit quo dante coronam.

Talis pictura talisque superscriptio principi, quando alio anno circa Urbem fuerat, per fideles imperii delata cum vehementer displicuisset, amica prius invectione precedente, laudamentum a papa Adriano accepisse memoratur, ut 20 et scriptura pariter atque pictura talis de medio tolleretur, ne tam vana res summis in orbe viris litigandi et discordandi prebere posset materiam.

1 **lectis et** looks forward to the second ablative participle *expositis* (on which *per...interpretatione* depends).

Reinaldum: Rainald von Dassel (see section 19.III Intro.).

fida satis interpretatione: 'by means of...', 'in...'; *fida satis* suggests that Rainald explained in German, keeping closely to the Latin text.

2 **magna** looks forward to *indignatione* (depending on *commoti sunt*).

3 **tota...continentia** is the subject of *videbatur* (which governs *habere* and *preferre*).

5 **accenderat quod:** 'it had upset (lit. set on fire)...that...'.

dictum...acceperant: 'they had understood that it had been said that...' (introducing acc. + inf. *dignitatis...plenitudinem* (subject) *sibi* (i.e. to them)...*collatam* (sc. *esse*) *et insigne* (obj.)...*imperatorem* (subject) *suscepisse, nec ipsum* (i.e. the Pope) *penitere, si... provenire*).

8 **quanta** looks forward to *incrementa et commoda* (subject); the clause is introduced by the abl. abs. *habita consideratione* (which in this résumé parallels *considerantes* in the papal letters).

9 **per ipsum:** i.e. the Emperor.

10 **ad** governs *expositionem* (on which *horum verborum* depends) and *fidem* (governing *prefatae interpretationis*); the subject of *induxerat* is *quod...transmittere* (tr. 'what had...towards... was the fact that...').

11f. **quod...possedisse:** the structure is *a...affirmari*

('that it was...') introduced by *noverant* and followed by another acc. + inf. *imperium...et regnum* (objects)...*reges nostros* (subject)... *possedisse*.

13f. **idque...transmittere:** another acc. + inf. introduced by *affirmari*; the subject (unstated) is 'they' (i.e. 'the Romans') and the object *id* (i.e. 'this view').

14 **Lothario:** Lothair III, German King 1125–7, Emperor 1133–7.

17 **homo...papae:** i.e. does homage to the Pope for his *feudum*, the Empire.

quo dante: tr. 'on whose bequest he...'.

18f. **Talis...displicuisset:** a subordinate clause introduced by *cum* ('when'); tr. *talis* as 'this' throughout this sentence.

18 **principi** depends on *displicuisset*.

alio anno: the date was 1155.

19 **delata** picks up *Talis pictura talisque superscriptio* and is qualified by *per...imperii* ('by men faithful to...').

19f. **amica...precedente:** 'after a...had...' (see G.20(a)).

20 **laudamentum...memoratur:** subject (unstated) 'the Emperor'.

ut expands *laudamentum* (tr. 'requiring that...').

22 **summis** looks forward to *viris* (dat. with *prebere...materiam*) and *in orbe* qualifies the phrase. **litigandi et discordandi** depend on *materiam* (tr. 'for...and...').

(iv) *The turbulent atmosphere created by this letter among Frederick's nobles is stoked up by a claim from one of the ambassadors of papal superiority. He is threatened with death by Otto von Wittelsbach, count palatine of Bavaria. Frederick calms the meeting and orders the legates to be sent directly back to Rome.*

His omnibus in unum collatis, cum strepitus et turba inter optimates regni de tam insolita legatione magis ac magis invalesceret, quasi gladium igni adderet, dixisse ferunt unum de legatis: 'A quo ergo habet si a domno papa non habet imperium?' Ob hoc dictum eo processit iracundia ut unus eorum, videlicet Otto palatinus comes de Baioaria, ut dicebatur, exerto gladio cervici illius   5 mortem intentaret.

At Fridericus auctoritate presentiae suae interposita tumultum quidem compescuit, ipsos autem legatos securitate donatos ad habitacula deduci ac primo mane via sua proficisci precepit, addens in mandatis ne hac vel illac in

territoriis episcoporum seu abbatum vagarentur, sed recta via, nec ad dexteram 10
nec ad sinistram declinantes, reverterentur ad Urbem.

1 **His omnibus...collatis:** 'when all these things...' (tr. in unum 'together').

1f. **de...legatione:** 'from...' (i.e. 'because of...').

2 **quasi...adderet:** 'as if to...' (the subject is to be inferred from the following *unum*).

3 **dixisse** is introduced by *ferunt* ('they say') and has *unum de* ('one of...') as subject.

habet: subject (unstated) 'the Emperor'.

4 **eo** ('to such an extent') looks forward to *ut*.

5 **illius:** i.e. the legate who had claimed papal superiority.

7 **auctoritate** looks forward to *interposita* (abl. abs.) and governs *praesentiae suae*.

8f. **ipsos...proficisci** depends on *precepit* ('he ordered them...to...': see G.17(b), 23(a)).

9 **via sua:** 'on their way' (see G.11(e)(iii)).

ne has two verbs, *vagarentur* and *reverterentur*.

hac vel illac: 'this way or that' (i.e. off the specified route).

(v) *An imperial letter addressed to the Pope is sent out to Frederick's subjects expressing his anger at the papal message brought to Besançon. At the outset the claim is made that it is God who has given power to Frederick and that it is a matter of great sadness that a poison which may produce a schism seems to be emanating from the head of the Church. Frederick describes what happened at Besançon from his viewpoint. The letter ends with a refutation of papal claims to confer power, based on 1 Peter 2.17: 'Fear God, but honour the king', and an appeal to the Pope not to sully the honour of the Empire.*

As business proceeded at the Besançon court, the papal legates returned to Rome and encouraged the Pope to make a response. The Curia was split on the issue. The Pope wrote an open letter to the German archbishops and bishops about the issue. In the first part he states that any slight on the Church should quickly be corrected and follows this observation with his view of the incident at Besançon, which he says arose from the use of the term beneficium, and the resulting imperial ban on travel to Rome through German territories. He comforts himself that this action was not taken on the advice of the recipients of this letter. In the extract, he asks his prelates to bring Frederick back into line and gain satisfaction for Rainald's and Otto's blasphemies. He should follow the path of other Catholic Emperors.

Quocirca, fratres, quoniam in hoc facto non solum nostra, sed vestra et omnium aecclesiarum res agi dinoscitur, karitatem vestram monemus et exhortamur in Domino quatinus opponatis vos murum pro domo Domini et prefatum filium nostrum ad viam rectam quam citius reducere studeatis, attentissimam sollicitudinem adhibentes, ut a Reinaldo cancellario suo et 5
palatino comite, qui magnas blasphemias in prefatos legatos nostros et matrem vestram sacrosanctam Romanam aecclesiam evomere presumpserunt, talem et tam evidentem satisfactionem faciat exhiberi, ut, sicut multorum aures

amaritudo sermonis eorum offendit, ita etiam satisfactio multos ad viam rectam
debeat revocare. Non acquiescat idem filius noster consiliis iniquorum,   10
consideret novissima et antiqua et per illam viam incedat per quam Iustinianus
et alii katholici imperatores incessisse noscuntur. Exemplo siquidem et
imitatione illorum et honorem in terris et felicitatem in caelis sibi poterit
cumulare.

*If they achieve this, they do a service to the Church and its liberty. They should let
Frederick know that the Church is built upon a rock and cannot be shaken whatever
hurricanes strike it. They must advise him of this and bring him to a better
understanding of the issue.*

1f. **nostra...vestra...aecclesiarum** looks forward
to *res* ('business', 'interest').
2 **agi dinoscitur:** lit. 'it is recognized as being
conducted', tr. 'is clearly at stake'.
3 **quatinus:** 'to...' (indirect command: see
G.23(d)).
murum: sc. 'as'.
4 **prefatum...nostrum:** i.e. the Emperor (obj. of
reducere).
quam citius: 'as quickly as possible' (see
G.12(a)).

5f. **ut a...comite:** the construction is completed by
talem...satisfactionem (governing *a...comite*) *faciat*
('cause to...': see G.17(c)) *exhiberi*.
6 **magnas blasphemias** is the object of *evomere*
(governed by *presumpserunt*).
8 **multorum aures:** obj. of *offendit*.
10 **debeat revocare:** 'may recall' (*debeo* + inf. used
for the subjunctive of *revocare*: see G.25(c)).
11 **novissima et antiqua:** Ps. 138.5 (*Ecce, Domine,
tu cognovisti omnia, novissima et antiqua*).
Iustinianus: Roman Emperor from 527 to 565.

(vi) *The German prelates put to the Pope the difficulty of the situation. The dispute
threatens to escalate, since the claims in the papal letter to Besançon simply could not
be countenanced by the Emperor or his nobles. This anger has meant that they have
been unable to sustain the papal position. However, they have taken the lead offered
by the papal letter to them and warned the king of the consequences of the situation.
His reply is basically as follows, that God has exalted the Church through putting
the Empire at the head of the world. Now, against God's will, the Church is trying
to destroy the Empire. In conclusion the prelates ask the Pope to write in a softer
tone to avoid a clash between Church and Empire.*

*Hadrian thinks again and sends two envoys more sympathetic to the imperial
cause to Frederick at Augsburg. After a perilous journey during which, possibly at
the instigation of Rainald, they are captured and held to ransom, they arrive and
after a salutation marked by its humility and modesty, they present Hadrian's reply.
'Since I became Pope I have studiously given honour to you. So I was very
surprised by the treatment of my legates to Besançon.'*

The extract contains an explanation of precisely what was meant by the term
beneficium *and the phrase* contulimus tibi insigne imperialis coronae.

Occasione siquidem cuiusdam verbi, quod est 'beneficium', tuus animus, sicut dicitur, est commotus, quod utique nedum tanti viri, sed nec cuiuslibet minoris animum merito commovisset. Licet enim hoc nomen, quod est 'beneficium', apud quosdam in alia significatione quam ex inpositione habeat assumatur, tunc tamen in ea significatione accipiendum fuerat, quam nos ipsi posuimus et quam 5 ex institutione sua noscitur retinere. Hoc enim nomen ex 'bono' et 'facto' est editum, et dicitur beneficium aput nos non feudum, sed bonum factum; in qua significatione in universo Sacrae Scripturae corpore invenitur, ubi ex beneficio Dei, non tamquam ex feudo, sed velut ex benedictione et bono facto ipsius gubernari dicimur et nutriri. Et tua quidem magnificentia liquido recognoscit, 10 quod nos ita bene et honorifice imperialis dignitatis insigne tuo capiti imposuimus, ut bonum factum valeat ab omnibus iudicari. Unde quod quidam verbum hoc et illud, scilicet 'contulimus tibi insigne imperialis coronae', a sensu suo nisi sunt ad alium retorquere, non ex merito causae, sed de voluntate propria et illorum suggestione, qui pacem regni et aecclesiae 15 nullatenus diligunt, hoc egerunt. Per hoc enim vocabulum 'contulimus' nil aliud intelligimus nisi quod superius dictum est 'imposuimus'.

Frederick was mollified, but asked the legates to settle a number of practical disputes, which Rahewin comments were to lead to a new rupture. The legates assured Frederick that the Pope had no intention of detracting from the dignity of the Empire, and were sent on their way with the sign of peace and gifts.

1 **Occasione** depends on *est commotus.*
2 **utique nedum...nec:** 'never mind...not even' (*tanti viri* and *cuiuslibet minoris* (sc. *viri*) depend on *animum*, obj. of *commovisset*).
3 **Licet** ('although') looks forward to *assumatur.*
4 **ex inpositione:** 'from its...(sc. by us)'.
  tunc: i.e. at Besançon.
5 **accipiendum fuerat:** 'ought to have been taken' (see G.4(a)).
7 **non...factum:** it is probable that Pope Hadrian and Cardinal Roland deliberately engineered this challenge to imperial power, reserving the position now taken up by the Pope by the ambiguity of the word *beneficium.* See section 19.III Intro.

8 **in universo** looks forward to *dicimur* (governing *gubernari...et nutriri*).
10 **tua...magnificentia:** i.e. 'you, Frederick' (cf. *tuae sublimitatis* in section 19.3 (ii)).
11 **imperialis dignitatis** is governed by *insigne* (object of *imposuimus*).
12 **valeat...iudicari:** 'it can be...' (*valeo* + inf. used for the subjunctive of *iudicari:* see G.25(c)).
  quod ('the fact that') looks forward to *nisi sunt* (from *nitor*)...*retorquere* (objects *verbum hoc et illud* (sc. 'saying')).
14f. **non ex...sed de...suggestione** looks forward to *hoc egerunt* (*de* 'through' governs both *voluntate* and *suggestione*).
16f. **nil aliud...nisi quod...est:** 'nothing other than what was expressed above as...'.

Section 20
Court literature

It is difficult to produce for the twelfth century a meaningful categorization of what we might today call literary works. Poetry served a number of purposes, including as well as entertainment the presentation of historical narrative, theological controversy and philosophical reflection (see section 18.4). Prose also crossed the boundary between the utilitarian and the amusing (e.g. Walter Map's *De nugis curialium* 'Courtier's trifles'). The best that can be said is that the more vigorous intellectual atmosphere provided space for the production and consumption of literary material which aimed to divert rather than primarily to instruct (though this object was never far away). It was in the regal and the episcopal courts that writers found their talents welcome and a society which would reward the effort of composition of lighter as well as more profound works in the traditional language. The lyric poetry of the period, composed to be sung, contains much of real value. The satirical verse is often pungent and at the same time unspecific. Epic poetry of classical depth is produced. However, the primary impression one gets is of a highly sophisticated society which understands very well how and when to make jokes about subjects (such as the sin of lust) which everyone knew were circumscribed by very clear theological laws.

1. Andreas Capellanus (*fl.* 1180)

The author of the treatise *De amore* calls himself at one point in the work 'Chaplain to the royal court'. This he may well have been, but the treatise itself and other external evidence suggests that at the time of its composition, *c.*1186, he was a dignitary at the court of Marie, countess of Champagne, in Troyes. Marie was a great patron of vernacular romance.

In particular, she encouraged the poet Chrétien de Troyes to deal with the adulterous love of Lancelot and Guinevere in his *Le chevalier et la charrette*, which embodies in its narrative the theory found in Andreas' treatise. It seems very likely that the playful treatment of the themes of love, sex and marriage according to a theory which dances on the margins of scholastic argumentation, Christian polemic and classical poetry (Ovid's *Ars amatoria* gives the work its structure) was a speciality of Marie's circle. *De amore*, however, must have been written primarily for a scholarly, that is clerical, audience, presumably to provide the sort of amusement in prohibited matters which is even now occasionally found at the dinner tables of celibate priests.

The treatise consists of three books. In the first a definition of love is given, its nature is discussed and a brief account is given of how to win it. This is followed by a series of eight dialogues on questions of love between women and men of varying social status. Book 2 tells how to preserve love. Book 3 contains a condemnation of love, returning to the standard Christian views on matters such as adultery. The essentially light-hearted approach to secular love of the first two books has many elements in common with love poetry of the period. In that sense, *De amore* makes a good introduction to collections such as *Carmina Burana* (see section 20.2 below). Andreas writes an elegant Latin. He demonstrates a wide knowledge of Ovid in particular, but knows some other classical writers at first hand also.

See further: *Andreas Capellanus on Love*, ed. and tr. by P. G. Walsh, London, 1982.

(i) *The love of nuns is to be avoided at all costs, and the man who ignores this injunction is to be held in contempt.*

Sed sollicitus quaerere posses quid de monacharum fateamur amore. Sed dicimus earum solatia tanquam animae pestem penitus esse vitanda, quia maxima inde coelestis sequitur indignatio patris, et publica inde iura potenter armantur et supplicia minantur extrema, et totius ex hoc crescit in populo mortificativa infamia laudis. Immo et in ipsius praecepto monemur amoris, ne   5
illius mulieris eligamus amorem cuius de iure nuptias nobis interdicitur affectare. Sed si aliquis sui ipsius et iuris utriusque contemptor monialis quaerat amorem, ab omnibus meretur contemni et est tanquam detestabilis belua fugiendus. Non de ipsius potest fide immerito dubitari, qui propter momentaneae delectationis actus gladii non veretur incurrere crimen nec Deo   10
vel hominibus fieri scandalum erubescit. Monacharum igitur penitus con-temnamus amorem et earum solatia quasi pestifera refutemus.

---

1 **sollicitus...posses:** lit. 'you might be able eagerly to ask', i.e. 'you might be eager to know...'.

de looks forward to *amore* (and the phrase governs *monacharum*).

2 **earum solatia** looks forward to *penitus esse vitanda.*

3 **maxima** looks forward to *indignatio* and governs *coelestis...patris*.

inde: (with *sequitur*) 'from this' (with *armantur, minantur*) 'against this'.

4 **supplicia** looks forward to *extrema*, obj. of *minantur*.

totius looks forward to *laudis*, which depends on *mortificativa infamia* (tr. 'infamy which kills your whole reputation').

5 **in** looks forward to *praecepto*, on which *ipsius...amoris* depends.

6 **illius mulieris** depends on *amorem*.

cuius looks forward to *nuptias* (object of *affectare*); *interdicitur* is impersonal passive ('it is...').

7 **sui...utriusque** depends on *contemptor*, in apposition to *aliquis* (the two laws are canon law –

see section 16.3 Intro. – and the laws of the state).

monialis (gen.) looks forward to *amorem*.

8 **quaerat:** tr. 'seeks' (irregular condition: see G.28(b)).

et est looks forward to *fugiendus*.

9 **Non...dubitari:** lit. 'It cannot undeservedly be doubted about...', i.e. 'It is right to have doubts about...'.

de looks forward to *fide* (governing *ipsius* 'of him...', looking forward to *qui*).

propter looks forward to *actus* (on which *momentaneae delectationis* depends).

10 **gladii** looks forward to *crimen* ('a crime involving (a sentence to death by) the sword').

11 **Monacharum** looks forward to *amorem*.

(ii) *Not that it is impossible. But Andreas warns his dedicatee off by the example of his own close encounter.*

Non autem haec dicimus, quasi monacha non possit amari, sed quia utriusque inde provenit damnatio mortis. Et ideo ad ipsarum sollicitationem pertinentia verba te volumus penitus ignorare. Nam tempore quodam quum quandam monacham nobis pervenerit opportunitas alloquendi, monacharum sollicitationis doctrinae non ignari facundo artis eam sermone coegimus nostrae acquiescere   5
voluntati; et nos tanquam mentis caecitate prostrati et quid deceret nullatenus recolentes, quia 'Quid deceat, non videt ullus amans' et iterum 'Nil bene cernit amor, videt omnia lumine caeco', statim coepimus ipsius attrahi pulchritudine vehementi et dulciore facundia colligari. Interim tamen eam qua ducebamur vesaniam cogitantes a praedicta mortis dormitione summo sumus excitati labore.   10
Et quamvis multum credamur in amoris arte periti et amoris praedocti remedia, vix tamen eius novimus pestiferos laqueos evitare et sine carnis nos contagione removere.

Cave igitur, Gualteri, cum monialibus solitaria quaerere loca vel opportunitatem desiderare loquendi quia, si lascivis ludis locum ipsa persenserit aptum, tibi   15
non crastinabit concedere quod optabis et ignita solatia praeparare, et vix unquam poteris opera Veneris evitare nefanda scelera sinistra committens. Nam quum nos, omni astutos ingenio et qualibet amoris doctrina vigentes, earum coegit vacillare suavitas, qualiter sibi tua imperita poterit obstare iuventus? Amor igitur talis tibi sit fugiendus, amice.   20

1 **utriusque** looks forward to *mortis* ('to...', dependent on *damnatio*: i.e. it is not only a capital crime on earth, it is also a mortal sin and leads

to damnation after death).

2 **ad** looks forward to *sollicitationem*, which depends on *pertinentia* (with *verba*, obj. of *ignorare*).

3f. **quandam monacham** is the object of *alloquendi* (which depends on *opportunitas*).

4f. **doctrinae** depends on *non ignari*, **sollicitationis** on *doctrinae* and **monacharum** on *sollicitationis*.

5 **facundo** looks forward to *sermone*, upon which *artis* depends.

nostrae looks forward to *voluntati* (indir. obj. of *acquiescere*).

6 **quid deceret** is introduced by *nullatenus recolentes* (agreeing with *nos*).

7 **Quid...amans:** Ovid, *Heroides* 4.154.

7f. **Nil...caeco:** Pseudo-Ovid, *Remedia* 51.

8 **ipsius** depends on *pulchritudine vehementi* and *dulciore facundia*.

9 **eam** looks forward to *vesaniam* (picked up by *qua ducebamur*), object of *cogitantes*.

10 **summo** looks forward to *labore* (governed by *sumus excitati*).

11 **multum** qualifies *periti* (sc. *esse* with *credamur*).

amoris looks forward to *remedia*; **praedocti** governs *remedia* ('in...').

12 **eius** (i.e. 'love's') depends on *pestiferos laqueos*.

novimus: 'know how to...'.

sine looks forward to *contagione* (on which *camis* depends).

14 **Cave** ('take care not to...') governs *quaerere* and *desiderare*.

Gualteri: 'Walter', the young friend to whom the precepts are supposedly addressed. The search for a real person behind this name seems fruitless.

solitaria looks forward to *loca*.

13f. **opportunitatem** looks forward to *loquendi*.

15 **lascivis ludis** depends on *aptum* (with *locum*: tr. 'that the place is...').

ipsa: i.e. 'the nun'.

17 **opera** looks forward to *nefanda* (governing *Veneris*), while *scelera sinistra* is the object of *committens*.

18 **nos** is the object of *eanum...suavitas* and is picked up by *astutos* (qualified by *omni...ingenio*: 'in...') and *vigentes* (qualified by *qualibet...doctrina*).

19 **sibi:** 'them' (see G.11(e)(i)).

tua imperita looks forward to *iuventus* (subject of *poterit obstare*).

(iii) *Love is not for sons of the soil. Toil is their lot. They should not receive instruction in love.*

Sed ne id quod superius de plebeiorum amore tractavimus, ad agricultores crederes esse referendum, de illorum tibi breviter amore subiungimus. Dicimus enim vix contingere posse quod agricolae in amoris inveniantur curia militare, sed naturaliter sicut equus et mulus ad Veneris opera promoventur, quemad-modum impetus eis naturae demonstrat. Sufficit ergo agricultori labor assiduus et vomeris ligonisque continua sine intermissione solatia. Sed etsi quandoque licet raro contingat eos ultra sui naturam amoris aculeo concitari, ipsos tamen in amoris doctrina non expedit erudire ne, dum actibus sibi naturaliter alienis intendunt, humana praedia, illorum solita fructificare labore, cultoris defectu nobis facta infructifera sentiamus.

5

10

1f. **Sed...referendum:** the structure is *ne...crederes*, which introduces *id...ad agricultores esse referendum*; *quod...tractavimus* picks up *id*.

2 **de illorum** looks forward to *amore*.

3 **contingere posse:** impersonal 'that it...'.

in amoris looks forward to *curia*.

4 **sicut equus et mulus:** the example comes from Tobias 6.17.

5 **impetus** governs *naturae*.

6 **vomeris ligonisque** look forward to *continua...solatia* (a second subject of *sufficit*).

7 **licet raro:** 'albeit...'.

ultra looks forward to *naturam*, upon which *sui* depends.

amoris depends on *aculeo*.

ipsos is the object of *erudire*.

8f. **ne...sentiamus:** the basic structure is *ne, dum...intendunt...sentiamus*; *sibi* 'to them' de-

pends on *alienis*; *sentiamus* introduces an acc. +
inf. clause *humana praedia...facta* (sc. *esse*) in-

fructifera; *praedia* is picked up by *solita*; *illorum...labore* ('by...') depends on *fructificare*.

(iv) *If you fancy a peasant, then don't beat about the bush and be sure to use force.*

Si vero et illarum te feminarum amor forte attraxerit eas pluribus laudibus
efferre memento et, si locum inveneris opportunum, non differas assumere
quod petebas et violento potiri amplexu. Vix enim ipsarum in tantum exterius
poteris mitigare rigorem, quod quietos fateantur se tibi concessuras amplexus
vel optata patiantur te habere solatia, nisi modicae saltem coactionis medela   5
praecedat ipsarum opportuna pudoris. Haec autem dicimus non quasi
rusticanarum mulierum tibi suadere volentes amorem, sed ut, si minus provide
ad illas provoceris amandum, brevi possis doctrina cognoscere quis tibi sit
processus habendus.

1 **illarum** looks forward to *feminarum*, dependent
   on *amor*.
   eas is the object of *efferre*.
2 **locum** looks forward to *opportunum*.
   non differas: 'do not...' (jussive subjunctive:
   RLGVE 152. See also G.23(c)).
3 **violento** looks forward to *amplexu* ('by means
   of...').
   ipsarum depends on *rigorem*, obj. of *mitigare*
   (qualified by *exterius*).
   in tantum ('so much') looks forward to *quod*
   ('that...': result, see G.26(b)).
4 **quietos** looks forward to *amplexus*, obj. of
   concessuras (sc. *esse*), verb in the acc. + inf.
   introduced by *fateantur*.

5 **optata** looks forward to *solatia* (obj. of *habere*).
   modicae...coactionis depends on *medela*.
6 **opportuna** picks up *medela* and governs *pudoris*
   ('convenient for their modesty'); i.e. force is
   the only medicine for their modesty.
7 **rusticanarum mulierum** looks forward to
   amorem, object of *suadere*. See below 20.2(ii)
   for a poem in which the love of peasant-
   women appears to be approached according
   to Andreas' advice.
8 **ad illas** looks forward to *amandum* (*illas* is the
   object of *amandum*).
   brevi looks forward to *doctrina*.
   quis looks forward to *processus* (the verb is
   sit...habendus).

2. Carmina Burana

Poetic anthologies are a common phenomenon of the Middle Ages. The
eleventh-century *Cambridge Songs* fall into this category (see section 15.1),
as do the Arundel Lyrics, preserved in a late fourteenth-century miscellany,
but containing poetry of the twelfth century (edited C. J. McDonough,
Toronto, 1984). By far the most famous collection of this sort is the Codex
Buranus, discovered in 1803 in the Bavarian monastery of Benediktbeuern.
The manuscript was written around 1230, at the court of a prelate rather
than in the monastery where it was found. Its contents, however, reach
back into the eleventh and twelfth centuries. The 228 poems were
assembled by three different compilers, who by and large kept poems of the

same type together, satirical and moralizing first, then love-songs, then drinking and party songs. However, there is a miscellany in the middle, which has no particular theme. The collection ends with two religious plays. As well as anonymous material, which may well have been copied from memory or dictation, the collection takes poems from well-known writers such as Peter of Blois (see section 20.3), the Archpoet (see section 20.4), and Walter of Châtillon (see section 20.5). The selection originally had a musical basis, but only ten of the texts were given neumes by the scribe who wrote them down. Another twenty tunes were inserted by later hands. The music for part of 20.2 (i) below (*Exiit diluculo*) survives in a fourteenth century manuscript from Diessen, and for all of it, with religious words composed to it, in one of the same period from Spain. Recordings of the surviving music are available in the series Das Alte Werk (Telefunken-Decca SAWT 9455-A Ex (1965) and SAWT 9522-A (1968) and on two recent CDs (L'Oiseau lyre 425 117-2 (1989)).

Of the three poems chosen here, two are from the love-song section and one is from the miscellany. Numbers (i) and (ii) are pastourelles, a genre which involves a love-encounter with a shepherdess. Number (iii) is from the miscellaneous section of the collection. It is the lament of a swan who is being roasted, best known nowadays as one of the *Carmina Burana* of Carl Orff. All these poems are in rhythmical verse (see section 5 Intro. for notation).

See further: P. Dronke, *Medieval Latin and the Rise of the European Love Lyric*, Oxford, 1968.

(i) *A pastourelle; the love of clerics and peasants.*

The metre is stanzas of 7pp, 6p, 7pp, 6p, with rhymes ABAB x 2, CDCD and an extra syllable in the last line of the final stanza.

> Exiit diluculo
> rustica puella
> cum grege, cum baculo,
> cum lana novella.

> Sunt in grege parvulo   5
> ovis et asella,
> vitula cum vitulo,
> caper et capella.

Conspexit in caespite
scolarem sedere: 10
'quid tu facis domine?
veni mecum ludere.'

9 **Conspexit:** the subject is *rustica puella*. This stanza was regarded as spurious by the editor of the standard modern edition. But the music in the fourteenth-century Spanish ms. shows that it was conceived as part of the same poem.

10 **sedere:** tr. 'sitting'. The *scolarem* is a clerk, therefore in religious orders and supposedly celibate. Debates about the relative value of loving clerics or soldiers are also part of the repertoire of twelfth-century lyric.

12 **ludere:** 'to...' (inf. of purpose: see G.17(a)).

(ii) *Andreas Capellanus' advice on peasant women heeded?*

The metre is stanzas of 8p x 5, 6p, with rhymes AAAAAAB x 2, CCCCCCB, DDDDDDB, EEEEEEB, FFFFFFB.

Vere dulci mediante
non in Maio, paulo ante,
luce solis radiante,
virgo vultu elegante
fronde stabat sub vernante   5
canens cum cicuta.

Illuc veni fato dante.
nympha non est forme tante,
equipollens eius plante!
que me viso festinante   10
grege fugit cum balante,
metu dissoluta.

Clamans tendit ad ovile.
hanc sequendo precor: 'sile!
nichil timeas hostile!'   15
preces spernit, et monile
quod ostendi, tenet vile
virgo, sic locuta:

'Munus vestrum,' inquit, 'nolo,
quia pleni estis dolo!'   20
et se sic defendit colo.
comprehensam ieci solo;

clarior non est sub polo
vilibus induta!

Satis illi fuit grave,   25
michi gratum et suäve.
'quid fecisti,' inquit, 'prave!
ve ve tibi! tamen ave!
ne reveles ulli cave,
ut sim domi tuta!   30

Si senserit meus pater
vel Martinus maior frater,
erit michi dies ater;
vel si sciret mea mater,
cum sit angue peior quater,   35
virgis sum tributa!'

1, 3 **Vere...mediante, luce...radiante:** ablative absolutes, setting the scene, the first temporally, the second meteorologically. Subject (*virgo*) and verb (*stabat*) follow this introduction.

4 **elegante:** this form is used (for *eleganti*) because of the rhyme (see G.7(a)).

5 **fronde** looks forward to *sub vernante*.

6 **fato dante:** 'because...'.

7 **forme tante** = *formae tantae* (see O.1).

8–9 tr. lit. 'there is no nymph of such great beauty as to come up to her foot', i.e. (perhaps) 'not even a nymph can match the beauty of her mere foot' (her foot alone is more beautiful than any nymph).

9 **plante** = *plantae* (see O.1).

10 **que:** 'she'.
me...festinante: abl. abs. ('when she had seen me hurrying...').

11 **grege** looks forward to *cum balante*.

14 **sequendo:** '...ing' (as though agreeing with subject of *precor*: see G.18).

15 **timeas:** 'fear' (jussive subjunctive: see *RLGVE* 152).

16f. **spernit, tenet:** the subject is *virgo*.

22 **comprehensam:** sc. *virginem* (tr. 'when I had...').
solo: dat. expressing place to where (see G.16(a)).

24 **vilibus induta:** 'than a woman dressed in cheap clothing' (*induta* is abl. of comparison with *clarior*).

25 **Satis** looks forward to *grave, gratum* and *suave*.

27 **prave:** vocative.

29 **ne...ulli** is introduced by *cave*.

34 **sciret:** 'were to...'.

35 **cum:** 'since she...'.

36 **sum tributa:** tr. 'I would be...' (irregular condition: see G.28(b)).

(iii) *The roasting swan.*

The metre is stanzas of 8pp x 3 with rhyme AAA, CCC, etc., plus a refrain
of 4p x 2 and 6pp, with rhyme BBB.

1 Olim lacus colueram,
  olim pulcher exstiteram,
  dum cygnus ego fueram.
  miser! miser!
  modo niger   5
  et ustus fortiter!

2 Eram nive candidior,
  quavis ave formosior;
  modo sum corvo nigrior.
  miser! miser!   10
  modo niger
  et ustus fortiter!

3 Me rogus urit fortiter,
  gyrat, regyrat garcifer;
  propinat me nunc dapifer.   15
  miser! miser!
  modo niger
  et ustus fortiter!

4 Mallem in aquis vivere,
  nudo semper sub aere,   20
  quam in hoc mergi pipere.
  miser! miser!
  modo niger
  et ustus fortiter!

5 Nunc in scutella iaceo   25
  et volitare nequeo;
  dentes frendentes video −
  miser! miser!
  modo niger
  et ustus fortiter!   30

1f. **colueram, exstiteram, fueram** should all be
    translated as simple past tenses (see G.9(c)).
    They are probably used for the rhyme-scheme.
5f. **niger/et ustus:** sc. *sum.*
15 **propinat me:** sc. 'before the guests'.

20 **nudo** looks forward to *sub aere.*
21 **in hoc** looks forward to *pipere.*
27 **dentes frendentes:** those of the diners who are
    about to consume the swan.

3. Peter of Blois (*c*.1135–1212)

Born of aristocratic stock in Blois around 1135, Peter studied law at Bologna and was writing verse already as a young scholar at Tours. He became tutor to William II in Palermo, but had to leave in 1168. Eventually, he became secretary and chaplain to Henry II, on whose behalf he fulfilled several important diplomatic missions. It was probably at Henry's behest that he put together a collection of his letters. Upon Henry's death in 1189 he became the secretary of his wife Eleanor of Aquitaine. He was involved in the correspondence surrounding attempts to free her son, Richard the Lionheart, from his captivity in Germany.

His contemporary Walter of Châtillon (see section 20.5) names Peter as one of the four main Latin poets of the time. Although there are only eight poems ascribed to him by the manuscripts, recent scholarship assigns him about fifty-two extant pieces. These include love-songs, moral–satirical songs, political poems, religious lyrics, poems of repentance and poetic debates. Some appear in the *Carmina Burana*, others in the Arundel Lyrics (see section 20.2 Intro.). The debate reproduced here between a courtier and an individual who warns against the court, is reflected in two letters in Peter's own collection (nos. 14 and 150), in which he takes up respectively each of the positions of his poetic argument.

See further: P. Dronke, *The Medieval Poet and his World*, Rome, 1984, 281–339.

The poem is made up of 11 stanzas each of a different rhythmic structure and different rhyme-scheme.

> *Dehortans:*
> Quod amicus suggerit
> fer cum paciencia:
> desere palacia,
> nam curia
> curis, immo crucibus   5
> et mortibus
> semper est obnoxia.
>
> Figura mundi preterit;
> homo cum interierit
> non sumet secum omnia: 10
> dies hunc peremptoria

comprehendet,
nec descendet
eius cum eo gloria.

Curialis:
Quicquid dicas, hodie   15
curie
iuvant me delicie,
quarum prebent copie
quod in votis sum perplexus;
quo me vertam nescio   20
pre gaudio,
dum ad usum glorie
michi cedit omnis sexus,
etas et condicio –
totus feror in amplexus   25
voluptatis obvie.

Tenent nos in curia
cultus delicacior,
cibus exquisicior
et laucior,   30
et timeor, nec timeo,
et augeo
parentum patrimonia,
et intono magnalia;
me divitum consilia,   35
me tenent accidencia
dignitatum,
quas magnatum
largitur amicicia.

Dehortans:
Nexus abrumpe curie,   40
deo te totum immola:
tempus indulget venie
ficulnee
parabola;
Rachel abscondat ydola   45
sub fimo penitencie:
sumptus perdis et operas

si differas
oblatam tibi graciam,
vincis, regnas et imperas   50
si tangas Christi fimbriam
et ydriam
Samaritane deseras.

Curialis:
Stulti sunt qui miseri
volunt sponte fieri: 55
non est inpaciens
Christi clemencia,
sera sufficiens
est penitencia!
tu verba garriens,   60
Davi, non Edipi
presagis pessima
michi novissima –
sed sic intercipi
non potest anima,   65
nec laus est ultima
placere principi.

Dehortans:
Quid te iuvat vivere
si vis vitam perdere?
in anime   70
dispendio
nulla est estimacio:
si vis ut te perhennibus
absorbeant suppliciis
mors et inferna palus,   75
confidas in principibus
et in eorum filiis,
in quibus non est salus.

Curialis:
Grata est in senio
religio,   80
iuveni non congruit;
carnis desiderio

consencio,
nullus enim odio
carnem suam habuit.   85
neminem ab inferis
revertentem vidimus –
certa non relinquimus
ob dubia;
sompniator animus   90
respuens presencia
gaudeat inanibus –
quibus si credideris,
expectare poteris
Arturum cum Britonibus!   95

Dehortans:
Divicie
tam anxie
quas adquiris cum tormento,
ut sompnium
surgencium   100
evanescunt in momento:
sine fine
tanquam spine
pungunt, angunt, lacerant –
scis quid tibi conferant?   105
quod servus es servorum
dum in his te crucias
ut servias
clientum libidinibus
et ventribus   110
equorum.

Curialis:
Cur arguor
si perfruor
bonis que manus domini
dedit ad usum homini?   115
quociens voluero
miser esse potero:
si michi soli vixero,
toti sum mundo perditus –

benignus dei spiritus 120
non dedit ista celitus
ut in dolo nos eludat
et per ista nos detrudat
in puteum interitus!

Dehortans:
O vanitatum vanitas, 125
que est ista securitas
inter hastas hostium
frendencium?
astat mors in ianuis
et diffluis 130
in omne desiderium.
sed irruet calamitas
repente super impium,
voluptatumque brevium
mutabitur iocunditas 135
in eternum supplicium.

1 **Quod...suggerit** ('What...') is the object of *fer*.
4 **curia** looks forward to *est obnoxia* (which governs *curis...mortibus*).
11 **dies** looks forward to *peremptoria* (i.e. the day of death).
  hunc refers back to *homo*.
14 **eius** (i.e. of the man) depends on *gloria* (subject of *descendet*).
16 **curie** (= *curiae*: see O.1) depends on *delicie* (= *deliciae*, nom.: see O.1).
18 **copie** (= *copiae*: see O.1) depends on *quarum* (antecedent *delicie*).
19 **quod...sum perplexus**: 'what I embraced...', i.e. 'what I wished for'.
20 **quo...vertam** (deliberative subjunctive: *RLGVE* 152 Note 1) is introduced by *nescio*.
22 **dum**: 'because' (see G.30(a)).
  ad usum glorie (= *gloriae*: see O.1): 'to make use of my...'.
25 **totus**: 'completely'.
26 **obvie** = *obviae* (see O.1).
27 **Tenent** has two subjects, *cultus* and *cibus* (supply *et* before *cibus*).
35 **me** is the object of *tenent* and *consilia* is its first subject (the second being *accidencia*: this word evokes the

vocabulary of Aristotelian philosophy, in which an accident is only a secondary characteristic of matter; there is some irony here).
38f. **magnatum** depends on *amicicia*.
40 **Nexus** (acc.) governs *curie* (= *curiae*: see O.1).
42 **tempus** governs *venie* (= *veniae*: see O.1), and is the object of *indulget*; the subject is *ficulnee* (= *ficulneae*: see O.1) *parabola*. The parable occurs in Lk 21.29f. as a warning of the nearness of the end of time and the kingdom of God.
45f. **Rachel...penitencie** (= *penitentiae*: see O.1, O.2): *abscondat* 'let...' (jussive subjunctive: *RLGVE* 152). The reference is to Gen. 31.19 and 34, which had been allegorized in biblical commentaries as the Church burying worship of idols in penitence.
47 **sumptus**: first object of *perdis* (note that the subjunctives *differas, tangas* and *deseras* in the *si* clauses of ll.48 and 51 should be translated as ordinary present tenses: see G.28(b)–(c)); the object of *differas* is *graciam* (qualified by *oblatam tibi*).
51 **Christi fimbriam**: Mt 9.20 and 14.36 tell of people cured by touching the hem of Christ's garment.

52f. **ydriam Samaritane** (= *Samaritanae*: see O.1):
the story of the Samaritan woman who is asked
by Jesus for water and who eventually ends up
by leaving her water jar to tell people that he is
the Christ is told at Jo 4.7–30. In biblical
commentary her action was allegorized as
laying aside the burdens of wordly life and
the rejection of greed for worldly things.

54 **qui**: 'those who...'.
miseri is the complement of *fieri*.

58f. **sera** looks forward to *penitencia* (subject of *est*).

60f. **Tu...Edipi**: *Davi* and *Edipi* depend on *pessima...novissima*. In Terence, *Andria* 194, the
wily slave Davus pretended not to compre-
hend his master's threats in replying to them
'I'm Davus, not Oedipus' (so I can't, like
Oedipus, unravel an enigma). The threats
turn out to be futile. Here, then, the courtier
refutes the warnings given to him by his
opponent by claiming that they belong to
comedy rather than tragedy, and will not
therefore have the dire outcome claimed.

63 **novissima**: lit. 'last things', i.e. 'death'.

67 **placere principi**: complement of *est*. The idea
is borrowed from Horace, *Epistles* 1.17.35:
principibus placuisse viris non ultima laus est 'It is
not the lowest praise that one has pleased
leading men'. Note that the courtier uses
pagan allusions to counter the biblical wisdom
of the opponent.

70 **in** looks forward to *dispendio* (which governs *anime
= animae*: see O.1). The moral of ll.68–72, that
the soul is priceless, is based on Mt 16.26: *Quid
enim prodest homini, si mundum universum lucretur,
animae vero suae detrimentum patiatur? Aut quam
dabit homo commutationem pro anima sua?* 'What
does it profit a man if he gain the whole world
but suffers the loss of his own soul? Or what
shall a man exchange for his soul?' (cf. Mk 8.36–
7). The *vitam* of L. 69 is eternal life with Christ
after death.

73 **perhennibus** looks forward to *suppliciis*.

76f. **confidas...salus**: *confidas* (tr. 'trust') is jussive
subjunctive (*RLGVE* 152). The message here
derives from Ps. 145.2–3: *Nolite confidere in
principibus, in filiis hominum in quibus non est
salus* 'Do not trust in princes, in the sons of
men in whom there is no salvation'.

84f. **nullus...habuit**: *odio* looks forward to *habuit*

(obj. *carnem suam*). The *curialis* cheekily uses
St Paul against the religious arguments of the
preceding stanza (Ephesians 5.29: *Nemo enim
unquam carnem suam odio habuit* 'For no one
ever hated his own flesh'). But Paul was
speaking about marital fidelity ('Men ought
to love their wives as they do their own
bodies', v. 28).

86f. The *curialis* is thinking of pagan myths (Orpheus,
Theseus and Hercules all made descents to
Hades and returned). He rightly rejects them
as mere tales. But his audience will know that
the Resurrection of Christ was not a myth like
these. His support for the life of the world is
thus tantamount to blasphemy.

90 **sompniator**: a noun used as an adjective with
animus.

92 **gaudeat**: 'let it...' (jussive subjunctive: *RLGVE*
152).

93 **quibus** looks forward to *credideris*, and falls inside
the *si* clause.

94f. The Celts (*Britones*) believed that one day their
ancient king, Arthur, would return to save
them. This belief was regularly ridiculed (for
example, by Peter in a letter and by Joseph of
Exeter in his epic poem *Ilias*).

96 **Divicie** is picked up by *quas...tormento* (take *tam
anxie* with *adquiris*) and looks forward to
evanescunt (of which it is the subject).

100 **surgencium** (= *surgentium*: see O.2): 'of people
who...'.

103 **spine** = *spinae* (see O.1).

106 **quod...servorum**: 'that...' (result: see G.26(a)–
(b)). There is perhaps irony in the fact that the
Pope regularly styled himself *servus servorum
Dei* (note the consequent religious undertone
of *crucias*).

111 **equorum**: this may = *aequorum* ('of your peers'),
but since the *curialis* is here viewed as a rich
man and a *patronus*, it seems more likely that he
is using his wealth to feed retainers and
hunting horses.

114f. **bonis...homini**: the gift of God to man of the
good things of the earth is perhaps a reference
to Gen. 1.29–30: *Dixitque Deus: 'Ecce dedi vobis
omnem herbam...'* 'And God said, "Behold, I
have given you every plant...".' If so, the
curialis in his reply picks up the reference to
hunting in l. 111, since one of the things God

gave to man was the beasts of the earth for food.

119 **toti** looks forward to *mundo*, and **sum** to *perditus*. The *curialis* appears to be arguing that his sociable existence is preferable to the recommended Christian type of monastic solitude,

'dying to the world', as it was called.

122 **in dolo: 'by...'** (see G.15(a)(ii)).

124 **in...interitus:** the phrase is from Ps. 54.24.

125 **O...vanitas:** Ecclesiastes 1.2 (also 12.8).

134 **voluptatumque brevium** looks forward to *iocunditas* (on which it depends).

4. The Archpoet (*fl.* 1160)

Generally regarded as the most important Latin lyric poet of the Middle Ages, the Archpoet, whose real name is unknown, perhaps received his nickname from the fact that his patron was Rainald von Dassel, the archbishop of Cologne and archchancellor of Frederick Barbarossa (see further section 19.3). He was the son of a knight, born around 1130, and fades from the record after Rainald's death in 1167. Ten of his poems survive, eight of which are addressed to Rainald. One of these is the most famous lyric of the Middle Ages, the confession *Estuans intrinsecus ira vehementi* 'Burning inside with violent rage' (which can be found in *Love Lyrics from the Carmina Burana*, ed. and trans. P. G. Walsh, Chapel Hill and London, 1993). Another is a refusal of a request to write an epic dealing with the campaigns of Frederick Barbarossa. But one of the two poems not addressed directly to Rainald is a panegyric of Barbarossa. This pair recalls a similar strategy in Horace (*Odes* 4.14–15), and it is no surprise to find Rainald called 'Maecenas' by John of Salisbury upon his death. The Archpoet played Horace to Rainald's Maecenas. His ironic tone and his constant use of biblical parody make it rather difficult to be confident about the presence of any real-life situations in the works addressed to Rainald. However, the panegyric of Barbarossa is clearly a seriously-meant piece, and it is probable that Rainald's patronage of the Archpoet had some political significance.

It has been suggested that the poem printed here has a serious political function, despite its apparently personal appeal to the archbishop to recall the poet from an exile imposed on him because of his evil life. In April 1164, Barbarossa's anti-Pope Victor died. Frederick wished to end the schism, but Rainald had already had Paschal III appointed. In July 1164, Rainald visited Vienne, in Burgundy, to try to win over the Burgundian bishops to continued opposition to the offical Pope, Alexander III, and to obtain imperial troops. *Fama tuba dante sonum* seems to have been composed for public performance during this visit. Its learned allusions link Nineve(h) to Vienne (by anagram, cf. *agens/Agnes* in section 8.4(b)), represent Rainald as a Christ-like judge who will come on the Last Day with forgiveness in his heart, and represent the poet as a Jonah appealing to God for release from the whale so that he can preach repentance to the Ninevites. The message, then, is that the people and bishops of Vienne should repent of their opposition to Rainald, listen to the words of his errant *vates* ('poet/prophet') and be certain of receiving his pardon. In addition, as a cultural product, this composition of a German for a German prelate proclaims itself in no way inferior to works produced by Latin poets from a Romance-speaking area such as Burgundy.

See further: F. Cairns, 'The Archpoet's "Jonah-Confession" (Poem II): literary, exegetical and historical aspects', *Mittellateinisches Jahrbuch*, 18 (1983), pp. 168–93.

The poem is arranged in stanzas of varying length, made up of lines of 8p which rhyme with every other line in the stanza.

> Fama tuba dante sonum,
> excitata vox preconum
> clamat viris regionum
> advenire virum bonum,
> patrem pacis et patronum   5
> cui Vienna parat tronum.
> multitudo marchionum,
> turba strepens istrionum
> iam conformat tono tonum.
> genus omne balatronum   10
> intrat ante diem nonum,
> quisquis sperat grande donum.
> ego caput fero pronum,
> tanquam frater sim latronum,
> reus, inops racionum,   15
> sensus egens et sermonum.
>
> Nomen vatis vel personam
> manifeste non exponam,
> sed quem fuga fecit Ionam,
> per figuram satis bonam   20
> Ione nomen ei ponam.
>
> Lacrimarum fluit rivus,
> quas effundo fugitivus
> intra cetum semivivus,

tuus quondam adoptivus.   25
sed pluralis genetivus,
nequam nimis et lascivus,
michi factus est nocivus.

Voluptate volens frui
conparabar brute sui   30
nec cum sancto sanctus fui,
unde timens iram tui,
sicut Ionas Dei sui,
fugam petens fuga rui.

Ionam deprehensum sorte   35
reum tempestatis orte,
condempnatum a cohorte
mox absorbent ceti porte.
sic et ego dignus morte
prave vivens et distorte,   40
cuius carnes sunt absorte,
sed cor manet adhuc forte.
reus tibi vereor te
miserturum michi forte.

Ecce Ionas tuus plorat,   45
culpam suam non ignorat,
pro qua cetus eum vorat,
veniam vult et inplorat,
ut a peste, qua laborat,
solvas eum, quem honorat,   50
tremit, colit et adorat.

Si remittas hunc reatum
et si ceto das mandatum,
cetus, cuius os est latum,
more suo dans hiatum   55
vomet vatem decalvatum
et ad portum destinatum
feret fame tenuatum,
ut sit rursus vates vatum
scribens opus tibi gratum.   60
te divine mentis fatum

ad hoc iussit esse natum,
ut decore probitatum
et exemplis largitatum
reparares mundi statum.   65

Hunc reatum si remittas,
inter enses et sagittas
tutus ibo, quo me mittas,
hederarum ferens vittas.
non timebo Ninivitas   70
neque gentes infronitas.
vincam vita patrum vitas
vitans ea, que tu vitas,
poetrias inauditas
scribam tibi, si me ditas.   75

Ut iam loquar manifeste,
paupertatis premor peste
stultus ego, qui penes te
nummis, equis, victu, veste
dies omnes duxi feste,   80
nunc insanus plus Oreste
male vivens et moleste,
trutannizans inhoneste
omne festum duco meste,
res non eget ista teste.   85

Pacis auctor, ultor litis,
esto tuo vati mitis
neque credas inperitis!
genetivis iam sopitis
sanccior sum heremitis.   90
quicquid in me malum scitis,
amputabo, si velitis,
ne nos apprehendat sitis.
ero palmes et tu vitis.

1f. **Fama** and **vox** are both subjects of *clamat* (supply *et* between them); *tuba dante* is abl. abs. (*sonum* is obj. of *dante*); *clamat* introduces the acc. + inf. *advenire virum bonum*; *patrem...et patronum* is in apposition to *virum*.

7f. **multitudo** and **turba** are both subjects of *conformat* (supply *et* between them).

10f. **genus** and **quisquis...donum** are both subjects of *sperat* (supply *et* between them).

11 **ante diem nonum:** i.e. on the Ides. Rainald seems to have entered Vienne on July 7. A case has been made for allusion here to the *dies octavus*, 'the eighth day', another name for the *Dies Irae* or Day of Judgement. If so, Rainald

comes to Vienne as Christ will come on that last day, to judge the quick and the dead.

15f. Supply *et* before *reus* and *inops* and *egens* (tr. 'a person lacking...').

19 **quem...Ionam** is picked up in l. 21 by *nomen ei ponam* ('upon the one whom exile made a Jonah, I shall place the name of Jonah').

20 **Per figuram:** the use of allegory was one of the central modes of biblical exegesis (see section 3 Intro.). Jonah could be seen as a figure of the sinner, whose separation from God is imaged by Jonah's time in the belly of the whale. Jonah upon his release becomes the prophet of God to the people of Nineve(h), an anagram of Vienne. Hence the poet, by ascribing to himself a sinful disposition which led to exile from Rainald's presence, could use the Jonah *figura* to present himself as Rainald's redeemed prophet to the modern Ninevites, the people of Vienne. In addition to the figurative interpretation, there are allusions in the poem to details of the Jonah story as related in the Book of Jonah (e.g. his flight 1.3, his fear of the wrath of his Lord, 1.9, his lamentation, 2.3, 4.10, his ingestion by the whale and his escape, 2.1–11), and to aspects emphasized by medieval biblical exegesis.

22 **Lacrimarum** depends on *rivus* and is picked up by *quas...adoptivus*.

26 **pluralis genetivus:** 'my plural genitive', i.e. my lustful genitals. Such grammatical innuendo is quite common (see also l. 89).

29 **Voluptate** depends on *frui*.

30 **brute** (= *brutae*: see O.1) **sui:** cf. 2 Peter 2.22: *sus lota in volutabro luti* 'a pig wallowing in its own mud-pool'.

31 **cum sancto sanctus:** 2 Kings (= 2 Samuel) 22.26: *Cum sancto sanctus eris* 'With the holy you will be holy'.

32f. **unde...sui:** the poet pretends that, like Jonah fleeing to Tarshish when asked to preach to the Ninevites, he feared Rainald's just wrath at his sinful life and ran away.

35f. **Ionam** is the object of *absorbent* (subject *ceti porte* = *portae*: see O.1); the phrases *deprehensum* (picking up *Ionam*)...*orte* and *condempnatum* (also agreeing with *Ionam*) *a cohorte* tell Jonah's story: tr. 'having been...as...' (*sorte* refers to the lottery in which Jonah was selected as the

cause of the storm; *reum* governs *tempestatis orte* = *ortae*: see O.1), 'and having been...' (*cohors* refers to the other people on board Jonah's ship).

39 **Sic...morte:** sc. *sum*.

40 **vivens:** 'having...ed' (see G.20(a)).

41 **cuius...absorbe** (= *absorptae*: see O.1): sc. 'I' ('whose...'). Like Jonah, his flesh has been swallowed by a whale, which in his case represents his poverty.

43 **tibi** depends on *reus*.

43f. **vereor** is qualified by *forte* (adv.) and introduces the acc. + inf. *te miserturum* (sc. *esse*) *michi* ('that you will not...').

46 Supply *et* before *culpam...ignorat*.

48 Supply *sed* before *veniam vult*.

49 **a peste:** in his role as Jonah, the poet is still in the belly of the whale. i.e. his poverty.

50f. **quem...adorat:** '(you) whom he...'. Rainald is assimilated to God on the Day of Judgement, with the power to forgive or to condemn to perpetual torment.

52 **remittas:** the subjunctive mood is not significant; tr. as indicative (cf. *das* in l. 53).

56f. **vomet...gratum:** This sequence mirrors what happens to Jonah, viz. the whale vomits him up onto dry land (Book of Jonah 2.11) and he goes to prophesy to the Ninevites. The detail *decalvatum* comes from the iconographic tradition: Jonah is depicted as bald because he had shaved his head as a sign of penitence.

58 **feret:** sc. 'him'.
fame tenuatum ('made thin by...') .

61 **divine** (= *divinae*: see O.1) **mentis** depends on *fatum* (subject of *iussit*).

63f. **decore probitatum** and *exemplis largitatum* both refer forward to *mundi statum*: tr. 'when it has been...ed by your...and...ed by your..., you may...the *mundi statum*'.

69 **hederarum** depends on *vittas*: God grows for Jonah a vine (Book of Jonah 4.6), which for the exegetic tradition images security. But for the Archpoet, the ivy has also the pagan significance of a garland with which poets are crowned and thus recognized.

72f. **vita:** 'with my...'. Note the puns on *vita* and *vitare*.

77 **paupertatis** depends on *peste*.

81 Supply *sed* before *nunc*.

plus qualifies *insanus* and *Oreste* is abl. of comparison (Orestes was driven insane by the Furies after killing his mother Clytemnestra in revenge for her murder of his father Agamemnon).

85 **res** is qualified by *ista* (*eget* governs *teste*).

88 **credas:** 'believe' (jussive subjunctive: see *RLGVE* 152).

89 **genetivis iam sopitis:** 'now that my genitals...' (cf. l. 26).

90 **sanccior** = *sanctior* (see O.2).

91f. **quicquid** qualifies *malum* (obj. of *scitis*). The notion of cutting off the limb that offends

you (here presumably the Archpoet's *genetivus*) is from Mt 5.29–30. But *amputare* is also used in viticulture, meaning 'prune', so that the point of l. 93 is that the poet will prune himself so as to be more fruitful, as a pruned vine brings forth more grapes and so makes more wine (so banishing the possibility of thirst). Line 94 contains a reference to Jo 15.5: *Ego sum vitis, vos palmites*, which is suggested by the preceding image but means that he will depend upon Rainald like Christ's disciples upon Christ.

5. Walter of Châtillon (*fl.* 1170)

Walter was born near Lille, possibly around 1135. He studied at Paris and Rheims with Stephen of Beauvais, and later become a *magister* himself at Laon and at Châtillon, where he composed some lyric verse. He then left teaching for law, which he studied at Bologna. On going back to France, he became a protégé of William of the White Hands, archbishop of Rheims (1176–1202), who brought him to this city as a notary and public orator. It was to this prelate that Walter's major work, the *Alexandreis*, a ten-book epic of some 5,500 hexameters, was addressed, with the initials of the ten books spelling his name in Latin (GVILLERMVS). The reward for this labour was a canonry, probably at Amiens. Two traditions exist concerning his death. He died either of leprosy or of self-inflicted scourgings. The date of his death is unknown. It is still thought by some that he is identical with a Walter of Lille mentioned by John of Salisbury, who was intimately connected with the court of Henry II. In that case his connection will have ended in 1170 after Becket's murder (see section 19.I).

Walter wrote prose and poetry. His *Tractatus contra Iudaeos* ('Tract against the Jews') shows him dealing with a common topic of the period. His rhythmical poetry is often satirical, attacking in particular the Church of his day. The *Alexandreis*, however, is a thoroughly classical poem, designed to fill a gap left by ancient Roman poets. Walter's knowledge of pagan literature was exceptionally broad and deep. His main sources for the story are Quintus Curtius, Justin and Julius Valerius, but he constantly alludes to classical poetry, especially Virgil, Ovid and Lucan. Although some mss. report that it was begun in 1170, it is more likely that it was not started until Walter's patron became archbishop in 1176. The poem was an immediate success, being echoed in Henry II's epitaph (1189), and criticized by Alan of Lille in his *Anticlaudianus* (see section 18.4). By the thirteenth century, it was a school text.

Books I–VII are mostly occupied by an account of the conquest of Persia, which climaxes in book VII with the murder of Darius by his own followers (the subject of this extract and his burial in pomp by Alexander. Books VIII–IX recount the victories over the Scythians and the Indian Porus. Book X relates how Nature's agency leads to Alexander's death at the hands of Treachery.

See further: R. Telfryn Pritchard, *Walter of Châtillon, the Alexandreis*, Toronto, 1986.

(i) *The Macedonians search for Darius, but his wounded chariot-horses have transported him, barely alive, to a place near a fountain. Here he is discovered by a thirsty Macedonian, Polistratus, to whom Darius entrusts a final message to Alexander.*

Singula scrutantur Persarum plaustra nec usquam	235
dedecus inueniunt fati regale cadauer.	
regis enim trito deserto calle iugales,	
pectora confossi iaculis, in ualle remota	
constiterant, mortem Dărĭique suamque gementes.	
haut procul hinc querulus lasciuo murmure riuus	240
labitur et uernis solus dominatur in herbis.	
patrem riuus habet fontem qui rupe profusus	
purus et expressis per saxea uiscera guttis	
liquitur et siccas humectat nectare glebas.	
ad quem uir Macedo post Martem fessus anhelo	245
ore Polistrātus sitis incumbente procella	
ductus, ut arentes refoueret flumine fauces,	
curriculum Dărĭi uitam exhalantis opertum	
pellibus abiectis iumentaque saucia uidit.	
uidit et accedens confossum uulnere multo	250
inuenit Dărĭum turbatum lumina, mortis	
inter et extremae positum confinia uitae...	

235 **Singula** looks forward to *plaustra* (governing *Persarum*). The subject of *scrutantur* is 'the Macedonians'.

236 **dedecus** looks forward to *fati*, and *regale cadauer* is in apposition to it.

237f. **regis** depends on *iugales*, picked up by *confossi* (tr.

pectora 'in their...'), subject of *constiterant* in l. 239.

239 **suamque:** sc. *mortem*.

240 **querulus** looks forward to *riuus* and governs *lasciuo murmure* ('with...').

241 **uernis** looks forward to *in herbis*.

243 **expressis** looks forward to *guttis* (abl. abs.).

244 **siccas** looks forward to *glebas*, obj. of *humectat*.

245 **ad quem:** i.e. the *fons* just described.
   anhelo looks forward to *ore* in 246.

246f. **sitis** depends on *procella*, which in turn depends
   on *ductus* (picking up *uir Macedo...Polistratus*
   (the main verb is *uidit* in l. 249).

247 **arentes** looks forward to *fauces* (obj. of *refoueret*).

248f. The structure is *curriculum* (obj.) *Darii...exhalantis*
   (depends on *curriculum*) *opertum* (picks up

curriculum and is expanded by *pellibus abiectis*
'by...') *iumentaque saucia* (second obj.) *uidit*
(main verb, subject *uir Macedo...Polistratus*).

250 **confossum** looks forward to *Darium* in Ll. 251
   (obj. of *inuenit*).

251 **turbatum lumina:** lit. 'troubled in his eyes', i.e.
   'with troubled eyes'.

251f. **mortis** depends on *confinia* (as does *extre-
   mae...uitae*), which is governed by *inter*; *positum* picks up *Darium* in l. 251.

(ii) *Darius, after expressing his dying wish that Alexander should rule the world,
gives Polistratus his hand as a pledge to Alexander and shuffles off his mortal coil.*

'hoc unum superos uotis morientibus oro
infernumque Chaos, ut euntibus ordine fatis   295
totus Alexandro famuletur subditus orbis,
magnus et in magno dominetur maximus orbe,
utque michi iusti concesso iure sepulchri
a rege extremi non inuideantur honores.'
sic ait et dextram tamquam speciale ferendam   300
pignus Alexandro Greco porrexit, eique
letifer irrepsit per membra rigentia sompnus,
et sacer erumpens luteo de carcere tandem
spiritus, hospicium miserabile carnis abhorrens,
prodiit et tenues euasit liber in auras.   305

294 **hoc unum** and **superos** (joined by *infernum...Chaos* in l. 295) are the two objects of
   oro ('ask X for Y': *hoc unum* = Y and looks
   forward to *ut...orbe/utque...honores*).

295 **euntibus** looks forward to *fatis* (abl. abs.).

296 **totus** looks forward to *orbis*, subject of *famuletur.*

297 **et** is postponed and actually joins on a second verb
   (*dominetur*), whose subject is *Magnus* (*Alexander*); *in magno* looks forward to *orbe*; tr. *maximus*
   'as the greatest (sc. ruler)' and note the word
   play with *Magnus, magno* and *maximus.*

298–9 **michi** ('to...') depends on *concesso iure* (abl. abs.:
   iure governs *iusti...sepulchri*); *a rege* supplies the

agent to *inuideantur, extremi* looks forward to
honores (i.e. 'a funeral').

300f. **speciale** looks forward to *pignus* (tr. 'as a...').

301 **Greco:** i.e. *Polistrato* (*Alexandro* is indir. obj. of
   porrexit).
   ei: tr. 'his' (with *per membra rigentia*).

302 **letifer** looks forward to *sompnus* (subject of
   irrepsit).

303f. **sacer** looks forward to *spiritus* (picked up by
   abhorrens, obj. *hospicium miserabile carnis* and
   subject of *prodiit* and *euasit*); *luteo* looks forward to *de carcere*; *tenues* looks forward to *in
   auras.*

(iii) *Walter expostulates upon the way the soul is enticed from felicity by the desire
for the transient things of the world. If only it were different, crimes like that of
Bessus – and others which are more recent – would not occur.*

Felices animae, dum uitalis calor artus
erigit infusos, si pregustare daretur
que maneant manes decurso tempore iustos
premia, que requies, et quam contraria iustis
impius exspectet: non nos funestus habendi   310
irretiret amor, nec carnis amica libido
uiscera torreret; sed nec prediuite mensa
patrum sorberēt obscenus iugera uenter;
sed neque ferrato detentus carcere Bachus
frenderet horrendum fracturus dolia, nec se   315
inclusum gemeret sine respiramine Liber;
non adeo ambirent cathedrae uenalis honorem
Symonīs heredes; non incentiua malorum
pollueret sacras funesta Pecunia sedes;
non aspiraret, licet indole clarus auiti   320
sanguinis, inpubes ad pontificale cacumen
donec eum mores, studiorum fructus, et etas
eligerent, merito non suffragante parentum;
non geminos patres ducti liuore crearent
preficerentque orbi sortiti a cardine nomen;   325
non lucri regnaret odor; peruertere formam
iudicii nollet corruptus munere iudex;
non caderent hodie nullo discrimine sacri
pontifices, quales nuper cecidisse queruntur
uicinae modico distantes equore terrae.   330
sed quia labilium seducta cupidine rerum,
dum sequitur profugi bona momentanea mundi,
allicit illecebris animam carŏ, non sinit esse
principii memorem uel cuius ymaginis instar
facta sit aut quorsum resoluta carne reuerti   335
debeat. inde boni subit ignorantia ueri.
inde est quod spreta cupimus rationis habena
quod natura negat, facinusque paratus ad omne
non reueretur homo quod fas et iura uerentur.
inde est quod regni flammatus amore satelles,   340
non reuerens homines, non curans numina, Bessus
et patris et domini fatalia fila resoluit.
te tamen, o Dari, si que modo scribimus olim
sunt habitura fidem, Pompeio Francia iuste
laudibus equabit, uiuet cum uate superstes   345
gloria defuncti nullum moritura per euum.

306 **Felices animae:** sc. 'Would be'.
artus (obj. of *erigit*) is picked up by *infusos* ('infused by it', i.e. *uitalis calor*).

307 **daretur:** 'it were permitted (sc. them)'.

308–9 **que** looks forward to *premia* (first subject of *maneant*; the second is *que requies*); *manes* is picked up by *iustos* (obj. of *maneant*).

309 **quam contraria:** 'what contrary things from...' (obj. of *exspectet*); *iustis* is dative after *contraria*).

310f. All the imperfect subjunctive verbs (*irretiret, torreret, sorberet, frenderet*, etc.) are expressing apodoses to the *si...daretur* clause of l. 307; tr. 'would (not)...' in every case.

310f. **funestus** looks forward to *amor* (governing *habendi*).

311 **carnis amica** is in apposition to *libido* (subject of *torreret*).

313 **patrum** depends on *iugera* (object of *sorberet*).

314 **ferrato** looks forward to *carcere* (dependent on *detentus*).
Bachus: god of wine, and thus wine itself.

315 **frenderet horrendum:** 'grind (sc. his teeth) horribly'.

315f. **se inclusum:** sc. *esse* (acc. + inf. introduced by *gemeret*, subject *Liber*, another name for Bacchus).

317 The subject of *ambirent* is *Symonis heredes*, its object *honorem* (on which *cathedrae uenalis* depends). Simony was the sin of buying the power of the Holy Spirit (deriving from the offer made to the Apostles by Simon Magus in Acts 8.18–20). In an age when bishoprics carried wealthy benefices and hence political power, the practice and the accusation were common (see Part Three Intro.).

318f. **incentiua malorum** ('that incites to...') is in apposition to *funesta Pecunia* (subject of *pollueret*); *sacras* looks forward to *sedes*.

320f. The basic structure is *non aspiraret...inpubes* ('a minor') *ad...cacumen*; *indole* ('in...') depends on *clarus*, and governs *auiti sanguinis*. The sin berated here is nepotism (as exemplified by William of Champagne, only 29 when elected bishop of Chartres).

323 **merito** governs *parentum* (and is part of an abl. abs. with *non suffragante*).

324f. The subject is *sortiti a cardine nomen* 'those who have taken their name from the word *cardo* ('hinge')', a periphrasis for *cardinales*, who were

by this date responsible for electing the Pope; *ducti liuore* refers to them; the object of the verbs *crearent* and *preficerent* is *geminos patres*, referring to the Popes and anti-Popes chosen by the electoral college during the schism of 1159–77 (see section 19.III).

326 **lucri** looks forward to *odor* (subject of *regnaret*).

326f. **peruertere** is governed by *nollet*, whose subject is *corruptus...iudex*.

328 **nullo discrimine:** 'indiscriminately'.

329f. **quales...cecidisse** is acc. + inf. introduced by *queruntur* (from *queror* 'I complain'), whose subject is *terrae* (qualified by *uicinae* and *distantes*, the latter amplified by *modico...equore*). The reference is to the murder of Thomas Becket (1170: see section 19.I) and that of Robert, archbishop of Cambrai (1174).

331 **seducta** looks forward to *caro* in l. 334 (the subject of *dum...sequitur, allicit* and *non sinit*), and is qualified by *cupidine*, which governs *labilium...rerum*.

332 **profugi** looks forward to *mundi*.

333 **esse:** sc. *animam* (picked up by *memorem*).

334f. **cuius** depends on *memorem* (as does *principii*): tr. 'remember in whose likeness...'; *resoluta came* is abl. abs. ('when...'). The soul is made in God's image and after death should return to him if it and the body in which it was housed have been good.

336 **ignorantia** is the subject and on it depend *boni* (noun)...*ueri*.

337 **spreta** looks forward to *habena* (which governs *rationis*), abl. abs. 'rejecting...'.

338 **quod:** 'what...'.

338f. The subject is *homo*, preceded by the participle *paratus* agreeing with it and governing *facinus...ad omne*, and the verb *reueretur, quod:* 'what'.

340f. The subject is *satelles*, qualified by the preceding *flammatus* (governing *regni...amore*), and picked up by *reuerens* and *curans*; *Bessus* is in apposition to *satelles*; *patris* and *domini* depend on *fatalia fila* (obj. of *resoluit*).

343f. **te** is the object of *equabit* (*Pompeio* 'with...', *laudibus* 'in...'); *que* is obj. of *scribimus* and subject of *sunt habitura*; *olim:* 'in the future' (with *sunt habitura*); supply *et* before *uiuet* (subject *gloria defuncti*, picked up by *moritura*); *nullum* looks forward to *per euum*. Pompey, the

Roman general (106–48 BC), was the opponent of Caesar in the Civil War (see *RL Text*
6C). The reference here is to the popularity of

Lucan's *Bellum Ciuile*, the epic which glorifies
the losing general just as Walter does in his.
Walter hopes for esteem equal to Lucan's.

6. Nigel Whiteacre (*c*.1130–*c*.1207)

A younger contemporary of John of Salisbury (see section 16.1), Nigel was
a monk and possibly precentor at Christ Church, Canterbury. He visited
Normandy and Paris. His patron was William of Longchamps, chancellor of
Henry II, later bishop of Ely and regent of England during Richard
Lionheart's absence on crusade. Nigel's chief concern in his surviving
works is clerical ambition and secularization. He wrote a *Tractatus contra
curiales et officiales clericos* ('Tract against courtiers and clerical officials'), aimed
especially at clerks in the royal and episcopal chancery and at students of
medicine at Montpellier and Paris and of law at Bologna.

Some of the same targets are attacked in his masterpiece *Speculum
stultorum* ('The mirror of fools'), written 1179–80. The central character of
this elegiac poem of around 3,900 lines is an ass named Burnellus.
Discontented with his lot and aiming to increase the length of his tail in
proportion to that of his ears, he travels to Salerno (famous for medical
studies). His later adventures take him to Lyons, Paris and Bologna, where
he studies law. He then joins the English and plans to found a new
monastic order, adapted to human weakness (this is the passage printed
here). Finally he is found again by his former master Bernard. In a preface,
Nigel suggests that the meaning of the poem is to be sought by the reader
by allegorization. The ass stands for the ambitious cleric or monk who
strives for a high position in the Church. However, the allegory is by no
means wooden, and it may well be that such rare authors as Petronius and
Apuleius helped Nigel in constructing this picaresque fable.

See further: A. G. Rigg, *A History of Anglo-Latin Literature, 1066–1422*,
Cambridge, 1992.

*After detailed consideration of the religious orders which he could join Burnellus the
ass decides to concoct a new order to suit his lifestyle which draws on advantageous
features of the others. He will then obtain leave from the Pope for its establishment.*

NOVUS ORDO BURNELLI FACTUS DE ALIIS ORDINIBUS

'talia dum mecum tacitus consideró, vitam
  nesció quam possim constituisse mihi.
tutius ergó puto nec non consultius esse   2415

ut statuam leges ordinis ipse novi.
qui meus ordo meo nomen de nomine sumat,
    nomen in aeternum vivat ut inde meum.
sic igitur fiet de quolibet ordine sumam
    quod melius fuerit commodiusque mihi.   2420
ordine de Templi sumamus equos gradientes
    leniter, ut lenis sit meus ordo mihi.
ut mihi mentiri liceat quocumque locorum,
    fratribus ex aliis hoc retinere volo.
ut feria sexta liceat mihi pinguibus uti,   2425
    haec Cluniācensis conferat ordo mihi.
fratribus ex albis satis est et sufficit illud,
    ut liceat braccis nocte carere meis.
Grandimontanos in eo quod multa loquuntur
    multum commendo, quod retinere volo.   2430
Carthŭsiae fratres in eo decernŏ sequendos,
    missa quod in mense sufficit una satis.
Canonicos nigros carnes comedendo sequamur,
    ne quid ab hȳpocrisi contrahat ordo meus.
Praemonstratenses statuo de jure sequendos   2435
    in molli tunica multiplicique toga.
ordine de reliquo placet, ut persona secunda
    foedere perpetuo sit mihi juncta comes.
hic fuit ordo prior et conditus in Paradiso;
    hunc Deus instituīt et benedixit ei.   2440
hunc in perpetuum decrevimus esse tenendum,
    cujus erat genitor cum genetrice mea;
et genus omne meum semper fuit ordinis hujus,
    quo genus humanum deficiente cadet.
ordine de sacro velatarum mulierum   2445
    accipiam, zonam semper abesse meam;
cingula lata mihi non sunt bona, sed neque ventri
    conveniunt grosso cingula stricta meo.
est et adhuc aliūd in eis quod in ordine nostro
    apponi volumus, cum locus aptus erit.   2450
quid de Simplingham, quantum, vel qualia sumam,
    nescio, nam nova res me dubitare facit.
hoc tamen ad praesens nulla ratione remittam,
    namque necesse nimis fratribus esse reor,
quod nunquam nisi clam nulloque sciente sorori   2455
    cum quocunque suo fratre manere licet.

sunt etiam quaedam quae si non nunc meminisse
possumus ad praesens, posteă tempus erit.
ergo nil restat nisi confirmatiŏ sola
pontificis summi, quam dabit ipse libens.   2460
nam qui justa petunt, nulla ratione repulsam
a domino papa sustinuisse solent.
illuc ergŏ decet primo divertere, papam
et fratres humili sollicitare prece.'

2413 **talia** is within the *dum* clause and is the object of
 considero.
 vitam is the object of *constituisse* and should be
 taken with *quam* as the object of *nescio*.
2414 **constituisse**: tr. as present infinitive (the form is
 chosen for metrical reasons).
2415 **tutius** looks forward to *esse*; the acc. + inf. is
 introduced by *puto* (subject is 'it').
2416 **ordinis** is picked up by *novi*.
2417 **qui**: 'this'.
 meo looks forward to *de nomine*.
2418 Everything in this line is introduced by *ut*.
 nomen (subject) is picked up by *meum*.
2419 **fiet...sumam:** 'it will happen (sc. that) I shall
 take...'.
2420 **quod:** 'what'.
2421 **ordine** is governed by *de* and governs *Templi*;
 gradientes: tr. 'which...'. The order of the
 Knights of the Temple originated in the reign
 of Baldwin I, king of Jerusalem (1100–18) as a
 small group of knights, formed by Hugh de
 Payns (a Burgundian) and Godfrey of St Omer,
 and dedicated to protecting pilgrims on the
 road to Jerusalem. They were under the vows
 of chastity, obedience and poverty, like regular
 canons. Under Baldwin II (1118–31) they
 received a house near the Temple of Solomon, hence their name. Since Burnellus is an
 ass, he will be well pleased if the order has a rule
 obliging four-legged animals to go slowly.
2422 **mihi** depends on *lenis*.
2423 **ut:** 'that...' (it is picked up by *hoc*, object of *retinere*
 volo: the same construction is used in ll. 2425–
 6, with *ut* picked up by *haec*).
 quocumque locorum: lit. 'in whatever of
 places', i.e. 'wherever I am'.
2425f. see note on l. 2423 above.

2425 **feria sexta:** Friday was a meatless day.
 Cluniacensis looks forward to *ordo* (subject of
 conferat: 'let...' (jussive subjunctive: *RLGVE*
 152)). In fact, the reform set in train at Cluny
 (founded 910: see map 2) had been based upon
 strict adherence to the Rule of St Benedict (see
 section 1.1), including complete abstention
 from meat. The three-course dinner consisted
 of (1) dried beans, (2) vegetables, (3) fish or
 eggs. The vegetables were cooked in animal fat
 except on Ember Days and during Lent, and
 this is the point of attack here.
2427 **fratribus** is governed by *ex*. The *fratres albi* are the
 Cistercians, whose Order was founded in 1098
 (see map 2 and section 17.2). The name derives
 from their undyed woollen garment. They
 were allowed to remove their undertrousers
 at night, a fact satirized also by other writers.
2428 **braccis** (obj. of *carere*) is picked up by *meis*.
2429f. **Grandimontanos** is the object of *commendo*.
 in eo...quod: 'in this feature, that...' (*quod...*
 loquuntur is quoted from Cato's *Disticha*
 (2.20.2), a popular school text).
2430 **quod:** 'and (sc. this is something) which...'. The
 order of Grandmont was founded by St
 Stephen of Tournai, who renounced the
 world and took up his dwelling on the hill
 of Muret near Limoges in 1076. The group
 which had gathered around him moved to
 Grandmont after his death. Its Rule, establishing a community with common buildings
 divided between *clerici* (concerned with worship and contemplation) and *conversi* (concerned with taking care of the community's
 physical needs) was approved by Pope Hadrian
 IV in 1156. In fact, their Rule specifies very
 strict observance of silence and lays great stress
 on solitude.

2431 **Carthusiae fratres:** the Carthusian order was established by Bruno of Cologne at Chartreuse near Grenoble in 1084, but was not fully recognized as an order until 1176. Its basic tenets were isolation from worldly affairs and complete poverty. The rarity of Masses at the Chartreuse is put down by Prior Guigo to the particular enthusiasm of the monks for silence and solitude.

sequendos: sc. *esse* (the acc. + inf. is introduced by *decerno* and its subject is *Carthusiae fratres*).

2432 **missa** (subject of *sufficit*, and within the *quod* clause) is picked up by *una*.

2433 **Canonicos nigros:** object of *sequamur* 'let us...' (jussive subjunctive: see *RLGVE* 152). These are the Austin Canons, whose order grew out of the eleventh-century reform movement. They wore a black cape which gave them their title. They followed the Rule of St Augustine, which emerged around 1063 and was based on a letter of St Augustine to a congregation of religious women. This did not forbid the consumption of meat.

2435 **Praemonstratenses** are the subject of the acc. + inf. (*sequendos*, sc. *esse*) introduced by *statuo*. The order was founded by Norbert of Xanten at Prémontré in 1120 (see map 2). It was constituted to follow the Rule of St Augustine and was much influenced by Cîteaux (see section 17.2) in its simplicity of dress, ritual and architecture, abstinence from meat and long fasts. The reference here is to the (white) woollen garments prescribed by their Rule (white in imitation of the angels of the Resurrection and woollen symbolizing penitence).

2437 **ordine** is governed by *de*. The remaining order is that of secular canons, priests attached to cathedrals or large churches organized in groups. No single Rule governed them, but the provisions relating to their way of life go back ultimately to a revision of the Rule of Chrodegang (816). Until the first half of the twelfth century, such priests were often married. But from the time of Gregory VII this had begun to be seen as an abuse. It is this custom which is attacked here.

2438 **sit** looks forward to *juncta*; *comes*: 'as a companion'.

2439f. Burnellus defends his concept of monastic marriage by reference to Gen. 2.24: 'Therefore a man shall leave his father and his mother and cleave to his wife and the two will be one flesh.'

2441 **hunc:** sc. *ordinem* (it is the subject of the acc. + inf. clause (*hunc...esse tenendum*) introduced by *decrevimus*.

2442 **cujus:** '(sc. a member) of which...'.

2444 **quo** looks forward to *deficiente* and picks up *genus* (tr. 'if this...').

2445 **ordine** is governed by *de*. The reference is to orders of nuns (because they are distinguished by taking the veil). Earlier they have been attacked for quarrelsomeness, vanity and sexual immorality.

2446 **zonam** is picked up by *meam*; tr. 'that...'. The absence of belts from the nun's wardrobe is mentioned earlier, but the custom remains obscure. For the ass Burnellus, of course, such a belt would normally keep on a saddle or panniers.

2447f. **ventri** is picked up by *grosso...meo* and depends on *conveniunt* (subject *cingula stricta*).

2450 **cum locus...erit** seems to indicate some convenience Burnellus will take from established practice among nuns once he has a proper location for his monastery. What it is, he does not say, but it would be reasonable to conjecture that he is indulging in innuendo. One of the charges levelled at nuns was sexual immorality. The nuns of Amesbury were expelled in 1177: their abbess was said to have had three children and the nuns to be living immoral lives.

2451 **Simplingham:** Sempringham. The order was founded by Gilbert of Sempringham in Lincolnshire in 1131. The houses were double monasteries, for Augustinian canons and nuns together. This accounts for Burnellus' comments in ll. 2453–6, though in fact a partition wall the length of the church divided the establishment to prevent visual contact even during services.

2453 **hoc** is picked up by ll. 2455–6 (*Quod...licet*).

nulla ratione: 'by no means'.

2454 **necesse...esse** is acc. + inf. introduced by *reor*.

2455f. **sorori** depends on *licet* (which governs *manere*).

2461 **qui:** 'those who'.

repulsam is the object of *sustinuisse* (depending on *solent*); tr. as present (the form is determined by the metre).

2463 **illuc:** i.e. 'to Rome'.

2464 **humili** looks forward to *prece*.

sollicitare: 'to...' (purpose: see G.17(a)).

Grammar

1–8: Morphology

1. As a general rule, the forms of Latin nouns, adjectives, adverbs and verbs remain the same as in CL.

2. The majority of changes occur within the system. That is, forms are taken from another declension (e.g. *pauperorum* for *pauperum*) or conjugation (e.g. *descendent* for *descendunt* in Egeria; CL *odi* – perfect in form, present in meaning – 'I hate' is conjugated as if *odio odire*). Or nouns move gender or declension: e.g. *thesaurum* n. instead of *-us* m. The shift from n.pl. to 1 f.s. is very noticeable in ML (continuing a trend of LL, e.g. *folia* 'leaf' 1f.s., for CL *folium* 2n.).

3. Many verbs change voice. These changes are not necessarily consistently made. E.g. deponent to active: e.g. *loquere, loquis* instead of *loqui, loqueris*.

4. New periphrastic tenses:
    (a) Past participle + *fui, fueram, fuero, fuerim, fuisse* (for CL *sum eram* etc.): e.g. *factum fuerat* 'it had been done' (Vulgate); *fuissent conlata* 'they had been brought together' (Bede). This usage is sanctioned by Donatus' Grammar, which was the main medium through which Latin was learned during the Middle Ages.
    (b) Present participle + *sum* is used instead of the CL tense: e.g. *erat cupiens* 'he desired' (Vulgate), for CL *cupiebat*; *erant circumcingentes* 'they were surrounding' (*Gesta Francorum*), for CL *circumcingebant*.
    (c) Infinitive + *habeo* is used to express the future tense: e.g. *dicere habet* 'he is going to say'; *haberetis...cognoscere* 'you would learn' (Egeria); *mihi cantare habes* 'you will sing to me' (Bede). The Romance future is formed on this basis: cf. e.g. *daras* 'you will give' (Fredegar) = *dare habes*.

(d) Modal verbs (*uelle, posse, coepi, debere, conari, dignari, uideri*) may be used simply to express tense: e.g. *accedere uolebamus* 'we arrived'; *potuimus peruenire* 'we arrived'; *coepimus egredere* 'we went out' (Egeria).

5. CL *fore* future infinitive is used for *esse*: e.g. *dicebat...astronomiam...fore ceteris digniorem* 'he said that astronomy was more worthy than the rest' (Johannes of Alta Silva).

6. (a) Hebrew names are often indeclinable (e.g. Goliath, Geth, Dauid, etc.). and the case either has to be inferred from the context or is indicated by a preposition. This usage is extended to Germanic, Celtic, Slavic and other non-Latin names (e.g. Alahis, Mocumin).

   (b) Some names are declined, often with Greek forms (see RLRGr H6). Names in *-as* are 1st declension (e.g. *Abdias* = Obadiah; *Satanas* 'Satan' – but also indecl. *Satan*). *Adam* is usually indeclinable but sometimes has gen.s. *Adae* (so *Abraham, Abrahae*. Cf. *Iuda* indecl. and *Iuda, -ae* f.). Hebrew plurals are quite common. The m. form is *-im*, the f. *-oth*, the dual *-ayim*. E.g. *Philistiim* (cf. *Cherubim, Seraphim*), *Sabaoth* ('hosts'). They can represent any case (e.g. *de Philistiim* abl.). But sometimes the Latinized form is used (e.g. *Philisthaei* for *Philistiim*). Jerusalem appears either as the indeclinable *(H)ierusalem* or as *Hierusolyma* f. or n.pl. (so that *Hierusolymis* means 'in Jerusalem'). The preposition *in* is used especially with indeclinable names to express 'in' and 'to'.

   (c) A few Hebrew common nouns are used. Some, like *(o)ephi* 'ephah' (a measure) are indeclinable; *amen* 'truth', 'faithfulness' is used adverbially (e.g. *amen dico tibi* 'Verily I say unto thee'). Others are given Latin endings: e.g. *siclus* 2m. 'shekel'; *sabbatum* (or pl. *sabbata*) 2n. 'sabbath'; *gehenna* 1f. 'Hell'; *pascha* 1f. (or n.indecl./ decl.pl. *paschata*) 'Passover', 'Easter'.

7. Note the following common changes in adjectives and pronouns:
   (a) The use of consonant-stem abl, s. (*-e*) for *i*-stem (*-i*) and vice versa, e.g. *conclaue* for *conclaui* 'room'; *ueteri* for *uetere* 'old'. This usage is especially common with comparative adjectives, e.g. *priori* for *priore* 'first' (cf. *a priori*), but *vespere* is CL also (Lewis & Short quote Caesar and Cicero).

   (b) The use of 2nd declension forms for pronouns: e.g. *alium* for *aliud*; *illum* for *illud*; *aliae* for *alius* (gen.s.f.); *alio* for *alii* (dat.s.m./n.); *illo* for *illi* (dat.s for *nulli* (dat.s.m./n.).

8. Adverbs are often combined with prepositions to make a new adverb
   or phrase. The words are sometimes run together, sometimes written
   separately: e.g. *insimul* = *simul* 'at the same time'; *a longe* (or *alonge*)
   'from a distance' (CL *procul, longe*); *pro tunc* 'at that time' (CL *eo
   tempore, tunc temporis*). See also G.13.

9–30: Syntax

See RLRGr L–V Intro. for CL rules. CL syntax in the widest sense, that is
both prose and poetic usage, is the basis of both LL and ML writing.

9. Tense (See RLRGr A–G Intro. (c) for CL rules). In general, the sharp
   CL distinctions are not always observed.
   (a) Imperfect is found instead of perfect: e.g. *at illa, cum audisset, uiro
       suo denuntiabat et ipsi consiliauit* 'but when she had heard this, she
       told her husband and advised him' (*Gesta Romanorum*).
   (b) Perfect is found instead of pluperfect: e.g. *et non apparuit, quia tulit
       eum Deus* 'And he appeared not, because God had taken him'
       (Vulgate).
   (c) Pluperfect is found instead of perfect: e.g. *sed ego dixeram* 'But I
       said' (Augustine).

10. Translation, especially of the Scriptures, produced many oddities which
    are due to literal rendering of the syntax of the text's original language.
    The major influences were Hebrew (via the Septuagint, the Greek
    version of the Old Testament) and Greek (visible already in Virgil and
    Horace; their influence brought Graecisms into LL and ML prose,
    since the grammars were full of poetic examples; direct translation from
    the Septuagint and the New Testament brought many other Graecisms
    into the language). Since the process was by nature *ad hoc*, it is not
    possible to give a full account here. For further details, see W. E. Plater
    and H. J. White, *A Grammar of the Vulgate*, Oxford, 1926, Chapters I
    and II. For Hebrew names and vocabulary, see G.6. For Greek
    declensions see RLRGr H6. Some examples are:
    (a) The genitive in phrases such as *in saecula saeculorum* 'for ever and
        ever' reflects the Hebrew way of expressing a superlative.
    (b) Greek, unlike CL, uses prepositional phrases directly to qualify
        nouns: e.g. *audio uocem de uicina domo* 'I heard a voice from a
        neighbouring house' (Augustine); *pro ueritate contumelia* 'an outrage
        undergone for the sake of the truth' (Gregory the Great).
    (c) Greek often uses the future participle to express purpose: cf.

celatura 'to hide' (Jerome). Also due to translation from Greek is the common use of present participles to express the past and a wider range of ideas than in CL. See G.20.

(d) *unus* is used to translate Greek τις 'someone' (CL *quidam*): e.g. *propheta unus* 'a prophet' (Vulgate); *unus quispiam* 'a man' (someone or other). See G.11(a)(i) and G.11(d).

11. Demonstratives and pronouns are used without the clear CL distinctions (see RLRGr I). E.g.:

(a) *ipse* CL 'very, actual, self' is used:

    (i) 'as a definite article: e.g. *in monte ipso* 'on the mountain' (Egeria). See G.11(d) and cf. G.10(d).

    (ii) indiscriminately for *is, hic, ille, iste*: e.g. *quidam prelatus... optimum equum habebat; frater autem eius...ualde desiderabat ipsum, ut uteretur illo* 'A certain prelate had an excellent horse; but his brother very much wanted it, so as to use it' (James of Vitry).

(b) *idem* CL 'the same' is used alone instead of *hic/is/ille*: e.g. *nam et ipsi duces nostri coeperunt de eadem lanugine colligere* 'And our leaders too picked some of this wool' (*Alexander Romance*).

(c) *is* CL 'this', 'that' (3rd person pronoun), *hic* CL 'this', *ille* 'that' and *iste* (2nd person pronoun) 'that of yours' are used interchangeably: e.g. *uos ascendite ad diem festum hunc: ego non ascendo ad diem festum istum* 'Go ye up to this feast: I go not up to this feast' (Vulgate); *gener eius, qui acceperat filiam illius* 'his son-in-law, who had taken (in marriage) his daughter' (Gregory of Tours).

(d) *hic* and *ille* are used to translate the Greek definite article: e.g. *respondit ille homo* 'The man replied' (Vulgate). See G.11(a)(i) and cf. G.10(d).

(e) *se* CL 'him/herself', 'themselves' and *suus* CL 'his', 'her', 'their' (referring to the subject). See RLRGr I1 Note 1, R1 Note 4, R2 Note 2, R3 Note 3, S2(b) Note 2, S2(d) Note for CL rules.

    (i) *se* is often used for *is* CL 'him/her/it them': e.g. *tristis igitur et desperans ad tertium amicum perrexit...sibique dixit* 'sad and desperate he went to the third friend and said to him' (James of Voragine). CL would haved written *ei*. This confusion, both ways round, also occurs in indirect statement: e.g. *se* (= *eos*) *profecturos...Renatus clamauerit* 'Renatus cried that they would set out' (Ambrose); *exinde coepit Iesus ostendere discipulis suis, quia oporteret eum ire Hierosolymam* 'Then Jesus revealed to his disciples that he (Jesus) must go to Jerusalem' (Vulgate).

(ii) CL expressions of reciprocity (e.g. *alius alium, alter alterum, inter se, inter nos* 'one another') are expressed with pronoun alone or combined with *inuicem, ad inuicem, uicissim* or *alteruter*: e.g. *ad inuicem dicentes* 'saying to one another' (Vulgate); (sc. two businessmen who) *se...solo auditu cognouerant* 'knew one another only by reputation' (Petrus Alfonsi); *meam offero et uestram expeto amicitiam ut nobis uicissim...prodesse curemus* 'I offer you my friendship and seek yours, so that we may take the trouble to help one another' (Lupus of Ferrières); *dicentes ad alterutrum* 'saying to each other' (Vulgate). The dative 'to each other' is often expressed by *sibi uicibus*.

(iii) *suus* is often confused with *eius/eorum* (referring to a person other than the subject): e.g. *de uagina sua* 'from its sheath' (Vulgate); *puella...ipsum a uinculis liberauit et cum eo ad patriam suam fugit* 'The girl freed him from his chains and fled with him to his native land' (*Gesta Romanorum*).

(f) There is considerable confusion with the CL pronouns and pronominal adjectives. For example, *aliquis* 'someone' is used after negatives instead of *quisquam* 'anyone': e.g. *nec praesumat aliquis* 'And let no one presume' (Benedict).

12. Comparison of adjectives (see RLRGr J for CL rules). In general, the CL system is used correctly. But the following deviations occur:

(a) comparative for superlative: e.g. *maior* (CL *maximus*) *his* 'the greatest among these' (Vulgate); *uirum meliorem* (CL *optimum*) *et nobiliorem* (CL *nobilissimum*) *omnium* 'the best and noblest of men' (Regino of Prüm).

(b) superlative expressed by *nimis, satis, multum, bene, fortiter, ualde, maxime* + positive: e.g. *pulchra nimis* 'very beautiful' (Vulgate); *multum mirabilis* 'very wonderful' (Augustine).

(c) comparative for positive: e.g. *aliis...uerbis pluribus* 'with many other words (Vulgate).

13. Adverbs (see G.8 for changed formation). The following are common replacements for CL adverbs: *secundo, iterato* = CL *iterum* 'again'; *nouissime* = CL *postremo* 'at last', 'finally'; *de facili* = CL *facile* 'easily'; *a praesenti* = CL *statim* 'at once'; *nimium* (CL 'too much') = CL *multum* 'much'; *inde* (CL 'thence') = CL *ibi* 'there' (and in LL often = 'by that means', 'about it', 'from it', etc.: e.g. *quia et hic inde uiuitur, et in futuro inde gaudetur* 'because we live by that means (sc. goodness) here and we

shall rejoice because of it in the future' (Caesarius of Arles). So also *aliunde* can mean 'about something else' (Caesarius); *minus* (CL 'less') = CL *non* 'not'; *continue* (CL *continuo* 'at once') = CL *continenter,* 'continuously'; *festinato* = CL *festinanter* 'hastily'; *nimis parum* = CL *parum* 'too little'; *a mane* = CL *mane* 'in the morning' (see G.8); *latialiter, litteraliter* = CL *Latine* 'in Latin'.

14. Connecting particles often lose their specific CL force and mean 'and' or signify transition: e.g. CL *siquidem* 'inasmuch as', *uerumtamen* 'but even so' are commonly used for transition, e.g. 'Now...' (section 7.2(a)(iii) l.1 (but note also *nam, namque, uero, autem*).

15. Prepositions (see RLRGr K):
    (a) are used where CL uses case alone:
        (i) *in* + abl. for CL abl. to express time 'when': e.g. *in hac die* 'on this day' (Gregory of Tours).
        (ii) *de, cum, in* + abl. are used to express CL ablative of means: e.g. *uictus itaque monachus a prece pauperis* 'So the monk, defeated by the prayer of the poor man' (Johannes Monachus); *trinum Deum uenerantes tribus in muneribus* 'worshipping the Three-in-One God with three gifts' (twelfth-century liturgical play): this usage is a Hebraism, introduced by the Vulgate, due to the use in Hebrew of prepositions to express instrument (its nouns are virtually uninflected); *replebis me iucunditate cum facie tua* 'You will fill me with joy with your presence' (Vulgate).
    (b) There are many changes in the constructions used after verbs and adjectives involving prepositions. Such constructions may be checked using the LL and ML dictionaries listed at pp. 376–7.
    (c) Indifference to case after prepositions:
        (i) Prepositions with abl. (*de, cum, in*) are often used with acc.: e.g. *simul cum monazontes* 'along with the monks' (Egeria).
        (ii) Note the tendency to use *in* + abl. for *in* + acc.: e.g. *in quo* = *in quem* 'into which', in *eodem campo* = *in eundem campum* 'into the same plain' (Egeria).
    (d) Many prepositions acquire new meanings. E.g. *de* CL 'about', 'from' is used to mean 'of' (partitive: CL *ex* + abl.): e.g. *quamdiu non feceritis uni de minoribus his* 'as long as you have not done it to one of the least of these' (Vulgate); *frustella de argento* 'small pieces of silver' (Egeria).

16. Changes of case construction with verbs, adjectives and prepositions are exceedingly common. See RLRGr L for CL rules. See G.15 above for the use of prepositions. Such usages are best checked by means of the dictionaries listed at pp. 376–7.

   (a) Dative is used instead of CL preposition after verbs of motion, sending, bringing, etc. (as in CL poetry): e.g. *optatae tranquillitati nauem perducere* 'to bring the ship to the longed for calm' (Augustine).

   (b) Dative of the agent (common in CL poetry) is often used in prose: e.g. *inutiliter...eis geruntur egregia* 'to no purpose are outstanding deeds done by them' (John of Salisbury).

   (c) The ablative is commonly used to express duration of time as opposed to CL accusative. e.g. *quadraginta diebus* 'for forty days' (Egeria); *non potestis uiuere nisi dimidio anno* 'you cannot live but for half a year more' (James of Vitry).

17. Infinitives (see RLRGr M for CL rules):

   (a) Infinitive to express purpose (a Graecism common in CL poetry: e.g. *uenerat aurum petere* 'he had come to look for the gold' (Plautus)) becomes more common: e.g. *inposuerunt illi crucem portare* 'They put the cross on him to carry' (Vulgate); *abiit quaerere* 'he went off to seek' (Benedict). See G.27 for other purpose constructions.

   (b) Infinitive expressing indirect command becomes common: e.g. *hic roget sacerdos circumstantes orare pro anima defuncti* 'Here the priest is to ask those present to pray for the soul of the deceased' (Sarum Burial Service). See also G.23(a).

   (c) Infinitive is used after *facio* 'I cause' (CL *ut* + subj.): e.g. *fecit percuti* 'he caused him to be struck' (Cassiodorus); *nauem parari fecit* 'He caused a ship to be got ready' (*Gesta Romanorum*).

   (d) *ualeo* + inf. (CL 'I have the strength to') is increasingly used as a mere synonym for *possum*: e.g. *celare non ualens* 'not able to hide' (Regino of Prüm). In LL *ualet* is used as an impersonal verb meaning 'it is possible'.

18. The gerund (See RLRGr N for CL rules) is often used in the ablative instead of any case of the present participle: e.g. *non aliter Mauros timidos fugitando per urbem/insequitur/gladius undique morsque pauor* 'Just the same the sword, death and panic followed the Moors as they fled through the city' (Ermoldus Nigellus). *fugitando* for *fugitantis* (acc. pl. m. with *Mauros*).

19. Gerundive (see RLRGr O for CL rules) is sometimes used as a future

passive participle ('going to be...ed'): e.g. *tum clericus, qui se deprehendendum...timeret* 'then the clerk, since he thought he was going to be caught' (William of Malmesbury). This usage is sanctioned by Donatus' Grammar.

20. Participles (See RLRGr P for CL rules):
   (a) The present participle is commonly used to express past tense: e.g. *proficiscens* 'having set out' (Vulgate).
   (b) The present participle is more often used with circumstantial force than in CL, to express time ('when...ing'), manner/means ('by...ing'), continuity ('continuing...ing'), cause ('in...ing'), concession ('although...ing'), condition ('if...ing') and purpose ('to...'): e.g. *diuidentes ueri uestimenta eius* 'when dividing up his clothes' (Vulgate); *porro milites armati subsequantur, capientes si quos uiderint uel mulieres ad aspectum cadaueris lacrimari* 'furthermore, let armed soldiers follow after, to catch any men or women they have seen weeping at the sight of the corpse' (Johannes of Alta Silva).

21. Indirect speech (see RLRGr R for CL rules) is the area where the greatest and commonest changes occur. Nonetheless, the CL constructions are still used side by side with the new syntax.

22. Indirect Statement:
   (a) Indirect statement is very commonly expressed by a subordinate clause with a finite verb in indicative or subjunctive, introduced by various conjunctions. The commonest are: *quod* CL 'the fact that', *quia* CL 'because', *quoniam* CL 'since', *ut* CL 'how', 'that'. Less frequent are: *qualiter* CL 'how', *quomodo* CL 'how', *quatenus* CL 'as far as', 'since'. E.g. *feruntque alii ut...euangelium in ecclesia eum legere fecissent* 'and others claim that he had made him read the gospel in church' (Chronicle of Salerno); *ignoras quoniam benignitas Dei ad paenitentiam te adducit?* 'Do you not know that the kindness of God leads you to repentance?' (Vulgate); *intelligitis quomodo in parabolis posita sunt multa* 'you know that many things have been expressed in parables' (Barnabas).
   (b) Verbs of hoping, promising and swearing (*sperare, promittere, iurare*) sometimes take plain infinitive: e.g. *sperabat signum aliquod uidere* 'he hoped to see a sign' (Vulgate). Sometimes the acc. + inf. is used, but with present infinitive (contrast CL future infinitive): e.g. *iurasset illi Deus de fructu lumbi eius sedere* 'God had sworn to him that the fruit of his loins would sit' (Vulgate).

23. Indirect command. There are three main types of deviation from CL: in construction, in negation and in conjunction:

(a) The CL construction *ut* (*ne*) + subj. is often replaced by the plain infinitive: e.g. *praecepi paucas sagittas iactare* 'I told (them) to fire a few arrows' (*Alexander Romance*). See also G.17(b).

(b) CL *ne* for the negative in indirect commands is often replaced by *ut non* (reserved in CL for result clauses): e.g. *postulasti...ut...non tacerem* 'you asked me not to keep quiet' (Jerome).

(c) In direct commands also, where CL would use *ne* + subj., *non* + subj. is often used: e.g. *et non intres in iudicium cum seruo tuo* 'And enter not into judgement with thy servant' (Vulgate).

(d) Indirect command is sometimes introduced by *quod* or *quatenus*: e.g. *tortuca...rogauit aquilam quod portaret eam in altum* 'A tortoise asked an eagle to carry her into the air' (Odo de Cerinton); *obsecrans eum...quatenus puerum...instrueret* 'begging him to teach the boy' (Johannes of Alta Silva).

24. Direct and indirect questions:

(a) In direct questions, the interrogative words *numquid* '?' and *utquid* 'why?' become very common: e.g. *utquid iubes, pusiole, quare mandas, filiole...?* 'Why do you command, little one, why do you instruct, my son...' (Gottschalk of Orbais).

(b) Indicative is often used in indirect questions, as in Plautus (CL subj.): e.g. *non sciunt quid faciunt* 'they know not what they do' (Vulgate).

(c) *si* is often found for *num* in indirect questions (as in early Latin): e.g. *Pilatus...interrogauit si homo Galilaeus esset* 'Pilate asked whether the man was a Galilean' (Vulgate).

25. Subjunctive (see RLRGr S for CL rules):

(a) Many subordinate clauses taking subjunctive in CL are varied in three ways: (i) their conjunction is altered, (ii) they have an indicative verb, (iii) the tense of the verb ignores CL rules of sequence (see RLRGr Intro. A–G(a)). CL constructions continue side by side with these variations.

(b) The sharp CL distinctions between indicative and subjunctive are blurred. Indicative is often used where CL used subjunctive and vice versa. This blurring is well illustrated by the use of indicative and subjunctive in parallel subordinate clauses: e.g. *praeter quod...crebro febribus corripiebatur* (indic.)..., *ad extremum etiam uno pede claudicaret* (subj.) 'except that he was frequently seized by fevers (and) also near the end limped with one foot' (Einhard). See also G.26(a), 26(b).

(c) *debeo* 'I ought', *oportet* 'it behoves', *uolo* 'I wish', *possum, ualeo* 'I am able' + inf. are often used to reinforce the subjunctive: e.g. *ut quos morituros conspexerit, debeat baptizare* 'in order that he may baptize any he sees are going to die' (Gregory the Great). CL *ut baptizet.*

26. Result (consecutive) clauses (see RLRGr S2(a) for CL rules):
   (a) Indicative is common in result clauses: e.g. *tantam altitudinem ascendi ut sicut area uidebatur esse terra sub me* 'I climbed so high that the earth beneath me seemed like a threshing floor' (Leo of Naples). See also (b) below.
   (b) *quod* (and very occasionally *quatenus*) is used for *ut* (with subjunctive or indicative): e.g. *et tunc defecit illis cibus ita quod non remansit eis quicquam* 'and then their food ran out so that they had nothing left' (Petrus Alfonsi).

27. Purpose (final) clauses (see RLRGr S2(b) for CL rules):
   (a) For infinitive of purpose, see G.17(a).
   (b) *quod, quatenus* and occasionally *qualiter* and *quemadmodum* are used instead of *ut*: e.g. *misit...nuntios ad imperatorem ut...ei treugam concederet quod cum eo personaliter loqui posset* 'He sent messengers to the emperor to (get him to) give him a truce so that he could talk to him in person' (*Gesta Romanorum*).
   (c) *quo* is used for *ut* without a comparative (see RLRGr S2 Note 3 for CL construction).
   (d) *ut non, ut nullus* are used instead of CL *ne, ne quis,* etc.: e.g. *ut non cognoscerentur simul* 'so as not to be recognized together' (Gregory of Tours).

28. Conditions. The rules of CL, especially for unreal conditions (see RLRGr S2(c), R4(b)) are often ignored.
   (a) Sometimes the imperfect subjunctive is found in unreal future conditions (for CL present): e.g. *uos...grauis persona estis et si forte caderetis, multum laedi possetis* 'You are a heavy person and if you were to fall you could be hurt' (James of Vitry).
   (b) Subjunctive is very often found in the protasis with indicative in apodosis: e.g. *si...sapienter...intelligamus...inueniemus* 'If we understood wisely, we would find' (Leo); *si...loquar...et...non habeam, factus sum* 'If I speak...and have not..., I am made...', *si*

habuero...et nouerim..., nihil sum 'If I have...and know..., I am nothing' (Vulgate).

(c) Present subjunctive is found for indicative in the protasis of open conditions: e.g. *si...haec fiant in capite quid fit in membris?* 'If these things happen in the head, what goes on among the limbs?' (Roger Bacon). CL *fiunt*.

29. Temporal clauses (see RLRGr T for CL rules): *dum* CL 'while' is often used with subjunctive (= *cum*): *et dum hortaretur iuuenem, subito itroiuit filia regis* 'And while he was encouraging the young man, suddenly the king's daughter entered' (*History of Apollonius of Tyre*).

30. Causal clauses (see RLRGr U for CL rules):
   (a) *dum* CL 'while' is used to mean 'since', with indicative or subjunctive: e.g. *dum conscientiae bono fruitur, uetuit* 'because she enjoyed the advantage of a good conscience, she forbade'(Jerome).
   (b) *dum* is also used to describe 'manner' or 'means': e.g. *dum in suum mentitur sanguinem, accusauit* 'by lying against his own life, he accused' (Jerome).
   (c) *ex quo* 'since', *pro eo quod* 'because' and *eo quod* 'because' are regularly used for CL *quod, quia, quoniam*.

Orthography

O.0 Some modern texts and anthologies use the standard classical Latin spellings, but others (e.g. the Toronto Medieval Latin Texts series: see Introduction) retain the vagaries of medieval orthography. Consistency of spelling cannot necessarily be expected even within the same text (for example, we find *hostium* and *ostium* 'door'in the same twelfth-century work).

Spelling errors sometimes indicate sound changes, but the correlation is not automatic (it depends upon a knowledge of phonology and educational history – a scribe may be writing what he has *seen*). Pronunciation was taught in the schools (see M. Bonioli, *La pronuncia del Latino nelle scuole, dall'antichità al Rinascimento*, Turin, 1962). But local dialects and languages dictated the *actual* sounds produced. So we may say that the spelling *ci* for *ti* and vice versa (see O.2) indicates, along with other evidence, that this combination was pronounced *tsi*. However, in Ireland, for example, *c* would have been pronounced *k*, and an attempt by an Irishman to imitate continental pronunciation of *ci* or *ce* would have led to his substitution of *s*, because Old Irish did not possess the phoneme *ts*. It is better to say that pronunciation *affects* spelling, then, than that spelling is a guide to pronunciation.

O.1 *e* is written for *ae* and *oe*. The spelling can cause confusion, e.g. *ille* could be nom.s.m. or nom.pl.f. = *illae*; *equus* = horse, or is it *aequus* 'peer'? Quite often *ae* is written where *e* is correct, e.g. *praecipuae* = CL *praecipue* 'especially'; *aecclesia* = *ecclesia* 'church'.

O.2 *ci* is written for *ti*, or *ti* is written for *ci* where a vowel follows (see O.0). E.g. *eciam* = *etiam* 'also'; *fatio* = CL *facio* 'I make, do'.

O.3   The letter *h*:
      (a) is added to *c*, *t* or *p*. (e.g. *charitas* = *caritas* 'love') or removed
           from *ch*, *th* or *ph* (e.g. *spera* = *sphaera* 'sphere').
      (b) has *c* added to it. E.g. *michi* = *mihi* 'to me'.
      (c) is omitted or is inserted: (i) at the beginning of words, e.g. *ac* =
           CL *hac* 'this' (abl.s.f.), *hortus* = *ortus* 'having arisen' (p.p. of *orior*)
           (ii) in the middle of words, e.g. *aduc* = *adhuc* 'up to now',
           perhennis = *perennis* 'everlasting'.

O.4   *p* is added, usually to *mn*. E.g. *columpna* = *columna* 'column'.

O.5   *y* is written for *i* (and vice versa). E.g. *epytafium* = *epitaphium* 'epitaph'.

O.6   *f* is written for *ph* and vice versa. E.g. *prophanus* = *profanus* 'profane'.

O.7   Single consonants are often doubled, or double consonants are often
      made single. E.g. *bellua* = *belua* 'monster'; *imo* = *immo* 'nay, rather'.

O.8   *v* and *f* are confused. E.g. *pontevecem* = *pontificem* (Fredegar) (cf.
      O.13).

O.9   Procope, syncope and apocope (respectively, the loss of initial,
      medial and final syllable) may occur. E.g. *Strumentum* (=
      instrumentum: *Tablettes Albertini*), *dedcauit* (= *dedicauit*: an inscription
      from Gaul); *barbar* (= *barbarus*: *Appendix Probi*).

O.10 Progressive nasalisation of all vowels leads to uncertainty in applying
      nasal consonants (*m*, *n*) and may result in incorrectly-written singular
      case-endings (e.g. *per nostra ordenacione* = *per nostram ordinationem*).

O.11 *i* is written for *e* and vice versa. E.g. *quatinus* = *quatenus* 'that'.

O.12 *o* is written *u*, and vice versa. E.g. *clericus* = *clericos* 'clerks' (acc.pl.).

O.13 *b* and *u(v)* are confused. E.g. *bemacula* = *uemacula* 'handmaiden'
      (Aldhelm).

O.14 *di* before a following vowel or diphthong is written *z*. E.g. *zabolus* =
      diabolus 'devil'.

O.15 *nct* is written *nt*. E.g. *santus* = *sanctus* 'saint'.

O.16 *x* (and *cx*, *cxs*, *xs*) is written *s* and vice versa. E.g. *mox* = *mos* 'custom' (*Chronicon Salernitanum*).

O.17 *g* is written for *c* and vice versa. E.g. *ogra* = *ocra* (*ochra*) 'ochre' (Theophilus).

O.18 *pt* is written *bt*. E.g. *scribtura* = *scriptura* 'scripture, writing'. CL also.

O.19 *t* is written *d* and vice versa. E.g. *set* = *sed* 'but'. CL also.

O.20 *ct* is written for *th*. E.g. *auctentice persone* = *authenticae personae* 'of the person in authority' (Richard FitzNigel).

O.21 Dissimilation: the prefix is written in its normal form, e.g. *impendia* becomes *inpendia*. The tendency to write the original form of the prefix becomes well established in ML. Sometimes incorrect dissimilation occurs, e.g. *menbra* = *membra* 'limbs' (twelfth–thirteenth-century ms. of Hugh Primas).

O.22 Prosthesis: adding on to the first syllable. There is a tendency for a vowel (*i* or *e*) to be added before the combinations *sp*, *sc*. *h* is sometimes added as well, e.g. *hispatium* = *spatium* 'distance' (Egeria).

Note on vocabulary

This vocabulary contains only words in the selected texts, in the following categories:

(i) those not found in the medium-sized Cassell's classical Latin dictionary (5th edn, ed. D. P. Simpson, London, 1987).

(ii) words found in the above dictionary which have new meanings in LL or ML.

(iii) words which appear in these texts spelled in a way different from their Classical Latin form. These words are glossed fully if they belong to categories (i) or (ii), but otherwise are simply glossed with their classical form (which can then be looked up in the dictionary). The most important spelling changes are listed in Orthography, to which these words are cross-referred in the form O.1 etc.

(iv) names of people and places are, generally speaking, glossed in the commentaries, not here.

Further study: note on dictionaries

No one dictionary will solve all the problems likely to be encountered in reading ML texts. Much depends upon the *register* (legal document, chronicle, theological text, quantitative verse, etc.). If your own dictionary fails you, the following procedure is recommended:

1. Consult Lewis and Short, *A Latin Dictionary*, Oxford, 1879 (reprinted 1962 etc.). This contains vocabulary from many LL authors, including the Vulgate.
2. If the word is not there, or the senses do not suit the context, try A. Souter, *A Glossary of Later Latin to 600 AD*, Oxford, 1949.
3. A library which has 2 should also have A. Blaise, H. Chirat, *Dictionnaire latin–français des auteurs chrétiens*, Turnhout, 1962, which you should also

try. Translations are in French, but it gives much more detail, especially on verb constructions.

4. If 1–3 fail you, then try the following, each of which has its own particular area of concern:

   (a) R. E. Latham, *Revised Medieval Latin Word-List from British and Irish Sources*, London, 1965 (good for problems encountered in reading historical documents).

   (b) J. F. Niermeyer and C. Van de Klieft, *Mediae latinitatis lexicon minus*, Leiden, 1976 (translations in English and French: especially good for technical legal vocabulary).

   (c) A. Blaise, *Dictionnaire latin–français des auteurs du moyen-âge. Lexicon latinitatis medii aevi, praesertim ad res ecclesiasticas investigandas pertinens*, Turnhout, 1975 (Corpus Christianorum, Continuatio Medievalis). (French translations: concentrates on ecclesiastical vocabulary.)

5. Beyond these aids are the older dictionaries and the specialist dictionaries currently being produced by individual national academies. Details of many of these are available in R. C. Van Caenegem, *Guide to the Sources of Medieval History*, Amsterdam/New York/London, 1978, pp. 276 and 278.

6. Place names are often problematic. For these try *Orbis Latinus: lexicon lateinischer geographischer Namen des Mittelalters und der Neuzeit*, ed. H. Plechl, S.-C. Plechl, 3 vols., Brunswick, 1972.

Vocabulary

A

a see *facie*
abbas abbat-is 3m. abbot
abbati-a ae 1f. monastery, abbey
abbatiss-a ae 1f. abbess
abenae = *habenae* (see O.3(c))
abeo = *habeo* (see O.3(c))
ablatio ablation-is 3f. removal
ablatus part. from *aufero*
abominabil-is e accursed
absolutio absolution-is 3f. release
abyss-us i 2f. abyss, unfathomable
  depth
acceptabil-is e acceptable, welcome
accidenci-a/ accidenti-a um 3n.pl.
  accidents (secondary qualities)
accubit-us us 4m. bed, couch
accula = *accola:* (see O.12)
acr-a ae 1f. acre
acredo acredin-is 3f. bitterness
acsi as if
actualiter actively, practically
ad (+ acc.) for the purpose of (= *in* +
  acc.)
adcl- see *accl-* (see O.21)
ademptor ademptor-is 3m. depriver
ademptus part. from *adimo*
adimpleo 2 I accomplish, fulfil
adinuenio 4 I invent, devise
adinventio adinvention-is 3f. invention

adiutori-um i 2n. help, aid
adju- = *adiu-*
adolescentula = *adulescentula* (see O.12)
adplene completely
adque = *atque* (see O.19)
adsimilo = *adsimulo*
adsimulo 1 I compare
aecclesia = *ecclesia* (see O.1)
aecclesiasticus = *ecclesiasticus* (see O.1)
aeclisia = *ecclesia* (see O.1, O.7 and
  O.11)
aedificatio aedification-is 3f. instruction
aedifico 1 I instruct, edify
aejectus = *eiectus* (*eicio*) (see O.1)
aepiscopatus = *episcopatus* (see O.1)
aeternal-is e eternal
aethral-is e of the upper air
agap-e es f. (Christian) love, charity
  (Greek)
agi-us a um holy (Greek *hagios*)
agnitus part. from *agnosco*
agon agon-is 3m. suffering, passion
agricol-a ae 1f. peasant
agricultor agricultor-is 3m. peasant
alacriter speedily
aliquandiu = *aliquamdiu*
Alleluia Hallelujah! praise the Lord!
almitas almitat-is 3f. benignity
aln-us i 2m. wooden boat, dugout
altar-e is 3n. altar

altithron-us a um seated on high
amabo please (tell me)
ambiciosus = *ambitiosus* (see O.2)
ambrosian-um i 2n. (Ambrosian) hymn
Amen truly, so be it, Amen (Hebrew
  'truth', 'true')
amenus = *amoenus* (see O.1)
amicicia = *amicitia* (see O.2)
amm- see *adm-* (O.21)
ammirali-us i 2m. emir, governor
Anastas-is Anastas-is 3 Church of the
  Resurrection (Greek)
anathema anathemat-is 3n. cursing,
  anathema
anathematizo 1 I curse
ancella = *ancilla* (see O.11)
ancellula = *ancillula* (see O.11)
anchello = *anhelo* (see O.3(b))
angel-us i 2m. angel (Greek
  'messenger')
angelic-us a um of angels, angelic
Angligen-a ae 1m. Englishman
Angl-us a um English
ann- see *adn-*
anniversari-us i 2m. anniversary
antiphon-a ae 1f. antiphon, psalm
  (sung responsively)
antistes antistit-is 3m. bishop
anxio 1 I am anxious
apices apic-um 3m.pl. letters
apoplexi-a ae 1f. apoplexy (Greek)
apostat-a ae 1f. apostate, rebel (Greek)
apostolic-us a um apostolic (Greek); i
  2m. the Pope
apostol-us i 2m. apostle (Greek 'one
  sent out')
aput = *apud* (see O.19)
arbitri-um i 2n. free will
arbuscul-um i 2n. (small) tree
archangel-us i 2m. archangel
archiepiscop-us i 2m. archbishop

archos m. God (Greek)
arctus = *artus*
aroma aromat-is 3n. spice (Greek)
arr- see *adr-*
ass- see *ads-*
assertio assertion-is 3f. assertion
assimilo = *adsimulo* (q.v.)
asso 1 I roast
asto = *adsto*
astruo 3 I affirm, declare, prove
atom-us i 2m. individual (Greek: =
  Latin *indiuiduus*)
atri-um i 2n. graveyard
auctus part. from *augeo*
audenter boldly
augment-um i 2n. extension
auliga = *aulicus*
auricalcum = *orichalcum*
auspicor 1 dep. I begin
aut(h)entic-us a um authoritative

B
Bachus = *Bacchus* (see O.7)
baiolo = *baiulo* (see O.12)
baj = *bai-*
balista (= *ballista*: see O.21) *ae* 1f.
  slingshot
bann-a leuc-a ae 1f. area of jurisdiction
  (Fr. *banlieue*)
bann-us i 2m. ban
baptisma baptismat-is 3n. baptism
baptist-a ae 1m. baptist, baptizer
basilic-a ae 1f. church
basilisc-us i 2m. basilisk
benedico 3 -*dixi* -*dictus* I bless (+ dat.
  or acc.)
benedictio benediction-is 3f. blessing,
  benediction
benedict-us a um blessed
benefacio 3/4 -*feci* -*factus* I do good to
  (+ dat.)

benefici-um i 2n. benefice; fief (= *feudum*)

beneplacit-um i 2n. pleasure, will

benivole = *benevole* (see O.11)

berbices = *vervices* (*vervex vervicis*) (see O.13)

berna = *verna* (see O.13)

biber-a ae 1f. glass

bibl-us i 2m. book (Greek)

biduan-us a um lasting two days

bilua = *belua* (see O.11)

bisacut-a ae 1f. two-edged axe, twibill

bisante-us i 2m. bezant (gold coin)

blad-um i 2n. corn, grain (wheat)

blandiciae = *blanditiae* (see O.2)

blasphemi-a ae 1f. blasphemy

blasphemo 1 I revile, blaspheme

bordari-us i 2m. bordar, bordage-tenant, smallholder

botrus f. cluster (= 'grape' in Greek)

bracc-ae arum 1f.pl. underpants

brachium = *bracchium* (see O.7)

bratteola = *bracteola*

bravi-um i 2n. prize (= *brabium* (see O.13): Greek)

brumali-us a um wintry

burgenses burgensi-um 3m.pl. townsfolk, burghers

C

caement-um i 2n. floor

caenubium = *coenobium* (see O.1 and O.12)

caeremonia = *caerimonia* (see O.11)

caeteri etc. = *ceter-* (see O.1)

camer-a ae 1f. room, chamber

campan-um i 2n. bell

cancellari-us i 2m. chancellor

cancell-us i 2m. screen, enclosure; pl. (chancel) railings

canicies = *canities* (see O.2)

cannon = *canon* (see O.7)

canon canon-is 3m. Rule

canonic-us i 2m. clergyman

cantic-um i 2n. canticle

capitell-um i 2n. capital (of a column)

capitular-e capitular-is 3n. rescript, order

capitul-um i 2n. chapter

captuosus = *captiosus*

caput capit-is 3n. chapter

cardinal-is cardinal-is 3m. cardinal

carnal-is e fleshly, carnal

carpentari-us i 2m. carpenter

carruc-a ae 1f. plough, plough-team

carta = *charta* (see O.3(a))

cartul-a ae 1f. (little) charter, deed, document

casat-us i 2m. farm (= *colonia, mansus*)

cassabundus = *casabund-us a um* tottering (see O.7)

castell-um i 2n. castle

castrametor 1 dep. I pitch a camp

cata (+ acc.) along with (Greek)

catacuminus = *catechumenus*

catalog-us i 2m. catalogue, list

catechumin-us/catacumin-us i 2m. catechumen (receiving elementary instruction)

cathedr-a ae 1f. bishop's position

cathena = *catena* (see O.3(a))

catholic-us a um catholic, orthodox, universal; 2m. a catholic

caupall-us i 2m. boat

caus-a ae 1f. matter (cf. It. *cosa*, Fr. *chose*)

cavefacio 3/4 *-feci* I beware

cecidisse inf. from *cado*

cecinit pf. of *cano*

cecus = *caecus* (see O.1)

cedes = *caedes* (see O.1)

cedrin-us a um of cedar

celerari-us (= *cellerarius*: see O.7) *i* 2m. cellarer

celitus = *caelitus* (see O.1) from heaven

cellari-um i 2n. store-room, pantry

celsitudo celsitudin-is 3f. highness (title)

celum = *caelum* (see O.1)

cenodoxi-a ae 1f. vanity, conceit

censur-a ae 1f. majesty, censure

cepi sometimes = *coepi* (see O.1)

cepta = *coepta* (see O.1)

cere-us i 2m. waxlight

cerimonia = *caerimonia* (see O.1)

certitudo certitudin-is 3f. certainty

Cesar = *Caesar* (see O.1)

cesius = *caesius* (see O.1)

ces-us = *caes-us* part. from *caedo* (see O.1)

charitas = *caritas* (see O.3(a))

chart-a/cart-a ae 1f. charter, deed, document

chor-us i 2m. choir

c(h)risma c(h)rismat-is 3n. consecrated oil

cimba = *cumba*

cimentari-us = *caementarius i* 2m. stonemason

circumcingo 3 *-cinxi -cinctus* I surround, enclose

circumquaque on every side

clamis = *chlamys* (see O.5)

claustr-um i 2n. cloister

clemencia = *clementia* (q.v.: see O.2)

clementi-a ae 1f. mercifulness (as title)

cleric-us i 2m. priest

cler-us i 2m. clergy

cliens client-is 3m. dependant, companion, household monk

clima climat-is 3n. region

climacter climacter-is 3n. climacteric (critical point)

clypeus = *clipeus* (see O.5)

coactio coaction-is 3f. force

coadiutor coadiutor-is 3m. co-author, helper

coaetern-us a um coeternal

coapto 1 I compare

cocle-ae arum 1f.pl. spiral staircase

cocus = *coquus*

coelestis = *caelestis*

coenobi-um/caenubi-um i 2n. monastery

coepiscop-us i 2m. fellow-bishop

cognomino 1 I name

cognor = *conor*

collatio collation-is 3f. supper

collectane-us i 2m. collection

colligo 3 I deduce, conclude

columpna = *columna* (see O. 4)

comes comit-is 3m. count

comet-a ae 1f. = *cometes*

comitat-us us 4m. county (district administered by a *comes*)

comitiss-a ae 1f. countess

comitto = *committo* (see O.7)

commentariens-is commentariens-is 3m. secretary, recorder

commentator commentator-is 3m. commentator

commessatio = *comissatio* (see O.7 and O.11)

commilito commiliton-is 3m. fellowmonk

communico 1 I share (+ dat.: of Holy Communion)

communio communion-is 3f. company, communion, Eucharist

compassio compassion-is 3f. suffering

compater compatr-is 3m. first cousin

compatior 3 *compassus* I suffer with, pity

competens competent-is corresponding

competent-es ium 3m.pl. catechumens

completori-um i 2n./ or *-i orum* 2m.pl. compline (last service) *complex complic-is* 3m. confederate, ally

comprobo 1 I record

computatio computation-is 3f. reckoning, computation

concavitas concavitat-is 3f. hollow, cavity

concio = *contio* (see O.2)

conclusio conclusion-is 3f. confinement

concubinal-is e with a concubine

concupiscentia ae 1f. desire, longing

condempno = *condemno* (see O.4)

condict-us a um promised

conditio = *condicio* (see O.2)

condoleo 2/*condolesco* 3 -*dolui* I pity (+ dat.)

confedero (= *confoedero*: see O.1) 1 I join

confertus part. from *confercio*

confessio confession-is 3f. burial-place

confirmacio = *confirmatio* (see O.2)

conflict-us us 4m. conflict

conforto 1 I strengthen

confoveo 2 I cherish

confractio confraction-is 3f. breaking

congaudeo 2 I rejoice with another, rejoice greatly in (+ dat.)

congregatio congregation-is 3f. congregation, society

coniux = *coniunx*

conj- = *coni-*

conlimino 1 I join together

conloquium = *colloquium*

conprovincial-is e belonging to the same region

consencio = *consentio* (see O.2)

consepelio 4 I bury with

consequenter continuing

consuliturus = *consulturus*

contestor 1 dep. I testify

continenti-a ae 1f. contents

contribul-us i 2m. fellow-tribesman,

man of the same religion, compatriot

contritio contrition-is 3f. grief, contrition

contropabil-is e metaphorical

contul-us i 2m. (little) pole

convaleo 2 I get better

conversatio conversationis 3f. way of life

conversio conversion-is 3f. conversion

convinco 3 I convince

convitium = *convicium* (see O.2)

cooperor 1 dep. I work together with, help

coquin-a ae 1f. kitchen

cordetenus from the heart, deeply

corpulenti-a ae 1f. mass

correptio correption-is 3f. seizing, reproof

corruptio corruption-is 3f. corruption

coruscatio coruscation-is 3f. glittering, brightness

cottidie = *cotidie* (see O.7)

crastino 1 I put off, postpone

creatur-a ae 1f. creature

crebro = *cribro* 1 I sieve (see O.11)

crepido crepidin-is 3f. end

crevisse pf. inf. from *cresco*

cripta = *crypta* (see O.5)

crisma (= *chrisma*, Greek: see O.3(a)) *crismat-is* 3n. consecrated oil

crucifigo 3 -*fixi* -*fixus* I crucify

cuju- = *cuiu-*

cult-us us 4m. dress, clothing

curi-a ae 1f. court

curial-is curial-is 3m. courtier

curricul-um i 2n. cycle

cursor cursor-is 3m. runner (tr. as adj. 'swift')

custus = *custos* (see O.12)

cypressin-us a um of cypress wood

cypr-us i 2f. henna, henna-blossom

D

dampn- = *damn-* (see O.4)
dampnabil-is (= *damnabilis*: see O.4) *e*
  reprehensible
dapifer i 2m. waiter
de (+ abl.) with, of; (+ acc.) from
  (see G.15(a)(ii))
dealbo 1 I make white, dress in white
deambulatori-um i 2n. gallery
decaeptus = *deceptus* (see O.1)
decalvo 1 I make bald
decan-us i 2m. dean
deceptio deception-is 3f. deceit,
  deception
decrevisse pf. inf. of *decresco*
defloro 1 I excerpt
deflu-um i 2n. downpour
degrado 1 I reduce to a lower rank
dehonestas dehonestat-is 3f. dishonour
deitas deitat-is 3f. divinity, divine
  nature
dej- = *dei-*
delicacior = *delicatior* (see O.2)
deluculum = *diluculum* (see O.11)
denari-us i 2m. penny, coin
densitas densitat-is 3f. density
denuntio 1 I order
depromo 3 I declare
deputo 1 I cut down, allot
derelict-a ae 1f. widow
desepelio 4 I disinter
desevio = *desaevio* (see O.1)
desiderans desiderant-is longed for,
  loving
detentus part. from *detineo*
detestor 1 dep. I detest, hate
detons-us a um given the (monk's)
  tonsure
diabolic-us a um of the Devil
diabol-us/zabolus i 2m. the Devil
diacon-us i 2m./*diacon diacon-is* 3m.

deacon
dialectic-a ae 1f. logic
dialectic-us i 2m. teacher of logic
dial-is e divine
dibeo = *debeo* (see O.11)
dico 3 *dixi dictus* I sing, chant
dilacio = *dilatio* (see O.2)
dilapido 1 I squander, throw into (+
  dat.)
dilato 1 I defer, postpone
dilectio dilection-is 3f. love
dilector dilector-is 3m. worshipper
dilubrum = *delubrum* (see O.11)
dimersurus = *demersurus* fut. part. of
  demergo (see O.11)
dio(e)ces-is dio(e)ces-is 3f. (bishop's)
  diocese (see O.1)
directane-us a um without response
  (i.e. alternate chanting)
discisco = *descisco* (see O.11)
discucio = *discutio* (see O.2)
dispensatio dispensation-is 3f.
  dispensation
disr- = *dir-*
disseminatio dissemination-is 3f.
  dissemination
dissonanti-a ae 1f. discrepancy
distorte perversely
distruo = *destruo* (see O.11)
diuorcium = *diuortium* (see O.2)
divicie = *divitiae* (see O.2, O.1)
divisim separately
dodrans dodrant-is 3m. three-quarters
  (later: tidal-wave, flood)
dominic-a ae 1f. Sunday
dominic-us a um the Lord's (see also
  mensa); belonging to a master
dominor 1 dep. I induce (+ dat.)
Domin-us i 2m. God
domn- = *domin-* (see O.9)
domn-us (= *dominus*: see O.9) great

donari-um i 2n. gift, endowment
dormitio dormition-is 3f. sleep, death
dubietas dubietat-is 3f. doubt
ducat-us us 4m. guidance, escort, duchy
dum (+ subj.) when, since, by ...ing
   (see G.29, 30(a), 30(b))
duodenni-um i 2n. space of 12 years
dur-us a um bad
dux duc-is 3m. duke

E

ebdomad-a/hebdomad-a (see O.3(c)) *ae*
   1f. week
ebdomadari-us i 2m. monk assigned a
   duty for a week
ecclesi-a/eclesi-a/aecclesi-a/aeclisi-a/
   exclesi-a ae 1f. assembly, church
ecclesiastic-us/aecclesiastic-us a um of the
   Church, ecclesiastical
eciam = etiam (see O.2)
eclesia = ecclesia (see O.7)
econtra = contra on the other hand,
   instead
Edipus = Oedipus (see O.1)
eger = aeger (see O.1)
eginus = egenus (see O.11)
egritudo = aegritudo (see O.1)
egrotus = aegrotus (see O.1)
eju- = eiu-
elatio elation-is 3f. pride
elegere = eligere (see O.11)
eleison/eleyson have mercy (Greek)
elemosin-a ae 1f. charity, kindness, alms
eleuo 1 I build, put up
eleyson = eleison (q.v.)
elongo 1 I remove, postpone
eloqui-um i 2n. (fine) word
emitari = imitari (see O.11)
emorrois (= *haemorrhois haemorrhoid-is* 3f.
   (see O.3(c), O.1)) poisonous snake
emulus = aemulus (see O.1)

enarithn-us i 2m. individual
enigma = aenigma (see O.1)
enormitas enormitat-is 3f. enormous size
Ephrathe-us i 2m. an Ephrathite
episcopat-us/aepiscopatus us 4m
   episcopate, bishopric
episcop-us i 2m. bishop
epylentic-us = epileptic-us i m. adj.
   epileptic
epytafi-us (= *epitaphius*: see O.5, O.6)
   i 2m. tomb, tombstone (?)
eques equit-is 3m. knight
equipollens (= *aequipollens*: see O.1) of
   equal value (to: dat.)
equitat-us us 4m. horse
equo = aequo (see O.1)
equor = aequor (see O.1)
equs = equus
equus might be *aequus* (see O.1)
erba = herba (see O.3(c))
ereus = aereus (see O.1)
ergastul-um i 2n. prison
es = aes (see O.1)
esse n. being, existence
essenti-a ae 1f. existence, actuality
essentialiter in essence, actually
estimacio = aestimatio (see O.1, O.2)
estimo = aestimo (see O.1)
es-us us 4m. eating
etas = aetas (see O.1)
eternus = aeternus (see O.1)
ether = aether (see O.1)
Ethiopis = Aethiopis (see O.1)
ethnic-us i 2m. pagan
euacuo 1 I empty (out), cancel, lay
   aside
euangeli-a ae 1f. or *-um i* 2n. gospel
euangelic-us a um (of the) gospel
euangelizo 1 I preach the gospel (to: +
   dat.)
eus = Heus (see O.3(c))

euum = *aeuum* (see O.1)

evacuo see *euacuo*

evagino 1 I unsheath

evectio evection-is 3f. transport, course
(of the sun), promotion

exa- see also *exsa-*

exardeo 2 I am inflamed/encouraged

excavo 1 I demoralize

excellenti-a ae 1f. excellency (title)

exclesia = *ecclesia* (q.v.)

excommunicatio excommunication-is 3f.
excommunication

excommunicat-us i 2m. an
excommunicate

excommunico 1 I excommunicate

excurs-us us 4m. course, way (or sally,
attack)

exi- see *exsi-*

exicium = *exitium* (see O.2)

existens existent-is existing, being

existenti-a ae 1f. being, existence

existo 3 I am, exist

exorbito 1 I turn aside from

exp- see also *exsp-*

expaveo 2 I am very afraid (of)

expectatio expectation-is 3f.
contemplation

expletio expletion-is 3f. completion

expulsus part. from *expello*

exquisicior = *exquisitior* (see O.2)

ext- see also *exst-*

extimeo 2 I fear greatly

extimplo = *extemplo* (see O.11)

exu- see also *exsu-*

F

fabell-a ae 1f. little bean

fabric-a ae 1f. building, structure

fabulor 1 dep. I say

facie: a facie (+ gen.) before (lit. from
the face of: Hebraism)

facio 3/4 *feci factus* I make x (acc.) do
Y (inf.): see G.17(c)

factur-a ae 1f. making, piece of
handiwork

falanx = *phalanx* (see O.6)

falsitas falsitat-is 3f. falsehood

famen famin-is 3n. speech, word

familiar-is e private, familiar

famolus = *famulus* (see O.12)

fari-us a um Arab

fassus part. from *fateor*

fatesco = *fatisco* (see O.11)

fatigacio = *fatigatio* (see O.2)

fatigi-um i 2n. trouble, pains

fatimen fatimin-is 3n. word

fec- see *fex*

fedo = *foedo* (see O.1)

fedus = *foedus* (see O.1)

fenestell-a ae 1f. little window

feri-a ae 1f. day: *quarta f.* =
Wednesday; *sexta f.* = Friday)

feste in festive mood

festuc-a ae 1f. mote

feud-um i 2n. fief, fee

fex fec-is = *faex faec-is* (see O.1)

ficulne-a ae 1f. fig-tree

fidel-es ium 3m.pl. the faithful (i.e.
Christians)

figur-a ae 1f. example, allegory

figuraliter figuratively, symbolically

figuratio figuration-is 3f. parable

fimbri-a ae 1f. hem

firm-a ae 1f. revenue

fixus part. from *figo*

flagicium = *flagitium* (see O.2)

flammatic-us a um fiery (CL *flammeus*)

flexus part. from *flecto*

fluius = *fluuius*

focilo = *focillo* (see O.7)

fol OFr. 'fool'

fore = *esse* (see G.5)

formell-a ae 1f. mould, round
formidabiliter terrifyingly
formonsus = *formosus*
fornicari-us i 2m. fornicator; adj.
   fornicatory
fornicor 1 dep. I fornicate
fraglo = *fragro*
frame-a ae 1f. sword
fratr-es um 3m.pl. monks, brothers
fraudolentus = *fraudulentus* (see O.12)
frontispici-um i 2n. countenance
fructifico 1 I bear fruit
functus part. of *fungor*

G

garcifer i 2m. servant, boy (cf. Fr.
   garçon?)
gavisus part. from *gaudeo*
Gehenn-a ae 1f. Hell (Hebrew)
generatio generation-is 3f. generation,
   begetting
Genes-is Genes-is 3 the book of Genesis
genitali-a genitali-um 3n.pl. genitals
genitus part. from *gigno*
gentil-es ium 3m.pl. pagans, heathen
gentil-is e heathen
genui pf. parf. of *gigno*
giro/gyro 1 I whirl round, turn
glorifico 1 I glorify
grabe = *grave* (see O.13)
gracia = *gratia* (q.v.: see O.2)
grandevus = *grandaevus* (see O.1)
grassatrix f.adj. marauding
gratanter gladly
grati-a/graci-a ae 1f. grace (of God)
Grecus = *Graecus* (see O.1)
gross-us a um thick, fat
gyro/giro 1 I turn, whirl round

H

habeo 2 + inf. forms future tense: see
   G.4(c)

habitacul-um i 2n. home, dwelling
habundantia = *abundantia* (see O.3(c))
habunde = *abunde* (see O.3(c))
h(a)eres-is h(a)eres-is 3f. heresy
haeretic-i orum 2m.pl. heretics
halienus = *alienus* (see O.3(c))
hebraic-us a um Hebrew
hec = *haec* (see O.1)
hedus = *haedus* (see O.1)
heremit-a ae 1m. (= *eremita*: see
   O.3(c)) hermit, monk
heres-is (= *haeresis*: see O.1) *heres-is* 3f.
   heresy
heretic-us (= *haereticus*: see O.1) *i* 2m.
   heretic
hid-a ae 1f. hide (measure of land)
Hierosolym-a orum 2n.pl./*Hierusalem*/
   Jerusalem indecl. Jerusalem
hii = *hi*
hilariter = *hilare*
hinnulus = *hinnuleus* a young roebuck
histe = *iste* (see O.3(c))
honorificenti-a ae 1f. honour
hor-a ae 1f. canonical hour (e.g.
   prime, terce, etc.)
hospicium = *hospitium* (see O.2)
hostiarius = *ostiarius* (see O.3(c))
huju- = *huiu-*
humi on the ground
humilio 1 I abase, humble
humilitas humilitat-is 3f. humility
humitenus towards the ground
hundred-um i 2n. hundred
hyemps/hyems = *hiems* (see O.4)
hymn-us/ymn-us i 2m. hymn
hypocris-is hypocris-is f. hypocrisy,
   pretended sanctity
hypocrit-a ae 1m. hypocrite
Hyspania = *Hispania* (see O.5)

I

iacul-us i 2m. serpent (that darts from
a tree)
iamiam already
idem eadem idem aforementioned
idol-um/ydol-um i 2n. graven image,
idol
idum-a ae 1f. hand (Hebrew)
Ieronymus = Hieronymus (see O.3(c))
Jerome
Ies-us u m. Jesus
igitur therefore (often *first* word)
ignabus = ignauus (see O.13)
ignit-us a um fiery
illico = ilico (see O.7)
immarcescibil-is e unfading
immoderanci-a (= immoderanti-a: see
O.2) *ae* 1f. intemperance
imo = immo (see O.7)
imperatrix imperatric-is 3f. empress
imperial-is e imperial
impossibil-is e impossible
impossibilitas impossibilitat-is 3f.
impossibility
impugnator impugnator-is 3m. assailant,
enemy
in (+ acc.) as, (+ abl.) into, (+ abl.)
with (see G.15(a)(ii))
inaedia = inedia (see O.1)
inb-; see *imb-* (O.21)
incarnatio incarnation-is 3f. incarnation
incensor incensor-is 3m. inciter
incentiu-us a um that incites (to: gen.)
incircumcis-us a um uncircumcised (i.e.
not Jewish)
incircumscript-us a um infinite
incolomis = incolumis (see O.12)
incomparabiliter incomparably
inconsolabiliter inconsolably
inconvulsibil-is e unalterable
incorrigibil-is e incorrigible, incurable

increpatio increpation-is 3f. rebuke
incurabil-is e incurable
indictio indiction-is 3f. period of 15
years, indiction
indubie certainly
inestimabil-is = inaestimabilis (see O.1)
infantul-us i 2m. baby
infernal-is e infernal, below the earth
infern-um i 2n. Hell
infero -ferre -tuli -latus I say, speak
infestatio infestation-is 3f. disturbance,
molestation
infra (+ acc.) within (= *intra*)
infronit-us a um (= *infrunitus:* see
O.12) silly, tasteless
infructifer a um unfruitful
infulat-us a um adorned (with)
ingeniol-um i 2n. small intellect (dim.
of *ingenium*)
ingenit-us a um unbegotten
inhereo = inhaereo (see O.1)
iniquitas iniquitat-is 3f. sin
init-us part. of *ineo*
inj- = ini-
inlitus part. from *inlino*
inluminatio inlumination-is 3f.
enlightening
inmaniter enormously
inobediens = inoboediens inoboedient-is
disobedient (see O.1)
inolit-us a um inveterate, normal
inpaciens = impatiens (see O.21, O.2)
inperium = imperium (see O.21)
inpinguo 1 I smear, make sleek
inplico = implico (see O.21)
inpositio inposition-is 3f. (= *impositio:*
see O.21) application
inpostmodum soon, in future (CL
postmodum)
inquid = inquit (see O.19)
inquio I say (= *inquam*)

inrationabil-is e irrational,
    unreasonable
insensat-us a um foolish
institutio institution-is 3f. creation,
    institution
instrument-a orum 3n.pl. title-deeds
intelligo = intellego (see O.11)
intendo 3 I observe, look (at), pay
    attention (to)
intentio intention-is 3f. intention
intent-us us 4m. purpose, intent
interemptus part. from *interimo*
intiger = integer (see O.11)
intimo 1 I make known
intono 1 I chant
intro (+ abl.) into; *de intro* (+ acc.)
    (from) within
inuicem = invicem (q.v.)
investitur-a ae 1f. investiture
invicem/inuicem with each other; *ad
    invicem* to one another (G.11(e)(ii))
invisibil-is e invisible
iocund- = iucund- (see O.12)
ipotes-is ipotes-is 3f. hypothesis
ipse a um the, this/that, he/she/it
    G.11(a)
Ispania = Hispania (see O.3(c))
Ispanius = Hispanus (see O.3(c))
Israhel -is 3m. or /*Israel* indecl. Israel
Israhelit-a ae 1m. Israelite
Israheliticus a um of Israel
iste a ud this/that (G.11(c))
istoria = historia (see O.3(c))
istrio istrion-is 3m. (= *histrio*: see
    O.3(c)) actor, minstrel
iterato again, a second time (G.13)
Iudae-us i 2m. a Jew
Iud-as ae/Iuda indecl. Judah
iugiter constantly
iusticia = iustitia (see O.2)
iustitiari-us i 2m. justice, judge

iuvencul-us i 2m. young man
iuxta (+ acc.) according to, in
    accordance with

J
j- see *i-*
jussio jussion-is 3f. (= *iussio*) command

K
k- see *c-*
kyrie/quirie O Lord (Greek)

L
labil-is e transient
lacer-us a um mangling
lacrym- = lacrim- (see O.5)
lacto 1 I give suck
laetalis = letalis (see O.1)
laic-us i 2m. lay person; adj. lay
lamento = lamentor (see G.3)
lat- part. from *fero*
laucior = lautior (see O.2)
laudament-um i 2n. permission
lebo = levo (see O.13)
ledo = laedo (see O.1)
lesio lesion-is 3f. (= *laesio*: see O.1)
    injury
letania = litania (q.v.) (see O.11)
letifico = laetifico (see O.1)
letor = laetor (see O.1)
letus = laetus (see O.1)
leuca see *banna*
leuo 1 I build
leuug-a ae 1f. league, mile, measure of
    land
levigo 1 make smooth, lighten
libr-a ae 1f. pound (weight or money)
licencia = licentia (see O.2)
liciatori-um i 2n. weaver's beam
licinicon the tenth hour (when candles
    are lit for Vespers)

linio = *lino*

litani-a/letani-a ae 1f. prayer; litany

lith-us i 2m. stone (Greek)

litteratori-us a um grammatical, of grammar

littor- = *litor-*, from *litus* (see O.7)

litu-us i 2m. bishop's crozier

locul-us i 2m. tomb, bier, bookcase, scabbard

locutio locution-is 3f. conversation, expression

loetifer = *letifer* (see O.1)

longeuus = *longaeuus* (see O.1)

loquutus = *locutus*

loric-a ae 1f. chain-mail

lucernar-e is 3n. = *licinicon*

lucernar-is e Vesper, by candlelight

Lucifer i 2m. Lucifer, the Devil

luct-a ae 1f. wrestling

luminar-e luminar-is 3n. light

lunul-a ae 1f. little moon

M

machumari-a ae 1f. mosque

madido 1 I moisten

magnali-a magnali-um 3n.pl. miracles, mighty works

magnas magnat-is 3m. great man, noble, magnate

magnifico 1 I acknowledge (the) greatness (of)

maj- = *mai-*

manduco 1 I eat

mani-a ae 1f. madness (Greek)

manifeste = *manifesto* clearly

mansio mansion-is 3f. home

manubi-a arum 1f.pl. prize

marchi-a ae 1f. march, borderland (governed by a *marchio*)

marchio marchion-is 3m. margrave, marquis

marsupium = *marsuppium* (see O.7)

martiri-um/martyri-um i 2n. martyrdom (see O.5)

martyr martyr-is 3m. martyr

matutin-ae arum 1f.pl or -*um i* 2n. morning prayers, matins

medel-a ae 1f. healing

medio/medior 1/1 dep. I am in the middle

melliflu-us a um honeyed, mellifluous

memento remember (imper. of *memini*)

memorat-us a um aforementioned

mensa dominica the altar at Mass, the Lord's table

mercatio mercation-is 3f. price

mercimoni-um i 2n. market

mereo = *maereo* (see O.1)

meror = *maeror* (see O.1)

mestus = *maestus* (see O.1)

metor 1 dep. I stay

michi = *mihi* (see O.3(b))

miles milit-is 3m. knight

millen-i ae a a thousand

ministeri-um i 2n. job, office, minister

ministro 1 I serve (+ dat.)

minor 1 dep. I brandish

minsis = *mensis* (see O.11)

mirabil-e mirabil-is 3n. miracle

mirand-a orum 2n.pl. miracles

miserturus fut. part. from *misereor*

miss-a ae 1f. (or pl.) dismissal, Mass, Eucharist

misticus = *mysticus* (see O.5)

misus = *missus* (see O.7)

mixt-um i 2n. diluted wine

molendin-um i 2n. mill

momentane-us a um momentary, brief

monach-a ae 1f. nun

monach-us i 2m. monk

monasteri-um/monastirium i 2n. monastery

monastic-us a um monastic
monazon monazont-is 3m. monk
monet-a ae 1f. money
monial-is monial-is 3f. nun
montane-a ae 1f. mountain
monument-um i 2n. tomb
moraliter figuratively, ethically
mortificativ-us a um destructive,
    mortifying
multiplicitas multiplicitat-is 3f.
    polyvalence, variety of meaning
mundan-us a um worldly
mundo 1 I cleanse, purify
munitio munition-is 3f. castle
murenul-a ae 1f. small necklace
murrh-a ae 1f. myrrh
mursus = morsus (see O.12)
musitatio musitation-is 3f. murmuring

N
nactus part. from *nanciscor*
natal-e natal-is 3n. anniversary (of a
    martyr's death); *natale domini*
    Christmas
natatilis e able to swim
nativitas nativitat-is 3f. birth
natur-a ae 1f. substance
nauigeri-um i 2n. voyage
nautor nautor-is 3m. sailor, captain
necessari-a orum 2n.pl. necessities
neglig- = negleg- (see O.11)
negocium = negotium (see O.2)
neguciator = negotiator (see O.12, O.2)
nept-is nept-is 3f. niece
nequissimus sup. of *nequam*
nichil = nihil (see O.3(b))
nichilominus = nihilominus (see O.3(b))
nichilum = nihilum (see O.3(b))
nimie excessively
Ninivit-a ae 1m. Ninevite
nominal-is e nominalist

non-a ae 1f. nones (prayer at the ninth
    hour)
Noric-us i 2m. a Norse, Norwegian
Normannic-us a um Norman
Normann-us i 2m. a Norman
notant-es ium 3m.pl. officials
notari-us i 2m. notary, lawyer
nouiter recently
nox noct-is 3f. eve
nugacitas nugacitat-is 3f. frivolous
    advances
nugax nugac-is 3m. fornicator
nullatenus by no means
numerositas numerositat-is 3f. multitude
numquid indicates a question (see
    G.24(a))
nunci- = nunti- (see O.2)
nunquid = numquid
nus = nos (see O.12)
nutabund-us a um tottering
nutrici-us i 2m. tutor

O
obediens = oboediens (see O.1)
obj- = obi-
oblatam part. from *offero*
oblatio oblation-is 3f. offering
obnubilatio obnubilation-is 3f.
    obscuration
obsecundo 1 I obey
obtenebro 1 I darken
obtimates = optimates (q.v.: see O.18)
obto = opto (see O.18)
obvio 1 I meet
occidental-is e western
octav-a ae 1f. octave (7th/8th day after
    a feast)
odio = odi (see G.3)
odio habeo I hate x (acc.)
oephi/ephi indecl. ephah (a Hebrew
    dry measure) (see G.6(c))

offendicul-um i 2n. stumbling-block
official-is official-is 3m. official,
    attendant
operatio operation-is 3f. divine service,
    grace
opertori-um i 2n. cover
opertur-a ae 1f. roof
opifex opific-is 3m. creator
opitulatio opitulation-is 3f. help
oportunus = opportunus (see O.7)
oppressor oppressor-is 3m. oppressor
opteneo = obtineo (see O.18, O.11)
optimat-es ium 3m.pl. magnates, nobles
optineo = obtineo (see O.18)
optulit = obtulit (*offero*: see O.18,
    O.11)
oracio = oratio (q.v.: see O.2)
oracul-um i 2n. imperial rescript
oratio oration-is/oracio oracion-is 3f.
    prayer (see O.2)
oratori-um i 2n. place of prayer
ordenacio = ordinatio (q.v.: see O.11,
    O.2)
ordinatio ordination-is 3f. order
ordo ordin-is 3m. monastic order
oriental-is e eastern
orror = horror (see O.3(c))
orthodox-us i 2m. a person of the true
    Church, orthodox Christian
orthograph-us i 2m. authority on
    correct spelling
ostentament-um i 2n. sign, mark

P

paciencia = patientia (see O.2)
pactus part. from *pango*
pagan-us i 2m. pagan
palacium = palatium (see O.2)
palatin-us a um (count) palatine
palm-us i 2m. palm
pap-a ae 1m. pope

parabol-a ae 1f. parable
paradis-us i paradys-us i 2m./ paradise
    (see O.5)
parascev-e -es day of preparation
    (before Passover sabbath: Greek)
parasit-us i 2m. deceiver
Parisius indecl. Paris, to Paris, in Paris
paro 1 I learn by heart
parthen-a ae 1f. nun (Greek)
participatio participation-is 3f. sharing
parvolus = parvulus (see O.12)
parvul-us/parvolus i 2m. little boy
pasch-a ae 1f. (or n.indecl. or *pascha*
    paschat-is) Easter
paschal-is e of Easter
pascu-a ae 1f. pasture
passio passion-is 3f. passion (especially
    Christ's)
pastor pastor-is 3m. bishop
pastoral-is e of a bishop
pastus part. from *pasco*
patr-es patr-um 3m.pl. fathers (of the
    Church)
patriarch-a ae 1m. patriarch
patriarchi-um i 2n. papal palace
patrici-us i 2m. patrician (an honorific
    title)
pauso 1 I rest
pavifactus = pavefactus (see O.11)
peccator peccator-is 3m. sinner
pedetentim = pedetemptim
pej- = pei-
pene = paene (see O.1)
penitencia = paenitentia (see O.1, O.2)
penitet = paenitet (see O.1)
per (+ acc.) because of (= *propter*)
perauid-us a um eager
percanto 1 I finish singing, sing
    through
percelebro 1 I celebrate in full
percerte certainly, for sure

perdico 3 -dixi -dictus I finish saying
perditio perdition-is 3f. ruin
peremptor peremptor-is 3m. murderer
peremptori-us a um of destruction
perentor = peremptor (q.v.)
perfid-i orum 2m.pl. heretics
pergam-a orum 2n.pl. citadel
perhennis = perennis (see O.3(c))
perigrinus = peregrinus (see O.11)
permixtio permixtion-is 3f. mixing up
perplexor 3 dep. -plexus I embrace
persolbo = persolvo (see O.13)
pertinaci-a ae 1f. cruelty, wrath
pervicatia = pervicacia (see O.2)
Pharisae-us i 2m. Pharisee
Pharius = Parius (see O.3(a))
Phebus = Phoebus (see O.1)
Philisthae-us a um Philistine
Philistim nom.pl./Philistin-i orum
    2m.pl. Philistines
philosophic-us a um philosophical, of
    philosophy
piacular-is e sinful, requiring atonement
pignus pignor-is 3n. child (lit. pledge
    (of love))
pigretudo pigretudin-is 3f. slothfulness,
    laziness
pigrito 1 I am slow
pigritor 1 dep. I am slow
pil-a ae 1f. pill
pilul-a ae 1f. pill, pellet
pisinn-us i 2m. small boy
planet-a ae 1f. chasuble
planto 1 I set
plasma plasmat-is 3n. creature
plenitudo plenitudin-is 3f. fullness
pocius = potius (see O.2)
podi-um i 2n. scaffolding, centring
poenal-is e painful, injurious
poenitudo poenitudin-is 3f. repentance
poetri-a ae 1f. poetry, poem

polyandri-um i 2n. tomb, cemetery
pontifex pontific-is 3m. bishop, pontiff
pontifical-is e of a bishop, of the Pope
pontificat-us us 4m. see, bishopric,
    episcopal office
portiuncul-a ae 1f. little bit
possibilitas possibilitat-is 3f. possibility
posthumus = postumus (see O.3(a))
poto might = puto (see O.12)
praecaeptum = praeceptum (see O.1)
praeceptio praeception-is 3f. diploma
praecipuae = praecipue (see O.1)
praecordial-is e heartfelt, sincere
praedestinatio praedestination-is 3f.
    predestination
praedicament-um i 2n. category (of
    Aristotle)
praedicatio praedication-is 3f. preaching
praedicator praedicator-is 3m. preacher
praedico/predico 1 I preach
praedict-us/predict-us a um aforesaid
praefat-us/prefat-us a um
    aforementioned
praefect-us/prefect-us i 2m. count
praelacio praelacion-is 3f. authority
praelibo 1 I taste beforehand
praeposit-us i 2m. abbot; (later) provost
    (2nd to abbot)
praerogativ-a/prerogativ-a ae 1f. right (of
    first vote), prerogative
praesagmen praesagmin-is 3n. presage,
    word (?)
praesencia = praesentia (see O.2)
praestulor = praestolor (see O.12)
praesul praesul-is 3m. prelate
praesumpcio (= praesumptio: see O.2)
    praesumpcion-is 3f. audacity
praesumptuose boldly, presumptuously
pre = prae (see O.1)
pre- = see under prae- if not listed
    (see O.1)

preampl-us a um very large
prebeo = *praebeo* (see O.1)
precedo = *praecedo* (see O.1)
precello = *praecello* (see O.1)
preceps precipit-is = *praeceps praecipit-is* (see O.1)
precipio = *praecipio* (see O.1)
precipue = *praecipue* (see O.1)
precium = *pretium* (see O.2)
preclarus = *praeclarus* (see O.1)
preco = *praeco* (see O.1)
predecessor (= *praedecessor.* see O.1)
   predecessor-is 3m. predecessor
predicare = *praedicare* (q.v.) (see O.1)
predictus = *praedictus* (see O.1)
predives = *praedives* (see O.1)
preeo = *praeeo* (see O.1)
prefatus = *praefatus* (see O.1)
prefectus = *praefectus* (q.v.) (see O.1)
prefero = *praefero* (see O.1)
preficio = *praeficio* (see O.1)
pregusto = *praegusto* (see O.1)
prelatur-a ae 1f. prelacy, preferment
prelat-us i 2m. prelate, Church dignitary
prelium = *proelium* (see O.1)
premineo = *praeemineo* (see O.1)
premissa from *praemitto* (see O.1)
premitto = *praemitto* (see O.1)
premium = *praemium* (see O.1)
preparo = *praeparo* (see O.1)
prepedio = *praepedio* (see O.1)
prependul-us (= *praependulus:* see O.1) *a um* hanging, in mid-air
prepondero = *praepondero* (see O.1)
prerogativa = *praerogativa* (q.v.) (see O.1)
preruptus = *praeruptus* (see O.1)
presagio = *praesagio* (see O.1)
presagium = *praesagium* (see O.1)
presbiter = *presbyter* (q.v.) (see O.5)

presbyter/presbiter i 2m. elder, priest
presencia = *praesentia* (see O.1, O.2)
presens = *praesens* (see O.1)
presento 1 I show, display, present
preses = *praeses* (see O.1)
presideo = *praesideo* (see O.1)
prestantius = *praestantius* (see O.1)
presto = *praesto* (see O.1)
prestolor = *praestolor* (see O.1)
presul = *praesul* (q.v.) (see O.1)
presumo = *praesumo* (see O.1)
presumptor (= *praesumptor.* see O.1)
   presumptor-is 3m. presumptuous person
pretendo = *praetendo* (see O.1)
preter = *praeter* (see O.1)
preterea = *praeterea* (see O.1)
pretereo = *praetereo* (see O.1)
prevenio = *praevenio* (see O.1)
prim-a ae 1f. prime (prayers at the first hour)
primat-es ium 3m.pl. nobles, leading men
primogenit-us a um first-begotten
principaliter chiefly, primarily, in the first instance
prior prior-is 3m. abbot
privilegi-um i 2n. privilege, charter, bull
problema problemat-is 3n. riddle, problem
processio procession-is 3f. procession
prodicio = *proditio* (see O.2)
profect-us us 4m. progress
proficu-us a um beneficial
profunditas profunditat-is 3f. depth
promtus = *promptus*
propalo 1 I make public, divulge
prophet-a ae 1m. prophet
prophetal-is e prophetic
propheti-a ae 1f. prophecy

prophetic-us a um prophetic
propheto 1 I prophesy
propicius = *propitius* (see O.2)
propino 1 I serve, give
propitiatio propitiation-is 3f.
   propitiation, forgiveness
propositiuncul-a ae 1f. tiny proposition
proprietas proprietat-is 3f. property
propri-us a um natural
prosator prosator-is 3m. progenitor,
   ancestor
protoplast-us a um first-created
provide = *providenter* with
   forethought
provinci-a ae 1f. region, district
provulgo 1 I publish, make known
psallo 3 I chant (the Psalms)
psalmist-a ae 1m. psalmist
psalmodi-a ae 1f. psalm-singing
psalm-us i 2m. psalm
psalteri-um i 2n. psaltery, the Psalms
pseudo false
pseudoloqu-us i 2m. liar
pseudophilosoph-us i 2m. false
   philosopher
purificatio purification-is 3f. Purification
   (feast of), Candlemas
purpuro 1 I dye purple
pusillanimitas pusillanimitat-is 3f.
   faintheartedness
putredo putredin-is 3f. rottenness

Q

Quadragesim-a ae 1f. Lent
quadriflu-us a um with four streams
quaestio quaestion-is 3f. question
quaestor quaestor-is 3m. treasurer
qualiter that (see G.22(a)), how
quandiu = *quamdiu*
quantotius (= *quantocius*) as quickly as
   possible

quatenus in order that, so that, that, to
   (see G.22(a), G.23(d), G.26(b),
   G.27(b))
quatinus = *quatenus* (q.v.) (see O.11)
que = *quae* (see O.1)
quedam = *quaedam* (see O.1)
quero = *quaero* (see O.1)
questio = *quaestio* (q.v.: see O.1)
quia that (see G.22(a))
quirie = *kyrie*
quo in order that (without
   comparative: see G.27(c))
quociens = *quotiens* (see O.2)
quod as, that (see G.22(a))
quoniam that (see G.22(a))
quum = *cum*

R

racio = *ratio* (see O.2)
radico 1 I take root
rancor rancor-is 3m. grudge
rasur-a ae 1f. scraping
rationabiliter rationally
reat-us us 4m. guilt, charge
recordacio = *recordatio* (see O.2)
redemo = *redimo* (see O.11)
redemptio redemption-is 3f. redemption,
   redeemer
redemptor redemptor-is 3m. redeemer
refecturi-um (= *refectorium*: see O.12) i
   2n. refectory
regali-a regali-um 3n. imperial
   privileges
regenero 1 I regenerate
regiro = *regyro* (q.v.) (see O.5)
regular-is e canonical, of a (monastic)
   rule
regyro/regiro 1 I turn back, wheel
   round
relampo 1 I shine out
relatiue relatively

relegio = religio (see O.11)
relevatio relevation-is 3f. relief
ren renis 3m. inmost thoughts/feelings
renuncio = renuntio (see O.2)
reparatio reparation-is 3f. restoration,
    healing, redemption
repp- often = rep- (see O.7)
represento = repraesento (see O.1)
reprobo 1 I condemn
reprob-us a um false, spurious, unsound
repulsio repulsion-is 3f. repulsion
resalio 4 I leap back
rescript-um i 2n. rescript, copy
respiramen respiramin-is 3n. respite (=
    respiramentum)
responsori-um i 2n. response
resulto 1 I re-echo (trans.)
resurrectio resurrection-is 3f. resurrection
retributor retributor-is 3m. requiter,
    recompenser
rettulit = retulit (see O.7)
revellacio = rebellatio (see O.13, O.2)
rhythm-us i 2m. poem in a rhythmic
    (non-classical) metre
rignum = regnum (see O.11)
rigo 1 I water, bedew, make wet
rot-a ae 1f. court; sphere
rotul-us i 2m. roll
rudiloqu-us i 2m. detractor
rugio 4 I roar
rugit-us us 4m. roaring

S

sabbat-um i 2n. the Sabbath, Saturday
sacerdos sacerdot-is 3m. bishop
sacrament-a orum 2n.pl. sacraments
sacrament-um i 2n. sacred power,
    sacrament
sacrifici-um i 2n. offering, Eucharist
sacrist-a ae 1f. sacristan, sacrist
saecular-is e secular

saecul-um i 2n. the present world; in
    saecula saeculorum for ever
sagen-a ae 1f. large fishing-net, seine
sagita = sagitta (see O.7)
sagito = sagitto (see O.7)
salivar-e salivar-is 3n. bit
saltim = saltem (see O.11)
saluator (salvator) saluator-is 3m. saviour
salus salut-is 3f. eternal life, salvation,
    conversion
salutar-is e of salvation
salvo 1 I save
sanctimonial-is sanctimonial-is 3f. nun
sanct-us i 2m. saint
sarcofagus = sarcophagus (see O.6)
satago 3 I endeavour (+ inf.)
Satan-as ae m. the Devil, Satan
satis = nimis very (see G.12(b))
scalor = squalor
scandal-um i 2n. obstacle, stumbling-
    block, scandal, abuse
sc(h)isma sc(h)ismat-is 3n. schism (see
    O.3(b))
sc(h)olar-is sc(h)olar-is 3m. student,
    scholar (see O.3(b))
scissio scission-is 3f. division, schism
scola = schola (see O.3(b))
scotic-us a um Irish
scrib-a ae 1m. scribe (Jewish doctor of
    the Law)
scriptur-ae arum 1f. the Scriptures
scutat-us a um armed with a shield
se him/her/it/them (= eum etc.: see
    G.11(e)(i))
secul- = saecul- (q.v.) (see O.1)
secundo again, a second time
secus (+ acc.) near
sedicio = seditio (see O.2)
segnicies = segnities (see O.2)
semet strengthened form of se
senodalis = sinodalis (q.v.)

sensualiter corporeally

sentencia = *sententia* (see O.2)

sepe = *saepe*: see O.1

sept-um (= *saept-um*: see O.1) *i* 2n. precinct

sepultor sepultor-is 3m. burier

sequestro 1/ *-or* 1 dep. I separate

serenitas serenitat-is 3f. serenity

serpentin-us a um of a serpent

seruitor seruitor-is 3m. attendant

seru-us i 2m. serf, villein

sevicia = *saevitia* (see O.1, O.2)

sevus = *saevus* (see O.1)

sext-a ae 1f. sext

sicer-a ae 1f. liquor, strong drink, spirits

sicl-us i 2m. shekel (Hebrew)

sigillabil-is e able to make an impression

sigillans sigillant-is making an impression

sigillo 1 I make an impression

sigill-um i 2n. seal

signacul-um i 2n. seal

signo 1 I make the sign of the Cross

simoniach-us i 2m. simoniac

sinax-is (synaxis) sinax-is f. gathering, assembly, Eucharist

sinodal-is (also *senodalis* = *synodalis*) *e* of a synod

siquidem certainly, indeed, without doubt, therefore

sirpus = *scirpus*

sixtus = *xystus* (q.v.) (see O.16, O.5)

soboles = *suboles* (see O.12)

solemneter = *sollemniter* (see O.11)

solid-us i 2m. shilling

sollempniter = *sollemniter* (see O.4)

sollicitatio sollicitation-is 3f. seduction

solummodo only

sompn- = *somn-* (see O.4)

sophistice sophistically

sophistic-us i 2m. sophist

soror-es um 3f.pl. nuns, sisters

spacium = *spatium* (see O.2)

speci-es ei 5f. goods

specimen specimin-is 3n. beauty

spiculator = *speculator* (see O.11)

spiracul-um i 2n. breath

spirital-is e spiritual

spiritual-is e spiritual

spondali-a spondali-um 3n.pl. parapets

spretus part. from *sperno*

spreui pf. of *sperno*

spuri-us a um illegitimate

stacio = *statio* (see O.2)

stol-a ae 1f. stole, vestment

stranguillo = *strangulo*

subiect-um i 2n. subject (logic)

subiugal-is subiugal-is 3m. beast of burden, horse

subiugo 1 I subjugate

subj- = *subi-*

sublimo 1 I praise, raise, elevate

subreptio subreption-is 3f. plot

subsanno 1 I mock, deride

subsistenti-a ae 1f. being, substance, essence

substento = *sustento*

subterfugi-um i 2n. subterfuge, evasion

suffragi-um i 2n. prop, aid

suffult-us us 4m. support

suficientissime (= *sufficientissime*: see O.7) very adequately

suggestio suggestion-is 3f. suggestion

sulphurius = *sulfureus* (see O.6, O.11)

super (+ acc.) concerning, on

supericio 3/4 *-ieci -iectus* I throw on top

superno 1 I float on the surface

superscriptio superscription-is 3f. inscription

supervestio 4 I clothe
supplimentum = *supplementum* (see
  O.11)
supradict-us a um aforementioned
surreptio surreption-is 3f. deception,
  trickery
susum = *sursum*
su-us a um his, her, their (= *eius,*
  eorum: see G.11(e)(iii))
synod-us i 2f. synod

T

tabul-a ae 1f. gong; pl. castanets
taliter in such a way
temet strengthened form of *te*
temporal-is e worldly
tenebresco 3 I become dark
tenor tenor-is 3m. sense
tercia = *tertia* (see O.2)
terren-us a um earthly
tersus part. from *tergeo*
terti-a ae 1f. terce
tertio three times
testament-um i 2n. Testament (Old or
  New)
Teutonic-us a um German
thelone-um (= *telon-ium/-eum*) *i* 2n.
  toll
theologic-a orum 2n.pl. theology
thom-us i 2m. (= *tomus*: see O.3(a))
  volume
thorus = *torus* (see O.3(a))
titillatio titillation-is 3f. titillation
titul-us i 2m. church
tog-a ae 1f. cassock
torridul-us a um a little burnt
tortus part. from *torqueo*
tractat-us us 4m. (or *um i* 2n.) treatise
traditio tradition-is 3f. tradition
tradux traduc-is 3m. transmission
transmutatio transmutation-is 3f. change

tribulatio tribulation-is 3f. trouble,
  tribulation
tribulo 1 I torment
trico 1 I lag behind
triduan-us a um for three days
trinitas trinitat-is 3f. trinity, the Trinity
tripudi-um i 2n. jubilation, jubilant
  dance
tristeg-a ae 1f. bell-scaffold (lit. third
  storey)
tritus part. from *tero*
tronus = *thronus* (see O.3(a))
tropice figuratively
tropic-us a um figurative
trutannizo 1 I am a beggar
tumb-a ae 1f. tomb, sepulchre
turbulenti-a ae 1f. trouble
Turc-i orum 1m.pl. Turks

U

uaccin-us a um cow-like, stupid
uel and
uesper-a/vesper-a ae 1f. Vespers
uigili-ae nocturn-ae arum 1f.pl. vigils
  (the night office)
uillan-us i 2m. villein, customary
  tenant, villager, villain (OFr)
ulcio = *ultio* (see O.2)
ulcus ulcer-is 3n. torment
ullatenus in any respect whatever
umbr-a ae 1f. trick
unanim-is e of one mind
uncin-us i 2m. hook
unianimis = *unanimis* (q.v.)
unigenit-us a um only-begotten
universitas universitat-is 3f. whole body,
  college
unusquisque each individual
usque (+ acc.) as far as, (+ abl.) until
usquedum until
usquequo how long? until when?

ustus part. from *uro*
usy-a ae 1f. substance (Greek)
utili-a utili-um 3n.pl. requirements
utique by any means
utrumnam whether

V

vacco = *vaco* (see O.7)
vademonium = *vadimonium* (see O.11)
vaesanio 4 (= *vesanio*: see O.1) I am
    insane
valens valent-is 3m. value
valeo 2 I am able (+ inf.)
vass-us i 2m. vassal
ve = *vae* (see O.1)
vel = *uel* (q.v.)
velat-us a um veiled (i.e. nuns)
vel-um i 2n. veil
venacio = *venatio* (see O.2)
venalitas venalitat-is 3f. venality
ventilo 1 I discuss, examine
veraciter truthfully
Veritas Veritat-is 3f. Christ
vesper-a ae 1f. (or *-ae arum* pl.)
    Vespers
vespere in the evening: see G.7(a)
vesperin-us a um = *vespertinus*
vexacio = *vexatio* (see O.2)
vicium = *vitium* (see O.2)

vigili-a ae 1f. vigil (night spent in
    prayer)
vilanus = *uillanus* (q.v.)
vill-a ae 1f. town; *villa publica* royal
    palace
virtus virtut-is 3f. power
virtut-es virtut-um 3f.pl. miracles
visceratenus moved to my inwards
visibil-is e visible
vivifico 1 I restore to life
vocison-us a um loud
volatil-e is 3n. bird
volt-a ae 1f. vault, severy
volut-us a um vaulted

X

Xp- = *Chr-* (Greek)
xyst-us/sixtus i 2m. cloisters

Y

ydolum = *idolum* (see O.5)
ydria = *hydria* (see O.3(c))
ymago = *imago* (see O.5)
ymnus = *hymnus* (see O.3(c))

Z

zabulus = *diabolus* (see O.14)
zel-us i 2m. zeal, fervour, heat (Greek)
zizani-a orum 2n.pl. tares